Dictionary of Literary Biography

Dictionary of Literary Biography Documentary Series

Dictionary of Literary Biography Yearbooks

1980 edited by Karen L. Rood, Jean W. Ross, and Richard Ziegfeld (1981)

1981 edited by Karen L. Rood, Jean W. Ross, and Richard Ziegfeld (1982)

1982 edited by Richard Ziegfeld; associate editors: Jean W. Ross and Lynne C. Zeigler (1983)

1983 edited by Mary Bruccoli and Jean W. Ross; associate editor Richard Ziegfeld (1984)

1984 edited by Jean W. Ross (1985)

1985 edited by Jean W. Ross (1986)

1986 edited by J. M. Brook (1987)

1987 edited by J. M. Brook (1988)

1988 edited by J. M. Brook (1989)

1989 edited by J. M. Brook (1990)

1990 edited by James W. Hipp (1991)

1991 edited by James W. Hipp (1992)

1992 edited by James W. Hipp (1993)

1993 edited by James W. Hipp, contributing editor George Garrett (1994)

1994 edited by James W. Hipp, contributing editor George Garrett (1995)

1995 edited by James W. Hipp, contributing editor George Garrett (1996)

1996 edited by Samuel W. Bruce and L. Kay Webster, contributing editor George Garrett (1997)

1997 edited by Matthew J. Bruccoli and George Garrett, with the assistance of L. Kay Webster (1998)

1998 edited by Matthew J. Bruccoli, contributing editor George Garrett, with the assistance of D. W. Thomas (1999)

1999 edited by Matthew J. Bruccoli, contributing editor George Garrett, with the assistance of D. W. Thomas (2000)

2000 edited by Matthew J. Bruccoli, contributing editor George Garrett, with the assistance of George Parker Anderson (2001)

2001 edited by Matthew J. Bruccoli, contributing editor George Garrett, with the assistance of George Parker Anderson (2002)

Concise Series

Concise Dictionary of American Literary Biography, 7 volumes (1988–1999): *The New Consciousness, 1941–1968; Colonization to the American Renaissance, 1640–1865; Realism, Naturalism, and Local Color, 1865–1917; The Twenties, 1917–1929; The Age of Maturity, 1929–1941; Broadening Views, 1968–1988; Supplement: Modern Writers, 1900–1998.*

Concise Dictionary of British Literary Biography, 8 volumes (1991–1992): *Writers of the Middle Ages and Renaissance Before 1660; Writers of the Restoration and Eighteenth Century, 1660–1789; Writers of the Romantic Period, 1789–1832; Victorian Writers, 1832–1890; Late-Victorian and Edwardian Writers, 1890–1914; Modern Writers, 1914–1945; Writers After World War II, 1945–1960; Contemporary Writers, 1960 to Present.*

Concise Dictionary of World Literary Biography, 10 volumes projected (1999–   ): *Ancient Greek and Roman Writers; German Writers; African, Caribbean, and Latin American Writers; South Slavic and Eastern European Writers.*

F. Scott Fitzgerald's
Tender Is the Night:
A Documentary Volume

Dictionary of Literary Biography® • Volume Two Hundred Seventy-Three

F. Scott Fitzgerald's
Tender Is the Night:
A Documentary Volume

Edited by
Matthew J. Bruccoli
and
George Parker Anderson

A Bruccoli Clark Layman Book

GALE®

THOMSON

GALE

Detroit • New York • San Diego • San Francisco • Cleveland • New Haven, Conn. • Waterville, Maine • London • Munich

THOMSON

GALE

Dictionary of Literary Biography
Volume 273: F. Scott Fitzgerald's
Tender Is the Night:
A Documentary Volume
Matthew J. Bruccoli and George Parker Anderson

Advisory Board
John Baker
William Cagle
Patrick O'Connor
George Garrett
Trudier Harris
Alvin Kernan
Kenny J. Williams

Editorial Directors
Matthew J. Bruccoli and Richard Layman

LIBRARY OF CONGRESS CATALOGING-IN-PUBLICATION DATA

F. Scott Fitzgerald's Tender is the night: a documentary volume/ edited by Matthew J. Bruccoli and George Parker Anderson.
       p. cm. — (Dictionary of literary biography ; v. 273)
"A Bruccoli Clark Layman book."
Includes bibliographical references and index.
     ISBN 0-7876-6017-5
     1. Fitzgerald, F. Scott (Francis Scott), 1896–1940. Tender is the night.
     2. Fitzgerald, F. Scott (Francis Scott), 1896–1940. Tender is the night—
Criticism, Textual.
     I. Bruccoli, Matthew Joseph, 1931–
     II. Anderson, George Parker, 1957–
     III. Series.

PS3511.I9T4 2003
813'.52—dc21

2002155221

Printed in the United States of America
10 9 8 7 6 5 4 3 2 1

For Scottie.

Contents

Contents

Plan of the Series

The advisory board, the editors, and the publisher of the *Dictionary of Literary Biography* are joined in endorsing Mark Twain's declaration. The literature of a nation provides an inexhaustible resource of permanent worth. Our purpose is to make literature and its creators better understood and more accessible to students and the reading public, while satisfying the needs of teachers and researchers.

To meet these requirements, *literary biography* has been construed in terms of the author's achievement. The most important thing about a writer is his writing. Accordingly, the entries in *DLB* are career biographies, tracing the development of the author's canon and the evolution of his reputation.

The purpose of *DLB* is not only to provide reliable information in a usable format but also to place the figures in the larger perspective of literary history and to offer appraisals of their accomplishments by qualified scholars.

The publication plan for *DLB* resulted from two years of preparation. The project was proposed to Bruccoli Clark by Frederick G. Ruffner, president of the Gale Research Company, in November 1975. After specimen entries were prepared and typeset, an advisory board was formed to refine the entry format and develop the series rationale. In meetings held during 1976, the publisher, series editors, and advisory board approved the scheme for a comprehensive biographical dictionary of persons who contributed to literature. Editorial work on the first volume began in January 1977, and it was published in 1978. In order to make *DLB* more than a dictionary and to compile volumes that individually have claim to status as literary history, it was decided to organize volumes by topic, period, or

genre. Each of these freestanding volumes provides a biographical-bibliographical guide and overview for a particular area of literature. We are convinced that this organization—as opposed to a single alphabet method—constitutes a valuable innovation in the presentation of reference material. The volume plan necessarily requires many decisions for the placement and treatment of authors. Certain figures will be included in separate volumes, but with different entries emphasizing the aspect of his career appropriate to each volume. Ernest Hemingway, for example, is represented in *American Writers in Paris, 1920–1939* by an entry focusing on his expatriate apprenticeship; he is also in *American Novelists, 1910–1945* with an entry surveying his entire career, as well as in *American Short-Story Writers, 1910–1945, Second Series* with an entry concentrating on his short fiction. Each volume includes a cumulative index of the subject authors and articles.

Since 1981 the series has been further augmented by the *DLB Yearbooks,* which update published entries, add new entries to keep the *DLB* current with contemporary activity, and provide articles on literary history. There have also been nineteen *DLB Documentary Series* volumes, which provide illustrations, facsimiles, and biographical and critical source materials for figures, works, or groups judged to have particular interest for students. In 1999 the *Documentary Series* was incorporated into the *DLB* volume numbering system beginning with *DLB 210: Ernest Hemingway.*

We define literature as the *intellectual commerce of a nation:* not merely as belles lettres but as that ample and complex process by which ideas are generated, shaped, and transmitted. *DLB* entries are not limited to "creative writers" but extend to other figures who in their time and in their way influenced the mind of a people. Thus the series encompasses historians, journalists, publishers, book collectors, and screenwriters. By this means readers of *DLB* may be aided to perceive literature not as cult scripture in the keeping of intellectual high priests but firmly positioned at the center of a nation's life.

DLB includes the major writers appropriate to each volume and those standing in the ranks behind them. Scholarly and critical counsel has been sought in deciding which minor figures to include and how full their entries should be. Wherever possible, useful references are made to figures who do not warrant separate entries.

Each *DLB* volume has an expert volume editor responsible for planning the volume, selecting the figures for inclusion, and assigning the entries. Volume editors are also responsible for preparing, where appropriate, appendices surveying the major periodicals and literary and intellectual movements for their volumes, as well as lists of further readings. Work on the series as a whole is coordinated at the Bruccoli Clark Layman editorial center in Columbia, South Carolina, where the editorial staff is responsible for accuracy and utility of the published volumes.

One feature that distinguishes *DLB* is the illustration policy—its concern with the iconography of literature. Just as an author is influenced by his surroundings, so is the reader's understanding of the author enhanced by a knowledge of his environment. Therefore *DLB* volumes include not only drawings, paintings, and photographs of authors, often depicting them at various stages in their careers, but also illustrations of their families and places where they lived. Title pages are regularly reproduced in facsimile along with dust jackets for modern authors. The dust jackets are a special feature of *DLB* because they often document better than anything else the way in which an author's work was perceived in its own time. Specimens of the writers' manuscripts and letters are included when feasible.

Samuel Johnson rightly decreed that "The chief glory of every people arises from its authors." The purpose of the *Dictionary of Literary Biography* is to compile literary history in the surest way available to us—by accurate and comprehensive treatment of the lives and work of those who contributed to it.

The *DLB* Advisory Board

Introduction

Tender Is the Night, published nine years after *The Great Gatsby,* has been categorized by lazy critics as a "noble failure." That sloppy label has discouraged readers and deprived them of a masterpiece. The reputation and influence of *Tender* lag behind those for *Gatsby,* a classroom staple in high schools and colleges. The only literary power exercised by English teachers is through the works they assign for required reading. *Gatsby* is assigned because it is very teachable and lends itself to corny treatment: costume parties and chit-chat about the Roaring Twenties. Moreover, *Gatsby* is short; there is an outside chance that the students will read it. *Tender* is not taught in high schools and infrequently assigned in colleges because it is difficult to teach, requiring a level of experience lacking in teachers and their students. It is three times as long as *Gatsby.*

A variety of good and bad explanations have been adduced for the uncertain position in the F. Scott canon of his greatest and most profound novel. The first is that people who don't know what they are talking about automatically charge Fitzgerald with writing *Tender* drunk. He was a prominent alcoholic in a profession populated with alcoholics: if it weren't for the drunks, twentieth-century American literature would be scarcely worth studying. Fitzgerald was drinking during the time he worked on *Tender;* but he did not write the entire novel drunk. He explained to his editor, Maxwell Perkins, a year after publication:

> A short story can be written on a bottle, but for a novel you need the mental speed that enables you to keep the whole pattern in your head and ruthlessly sacrifice the sideshows as Ernest did in "A Farewell to Arms." If a mind is slowed up ever so little it lives in the individual part of a book rather than in a book as a whole; memory is dulled. I would give anything if I hadn't had to write Part III of "Tender is the Night" entirely on stimulant. If I had one more crack at it cold sober I believe it might have made a great difference. (11 March 1935 to Maxwell Perkins, *Dear Scott/Dear Max,* pp. 218–219)

Yet Scribners editor John Hall Wheelock stated that Fitzgerald was able to make delicate revisions on the *Tender* proofs when he was tight.

Two: that *Tender* was a victim of the Thirties leftists who associated Fitzgerald with the excesses of the Twenties and deprecated *Tender* during the Depression when proletarian fiction was fashionable. Three: that Fitzgerald worked on *Tender* so long that it changed in the process of writing. Four is a variant of explanation three: that the novel jelled in the early stages of composition, and the later sections do not match the early parts.

Five: that the flashback structure is flawed and confuses the reader. This is the most damaging and wrong-headed assertion. One function of this documentary volume is to provide evidence that permits serious readers to judge Fitzgerald's intentions and his achievement in *Tender,* particularly with regard to the structure. Vladimir Nabokov remarked that all great novels are mystery novels: the mystery the reader must solve is the structure.

Fitzgerald was at least partly responsible for the charge that *Tender* is structurally flawed. His broodings on the disappointing 1934 sale—three printings totaling 15,195 copies—of his novel prompted him to blame its poor reception on the 1925 opening section written from Rosemary Hoyt's point of view, followed by the 1917 flashback. Yet few critics cited the flashback as a flaw. The damage attributable to the structure resulted from the serialization of the novel—not from book publication. Breaking the complex novel into four monthly installments in *Scribner's Magazine* made it difficult for readers to hold the plan in their heads during the thirty-day intervals.

Near the end of his life Fitzgerald prepared his so-called "author's final version," posthumously published in 1951, in which he re-ordered the story in straight chronology. This revision or redaction edited by Malcolm Cowley does not rescue or improve *Tender.* Civilians and even critics have not embraced this edition.

Fitzgerald's original plans reproduced here reveal no uncertainty about the structure of *Tender:* the flashback was built into the novel from the time he began writing the Richard Diver version in 1931–1932. The structure is not to blame for readers' difficulty with *Tender;* but their difficulty is related to the structure. The time scheme or chronology is unclear because Fitzgerald neglected to provide necessary signals. The reader is uncertain when key events occur and how much time has elapsed between these events: When do the Divers take up residence at the clinic? When do they return to the Riviera? When does Diver leave the Riviera? The uncertain pacing obscures the velocity of Diver's decline. Reviewers who complained that the reasons for his collapse were not clear were probably expressing their uncertainty about the time scheme in *Tender*.

Related to the time-scheme problem are the many distracting detail errors—geography and foreign terms. These errors are partly attributable to Fitzgerald's custom of adding new material in the proofs, at the late stages of production when copy-editing was rushed. Although he used details deliberately and brilliantly, Fitzgerald mis-spelled the words.

A good reader should be able to respond to a great novel without help. But responding is not possessing. The reading experience is determined by what the reader brings to the novel. The more a reader knows about the author's life, times, career, and material, the more meaningful the novel will be. The time of *Tender* is now more than eighty years ago; the setting is Europe. Readers require the help provided here.

Great fiction is great social history, and Fitzgerald utilized social details deliberately. Serious writers write for readers who know the things that the writers know. They expect reader recognition of meaningful details. All details are meaningful in the work of competent writers.

A rewarding reading of any novel worth reading requires understanding of the author's intentions and techniques—as well as the material. This *DLB Documentary* volume provides resources for a fuller response to Fitzgerald's masterpiece. It assembles and organizes evidence not otherwise available in one place, thereby serving students, teachers, and the celebrated general reader. If deprived students can find this volume, they can read *Tender Is the Night* with comprehension, recognition, excitement, and pleasure. It is a crime to waste a masterpiece.

Readers who imagine that a work of literature means whatever they want it to mean and that literature provides a receptacle for the "free play" of their critical insights are enjoined to have nothing to do with this *Documentary* volume.

—Matthew J. Bruccoli

Acknowledgments

This book was produced by Bruccoli Clark Layman, Inc. Karen L. Rood is senior editor. George Parker Anderson was the in-house editor.

Production manager is Philip B. Dematteis.

Administrative support was provided by Ann M. Cheschi and Carol A. Cheschi.

Accountant is Ann-Marie Holland.

Copyediting supervisor is Sally R. Evans. The copyediting staff includes Phyllis A. Avant, Caryl Brown, Melissa D. Hinton, Philip I. Jones, Rebecca Mayo, Nancy E. Smith, and Elizabeth Jo Ann Sumner.

Editorial associates are Amelia B. Lacey, Michael S. Martin, Catherine M. Polit, and William Mathes Straney.

In-house prevetting is by Nicole A. La Rocque.

Permissions editor and database manager is Amber L. Coker.

Layout and graphics supervisor is Janet E. Hill. The graphics staff includes Zoe R. Cook and Sydney E. Hammock.

Office manager is Kathy Lawler Merlette.

Photography supervisor is Paul Talbot. Photography editor is Scott Nemzek.

Digital photographic copy work was performed by Joseph M. Bruccoli and Zoe R. Cook.

Systems manager is Marie L. Parker.

Typesetting supervisor is Kathleen M. Flanagan. The typesetting staff includes Patricia Marie Flanagan, Mark J. McEwan, and Pamela D. Norton. Freelance typesetters are Wanda Adams and Rebecca Mayo.

Walter W. Ross did library research. He was assisted by Jo Cottingham and the following other librarians at the Thomas Cooper Library of the University of South Carolina: circulation department head Tucker Taylor; reference department head Virginia W. Weathers; reference department staff Brette Barron, Marilee Birchfield, Paul Cammarata, Gary Geer, Michael Macan, Tom Marcil, Rose Marshall, and Sharon Verba; interlibrary loan department head John Brunswick; and interlibrary loan staff Robert Arndt, Hayden Battle, Alex Byrne, Bill Fetty, Marna Hostetler, and Nelson Rivera.

Permissions

Illustrations

Dictionary of Literary Biography® • Volume Two Hundred Seventy-Three

F. Scott Fitzgerald's
Tender Is the Night:
A Documentary Volume

Dictionary of Literary Biography

A Brief Life of F. Scott Fitzgerald

All serious fiction is transmuted autobiography, and F. Scott Fitzgerald was among the most autobiographical writers. Tender Is the Night became the novelized history of his life during the years he worked—or should have been working—on it. Familiarity with the shape of his career facilitates recognition of the connections between his works and his life. This brief biography, adapted from F. Scott Fitzgerald: A Life in Letters *(1994), provides a reliable overview of a reputation that has been distorted by gossip and guesses.*

The dominant influences on F. Scott Fitzgerald were aspiration, literature, Princeton, Zelda Sayre Fitzgerald, and alcohol.

Francis Scott Key Fitzgerald was born in St. Paul, Minnesota, on 24 September 1896, the namesake and second cousin three times removed of the author of the national anthem. Fitzgerald's given names indicate his parents' pride in his father's ancestry. His father, Edward, was from Maryland, with an allegiance to the old South and its values. Fitzgerald's mother, Mary (Mollie) McQuillan, was the daughter of an Irish immigrant who became wealthy as a wholesale grocer in St. Paul. Both were Catholics.

Edward Fitzgerald failed as a manufacturer of wicker furniture in St. Paul, and he became a salesman for Procter & Gamble in upstate New York. He was dismissed in 1908: when his son was twelve the family returned to St. Paul and lived comfortably on Mollie Fitzgerald's inheritance. Fitzgerald attended the St. Paul Academy; his first writing to appear in print was a detective story in the school newspaper when he was thirteen.

During 1911–1913 he attended the Newman School, a Catholic prep school in New Jersey, where he met Father Siguorney Fay, who encouraged his romantic ambitions for personal distinction and achievement. As a member of the Princeton class of 1917, Fitzgerald neglected his studies for his literary apprenticeship. He wrote the scripts and lyrics for the Princeton Triangle Club musicals and was a contributor to the *Princeton Tiger* humor magazine and the *Nassau Literary Magazine.* On academic probation and unlikely to graduate, Fitzgerald joined the army in 1917 and was commissioned a second lieutenant in the infantry. Convinced that he would die in the war, he rapidly wrote a novel, "The Romantic Egoist"; the letter of rejection from Charles Scribner's Sons praised the novel's originality and asked that it be resubmitted when revised.

In June 1918 Fitzgerald was assigned to Camp Sheridan, near Montgomery, Alabama. There he fell in love with a celebrated belle, eighteen-year-old Zelda Sayre, the daughter of an Alabama Supreme Court judge. The romance intensified Fitzgerald's hopes for the success of his novel, but after revision it was rejected by Scribners a second time. The war ended before he was sent overseas; after his discharge in 1919 he went to New York City to seek his fortune in order to marry. Unwilling to wait while Fitzgerald succeeded in the advertisement business and unwilling to live on his small salary, Zelda broke their engagement.

Fitzgerald quit his job in July 1919 and returned to St. Paul to rewrite his novel as *This Side of Paradise;* it was accepted by editor Maxwell Perkins of Scribners in September. Set mainly at Princeton and described by its author as "a quest novel," *This Side of Paradise* traces the aspirations and loves of Amory Blaine.

In the fall–winter of 1919 Fitzgerald commenced his career as a writer of stories for the mass-circulation magazines. Working through agent Harold Ober, Fitzgerald interrupted work on his novels to write money-making popular fiction for the rest of his life. *The Saturday Evening Post* became Fitzgerald's best story market, and he was regarded as a "*Post* writer." His early commercial stories about young love introduced a fresh character: the independent, determined young American woman who appeared in "The Offshore

Pirates" and "Bernice Bobs Her Hair." Fitzgerald's more ambitious stories, such as "May Day" and "The Diamond as Big as the Ritz," were published in *The Smart Set,* which had a small circulation.

The publication of *This Side of Paradise* on 26 March 1920 made the twenty-four-year-old Fitzgerald famous almost overnight, and a week later he married Zelda in New York. They embarked on an extravagant life as young celebrities. Fitzgerald endeavored to develop a solid literary reputation, but his playboy image impeded the proper assessment of his work.

After a riotous summer in Westport, Connecticut, the Fitzgeralds took an apartment in New York City; there he wrote his second novel, *The Beautiful and Damned,* a naturalistic chronicle of the dissipation of Anthony and Gloria Patch. When Zelda became pregnant they took their first trip to Europe in 1921 and then settled in St. Paul for the birth of their only child; Frances Scott (Scottie) Fitzgerald was born on 26 October 1921.

Fitzgerald expected to become affluent from his play, *The Vegetable;* in the fall of 1922 they moved to Great Neck, Long Island, in order to be near Broadway. The political satire—subtitled "From President to Postman"—failed at its tryout in November 1923, and Fitzgerald wrote his way out of debt with short stories. The distractions of Great Neck and New York prevented Fitzgerald from making progress on his third novel. During this time his drinking increased. Fitzgerald was an alcoholic, but he wrote sober. Zelda regularly got "tight" but she was not an alcoholic. There were frequent domestic rows.

Literary opinion-makers were reluctant to accord Fitzgerald full marks as a serious craftsman. His reputation as a drinker inspired the myth that he was an irresponsible writer; yet, he was a painstaking reviser whose fiction went through layers of drafts. Fitzgerald's clear, lyrical, colorful, witty style evoked the emotions associated with the time and place. As a social historian Fitzgerald became identified with "The Jazz Age" that he named: "It was an age of miracles, it was an age of art, it was an age of excess, and it was an age of satire." When critics objected to Fitzgerald's concern with love and success, his response was: "But, my God! It was my material, and it was all I had to deal with." The chief theme of Fitzgerald's work is aspiration—the idealism he regarded as defining American character. Another major theme was mutability of loss.

The Fitzgeralds went to France in the spring of 1924 seeking tranquility for his work. He wrote *The Great Gatsby* during the summer and fall in Valescure near St. Raphael, but the marriage was damaged by Zelda's involvement with a French naval aviator. The extent of the affair—if it was in fact consummated—is not known. On the Riviera the Fitzgeralds formed a close friendship with Gerald and Sara Murphy.

The Fitzgeralds spent the fall and winter of 1924 in Rome, where he revised *The Great Gatsby;* they were en route to Paris when the novel was published in April. *The Great Gatsby* marked a striking advance in Fitzgerald's technique, utilizing a complex structure and a controlled narrative point of view. Fitzgerald's achievement received critical praise, but sales of *Gatsby* were disappointing, though the stage and movie rights brought additional income.

In Paris Fitzgerald met Ernest Hemingway—then unknown outside the expatriate literary circle—with whom he formed a friendship based largely on his admiration for Hemingway's personality and genius. The Fitzgeralds remained in France until the end of 1926, alternating between Paris and the Riviera.

Fitzgerald made little progress on his fourth novel, a study of American expatriates in France provisionally titled "The Boy Who Killed His Mother," "Our Type," and "The World's Fair." During these years Zelda's unconventional behavior became increasingly eccentric.

The Fitzgeralds returned to America to escape the distractions of France. After a short, unsuccessful stint of screenwriting in Hollywood, Fitzgerald rented "Ellerslie," a mansion near Wilmington, Delaware, in the spring of 1927. The family remained at Ellerslie for two years interrupted by a visit to Paris in the summer of 1928, but Fitzgerald was still unable to make significant progress on his novel. At this time Zelda commenced ballet training, intending to become a professional dancer. The Fitzgeralds returned to France in the spring of 1929, where Zelda's intense ballet work damaged her health and estranged them. In April 1930 she suffered her first breakdown. Zelda was treated at Les Rives de Prangins clinic in Switzerland until September 1931, while Fitzgerald lived in Swiss hotels. Work on the novel was again suspended as he wrote short stories to pay for her psychiatric treatment.

Fitzgerald's peak story fee of $4,000 from *The Saturday Evening Post* may have had the purchasing power of $30,000 to $40,000 in 2003 dollars. Nonetheless, the popular view of his affluence is distorted. Fitzgerald was not among the highest-paid writers of his time; his novels earned comparatively little, and most of his income came from 160 magazine stories. During the 1920s his income from all sources averaged under $25,000 a year—good money at a time when a schoolteacher's average annual salary was $1,299, but not a fortune. The Fitzgeralds spent money faster than he earned it; the author who wrote so eloquently about the effects of money on character was unable to manage his own finances.

The Fitzgeralds returned to America in the fall of 1931 and rented a house in Montgomery. Fitzgerald made a second unsuccessful trip to Hollywood in 1931. Zelda suffered a relapse in February 1932 and entered Johns Hopkins Hospital in Baltimore. She spent the rest of her life as a resident or outpatient of sanitariums.

In 1932, while a patient at Johns Hopkins, Zelda rapidly wrote *Save Me the Waltz*. Her autobiographical novel generated considerable bitterness between the Fitzgeralds, for he regarded it as preempting the material that he was using in his novel-in-progress. Fitzgerald rented "La Paix," a house outside Baltimore, where he completed his fourth novel, *Tender Is the Night*. Published in 1934, his most ambitious novel was a commercial failure, and its merits were matters of critical dispute. Set in France during the 1920s, *Tender Is the Night* examines the deterioration of Dick Diver, a brilliant American psychiatrist, during the course of his marriage to a wealthy mental patient.

The 1935–1937 period is known as "the crack-up" from the title of an essay Fitzgerald wrote in 1936. Ill, drunk, in debt, and unable to write commercial stories, he lived in hotels around Asheville, North Carolina, where in 1936 Zelda entered Highland Hospital. Fitzgerald went to Hollywood alone in the summer of 1937 with a six-month Metro-Goldwyn-Mayer contract at $1,000 a week. He received his only screen credit for adapting *Three Comrades* (1938), and his contract was renewed for a year at $1,250 a week. Although Fitzgerald paid off his debts, he was unable to save. His trips East to visit Zelda were disastrous. In California Fitzgerald formed a relationship with movie columnist Sheila Graham. After M-G-M terminated his contract at the end of 1938, Fitzgerald worked as a freelance screenwriter and sold short-short stories to *Esquire*. He began his Hollywood novel, *The Love of the Last Tycoon*, in 1939 and had written more than half of a working draft when he died of a heart attack in Graham's apartment on 21 December 1940. Zelda Fitzgerald perished in a fire in Highland Hospital in 1948.

F. Scott Fitzgerald died believing himself a failure. The obituaries were condescending, and he seemed destined for literary obscurity. The first phase of the Fitzgerald resurrection—"revival" does not properly describe the process—occurred between 1945 and 1950. By 1960 he had achieved a secure place among America's enduring writers. Where he wanted to be. Where he belongs. (Copyright ©1994; courtesy of Charles Scribner's Sons)

–M. J. B.

Tender Is the Night Chronology

1924

May	Fitzgeralds sail for France.
June	Fitzgeralds rent Villa Marie, Valescure.
Summer	Fitzgeralds meet Gerald and Sara Murphy at Cap d'Antibes.
October	Fitzgeralds arrive in Rome, where they stay until January 1925.

1925

February	Fitzgeralds travel to Capri and stay at Hotel Tiberio.
14 March	Publication of "Love in the Night" in *The Saturday Evening Post*.
10 April	Publication of *The Great Gatsby*.
Late April	Fitzgeralds move to Paris; rent apartment at 14 rue de Tilsitt.
May	Fitzgerald meets Ernest Hemingway in the Dingo Bar.
Summer	Fitzgerald begins planning the novel that will become *Tender Is the Night*.
circa 10 July	Fitzgerald reports in a letter to Maxwell Perkins, "The Novel has begun." He probably started writing the Francis Melarky version in late 1925–early 1926; working titles are "The Boy Who Killed His Mother," "The World's Fair," "Our Type," and "The Melarky Case."
August	Fitzgeralds leave Paris for month at Cap d'Antibes, then return to Paris.
10 October	Publication of "A Penny Spent" in *The Saturday Evening Post*.

1926

January	Zelda Fitzgerald takes "cure" at Salies-de-Béarn.
26 February	Publication of *All the Sad Young Men,* Fitzgerald's third collection of short stories.
Early March	Fitzgeralds return to Riviera and rent Villa Paquita at Juan-les-Pins.
May or June	Fitzgeralds move to Villa St. Louis, Juan-les-Pins.
December	Fitzgeralds return to America.

1927

January–February	First Hollywood trip: Fitzgerald works on "Lipstick" (unproduced) for United Artists; they meet Lois Moran.
March	Fitzgeralds rent "Ellerslie," near Wilmington, Delaware, where they stay until March 1928. Zelda Fitzgerald begins ballet lessons.
20 August	Publication of "Jacob's Ladder" in *The Saturday Evening Post*.

17 December	Publication of "A Short Trip Home" in *The Saturday Evening Post*.

1928

3 March	Publication of "Magnetism" in *The Saturday Evening Post*.
April	Fitzgeralds return to Europe and rent apartment at 58 rue de Vaugirard, Paris, where they stay until August.
28 April	Publication of "The Scandal Detectives" in *The Saturday Evening Post*, first of eight-story Basil Duke Lee series.
October	Fitzgeralds return to America and rent "Ellerslie" until March 1929.

1929

2 March	Publication of "The Last of the Belles" in *The Saturday Evening Post*.
March	Fitzgeralds return to Europe; they travel from Genoa along Riviera. In April, they settle in Paris in an apartment on rue Mézières.
8 June	Publication of "The Rough Crossing" in *The Saturday Evening Post*.
June	Fitzgeralds rent Villa Fleur des Bois, Cannes.
	Fitzgerald works on "new angle": the Kelly version.
October	Fitzgeralds return to Paris by way of Provence; take apartment at 10 rue Pergolèse.
19 October	Publication of "The Swimmers" in *The Saturday Evening Post*.

1930

Early	Fitzgerald returns to work on the Melarky version.
18 January	Publication of "Two Wrongs" in *The Saturday Evening Post*.
February	Fitzgeralds travel to North Africa.
5 April	Publication of "First Blood" in *The Saturday Evening Post*, first of five-story Josephine Perry series.
23 April	Zelda Fitzgerald enters Malmaison Clinic outside Paris; discharges herself on 11 May.
22 May	Zelda Fitzgerald enters Val-Mont Clinic at Glion, Switzerland.
5 June	Zelda Fitzgerald enters Les Rives de Prangins clinic at Nyon, Switzerland.
Summer and Fall	Fitzgerald commutes between Paris and Switzerland; in fall settles at Hotel de la Paix in Lausanne.
11 October	Publication of "One Trip Abroad" in *The Saturday Evening Post*.

1931

26 January	Death of Edward Fitzgerald. Fitzgerald returns alone to America to attend burial.
31 January	Publication of "The Hotel Child" in *The Saturday Evening Post*.
Winter–Spring	Fitzgerald commutes between Paris and Switzerland.
26 February	Publication of "Babylon Revisited" in *The Saturday Evening Post*.
16 May	Publication of "Indecision" in *The Saturday Evening Post*.

July	Fitzgeralds spend two weeks at Lake Annecy, France.
15 August	Publication of "Emotional Bankruptcy" in *The Saturday Evening Post*.
15 September	Zelda Fitzgerald is discharged from Les Rives de Prangins clinic. Fitzgeralds return to America; rent house at 819 Felder Avenue in Montgomery, Alabama.
November–December	Second Hollywood trip: Fitzgerald goes to Hollywood alone to work on rejected screenplay "Red-Headed Woman" for Metro-Goldwyn-Mayer.
17 November	Death of Judge Sayre.

1932

Early	Fitzgerald plans Dick Diver version of *Tender Is the Night*.
January	Zelda Fitzgerald suffers relapse.
12 February	Zelda Fitzgerald enters Phipps Psychiatric Clinic of Johns Hopkins Hospital in Baltimore.
March	Zelda Fitzgerald completes first draft of her novel, *Save Me the Waltz*, while at Phipps Clinic.
20 May	Fitzgerald rents "La Paix" at Rodgers Forge, Towson, outside Baltimore, where he writes most of *Tender Is the Night*. Working titles: "The Drunkard's Holiday," "Dr. Diver's Holiday," "Richard Diver."
26 June	Zelda Fitzgerald is discharged from Phipps; joins family at "La Paix."
27 August	Publication of "What a Handsome Pair!" in *The Saturday Evening Post*.
7 October	Publication of *Save Me the Waltz*.

1933

December	Fitzgerald rents house at 1307 Park Avenue, Baltimore.

1934

January–April	Serialization of *Tender Is the Night* in *Scribner's Magazine*.
12 February	After third breakdown, Zelda Fitzgerald returns to Phipps Clinic.
12 April	Publication of *Tender Is the Night*.

Backgrounds

The Great Gatsby *elicited the best reviews F. Scott Fitzgerald ever received—as well as uncomprehending reviews about the triviality of the characters. Fitzgerald's third novel was an extraordinary advance over his previous novels. The control of point of view, structure, and narrative voice promised more brilliant novels to come. The sales of twenty thousand copies were disappointing; but the income from stage and movie rights came to about $20,000 (perhaps $150,000 to $200,000 in 2003 dollars). At twenty-nine Fitzgerald was positioned to undertake his best work. Instead he squandered the opportunity in dissipation and extravagance, writing short stories for ready money and then writing stories to pay his wife's medical bills after 1929.*

In the nine years between the publication of The Great Gatsby *(1925) and* Tender Is the Night *(1934), Fitzgerald worked on three plot versions of the novel that was finally published: the Melarky version, which deals with a young man who murders his mother; the Kelly version, in which a successful young movie director sails to Europe; and, finally, the Diver version, which was published. Although Fitzgerald created different characters for each of the versions, he nevertheless was working with the same themes and much of the same material throughout his long composition process: in each version he was interested in showing the disintegration of a promising American man against a European backdrop.*

The Melarky Version

As planned in 1925–1926, the central figure in the matricide version is Francis Melarky, a twenty-one-year-old Southerner who is touring Europe, against his will, with his mother. The narrative opens with their arrival on the Riviera; at this point Francis has already been involved in a drunken brawl in Rome and been beaten by the police. Before that he had been dismissed from West Point and had then worked as a technician in Hollywood—although the nature of his work remains vague—where he had become involved with an actress. Melarky has a quick and violent temper, which his domineering mother triggers by reminding him of his past failures. Her attempts to control him have alienated Francis, so that she resorts to deceit in order to manage him.

Sources for Francis Melarky
Matthew J. Bruccoli

The Great Gatsby was completed in November of 1924 at Valescure on the French Riviera and revised in Rome. It was published in April 1925. There is no evidence that Fitzgerald began writing his fourth novel until late in 1925. He had borrowed money from Scribners against the royalties of *The Great Gatsby,* and the disappointing sales—about 25,000 copies—did little more than discharge his debt. His immediate conern was to raise money by writing short stories. In 1925 he published eight stories. One of these, "Love in the Night," includes writing about the vanished Russian colony on the Riviera, which was incorporated into *Tender Is the Night.*

The Fitzgeralds spent November and December of 1924 in Rome, which they abhorred, and then went to Capri where they stayed through March. They spent the spring and early summer of 1925 in Paris; this was a time of heavy drinking and little work for Fitzgerald. His difficult friendship with Ernest Hemingway began in Paris. Fitzgerald's experiences of 1924 and 1925 were written into the Melarky story, and some public events of the period supplied him with the idea for the matricide plot. In January of 1925 Dorothy Ellingson, a sixteen-year-old San Francisco girl, murdered her mother during a quarrel about the daughter's wild living. The European papers treated the case as a manifestation of the collapse of Prohibition society. Fitzgerald mentioned Ellingson to Harold Ober, his agent, as a source for his new novel. The Ellingson case followed the Leopold-Loeb case of 1924, another sensational murder, which also interested Fitzgerald. He may also have been influenced in his choice of material by Theodore Dreiser's *An American Tragedy,* published in 1925.

That Fitzgerald had discussed this material with Ernest Hemingway is shown by a kidding letter he wrote Fitzgerald in 1926:

Poster by Kimberly Hamner for the University of South Carolina Fitzgerald Centenary celebration, showing the author against a Riviera scene (Bruccoli Collection of Fitzgerald, Thomas Cooper Library, University of South Carolina)

I have tried to follow the outline and spirit of the Great Gatsby but I feel I have failed somewhat because of never having been on Long Island. The hero, like Gatsby, is a Lake Superior Salmon Fisherman. (There are no salmon in Lake Superior.) The action all takes place in Newport, R. I., and the heroine is a girl named Sophie Irene Loeb who kills her mother. The scene in which Sophie gives birth to twins in the death house at Sing Sing where she is waiting to be electrocuted for the murder of the father and sister of her, as then, unborn children I got from Dreiser but practically everything else in the book is either my own or yours. I know you'll be glad to see it. The Sun Also Rises comes from Sophie's statement as she is strapped into the chair as the current mounts.[1]

Another source of material for Fitzgerald's new novel was his friendship with Gerald and Sara Murphy. A sophisticated American couple who had pioneered the summer Riviera, the Murphys were splendid hosts and party-givers. Their friends included John Dos Passos, Archibald MacLeish, and Philip Barry (the setting of *Hotel Universe* is said to be based on the Murphys' Villa America at Cap d'Antibes, which supplied the ambience for the Divers' Villa Diana). They represented American expatriate life at its richest, and Fitzgerald, who was in Antibes in August of 1925, was fascinated by the Murphys. He paid court to Sara Murphy—as he did with all attractive women—and he identified himself with Gerald Murphy. So complete was this identification that when Murphy remarked after reading *Tender Is the Night* that he was puzzled by the combination of himself and Fitzgerald in the character of Dick Diver, Fitzgerald assured him that it was not a problem because he and Murphy were, in fact, the same person. Evidence of the way Fitzgerald borrowed qualities from Murphy for both himself and Dick Diver is provided by a passage in "Handle with Care" (1936): "That a fourth man had come to dictate my relations with other people when these relations were successful: how to do, what to say. How to make people at least momentarily happy. . . . This always confused me and made me want to go out and get drunk, but this man had seen the game, analyzed it and beaten it, and his word was good enough for me." The parallels between Murphy and Dick Diver troubled Hemingway, who warned Fitzgerald after *Tender Is the Night* was published about the self-pity involved in interpolating Fitzgerald's own anxieties into a portrait of Murphy. The Murphys were written into the novel from the start as the Rorebacks or the Pipers, and ultimately they supplied many of the external or social traits of Dick and Nicole Diver. The dedication page of *Tender Is*

the Night reads: "TO GERALD AND SARA MANY FÊTES".

As Fitzgerald worked at converting the Murphys into characters in his novel, he shared his insights into their personalities with them. By the summer of 1929 the strain of being analyzed became so great that Sara Murphy warned Fitzgerald that he was endangering their friendship:

[Y]ou can't expect anyone to like or stand a Continual feeling of analysis + sub-analysis + criticism—on the whole unfriendly—such as we have felt for quite awhile. It is definitely in the air,—+ quite unpleasant. It certainly detracts from any gathering,—+ Gerald, for one, simply curls up at the edges + becomes someone else in that sort of atmosphere. And last night you even said, "that you had never seen Gerald so silly + rude." It's hardly likely that I should Explain Gerald,—or Gerald me—to you. If you don't know what people are like it's your loss—and if Gerald was "rude" in getting up + leaving a party that had gotten quite bad,—then he was rude to the Hemingways & MacLeishes too. No, it is hardly likely that you would stick at a thing like Manners—it is more probably some theory you have,—(it may be something to do with the book.)—But you ought to know at your age that you Can't have Theories about friends—If you Can't take friends largely, + without suspicion—then they are not friends at all—We cannot—Gerald + I—at our age—+ stage in life—be bothered with Sophomoric situations—like last night. We are very simple people—(unless we feel ourselves in a collegiate quagmire)—and we are literally + actually fond of you both—(There is no reason for saying this that I know of—unless we meant it.)

And so—for God's sake take it or leave it,—as it is meant,—a straight gesture, without subtitles—[2]

According to Theodore Chanler, a composer who was studying abroad in 1925, an incident in which the Murphys figured supplied Fitzgerald with the idea for the earliest form of the novel. Chanler had been befriended by the Murphys and the poet Archibald MacLeish, and although he enjoyed their company, he found himself growing increasingly dissatisfied with the irregularity of his life in France—especially with his drinking—and decided to break with his friends. In this mood he informed the Murphys and the MacLeishes that he was tired of them. Chanler reported this incident to Fitzgerald, who spoke of it as the basis for a novel about a talented young American who is taken up by a glamorous expatriate group and experiences a breakdown. This is the story of Francis Melarky with the matricide omitted.

Another American abroad may have added to the picture Fitzgerald was then forming of Francis

The Fitzgeralds' passports (Bruccoli Collection of Fitzgerald, Thomas Cooper Library, University of South Carolina)

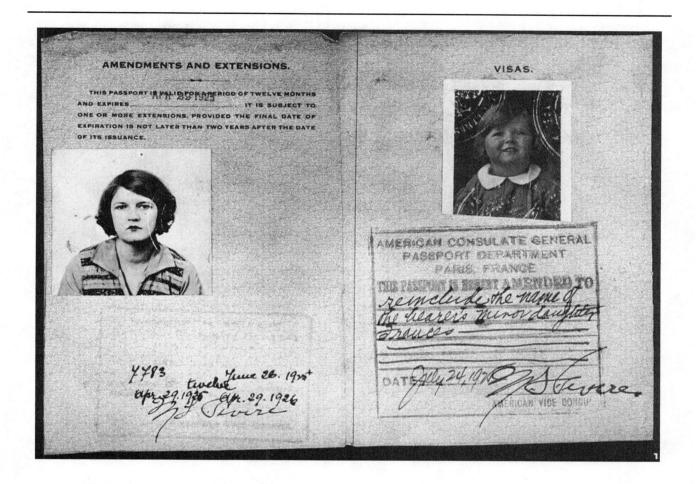

Melarky. While at Princeton Fitzgerald had admired Walker Ellis. A member of the class of 1915, Ellis had a brilliant undergraduate career. He was elected to Phi Beta Kappa and was Commencement Ivy Orator, but to Fitzgerald his greatest distinction was the presidency of the Triangle Club. Fitzgerald's first Triangle show, *Fie! Fie! Fi-Fi!,* was written in collaboration with Ellis, although Fitzgerald actually did most of the work. After taking a law degree at Harvard, Ellis served as a pilot in the war, but after 1918 failed to fulfill the promise of his college years. He abandoned the law for acting, and in 1925 went to Europe. Like Francis Melarky, he was a Southerner and seems to have had a difficult relationship with his mother. Walker Ellis was on the Riviera at the time Fitzgerald was, and Gerald Murphy recalls that "He was much on Scott's mind. He spoke often of him to me."

While they were in Rome in 1924, the Fitzgeralds became friendly with the Americans who were working on the movie *Ben-Hur*. The information about the motion-picture industry that Fitzgerald picked up from the *Ben-Hur* crew may have supplied the background he needed for the characterization of Francis Melarky as a motion-picture technician.

At the same time that Fitzgerald's imagination was stimulated by Chanler, Ellis, the Ellingson case, and the motion-picture industry, some of his more personal experiences contributed to his plan for the new novel. The Fitzgeralds attended the *Ben-Hur* studio Christmas party, after which he got into a nightclub brawl by volunteering his opinions of Italians. On another occasion Fitzgerald fought with taxi drivers and was beaten by the police. These episodes formed the basis for Francis Melarky's experiences in Rome and were later combined into one of the strongest episodes in *Tender Is the Night*. Fitzgerald's intense dislike of Italians colored his treatment of them from the inception of his novel.

Richard Loeb and Nathan Leopold at the time of their murder trial in 1924

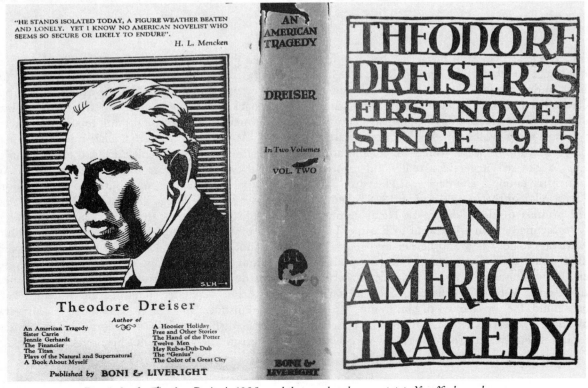

Dust jacket for Theodore Dreiser's 1925 novel that was based on an upstate New York murder case

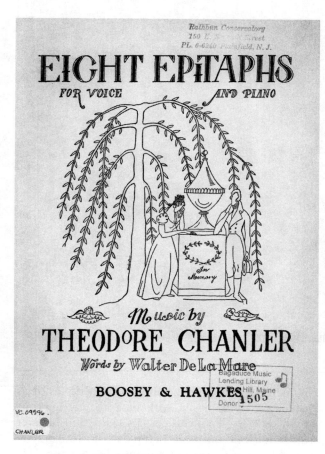

Cover for Chanler's 1939 composition, a cycle based on
Walter de la Mare's imaginary gravestone inscriptions

A Model for Melarky

Theodore Chanler (1902–1961), the young man whose rejection of the Murphys and the MacLeishes may have inspired Fitzgerald's creation of Francis Melarky, had a distinguished career as a composer and music critic. A student of Ernest Bloch at the Cleveland Institute and Nadia Boulanger in Paris, Chanler was best known for his art songs, especially Eight Epitaphs. *He was a contributor to* Modern Music *and wrote criticism for* The Boston Herald *and* The New York Herald Tribune. *Chanler taught at the Peabody Conservatory of Music and* The Longly School in Boston.

Theodore Chanler

The many accomplishments at Princeton of Walker M. Ellis, a possible model for Melarky, were listed in the 1915 Nassau Herald.

WALKER MALLAM ELLIS. He was born in New Orleans on April 29, 1893, and has always lived in New Orleans.

He is the son of Caswell Ellis and Ellen Elizabeth Mallam. His father is a cotton broker. He has three brothers and two sisters.

Ellis prepared at Dixon Academy, Dixon, La., and Hill School, Pottstown, Pa. At Hill School he was a member of the dramatic club, editor of the paper and member of the gym team.

In Princeton, he was president of the Triangle Club. Member of the Glee Club. Senior Council. Ivy Orator. Master of Ceremonies. University Cottage Club. Whig Hall. Contributor to the *Nassau Literary Magazine*. Junior French Prize. Washington's Birthday Orator, Sophomore Year. Phi Beta Kappa. In politics, he is a Democrat.

Throughout College, he has roomed in 8 National Bank Building; Freshman Year, with Jenkins, '14; Sophomore Year, with R. B. Dort, Ex-'13; Junior and Senior Years, with Riegel.

He expects to take up law, and will attend the Harvard Law School next year. His permanent address is: Care of C. P. Ellis, New Orleans, La.

In examining so subjective a writer's selection of a matricide plot, it is obligatory to consider the author's feelings about his own mother. It is true that relations between them were strained and that Fitzgerald was often embarrassed by his mother. Molly Fitzgerald was a mildly eccentric woman whom her son hyperbolically described in 1926 as "a neurotic, half insane with pathological nervous worry." She had spoiled him as a child, and he later came to feel that this upbringing had at least contributed to his egocentric and unhappy adolescence. He was also grateful to his mother for her devotion to him. *Tales of the Jazz Age* is dedicated to her; when she died in 1936, he wrote the story "An Author's Mother," in which she is sympathetically portrayed as a confused woman, very proud of her author son. At the time Fitzgerald was working on the matricide story, his mother visited him in Paris. Though he expected to be embarrassed by her, her behavior was unexceptionable.

Crucial to an assessment of Molly Fitzgerald's influence on the matricide material is whether or not she served as a recognizable model for Charlotte Melarky, Francis's mother. The domineering Mrs. Melarky is unlike the rather pathetic Mrs. Fitzgerald. Nor is there anything to indicate that Fitzgerald was obsessed by the theme of matricide. At the time he was working on the Melarky story, he wrote a comic ballad about matricide:

In a 15 February 1960 letter to Matthew J. Bruccoli, Gerald Murphy recalled Fitzgerald's interest in Walker Ellis.

Walker Ellis <u>was</u> on the Riviera at the time Scott was. We all knew him—and his discomforting habits. Scott was struck by the contrast between his spectacularly 'successful' career at Princeton and his later life of dissipation (which your letter lists accurately.). It would seem that the wild character you speak of was drawn from Ellis, as he was much on Scott's mind. He spoke often of him to me.

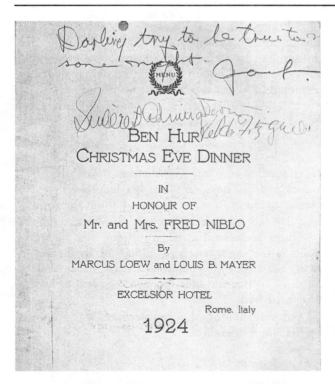

Menu for dinner honoring Fred Niblo, who directed Ben-Hur, *signed by Zelda Fitzgerald (Bruccoli Collection of Fitzgerald, Thomas Cooper Library, University of South Carolina)*

Just a boy that killed his mother
I was always up to tricks
When she taunted me I shot her
Through her chronic appendix.

Fitzgerald entertained his friends by reciting this poem, and his willingness to burlesque the theme of his novel can be interpreted as an indication that he had developed doubts about the material, which was alien to his creative temperament. This suspicion is supported by his otherwise inexplicable selection of the name Francis Melarky for the protagonist of a novel that was not to be satiric. The name is doubly puzzling because the given name identifies the character with the author, whereas the surname ridicules him. "Melarky" was a slang term for something fake or unbelievable. Fitzgerald was extremely careful about the names of his characters and often chose names which indicate their personalities—Jay Gatsby, Dick Diver, Anthony Patch, Monroe Stahr. None of the other people in the Melarky version take any notice of the name, although they do jibe at Albert McKisco's ordinary name.

Fitzgerald worked on the Melarky-matricide version through repeated interruptions from 1925 to 1930. It had four tentative titles. *Our Type* and *The*

Lobby card for the 1925 movie showing Carmel Myers as Iras and Francis X. Bushman as Messala

World's Fair were the earliest; later Fitzgerald considered *The Melarky Case* and *The Boy Who Killed His Mother,* which was suggested by his wife.

Notes

1. Matthew J. Bruccoli, *Fitzgerald and Hemingway: A Dangerous Friendship* (Columbia, S.C.: Manly, 1999), pp. 58–59.
2. *Correspondence of F. Scott Fitzgerald,* edited by Matthew J. Bruccoli and Margaret M. Doggan with the assistance of Susan Walker (New York: Random House, 1980), pp. 190–191.

The Dorothy Ellingson Case

In January 1925 Dorothy Ellingson, a sixteen-year-old in San Francisco, murdered her mother with a pistol after a series of quarrels about the girl's partying. The crime received coverage in America as well as Europe. The following story of the murder carried a subhead: "Dispute Between His Mother and Sister Over Parties, Night Before, Is Told by Brother."

S.F. Woman Slain; Daughter, 16, Missing
The San Francisco Examiner, 14 January 1925, pp. 1–2

The howling of a gray cat, mute witness of its mistress' murder, disclosed last night a mystery that sent police searching through the haunts of wayward girls for a 16-year-old miss, beautiful, with flaming bobbed hair and a determination to live her own life.

Somewhere this young girl, Dorothy Ellingson, former ward of the Juvenile Court, was following last night her self-appointed path that led away from the humble home at 256 Third avenue.

In the bedroom of that home lay the body of her mother, Mrs. Annie Ellingson, dead, a bullet in the back of her head.

SON FINDS BODY.

Her son, Earl Ellingson, 25, a wholesale drug clerk, had returned home from work to find her there, prone upon the bed, partially dressed.

He was first attracted by the low call of the cat which ran wide eyed from the room as he opened the bedroom door.

A .45 caliber revolver was found in the bathroom upon a trunk. Two cartridges had been discharged.

The second bullet went wide of its mark and imbedded itself in a wall near a framed motto which read, "I Will Never Leave Thee Nor Forsake Thee."

Ellingson's next discovery was that his young and beautiful sister, Dorothy, was missing. Her clothes had been hurriedly packed. A trunk had been partially emptied and the contents evidently crammed into a suitcase which was gone.

Beside the trunk were heaped childish playthings, a doll and other keepsakes.

MONEY TAKEN.

The mother's purse, empty, lay upon the dresser, rifled of a small quantity of silver and a $25 money order. The contents of her handbag had also been emptied hastily and scattered about the room.

Detectives, reconstructing the scene of the shooting, declared that the murderer had evidently stood in the doorway. Mrs. Ellingson, in the act of lacing her shoes, was bending over with her back to the door. When the shot was fired she fell backward across the bed.

Beside her on the counterpane was found a verse from a calendar:

Let the old life be covered by the new,
The old past, so full of sad mistakes,
Let it be wholly hidden by the new—
By deeds as white as silken flakes.

This was regarded by the investigators as a gift from the daughter, a subtle promise with the new year of better understanding and better behavior.

Only the night before, according to the son, Earl, there had been a bitter quarrel between Mrs. Ellingson and her daughter over Dorothy's determination to attend a certain party.

A letter was found last night from a former sweetheart sent from Los Angeles to Dorothy and inviting her to come on down at once where happiness and her own free way awaited her.

Police immediately dispatched a full description to Los Angeles where a search was made through the various hotels.

GIRL SOUGHT FREEDOM.

Back of the grim tragedy in the Third avenue home is the story of the young girl's constant battle against parental restraint, her desire to drink to the full of life as she had pictured it.

A number of love stories were found in her room, while a volume of "Little Women," a Christmas present from her brother, lay with leaves uncut.

From her father, Joseph Ellingson, a tailor, the police learned the pitiable tale of the parental attempt to keep the girl at home and away from cafes and night life.

'JAZZMANIAC' HELD PRODUCT OF ENVIRONS

U. C. Psychologist Says Missing Girl in Murder Case Is Only One of Many of Her Type

Headline from the 15 January 1925
San Francisco Examiner

A month ago the parents separated for the reason, said Ellingson, that he could no longer countenance his daughter's constant absence from home and the mother's defense of her.

There were times, according to the father, when Dorothy would remain away for two nights at a time. He declared that she would register at downtown hotels under assumed names, using "Mrs. Dorothy De Wolfe and Mrs. Dorothy Renero" as her favorite titles.

Gay parties, jazz, and occasionally liquor were the lure that drew her away from them, he said.

"I suppose we were too old fashioned," he sobbed last night. "But I never believed it would lead to this."

An older woman, known as "Gussie," was said by police to have been Dorothy's companion on many of these parties. The father gave the detectives the names of several of the girl's men friends, who will be quizzed when found.

On Monday night, the occasion of the quarrel between mother and daughter, a mysterious telephone conversation occurred between the girl and a man.

Dorothy, according to her brother's account of the incident, had been sitting morose and sullen after the quarrel when the phone rang. Mrs. Ellingson answered and called her daughter.

A sprightly exchange of greetings and reference to "that party last Saturday night" occurred, then Dorothy is said to have remarked:

"Oh, don't worry about that. I am expecting a change very soon."

The mother upbraided her daughter for these continued conversations, protesting that she never invited her men friends to the house but persisted in meeting them at cafes or in a little music store on Clement street.

SLEPT TOGETHER.

Later their disagreement was patched up and mother and daughter retired for the night sleeping together in the same bed that the next day was to be the last resting place of the murdered woman.

Mrs. Ellingson arose yesterday morning as was her wont and cooked her son's breakfast. When he left home, Dorothy was still in bed. She had promised to seek a position that day and there was a cheerful atmosphere after the storm of the night before.

It was Ellingson's revolver that was used in the slaying. He had always kept it in his bureau drawer and to his knowledge none knew of its existence save members of the family. The father, since the separation a month ago, had taken rooms elsewhere.

Two bullets were fired from the gun. One missed and lodged in the wall above the bending figure of the woman, who apparently was shot from the rear, without ever seeing the murderous form in the doorway.

Ellingson, senior, recalled last night that his daughter's chafing at home restraint had begun at the age of 12, when she ran away from home.

HASTY DEPARTURE.

From the testimony of a neighbor and other evidence it is believed the shooting occurred at 9 o'clock yesterday morning. One shot was heard by Mrs. Julia Ur, 258 Third avenue.

Dorothy's departure was evidently made in haste. A table knife was found beside a bank, from which an attempt had been made to extract a few coins. The mother's empty handbag was on the floor, and some of the girls own clothes had been tossed from the trunk.

No one saw her leave the house, but it is believed she was dressed in a dark blue suit and wore a long black cape. With a stylish, somewhat mature figure and her flaming red hair, the girl was said to be a striking figure easily recognized by friends.

* * *

Spirit of Jazz Will Drag Race to Level Of Savages, Says Sage

Headline for the 27 January 1925 San Francisco Examiner *article in which horticulturalist Luther Burbank is interviewed*

Ellingson was quickly apprehended and confessed to the crime.

Dorothy Ellingson Egotist
Who Thinks Only About Herself
Annie Laurie
The San Francisco Examiner, 16 January 1925, pp. 1, 3

Did you ever see a little bedraggled moth trying to struggle up out of the dew—on a dark, rainy morning?

Not a clean moth, not a bright, gay moth, but a drab, besmirched little thing with drooping wings and all the beauty and all the joy gone out of life and out of its own frivolous, vain little body.

That's what Dorothy Ellingson made me think of when she sat on the edge of a chair in the district attorney's office yesterday and told the police and the reporters and the visiting philanthropists, and whoever happened to look into the room, all about how she murdered her mother and why she murdered her mother and how she came to be the "*life of the party*" at a low dance on the night after she had read in the paper that her mother was actually dead.

Not a beauty, Dorothy Ellingson, no matter what the enthusiastic describers can say, but not ugly, either—a mop of reddish hair, not any too well kept, rather good features, a pair of sly eyes, shallow and deceitful, a secretive smile, a good, muscular, sturdy little figure, a soft pleasant voice, and a constant, never-ending, never-changing smile.

A Mona Lisa smile, full of cunning and full of guile and full of the strange, secretive pride of her strange, secretive heart.

BEDRAGGLED CREATURE
OUT OF SLUMS

A cheap Mona Lisa, in a cheap little pink waist, and a sport skirt, neat, not too expensive, shoes, and a lampshade hat pulled down over her eyebrows in the correct flapper fashion.

No earrings, no bracelets, no rings, no dingles dangles of any sort, just a bedraggled little creature out of the slums—that's what she looks and that in my mind is what she is, although she lived at home and had a good mother and a splendid brother and a father who is at least honest and industrious.

Not at all excited, not at all moved, not in the least remorseful—so she seemed as she leaned her sharp little elbows on the arms of her chair and answered quite deliberately and quite calmly a dozen different kinds of questions.

On the table at the side of her lay the little diary which has been so much quoted—nothing in the diary that I could see except a lot of silly quotations and a few little paragraphs about parties and "*sweeties,*" as the jargon goes.

"Jazz Girl" Faces Trial for Murder

Headline from the 30 January 1925 San Francisco Examiner.
Ellingson was sentenced to a ten-year prison term.

Perhaps the shorthand notes in the diary really mean something–Dorothy Ellingson loves to make those who interview her think so anyway, and is a little vain about it–and a little pleased to be the author of a mystery no matter how sordid or how meaningless.

"Yes," said Dorothy, tilting her youthful head on one side in what is evidently a cultivated attempt at coquetry—

Yes, I killed my mother; they all know it now, so I might as well confess. She made me mad, so I killed her.

"SO I JUST GOT THE GUN AND SHOT HER"

She was always at me about going to wild parties and she didn't like any of my friends and she said if I went out again that night she would call up the police and have them arrest me, and she said she would bar the door and never let me in again, and so *I just went into the other room and got the gun and when her back was turned I shot her.*

I didn't know whether I killed her or not–I guess I didn't care. I was mad–and you know when you're mad–

The secretive smile was particularly in evidence just then and the sly eyes gleamed a little– *"when you're mad, you'll do most anything."*

Evidently an article of the code in her strange, squalid world of cheap cafes and "wild parties"– "when you're mad you'll do most anything."

"So I just grabbed a few things and left," she said. "I got a room to stay in and then I went to a party. Yes, I had a good time at the party. I love to dance and the music was certainly swell–every once in a while it would come over me what I had done and I would get *sort of cold and feel sort of queer,* as if it was all in a play or a book or something.

"But I just went on dancing and singing and jazzing things up the same as I always do.

"I didn't know whether my mother was really dead or not, but I knew I had hit her.

"Jazz Best Medicine In the World"

"On Wednesday morning the landlady showed me a paper with the picture of my mother and myself–it made me feel queer."

Queer–yes, that is the word she used. It made her feel queer to see the picture of herself and the mother she had murdered–but not "queer" enough to make her confess, not "queer" enough to drive her home through the terrible streets, home to the poor little house where the mother who loved her better than she loved her life lay dead, murdered by the hand of her own child.

"I went to another party Wednesday night– sure I did–I didn't feel right and *jazz is the best medicine in the world!*"

"When I got home Wednesday night I was tired and I went to bed and to sleep. I didn't seem to remember much about anything–I didn't want to remember, so I just hummed the jazz music over and over to myself and went to sleep, but when the bell rang downstairs way late in the night I knew they were after me.

"I knew it just as well as if I had heard them calling my name, and when they came in I sat up in bed and said I'd go with them.

"They were mad at me at first because I was slow getting dressed; they needn't have been mad, I had mascara on my eyelashes and it got in my eyes and they smarted, and I had to wash my face and get the makeup off. I hadn't stopped to do it when I came in from the party.

"And that's all there is to tell.

"And So I Got Mad And Killed Her"

"I didn't plan to kill mama; she wouldn't let me go to the party–I wanted to dance and she tried to stop me and so I got mad and I killed her. Oh, you know how a person is when they get mad.

"Yes, mama was a good woman; I guess she was the best mother in the world.

"She was always doing things for me and trying to make me happy.

"I loved my mother; she always stood between me and my father's temper. My father's a Norwegian, you know, and when he gets mad—And my mother was a great reader, just as I am, and we used to talk books over, poetry and novels—

"I wrote a few little stories myself sometimes when I felt romantic, and mama always thought I would be a great writer some day—*you know how mothers are.*

"I didn't think so: I didn't care much about that; I wanted to have a good job and lots of friends and be going all the time—yes, I guess you'd call me a 'JAZZ BABY'—if you ever use such words—mama didn't.

"Mama was awfully innocent. She didn't seem to know a thing about life at all; she was just like a little girl about some things—you could fool her awful easy. She *wasn't wise.*

"I fooled her all the time.

"Why, when I was fourteen I used to be out of school two and three weeks at a time jazzing around with some boys I knew. The called 'em the 'Mission gang'—we used to go out to the beach all the time, and mama thought I was in school.

"The principal of the school was a bonehead and it was easy to put it over on him, too.

"I don't see how people can live in the world and be so innocent, do you?"

Right and Wrong
—Only Words

And little, bedraggled, shallow-eyed, secretive, egotistical Dorothy Ellingson, who murdered her good mother because her mother was trying to make a good girl of her, looked at me with what she tried to make a confidential and understanding smile.

"Dorothy," I said, "do you really feel as calm and as quiet in your deepest heart as you pretend to feel right now?"

The girl veiled her secretive eyes, turned her strange and almost classic head a little to one side, looked at me as if trying to calculate what I wanted her to say, and spoke for the first time with a little tremor in her voice.

"No," she said, "I guess I don't. I guess I'm just trying to be calm—I don't want to get excited again—you know what a person might say or do when they get excited."

Not one word of remorse, not one look of shuddering misery, not one bowing of the head in shame when all the hideous, sordid, cruel, degrading story of her degraded childhood and her besmirched youth came out.

Dorothy Ellingson speaks as lightly of the most fearful degradation as if she were talking of an ice cream soda party at the home of some nice girl from one of her classes in a clean, decent school.

Right and wrong, bad and good, disgraceful and honorable—these words are to her apparently *nothing but words.*

Honor, self-respect, pride, modesty, reserve, self-control, duty, loyalty—what do they stand for in her life? I doubt if she has ever even dreamed of them.

Jazz, automobiles, the moving pictures, chop suey restaurants, the snarling whine of the saxophone, the teasing wall of violin strings, bright lights, loud laughter—these are the things Dorothy Ellingson loves and these are the things she understands.

Her own pleasure, her own wild way, her own determined will—these are what she wanted and what she was bound to have, no matter what price she paid.

And now that she has paid the price and that her poor, loving mother is dead and gone, what is going to become of the bedraggled, besmirched little moth who fluttered her poor, feeble little wings with such a sordid imitation of gaiety?

All the jazz friends have hurried into hiding.

And there is neither the whine of the saxophone nor the teasing wail of the violin for Dorothy Ellingson any more.

What Does Father
Know of Child?

Whose fault is it that such strange, perverted little egotists are born and raised and allowed to work their wild will on any one who happens to stand in their way?

Joseph Ellingson, the father—a mighty-shouldered man he is—does he understand the dark heart of this strange child of his better than the gentle mother who loved her so dearly could ever possibly have understood it?

Is that why Joseph Ellingson went so wild in his rages when he heard that his daughter was staying out at night and would not tell where she had been?

Earl Ellingson, the brother of Dorothy, what a fine, strapping, tall, broad-shouldered, manly fellow he is—he made a good record for himself in the A. E. F., a good record at his work, a good record among the neighbors, and at home he was a loyal, devoted and most loving son to the loyal, devoted and loving woman who lies so cold in death today.

Shot down by the girl she brought into the world and did her gentle, loving best to hold in some kind of control!

Earl Ellingson and his father were waiting outside the door to see Dorothy yesterday when she was putting her head on one side and telling without the quiver of an eyelash of the way she shot her mother and how it is when you are "mad."

The girl did not want to see her father and her brother.

I wonder why they wanted to see her?

"How the poor mother's loving heart would yearn if she knew of that meeting and how she would try to step in between the just anger of her husband and her son and the selfish, hard-hearted, egotistical, shallow-minded, high-tempered little "JAZZ BABY" who was the bone of her bone, the flesh of her flesh and the very core of her sore and tormented heart.

"After your mother, who do you love?
"After your father, who do you love?"

How did it go, the cheap little song they used to sing in all the prisons from one end of the country to the other when it was the cheap and popular vogue?

"After your own dear folks at home,
"Tell me, who do you love?"

If Dorothy Ellingson answered the crude question in the crude refrain, and answered it truthfully, I'm very much afraid she would have to say:
"MYSELF!"

Ring Lardner

Ring Lardner—vernacular humorist, short-story writer, and sports reporter—and Fitzgerald formed a close friendship when both were living in Great Neck, Long Island, 1922–1924. Lardner remarked that "Mr. Fitzgerald is a novelist and Mrs. Fitzgerald is a novelty." Fitzgerald dedicated All the Sad Young Men *(1926) to the Lardners. An alcoholic, Lardner was the source for Abe North. The subhead for the following obituary read "'You Know Me Al' Letter Writer, 48, Revolutionized Sports Reporting."*

Ring Lardner, Humorist and Author, Dead
New York Herald Tribune, 26 September 1933, pp. 1, 19

EAST HAMPTON, L. I., Sept. 25.—Ring Lardner, creator of "You Know Me, Al," died at 11 o'clock tonight at his home here. He was forty-eight years old.

Mr. Lardner had been in poor health since 1931. Heart disease, complicated by other ailments, caused his death. He had been living in East Hampton for about three years, having moved here from Great Neck.

One of the physicians who had attended Mr. 'ardner said tonight that he has been permitted to continue his writing "because he wasn't happy unless he was working." In recent months he had contributed regularly to 'The New Yorker," generally under the date line, "No Visitors, N. Y.," all the pieces being devoted to the radio, of which he had become as diligent a student as he had been of baseball in earlier years.

Members of his family were with Mr. Lardner when he died. Surviving are his wife, the former Ellis Abbott, of Goshen, Ind.; four sons, John Abbott, James Phillips, Ring W. jr. and David Ellis Lardner; two sis-

Ring Lardner

```
A CHRISTMAS WISH—AND WHAT CAME OF IT.

Of all the girls for whom I care,
And there are quite a number,
None can compare with Zelda Sayre,
Now  wedded to a plumber.

I knew her when she was a waif
In southern Alabama.
Her old granddaddy cracked a safe
And found therein her grandma.

A Glee Club man walked up New York
For forty city blocks,
Nor did he meet a girl as sweet
As Mrs. Farmer Fox.

I read the World, I read the Sun,
The Tribune and the Herald,
But of all the papers, there is none
Like Mrs. Scott Fitzgerald.

God rest thee, merry gentleman!
God  shrew thee, greasy maiden!
God love that pure American
Who married Mr. Braden.

If it is dark when home I go
And safety is imperilled,
There's no  policeman that I know
Like Zelda Sayre  Fitzgerald.

I met her at the  football game;
'Twas in the Harvard  stadium.
A megaphone announced her name:
"It's Mrs. James S. Braden!"

So here's my Christmas wish for you:
I worship Leon Errol,
But the funniest girl I ever knew
Is Mrs. Scott Fitzgerald.
```

A poem Lardner wrote for Zelda Fitzgerald
(*from* The Romantic Egoists)

ters, Mrs. Richard Tobin, of Douglaston, Queens, and Miss Lena Lardner, and three brothers, Rex Lardner, of Great Neck; Henry Lardner, of Niles, Mich., and William Lardner, of Duluth, Minn.

Flunked Everything but Rhetoric

Ringgold Wilmer Lardner, better known as Ring Lardner, one of America's greatest humorists and short story writers, was born on March 6, 1885, in Niles, Mich., the youngest of the five children of Henry and Lena Bogardus Phillips Lardner. His parents intended for him to become a mechanical engineer, so after being graduated from Niles High School in 1901 he entered Armour Institute of Technology, Chicago, the following fall. Not endowed with a gift for science, he "graduated in February," failing in everything but rhetoric.

On his return he became the Michigan Central freight agent at Niles at $1 a day, wrestling merchandise in the hot summer sun. Fate, however, robbed the railroad of a potential conductor, but saved the nation a great writer. Lardner was discharged for absentmindedly sending a consignment of cream cheese to Jackson instead of Battle Creek.

His next job was that of bookkeeper, collector and general handy man in the local gas office at $6 a week. Years later he drew upon his memories of the gas office for a short story called "The Maysville Minstrel."

Stole First Newspaper Job

"I thought I was getting away with murder in that gas office," he once said. "The work was so

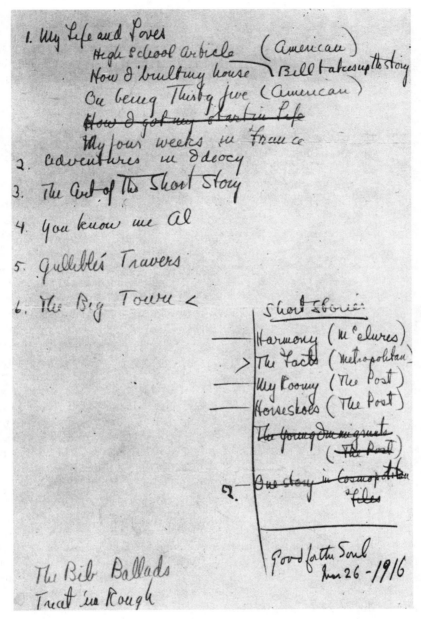

*The back of a menu on which Fitzgerald and Maxwell Perkins listed possible titles for Ring Lardner's first book
published by Scribners (Scribner Archives, Princeton University Library)*

much easier there than that I had to do at the freight station. After working there I met a representative of 'The South Bend (Ind.) Times,' who had come to Niles to sign up my brother Rex. I knew that he was tied up in contracts with 'The Niles Sun' and 'The Kalamazoo Gazette,' so I stole the job. I got $12 a week and worked there for two years.

"My first assignment was to cover the wedding of Mr. and Mrs. Clement Studebaker, of the automobile family, which formed the backbone of South Bend's social existence. I amazed my editor by com-ing back with exactly five lines of news. He didn't fire me, but assigned me to cover a musical show that opened that evening. Instead of giving the entertainment the boost customary and expected of all small town theatrical critics, I roasted the piece to death.

"This brought an avalanche of criticism down on my head from the owner of the theater, Joseph E. Howard, who also owned and wrote the show. I survived the storm, however, and the boss put me to work covering the state league ball games.

*Dust jacket for Lardner's 1924 collection that Fitzgerald
persuaded Maxwell Perkins to publish*

He Had a Lovely Time

"Altogether I had a lovely time on that paper. In the morning I covered the police stations and courts. Then I would drop over to the Circuit Court to get the divorce news. In the afternoon I went to the ball park. The press box was a little sewing table right out on the field and I had a grand time ducking foul balls. When fouls were few the players would come up and abuse me for not praising them enough in my stories. In the evenings I covered shows. Then I would go to the office to write the day's events.

"The second year I took my vacation in the fall so I could attend the World Series between the Cubs and the Detroit Tigers. When in Chicago I thought I ought to get a job on a big paper. I ran into Hughey Fullerton and he recommended me to 'The Inter-Ocean,' a daily which has since passed away.

"There I got a job at $17.50 a week and wrote football. One of my first assignments was to cover the Carlisle Indians, who were running through signals at Lake Forest in preparation for a game with Chicago the following Saturday. I was standing on the field with Glenn Warner, their coach, when we heard some girls behind us talking. One said, 'He must have some white blood in him.' They were talking about me.

"After a while I was offered $25 by 'The Chicago Examiner' to go South with the White Sox for the spring training. That was in 1908. I sent back some comic sketches of the ball players which the sports editor threw away. I don't blame him. They were terrible. I admit it. After that I went with 'The Chicago Tribune.'

Married, Changed Jobs Again

"In 1911 I married Miss Ellis Abbott, of Goshen, Ind., and found a job with a weekly in St. Louis called 'The Sporting News,' so I wouldn't have to work nights or go out of town.

"After that I worked on 'The Boston American' and then on 'The Chicago American' as copy reader. My copy reading days ended when I printed a story that Tom Shevlin was dead. It later developed that it was Shevlin's father who had passed on. After a brief spell on 'The Chicago Herald-Examiner' I went to 'The Chicago Tribune,' where from 1913 to 1919 I conducted the 'In the Wake of the News' column.

"While on 'The Tribune' I met a ball player who couldn't read or write and used to bring me letters from his wife to read and answer. The fellow was a great alibi artist and always had an excuse for not sending the money she continually pleaded for and most likely needed.

"We had a lot of fun kidding him on dining cars during the out-of-town trips the team made. He was a terrible eater, but never knew what to order, as he couldn't read the menus. He'd wait for us to order and then say, 'I'll take the same.' When we knew he was starving we'd wait till he was seated at the table and then decide not to order anything."

The Birth of Jack Keefe

Out of this voracious, illiterate alibi artist grew Jack Keefe, composer of the "You Know Me, Al" letters which Lardner began sending to "The Saturday Evening Post" in 1914 at the suggestion of the late Charles E. Van Loan. The series took the country by storm and founded a new school of sports writing. For the first time in America a realistic picture of a professional athlete was drawn. Previously, sports writers had eulogized ball players as flashing-limbed young Mercuries. Lardner changed all that. In his wake grew up the new debunking school of sports criticism—the McGeehans, the Peglers, the Joe Williamses.

Lardner left "The Chicago Tribune" after the war, moved to Great Neck, and went to work for the Bell Syndicate.

There are two distinct phases in Lardner's writing. The first was devoted entirely to rather broad humor ranging from "Bib Balads" in 1915 to "Symptoms of Being Thirty-five" and "The Big Town" in 1921. The main body concerns the adventures of Jack Keefe, the White Sox pitcher, and his wife, Florrie, as recounted in the delightfully analphabetic epistles to Al. Other books of this period, all collections of the author's magazine work, are "You Know Me Al" (1915), "Gullible's Travels" and "Own Your Own Home" (1917), "Treat 'Em Rough," "The Real Dope" and "My Four Weeks in France" (1918) and "The Young Immigrunts" (1919).

Put in Ranks of the Great

Lardner achieved tremendous popularity. At the Democratic convention of 1920 in San Francisco the Missouri delegation cast one-half vote for him. Carl Van Doren in an essay written at this time pointed out that Lardner was perhaps the only writer for the popular magazines whose productions were uniformly excellent. Dr. Van Doren was somewhat amazed that Lardner never wrote trash. Gilbert Seldes in "The Seven Lively Arts" discussed him from an esthetic standpoint.

It was not until 1924, however, when "How to Write Short Stories," another collection of magazine pieces, was published, that critics realized that Lardner was not only an excellent humorist, but a great writer of short stories. This book and "The Love Nest," brought out two years later, established him as one of the foremost artists of our time. Some of the stories in these two books, notably "Haircut," "Champion," "The Golden Honeymoon," "Some Like Them Cold" and "My Roomy," have become classics.

A new bitterness seemed to have come over the Lardner of the later phase. The late William Bolitho wrote of him: "Ring Lardner, commonly referred to as a humorist, is the greatest and sincerest pessimist America has produced." Many critics pointed out, however, that while Lardner etched bores, morons and swine his acid was tinctured with a great pity.

In 1929 the "Roundup"

During this second phase of his work, the bitter short stories were interspersed with pieces of nonsense so wild, so cacknevey and so funny that to read them made the body protest in pain. There was a series of dadaistic plays—"I Gaspiri, or The Upholsterers," (translated from the Bukovinian by Caspar

Redmonds), "The Tridget of Greva," and "Cora, or Fun at the Spa," and "Clemo Uti, the Waterlilies" that were dangerous to have about the house. There was a series of burlesqued bedtime stories written when the idea was new but still mightily amusing. And there was that epitome of low comedy, "The Story of a Wonder Man" which came out in 1927 and will remain the most deliciously crazy work for a long time to come.

In that amazing autobiographical work the author tells how he was born in Niles, Mich., during Have-a-Baby Week, how he [was] once a sports writer for "The Rabies" and interview[ed] Paul Whelton, the inventor of straw; how he later become one of the show places of Long Island; and how he was the Don Juan of his day and carried on with such belles as Livid Taylor, Emma Geezle, Dolly Madison, Jane Austen and the Laplander, Hugga Mugga.

In 1929 all of his short stories were collected in one volume under the title of "Roundup." The work achieved nation-wide critical acclaim, and was a Literary Guild selection. That same year, "June Moon," a comedy written with George S. Kauffman, was produced and enjoyed a long run. "Elmer the Great," a play about a ball player, on which George M. Cohan collaborated, had been produced two years earlier. Lardner also wrote a number of musical comedy skits, furnishing many for several editions of the Ziegfeld "Follies."

Only One Known Enemy

Personally, Ring Lardner was one of the most beloved men who ever worked on a newspaper or wrote for a magazine. The only enemy he was known to have had was a clerk in the municipal clerk's office in Chicago. After he had moved to New York, Lardner wrote that when he was in Chicago he always took a room in the Hotel Sherman, which enabled him to look on the City-County Building so that he could see "how the other half lives." The clerk became angry and issued a capias for Lardner's arrest for the alleged failure to pay a $50 fine for speeding six years previously.

Lardner's generosity was proverbial, and when he achieved affluence he continually spent large sums backing unsuccessful plays and musical comedies written by his friends, paying for the education of struggling musicians, and helping out almost any one who approached him.

For so successful a writer he was astoundingly modest. The praises of the highbrow critics always made him feel rather uncomfortable.

"It may shock Mr. Lardner," one wrote, "to know that he has done in little what Mr. Joyce has done on a grand scale in 'Ulysses.'"

To which the reply was:

"The reason Joyce or anyone takes more space than I do is because they aren't half so lazy. I haven't read 'Ulysses' because some one discouraged me by saying it was too long or too expensive. I forget which. It must be fun to be suppressed, because then one wouldn't have to work. None of my writing is fun to do except nutty things."

But much as he loathed the sweat of writing, he was successful from the start; the very first "You Know Me Al" letters were snapped up by "The Saturday Evening Post." The only unsaleable piece he ever wrote for a magazine was one ordered by the late John Siddall, author of "The American Magazine," which at the time specialized in "success" stories. As he had not conveniently come up from the gutter, Lardner decided that he would write on "My Success as a Song Writer." Computing his time as worth 10 cents an hour, he figured that he had lost something like $4,300 in attempting to compose songs. Siddall, however, couldn't understand the story and sent it back.

"The Saturday Evening Post," after Lardner had been one of its biggest authors for years, turned down "Harmony," "The Golden Honeymoon" and "Champion," but the first two were eagerly snapped up by Ray Long, then editor of "The Cosmopolitan," who signed up Lardner for his entire output of short stories.

Lardner was a member of the New York Athletic Club, the Lambs, the Friars, the Dutch Treat Club, the Players, the Coffee House Club, and the North Hempstead Country, the Soundview Golf, the Coldstream Golf and the Lakeville Golf Clubs.

* * *

COPY

We combed Fifth Avenue this last month
A hundred times if we combed it onth,
In search of something we thought would do
To give to a person as nice as you.

We had no trouble selecting gifts
For the Ogden Armours and Louie Swifts,
The Otto Kahns and the George E. Bakers,
The Munns and the Rodman Wanamakers.

It's a simple matter to pick things out
For people one isn't so wild about,
But you, you wonderful pal and friend, you!
We couldn't find anything fit to send you.

THE RING LARDNERS

Xmas 1927 or 1928
I forget which
757

A poem Lardner wrote for the Fitzgeralds
(*from* The Romantic Egoists)

Before Tender Is the Night *was published, Fitzgerald wrote this tribute to Lardner for* The New Republic; *it was collected in* The Crack-Up *(1945).*

Ring
F. Scott Fitzgerald
The Crack-Up, pp. 34–40

October, 1933

For a year and a half, the writer of this appreciation was Ring Lardner's most familiar companion; after that, geography made separations and our contacts were rare. When my wife and I last saw him in 1931, he looked already like a man on his deathbed—it was terribly sad to see that six feet three inches of kindness stretched out ineffectual in the hospital room. His fingers trembled with a match, the tight skin on his handsome skull was marked as a mask of misery and nervous pain.

He gave a very different impression when we first saw him in 1921—he seemed to have an abundance of quiet vitality that would enable him to outlast anyone, to take himself for long spurts of work or play that would ruin any ordinary constitution. He had recently convulsed the country with the famous kitten-and-coat saga (it had to do with a world's series bet and with the impending conversion of some kittens into fur), and the evidence of the betting, a beautiful sable, was worn by his wife at the time. In those days he was interested in people, sports, bridge, music, the stage, the newspapers, the magazines, the books. But though I did not know it, the change in him had already begun—the impenetrable despair that dogged him for a dozen years to his death.

He had practically given up sleeping, save on short vacations deliberately consecrated to simple pleasures, most frequently golf with his friends, Grantland Rice or John Wheeler. Many a night we talked over a case of Canadian ale until bright dawn, when Ring would rise and yawn: "Well, I guess the children have left for school by this time—I might as well go home."

The woes of many people haunted him—for example, the doctor's death sentence pronounced upon Tad, the cartoonist, (who, in fact, nearly outlived Ring)—it was as if he believed he could and ought to do something about such things. And as he struggled to fulfill his contracts, one of which, a comic strip based on the character of "the busher," was a terror, indeed, it was obvious that he felt his work to be directionless, merely "copy." So he was inclined to turn his cosmic sense of responsibility into the channel of solving other people's problems—finding someone an introduction to a theatrical manager, placing a friend in a job, maneuvering a man into a golf club. The effort made was

Ring Lardner with his wife, Ellis

often out of proportion to the situation; the truth back of it was that Ring was getting off—he was a faithful and conscientious workman to the end, but he had stopped finding any fun in his work ten years before he died.

About that time (1922) a publisher undertook to reissue his old books and collect his recent stories and this gave him a sense of existing in the literary world as well as with the public, and he got some satisfaction from the reiterated statements of Mencken and F. P. A. as to his true stature as a writer. But I don't think he cared then—it is hard to understand but I don't think he really gave a damn about anything except his personal relations with a few people. A case in point was his attitude to those imitators who lifted everything except the shirt off his back—only Hemingway has been so thoroughly frisked—it worried the imitators more than it worried Ring. His attitude was that if they got stuck in the process he'd help them over any tough place.

Throughout this period of huge earnings and an increasingly solid reputation on top and beneath, there were two ambitions more important to Ring than the work by which he will be remembered; he wanted to be a musician—sometimes he dramatized himself ironically as a thwarted composer—and he wanted to write shows. His dealings with managers would make a whole story: they were always commissioning him to do work which they promptly forgot they had ordered, and accepting librettos that they never produced. (Ring left a short ironic record of Ziegfeld.) Only with the aid of the practical George Kaufman did he achieve his ambition, and by then he was too far gone in illness to get a proper satisfaction from it.

The point of these paragraphs is that, whatever Ring's achievement was, it fell short of the achievement he was capable of, and this because of a cynical attitude toward his work. How far back did that attitude go?—back to his youth in a Michigan village? Certainly back to his days with the Cubs. During those years, when most men of promise achieve an adult education, if only in the school of war, Ring moved in the company of a few dozen illiterates playing a boy's game. A boy's game, with no more possibilities in it than a boy could master, a game bounded by walls which kept out novelty or danger, change or adventure. This material, the observation of it under such circumstances, was the text of Ring's schooling during the most formative period of the mind. A writer can spin on about his adventures after thirty, after forty, after fifty, but the criteria by which these adventures are weighed and valued are irrevocably settled at the age of twenty-five. However deeply Ring might cut into it, his cake had exactly the diameter of Frank Chance's diamond.

Here was his artistic problem, and it promised future trouble. So long as he wrote within that enclosure the result was magnificent: within it he heard and recorded the voice of a continent. But when, inevitably, he outgrew his interest in it, what was Ring left with?

He was left with his fine linguistic technique—and he was left rather helpless in those few acres. He had been formed by the very world on which his hilarious irony had released itself. He had fought his way through to knowing what people's motives are and what means they are likely to resort to in order to attain their goals. But now he had a new problem—what to do about it. He went on seeing, and the sights traveled back to the optic nerve, but no longer to be thrown off in fiction, because they were no longer sights that could be weighed and valued by the old criteria. It was never that he was completely sold on athletic virtuosity as the be-all and end-all of problems; the trouble was that he could find nothing finer. Imagine life conceived as a business of beautiful muscular organization—an arising, an effort, a good break, a sweat, a bath, a meal, a love, a sleep—imagine it achieved; then imagine trying to apply that standard to the horrible complicated mess of living, where nothing, even the greatest conceptions and workings and achievements, is else but messy, spotty, tortuous—and then one can imagine the confusion that Ring faced on coming out of the ball park.

He kept on recording but he no longer projected, and this accumulation, which he has taken with him to the grave, crippled his spirit in the latter years. It was not the fear of Niles, Michigan, that hampered him—it was the habit of silence, formed in the presence of the "ivory" with which he lived and worked. Remember it was not humble ivory—Ring has demonstrated that—it was arrogant, imperative, often megalomaniacal ivory. He got the habit of silence, then the habit of repression that finally took the form of his odd little crusade in the *New Yorker* against pornographic songs. He had agreed with himself to speak only a small portion of his mind.

The present writer once suggested to him that he organize some *cadre* within which he could adequately display his talents, suggesting that it should be something deeply personal, and something on which Ring could take his time, but he dismissed the idea lightly; he was a disillusioned idealist but he had served his Fates well, and no other ones could be casually created for him—"This is something that can be printed," he reasoned; "this, however, belongs with that bunch of stuff that can never be written."

He covered himself in such cases with protests of his inability to bring off anything big, but this was specious, for he was proud man and had no reason to rate his abilities cheaply. He refused to "tell all" because in a crucial period of his life he had formed the habit of not doing it—and this he had elevated gradually into a standard of taste. It never satisfied him by a damn sight.

So one is haunted not only by a sense of personal loss but by a conviction that Ring got less percentage of himself on paper than any other American of the first flight. There is *"You Know Me, Al,"* and there are about a dozen wonderful short stories (my God, he hadn't even saved them—the material of *How to Write Short Stories* was obtained by photographing old issues in the public library!), and there is some of the most uproarious and inspired nonsense since Lewis Carroll. Most of the rest is mediocre stuff, with flashes, and I would do Ring a disservice to suggest it should be set upon an altar and worshipped, as have been the most casual relics of Mark Twain. Those three volumes should seem enough—to everyone who didn't know Ring. But I venture that no one who knew him but will agree that the personality of the man overlapped it. Proud, shy, solemn, shrewd, polite, brave, kind, merciful, honorable—with the affection these qualities aroused he created in addition a certain awe in people. His intentions, his will, once in motion, were formidable factors in dealing with him–he always did every single thing he said he would do. Frequently he was the melancholy Jaques, and sad company indeed, but under any conditions a noble dignity flowed from him, so that time in his presence always seemed well spent.

On my desk, at the moment, I have the letters Ring wrote to us; here is a letter one thousand words long, here is one of two thousand words–theatrical gossip, literary shop talk, flashes of wit but not much wit, for he was feeling thin and saving the best of that for his work, anecdotes of his activities. I reprint the most typical one I can find:

"The Dutch Treat show was a week ago Friday night. Grant Rice and I had reserved a table, and a table holds ten people and no more. Well, I had invited, as one guest, Jerry Kern, but he telephoned at the last moment that he couldn't come. I then consulted with Grant Rice, who said he had no substitute in mind, but that it was a shame to waste our extra ticket when tickets were at a premium. So I called up Jones, and Jones said yes, and would it be all right for him to bring along a former Senator who was a pal of his and had been good to him in Washington. I said I was sorry, but our table was filled and, besides, we didn't have an extra ticket. "Maybe I could dig up another ticket somewhere," said Jones. "I don't believe so," I said, "but anyway the point is that we haven't room at our table." "Well," said Jones, "I could have the Senator eat somewhere else and join us in time for the show." "Yes," I said, "but we have no ticket for him." "Well, I'll think up something," he said. Well, what he thought up was to bring himself and the Senator and I had a hell a time getting an extra ticket and shoving the Senator in at another table where he wasn't wanted, and later in the evening, the Senator thanked Jones and said he was the greatest fella in the world and all I got was goodnight.

"Well, I must close and nibble on a carrot. R.W.L."

Even in a telegram Ring could compress a lot of himself. Here is one: WHEN ARE YOU COMING BACK AND WHY PLEASE ANSWER   RING LARDNER

This is not the moment to recollect Ring's convivial aspects, especially as he had, long before his death, ceased to find amusement in dissipation, or indeed in the whole range of what is called entertainment–save for his perennial interest in songs. By grace of the radio and of the many musicians who, drawn by his enormous magnetism, made pilgrimages to his bedside, he had a consolation in the last days, and he made the most of it, hilariously rewriting Cole Porter's lyrics in the *New Yorker*. But it would be an evasion for the present writer not to say that when he was Ring's neighbor a decade ago, they tucked a lot under their belts in many weathers, and spent many words on many men and things. At no time did I feel that I had known him enough, or that anyone knew him–it was not the feeling that there was more stuff in him and that it should come out, it was rather a qualitative difference, it was rather as

though, due to some inadequacy in one's self, one had not penetrated to something unsolved, new and unsaid. That is why one wishes that Ring had written down a larger proportion of what was in his mind and heart. It would have saved him longer for us, and that in itself would be something. But I would like to know what it was, and now I will go on wishing–what did Ring want, how did he want things to be, how did he think things were?

A great and good American is dead. Let us not obscure him by the flowers, but walk up and look at that fine medallion, all abraded by sorrows that perhaps we are not equipped to understand. Ring made no enemies, because he was kind, and to many millions he gave release and delight.

Abe North's Day in the Ritz Bar

One of the three substantial cuts Fitzgerald made between the text of his novel published as a serial in Scribner's Magazine and its publication in book form was an extended account of Abe North's experiences in the Ritz Bar. The revised version of this episode became chapter 23 of Book I.

The famous Paul, master of ceremonies, had not arrived, but Claude, who was checking stock, broke off his work with no improper surprise to make Abe a pick-me-up. Abe sat on a bench against a wall and examined the empty room more thoroughly than ever he had before–the faded rose carpet, the olive frame of a great mirror, the green upholstery, the yellow pillars matching the yellow walls, the clock, disregarded now as it ticked away the morning.

The drink Claude served him was a "Dashdeller," invented one day, years ago, for himself and Herman Dashdeller–it consisted of a jigger of gin shaken up with a jigger of cuantro with the addition of minor perfumes and charged water. Abe took two of them and began to feel better–so much better that he mounted to the barber's shop and was shaved. When he returned to the bar Paul had arrived–in his custom-built car, from which he had disembarked correctly at the Boulevard des Capucines. Paul like Abe and came over to talk. . . .

Other clients had meanwhile drifted in to the bar: first came a huge Dane whom Abe had somewhere encountered. The Dane took a seat across the room, and Abe guessed he would be there all the day, drinking, lunching, talking or reading newspapers. He felt a desire to out-stay him.

The Ritz Hotel (white awnings) in the Place Vendome, Paris

It was eleven and the college boys had begun to drift in, stepping gingerly lest they tear one another bag from bag—Abe saw Collis Clay among them.

He watched Collis's conduct with amusement: Collis strode to the bar looking neither to left nor to right; he commanded a drink, and only then did he turn to search the room for friends. Out of the corner of his eye, he perceived Abe, but apparently decided that he did not know him well enough to come over; however an equivalent young man, who had entered with equivalent caution, was recognized as a pal, and with diffidence forgotten and confidence restored the pair of them sat down in the centre of the room—even bawled for a prominent barman to come and shake dice with them.

Many people were entering now. Meanwhile Abe was kept busy inventing excuses for the chasseur as to why he could not go to the phone to answer calls from a Mr. Crawshaw. Then he had the chasseur telephone to the Divers; by the time he was in touch with them he was in touch also with other friends—was feeling the bite of the "Dash-dellers." His hunch was to put them all on the phone at once—the result was somewhat general. From time to time his mind reverted to the fact that he ought to go over and get Freeman out of jail but he shook off all facts as parts of the nightmare.

By one o'clock the bar was jammed; there were coteries of alcoholics, journalists, South Americans, innumerable collegians, a sprinkling of sponges; every table was occupied—clients stood in double ranks at the bar. An American gossip sheet was hawked through the room, but before the vender had completed his round, he was knifing through sardines; amidst the consequent mixture of voices the staff of waiters functioned, pinning down their clients to the facts of drink and money.

"That makes two stingers . . . and one more . . . two martinis and one . . . nothing for you, Mr. Quarterly . . . that makes three rounds. That makes seventy-five francs, Mr. Quarterly. Mr. Schaeffer said he had this—you had the last . . . I can only do what you say . . . thanks vera-much."

In the confusion Abe had lost his seat; now he stood gently swaying and talking to some of the peo-

The Ritz Bar (photo on left, Agence France-Presse), where Abe North prolongs
"his state of irresponsibility" (p. 133)

ple with whom he had involved himself. A terrier ran a leash around his legs but Abe managed to extricate himself without upsetting and became the recipient of profuse apologies. Presently he was invited to lunch, but declined. It was almost Briglith, he explained, and there was something he had to do at Briglith. A little later, with the exquisite manners of the alcoholic that are like the manners of a prisoner or a family servant, he said good-bye to an acquaintance, and turning around discovered that the bar's great moment was over as precipitately as it had begun.

Across from him the Dane and his companions had ordered luncheon. Abe followed the pattern except that he paid his check. After lunch—that he scarcely touched, though he envied the appetite of the correspondent Scandinavian—he watched the preparations for the afternoon. The glasses for champagne cocktails were banked in battalions on the bar—a majority of them destined for the women's side across the hall. At three-thirty the staff would begin to fill these glasses; a hundred could be served while another hundred was made up. The barman serving the women's side had an extraordinary face—hard and handsome.

Drifters came in the off hours, two to four, and there were a few business meetings. The Dane sat alone with his paper, deserted, speaking only to the waiters. Abe had not a paper; he sat, and each time he found a glass empty before him he ordered a new drink concocted from a brandy base that he called "L'Elixir Aux Nids d'Irondell." He was happy living in the past. The drink made past happy things contemporary with the present, as if they were still going on, contemporary even with the future as if they were about to happen again. . . .

He had been absent an hour, and during that time a change had taken place; the chatter from the women's side now reached out to the Rue Cambon, it roared into Abe's ears in the hall—and as he turned into the men's bar, he came upon its very personification: a woman, half concealed by the protecting screen, stood looking uncertainly toward the jam of males and wobbling an unconfident finger at it. She was conscious of being out of place; she could see the coldly disgusted looks in such eyes as she managed to meet; yet she was not able to muster the grace to quit. Only Claude's loud "Excuse *me!*" as he passed her with a tray served to discourage her—by the time Abe had collapsed on a bench she was gone.

A man had entered in a battered derby with a cane improvised from wire and was playing Charlie Chaplin; Paul gave orders that he was not to be served. After another pair of "Elixirs" Abe himself was in shining shape; he told his next companions

Ashtrays from the Ritz (Bruccoli Collection of Fitzgerald, Thomas Cooper Library, University of South Carolina)

an Odyssean version of how he had missed his ship. He was not having a good time but across the room his Danish antagonist was at his mellowest, telling stories and snickering aloud at them exactly as if he were a real person, instead of Hamlet's father in a few short minutes that approximated life.

A little before seven began the drift away. The chasseur was constantly on the telephone making last-minute engagements or consoling deserted wives. The blue, brown and slate had faded from the picture, and the tone was black and white. There was no further noise across the hall. The Dane, once more alone, had ordered dinner—a certain relation had sprung up between them, including some petulance on the part of the Dane about Abe's staying so long without even a newspaper. The Dane had read parts of his own newspapers many time over.

Abe North's Death

From "Bennett Cerf's Fan Letter on Tender Is the Night*: A Source for Abe North's Death":*

One of the documents F. Scott Fitzgerald preserved in his *Tender Is the Night* scrapbook is an undated 1934 letter from Bennett Cerf to Maxwell Perkins, which reads in part: " 'Tender Is the Night' is a haunting book, + reastablishes Fitzgerald, I think, way up there among the stars. I found the end so distressing that it's been bothering me for two days. Felt I knew Dick Diver personally, + the spectacle of that gal sucking all the insides from him, + then tossing off the empty skin pained me deep down. The book is so packed with incidents that I keep recalling them all the time."

Cerf's letter goes on to offer sources for characters and events in the novel, noting that a "chap named Winant" died at the Princeton Club after a speakeasy brawl. In *Tender* Abe North is "'beaten to death in a speakeasy in New York. He just managed to crawl home to the Racquet Club to die—' " (pp. 259–260).

The 4 May 1928 *New York Times* carried the report that Cornelius R. Winant, Princeton, '18, died in the Princeton Club. Winant was believed to have been beaten in a speakeasy before reaching the club. The autopsy assigned his death to a hemorrhage and alcoholism. As a member of the classes of 1917 and 1918, Fitzgerald would have known Winant.

—Fitzgerald/Hemingway Annual 1979,
pp. 229–230

At eight an American came in, looked at Abe, and then at the Dane, and took a table as far as possible removed from either. When, presently, another man joined him he arose and bowed. The acoustics were such that Abe overheard the beginning of the conversation:

"I asked you to meet me here because—"

"Cut out the preliminaries. What's it all about?" "Just this—I'll mix it up with you anywhere, at any time, with any weapons. But I didn't like it last night."

"Well, why didn't you say?"

"I'm not standing it any more. What you and Nancy do is—"

They saw simultaneously that they were overheard and their voices dropped back into obscurity.

It was dull in the bar—a few men in evening clothes came in wanting quick cocktails. Even the Dane was demanding a check, which he signed, and joked meanwhile with a not especially receptive waiter. He gave Abe a viking stare as he went out; after a few minutes Abe tried to leave but his legs would not support him, so he settled as inconspicuously as he could in the corner of his bench and fell asleep. Paul had long departed. The room was again a faded rose and two yellow pillars matching the walls. The one attendant was in the service room adjoining, so Abe was alone.

Paris

From the beginning of his work on the Melarky version Fitzgerald intended to use Paris as one of the settings of his novel. In the following excerpt a French scholar examines Fitzgerald's use of the city in his stories and in Tender Is the Night.

Fitzgerald in Paris
André Le Vot
Fitzgerald/Hemingway Annual 1973, pp. 49, 64–65, 66

During a span of ten years, from his first brief visit to Europe in May 1921 to the moment he left for good in September 1931, Fitzgerald lived for about four and a half years abroad, out of which three years were spent in France—two-thirds of which, roughly twenty-two months, in Paris, the same amount of time he spent in the States during the seven years between 1924 and 1931.

. . . .

This brings us to the question of the extent to which the streets and the monuments, the mood and the atmosphere of Paris play a part in Fitzgerald's work. That he was familiar with the city is obvious, with the Right Bank and the Left Bank alike. First the Murphys, then many others served as knowledgable guides to the places of interest. He became a famous figure at the Ritz, place Vendôme, and the near-by Crillon, place de la Concorde. The head barman of the Ritz, Frank, who died in 1957 and was replaced by George, a bell-boy in the twenties, seems to have remembered him well, whatever Hemingway may say about being the *one* who was never forgotten. He was also on familiar terms with Julien at Ciro's, on the Champs-Elyseés. Not long ago Maurice, Julien's brother, could show the small back room which was his favorite dining place. Another restaurant, Voisin, near the Smith bookstore, was also a favorite and appears in *Tender*. In Montmartre he would haunt Zelli's, rue Fontaine, which was the meeting place of the American journalists, or Bricktop's with its black performers, or le Perroquet, on the first floor next to the Casino de Paris. Those were the show places but he also knew the small bistros of the Left Bank where he would spend hours with Chamson, or the famous cafés of Montparnasse, le Dôme, la Coupole, le Select.

Still very little of this inside knowledge appears in his fiction. Some fifty pages in *Tender in the Night* and a handful of stories, among which only three, "The Bridal Party," written in May 1929, "Babylon," written in December 1930, and "News of Paris, Fifteen Years Ago," written in 1940, have Paris exclusively as a background. To these we may add the beginning of "The Swimmers" (written in July 1929), the end of "One Trip Abroad" (August 1930), a few scenes in "A New Leaf" (April 1931), "The Intimate Strangers" (June 1935), "A Penny Spent" (July 1925), "Not in the Guide Book" (February 1925).

In the stories specifically devoted to Paris, the atmosphere is wonderfully evocative, the various moments of the day, the quality of the light, the charm of twilight on the old monuments, all that recaptures with felicity the immediacy of the there and the now. One sentence out of "A Penny Spent" will illustrate that intense poetical feeling for the city: "One thing is certain—that before you melt out into the green-and-cream Paris twilight you will have the feel of standing for a moment at one of the predestined centers of the world."

His topography is practically faultless and I have been able to find only one little mistake. In the story "The Swimmers," and in *Tender* at the beginning of the description of the party in which Dick and Rosemary encounter the lesbians, the places are described in about the same terms, which cannot apply to the street where they are set, rue Monsieur. In the first instance: "Home was fine high-ceiling apartment hewn from the palace of a Renaissance cardinal in the Rue Monsieur"; in the second case: "It was

*Fitzgerald, Scottie, and Zelda on shipboard, 1927 or 1928 (Bruccoli Collection of Fitzgerald,
Thomas Cooper Library, University of South Carolina)*

a house hewn from the frame of Cardinal de Retz's palace in the Rue Monsieur . . ." Now rue Monsieur is part of the Faubourg St Germain which was built in the eighteenth century; at the time of the Renaissance there were only fields belonging to the Abbaye and the University. And of course the Cardinal de Retz lived in the seventeenth century. Fitzgerald who certainly was familiar with the area (Michael Arlen's apartment was a hundred yards from the rue Monsieur, 11 rue Masseran, on the other side of the Boulevard des Invalides) may have thought of the Hôtel de St. Simon, nº 3, or the small "folie" at nº 7 where Paul Bourget, whom he knew, lived for a long time. But both are definitely eighteenth century buildings.

. . . .

The picture Fitzgerald has given of Paris is a true and precise one, although limited in scope, and dealing chiefly with the international set. Nothing in it is evocative of the French problems or the French way of life. If it uses a true fact from the chronicle of the Twenties, such as the murder in the Gare St. Lazare which appears in *Tender,* it is sure to be a *fait divers* dealing with the only types of people he was bound to meet and to know: in that case the actual shooting of an Englishman, Raymond de Trafford, by his American mistress, the Countess de Janze. The deceptively French-sounding names are in a way here symbolic of the thin disguise under which Anglo-Saxon attitudes asserted themselves in a city which was nothing but a dream setting for compulsions and passions born elsewhere.

This city might just as well have been London or Rome, a mere backdrop for Fitzgerald's imagination, a stimulus for his sensibility, playing the role New York had played from 1922 to 1924 before he came to France. With the difference perhaps that, just as was the case for some other exiles, it possessed some quality of freedom and excitement which had been blunted in the native country.

* * *

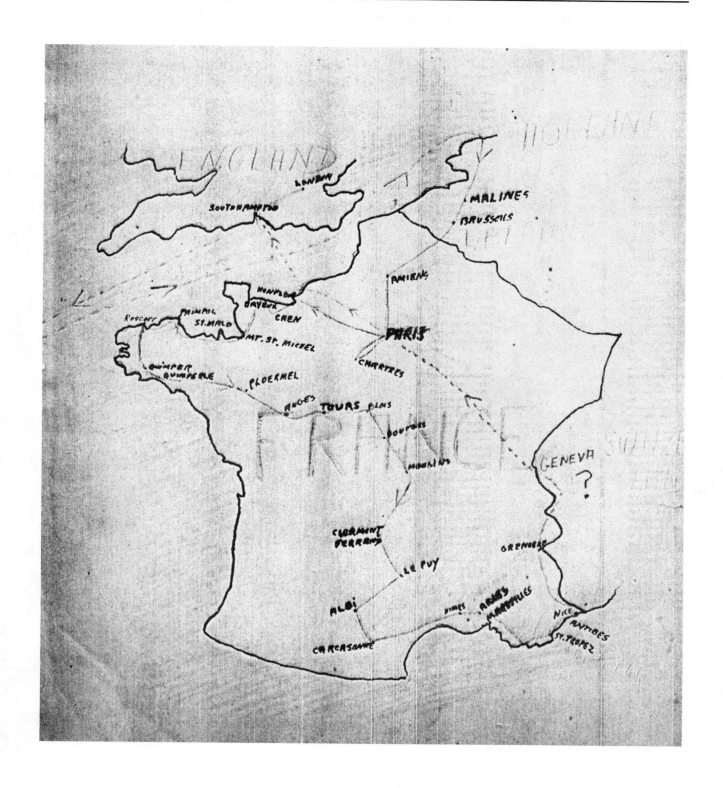

Map drawn by Fitzgerald for his daughter (Bruccoli Collection of Fitzgerald,
Thomas Cooper Library, University of South Carolina)

Exposition des Arts Décoratifs

ILLUMINATIONS DE LA TOUR EIFFEL exécutées et animées par LES ETABL^{nts} JACOPOZZI

The Eiffel Tower illuminated for the 1925 Art Deco exposition, mentioned in chapter 14 of Book I: "When they reached Paris Nicole was too tired to go on to the grand illumination at the Decorative Arts Exposition as they had planned" (p. 79).

In the following excerpts from Where Paris Dines *(1929), Julian Street discusses two of the establishments referenced in* Tender Is the Night. *Voisin, which Fitzgerald describes in chapter 12 of Book I, is the first Paris setting in the novel.*

Voisin
261 Rue St. Honoré

FOR more years than are covered by my memories of Paris, the Restaurant Voisin, at the corner of the Rue St. Honoré and Rue Cambon, has stood as an example of all that an ancient and aristocratic Parisian restaurant should be. Established in 1813, in a building belonging to a convent, the grounds of which formerly occupied the entire neighbourhood,

it has never moved from its location, and had, until 1926, changed hands but twice. In that year, however, Monsieur Braquessac, long and widely known as its proprietor, died at the age of eighty-two, and the restaurant has since been conducted by his nephew.

. . . .

However matters may have stood forty-odd years ago, there exists in Paris to-day no restaurant building more redolent than Voisin's of old times and old traditions. Its panelled rooms are distinguished by an air of the most extreme simplicity, its cuisine and cellars are famous, so are its private dining rooms, and so are its high prices.

. . . .

Voisin's has long been known as a rendezvous of the French nobility, of diplomats, and of gourmets and amateurs of wine from all over the world. Its cuisine is impeccable, and its cellars are the best in Paris, including, as they do, practically all the greatest wines of France in all their greatest years. Certain wines can be had at Voisin's which are elsewhere unobtainable, among them rare old Château d'Yquem in magnums which cost a fortune and are worth it, just as a Leonardo or Stradivarius is worth whatever it may cost.

* * *

In chapter 21 of Book II the Divers walk "into a warm strident Paris night, snatching a vermouth and bitters in the shadow by Fouquet's bar" (p. 124).

Fouquet
99 Avenue des Champs Elysées

SITUATED on the second floor, above a pleasant café-bar where amusing people meet at the sad hour of the afternoon to cheer themselves, Fouquet's dining rooms, with their yellow panelled walls, yellow silk curtains, and agreeable lighting, have an air at once intimate and smart.

The clientele of the place is diverting. A sedate old French couple will be dining at one table, Americans at the next, South Americans beyond them, and throughout the room, in the racing season, will be sporting men with their pretty and vivacious feminine companions chatting gaily back and forth.

Published Weekly

The Curtis Publishing Company

Cyrus H. K. Curtis, President

George H. Lorimer, First Vice-President
John B. Williams, Second Vice-President
Walter D. Fuller, Second Vice-President
and Secretary, Philip S. Collins, Second
Vice-President and Treasurer
Fred A. Healy, Second Vice-President
and Advertising Director

Independence Square, Philadelphia

THE SATURDAY EVENING POST

Founded A°D¹ 1728 *by* Benj. Franklin

Copyright 1931, by The Curtis Publishing Company in the United States and Great Britain. Title Registered in U.S. Patent Office and in Foreign Countries. Entered as Second-Class Matter at the Post-Office Department, Ottawa, Can.

George Horace Lorimer
EDITOR

Thomas B. Costain, A. W. Neall,
Wesley Stout, B. Y. Riddell,
Merritt Hulburd, W. Thornton Martin,
Associate Editors

Entered as Second-Class Matter, November 18, 1879, at the Post Office at Philadelphia, Under Act of March 3, 1879. Additional Entry at Columbus, O., St. Louis, Mo., Chicago, Ill., Indianapolis, Ind., Saginaw, Mich., Des Moines, Ia., Portland, Ore., Milwaukee, Wis., St. Paul, Minn., San Francisco, Cal., Kansas City, Mo., Savannah, Ga., Denver, Colo., Louisville, Ky., Houston, Tex., Omaha, Neb., Ogden, Utah, Jacksonville, Fla., New Orleans, La., Portland, Me., and Los Angeles, Cal.

Volume 203   5c. THE COPY   PHILADELPHIA, P.A., FEBRUARY 21, 1931 $2.00 By Subscription (52 issues)   Number 34

BABYLON REVISITED

By F. SCOTT FITZGERALD

ILLUSTRATED BY HENRIETTA McCAIG STARRETT

*"But You Won't Always Like Me Best, Honey. You'll Grow
Up and Meet Somebody Your Own Age and Go Marry Him and Forget You Ever Had a Daddy"*

"AND where's Mr. Campbell?" Charlie asked.

"Gone to Switzerland. Mr. Campbell's a pretty sick man, Mr. Wales."

"I'm sorry to hear that. And George Hardt?" Charlie inquired.

"Back in America, gone to work."

"And where is the snow bird?"

"He was in here last week. Anyway, his friend, Mr. Schaeffer, is in Paris."

Two familiar names from the long list of a year and a half ago. Charlie scribbled an address in his notebook and tore out the page.

"If you see Mr. Schaeffer, give him this," he said. "It's my brother-in-law's address. I haven't settled on a hotel yet."

He was not really disappointed to find Paris was so empty. But the stillness in the bar was strange, almost portentous.

It was not an American bar any more—he felt polite in it, and not as if he owned it. It had gone back into France. He had felt the stillness from the moment he got out of the taxi and saw the doorman, usually in a frenzy of activity at this hour, gossiping with a *chasseur* by the servants' entrance.

Passing through the corridor, he heard only a single, bored voice in the once-clamorous women's room. When he turned into the bar he traveled the twenty feet of green carpet with his eyes fixed straight ahead by old habit; and then, with his foot firmly on the rail, he turned and surveyed the room, encountering only a single pair of eyes that fluttered up from a newspaper in the corner. Charlie asked for the head barman, Paul, who in the latter days of the bull market had come to work in his own custom-built car—disembarking, however, with due nicety at the nearest corner. But Paul

was at his country house today and Alix was giving him his information.

"No, no more. I'm going slow these days."

Alix congratulated him: "Hope you stick to it, Mr. Wales. You were going pretty strong a couple of years ago."

"I'll stick to it all right," Charlie assured him. "I've stuck to it for over a year and a half now."

"How do you find conditions in America?"

"I haven't been to America for months. I'm in business in Prague, representing a couple of concerns there. They don't know about me down there." He smiled faintly. "Remember the night of George Hardt's bachelor dinner here? . . . By the way, what's become of Claude Fessenden?"

Alix lowered his voice confidentially: "He's in Paris, but he doesn't come here any more. Paul doesn't allow it. He ran up a bill of thirty thousand francs, charging all his drinks and his lunches, and usually his dinner, for more than a year. And when Paul finally told him he had to pay, he gave him a bad check."

Alix pressed his lips together and shook his head.

"I don't understand it, such a dandy fellow. Now he's all bloated up ——" He made a plump apple of his hands.

A thin world, resting on a common weakness, shredded away now like tissue paper. Turning, Charlie saw a group of effeminate young men installing themselves in a corner.

"Nothing affects them," he thought.

"Stocks rise and fall, people loaf or work, but they go on forever." The place oppressed him. He called for the dice and shook with Alix for the drink.

"Here for long, Mr. Wales?"

"I'm here for four or five days to see my little girl."

3

First page of one of the few stories that Fitzgerald set in Paris, in which Charlie Wales returns to the city to regain custody of his daughter, Honoria (Bruccoli Collection of Fitzgerald, Thomas Cooper Library, University of South Carolina)

Morley Callaghan (from the dust jacket for his 1928 novel
Strange Fugitive; *Bruccoli Collection, Thomas*
Cooper Library, University of South Carolina)

Fitzgerald evidently transformed something of his own experience into the episode that involves Abe North and Jules Peterson, the black man who takes Abe's part in "the early morning dispute in Montparnasse."

[Peterson] had accompanied Abe to the police station and supported his assertion that a thousand-franc note had been seized out of his hand by a Negro, whose identification was one of the points of the case. Abe and Jules Peterson, accompanied by an agent of police, returned to the bistro and too hastily identified as the criminal a Negro, who, so it was established after an hour, had only entered the place after Abe left. The police had further complicated the situation by arresting the prominent Negro restaurateur, Freeman, who had only drifted through the alcoholic fog at a very early stage and then vanished. The true culprit, whose case, as reported by his friends, was that he had merely commandeered a fifty-franc note to pay for drinks that Abe had ordered, had only recently and in a somewhat sinister rôle, reappeared upon the scene.

—Tender Is the Night, p. 139

In the novel this incident leads to Peterson's murder and Nicole's relapse, revealing to Rosemary "what Violet McKisco had seen in the bathroom at Villa Diana" (p. 148).

A Recollection of Fitzgerald

The Canadian writer Morley Callaghan remembers an evening with Fitzgerald in Paris.

Scott had asked me what I had been working on, and I had told him I had taken away from Perkins some chapters of a novel. Very inferior stuff, I had decided. I didn't want to publish it. Scott had insisted I show these chapters to him. I was to call in late one particular evening. Loretto had come with me, but she wouldn't go into the Fitzgerald place. Scott might want to sit around drinking, and Zelda might want to stay up too, she said. I could tell Scott I had to meet her at the Deux Magots.

Zelda came to the door. As soon as I saw her I knew I shouldn't have been there. Pale, haggard, dark patches under her eyes, she stared at me vaguely, then tried to smile and failed. I can remember the way the overhead hall light glinted on her blond head. "Hello, Morley," she said reluctantly. I asked for Scott. Then she told me in a worried tone that she and Scott had had no sleep for twenty-four hours. Some trouble over the theft of Scott's wallet in a night club. Forget I had called, I said hastily. As she nodded gratefully and I went to go, I heard Scott's voice. "Who is it?" he called out loudly from the back of the apartment. "Who is it?" he yelled again, more insistently. Shaking my head, I would have fled. But she put out her hand, sighing wearily. No, I had better speak to him, she whispered. "It's Morley," she called. He answered firmly, "Tell him to come in."

It must have been a kitchen that we entered. It was impossible to look around. My eyes went straight to the table where Scott was stretched out naked except for his shorts; a French maid was rubbing his legs and kneading the muscles gently with practiced fingers. "Hello," he said, turning his head, but remaining prostrate. "Sit down," and he half groaned. I stared at him as Zelda did, standing beside me. She had a deep perplexed frown. Her obvious anguish made me hesitate to sit down. I thought Scott was drunk. "I'll just pick up that manuscript," I said soothingly. "I'll see you tomorrow, Scott." "No. I'll give it to you myself," he said. But he didn't move. Again he groaned wearily. Then I saw that he wasn't drunk; he was half numb with exhaustion. The nerves in his legs kept twitching. He told me what had happened.

Years later, I realized that I had walked in on the aftermath of the scene he wrote about in *Tender Is the Night*. Last night he had been in a night club, he said. His wallet had been stolen. He had accused a Negro, the wrong Negro, and the police had come; there had been a humiliating scene, then long hours of police interrogation as he tried to undo his false accusation yet prove his wallet had actually been stolen. The accused man and his friends had turned ugly. Dawn had come. The questioning, the effort to make an adjustment, had gone on, and he had despaired of ever getting out of the humiliating dilemma. Just an hour ago he had got home, having had no sleep. He was so exhausted he could hardly move.

—That Summer in Paris, pp. 190–192

Rome

Rome was the setting for what might have been Fitzgerald's first writing on his novel, the episode of the Francis Melarky beating by police, which Fitzgerald initially wrote as a prologue. In Tender Is the Night *the episode became the last two chapters of Book II.*

The Hotel Quirinale, where Dick Diver and Rosemary Hoyt consummate their affair

Hotel Excelsior in Rome, where Baby Warren stays

After Dick is beaten by the police and jailed, Baby Warren is roused from her sleep at the Hotel Excelsior to come to his rescue. At the end of Book II, he is treated by a doctor "whose stern manner revealed him as one of that least palpable of European types, the Latin moralist."

In his room in the Quirinale the doctor washed off the rest of the blood and the oily sweat, set his nose, his fractured ribs and fingers, disinfected the smaller wounds and put a hopeful dressing on the eye. Dick asked for a quarter of a grain of morphine, for he was still wide awake and full of nervous energy. With the morphine he fell asleep; the doctor and Collis left and Baby waited with him until a woman could arrive from the English nursing home. It had been a hard night but she had the satisfaction of feeling that, whatever Dick's previous record was, they now possessed a moral superiority over him for as long as he proved of any use.

—Tender Is the Night, p. 306

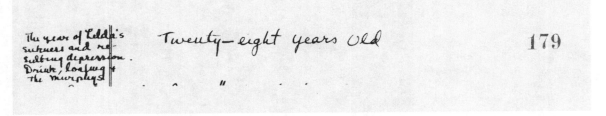

Fitzgerald's summation of the September 1924–September 1925 year, from his Ledger

The Murphys and the Riviera

Fitzgerald's first mention of Gerald and Sara Murphy is a Ledger *entry for August 1924, although they could have met as early as May in Paris. Gerald's sister Esther, whom the Fitzgeralds had known in America, or Donald Ogden Stewart, who had met the Murphys in Paris in 1923, probably provided the introduction. Critic Gilbert Seldes and his wife, on the Riviera during their wedding trip in August, in 1924, visited the Fitzgeralds and the Murphys, who were staying at Cap d'Antibes, thirty miles east of Valescure. The Murphys became the Fitzgeralds' cherished friends in France and remained devoted to them.*

Gerald and Sara Murphy were an American couple of independent means who had determined to make an art of life, taking for their motto the Spanish saying "Living well is the best revenge." Gerald was the son of the owner of the Mark Cross luxury leather-goods store; Sara was one of the admired Wiborg sisters from Cincinnati, daughters of a wealthy ink manufacturer. Gerald had graduated from Yale in 1912—where he had been tapped for the Skull and Bones senior society—and had worked in the family business, which he hated. Sara had spent much of her childhood touring Europe with her mother and had been presented at the Court of St. James in 1914. They were married in 1915. After Gerald was discharged from the army (he was trained as a pilot but never got overseas), the Murphys decided to make a break with American commercial life and family pressures. He studied landscape architecture at Harvard, and in 1921 they settled in France with their three children to live well.

Eight years older than Fitzgerald, Gerald was handsome, witty, and charming. Sara matched his intelligence and was direct in her speech. Although the Murphys lived in luxury, with great originality and impeccable taste, they were not big rich. Gerald invaded his capital to maintain their good life, and Sara's income was $7,000 a year. Their houses in Paris and at Cap d'Antibes were beautifully furnished and run by competent servants. Both of the Murphys were seriously interested in the arts. They studied painting with Natalie Goncharova and were active supporters of the Russian and Swedish ballets in Paris. Their close friends included Pablo Picasso, Philip Barry, Cole Porter, John Dos Passos, Archibald MacLeish, and Fernand Léger. Between 1922 and 1930 Gerald Murphy completed ten paintings that combined minute detail with Cubist techniques. His first work was a large-scale arrangement of a safety razor, a fountain pen, and a matchbox; art historians have credited him with anticipating the pop art school. Fitzgerald admired Murphy's virtuosity with people and felt that their shared Irish backgrounds provided a link between them. In Tender Is the Night *he transferred Murphy's "power of arousing a fascinated and uncritical love" to Dick Diver: ". . . people believed he made special reservations about them, recognizing the proud uniqueness of their destinies, buried under the compromises of how many years."*

Gerald and Sara Murphy (courtesy of Honoria Murphy Donnelly)

Sara Murphy sunning her pearls. In Tender Is the Night, *Nicole Diver is initially described on the beach: "Her bathing suit was pulled off her shoulders and her back, a ruddy, orange brown, set off by a string of creamy pearls, shone in the sun" (p. 7, courtesy of Honoria Murphy Donnelly).*

Gerald Murphy raking the beach. Rosemary's first impression of Dick Diver is when he is "giving a quiet little performance" for his friends: "he moved gravely about with a rake, ostensibly removing gravel and meanwhile developing some esoteric burlesque held in suspension by his grave face" (p. 7; from The Romantic Egoists*).*

On the Plage de la Groupe, left to right: Dorothy Parker, Robert Benchley, Honoria Murphy, and Gerald Murphy (courtesy of Honoria Murphy Donnelly)

Murphy with Pablo Picasso (courtesy of Honoria Murphy Donnelly)

Murphy's first painting, "Razor," 1924 (Dallas Museum of Art)

Murphy's sign for his Riviera home, 1924 (Estate of the artist)

THE FITZGERALDS ON THE RIVIERA

The Fitzgeralds lived at several locations on the French Riviera between 1924 and 1929:

June–Sept. 1924: Villa Marie, Valescure, St. Raphaël

August 1925: Cap d'Antibes

March–Dec. 1926: Villa Paquita and then Villa St. Louis, Juan-les Pins

June–Sept. 1929: Villa Fleur des Bois, Cannes

Fitzgerald wrote or rewrote The Great Gatsby *at Valescure, but he was unable to make substantial progress on his next novel, which is set on the Riviera. There were many distractions and many interesting visitors including Ernest Hemingway, Charles MacArthur, Archibald MacLeish, Robert Benchley, and Dorothy Parker—most of whom were serious drinkers.*

Fitzgerald, Zelda, Scottie, and nanny (Bruccoli Collection of Fitzgerald, Thomas Cooper Library, University of South Carolina)

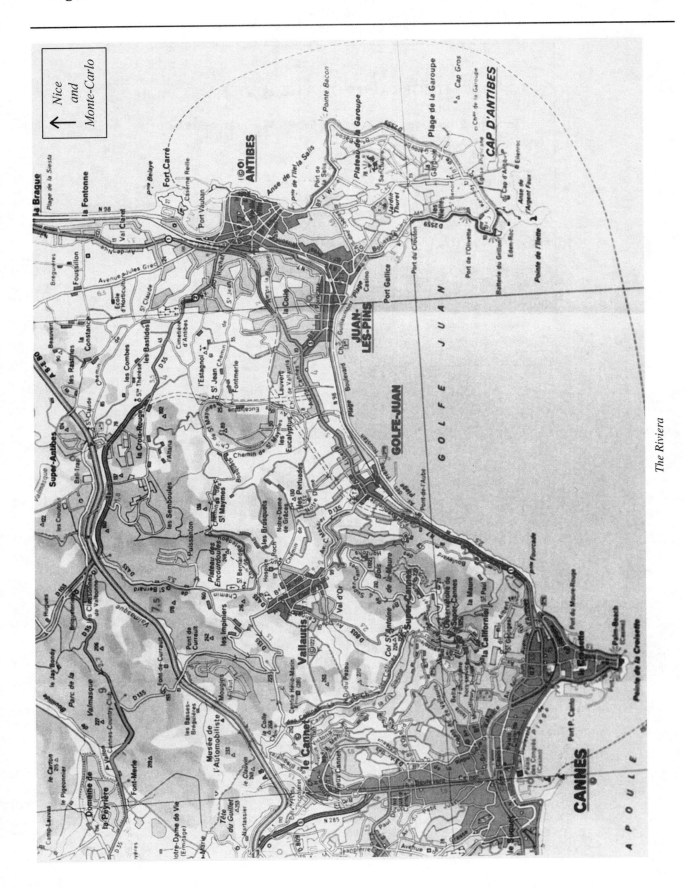

The Riviera

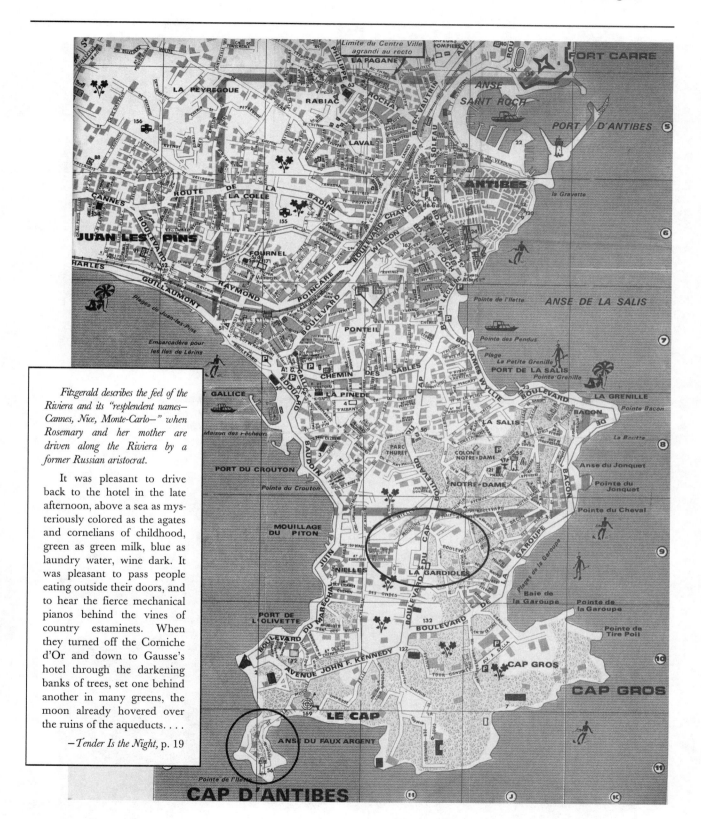

Fitzgerald describes the feel of the Riviera and its "resplendent names— Cannes, Nice, Monte-Carlo—" when Rosemary and her mother are driven along the Riviera by a former Russian aristocrat.

It was pleasant to drive back to the hotel in the late afternoon, above a sea as mysteriously colored as the agates and cornelians of childhood, green as green milk, blue as laundry water, wine dark. It was pleasant to pass people eating outside their doors, and to hear the fierce mechanical pianos behind the vines of country estaminets. When they turned off the Corniche d'Or and down to Gausse's hotel through the darkening banks of trees, set one behind another in many greens, the moon already hovered over the ruins of the aqueducts. . . .

—Tender Is the Night, p. 19

Contemporary map with a section of the Boulevard du Cap renamed Avenue John F. Kennedy. The Murphy's villa was inland, on Chemin des Mougins; the Grand Hôtel du Cap is on the Pointe de l'Ilette.

*Fitzgerald's annotation on a postcard of the Grand-Hôtel du Cap, the model for Gausse's Hôtel des Étrangers
(Bruccoli Collection of Fitzgerald, Thomas Cooper Library, University of South Carolina)*

*Zelda Fitzgerald's annotation on a postcard showing the view from the front of the hotel, located at the tip of Cap d'Antibes
(Bruccoli Collection of Fitzgerald, Thomas Cooper Library, University of South Carolina)*

The Café des Allées in Cannes, which Fitzgerald utilized as the Café des Allies, "where the trees made a green twilight over the tables"
(p. 18; Bruccoli Collection of Fitzgerald, Thomas Cooper Library, University of South Carolina)

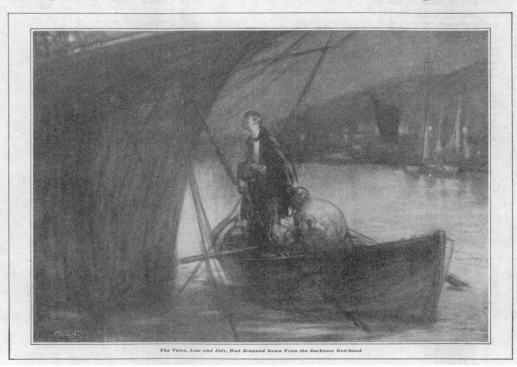

Illustration for the first story Fitzgerald set on the Riviera (Bruccoli Collection of Fitzgerald,
Thomas Cooper Library, University of South Carolina)

Railroad travel poster (Bruccoli Collection of Fitzgerald, Thomas Cooper Library, University of South Carolina)

(courtesy of Honoria Murphy Donnelly)

The Divers' Villa Diana

The Divers' Villa Diana combines the ambience of the Murphy Villa America at Cap d'Antibes with the location of the villa of American composer Samuel Barlow at Eze.

The terraced garden (photograph by Edmond Uher)

Gerald Murphy (courtesy of Honoria Murphy Donnelly)

A view of Eze, the model for the fictional Tarmes, where the Divers built their villa (Bruccoli Collection of Fitzgerald, Thomas Cooper Library, University of South Carolina)

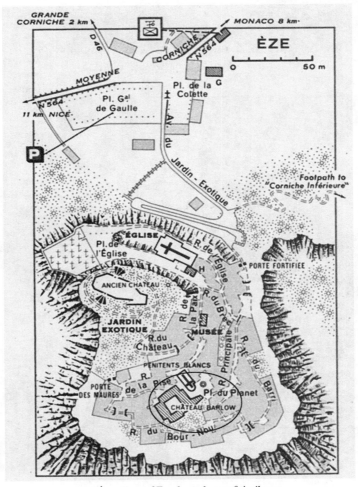

The village of Eze, located east of Antibes

Samuel Barlow, who composed the one-act opera Mon Ami Pierrot, *the first opera by an American to be performed at the Paris Opéra-Comique (1935). Fitzgerald might have alluded to Barlow's work when he has Earl Brady request "That song about 'Mon Ami Pierrot'" (p. 37) from the Diver children.*

In chapter 7 of Book I Fitzgerald describes the Divers' dinner party that Royal Dumphry years later remembers "as the most civilized gathering of people that I have ever known" (p. 318).

There were fireflies riding on the dark air and a dog baying on some low and far-away ledge of the cliff. The table seemed to have risen a little toward the sky like a mechanical dancing platform, giving the people around it a sense of being alone with each other in the dark universe, nourished by its only food, warmed by its only lights. And, as if a curious hushed laugh from Mrs. McKisco were a signal that such a detachment from the world had been attained, the two Divers began suddenly to warm and glow and expand, as if to make up to their guests, already so subtly assured of their importance, so flattered with politeness, for anything they might still miss from that country well left behind. Just for a moment they seemed to speak to everyone at the table, singly and together, assuring them of their friendliness, their affection. And for a moment the faces turned up toward them were like the faces of poor children at a Christmas tree. Then abruptly the table broke up—the moment when the guests had been daringly lifted above conviviality into the rarer atmosphere of sentiment, was over before it could be irreverently breathed, before they had half realized it was there.

—*Tender Is the Night*, p. 44

A view of Samuel Barlow's villa at Eze, which inspired Fitzgerald's description of the Divers' Villa Diana at Tarmes: "The villa and its grounds were made out of a row of peasant dwellings that abutted on the cliff—five small houses had been combined to make the house and four destroyed to make the garden" (p. 34; Bruccoli Collection of Fitzgerald, Thomas Cooper Library, University of South Carolina)

An interior view of Barlow's villa

A view of the frescoed dining room

The House of Samuel L. Barlow

The following magazine article reports that the building of the Barlow villa contributed to a renaissance at Eze.

Eze, or Eza, after a long sleep, has awakened to the songs of Italian masons. Eze is a town on a narrow strip of land, lying along the Mediterranean between Italy and Provence and isolated for centuries by its difficult geography. With the mountains on one side and the sea on the other, it has been regarded by historians and antiquarians as unworthy and unproductive. But, recently, it has blossomed into new beauty.

The new Corniche road, cut between the old sea road and the high mountain road, once the old Aurelian way, made this possible. For it is a road of easy access, with great beauty in its cypresses and gorse, its valerian and olive-trees and nightingales. And it leads to Eze, on a high butt of rock, Eze that was sleeping, like Brunhilda, waiting through the ages. Even the new road did not disturb the silent town, for the pyre of rock overlooks the road and its sycophant cafés and cottages.

The history of the coast is marked on this ancient town, and it bears old scars and crumbling armour. Its three gates, splendid stone memorials of the fierce pirate, Barbarossa, and his pillaging ravagers, are in ruins. Under the ruins lie Roman moneys, buried when Augustus built his white and golden Temple Monument at La Turbie, higher up in the mountains.

. . . .

Bits of the castle at Eze have stood through the centuries, and the town has clung to three sides of the hill in clusters and tiers of red and orange Roman tiles. Thirteen or fourteen hundred feet below, the Mediterranean stretches jade-green water all the miles across to Corsica.

And now, on this high promontory with all the Riviera from Nice to Toulon spread out before it, a new house has risen, as lordly and as massive as an old feudal castle. It is owned by Samuel L. Barlow, Esq., and it came to be through the mere chance of a picnic party.

The Barlow picnic party decided to buy some of the old houses in the narrow street. From dark doorways, donkeys brayed warning, but the Mayor was found and a sale arranged.

Soon Italian masons gathered, and a renaissance began. Water was pumped up into Eze. A house grew on the very edge of the promontory. Gardens were made to bloom with magnolias, lilies, and stock on the terraces.

Mr. Barlow's taste and energy have brought new beauty to Eze, and the old town has grown out of itself into a new self without too conscious a design or any jarring note.

In the house, one passes through a wrought-iron doorway at one end of the long stone-walled music-room into a dining-room in which are frescoes painted by Jan Juta and forming a saga of Eze and its countryside. Following the habits of the old Italian cinque-cento craftsmen, he has worked legendary, fantastic views of Eze straight into mortar. Mr. Juta, who has a studio in Paris, but is now in New York, has spent a great deal of time on the Riviera and is familiar with Eze and its history, its legends and romance.

The revival of fresco in house decoration has assumed a definite place in modern interiors. With the constant improvement in architectural taste and harmony of exterior and interior, mural space looms as a neglected possibility for beauty. Throughout the large rooms at Eze, Mr. Juta has used the long expanses of wall and ceiling to striking advantage.

—Vogue, 69 (1927): 69–70

Railroad travel poster (Bruccoli Collection of Fitzgerald, Thomas Cooper Library, University of South Carolina)

Postcards of the Riviera after it developed a fashionable summer season (Bruccoli Collection of Fitzgerald, Thomas Cooper Library, University of South Carolina)

A New Angle: Rex Ingram and the Kelly Version

In June 1929 Fitzgerald wrote to Perkins that he was working on a "new angle" on his novel. This comment almost certainly refers to the Kelly version, a two-chapter fragment in which American movie director Lew Kelly and his wife are traveling to Europe by ship. The Kelly version, which Fitzgerald abandoned to return to work on the Melarky story, may have been suggested by the career of Rex Ingram, the movie director, whom Lew Kelly resembles.

Kelly is Irish, a Yaleman, and has achieved great success early in life by hard work. He has artistic ambitions and hopes that his trip to Europe will enlarge his intellectual horizons. Rex Ingram (born Hitchcock) attended Trinity College, Dublin, and the Yale School of Fine Arts. He had worked at a series of jobs—in and out of the movies—before achieving resounding success as the director of The Four Horsemen of the Apocalypse *in 1921 when he was twenty-nine. Ingram followed this film with such successes as* The Prisoner of Zenda *(1922) and* Scaramouche *(1923) and then went to Europe in search of greater artistic freedom in making his films. He had a studio at Nice in 1927, where he made* Mare Nostrum *(1926) and* The Garden of Allah *(1927), which some critics regarded as pretentious. Ingram's career went into an eclipse with the introduction of sound movies. Fitzgerald was on the Riviera at the same time as Ingram, and it is more than likely that they met. There are only a few references to Ingram in Fitzgerald's letters and ledgers, but Ingram would have interested Fitzgerald.*

Director Rex Ingram, Fitzgerald's model for Lew Kelly in the Kelly draft and for Earl Brady in the published novel

Ingram's studio at La Turbie

"THE FOUR HORSEMEN
OF THE APOCALYPSE"
"EUGÉNIE GRANDET"
"LE SUPRÊME RENDEZVOUS"
"THE PRISONER OF ZENDA"

"WHERE THE PAVEMENT ENDS"
"SCARAMOUCHE"
"THE ARAB"
"MARE NOSTRUM"
"THE MAGICIAN"

TÉLÉPH. 50.81
51.97
57.08

ADR. TELEGR.
METROREX

REX INGRAM
PRODUCTIONS INC.
CINÉ STUDIO
SAINT AUGUSTIN. NICE, A.M. FRANCE

October 27th 1926.

Cher Maître:

For two nights Gatsby has shared my bed with
the Prophet Muhamed (this sounds queer) - but then as you
know Muhamed's "Gatsby" was the "Koran". You look so young
I would never have given you credit (feeling as I have, up
to now, that I was myself the only exception that proved the
rule). I am thankful I got this book of yours last week instead of twenty-five years after, having noticed in the fly
pages ads for the ouveries of F. Scott Fitz I find I have only
two more novels to read, two vols of short stories and a
treatise on Agriculture—otherwise F.S.F. might have shared
the fate of that Virgin set - uncut like Gatsbys - of George
Moore - and become, like Moore, part of a scheme of interior
decoration - for as you know I read about one Novel and the
Koran a year.

Gatsby is very fine: it is full of sentiment
without being sentimental - Gatsby was a sentimentalist but
on so heroic a scale that he was magnificent. Everyone of
your characters prove that the U.S.A. is uninhabitable - they
are all to the life. The great ambition of all successful
New-Yorkers is to keep a road house on Long-Island. Marcus
Loew admitted to me he was cutting down his beautiful timber
lands at Glen Cove to make a golf course for his week-end
guests -- (I understand he bought the Estate for the timber) -
his clients all threatening to patronize Zukors rival insti-
tution if they could'nt play golf. But Marcus has it on
Gatsby because everyone in the company is a relative, so I
am sure he will have a good funeral.

بسم الله الرحمن الرحيم
اخي

All for tonight.

Rex Ingram's letter to Fitzgerald (Princeton University Library)

Lobby card for movie in which Lois Moran made her first success (Bruccoli Collection of Fitzgerald,
Thomas Cooper Library, University of South Carolina)

Lois Moran

*Fitzgerald met actress Lois Moran when he
went to Hollywood in 1927 to write the unproduced movie "Lipstick." She was eighteen years
old and had recently made her first hit in* Stella
Dallas *(1925). They developed warm feelings
for each other, but there is no evidence that they
were romantically involved. Fitzgerald wrote
Moran into the Kelly version as a young actress
named Rosemary and into the Diver version as
Rosemary Hoyt.* Stella Dallas *became Rosemary's movie* Daddy's Girl *in* Tender Is the
Night.

(Bruccoli Collection of Fitzgerald, Thomas Cooper Library,
University of South Carolina)

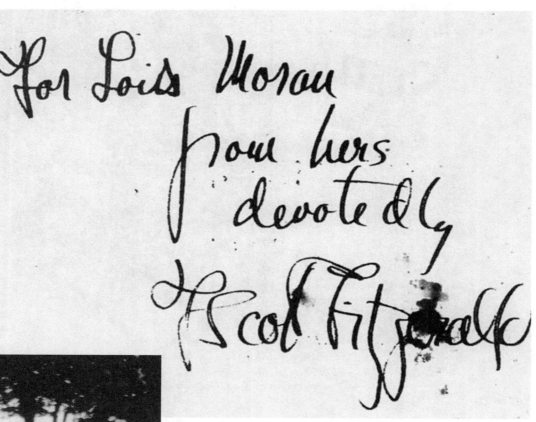

Fitzgerald with Moran at Ellerslie in 1927 (from The Romantic Egoists)

The Triumph of "Daddy's Girl"

In Paris, Rosemary arranges a private screening of "Daddy's Girl" for Divers, the Norths, and Collis Clay.

There she was—the school girl of a year ago, hair down her back and rippling out stiffly like the solid hair of a Tanagra figure; there she was—*so* young and innocent—the product of her mother's loving care; there she was—embodying all the immaturity of the race, cutting a new cardboard paper doll to pass before its empty harlot's mind.

—*Tender Is the Night,* pp. 90–91

Switzerland in Fitzgerald's story "One Trip Abroad" is described as "a country where very few things begin, but many things end."

Zelda Fitzgerald's Breakdown and the Diver Version

More than any other event, Zelda Fitzgerald's breakdown and subsequent diagnosis of schizophrenia provided the catalyst for the final stage of development of his novel—the Diver version—though more than two years passed between her 1930 collapse and Fitzgerald's written plan for the Diver plot. The concept of emotional bankruptcy became a key idea for Fitzgerald. He believed that people have a fixed amount of emotional capital; reckless expenditure results in early bankruptcy, leaving the person unable to respond to the events that require true emotion. There is no recoupment after emotional bankruptcy. Appropriately, Fitzgerald developed a theory of character in terms of a financial metaphor.

Ten years after her wedding Zelda Fitzgerald entered Malmaison clinic outside Paris. The admittance report reads:

Mrs. FITZ-GERALD entered on 23 April 1930 in a state of acute anxiety, restlessness, continually repeating: "This is dreadful, this is horrible, what is going to become of me, I have to work, and I will no longer be able to, I must die, and yet I have to work. I will never be cured, let me leave. I have to go see 'Madame' (dance teacher), she has given me the greatest joy that can exist, it is comparable to the light of the sun that falls on a block of crystal, to a symphony of perfume, the most perfect chord from the greatest composer in music."

Les Rives de Prangins

Zelda Fitzgerald was a patient at Les Rives de Prangins clinic at Nyon on Lake Geneva between Geneva and Lausanne during 1930–1931. Fitzgerald annotated these postcards for her parents to assure them that she was receiving the best—and most expensive—treatment. Prangins provided a model for the clinic that Diver and Gregorovious operate in Tender Is the Night.

For eighteen months now he had lived at the clinic—certainly one of the best-appointed in Europe. Like Dohmler's it was of the modern type—no longer a single dark and sinister building but a small, scattered, yet deceitfully integrated village—Dick and Nicole had added much in the domain of taste, so that the plant was a thing of beauty, visited by every psychologist passing through Zürich. With the addition of a caddy house it might very well have been a country club.

—Tender Is the Night, p. 238

" Les Rives de Prangins "

Five postcards annotated by Fitzgerald for his wife's family (Bruccoli Collection of Fitzgerald, Thomas Cooper Library, University of South Carolina)

"Les Rives de Prangins" *This is the view from Zelda's window*

(Bruccoli Collection of Fitzgerald, Thomas Cooper Library, University of South Carolina)

"Les Rives de Prangins" *On the grounds*   Le Bois

(Bruccoli Collection of Fitzgerald, Thomas Cooper Library, University of South Carolina)

(*Bruccoli Collection of Fitzgerald, Thomas Cooper Library, University of South Carolina*)

(*Bruccoli Collection of Fitzgerald, Thomas Cooper Library, University of South Carolina*)

Fitzgerald's captioned photo with Scottie in Switzerland
(*from* The Romantic Egoists)

The most interesting case that Dick Diver encounters at his clinic is an American painter who, once "exceptionally pretty," had become "a living agonizing sore." Her condition was "unsatisfactorily catalogued as nervous eczema" (p. 240). As Diver attends her, the painter searches for a reason for her affliction.

[H]er voice came up through her bandaged face afflicted with subterranean melodies:

"I'm sharing the fate of the women of my time who challenged men to battle."

"To your vast surprise it was just like all battles," he answered, adopting her formal diction.

"Just like all battles." She thought this over. "You pick a set-up, or else win a Pyrrhic victory, or you're wrecked and ruined—you're a ghostly echo from a broken wall."

—Tender Is the Night, p. 241

Fitzgerald's captioned photo of Zelda at the time of her discharge from Les Rives de Prangins (from The Romantic Egoists)

Songs of
Tender Is the Night

In chapter 5 of Book II, Nicole, still at Dohmler's clinic on the Zürichsee, tells Dick of the phonograph records her sister sent her from America.

"Do you know 'Hindustan'?" she asked wistfully. "I'd never heard it before, but I like it. And I've got 'Why Do They Call Them Babies?' and 'I'm Glad I Can Make You Cry.' I suppose you've danced to all those tunes in Paris?"

—Tender Is the Night, p. 178

At one meeting Nicole leads Dick "to the cache where she had left the phonograph, turned a corner by the workshop, climbed a rock, and sat down behind a low wall, facing miles and miles of rolling night" (p. 179).

"I've got one more record," she said. "—Have you heard 'So Long, Letty'? I suppose you have."

"Honestly, you don't understand—I haven't heard a thing."

Nor known, nor smelt, nor tasted, he might have added; only hot-cheeked girls in hot secret rooms. The young maidens he had known at New Haven in 1914 kissed men, saying "There!" hands at the man's chest to push him away. Now there was this scarcely saved waif of disaster bringing him the essence of a continent. . . .

—*Tender Is the Night*, p. 180

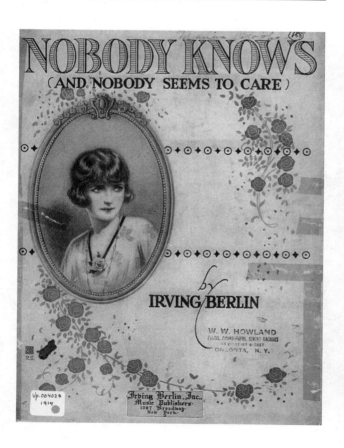

Postcard of the mountains that Dick Diver saw on his bicycle trip, just before he encountered Nicole on the funicular (Bruccoli Collection of Fitzgerald, Thomas Cooper Library, University of South Carolina)

Postcard of the mountain Dick Diver climbs after first kissing Nicole in Glion (Bruccoli Collection of Fitzgerald, Thomas Cooper Library, University of South Carolina)

After initially breaking off his romance with Nicole, Dick Diver sees little of her for weeks before meeting her by chance on the Glion funicular.

Mountain-climbing cars are built on a slant similar to the angle of a hat-brim of a man who doesn't want to be recognized. As water gushed from the chamber under the car, Dick was impressed with the ingenuity of the whole idea—a complementary car was now taking on mountain water at the top and would pull the lightened car up by gravity, as soon as the brakes were released.

. . . .

In the compartment above and in front of Dick's, a group of English were standing up and exclaiming upon the backdrop of sky, when suddenly there was a confusion among them—they parted to give passage to a couple of young people who made apologies and scrambled over into the rear compartment of the funicular—Dick's compartment. The young man was a Latin with the eyes of a stuffed deer; the girl was Nicole.

—*Tender Is the Night,* pp. 194, 195

A Swiss funicular (photograph by Michel Azéma)

*Fitzgerald's annotated photo of himself on the Western Front
(from* The Romantic Egoists)

The Great War and Dick Diver

Like Fitzgerald, Dick Diver was in uniform during World War I but did not see combat. The author and his character were nevertheless profoundly affected by the slaughter, as is clear from Dick's conversation with Abe North at the battlefield of Beaumont Hamel.

"See that little stream—we could walk to it in two minutes. It took the British a month to walk to it—a whole empire walking very slowly, dying in front and pushing forward behind. And another empire walked very slowly backward a few inches a day, leaving the dead like a million bloody rugs. No Europeans will ever do that again in this generation."

"Why, they've only just quit over in Turkey," said Abe. "And in Morocco—"

"That's different. This Western Front business couldn't be done again, not for a long time. The young men think they could do it but they couldn't. They could fight the First Marne again but not this. This took religion and years of plenty and tremendous sureties and the exact relation that existed between the classes. The Russians and Italians weren't any good on this front. You had to have a whole-souled sentimental equipment going back further than you could remember. You had to remember Christmas, and postcards of the Crown Prince and his fiancée, and little cafés in Valence and beer gardens in Unter den Linden and weddings at the mairie, and going to the Derby, and your grandfather's whiskers."

"General Grant invented this kind of battle at Petersburg in sixty-five."

"No, he didn't—he just invented mass butchery. This kind of battle was invented by Lewis Carroll and Jules Verne and whoever wrote 'Undine' and country deacons bowling and marraines in Marseilles and girls seduced in the back lanes of Württemberg and Westphalia. Why, this was a love battle—there was a century of middle-class love spent here. This was the last love battle."

"You want to hand over this battle to D. H. Lawrence," said Abe.

"All my beautiful lovely safe world blew itself up here with a great gust of high-explosive love," Dick mourned persistently. "Isn't that true, Rosemary?"

—Tender Is the Night, pp. 74–75

*Beaumont Hamel, November 1916 (Joseph M. Bruccoli Great War Collection,
Thomas Cooper Library, University of South Carolina)*

The Newfoundland Memorial at Beaumont Hamel (Joseph M. Bruccoli Great War Collection, Thomas Cooper Library, University of South Carolina)

Fitzgerald as a child with his father (Bruccoli Collection of Fitzgerald, Thomas Cooper Library, University of South Carolina)

The Death of Edward Fitzgerald

Fitzgerald's father died on 26 January 1931. In chapter 18 of Book II of Tender Is the Night *Fitzgerald writes of Dick Diver's reaction to the death of his father: "Dick loved his father—again and again he referred judgments to what his father would probably have thought or done" (p. 265). This sentence and the rest of the paragraph that follows are based on Fitzgerald's unfinished essay, "The Death of My Father":*

I loved my father—always deep in my subconscious I have referred judgements back to him, what he would have thought or done. He loved me—and felt a deep responsibility for me—I was born several months after the sudden death of my two elder sisters + he felt what the effect of this would be on my mother, that he would be my only moral guide. He became that to the best of his ability. He came from tired old stock with very little left of vitality and mental energy but he managed to raise a little for me.

In the summer father and son walked downtown together to have their shoes shined—Dick in his starched duck sailor suit, his father always in beautifully cut clerical clothes—and the father was very proud of his handsome little boy. He told Dick all he knew about life, not much but most of it true, simple things, matters of behavior that came within his clergyman's range.

—Tender Is the Night, pp. 265–266

Illustration from the story in which Fitzgerald created a character based on Bijou O'Connor, the model for Lady Caroline Sibly-Biers in Tender Is the Night *(Bruccoli Collection of Fitzgerald, Thomas Cooper Library, University of South Carolina)*

Bijou O'Connor, "The Hotel Child" and *Tender Is the Night*

Lady Caroline Sibley-Biers, who first appears in chapter 5 of Book III of Tender Is the Night, *was probably based in part on Bijou O'Connor, an Englishwoman who claimed to have had an affair with Fitzgerald in fall 1930 while Zelda was a patient in Les Rives de Prangins clinic. O'Connor was certainly the model in "The Hotel Child" for Lady Capps-Karr, a dissolute noblewoman. In January 1931 Fitzgerald wrote of these characters to his agent, Harold Ober: "Practi-cally the whole damn thing is true, bizarre as it seems. Lord Allington + the famous Bijou O'Connor were furious at me putting them in + as for the lovely Jewess (real name Mimi Cohn) I don't dare tell her" (As Ever, Scott Fitz−, pp. 174–175). In the novel Lady Caroline is characterized as "the wickedest woman in London" who bears "aloft the pennon of decadence, last ensign of the fading empire" (p. 349).*

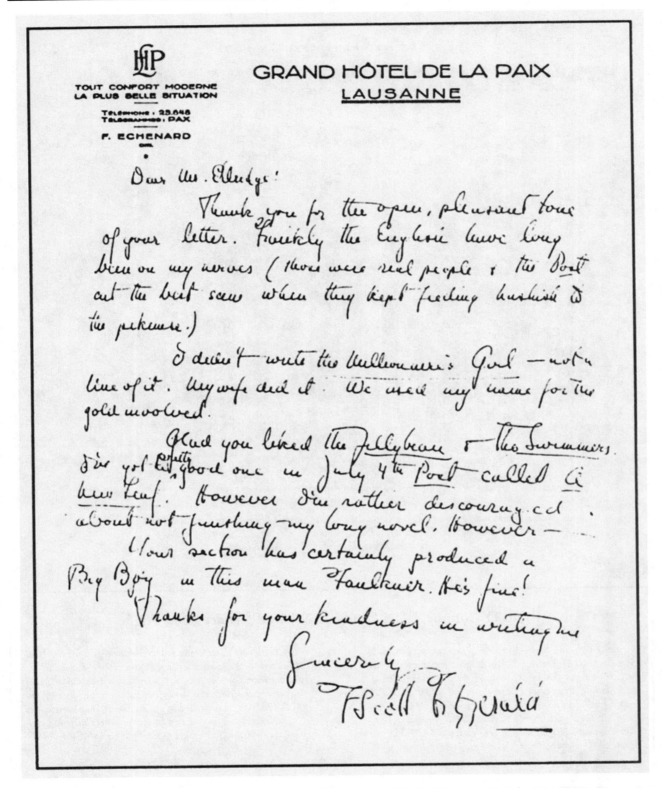

Fitzgerald's response to an admirer in which he alludes to the behavior of the English characters in "The Hotel Child"
(*Profiles in History* catalogue, 1989)

Save Me the Waltz

Zelda Fitzgerald's only novel, based on the Fitzgeralds' lives and written in a few months when her husband had been struggling to write his fourth novel for nearly seven years, increased the tension in the couple's marriage. Although the novel was not well received upon its initial publication in 1932, interest in the novel since its 1967 re-publication by Vernon Sternberg at Southern Illinois University Press has increased and been sustained.

The Composition and Publication of *Save Me the Waltz*
Matthew J. Bruccoli

Save Me the Waltz was written during January and February 1932 in Montgomery and at Phipps Clinic at Johns Hopkins Hospital; it was sent to Maxwell Perkins at Scribner's in March 1932.[1] The version that Perkins first saw had not been read by F. Scott Fitzgerald, for Zelda Fitzgerald was anxious to succeed without her husband's help or interference. The original manuscript and typescripts have disappeared; but the first draft appears to have been a much more personal document—more

Zelda Fitzgerald after the Fitzgeralds returned from Europe in 1931 (Bruccoli Collection of Fitzgerald, Thomas Cooper Library, University of South Carolina)

transparently about the Fitzgeralds' marriage. David Knight was originally named Amory Blaine after the hero of *This Side of Paradise,* who was an autobiographical character. When Fitzgerald did read the novel in typescript, he was disturbed on two counts: he felt it exposed too much of his private life; and he thought it drew upon material he had written for or intended for *Tender Is the Night,* which was then in progress.

The publication of *Save Me the Waltz* can be traced through Fitzgerald's correspondence. On 16 March—some four days after Zelda Fitzgerald sent the novel to Perkins—Fitzgerald instructed him not to decide anything until it was revised.[2] Although he clearly wanted his wife to have a success and praised the novel to Perkins, Fitzgerald was concerned that the original version would injure both of them—but especially him:

> Turning up in a novel signed by my wife as a somewhat anemic portrait painter with a few ideas lifted from Clive Bell, Leger, etc. puts me in an absurd & Zelda in a ridiculous position. The mixture of fact & fiction is calculated to ruin us both, or what is left of us, and I can't let it stand. Using the name of a character I invented to put intimate facts in the hands of the friends and enemies we have accumulated *en route* — my God, my books made her a legend and her single intention in this somewhat thin portrait is to make me a non-entity.[3]

He urged his wife to revise and no doubt helped her, but the extent of his labor is by no means clear in the absence of the working papers. It seems likely, though, that the assumption that he actually rewrote *Save Me the Waltz* is false. The available documents indicate that his work was advisory. On 25 March he wired Perkins that the novel would require only minor revisions and that it was a good novel; but three days later he informed Perkins that the whole middle section needed to be rewritten.[4] By 2 May he was able to report: "Zelda's novel is now good, improved in every way. It is new. She has largely eliminated the speakeasy-nights-and-our-trip-to-Paris atmosphere."[5] The letter warns Perkins against exciting her with too-generous praise.

On or about 14 May Fitzgerald sent the revised novel, stating:

> It is a good novel now, perhaps a very good novel — I am too close to tell. . . . (At first she refused to revise — then she revised completely, added on her own suggestion and has changed what was a rather flashy and self-justifying "true confessions" that wasn't worthy of her into an honest piece of work. She can do more with galleys but I can't ask her to do more now.) — But now praise will do her good, within reason.[6]

The typescript printer's copy for *Save Me the Waltz* and five sets of galley proofs are in the Fitzgerald Papers at the Princeton University Library. The typescript is clean copy, prepared by a typist, with only a few authorial corrections and printer's or editor's queries. The proof consists of two sets of very heavily revised – not just corrected – galleys, two duplicate sets, and one set of paged final galleys.

The two sets of revised galleys are drastically worked over, but almost all the marks are in Zelda Fitzgerald's hand. Fitzgerald did not systematically work on the surviving proofs: only eight of the words written on them are clearly in his hand.

Perhaps the wholesale revisions discouraged the proofreaders, or perhaps the author resisted editorial help – but whatever the reason, *Save Me the Waltz* is one of the most sloppily-edited novels ever produced by a distinguished American publisher.[7] Apart from authorial idiosyncracies of style and usage, there are hundreds of spelling errors that almost certainly affected reader response.

The size of the initial printing has not been determined, but it was probably a depression run of no more than 3,000 copies. Judging from the scarcity of copies, the run may have been smaller. *Save Me the Waltz* was not reprinted in America until 1967, but in 1953 Grey Walls Press published a new edition in England.

Notes

1. Zelda Fitzgerald to Maxwell Perkins, c. 12 March 1932. Scribner's files.

2. F. Scott Fitzgerald to Maxwell Perkins, 16 March 1932. Scribner's files.

3. Quoted in Andrew Turnbull, *Scott Fitzgerald* (New York: Scribner's, 1962), p. 207. This letter was presumably written to Zelda Fitzgerald's psychiatrist.

4. F. Scott Fitzgerald to Maxwell Perkins, 25 and 28 March, 1932. Scribner's files.

5. F. Scott Fitzgerald to Maxwell Perkins, before 2 May 1932. Quoted in *The Letters of F. Scott Fitzgerald,* ed. Andrew Turnbull (New York: Scribner's, 1963), pp. 226–227.

6. F. Scott Fitzgerald to Maxwell Perkins, c. 14 May 1932. Quoted in *Letters,* pp. 228–29. This letter warns Perkins not to discuss the novel with Ernest Hemingway, who had *Death in the Afternoon* coming out that season and who would regard *Save Me the Waltz* as competition. Fitzgerald's estimate of *Save Me the Waltz* was later revised downward. On 8 February 1936, he wrote Harold Ober: "Please don't have anybody read Zelda's book because it is a bad book!" (*Letters,* p. 402).

7. At least two reviews complained about the proofreading – *New York Times Book Review* (16 October) and *Bookman* (November). These and three other reviews all commented on the unusual word usage – *Boston Transcript* (30 November), *Saturday Review of Literature* (22 October), and *Forum* (December).

* * *

Beautiful and Damned
Geoffrey Hellman
The Saturday Review, 9 (22 October 1932): 190

THE most noticeable feature about this book is the steady stream of strained metaphor with which Mrs. Fitzgerald manages to make what should be a light novel a study in the intricacies of the English language. No phenomenon is too simple for her to obfuscate with the complexities of figure of speech. Her book rivals the cross-word puzzle page in point of obscurity. And her men and women are almost as badly off. They can never just have their own way about things simply and unostentatiously, but have to go around "splashing their dreams in the dark pool of gratification." And under no circumstances are they allowed to look at anything as *terre-à-terre* as a building or a tree; peering from train windows, they can distinguish only "the pink carnival of Normandy . . . the delicate tracery of Paris . . . the white romance of Avignon."

Once you have dug out these nuggets and put them away in your geology collection, you find you have been reading a book which evokes, quite effectively at times, those booming post-war years when tea-dancing at the Biltmore and champagne cocktails at the Paris Ritz were in the natural order of things not only for the children of the rich but for a large selection of *jeunesse* which did not consider itself particularly *dorée;* years when even artists made money. And more specifically, in this book, years when David Knight, a young painter, earned so much that he was able to take his family abroad and drift about expatriate Riviera beaches and Paris nightclubs.

It is with the disintegrating effect of this empty, rootless life on David's Southern-born wife, Alabama, that Mrs. Fitzgerald is chiefly concerned. Less plausible than her theme is her treatment thereof. To point to but one example of its implausibility, the desperation which prompts Alabama to turn to ballet-dancing with a group of dingy, impoverished people in Paris is anything but convincing on the part of a healthy young woman (which she has been shown to be) who has a husband whom she loves and a young daughter she adores. In short, Alabama is a poor vehicle for the neuroticism and dissatisfaction which she is suddenly called upon to exemplify. Typical of the other characters as well, this unconvincing motivation is part of the author's general inability to create full-bodied figures.

"Save Me the Waltz" belongs to that vast company of books of which some individual parts are greater than the whole. Particularly good is the episode of Alabama's parents' visit to the Knight home, where Mrs. Fitzgerald achieves a burlesque effect that is as amusing in itself as it is out of harmony with most of the rest of the book. But even here the inevitable metaphors rear their heads, doing their best to deflect attention from the humor that is this book's chief (if only occasional) redeeming feature.

* * *

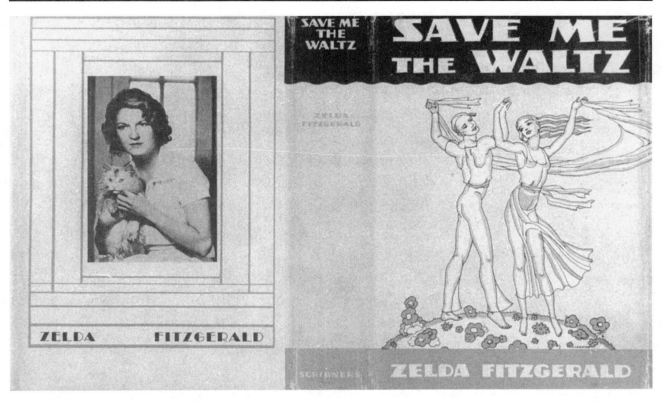

Dust jacket for Zelda Fitzgerald's only novel, which she wrote while she was a patient at Johns Hopkins Hospital
(Bruccoli Collection of Fitzgerald, Thomas Cooper Library, University of South Carolina)

On 28 May 1933 Fitzgerald, Zelda, and psychiatrist Dr. Thomas Rennie met at "La Paix" with a stenographer, who prepared a 114-page typescript. The angry discussion ranged over many of the fissures in the Fitzgerald marriage, but the crux was his insistence on veto power over her writing plans. Fitzgerald was concerned that she might preempt material that he had already written into Tender *or was planning to incorporate in the novel.*

The Fitzgeralds and the Psychiatrist: A Transcription of a Discussion

Sunday, May 28, 1933, 2:30 p.m.

Mr. Fitzgerald: Well, what I want to do briefly is talk over what goes through my head at night and why I am gradually being destroyed by the present situation. And in fact I think I can show you my whole line of reasoning and I would like that to be done in front of Dr. Rennie and also so there won't be any possible confusion I want a typescript of the whole thing of what is happening.

. . . .

I say I am a different sort of person than Zelda, that my equipment for being a writer, for being an artist, is a different equipment from hers. Her theory is that anything is possible and that a girl has just got to get along and so she has the right therefore to destroy me completely in order to satisfy herself. . . . She has certain experiences to report but she has nothing essentially to say. . . . The first time I met her I saw she was a drunkard. . . . Zelda was spoiled. She was made the baby and told that she had no obligations, that other people had obligations and so long as she was pretty she would never have to do anything except just be pretty. Then Zelda ceased being the prettiest person in the world as women inevitably will—and ceased to be so at twenty-five, though to me she is the most sexually attractive woman in the world. . . . I did not care whether you were a writer or not if you were any good. It is a struggle. It has been a struggle to me. It is self-evident to me that nobody cares about anything. It is a perfectly lonely struggle that I am making against other writers who are finely gifted and talented. You are a third-rate writer and a third-rate ballet dancer. . . . If you want to write modest things you may be able to turn out one collection of short stories. For the rest, you are compared to me is just like comparing—well, there is just not any comparison. I am a professional writer with a huge following. I am the high-

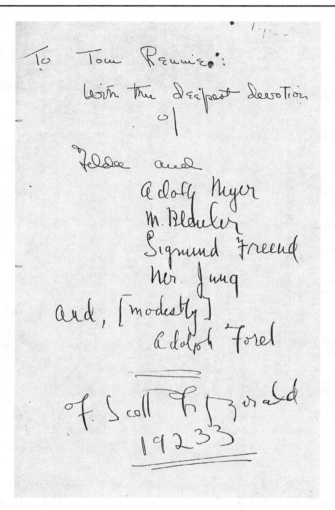

Zelda Fitzgerald's inscription to her psychiatrist in Rene Fülöp-Miller's The Mind and Face of Bolshevism *(1929).*
Fitzgerald added an inscription listing prominent psychiatrists (Bruccoli Collection of Fitzgerald,
Thomas Cooper Library, University of South Carolina).

est paid short story writer in the world. I have at various times dominated–

Zelda: It seems to me you are making a rather violent attack on a third-rate talent, then. . . . Why in the hell you are so jealous, I don't know. If I thought that about anybody I would not care what they wrote.

Fitzgerald: Because you are broaching at all times on my material just as if a good artist came into a room and found something drawn on the canvas by some mischievous little boy.

Zelda: Well, what do you want me to be?

Fitzgerald: I want you to do what I say. That is exactly what I want you to do and you know it. . . . Now, one of the agreements made between Dr. Adolph Meyer and Dr. Rennie and myself was that it was

extremely inadvisable for you to write any novels which were a resumé of your insanity or discussed insanity. I gave you a clipping one day about Nijinsky which I had in my files, and immediately you founded upon that the idea that you would write a novel about insanity. You have been sneakingly writing that novel for a period of some months. What good that could have brought you or given you, I don't know, against any wish of mine that you should [not] publish a book before I publish another book and with the use of my name. . . . I don't want you for your own sake to write a novel about insanity because you know there is certain psychiatric stuff in my books; and if you publish a book before me or even at the same time in which the subject of psychiatry is taken up and people see "Fitzgerald," why that is Scott Fitzgerald's wife. They read that and that spells the whole central point of being a novelist, which is being yourself. You picked up the crumbs I drop at the dinner table and stick them into books. . . .

8   *THE SATURDAY EVENING POST*   *January 18, 1930*

TWO WRONGS By F. Scott Fitzgerald

ILLUSTRATED BY H. WESTON TAYLOR

"What Shall I Do?" She Inquired, Quietly Laying Her Future in Bill's Hands

"LOOK at those shoes," said Bill— "twenty-eight dollars."

Mr. Brancusi looked. "Purty."

"Made to order."

"I knew you were a great swell. You didn't get me up here to show me those shoes, did you?"

"I am not a great swell. Who said I was a great swell?" demanded Bill. "Just because I've got more education than most people in show business."

"But then, you know, you're a handsome young fellow," said Brancusi dryly.

"Sure I am—compared to you anyhow. The girls think I must be an actor, till they find out. . . . Got a cigarette? What's more, I look like a man—which is more than most of these pretty boys round Times Square do."

"Good-looking. Gentleman. Good shoes. Shot with luck."

"You're wrong there," objected Bill. "Brains. Three years—nine shows—four big hits—one flop. Where do you see any luck in that?"

A little bored, Brancusi just gazed. What he would have seen—had he not made his eyes opaque and taken to thinking about something else—was a fresh-faced young Irishman exuding aggressiveness and self-confidence until the air of his office was thick with it. Presently, Brancusi knew, he would hear the sound of his own voice and be ashamed and retire into his other humor—the superior, quiet, sensitive one, the patron of the arts, modeled on the intellectuals of the Theater Guild. Bill McChesney had not quite decided between the two, and such blends are seldom complete before thirty.

"Take Ames, take Hopkins, take Harris—take any of them," Bill insisted. "What have they got on me? What's the matter? Do you want a drink?"—seeing Brancusi's glance wander toward the cabinet on the opposite wall.

"I never drink in the morning. I just wondered who was it keeps on knocking. You ought to make it stop. I get a nervous fidgets, kind of half crazy, with that kind of thing."

Bill went quickly to the door and threw it open.

interruption his other mood had come over him, and he resumed his conversation with Brancusi in the key of one hand in

He stared at her.

"Mr. Rogers told me ——"

"Come and have a spot of lunch with me," he said, and then, with an air of great hurry, he gave Miss Cohalan some quick and contradictory instructions and held open the door.

They stood on Forty-second Street and he breathed his preëmpted air—there is only enough air there for a few people at a time. It was November and the first exhilarating rush of the season was over, but he could look east and see the electric sign of one of his plays, and west and see another. Around the corner was the one he had put on with Brancusi—the last time he would produce anything except alone.

They went to the Bedford, where there was a to-do of waiters and captains as he came in.

"This is a ver' 'tractive restaurant," she said, impressed and on company behavior.

"This is hams' paradise." He nodded to several people. "Hello, Jimmy—Bill. . . . Hello there, Jack. . . . That's Jack Dempsey. . . . I don't eat here much. I usually eat up at the Harvard Club."

"Oh, did you go to Harvard? I used to know ——"

"Yes." He hesitated; there were two versions about Harvard, and he decided suddenly on the true one. "Yes, and they had me down for a hick there, but not any more. About a week ago I was out on Long Island at the Gouverneer Haights'—very fashionable people—and a couple of Gold Coast boys that never knew I was alive up in Cambridge began pulling this 'Hello, Bill, old boy' on me."

He hesitated and suddenly decided to leave the story there.

"What do you want—a job?" he demanded. He remembered suddenly that she had holes in her stockings. Holes in stockings always moved him, softened him.

"Yes, or else I've got to go home," she said. "I want to be a dancer—you know, Russian ballet. But the lessons cost so much, so I've got to get a job. I thought it'd give me stage presence anyhow."

"Hoofer, eh?"

"Oh, no, serious."

"Well, Pavlova's a hoofer, isn't she?"

"Oh, no." She was shocked at this profanity, but after a moment she continued: "I took with Miss Cambell—Georgia Berriman

Illustration from the story in which Fitzgerald examines the tension in a marriage when a husband's career falters while the wife's career begins to thrive. A similar pattern is evident in Tender Is the Night *as Nicole's growing strength and confidence seem to come at Dick's expense (Bruccoli Collection of Fitzgerald, Thomas Cooper Library, University of South Carolina).*

She wants to write a novel against everybody's advice and it is discovered about three weeks ago that she is doing it. . . . Everything that we have done is mine—if we make a trip—if I make a trip to Panama and you and I go around—I am the professional novelist and I am supporting you. That is all of my material. None of it is your material.

Dr. Rennie: We know that if you are writing a personal, individual study on a psychiatric topic, you are doing something that we would advise you right along not to do and that is not to write anything personal on psychiatric material.

Zelda: Well, Dr. Rennie, didn't we discuss some time ago and didn't I say to you that I was miserable because I could not write short things? . . . And didn't we decide that it would perhaps be better to go on and write long things?

Dr. Rennie: But didn't I also say very emphatically and haven't I said all along that for you to dabble with

Dust jacket for the first English edition, published in 1953 by Grey Walls Press (Bruccoli Collection of Fitzgerald, Thomas Cooper Library, University of South Carolina)

psychiatric material is playing with fire and you ought not to do it, and didn't you promise me really once that you put the psychiatric novel away for five years and would not touch it in that period?

Fitzgerald: Well, we have had no relations for more than three or four months. The fact of the thing is we have various social connections with each other, one of which I blame you chiefly for, this course you are taking, because I think that course is egotistic, and I think that I am trying to be social and you are trying to be individual; and that we cannot in these times, that everything is so hard and tough, that we cannot come to any understanding on that basis, and I have got all the worries that everybody also has of making a living and I find an enemy in the family, treachery behind my back, or what I consider that. I may be hypersensitive

to what I consider logical from the traditions of my profession.

Zelda: You think it is personally all right that you feel that way and you accuse me of everything in the world, with having ruined your life, not once, but over and over again.

Fitzgerald: When did that first happen?

Zelda: You did that last fall. You sat down and cried and cried. You were drunk, I will admit, and you said I had ruined your life and you did not love me and you were sick of me and wished you could get away, and I was strained and burdened. You said that when you came back from New York, also drunk, and that is the kind of life I am expected to live together with you, and make whatever adjustment I can.

Fitzgerald: What do you think caused these two things?

Zelda: It is impossible to live with you. I would rather be in an insane asylum where you would like to put me.

Fitzgerald: What do you think causes those things?

Zelda: I think the cause of it is your drinking. That is what I think is the cause of it. . . . Dr. Rennie, I am perfectly willing to put aside the novel, but I will not have any agreement or arrangements because I will not submit to Scott's neurasthenic condition and be subjected to these tortures all the time. I cannot live in this kind of a world, and I would rather live in any insane asylum. That is my ultimatum on the subject.

Fitzgerald: Our sexual relations were very pleasant and all that until I got the idea you were ditching me. They were all very nice to then, weren't they?

Zelda: Well, I am glad you considered them satisfactory.

Fitzgerald: I want you to stop writing fiction. . . . Whether you write or not does not seem to be of any great importance.

Zelda: I know. Nothing I do seems to be of any great importance.

 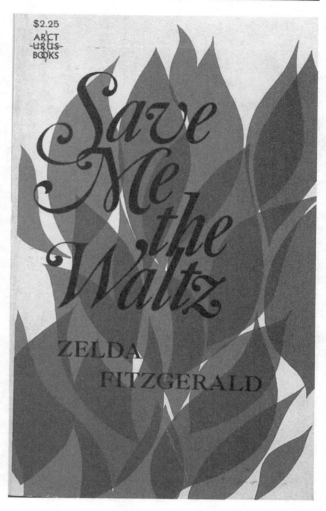

Dust jacket and cover for the 1967 Southern Illinois University Press edition of Save Me the Waltz, *which had been out of print in America for thirty-five years. Vernon Sternberg's Southern Illinois University Press edition triggered a reappraisal of the novel (Bruccoli Collection of Fitzgerald, Thomas Cooper Library, University of South Carolina).*

Fitzgerald: Why don't you drop it then?

Zelda: Because I don't want to live with you, because I want to live someplace that I can be my own self.

Fitzgerald: Would you like to go to law about it?

Zelda: Yes, I would. . . . I think honestly the only thing is to get a divorce because there is nothing except ill will on your part and suspicion.

Fitzgerald: I am perfectly determined that I am going to take three or four drinks a day. . . . And then the fact that if I ever stop drinking her family and herself would always think that that was an acknowledgement that I was responsible for her insanity, which is not so.

Zelda: What is the matter with Scott is that he has not written that book and if he will ever get it written, why, he won't feel so miserable and suspicious and mean towards everybody else.

Fitzgerald: It has got to be an unconditional surrender on her part. That is the only promise I can have. Otherwise I would rather go to law because I don't trust her. . . . The unconditional surrender is that it is necessary for her to give up the idea of writing anything. . . . the important point is that she must only write when under competent medical assistance I say that she can write. Now that sounds awfully egotistical, but it is the only way that I can ever organize my life again.

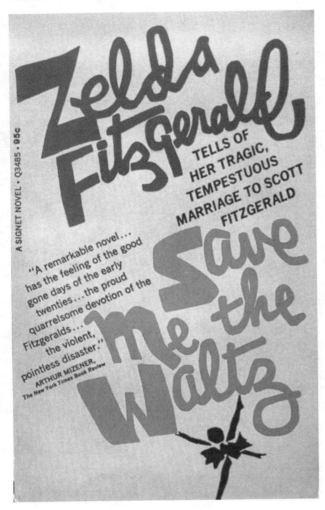
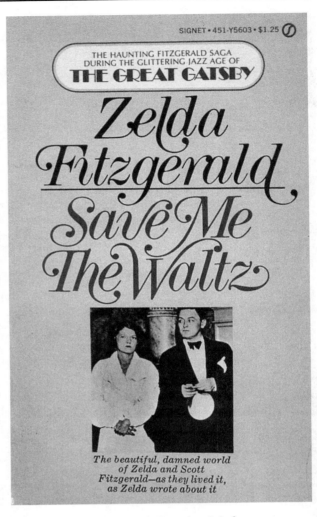

Covers for mass-market paperbacks published in 1968 and 1974, the latter of which was an inappropriate tie-in for the movie version of The Great Gatsby *(Bruccoli Collection of Fitzgerald, Thomas Cooper Library, University of South Carolina)*

Zelda: I want to write and I am going to write. I am going to be a writer, but I am not going to do it at Scott's expense if I can possibly avoid it. So I agree not to do anything that he does not want, a complete negation of self until that book is out of the way, because the thing is driving me crazy the way it is, and I cannot do that. And if he cannot adjust it and let me do what I want to do and live with me after that, I would rather do what I want to do.

Fitzgerald: The thing that used to crop up in the days before Zelda collapsed, she would continually make this statement, that she was working to get away from me. Now, you see, that sticks with me.

Zelda: Dr. Rennie, that is not true. . . . Here is the truth of the matter: that I have always felt some

necessity for us to be on a more equal footing than we are now because I cannot possibly—there is just something, one thing, that I simply cannot live in a world that is completely dependent on Scott when he does not care anything about me and reproachs me all the time. . . . I want to be able to say, when he says something that is not so, then I want to do something so good that I can say, "That is a goddamned lie," and have something to back it up—that I can say it.

Fitzgerald: Now we have found rock bottom.

Zelda: What is our marriage, anyway? It has been nothing but a long battle ever since I can remember.

Fitzgerald: I don't know about that. We were about the most envied couple in about 1921 in America.

Zelda: I guess so. We were awfully good showmen.

Fitzgerald: We were awfully happy. . . . You say that you will put off your writing another book, you will stop everything, and you have said that a number of times before in the presence of Dr. Rennie. And you did not mean it. You will start it up in twenty-four hours. You mean I will have to write this whole book in the next three months with the sense that you wait hating me, waiting for me to get away. That is not the social arrangement that I can live under. . . . I want my own way. I earned the right to my own way— . . .

Zelda: And I want the right of my own way.

Fitzgerald: And you cannot have it without breaking me so you have to give it up. It all comes to the same thing: I have to sacrifice myself for you, and you have got to sacrifice yourself for me, and no more writing of fiction.

Zelda: Of any kind?

Fitzgerald: If you write a play, it cannot be a play about psychiatry and it cannot be a play laid on the Riviera, and it cannot be a play laid in Switzerland, and whatever the idea is it will have to be submitted to me.

Zelda: Scott, you can go on and have your way about this thing and do anything until you finish the book, and when you finish the book I think we'd better get a divorce, and any decision you choose to make with regard to me is all right because I cannot live on those terms, and I cannot accept them.

***

Back Numbers
The Times Literary Supplement, 6 October 1967

Of Zelda Fitzgerald's one and only novel—written, in hospital, in a single inspired rush of six weeks—there can be no question. Despite a British reissue in 1953, the book has not been widely available. It remains an interesting adjunct to her husband's *Tender Is the Night* (which appeared two years later, covering much the same ground) and thus inevitably forms a footnote to the F. Scott Fitzgerald canon.

But it was precisely from the status of footnote that both Zelda and her novel needed rescuing:

> David's success was his own—he had earned his right to be critical—Alabama felt that she had nothing to give to the world and no way to dispose of what she took away.

The hope of entering Diaghilev's ballet loomed before her like a protecting cathedral.

David, alias Amory Blaine, was Scott himself. Alabama Beggs, the beauty from the Deep South, was Zelda—who had something to give to posterity, after all. Her narrative may be slipshod, moving awkwardly from tableau to tableau: the American South, New York, Long Island, the South of France, Paris, Naples, Switzerland. Her style tends to be highly charged, incandescent with verbal fireworks. As in some autobiographical novels, the pressure of memory does violence to both shape and language. And, like all novices, she is often pretentious. But her eyes and ears were rapacious. She presents the living texture of the age, its inconsequent chatter and shifts of sensation. Her picture of a Russian ballet school in Paris is particularly memorable.

For Zelda, New York's *prima* flapper *absolute,* in all else felt herself to be a failure. As a novelist's wife she desperately sought success in painting, ballet, and finally, during a nervous breakdown in the Johns Hopkins Hospital at Baltimore, in fiction, too. But

> by the time a person has achieved years, adequate for choosing a direction, the die is cast and the moment has long since passed which determined the future. We grew up founding our dreams on the infinite promise of American advertising. I *still* believe that one can learn to play the piano by mail and that mud will give a perfect complexion.

She was to learn not by mail, as it turned out, but her husband's art from her husband. And though, in the final analysis, Scott Fitzgerald was right in judging the novel "a bad book", it still brims with life, revealing more than most documentary tours of a decade when "people were tired of the proletariet—everybody was famous," and "all the other people who weren't well known had been killed in the war. . . ."

–Johns Hopkins Hospital Archives

***

Chews Gum–Shows Knees
Clarie Tomalin
New Statesman, 17 January 1969, p. 89

No publisher would have reprinted *Save Me the Waltz* again (there was an English edition in 1953) if it were not the work of Scott Fitzgerald's wife, and one that can be read as a gloss on his novel of the same period. Its sales in America in 1932 were slight—but then so were the sales of *Tender is the Night,* planned earlier, published two years later.

Covers for British mass-market paperbacks: left, for the first 1971 printing, and right, for the 1982 reprinting
(Bruccoli Collection of Fitzgerald, Thomas Cooper Library, University of South Carolina)

Who wanted to read about the Twenties during the Depression? 'A rather irritating type of chic' is what the NEW STATESMAN critic found in Scott's novel, which he had laboured at from 1925 to 1934, and continued to work on years later (in particular rearranging the sections of the book, much to its improvement). *Tender is the Night* is, for all its flaws and carelessness, something like a great book, showing us very clearly (since Fitzgerald's life is so well documented) the power of the artist to change particular personal experience into something utterly different; in the book, he is fair to all the characters and situations, as he couldn't be in life.

He himself was well aware of the fact and the cost of such artistry; he'd said to Zelda, when she took up ballet: 'I hope you realise that the biggest difference in the world is between the amateur and the professional in the arts,' and he showed some understandable bitter-

ness when she sent Maxwell Perkins her novel without letting him see it first. Perkins was his editor; *Save Me the Waltz* covered much of the same ground as what was already written and planned of his novel, which she'd seen. He wrote to Perkins: 'The mixture of fact and fiction is calculated to ruin us both, or what is left of us, and I can't let it stand.' It was indeed revised, more perhaps with an eye to content than style. A year later, in 1933, Scott told a psychiatrist that Zelda believed anything was possible, and used his material like a mischievous little boy drawing on an artist's canvas, with no awareness of 'the enormous moral business that goes on in the mind of anyone who writes anything worth writing.'

What strikes one forcibly about *Save Me the Waltz* is that most of the best passages are not concerned with the life she lived with her husband, David Knight, the character who represents him—Scott made her change the name from Amory Blaine, hero of his *This Side of Paradise*—is indeed a nonentity, as Scott complained, adding that *he* had made Zelda a legend. But he continued for the rest of his life to contribute to that legend, portraying her with a passionate regret for the love they had once shared; the generosity is his, as she acknowledged after his death.

Save Me the Waltz, written in six weeks during a schizophrenic breakdown, is in form a fairly conventionally shaped story about a Southern girl, Alabama, youngest daughter of Judge Beggs, a rigid, old-fashioned and domineering father. Here is the South, the period (First World War), the excitable sensibility of a young girl with nothing to do but shock her small-town world, and with all the means when a thousand young men in uniform arrive to amuse her. She falls in love with a youthful painter, marries in New York, dances, plays pranks; they're famous, and c-r-a-z-y about each other. There are terrible bits of purple writing, but we see what Zelda wants us to see. Later, on board ship for Europe and describing the Riviera and Paris world, the book sags; there is a baby, there are flirtations, love sours. Alabama takes up ballet, drives herself beyond all normal limits in her frenzy to succeed; she falls ill, and returns to the States for the death of her father. On his deathbed she frantically questions him about the pain of life; it is too late, he cannot answer. 'Ask me something easy,' he murmurs, uncharacteristically.

It could be claimed that the theme of the book is the presence of Judge Beggs in his daughter's life; her dreams of escape, her revolt against his authority and traditions, the failure of her husband to provide an equivalent moral presence; all relate to him. Alabama suffered cruelly as one of a generation of girls uneducated for anything but marriage, precipitated into a world their parents could not have foreseen. Her turning to ballet, which consumed time and energy and even her body with its physical demands – she was too old to start, too proud not to go at it like a tigress – expresses perhaps a belated respect for her father's belief in hard work, integrity and moral imperatives.

In plot, *Save Me the Waltz* (the title refers not to romantic memories of Scott but to her ambitions in the ballet) is almost entirely autobiographical, and it is part of the evidence of her ability and arresting personality. That she was jealous of Scott's fame and talent she acknowledged; that she wrote the book partly out of that jealousy, partly (as she took up painting and dancing) out of loneliness caused less by his work than by his compulsive gregariousness

and drinking – and partly to give *her* version–this is true.

She was, after all, still the same Zelda Sayre who had spent her last night in Alabama before her New York wedding lying awake and plotting with a friend ways to attract attention in New York, such as sliding down the banisters of the Biltmore; the same Zelda who'd inspired one of Scott's friends to write in his diary on first meeting her: 'Temperamental small town Southern belle. Chews gum – shows knees.' Exactly a year later, he was writing: 'She is without doubt the most brilliant and most beautiful young woman I've ever known.'

Fitzgerald and Keats

Fitzgerald best explained his love for Keats's poetry in a 3 August 1940 letter to his daughter.

Poetry is either something that lives like fire inside you—like music to the musician or Marxism to the Communist—or else it is nothing, an empty, formalized bore around which pedants can endlessly drone their notes and explanations. The Grecian Urn is unbearably beautiful with every syllable as inevitable as the notes in Beethoven's Ninth Symphony or it's just something you don't understand. It is what it is because an extraordinary genius paused at that point in history and touched it. I suppose I've read it a hundred times. About the tenth time I began to know what it was about, and caught the chime in it and the exquisite inner mechanics. Likewise with The Nightingale which I can never read through without tears in my eyes; likewise the Pot of Basil with its great stanzas about that two brothers, "Why were they proud, etc.", and The Eve of St. Agnes, which has the richest, most sensuous imagery in English, not excepting Shakespeare. And finally his three or four great sonnets, Bright Star and the others.

Knowing those things very young and granted an ear, one could scarcely ever afterwards be unable to distinguish between gold and dross in what one read. In themselves those eight poems are a scale of work for anybody who wants to know truly about words, their most utter value for evocation; persuasion or charm. For awhile after you quit Keats all other poetry seems to be only whistling or humming.

—F. Scott Fitzgerald: A Life in Letters, pp. 460–461

* * *

Fitzgerald chose a line from the fourth stanza of his favorite poem as his title.

Ode to a Nightingale
John Keats

MY heart aches, and a drowsy numbness pains
My sense, as though of hemlock I had drunk,
Or emptied some dull opiate to the drains
One minute past, and Lethe-wards had sunk:
'Tis not through envy of thy happy lot,
But being too happy in thine happiness,
That thou, light-wingèd Dryad of the trees,
In some melodious plot
Of beechen green, and shadows numberless,
Singest of summer in full-throated ease.

O for a draught of vintage! that hath been
Cool'd a long age in the deep-delvèd earth,
Tasting of Flora and the country-green,
Dance, and Provençal song, and sunburnt mirth!
O for a beaker full of the warm South!
Full of the true, the blushful Hippocrene,
With beaded bubbles winking at the brim,
And purple-stainèd mouth;
That I might drink, and leave the world unseen,
And with thee fade away into the forest dim:

Fade far away, dissolve, and quite forget
What thou among the leaves hast never known,
The weariness, the fever, and the fret
Here, where men sit and hear each other groan;
Where palsy shakes a few, sad, last grey hairs,
Where youth grows pale, and spectre-thin, and dies;
Where but to think is to be full of sorrow
And leaden-eyed despairs;
Where beauty cannot keep her lustrous eyes,
Or new Love pine at them beyond to-morrow.

Away! away! for I will fly to thee,
Not charioted by Bacchus and his pards,
But on the viewless wings of Poesy,
Though the dull brain perplexes and retards:
Already with thee! tender is the night,
And haply the Queen-Moon is on her throne,
Cluster'd around by all her starry Fays
But here there is no light,
Save what from heaven is with the breezes blown
Through verdurous glooms and winding mossy ways.

I cannot see what flowers are at my feet,
Nor what soft incense hangs upon the boughs,
But, in embalmèd darkness, guess each sweet
Wherewith the seasonable month endows
The grass, the thicket, and the fruit-tree wild;
White hawthorn, and the pastoral eglantine;
Fast-fading violets cover'd up in leaves;
And mid-May's eldest child,
The coming musk-rose, full of dewy wine,
The murmurous haunt of flies on summer eves.

John Keats, Fitzgerald's favorite poet (portrait by W. Hilton; National Portrait Gallery, London)

Darkling I listen; and, for many a time
I have been half in love with easeful Death,
Call'd him soft names in many a musèd rhyme,
To take into the air my quiet breath;
Now more than ever seems it rich to die,
To cease upon the midnight with no pain,
While thou art pouring forth thy soul abroad
In such an ecstasy!
Still wouldst thou sing, and I have ears in vain—
To thy high requiem become a sod.

Thou wast not born for death, immortal Bird!
No hungry generations tread thee down;
The voice I hear this passing night was heard
In ancient days by emperor and clown:
Perhaps the self-same song that found a path
Through the sad heart of Ruth, when, sick for home,
She stood in tears amid the alien corn;
The same that ofttimes hath
Charm'd magic casements, opening on the foam
Of perilous seas, in faery lands forlorn.

Forlorn! the very word is like a bell
To toll me back from thee to my sole self!
Adieu! the fancy cannot cheat so well
As she is famed to do, deceiving elf.
Adieu! adieu! thy plaintive anthem fades
Past the near meadows, over the still stream,
Up the hill-side; and now 'tis buried deep
In the next valley-glades:
Was it a vision, or a waking dream?
Fled is that music:—do I wake or sleep?

F. Scott Fitzgerald as John Keats

Richard L. Schoenwald

Boston University Studies in English, 3 (Spring 1957): 13–14

For Fitzgerald, Keats represented genius. Keats was everything that he sought so ardently to become: a great and famous writer. Keats and great writers did not merely enjoy success. He and they suffered too. Fitzgerald toiled, grew famous, and suffered. He learned that he could not have one side of what he considered Keats to have been without taking the other, the opposite, as well. He who gained the goodness and pleasure summed up in feelings of tenderness and awareness of acclaim had to endure the night's pain, sooner or later.

Fitzgerald created his own Keats and shaped his own nightingale ode. Both were anchored deep within. Very little time passed between the dropping of *Doctor Diver's Holiday* and the discovery of a new title. Very little time was needed. By the mid-thirties Fitzgerald had passed many days and nights with his Keats. He had added to the first image he had formed, that of the renowned artist. What he added was a way out of suffering, the burden of glory; he discovered this salvation in his reading of the ode. Union with the night, he came to believe, might bring the curtain down on tragedy, tragicomedy, farce that had played too long. It could end the miserable show called life.

Fitzgerald first made Keats into a model on which he would build his own being. Then the fullness of Keatsian destiny unrolled: days of greatness had to be followed by nights of searing pain. Yet these nights might end themselves by ending everything in a final slumber.

The theme of fated destruction reverberated from one end of Fitzgerald's life to the other. Absorption in Keats also stretched down the long way from the unknowing hopes of the adolescent who wanted to write to the knowing agonies of the man who could write. A little over a year before he died he took the concerns of a lifetime, to write and to live as he thought Keats had, out of his heart and exposed them to his daughter (August 3, 1940):

The Grecian Urn is unbearably beautiful, with every note as inevitable as the notes in Beethoven's *Ninth Symphony*. . . . It is what it is because an extraordinary genius paused at that point in history and touched it. I suppose I've read it a hundred times. About the tenth time I began to know what it was about, and caught the chime in it and the exquisite inner mechanics. Likewise with the *Nightingale,* which I can never read through without tears in my eyes. . . . For awhile after you quit Keats all other poetry seems to be only whistling or humming.

Fitzgerald's voice, calling up Keats, deepened and darkened until the compelling gloom of *Tender* was reached. Each time before this, when he named Keats or a nightingale, he acted out the ode and the poet's life as he then was reading them. He staged inside himself his own biography of Keats on the level to which his past experience drove him.

The young Fitzgerald read spottily, not too wisely, not really well. He went through Shelley, Swinburne, Tennyson among others. The fact that he read rather restrictedly argues for Keats's sticking with him. Malcolm Cowley, who ought to know, has said that Keats was his favorite author. In 1919 John Peale Bishop was already urging Fitzgerald to come chant Keats with him on New York streets. Discussing Fitzgerald in 1924, Edmund Wilson referred to "the capacity for pretty writing which he says he learned from Keats." He added that "With the seeds he took from Keats's garden (one of the best kept gardens in the world) he exfloreated so profusely that he blotted out the path of his own. . . ." The early connection between Keats and Fitzgerald resulted from fusing the young man eager to write prettily, and to lead an artistic life, with heavily romanticized pictures of Keats the meteoric poet. Fitzgerald said, each time he read Keats: I want to be like Keats; I am like Keats; I am Keats.

Tender Is the Night: Keats and Scott Fitzgerald

John Grube

Dalhousie Review (Winter 1964–1965): 180–182

Fitzgerald not only took the title of his novel from Keats' "Ode to a Nightingale," but places a quotation from the poem at the beginning of the book. Let us look for a moment at this section of the poem:

Already with thee! tender is the night,
And haply the Queen-Moon is on her throne,
Cluster'd around by all her starry Fays;
But here there is no light,
Save what from heaven is with the breezes blown
Through verdurous glooms and winding mossy ways.

That is the part of the poem he chose to quote and emphasize. Curiously enough he omits these two lines:

And haply the Queen-Moon is on her throne,
Cluster'd around by all her starry Fays;

We shall see that he had a reason for drawing attention to these two lines; he chose to make the moon, in her many aspects—queen, goddess, suggestive of madness—an important symbol in the book.

The novel, too, even in its structure is full of echoes of Keats' famous poem. Enwrapped in Nicole's money and beauty, Dr. Diver leaves the world of science and the intellect for the world of sense (". . . a drowsy numbness pains/My sense"), abandons his medical practice, and even forgets the promising research of his youth (". . . Lethe-wards had sunk"). The poem's word "opiate" has a medical touch, just as the parallel "hemlock," with its overtones of the death of Socrates, suggests the end of his rational life.

At this point Nicole's family buy him a half-interest in a private mental hospital, partly to restore his professional self-confidence and feelings of manliness. She names the house for incurable male patients The Eglantine (". . . the pastoral eglantine") and the corresponding house for female patients The Beeches: ("In some melodious plot/Of beechen green, and shadows numberless"). The "shadows numberless" of the poem become in the novel "those sunk in eternal darkness."

Dr. Diver often contrasts Nicole's innocence of human suffering with his own experience as a psychiatrist:

What thou among the leaves hast never known,
The weariness, the fever, and the fret
Here, where men sit and hear each other groan

Further, we are shown Dick on his daily medical rounds. There are the hopelessly old and senile ("Where palsy shakes a few, sad, last grey hairs"); the young, usually schizophrenic, who always touch his heart ("Where youth grows pale, and spectre-thin, and dies"); the formidably intelligent whose grief is that they can now think only in circles ("Where but to think is to be full of sorrow"); finally there are those who were once beautiful, twisted by despair until they become objects of profound pity and regret ("Where beauty cannot keep her lustrous eyes").

Soon Dick and Nicole tire of the Swiss mental home and again resume their search for the "hot, sweet south" (p. 91) where they had first found so much happiness ("Dance and Provençal song, and sunburnt mirth"). Settling in their villa, they become the glass of fashion and mould of form as Nicole increasingly attracts the admiration and attention of a large coterie. The men respond to her beauty, and in the process somewhat lose their manliness and cue for action ("The Queen-Moon is on her throne/

Cluster'd around by all her starry Fays"). At this point in the novel they are at the supposed peak of human happiness, surrounded by friends, good food, and particularly good wine ("With beaded bubbles winking at the brim/And purple-stained mouth"). But the wink turns into a leer as Dick goes on a serious drinking spree in Rome. His personality begins to crack, and he pursues a self-destructive course, sometimes violent as on the Roman holiday where he is seriously beaten up, sometimes simply alienating friends. But the death wish is there ("Darkling I listen; and for many a time/I have been half in love with easeful death"). He is more and more adrift on the "perilous" seas of "fancy", while Nicole is daily growing in health and vitality ("While thou art pouring forth thy soul abroad/In such an ecstasy").

Finally Nicole falls in love with Tommy Barban, a soldier of fortune; Dick and Nicole are divorced, and as Dr. Diver disappears to America at the end of the story, he is left only the haunting memory of her beauty. The corresponding lines of Keats' poem have a similar haunting quality and a theme of separation:

Adieu! Adieu! the plaintive anthem fades
Past the near meadows, over the still stream,
Up the hillside; now 'tis buried deep

In the next valley-glades:
Was it a vision, or a walking dream?
Fled is that music:—do I wake or sleep?

* * *

Tender Is the Night and The "Ode to a Nightingale"
William E. Doherty
Explorations of Literature (1966), pp. 191–197

It is true that the title *Tender Is the Night* was chosen late in the extended course of the book's writing; but it seems clear that Fitzgerald was conscious of the "Ode" not merely in the last stages of composition. The title is appropriate, though no one has said why. Yet, a moment's reflection will show that there is a good deal of Keatsian suggestiveness in *Tender Is the Night* in both decor and atmosphere—the Provençal summers of sunburnt mirth, the nights perfumed and promising, the dark gardens of an illusory world. But I suggest that there are parallels more significant than those of color and mood. The correspondences I offer in this case, when taken individually, might seem no more than coincidental; but considered in their cumulative weight, they indicate a calculated pattern of allusion beneath the literal surface of the novel which deepens the psy-

Fourth stanza of the earliest surviving manuscript of Keats's "Ode to a Nightingale"
(Fitzwilliam Museum, Cambridge University)

choanalytic rationale and adds context to the cultural analysis the book offers. In addition, the "Ode" appears to provide us with a sort of thematic overlay which clarifies unsuspected symbolic structures, essential to the understanding of the book.

I will begin with an admission that weakens my case. Fitzgerald dropped a reference to the nightingale from his second and subsequent version of the published novel. In the *Scribner's Magazine* version he wrote of "roses and the nightingales" that had become an essential part of the beauty of that "proud gay land," Provence. Why that observation was dropped, I cannot say; but its appearance, however brief, suggests that like Keats, Fitzgerald associated the south of France with the romantic bird. There is a second and more interesting reference which remained. It too connects the bird and the south of France. To understand its significance, one must consider it in context.

The Riviera, Mediterranean France, came to be, as Maxwell Geismar has pointed out, that apogee of ease and grace, that "psychological Eden" in which Fitzgerald and his heroes took refuge. None of his characters responds more fully to this environment than does Rosemary, coming as she does from the "salacious improvisations of the frontier." At the party at the Villa Diana, no guest is more enchanted by the life that seems promised there; she feels a sense of homecoming, feels drawn as if by magnetic lights. The spell of the party is still on her as she lies awake in her room "suspended in the moonshine, . . . cloaked by the erotic darkness." She is disturbed by

secret noises in the night: an "insistent bird" sings in the tree outside. She is not sure what bird it is, but the singing and the Divers seem to merge in her mind: "Beyond the inky sea and far up that high, black shadow of a hill lived the Divers. She thought of them both together, heard them still singing faintly a song like rising smoke, like a hymn, very remote in time and far away." But Rosemary is confused by it all; she cannot think as yet except through her mother's mind. Abe North identifies the bird for her:

"What are *you* doing up?" he demanded.
"I just got up." She started to laugh. . . .
"Probably plagued by the nightingale," Abe suggested and repeated, "probably plagued by the nightingale" (42).

The entire chapter, heavy with night imagery, seems to lead up to this identification. Rosemary has been brought up with the idea of work. Now she is on a summer's holiday, an emotionally lush interval between two winters of reality; and what she discovers is a world remote, romantic, something southern, a mysterious dark lure of life to which she responds—symbolized by the night bird. It is unreal; a duel will be fought; "up north the true world thundered by."

What I suggest is that the novel deals with characters who are plagued by the nightingale, those enamoured of the romantic illusion. Nicole seems to be the Nightingale.

Consider the scene in which Nicole sings to Dick. As she waits for Dick at the sanatorium, singing surrounds Nicole, summer songs of ardent skies and wild shade. The night, the woods, gardens, flowers are associated with Nicole throughout the novel. Here, the unknown seems to yield her up, "as if this were the exact moment when she was coming from a wood into the clear moonlight" (135). Dick responds to that illusion, wishes that she had no other background, "no address save the night from which she had come." She leads him to a secret copse. In this melodious plot she has hidden a phonograph. She plays for him "thin tunes, holding lost times and future liaison." Through song the two of them are transported out of the copse into another world. The journey is chronicled in ironic song titles. Finally Nicole herself sings to Dick. She supposes he has heard all these songs before. "'Honestly, you don't understand—I haven't heard a thing.' Nor known, nor smelt, nor tasted, he might have added" (136). Now here was this girl bringing him the essence of a continent, "making him a profound promise of herself for so little. . . . Minute by minute the sweetness drained down into her out of the willow trees, out of the dark world" (136). But there is danger in the promise of this "waif of disaster," in the song of this "young bird with wings crushed."

The brief transport from the world which the "Ode" details, the emotional adventure of climax and decline is suggested in this and in a number of other scenes in *Tender Is the Night*. Indeed, the pattern describes the very rhythm of the novel. The party at the Villa Diana, as Malcolm Cowley suggests, appears to be the high point in the story. The scene marks a change of mood; thereafter, the light romantic atmosphere is dispelled. We see there the Divers at their point of greatest charm—a "vision of ease and grace," commanding all the delicacies of existence. It is a high point for another reason. It is in this scene that the principals of the story make an escape from the prosaic and temporal world. In the rarified atmosphere of the party a moment is caught in which a delicate triumph over time is achieved.

The party is given out of doors in the garden, Nicole's garden. To Rosemary the setting seems to be the center of the world: "On such a stage some memorable thing was sure to happen" (29). The guests arrive under a spell, bringing with them the excitement of the night. Dick now seems to serve Nicole as prop man, arranging the set, dressing the trees with lamps. The guests are seated at Nicole's table:

There were fireflies riding on the dark air and a dog baying on some far-away ledge of the cliff. The table seemed to have risen a little toward the sky like a

---

Early in the evening that he is beaten in Rome, Dick Diver sits with Collis Clay in the Quirinale bar.

Dick evoked the picture that the few days had imprinted on his mind, and stared at it. The walk toward the American Express past the odorous confectioneries of the Via Nazionale, through the foul tunnel up to the Spanish Steps, where his spirit soared before the flower stalls and the house where Keats had died.

—*Tender Is the Night*, p. 288

---

mechanical dancing platform, giving the people around it a sense of being alone with each other in the dark universe, nourished by its only food, warmed by its only lights. And, as if a curious hushed laugh from Mrs. McKisco were a signal that such a detachment from the world had been attained, the two Divers began suddenly to warm and glow and expand, as if to make up to their guests, already so subtly assured of their importance, so flattered with politeness, for anything they might still miss from that country well left behind. Just for a moment they seemed to speak to everyone at the table, singly and together, assuring them of their friendliness, their affection. And for a moment the faces turned up toward them were like the faces of poor children at a Christmas tree. Then abruptly the table broke up—the moment when the guests had been daringly lifted above conviviality into the rarer atmosphere of sentiment, was over before it could be irreverently breathed, before they had half realized it was there.

But the diffused magic of the hot sweet South had withdrawn into them—the soft-pawed night and the ghostly wash of the Mediterranean far below—the magic left these things and melted into the two Divers and became part of them (34–35).

When we consider the care with which Fitzgerald dresses this scene, we sense an emphasis beyond what the mere events of the party would demand. This garden, the fireflies riding on the dark air, the summer evening, the wine-colored lanterns hung in the trees—the Romantic decor is there, and the Keatsian atmosphere: "the diffused magic of the hot sweet South . . . the soft-pawed night and the ghostly wash of the Mediterranean far below." There is no need to insist that these images have their antecedents in the "Ode"—in its "murmurous haunt of flies on summer eves," or its "warm south," its "tender night," its "charmed magic casements opening on perilous seas"; for the clearest parallel to the poem lies in the brief achievement of the precious atmosphere, achieved through the familiar Romantic formula of escape at the moment of emo-

The house where Keats died, located to the right of the bottom of the Spanish Steps (Bruccoli Collection of Fitzgerald, Thomas Cooper Library, University of South Carolina)

tional pitch—here ironically, a moment of social ecstasy, but suggesting inevitably the dynamics of the sexual event. The imagery itself reiterates the pattern: the fragile loveliness of Nicole's garden increases "until, as if the scherzo of color could reach no further intensity, it broke off suddenly in midair, and moist steps went down to a level five feet below" (26).

It seems unlikely that the material of the "Ode" was so immediate in Fitzgeral's mind that it would come to add to the novel a dimension of allusion of which he was unaware. We are willing to concede unlimited conscious subtlety to his contemporaries in the novel; but Fitzgerald, despite the evidence of his deliberate workmanship, is too often pictured by critics as a somewhat fatuous tool of the muse, whose mind was inferior to his talent. The intricacies of *Tender Is the Night* would suggest otherwise. Not only is the pattern of the momentary climax a repeated one in the novel; there occurs, too, the *recall to reality* that marks the ending of the "Ode." In the novel it is not the sound of a bell that signals the descent from bliss—or the word "forlorn" striking like a bell, tolling the poet back to his sole self; it is another sound heard three times in the

book: when Dick falls in love with Nicole, when Abe leaves on the train from Paris, and when Tommy becomes Nicole's lover. Each time a shot is heard, a loud report that breaks the illusion, signifies the end of happiness and the escape from self.

After Nicole leaves the sanatorium, Dick tries to avoid her; but she fills his dreams. Their chance meeting in the Alps ends in Dick's complete surrender of self: "he was thankful to have an existence at all, if only as a reflection in her wet eyes" (155). As in all her love situations, Nicole is triumphant, self-controlled, cool: "I've got him, he's mine" (155). The scene remains tender; it is raining, the appropriate weather for love in Fitzgerald's novels. But, "suddenly there was a booming from the wine slopes across the lake; like cannons were shooting at hail-bearing clouds in order to break them. The lights of the promenade went off, went on again. Then the storm came swiftly . . . with it came a dark, frightening sky and savage filaments of lightning and world-splitting thunder, while ragged, destroying clouds fled along past the hotel. Mountains and lakes disappeared--the hotel crouched amid tumult, chaos and darkness" (155–156).

This is not the storm of passion. Dick has come suddenly to his senses: "For Doctor Diver to marry a mental patient? How did it happen? Where did it begin?" The moment of passion and illusion is over. He laughs derisively. "*Big* chance—oh, yes. My God!—they decided to buy a doctor? Well, they better stick to whoever they've got in Chicago" (156). But Dick has committed himself to Nicole. His clear sight comes too late, and when the storm is over her beauty enters his room "rustling ghostlike through the curtains."

A loud shot sounds the ominous recall another time, in the Paris railway station. Here is departure and farewell; a gunshot cracks the air. Abe, on the train, waves good-by, unaware of what has happened. The shots do not mark the end of his happiness, for he has long been in misery, though they do forebode his violent death. It is the brief summer happiness of Dick—won in a desperate bargain with the gods—that is ending. It marks the end of a summer mirth for the Divers' group, the beginning of misfortune for Dick. Dick and his friends move out of the station into the streets as if nothing had happened. "However, everything had happened—Abe's departure and Mary's impending departure for Salzburg this afternoon had ended the time in Paris. Or perhaps the shots, the concussions that had finished God knew what dark matter, had terminated it. The shots had entered into all their lives . . ." (85).

The third of these recalls to reality occurs just after Tommy possesses Nicole. The entire account from the arrival of Tommy at the Villa Diana to the departure from the hotel presents a curious parallel to the ending of the "Ode." Tommy comes to Nicole like a worshipper before a mystery. His happiness intensifies: "And, my God, I have never been so happy as I am this minute" (194). But the time of joy is brief; the point of greatest happiness is a moment outside of self, a taste of oblivion. The ecstasy passes; disappointment and foreboding follow: "the nameless fear which precedes all emotions, joyous or sorrowful, inevitable as a hum of thunder precedes a storm." After the act, things begin to look tawdry to Tommy. He is edgy and apprehensive. Outside there are disturbing noises: "There's that noise again. My God, has there been a murder?" The final recall is heard. As they leave the room "a sound split the air outside: Cr-ACK-Boom-M-m-m! It was the battleship sounding a recall. Now, down below their window, it was pandemonium indeed . . ." (296–297). There is a rush to depart. Cries and tears are heard as the women shout farewells to the departing launch. The last ludicrous moments of the scene, the girls shouting their tearful good-byes from the balcony of Tommy's room, waving their underwear like flags, appear to be Fitzgerald's ironic counterpart to the adieu of the final stanza of the poem. The fading anthem of the "Ode" becomes the American National Anthem: "Oh, say can you see the tender color of remembered flesh?—while at the stern of the battleship arose in rivalry the Star-Spangled Banner" (297).

Writing *Tender Is the Night*

Knowledge of the gestation and composition of Tender Is the Night *clarifies Fitzgerald's intentions and enables the reader to judge the novel intelligently. Fitzgerald worked on his fourth novel from his twenty-ninth year to his thirty-eighth year. His writing of the novel was repeatedly interrupted for money-making short stories. It is impossible to understand Fitzgerald's work habits without accounting for the role of his commercial stories in his career—especially the two-way flow of passages between the stories and* Tender. *This section provides the most detailed examination of that process.*

An Overview of the Composition of *Tender Is the Night*
Matthew J. Bruccoli

On 1 May 1925—three weeks after publication of *The Great Gatsby*—F. Scott Fitzgerald wrote to his editor, Maxwell Perkins, from France: "The happiest thought I have is of my new novel—it is something really NEW in form, idea, structure—the model for the age that Joyce and Stien are searching for, that Conrad didn't find."[1] The novel that became *Tender Is the Night* was published in 1934 after evolving through three plot versions. It began as an examination of a young American, Francis Melarky, who murders his mother in France. Variously titled "The Boy Who Killed His Mother," "The World's Fair," and "Our Type," the matricide version did not progress beyond four chapters, although Fitzgerald worked on it with many interruptions until 1930. It is set on the Riviera and in Paris, where Melarky is taken up by an attractive American expatriate couple, Seth and Dinah Piper (or Roreback), and the alcoholic composer Abe Grant (or Herkimer). The Pipers were based on Fitzgerald's expatriate friends, the now-celebrated Gerald and Sara Murphy; Grant was modeled on Ring Lardner, Fitzgerald's friend. In a flashback chapter Melarky is beaten by the police in Rome. Fitzgerald first wrote the Melarky/matricide version in the third-person point of view and then with a narrator who functions much as Nick Carraway does in *The Great Gatsby*. These characters, except for the narrator, and events were salvaged for *Tender Is the Night*, with the Pipers and Grant as the Divers and North; and some of Melarky's experiences were transferred to Rosemary Hoyt, based on actress Lois Moran. Both Melarky and Rosemary serve as point-of-view characters through whose responses the reader learns about the Pipers and the Divers: Melarky falls in love with Dinah Piper, and Rosemary falls in love with Dick Diver.

In 1929 Fitzgerald wrote two chapters for a second plot version about American movie director Lew Kelly and his wife, Nicole, who are en route to Europe; on the ship is an aspiring actress named Rosemary. These manuscript chapters were apparently never typed, indicating that Fitzgerald lost interest in this approach early on. He probably returned to the Melarky plot in 1930, but work was interrupted by Zelda Fitzgerald's mental breakdown in April 1930 and her treatment in Switzerland—providing Fitzgerald with new material. The Fitzgeralds returned to America in September 1931.

Fitzgerald began replanning the final Dick Diver version in January 1932, but actual writing may not have begun until late spring or early summer 1932, when his wife was a patient in Baltimore. After years of delays, work progressed well, for the Diver version utilized personal experience Fitzgerald felt strongly about; moreover, he was under pressure to restore or reaffirm his standing as a serious novelist. The novel was ready for serialization in *Scribner's Magazine* at the end of 1933.

Tender Is the Night—which had as working titles "The Drunkard's Holiday," "Dr. Diver's Holiday," "Dr. Diver," and "Richard Diver"—traces the decline and failure of psychiatrist Dick Diver during his marriage to Nicole, a wealthy mental patient.

Fitzgerald's May 1925 message to Perkins attests that from the start he envisioned a structurally innovative work. He devised a flashback to reveal Diver's deterioration behind the mask of his charm and to expose the forces acting against his aspirations. There is no evidence that Fitzgerald was uncertain about this plan. The structure of the published book is the only one that survives in the drafts. Book I (25 chapters) occupies a couple of weeks in 1925 on the Riviera and in Paris—seen mainly from Rosemary's point of view. Book II (23 chapters) opens in 1917, returns to 1925 by the brilliant bridging device of Nicole's stream of consciousness in Chapter 10, and ends with Dick's 1928 beating in Rome. Book III (13 chapters) relates Dick's deterioration during 1928 and 1929—with the postscript chapter tracing his failure and anonymity: "in any case he is almost certainly in that section of the country, in one town or another."

GESTATION AND COMPOSITION OF *TENDER IS THE NIGHT*

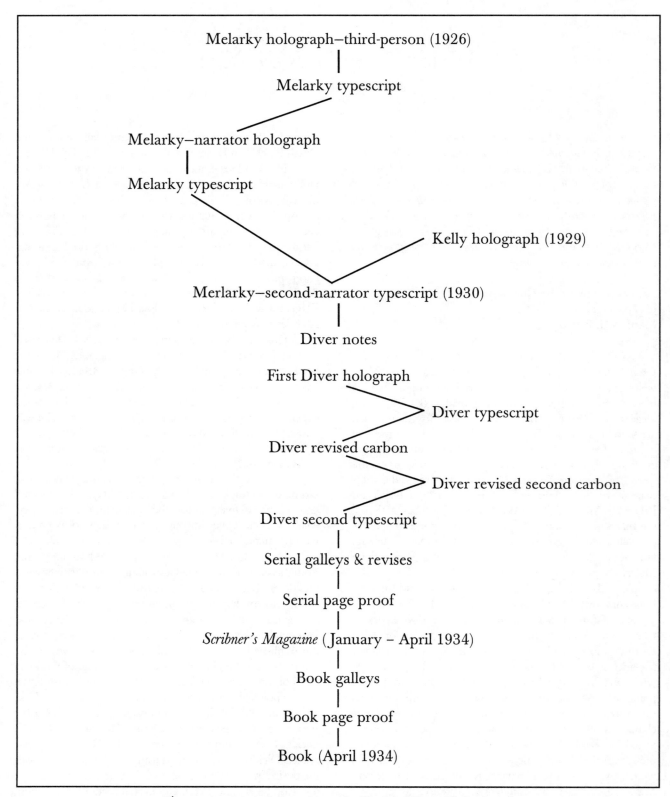

Melarky holograph–third-person (1926)

Melarky typescript

Melarky–narrator holograph

Melarky typescript

Kelly holograph (1929)

Merlarky–second-narrator typescript (1930)

Diver notes

First Diver holograph

Diver typescript

Diver revised carbon

Diver revised second carbon

Diver second typescript

Serial galleys & revises

Serial page proof

Scribner's Magazine (January – April 1934)

Book galleys

Book page proof

Book (April 1934)

The seventeen stages in the composition and publication of Fitzgerald's fourth novel

John Hall Wheelock

From the inception of the Melarky plot to publication of *Tender Is the Night,* the novel went through seventeen stages of rewriting and revision. Fitzgerald was a painstaking self-editor who improved his prose at every possible opportunity: he reworked the ribbon copy of the first typescript for the Diver version and two carbon-copies of that typescript. He regarded galleys and even page proof as an opportunity to perform further alterations—as shown by his revised proofs for the serial and book texts of *Tender.* Fitzgerald's revising was not nervous tinkering. He knew what he was doing to bring his work closer to the ideal novel that existed in his mind. Editor John Hall Wheelock stated that Fitzgerald was able to make delicate improvements in his proofs when obviously tight.

Note

1. *F. Scott Fitzgerald: A Life in Letters,* eds., Bruccoli and Judith S. Baughman (New York: Scribners, 1994), p. 108. Quotations from Fitzgerald's manuscripts retain his spellings.

The following essay is adapted from the preface to The Short Stories of F. Scott Fitzgerald *(New York: Scribners, 1989).*

Fitzgerald and the Slick-Magazine Short Story: Testing Material for *Tender Is the Night*
Matthew J. Bruccoli

F. Scott Fitzgerald's 160 short stories remain a misunderstood and underrated aspect of his career. They have been dismissed as hackwork and condemned for impeding his serious work. Certainly they are uneven; but Fitzgerald's best stories are among the best in American literature.

Fitzgerald was partly responsible for the continuing difficulty in properly assaying his stories. After an initial period of exuberance at what seemed instant celebrity and easy money, he came to resent the financial necessity of writing stories and the creative energy they drained from his novels. Fitzgerald's disparagement of his stories has persuaded critics to classify most of them as facile potboilers. But his bitterness was generated by the effort—not the ease—of writing fiction for the mass-circulation magazines. In the mid-Thirties, when Fitzgerald was having great difficulty in satisfying this market, he wrote in his *Notebooks:* "I have asked a lot of my emotions—one hundred and twenty stories. The price was high, right up with Kipling, because there was one little drop of something not blood, not a tear, not my seed, but me more intimately than these, in every story, it was the extra I had. Now it has gone and I am just like you now."[1] During this period of discouragement he explained to his agent, Harold Ober, that "all my stories are conceived like novels, require a special emotion, a special experience—so that my readers, if such there be, know that each time it'll be something new, not in form, but in substance (it'd be better for me if I could write pattern stories but the pencil just goes dead on me. . .)."[2] It is meaningful that Fitzgerald assessed his story capacity in terms of their emotional requirements.

Along with facility, Fitzgerald was charged with triviality because his stories did not deal with what critics—especially in the social-conscious Thirties—regarded as significant issues. There are no degrees of literary worth in material. A writer is his material, and it is as literary as he makes it. Fitzgerald never tried to be, or wanted to be, an experimental or avant-garde writer.

It is necessary to understand Fitzgerald's finances in order to evaluate the influence of his stories on his career. He did not make a fortune. The story income was supposed to provide writing time for novels, but he usually lived from story to story. Fitzgerald never had a blockbuster novel—not even *This Side of Paradise,* which sold 52,000 copies in his lifetime and earned about $15,000 in royalties. In 1929 eight *Post* stories brought Fitzgerald $30,000, while all of his books earned total royalties of $31.77 (including $5.10 for *Gatsby*).

Yet it is misleading to segregate Fitzgerald's stories as merely commercial. He was a professional writer, and everything that a professional gets paid for is commercial work. Fitzgerald was not unusual in combining remunerative magazine work with literary art. Before the time of huge advances and munificent subsidiary-rights deals, prominent novelists supplemented their book incomes with magazine work. Writers live by selling words, and Fitzgerald competed successfully in the toughest literary marketplace of his time: the high-paying mass-circulation slick-paper magazines. He became identified with *The Saturday Evening Post* where he published sixty-five stories—about 40 percent of his output—reaching a peak price of $4,000 in 1929. Readers for whom the old *Post* is even a memory will be surprised by the roster of its contributors, which included Willa Cather, Edith Wharton, William Faulkner, and Thomas Wolfe. The *Post* was the most widely read American magazine during the Twenties (2,750,000 copies per week). Harold Ober also placed Fitzgerald's work in most of the competing mass-circulation magazines: *Red Book, Liberty, Collier's, Metropolitan,* and *McCall's.* During his lifetime Fitzgerald was far better known and more widely read as a short-story writer than as a novelist.

All these magazines were aimed at family readership, but there is no evidence to support Ernest Hemingway's claim that Fitzgerald admitted he deliberately spoiled stories to make them salable. Although he wrote about the subjects that editors expected from him, his stories were rarely formulaic: "As soon as I feel I am writing to a cheap specification my pen freezes and my talent vanishes over the hill. . . ."[3] At the top of his form he was able to write popular stories that were honest Fitzgerald stories. His endings were not automatically happy, and he found ways to insert "a touch of disaster."

Fitzgerald did not have two mutually exclusive careers as a magazinist and as a novelist. It was one career, into which all of his work was integrated. Since Fitzgerald perforce wrote stories while he was working on novels, certain "cluster stories" introduce or test themes, settings, and situations that are fully developed in the novel. He routinely "stripped" passages from a story for reuse in a novel. The stories that belong to the gestation of *Tender* are: "One Trip Abroad," "Babylon Revisited," "The Bridal Party," "The Swimmers," "Jacob's Ladder," and "The Hotel Child."

Charles Scribner's Sons, Fitzgerald's only publisher during his lifetime, followed each of his novels with a volume of stories: *Flappers and Philosophers* (1920), *Tales of the Jazz Age* (1922), *All the Sad Young Men* (1926), and *Taps at Reveille* (1935)—a total of forty-five stories. Fitzgerald had scruples about collecting a story that had been stripped for use in a novel. These strippings are identified in *The Notebooks of F. Scott Fitzgerald* (1978). He maintained a distinction between magazine and book publication, insisting that inclusion of a story in one of his collections gave it permanence and literary standing. After he incorporated story material (ranging from phrases to paragraphs) into a novel, he declined to reprint that story as it had originally appeared. Either he rewrote the plundered passage or he designated the story as "buried"—not to be reprinted. In no case did Fitzgerald simply reprint the text of a magazine story.

Reading his stories in the order of their publication reveals Fitzgerald's delicate sense of history as he evokes the rhythms of the Jazz Age and the Depression. He was not a documentary writer; yet he was a brilliant social historian because of his capacity to convey, through style and point of view, the sense of time and place, the sense of being there. Thus he advised Scottie:

> But when in a freak moment you will want to give the low-down, not the scandal, not the merely <u>reported</u> but the <u>profound</u> essence of what happened at a prom or after it, perhaps that honesty will come to you—and then you will understand how it is possible to make even a forlorn Laplander <u>feel</u> the importance of a trip to Cartier's![4]

Notes

1. "Our April Letter," in *The Notebooks of F. Scott Fitzgerald,* edited by Matthew J. Bruccoli (New York & London: Harcourt Brace Jovanovich/Bruccoli Clark, 1978), p. 131.

2. *As Ever, Scott Fitz—: Letters Between F. Scott Fitzgerald and His Literary Agent Harold Ober, 1919–1940,* edited by Matthew J. Bruccoli and Jennifer Atkinson (Philadelphia & New York: Lippincott, 1972), p. 221.

3. To Zelda Fitzgerald, 18 May 1940. *The Letters of F. Scott Fitzgerald,* edited by Andrew Turnbull (New York: Scribners, 1963), pp. 117–118.

4. Undated. *The Letters of F. Scott Fitzgerald,* p. 101.

Writing the Melarky Version

Work on the third-person account of the Francis Melarky story was probably begun in Paris in the fall of 1925 and continued in the Pyrenees, where the Fitzgeralds stayed from January to April 1926. It was an ideal time for Fitzgerald to work on the novel, for he was temporarily free from financial pressures. The Great Gatsby *was made into a play that opened in February of 1926 and brought Fitzgerald about $18,000; Hollywood paid him $15,000 or $20,000 for the screen rights. Fitzgerald had been hurt by the poor sale of* The Great Gatsby, *and his ambition was to write a novel that would show the public that he was "much better than any of the young Americans without exception."*

No plot summary or outline survives for the matricide version; however, the general plan is clear up to a point. After his arrival on the Riviera, Francis is taken up by a brilliant group of Americans led by Seth and Dinah Roreback (also Rorebeck) or Piper. The most interesting of their friends is Abe Herkimer, an alcoholic composer who has squandered a strong talent. Herkimer and Francis act as seconds in a duel between Gabriel Brugerol and Albert McKisco, a writer. Francis attempts to secure work at an American movie studio in France, but his plans are frustrated by his mother, who considers movie people a bad influence on him. Having nothing better to do, he accepts the Rorebacks' invitation to go to Paris with them to see Abe off for America. In Paris, Francis falls in love with Dinah Roreback. She is flattered by his attentions and allows him a few kisses, but she does not develop any romantic feelings about him. At this point Fitzgerald abandoned the Melarky version, but from Fitzgerald's letters and from the recollections of his friends it appears that Francis would have suffered a nervous breakdown—probably from drinking—and then would have murdered his mother in a fit of rage. There is evidence that Fitzgerald considered two possible conclusions. One was to leave Francis in the hands of the law; and in February 1926 Fitzgerald requested legal information from Maxwell Perkins:

In regard to my novel. Will you ask somebody what is done if one American murders another in France. Would an American marshall come over for him? From his state of residence? Who would hold him meanwhile—the consul or the French police? Why isn't that so if one Italian kills another Italian in America?

Its important that I find this out and I can't seem to.

In a certain sense my plot is not unlike Dreisers in the American Tragedy. At first this worries me but now it doesn't for our minds are so different.

. . . .

I should be writing this afternoon but I'm nervous as hell and can't. Zelda is much better. My novel will be called <u>The World's Fair</u> or <u>Our Type</u>. I don't know which.[1]

Fitzgerald told Edmund Wilson that Melarky would have been hunted down and killed by a shot from a "squirrel gun."[2] According to Wilson, Fitzgerald considered it ironic that someone who had committed the grave crime of matricide should be punished with what Fitzgerald considered a childish weapon. Perhaps both episodes were to have been retained.

–Matthew J. Bruccoli

Notes

1. *Dear Scott/Dear Max,* edited by John Kuehl and Jackson R. Bryer (New York: Scribners, 1971), pp. 132–133.
2. Edmund Wilson to Matthew J. Bruccoli.

Correspondence, Spring 1925 to Summer 1929

The following excerpts from Fitzgerald's correspondence show a pattern of optimistic reports, promises, excuses, and apologies that persisted throughout his work on the Melarky and Kelly versions. The only installment of the Melarky manuscript that Fitzgerald sent to Perkins was the two chapters that accompanied his November 1928 letter.

Fitzgerald to Maxwell Perkins, circa 10 July 1925 Paris

The novel has begun. I'd rather tell you nothing about it quite yet.

–*F. Scott Fitzgerald: A Life in Letters,* p. 125

* * *

Fitzgerald to Perkins, circa 20 October 1925 Paris

There is no news. The novel progresses slowly + carefully with much destroying + revision.

–*Dear Scott/Dear Max,* p. 122

* * *

Marya Mannes was a young woman Fitzgerald had met on the Riviera who had written to him about The Great Gatsby.

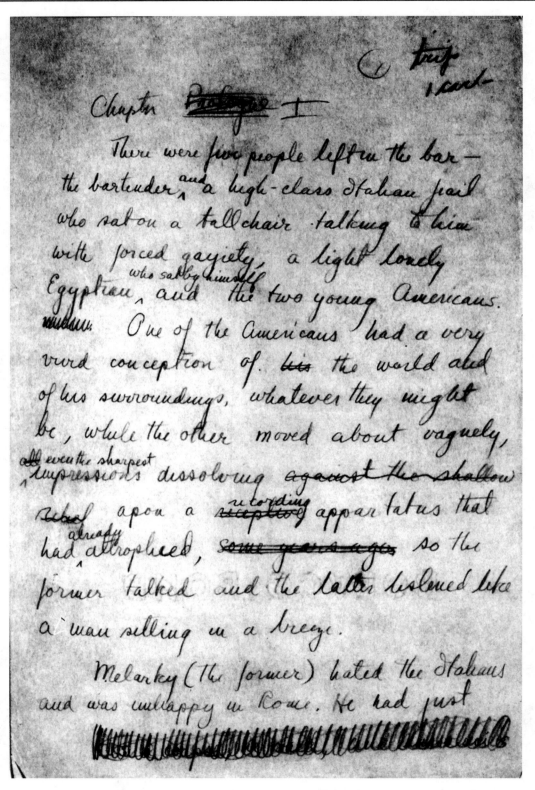

First page of the earliest Melarky draft, in which Francis Melarky is beaten in Rome
(Princeton University Library)

Chapter II

On the pleasant shore of the French Riviera, about half way between Marseilles and the Italian border, stands a large, proud rose-colored hotel. Its style is Second Empire, with a beam of the Crescent; deferential palms cool its flushed façade, and before it, in the position of a prayer-rug stretches a short dazzling beach. This summer many bungalows inhabited by people with nothing to conceal, cluster trustfully about it, but three years ago, at the time of the Melarky case, only the cupolos of a dozen old villas nodded like rotting water-lilies from the massed pines between Gauss' <u>Hotel des Etrangers</u> and Cannes, five miles away.

The hotel opened out to the beach where the sun thundered down in summer, and great planes from Corsica toured noisily ~~along~~ the sky. In the early morning the image of Cannes, the ~~white~~ and cream of old fortifications

First page of the second chapter of the Melarky manuscript, which became the opening of
Tender Is the Night *(Princeton University Library)*

**Fitzgerald to Marya Mannes, 21 October 1925
Paris**

You are thrilled by New York—I doubt you will be after five more years when you are more fully nourished from within. I carry the place around the world in my heart but sometimes I try to shake it off in my dreams. American's greatest promise is that something is going to happen, and after awhile you get tired of waiting because nothing happens to people except that they grow old, and nothing happens to American art because America is the story of the moon that never rose. Nor does the "minute itself" ever come to life either, the minute not of unrest and hope but of a glowing peace—such as when the moon rose that night on Gerald and Sara's garden and you said you were happy to be there. No one ever makes things in American with that vast, magnificent, cynical disillusion with which Gerald and Sara make things like their parties.

(They were here, last week, and we spent six or seven happy days together.)

My new novel is marvelous. I'm in the first chapter. You may recognize certain things and people in it.

—*The Letters of F. Scott Fitzgerald*, p. 488

**Fitzgerald to Perkins, circa 27 December 1925
Paris**

I write to you from the depths of one of my unholy depressions. The book is wonderful—I honestly think that when its published I shall be the best American novelist (which isn't saying a lot) but the end seems far away. When its finished I'm coming home for awhile anyhow

Maxwell Perkins

Maxwell Perkins, the legendary editor at Charles Scribners Sons, assembled the most celebrated stable of authors in American publishing. Fitzgerald was his first major discovery, and Perkins fought for publication of This Side of Paradise *in 1919. Ernest Hemingway came to Perkins and Scribners through Fitzgerald's intervention. Perkins is probably most closely identified with Thomas Wolfe, with whom he performed prodigious editorial labors. His last discovery was James Jones, but Perkins did not live to publish* From Here to Eternity.

In addition to Perkins's acclaimed editorial skills, his committment to authors—not a breed famed for gratitude—inspired their loyalty and trust. Perkins was Fitzgerald's unwavering friend during the period between The Great Gatsby *and* Tender Is the Night, *arranging advances while Fitzgerald was finishing* Tender. *He remained Fitzgerald's devoted friend after* Tender, *encouraging his work on the unfinished Hollywood novel,* The Love of the Last Tycoon.

Maxwell Perkins, who habitually wore a hat in his office

14 Rue de Tilsitt
Paris, France

Dear Gilbert :

Thank you a thousand times for your
enthusiasm about Gatsby. I believe I'd rather ~~stir your~~
~~discriminating enthusiasm~~ than anyone's in America, (did I tell you
this before?), and to be really believed-in again, to
feel "exciting", is tremendously satisfactory. My
new novel may be my last for ten years or so - that
is if it sells no better than Gatsby (which has only
gone a little over 20,000 copies) for I may go to
Hollywood + try to learn the moving picture
business from the bottom up.

We leave for Antibes on August 4th -
Zelda and I in our car (the same one) and nurse
+ baby by train. There we shall spend one month
growing brown and healthy — then return here
for the fall. Beyond January our plans are vague
Nice followed by Oxford or Cambridge for the summer
perhaps. Don Stuart has been here — he seemed
horribly pretentious to me and more than usually
wrong + in fact it was rather a shock to see the
change in him. I see Hemmingway a great deal and
~~be p~~ of left, something of Gerald — both of them are
thoroughly charming.

If you + Amanda come over in the spring we
may have a villa big enough for you to visit us in
Nice. God, I'm wild for the Riviera. Love from us to you
both
                                    Scott

Fitzgerald's letter to Gilbert Seldes refers to his new novel, June–July 1925 (Fire and Frost Catalogue, 1995)

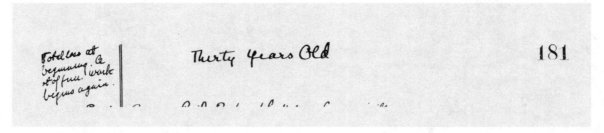

Fitzgerald's summary in his Ledger *of the year from September 1926 to September 1927*

though the thought revolts me as much as the thought of remaining in France. I wish I were twenty-two again with only my dramatic and feverishly enjoyed miseries. You remember I used to say I wanted to die at thirty—well, I'm now twenty-nine and the prospect is still welcome. My work is the only thing that makes me happy—except to be a little tight—and for those two indulgences I pay a big price in mental and physical hangovers.

. . . .

My novel should be finished next fall.
—*F. Scott Fitzgerald: A Life in Letters,* pp. 131, 132
* * *

Fitzgerald to Perkins, circa 8 May 1926
Juan-les-Pins

My book is <u>wonderful.</u> I don't think it'll be interrupted again. I expect to reach New York about Dec 10th with the ms. under my arm. I'll ask between $30,000 & $40,000 for the serial rights and I think Liberty will want it. So book publication would be late Spring 1927 or early fall.
—*Dear Scott/Dear Max,* p. 141
* * *

Perkins to Fitzgerald, 2 June 1927

I have been thinking much about the title, "The Boy Who Killed His Mother." I do not think it is sensational in any objectionable sense whatever, and its very simplicity and directness, almost literalness, give it a value, and a distinction from most of your other titles. At the same time, I am not at all sure about it. You will probably think of other titles in the meantime, so that there will be several to select from.
—*Dear Scott/Dear Max,* p. 148
* * *

Fitzgerald to Perkins, circa 1 January 1928
"Ellersie," Edgemoor, Delaware

Patience yet a little while, I beseech thee and thanks eternally for the deposits. I feel awfully about owing you that money—all I can say is that if book is serialized I'll pay it back immediately. I work at it all the time but that period of sickness set me back—made a break both in the book + financially so that I had to do those Post stories—which made a further break. Please regard it as a safe investment and not as a risk.
—*Dear Scott/Dear Max,* p. 148
* * *

Perkins to Fitzgerald, 3 January 1928

We feel no anxiety whatever about the novel. I have worried a little about the length of time elapsing between that and "The Great Gatsby".
—*Dear Scott/Dear Max,* p. 149
* * *

Fitzgerald to Perkins, circa 21 July 1928
Paris

The novel goes fine. I think its quite wonderful + I think those who've seen it (for I've read it around a little) have been quite excited. I was encouraged the other day, when James Joyce came to dinner, when he said, "Yes, I expect to finish my novel in three or four years more at the <u>latest</u>" + he works 11 hrs a day to my intermittent 8. Mine will be done <u>sure</u> in September.
—*F. Scott Fitzgerald: A Life in Letters,* p. 158
* * *

CHAPTER ~~XI.~~ I

On the pleasant shore of the French Riviera, about half way
between Marseilles and the Italian border, stands a large, proud, rose-
colored hotel. Its style is Second Empire, with a beam of the crescent;
deferential palms cool its flushed facade, and before it, like a prayer
rug, stretches a short dazzling beach.. This summer many new *little* houses, ~~of~~
~~mostly occupied by americans~~, *people with nothing to conceal,* cluster about it, but ~~five~~ *six* years ago at
the time of the Melarky case, only the cupolas of a dozen old villas
nodded, like rotting water-lilies, from the massed pines between <u>Gauss'</u>
<u>Hotel des Etrangers</u> and Cannes, five miles away.

The hotel opened out to the beach where the sun thundered
down in summer and sae-planes bound for Corsica roared over-head. In
the early morning the image of Cannes, the pink and cream of old fortifications, the purple Alp that bounded Italy, were cast across the water,
and lay wavering with the ripples and rings sent up by sea-plants through
the clear shallows. Before eight a man came down to the beach in a blue
bathrobe and with much preliminary application to his person of the chilly water, and some grunting and loud breathing, floundered for a minute
in the sea. When he had gone, beach and open bay were quiet for an hour.
On the horizon merchantmen crawled westward; bus-boys shouted in the hotel court; the dew dried upon the pines. In another hour the horns of
passing motors began to sound on the winding road behind the hotel, where
the Maures reach their crest and begin to slope gently down into the intricate civilization of avarice and glory, down into France.

*First page of the typescript for the original second chapter of the Melarky version that became the opening chapter
(Princeton University Library)*

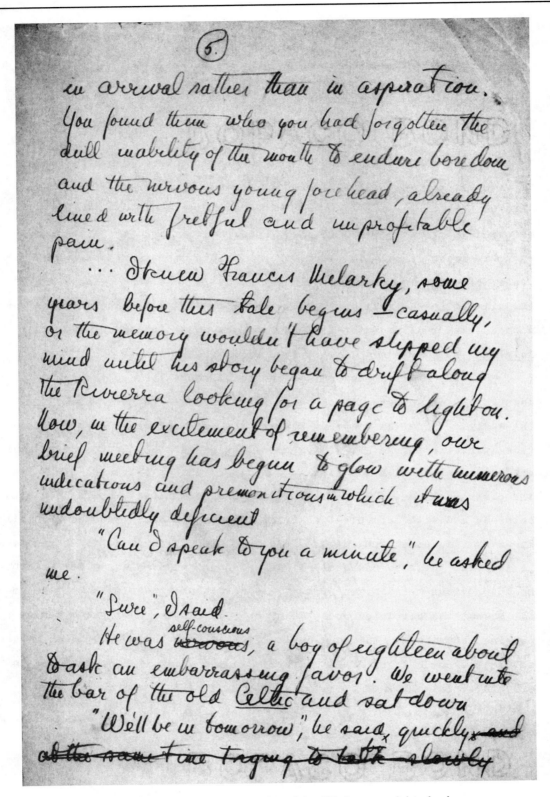

⑤

in arrival rather than in aspiration.
You found then who you had forgotten the
dull inability of the mouth to endure boredom
and the nervous young forehead, already
lined with fretful and unprofitable
pain.

… I knew Francis Melarky, ~~some~~
years before this tale begins — casually,
or the memory wouldn't have slipped my
mind until his story began to drift along
the Rivierra looking for a page to light on.
Now, in the excitement of remembering, our
brief meeting has begun to glow with numerous
indications and premonitions in which it was
undoubtedly deficient

"Can I speak to you a minute," he asked
me.

"Sure", I said.

self-conscious
He was ~~nervous~~, a boy of eighteen about
to ask an embarrassing favor. We went into
the bar of the old _Celtic_ and sat down

"We'll be in tomorrow", he said, quickly, ~~and
at the same time trying to talk slowly~~

Page from the Melarky–narrator holograph in which the narrator is introduced
(Princeton University Library)

Fitzgerald to Perkins, October/November 1928
Ellerslie

Am going to send you two chapters a month of the final version of book beginning next week + ending in Feb. Strictly confidential. [. . .] I think this will help me get it straight in my own mind–I've been alone with it too long.
　　　　　　　　–F. Scott Fitzgerald: A Life in Letters, p. 159

* * *

Fitzgerald to Perkins, November 1928
Ellerslie

It seems fine to be sending you something again, even though its only the first fourth of the book (2 chapters, 18,000 words). Now comes another short story, then I'll patch up Chaps. 3 + 4 the same way, and send them, I hope, about the 1st of December.

Chap I. here is good

Chap II. has caused me more trouble than anything in the book. You'll realize this when I tell you it was once 27,000 words long! It started its career as Chap I. I am far from satisfied with it even now, but won't go into its obvious faults. I would appreciate it if you jotted down any criticisms–and

---

A Reading at Ellerslie

In "A Weekend at Ellerslie" Edmund Wilson recalls Fitzgerald reading from his work in progress the morning after a dinner party at Ellerslie in February 1928.

I remember his sitting around in his bathrobe and reading to Gilbert Seldes and me what must have been one of the early Riviera chapters from his novel then in progress, which was to turn into *Tender Is the Night*. There was especially one dazzling passage with which he had evidently taken much pains and on which he must have counted to stun us. It presented a group of attractive girls–on a beach or in a room, I can't remember–but in any case floating and glowing in richest Fitzgerald glamor. "What do you think of that description?" he asked. We told him we thought it was splendid. "I read this chapter to Dos Passos, when he was here," he said, "and afterwards he said that he liked it 'all except that part,' he said, 'that's so wonderful.' I asked him what he meant, and he said, 'Oh, you know: that part that's so wonderful–that part that's so perfectly marvellous.'" This may have led him to leave it out, or he may have had to scrap it with his original subject, for I cannot now find this passage, in any form I can recognize, in *Tender Is the Night*.

　　　　　　　　–The Shores of Light, p. 381

Ellerslie, the mansion Fitzgerald rented in Edgemoor, Delaware, during 1927–1928 (Bruccoli Collection of Fitzgerald, Thomas Cooper Library, University of South Carolina)

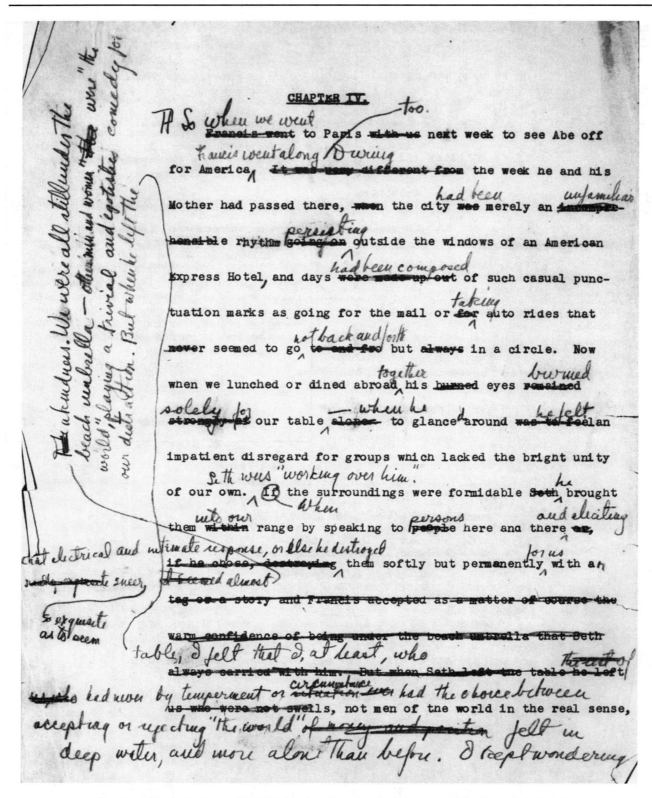

First page of the fourth chapter of the Melarky–narrator typescript, which corresponds to chapter 12 in Book I
of Tender Is the Night *(Princeton University Library)*

saved them until I've sent you the whole book, because I want to feel that each part is finished and not worry about it any longer, even though I may change it enormously at the very last minute. All I want to know now is if, in general, you like it + this will have to wait, I suppose, until you've seen the next batch which finishes the first half. (My God its good to see those chapters lying in an envelope!

—F. Scott Fitzgerald: A Life in Letters, pp. 159–160

* * *

Perkins to Fitzgerald, 13 November 1928

I have just finished the two chapters. About the first we fully agree. It is excellent. The second I think contains some of the best writing you have ever done—some lovely scenes, and impressions briefly and beautifully conveyed. Besides it is very entertaining, including the duel. There are certain things one could say of it in criticism, but anyhow I will make no criticism until I read the whole book, and so see the relationships of the chapters. I think this is a wonderfully promising start off. Send on others as soon as you can.

I wish it might be possible to get this book out this spring, if only because it promises so much that it makes me impatient to see it completed.

—Dear Scott/Dear Max, p. 154

* * *

Fitzgerald to Perkins, circa 1 March 1929
Ellerslie

I am sneaking away like a thief without leaving the chapters—there is a weeks work to straighten them out + in the confusion of influenza + leaving, I haven't been able to do it. I'll do it on the boat + send it from Genoa. A thousand thanks for your patience—just trust me a few months longer, Max—its been a discouraging time for me too but I will never forget your kindness and the fact that you've never reproached me.

—F. Scott Fitzgerald: A Life in Letters, p. 161

Fitzgerald's Stories and the Melarky Version

As a professional and as an artist, Fitzgerald's practice was to waste nothing. Every experience, every observation, every reflection was material for his writing. As he implied when he wrote of Ring Lardner's death, Fitzgerald believed a writer's object was to put "himself on paper"—as much as possible to write down "what was in his mind and heart." Inevitably Fitzgerald put some of his mind and heart into even his weakest stories, and he was loath to let the good writing pass with the mediocre into magazine morgues. The following essay examines the relationship of Fitzgerald's short-story work to his progress on the Melarky version.

Fitzgerald's Practice of Stripping Stories and the Melarky Version
George Parker Anderson

From the beginning of his career, Fitzgerald tried to write stories for and sell them to well-paying magazines—the so-called slick magazines, of which *The Saturday Evening Post* was the best paying—but since he also wanted to be, and be regarded as, a serious writer, the time he spent writing stories for the slicks was time lost to the work he cared most about. It is understandable and natural, then, that Fitzgerald would try to integrate his story- and novel-writing careers and that he wrote stories that he sometimes found to be of use to him in the composition of his novels.

Fitzgerald's lifelong practice of using his short work in his novels began with his first novel, *This Side of Paradise* (1920). In that pieced-together book—called by one reviewer "the collected works of F. Scott Fitzgerald published in novel form"[1]—Fitzgerald for the first and only time incorporated into an evolving novel the whole of a previously published story, "Babes in the Wood" (*Smart Set,* September 1919) making only minor changes. But in his work on *This Side of Paradise* Fitzgerald also initiated a more subtle practice that he employed in all of his subsequent novels: the excision of a meaningful phrase or passage from a previously written story, which he then revised and polished for the context of the novel—this is the practice Fitzgerald came to identify as *stripping* a story.

Of the thirty-four stories Fitzgerald published in magazines ranging from a college monthly to *The Saturday Evening Post* before the publication of *The Great Gatsby,* three—one incorporated wholesale, two stripped—were used in *This Side of Paradise;* one

STORIES WITH TEXTUAL LINKS TO THE MELARKY DRAFTS

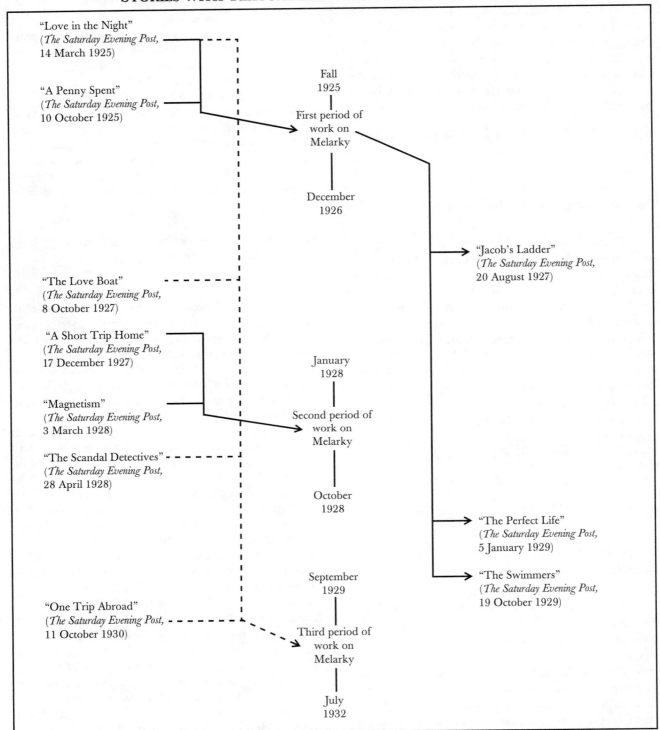

"Love in the Night"
(*The Saturday Evening Post*,
14 March 1925)

"A Penny Spent"
(*The Saturday Evening Post*,
10 October 1925)

Fall
1925

First period of
work on
Melarky

December
1926

"Jacob's Ladder"
(*The Saturday Evening Post*,
20 August 1927)

"The Love Boat"
(*The Saturday Evening Post*,
8 October 1927)

"A Short Trip Home"
(*The Saturday Evening Post*,
17 December 1927)

January
1928

"Magnetism"
(*The Saturday Evening Post*,
3 March 1928)

Second period of
work on
Melarky

"The Scandal Detectives"
(*The Saturday Evening Post*,
28 April 1928)

October
1928

"The Perfect Life"
(*The Saturday Evening Post*,
5 January 1929)

September
1929

"The Swimmers"
(*The Saturday Evening Post*,
19 October 1929)

"One Trip Abroad"
(*The Saturday Evening Post*,
11 October 1930)

Third period of
work on
Melarky

July
1932

Diagram showing the three time periods Fitzgerald worked on the Melarky version (central column) and the stories
textually connected with his progress. Fitzgerald stripped phrases or passages from the seven stories listed in the column
on the left and revised them for use in the Melarky version. The dotted lines show that during his third period of work,
between September 1929 and July 1932, Fitzgerald stripped "Love in the Night" again as well as three more
stories—"The Love Boat," "The Scandal Detectives," and "One Trip Abroad." Fitzgerald
took passages from the Melarky drafts for use in the three stories on the
right—"Jacob's Ladder," "The Perfect Life," and "The Swimmers."

story was stripped for *The Beautiful and Damned* (1922); and three stories were stripped for *The Great Gatsby* (1925). The author was growing increasingly disillusioned with the short-story market and in private remarks often denigrated his work for *The Saturday Evening Post*. As he began work on the book that became *Tender Is the Night*, Fitzgerald did not expect nine years to pass before publication of the novel–nor would he have expected his stories to play a significant role in its composition.

The relationship of Fitzgerald's stories to his progress on the Melarky version is complicated because the author not only stripped stories for his novel but also took passages from his novel in progress for his stories. From the fall of 1925 through December 1926, Fitzgerald wrote four chapters, in which Francis Melarky is beaten in Rome, becomes involved with a group of Americans on the Riviera, attends an elegant dinner party at the villa of Seth and Dinah Piper, and accompanies the Pipers on a visit to Paris, where he falls in love with Dinah Piper. Fitzgerald stripped two short passages from "Love in the Night" for the Riviera chapter and two phrases from "A Penny Spent" for this first phase of his work; he later used passages originating in this phase in three stories– "Jacob's Ladder," "A Perfect Life," and "The Swimmers."

When he returned to his novel sometime after January 1928, Fitzgerald stripped two paragraph-length descriptions from "Magnetism" and "A Short Trip Home." In November 1928, Fitzgerald sent Perkins his first two chapters but failed to send any more. In summer 1929 Fitzgerald put the Melarky version aside to work on the Kelly version of the novel, but it is clear that he returned to the Melarky material once he abandoned Kelly.

Fitzgerald no doubt worked sporadically on Melarky during the three-year period from September 1929 until perhaps as late as July 1932, the month before he began work on the Dick Diver plot–revising and rearranging the chapters, experimenting with point of view–but no evidence survives to show that he ever progressed beyond his initial four chapters. In this third period of work on the Melarky material Fitzgerald used previously stripped material from "Love in the Night" and "Magnetism" as well as taking new strippings from "Love in the Night," "The Love Boat," "A Short Trip Home," "The Scandal Detectives," and "One Trip Abroad."

Progress on the Melarky version came to a halt when the Fitzgeralds returned to America in

December 1926 and the author's finances forced him to devote himself to writing short stories. Nevertheless, the necessity to write for money that the author used as an excuse for his lack of progress on his novel led him to explore experiences that eventually changed his conception of the large work he was struggling to complete. From January 1927 to his temporary abandonment of the Melarky version in October 1928, Fitzgerald's useful writing–if "useful" is defined in terms of the author's progress toward the Diver version–is to be found in the stories that he wrote in the last half of 1927, especially "Jacob's Ladder," "Magnetism," and "A Short Trip Home," rather than in his direct writing on the Melarky version.

Upon returning from Europe, the Fitzgeralds almost immediately set out for Hollywood, where the author worked on a screenplay for United Artists in January and February. When the thirty-year-old Fitzgerald became attracted to an eighteen-year-old actress, Lois Moran, the flirtation provoked Zelda's jealousy and a quarrel between wife and husband. Several of Fitzgerald's subsequent stories–beginning with "Jacob's Ladder," the first major story Fitzgerald wrote after his return to America and the first to contain a passage taken from the Melarky drafts–explore the consequences of a mature man's attraction to a young girl.

Hoping to write and sell some stories quickly in the summer of 1927, Fitzgerald nevertheless seems to have written "Jacob's Ladder" in part to refine a scene in the novel. The development of the scene in the fourth chapter of the Melarky version is straightforward in the Melarky drafts. In the scene's initial appearance, Francis Melarky asks Dinah Piper to kiss him as they ride together in a taxi. Dinah obliges but is not emotionally involved in the kiss. In a revision of the episode, Fitzgerald extends the scene to show Dinah's involvement in the kissing. However, when he came to write "Jacob's Ladder," Fitzgerald reversed the gender roles in the kissing scene in the taxi. Instead of Francis wanting to be kissed by Dinah, it is a young girl, Jenny Delehanty, who desires the attention of an older man, Jacob Booth.

Whether or not Fitzgerald was aware of the fact, "Jacob's Ladder" marked the advent of the Rosemary Hoyt character and the beginning of his process of creating the Dick-Rosemary relationship. Fitzgerald's reliance on the story later–when he conceived the Diver version–is shown by the manifest similarities, both textual and thematic, between the story and the finished novel. In the story, Jacob Booth turns Jenny Delehanty into the movie starlet,

(13)

*and of he thought with a touch image of panic
that he ought to have stayed on the
Riverra and followed up Brady, and if
he realized that his mother had encouraged
him to come here with the Pipers because
it was they would be a good
influence on him and make him
gentle and well-ordered to —
well, there was Seth who would be so
a charming tongest and Dinah giving
off wave after wave of loveliness, simply in the starlit car of the taxi,
blooming away at his side. On the
pure parting of her lips no breath
hovered. He had never seen anything
so delicate as the texture of her skin,
tender and haunting and tender as
her eyes. No, nothing was being nothing was lost
nothing was slipping away, for beauty
gives back the image of one's highest
thoughts and looking at Dinah he*

Fitzgerald's first draft of the scene in which Francis Melarky and Dinah Piper kiss in a taxi. Fitzgerald conceived this scene to mark the moment when "Francis fell in love with Dinah." He used the highlighted phrases for the taxi scene in "Jacob's Ladder," a story published in The Saturday Evening Post, *20 August 1927 (Princeton University Library).*

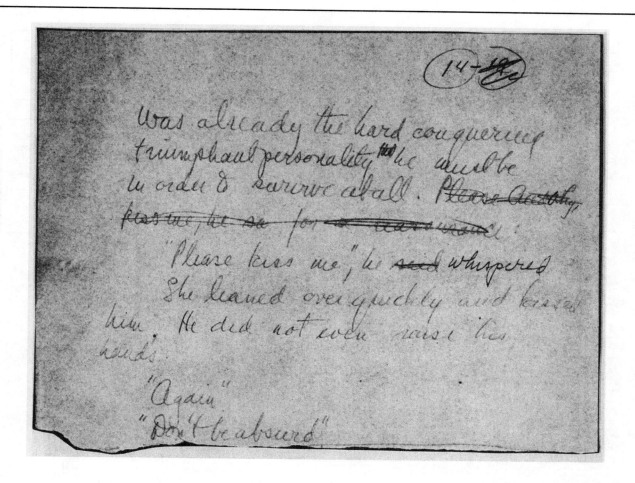

Jenny Prince, and then falls in love with the illusion he has created of her. In both story and novel, the older man's emptiness is manifested in jealousy for a young rival, though Jacob Booth endures his disappointment, while Dick Diver, the subject of more powerful and complicated tensions, cracks up. Fitzgerald consciously came to rely on the story so much that he found it impossible to revise the story collection *Taps at Reveille*. Writing of "Jacob's Ladder" to Lois Moran, he explained, ". . . I found that I had so thoroughly disemboweled it of its best descriptions for 'Tender is the Night' that it would be offering an empty shell."[2]

During all his struggles with the Melarky material, Fitzgerald stripped only ten passages from his stories. Although he made greater progress and relied more on his stories when he worked on the Kelly and Diver versions, it would be stretching the point to draw a direct correlation between the author's progress on his novel and his reliance on strippings. Bruccoli has accounted for Fitzgerald's poor progress by suggesting that the author, at least

subconsciously, might have doubted his Melarky-matricide plot and found it "alien to his creative temperament." However, the influence of Fitzgerald's short stories became demonstrably more important as the author began to explore plots that were closer to him emotionally. In such stories as "Jacob's Ladder" and "Magnetism," Fitzgerald was beginning to create the prototypical characters that became Dick Diver and Rosemary Hoyt, though years were yet to pass before he fully realized the contributions his popular stories could make to his novel.

Notes

1. *F. Scott Fitzgerald: The Critical Reception,* edited by Jackson R. Bryer (New York: Burt Franklin, 1978), p. 22.

2. *Correspondence of F. Scott Fitzgerald,* edited by Matthew J. Bruccoli and Margaret M. Duggan, with Susan Walker (New York: Random House, 1980), p. 400.

The description, "the pure parting of her lips," is unchanged from the Melarky drafts. Phrases from this passage were used in the novel for Rosemary's impression of Nicole's beauty (p. 43) and Dick's appreciation of Nicole (p. 180).

In the scene in which he is jealous of Rosemary's co-star Nicoterra, Dick is described as "a gruff red bird" (p. 285).

Fitzgerald revised this passage for the taxi scene in chapter 15 of Book I (p. 84 and p. 83).

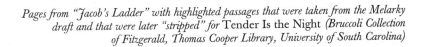

Pages from "Jacob's Ladder" with highlighted passages that were taken from the Melarky draft and that were later "stripped" for Tender Is the Night *(Bruccoli Collection of Fitzgerald, Thomas Cooper Library, University of South Carolina)*

Jenny Delehanty learned quickly; she let herself become grave and sweet and quiet as the night, and as they rolled over Queensboro Bridge into the city she was half asleep against his shoulder.

HE CALLED up Billy Farrelly next day. "I want to see you," he said. "I found a girl I wish you'd take a look at."

"My gosh!" said Farrelly. "You're the third today."

"Not the third of this kind."

"All right. If she's white, she can have the lead in a picture I'm starting Friday."

"Joking aside, will you give her a test?"

"I'm not joking. She can have the lead, I tell you. I'm sick of these lousy actresses. I'm going out to the Coast next month. I'd rather be Constance Talmadge's water boy than own most of these young ——" His voice was bitter with Irish disgust. "Sure, bring her over, Jake. I'll take a look at her."

Four days later, when Mrs. Choynski, accompanied by two deputy sheriffs, had gone to Auburn to pass the remainder of her life, Jacob drove Jenny over the bridge to Astoria, Long Island.

"You've got to have a new name," he said; "and remember, you never had a sister."

"I thought of that," she answered. "I thought of a name too—Tootsie Defoe."

"That's rotten," he laughed; "just rotten."

"Well, you think of one if you're so smart."

"How about Jenny—Jenny—oh, anything—Jenny Prince?"

"All right, handsome."

Jenny Prince walked up the steps of the motion-picture studio, and Billy Farrelly, in a bitter Irish humor, in contempt for himself and his profession, engaged her for one of the three leads in his picture.

"I know. You can tell when a guy wants to make you."

"What?"

"I don't mean he wanted to make me, handsome. But he's got that look about him, if you know what I mean." She distorted her lovely face with a wise smile. "He likes 'em; you could tell that this afternoon."

They drank a bottle of charged and very alcoholic grape juice.

Presently the head waiter came over to their table.

"This is Miss Jenny Prince," said Jacob. "You'll see a lot of her, Lorenzo, because she's just signed a big contract with the pictures. Always treat her with the greatest possible respect."

When Lorenzo had withdrawn, Jenny said, "You got the nicest eyes I ever seen." It was her effort, the best she

"You are the Most Beautiful Thing I Have Ever Seen," He Said, "But as it Happens, You are Not My Type and I Have No Designs on You at All"

Afterward, in the dark cave of the taxicab, fragrant with the perfume he had bought for her that day, Jenny came close to him, clung to him. He kissed her, without enjoying it. There was no shadow of passion in her eyes or on her mouth; there was a faint spray of champagne on her breath. She clung nearer, desperately. He took her hands and put them in her lap.

She leaned away from him resentfully.

"What's the matter? Don't you like me?"

"I shouldn't have let you have so much champagne."

"Why not? I've had a drink before. I was tight once."

"Well, you ought to be ashamed of yourself. And if I hear of your taking any more drinks, you'll hear from me."

"You sure have got your nerve, haven't you?"

"What do you do? Let all the corner soda jerkers maul you around whenever they want?"

"Oh, shut up!"

For a moment they rode in silence. Then her hand crept across to his. "I like you better than any guy I ever met, and I can't help that, can I?"

"Dear little Jenny." He put his arm around her again.

Hesitating tentatively, he kissed her and again he was chilled by the innocence of her kiss, the eyes that at the moment of contact looked beyond him out into the darkness of the night, the darkness of the world. She did not know yet that splendor was something in the heart; at the moment when she should realize that and melt into the passion of the universe he could take her without question or regret.

"I like you enormously," he said; "better than almost anyone I know. I mean that about drinking though. You mustn't drink."

"I'll do anything you want," she said; and she repeated, looking at him directly, "Anything."

The car drew up in front of her flat and he kissed her good night.

He rode away in a mood of exultation, living more deeply in her youth and future than he had lived in himself for years. Thus, leaning forward a little on his cane, rich, young and happy, he was borne along dark streets and light toward a future of his own which he could not foretell.

III

A MONTH later, climbing into a taxicab with Farrelly one night, he gave the latter's address to the driver. "So you're in love with this baby," said Farrelly pleasantly. "Very well, I'll get out of your way."

Jacob experienced a vast displeasure. "I'm not in love with her," he said slowly. "Billy, I want you to leave her alone."

"Sure! I'll leave her alone," agreed Farrelly readily. "I didn't know you were interested—she told me she couldn't make you."

(Continued on Page 57)

"They're all the same," he said to Jacob. "Shucks! Pick 'em up out of the gutter today and they want gold plates tomorrow. I'd rather be Constance Talmadge's water boy than own a harem full of them."

"Do you like this girl?"

"She's all right. She's got a good side face. But they're all the same."

Jacob bought Jenny Prince an evening dress for a hundred and eighty dollars and took her to the Lido that night. He was pleased with himself, and excited. They both laughed a lot and were happy.

"Can you believe you're in the movies?" he demanded.

"They'll probably kick me out tomorrow. It was too easy."

"No, it wasn't. It was very good—psychologically. Billy Farrelly was in just the one mood ——"

"I liked him."

"He's fine," agreed Jacob. But he was reminded that already another man was helping to open doors for her success. "He's a wild Irishman—look out for him."

could do. Her face was serious and sad. "Honest," she repeated herself, "the nicest eyes I ever seen. Any girl would be glad to have eyes like yours."

He laughed, but he was touched. His hand covered her arm lightly. "Be good," he said. "Work hard and I'll be so proud of you—and we'll have some good times together."

"I always have a good time with you." Her eyes were full on his, in his, held there like hands. Her voice was clear and dry. "Honest, I'm not kidding about your eyes. You always think I'm kidding. I want to thank you for all you've done for me."

"I haven't done anything, you lunatic. I saw your face and I was—I was beholden to it—everybody ought to be beholden to it."

Entertainers appeared and her eyes wandered hungrily away from him.

She was so young—Jacob had never been so conscious of youth before. He had always considered himself on the young side until tonight.

Fitzgerald initially stripped this passage for the Melarky version as the beginning of an encounter that would have been the means of making Francis aware of a movie crew's presence on the Riviera. Even in the Melarky version, Fitzgerald seems from the first to have intended the news vender as an omen of the disaster to follow. As finally worked into Ten-der Is the Night, *the news vender appears twice, first as a harbinger and then as a seal of disaster. He appears for the first time just as Dick is beginning to realize that he is losing the fine control he has always had over himself, that his infatuation with Rosemary is a "projection of some submerged reality" (p. 119) beyond his changing. Years later, the same "insistent American, of sinister aspect" (p. 399), interrupts Dick and Tommy Barban's negotiations on the Divers' divorce.*

THE SATURDAY EVENING POST 7

her with a stern, dignified, injured and, I thought, just exactly correct reproof in his expression. I followed.

Seated in the coupé—he had not dismounted to help Ellen out—was a hard thin-faced man of about thirty-five with an air of being scarred, and a slight sinister smile. His eyes were a sort of taunt to the whole human family—they were the eyes of an animal sleepy and quiescent in the presence of another species. They were helpless yet brutal, unhopeful yet confident. It was as if they felt themselves powerless to originate activity, but infinitely capable of profiting by a single gesture of weakness in another.

Vaguely I placed him as one of the sort of men whom I had been conscious of from my earliest youth as "hanging around"—leaning with one elbow on the counters of tobacco stores, watching, through heaven knows what small chink of the mind, the people who hurried in and out. Intimate to garages, where he had vague business conducted in undertones, to barber shops and to the lobbies of theaters—in such places, anyhow, I placed the type, if type it was, that he reminded me of. Sometimes his face bobbed up in one of Tad's more savage cartoons, and I had always from earliest boyhood thrown a nervous glance toward the dim borderland where he stood, and seen him watching me and despising me. Once, in a dream, he had taken a few steps toward me, jerking his head back and muttering: "Say, kid" in what was intended to be a reassuring voice, and I had broken for the door in terror. This was that sort of man.

Joe and Ellen faced each other silently; she seemed, as I have said, to be in a daze. It was cold, but she didn't notice that her coat had blown open; Joe reached out and pulled it together, and automatically she clutched it with her hand.

Suddenly the man in the coupé, who had been watching them silently, laughed. It was a bare laugh, done with the breath—just a noisy jerk of the head—but it was an insult if I had ever heard one; definite and not to be passed over. I wasn't surprised when Joe, who was quick tempered, turned to him angrily and said:

"What's your trouble?"

The man waited a moment, his eyes shifting and yet staring, and always seeing. Then he laughed again in the same way. Ellen stirred uneasily.

"Who is this—this——" Joe's voice trembled with annoyance.

"Look out now," said the man slowly.

Joe turned to me.

"Eddie, take Ellen and Catherine in, will you?" he said quickly. . . . . "Ellen, go with Eddie."

"Look out now," the man repeated.

Ellen made a little sound with her tongue and teeth, but she didn't resist when I took her arm and moved her toward the side door of the hotel. It struck me as odd that she should be so helpless, even to the point of acquiescing by her silence in this imminent trouble.

"Let it go, Joe!" I called back over my shoulder. "Come inside!"

Ellen, pulling against my arm, hurried us on. As we were caught up into the swinging doors I had the impression that the man was getting out of his coupé.

Ten minutes later, as I waited for the girls outside the women's dressing room, Joe Jelke and Jim Cathcart stepped out of the elevator. Joe was very white, his eyes were heavy and glazed, there was a trickle of dark blood on his forehead and on his white muffler. Jim had both their hats in his hand.

"He hit Joe with brass knuckles," Jim said in a low voice. "Joe was out cold for a minute or so. I wish you'd send a bell boy for some witch-hazel and court-plaster."

It was late and the hall was deserted; brassy fragments of the dance below reached us as if heavy curtains were being blown aside and dropping back into place. When Ellen came out I took her directly downstairs. We avoided the receiving line and went into a dim room set with scraggly hotel palms where couples sometimes sat out during the dance; there I told her what had happened.

"It was Joe's own fault," she said, surprisingly. "I told him not to interfere."

This wasn't true. She had said nothing, only uttered one curious little click of impatience.

"You ran out the back door and disappeared for almost an hour," I protested. "Then you turned up with a hard-looking customer who laughed in Joe's face."

"A hard-looking customer," she repeated, as if tasting the sound of the words.

"Well, wasn't he? Where on earth did you get hold of him, Ellen?"

"On the train," she answered. Immediately she seemed to regret this admission. "You'd better stay out of things that aren't your business, Eddie. You see what happened to Joe."

Literally I gasped. To watch her, seated beside me, immaculately glowing, her body giving off wave after wave of freshness and delicacy—and to hear her talk like that.

"But that man's a thug!" I cried. "No girl could be safe with him. He used brass knuckles on Joe—brass knuckles!"

"Is that pretty bad?"

She asked this as she might have asked such a question a few years ago. She looked at me at last and really wanted an answer; for a moment it was as if she were trying to recapture an attitude that had almost departed; then she hardened again. I say "hardened," for I began to notice that when she was concerned with this man her eyelids fell a little, shutting other things—everything else—out of view.

That was a moment I might have said something, I suppose, but in spite of everything, I couldn't light into her. I was too much under the spell of her beauty and its success. I even began to find excuses for her—perhaps that man wasn't what he appeared to be; or perhaps—more romantically—she was involved with him against her will to shield someone else. At this point people began to drift into the room and come up to speak to us. We couldn't talk any more, so we went in and bowed to the chaperons. Then I gave her up to the bright restless sea of the dance, where she moved in an eddy of her own among the pleasant islands of colored favors set out on tables and the south winds from the brasses moaning across the hall. After a while I saw Joe Jelke sitting in a corner with a strip of court-plaster on his forehead watching Ellen as if she herself had struck him down, but I didn't go up to him. I felt queer myself—like I feel when I wake up after sleeping through an afternoon, strange and portentous, as if something had gone on in the interval that changed the values of everything and that I didn't see.

(Continued on Page 55)

"Who is This—This——" Joe's Voice Trembled With Annoyance. "Look Out Now," Said the Man Slowly

Page from "A Short Trip Home," 17 December 1927, which Fitzgerald called his "first real ghost story" (Bruccoli Collection of Fitzgerald, Thomas Cooper Library, University of South Carolina), and page from a typescript showing how a passage was adapted first for the Francis Melarky version and then for the Dick Diver version (Princeton University Library)

ⓐ   *Insert for p. 39*

As he walked back ~~to his table~~ *along* he was accosted by a hard thin-

faced American of about thirty with an air of being scarred and

a slight sinister smile.   Even as ~~Francis~~ *Dick* gave him the light

he asked for he placed him as a type of man he had been conscious

of since earliest youth as hanging around tobacco stores with one

elbow on the counter and watching, through heaven knows what small

chink of the mind, the people who hurried in and out.   Intimate

to garages where he had vague business conducted in undertones,

to barber shops and the lobbies of theatres -- in such places, at

any rate, ~~Francis~~ *Dick* placed the type, if type it was.   Sometimes

the face bobbed in one of Tad's more savage cartoons and ~~Francis~~ *Dick*,

~~from earliest~~ *in early* boyhood, had always thrown an uneasy glance toward

the dim borderland of crime on which he seemed to stand.

                        How do you like Paris,
      "~~Can I join you~~, Buddy?"

                                                walked along
      Without waiting for an answer he ~~sat down and ordered~~

beside Dick
~~a glass of beer.~~

      "Where you from, ~~Buddy?~~" he asked encouragingly.

      "~~Tennessee~~." *I'm from Buffalo*

      "I'm from San Antone.   But I been over here ever since

the war."

In this passage, George Hannaford, an actor, accompanied by a producer, visits the studio where a young actress, Helen Avery, is playing a scene. Avery, like Rosemary Hoyt in Tender Is the Night, later is important for her role as a catalyst. Hannaford's interest in the young actress precipitates a conflict with his wife, Kay.

Although the importance of the scene is uncertain within the Melarky version since it is so fragmentary and undeveloped, the references to movies are integral to the finished novel. The stage building Rosemary enters with "glad familiarity" (p. 29) is part of a business that prepares paper dolls to pass before America's "empty harlot's mind" (p. 91)—and yet the novel shows that the movies are an expression of American immaturity rather than its cause.

Page from "Magnetism," 3 March 1928 (Bruccoli Collection of Fitzgerald, Thomas Cooper Library, University of South Carolina) and page from the Melarky typescript in which Francis visits Earl Brady's studio (Princeton University Library)

19.

He ~~las the way to~~ *opened* a small door in the big blank wall
of a stage building and with a sudden glad familiarity Francis *followed*
~~entered~~ *him* into its half darkness. Here and there figures spotted the
twilight, figures that turned up ashen faces to him, like souls in
purgatory watching the passage of a mortal through. There were
whispers and soft voices and, apparently from afar, the gentle
tremolo of a small organ. Turning the corner made by some flats,
they came upon the white crackling glow of a stage, where a French
actor ~~in evening clothes~~, his shirt-front, collar and cuffs tinted
a brilliant pink, and ~~a gold haired~~ *an* American leading woman stood
motionless face to face. They stared at each other with tired
dogged eyes as though they had been in the same position for hours.
And still for a long time nothing happened, no one moved. A bank
of lights went off with a savage hiss, went on again; the plaintive
tap of a hammer begged admission to nowhere in the distance; a blue
face appeared among the blinding lights above and called something
unintelligible into the upper blackness. Then the silence was broken
by a voice beside Francis.

"Baby, if you don't take off your stockings, you'll spoil
ten pairs *more* ~~more~~. That dress must weigh fifteen pounds"

Stepping backward the speaker ran against Francis and ~~turned~~.
~~He~~ looked questioningly at the studio manager who said, "Mr. Melarky".

"Hello, there. How are you?" ~~stood at his side~~

"We met at George Collins', Mr. Brady."

"Of course", He remembered. "Sure—you did a sequence for

Writing the Kelly Version

Fitzgerald informed Perkins in July: "I am working night + day on novel from new angle that I think will solve previous difficulties." He had almost certainly dropped the matricide story for a new plot about Lew and Nicole Kelly, a movie director and his wife who are going to Europe because he feels he has grown stale in Hollywood. Aboard the ship are a girl named Rosemary and her mother, who hope that Kelly will help Rosemary get a start in the movies. Lew Kelly was probably based on Rex Ingram, the director who had left Hollywood and set up a studio near Nice in 1927. Fitzgerald knew Ingram, who, like Kelly, was Irish and had attended Yale. The young actress introduces the Lois Moran-Rosemary Hoyt figure into the stream of composition.

At about the same time that Fitzgerald informed Perkins of the "new angle," he wrote his agent Harold Ober a practical letter about his plans for the summer of 1929, stating that he had enough money to work on the novel for two months. Even allowing for Fitzgerald's custom of exaggerating his progress, he must have made a good start on the Kelly version, for in August he wrote Reynolds that the novel would be three-quarters done by the end of September. This can be interpreted to mean that he had completed the two surviving chapters of the draft and expected to complete several more chapters by the end of September. In a letter received by Ober on September 1, Fitzgerald announced that he had another month to devote to the novel. Late in October, Fitzgerald reported to Ober that the novel was approaching completion.

Only two shipboard chapters, comprising about fifty manuscript pages, survive from the Kelly version. Reconstructing the stages of Tender Is the Night *is difficult because of Fitzgerald's exaggerated progress reports. He also claimed that he destroyed drafts, and Gerald Murphy reported to Bruccoli that he witnessed one such incident. There are no notes or outlines to indicate the direction of the story after the first two chapters. It is possible that Lew Kelly would have experienced a process of deterioration in Europe.*

The Kelly version represents a transitional stage between the matricide version and the Dick Diver version. The most obvious link is the names: Kelly is first called Melarky; and the names Nicole and Rosemary prefigure the female leads in Tender Is the Night. *Rosemary's method of gaining an entrée into the movies and her dependence on her mother's judgment were written into the published version. The description of the pier (taken from "The Rough Crossing") and Kelly's attempt to help the youth named Curly who had jumped overboard are in* Tender Is the Night—*but the Curly material was deleted after the novel was serialized. The opening of the Kelly version includes material that formed the basis for two important free-association passages in chapter 10 of Book II of* Tender Is the Night.

—Matthew J. Bruccoli

Correspondence, Fall 1929 to Spring 1930

Fitzgerald's 20,000-word claim in the following letter is high for fifty manuscript pages.

Fitzgerald to Hemingway, 9 September 1929 Cannes

Just taken another chapter to typists + its left me in a terrible mood of depression as to whether its any good or not. In 2½ mos. I've been here I've written 20,000 words on it + one short story, which is superb for me of late years. I've paid for it with the usual nervous depressions and such drinking manners as the lowest bistrop (bistrot?) boy would scorn. My latest tendency is to collapse about 11.00 and with tears flowing from my eyes or the gin rising to their level and leaking over, + tell interested friends or acquaintances that I haven't a friend in the world and likewise care for nobody, generally including Zelda and often implying current company—after which current company tend to become less current and I wake up in strange rooms in strange palaces. The rest of the time I stay alone working or trying to work or brooding or reading detective stories—and realizing that anyone in my state of mind who has in addition never been able to hold his tongue is pretty poor company. But when drunk I make them all pay and pay and pay.

. . . .

Your analysis of my inability to get my serious work done is too kind in that it leaves out dissipation, but among acts of God it is possible that the 5 yrs between my leaving the army + finishing <u>Gatsby</u> 1919-1924 which included 3 novels, about 50 popular stories + a play + numerous articles + movies may have taken all I had to say too early, adding that all the time we were living at top speed in the gayest worlds we could find.

Here's a last flicker of the old cheap pride:—the <u>Post</u> now pays the old whore $4000. a screw. But now its because she's mastered the 40 positions—in her youth one was enough.

—*F. Scott Fitzgerald: A Life in Letters*, p. 169

* * *

Hemingway to Fitzgerald, 13 September 1929

Oh Hell. You have more stuff than anyone and you care more about it and for Christ sake just keep on and go through with it now and dont please

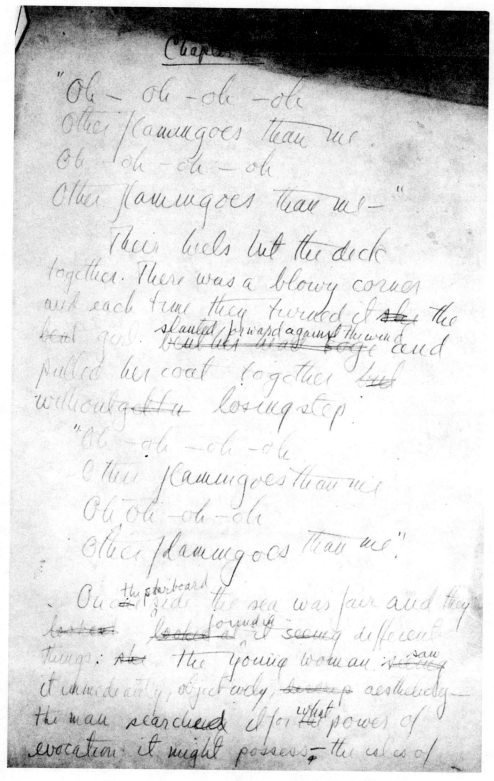

First page of the Kelly holograph, in which Lew and Nicole Kelly walk the deck of the ship, chanting a nonsense song (Princeton University Library)

write anything else until it's finished. It will be damned good—

(They never raise an old whore's price—She may know 850 positions—They cut her price all the same—So either you arent old or not a whore or both) The stories arent whoreing They're just bad judgement—you could have and can make enough to live on writing novels.

—Selected Letters, pp. 306–307

* * *

Fitzgerald to Perkins, circa 15 November 1929 Paris

For the first time since August I see my way clear to a long stretch on the novel, so I'm writing you as I can't bear to do when its in one of its states of postponement + seems so in the air. We are not coming home for Xmas, because of expense + because it'd be an awful interruption now. Both our families are raising hell but I can't compromise the remains of my future for that.

—F. Scott Fitzgerald: A Life in Letters, p. 171

* * *

Perkins to Fitzgerald, 30 November 1929

I could not be glader of anything than of hearing how well you are going forward now. I know the book will be a great book, and you will have the most ardent support from every man here when it is ready.

—Dear Scott/Dear Max, p. 160

* * *

Illustration from a story in which Fitzgerald treats adultery and divorce, unusual subjects for "family magazines" of the time
(Bruccoli Collection of Fitzgerald, Thomas Cooper Library, University of South Carolina)

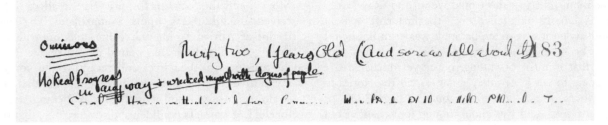

Fitzgerald's summary in his Ledger *of the year from September 1928 to September 1929*

Fitzgerald to Perkins, 21 January 1930
Paris

To begin with, because I don't mention my novel it isn't because it isn't finishing up or that I'm neglecting it–but only that I'm weary of setting dates for it till the moment when it is in the Post Office Box.

–*F. Scott Fitzgerald: A Life in Letters*, p. 173

* * *

Perkins to Fitzgerald, 14 March 1930

Harold Ober yesterday gave me reason to hope that a large part of your novel would be here before long. I'll tell you when we get that into our hands, and a publication date set, we'll let loose everything we have got in the way of salesmanship and advertising. Everyone here is impatient to get that book and what is more, there is no author who commands a more complete loyalty than you do.

–*Dear Scott/Dear Max*, pp. 165–166

* * *

Harold Ober (1881–1959) became Fitzgerald's agent for magazine sales at the Paul Revere Reynolds agency in 1919. Fitzgerald remained Ober's client when he established his own literary agency in 1929. Between 1919 and 1929 Fitzgerald's Saturday Evening Post *story fee rose from $400 to $4,000. Fitzgerald dealt directly with Maxwell Perkins at Scribners for book publications; but Ober served as Fitzgerald's magazine representative and banker until 1940–advancing payments for unsold stories. Anne and Harold Ober became Scottie Fitzgerald's surrogate parents, providing a home for her while she was at boarding school and Vassar. Harold Ober Associates became a prominent agency, with clients that included William Faulkner and J. D. Salinger.*

Fitzgerald to Harold Ober, 8 April 1930
Paris

Now–about the novel–the other night I read one great hunk of it to John Peale Bishop, and we both agreed that it would be ruinous to let Liberty start it uncompleted. Here's a hypothetical possibility. Suppose (as may happen in such cases) they didn't like the end + we quarreled about it–then what the hell! I'd have lost the Post, gained

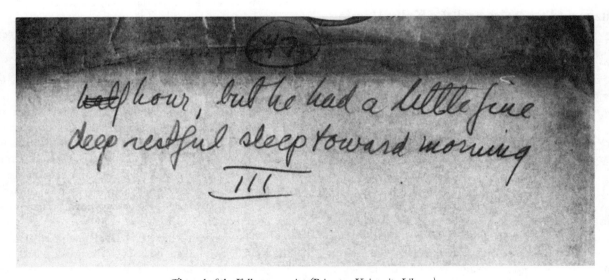

The end of the Kelly manuscript (Princeton University Library)

an enemy in <u>Liberty</u>—who would we turn to—Ray Long? Suppose Liberty didn't like even the first part + went around saying it was rotten before it was even finished. I want to be in New York if possible when they accept it for there's that element of cutting, never yet discussed—are they going to cut it Are they going to cut my stories to 5000 words or not? Are they going to pay $3500, or $4000. At one time I was about to send four chapters out of eight done to you. Then I cut one of those chapters absolutely to pieces. I know you're losing faith in me + Max too but God knows one has to rely in the end on one's own judgement. I could have published four lowsy, half baked books in the last five years + people would have thought I was at least a worthy young man not drinking myself to pieces in the south seas—but I'd be dead as Michael Arlen, Bromfield, Tom Boyd, Callaghan + the others who think they can trick the world with the hurried and the second rate. These <u>Post</u> stories <u>in</u> the <u>Post</u> are at least not any spot on me—they're honest and if their <u>form</u> is stereotyped people know what to expect when they pick up the <u>Post</u>. The novel is another thing—if, after four years I published the Basil Lee stories as a book I might as well get tickets for Hollywood immediately.

Well, that's how things are. If you'll have confidence in me I think you'll shortly see I knew what I was doing.

Scott Fitz—

Addenda

Zelda's been sick + not dangerously but seriously, + then I got involved in a wedding party + after 2 weeks just got to work on new story yesterday but 3000 words already done—about as many as I must owe you dollars.

—*As Ever, Scott Fitz*—, pp. 167–168

Fitzgerald's Stories and the Kelly Version

Fitzgerald stripped passages from four stories during his work on the Kelly version. Most of these strippings were minor, but the thematic and textual connections of "The Rough Crossing" to the Kelly material demonstrate that the story was important to the development of the novel.

The 'New Angle' of "The Rough Crossing"
George Parker Anderson

The comparison of "The Rough Crossing," the Kelly version, and *Tender Is the Night* reveals the intimate connections, beyond the actual stripping of material, between Fitzgerald's story and his ongoing work on the novel. Like "Jacob's Ladder" and "Magnetism" earlier, "The Rough Crossing" was one of the several stories inspired by Fitzgerald's experience with Lois

Moran, and the focus in the story is the effect of perceived unfaithfulness upon a marriage. The story begins as Adrian Smith, thirty-one, and his wife Eva, twenty-six, board the ship bound for Europe to escape the pressures of their lives and recapture the youthful joy in their marriage: "It was in the hope that there was some secret of graceful living, some real compensation for the lost, careless confidence of twenty-one, that they were going to spend a year in France"[1] (p. 14).

Although the Smiths are a loving couple, Fitzgerald in the beginning carefully hints at cracks in the foundation of their marriage. Adrian's career as a successful playwright has put a strain upon them as Eva "was often bored by the great streams of [people], of all types and conditions and classes that passed though Adrian's life" (p. 14). Even as Eva asks Adrian to tell her "what a good time we'll have, and how we'll be much better and happier, and very close always" and suggests that they "not get to know anybody, but just stay together," she knows "that the moment of utter isolation had passed almost before it had begun" (p. 12). While Adrian is infatuated with the young, admiring Betsy D'Amido—the obvious parallel of Lois Moran—Eva is sickened by jealousy, excessive drinking, and the storm that threatens the ship.

The story's genesis in the Lois Moran experience is clearly indicated by the central symbol of the story, Eva's pearls. After leaving Hollywood, the Fitzgeralds violently quarreled about Lois Moran, and Zelda threw her diamond and platinum wristwatch—the first expensive thing he had given her, in 1920—from the train window. In the story, the valuable gift is a string of "fine seed pearls" Adrian had given Eva as a birthday present the week before their voyage. Fingering the pearls before the ship leaves the dock, Eva tells Adrian she has promised herself to "try never to say a mean thing to you again" (p. 12). Later, when she notices Adrian's interest in Betsy D'Amido, Eva tries to remind him of their commitment through the pearls: "'Look Adrian,' She held up the string of pearls before clasping them on. 'Aren't they lovely?'" (p. 70). Finally, bewildered by the storm and drunkenly sure that she has lost Adrian, Eva believes that her husband's love demands a sacrifice: "Deliberately, she unclasped her pearl necklace, lifted it to her lips—for she knew that with it went the freshest, fairest part of her life—and flung it out into the gale" (p. 70). Although the Smiths' marriage is seemingly restored in the end and they tell themselves that the rough crossing was a passing nightmare, Adrian's reassurance that "there are better pearls in Paris" (p. 75)—as if their marriage can be mended by money alone—suggests their happiness is far from secure.

The similarities between "The Rough Crossing" and the Kelly version make it clear why Bruccoli points to the story as the inspiration for Fitzgerald's new approach to his novel. The Kelly fragment begins with Lewellyn Kelly,

STORIES WITH TEXTUAL LINKS TO THE KELLY DRAFT

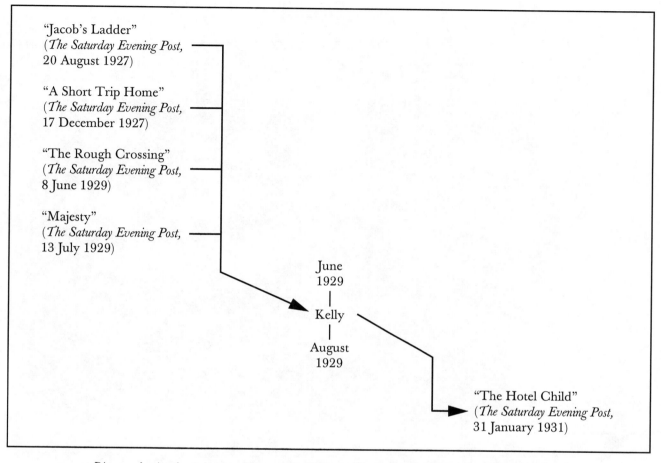

"Jacob's Ladder"
(*The Saturday Evening Post*,
20 August 1927)

"A Short Trip Home"
(*The Saturday Evening Post*,
17 December 1927)

"The Rough Crossing"
(*The Saturday Evening Post*,
8 June 1929)

"Majesty"
(*The Saturday Evening Post*,
13 July 1929)

June
1929
|
Kelly
|
August
1929

"The Hotel Child"
(*The Saturday Evening Post*,
31 January 1931)

Diagram showing the stories textually connected with Fitzgerald's work on the Kelly version. Fitzgerald stripped passages from the four stories on the left—"Jacob's Ladder," "A Short Trip Home," "The Rough Crossing," and "Majesty"—and revised them for use in the Kelly draft. After he abandoned the Kelly plot, he took two phrases from the Kelly material for "The Hotel Child."

twenty-seven, and his wife Nicole, twenty-four, already embarked upon a voyage to Europe. Like Adrian Smith, Lew Kelly is a celebrity, though his fame is much greater than Adrian's and attracts the attention of a seventeen-year-old aspiring actress:

> At the moment he was, save for Griffith, the most successful picture director in the United States. To Rosemary he was more than that—he was the gatekeeper of the promised land, the portal itself to all that was desirable.[2] (p. 302)

Although the strain upon the Kellys' marriage only just begins to develop in the fragment, the cracks in the foundation, as they were in the story, are apparent. Like Eva Smith, Nicole is so dependent on her husband she feels she always "must cling to his arm" (p. 283).

When Lew's attention is drawn to Rosemary, Nicole recalls "a small old scar":

> a flash of jealousy she had felt when he was attracted to just such a child two years before. It had been less than nothing but she was glad they were going away from a world where beauty literally went begging, where for all her own generous endowments she experienced intermittent moments of envy. (p. 303)

Also as in the story, the wife's drinking creates tension in the marriage. At the boring dinner party, Lew watches as Nicole drinks a fourth glass of champagne: "Momentarily, he hated her for taking such an easy escape tonight" (p. 310).

The Kelly fragment does significantly differ from the story, for the focus is more on Lew Kelly's character than on Lew and Nicole's marriage. Lew Kelly's purpose

The longest passage that Fitzgerald stripped from "The Rough Crossing" was the opening description of boarding the ship.

Opening page from the story that is related to the Kelly version, with a stripped passage highlighted
(Bruccoli Collection of Fitzgerald, Thomas Cooper Library, University of South Carolina)

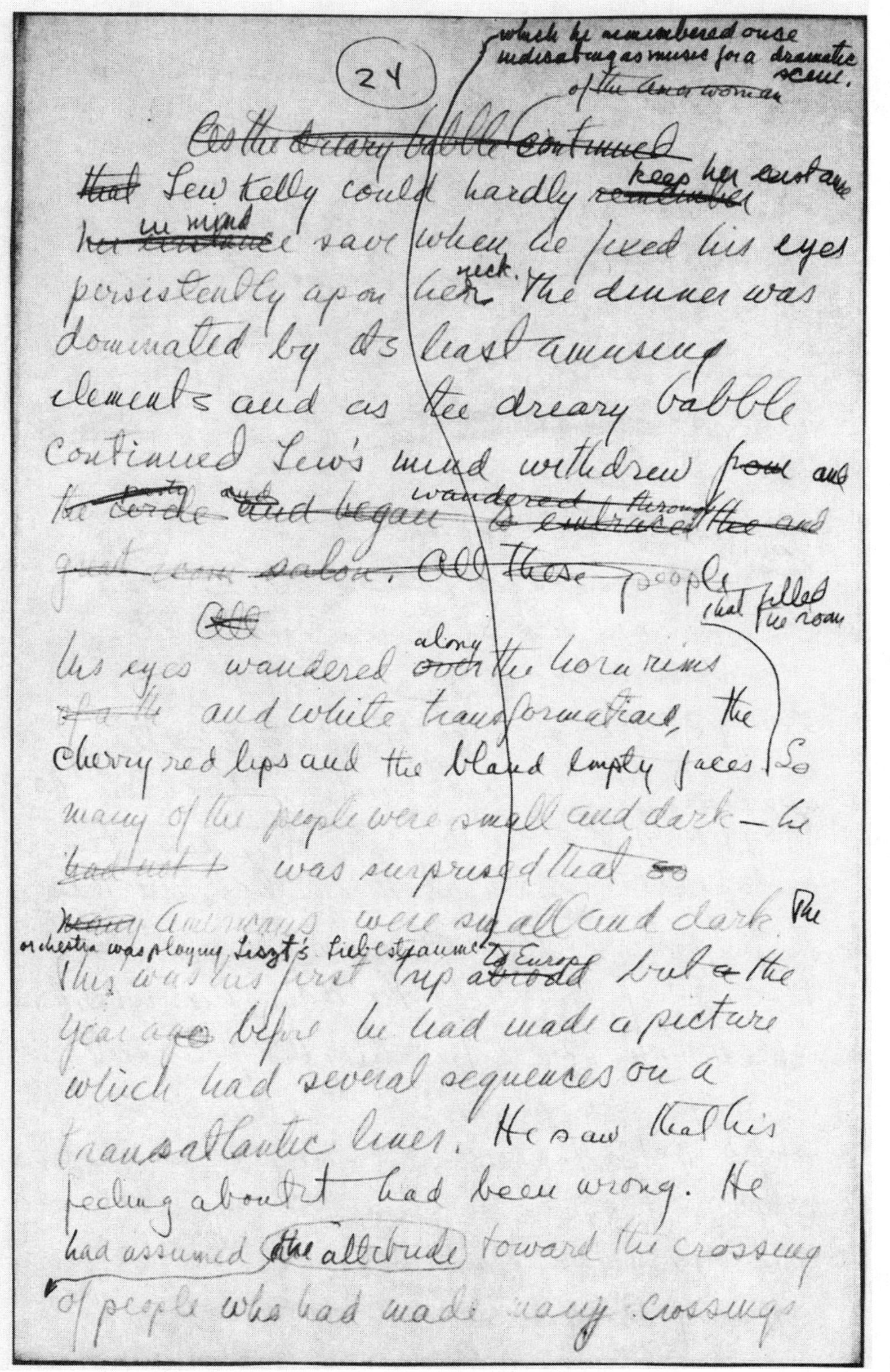

which he remembered once
indicated as music for a dramatic
scene.
of the cleaver woman

24

~~As the dreary babble continued~~

~~that~~ Lew Kelly could hardly ~~remember~~ keep her ~~costan~~
~~her costume~~ in mind save when he fixed his eyes
persistently upon her. neck. The dinner was
dominated by its least amusing
elements and as the dreary babble
continued Lew's mind withdrew ~~from~~ and
~~the table~~ ~~and began~~ wandered ~~through~~ ~~embraced the~~ and
~~just now salon.~~ ~~All those~~ ~~people~~
that filled
the room

~~Off~~

his eyes wandered along ~~over~~ the ~~liora~~ rims
~~of the~~ and white transformations, the
cherry red lips and the bland empty faces So
many of the people were small and dark — he
~~had not t~~ was surprised that ~~so~~
~~many~~ Americans were small and dark. The
orchestra was playing Liszt's Liebestraume
This was his first trip ~~abroad~~ to Europe but ~~the~~ the
year ~~ago~~ before he had made a picture
which had several sequences on a
transatlantic liner. He saw that his
feeling about it had been wrong. He
had assumed ~~the attitude~~ toward the crossing
of people who had made many crossings

Pages from the Kelly manuscript in which Fitzgerald used the opening of "The Rough Crossing." The stripping begins as Lew Kelly imagines how he should have filmed scenes set aboard a transatlantic liner in a movie he had made the previous year (Princeton University Library).

(25) remembered the departure,

and thus diminished the intensity of his effects. Always the first view was freshest and best and it was snobbish of him to assume that his audiences were travellers rather than to conduct them through the experience.

— He ~~remembered now~~ the long ~~roofed~~ piers covering a country that was no longer here and not yet there. It was ~~evening~~ ~~night~~ and the hazy yellow vault was full of shouting echoing voices. There was the rumble of trucks and the clump of trunks, the strident chatter of a crane and the first smell of the sea. He ~~and bugle and the nurse and baby~~ ~~They~~ hurried even though there was time. The past, the continent was behind them; the future was that glowing mouth in the side of the ship; the dim turbulent alley was too confusedly the present.

Up the gangplank + their vision of the world narrowed, they were citizens of a commonwealth smaller than Andorra. They were no longer sure of ~~anything~~. Curiously

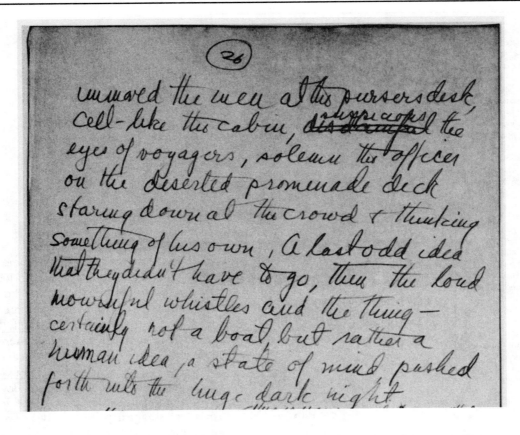

in going to Europe is not just to rest or escape but to find meaning, "to learn something" (p. 307):

> The idea of Europe seen from the sudden bareness he had discovered in their Hollywood house had seemed warm unified and clear, a movement from the diverse and thin toward the definite and concrete. (p. 329)

Insofar as the fragment advances the action, Kelly's restlessness is shown less by the slight interest he shows in Rosemary than by his reaction to the young man, Curly, who jumps overboard and intrudes "his personal tragedies upon three thousand people" (p. 294). Kelly quickly understands Curly's explanation as to why he jumped:

> "We'd been talking about jumping and suddenly, I don't know why, it didn't seem important whether I jumped or not. I didn't want to die but for just a moment life and death seemed just about the same, if you know what I mean."
> "Equally valuable."
> "Equally valuable, as if I wrote down the reasons and there were just as many reasons for dying as for living."
> (pp. 321–322)

Although Kelly recognizes Curly as "a scamp" and his own superiority to him "[i]n every element of character and achievement," the successful director is unable to surely feel "the gap between them" (*M&K II* 325). At the end of the fragment, Lew Kelly, without knowing "what relation he bore to Nicole or to the world" (*M&K II* 328–329), is looking to Europe for answers.

Since Fitzgerald decided to abandon the Kelly version for a return to Melarky, the "new angle" the story inspired apparently did not "solve previous difficulties" as the author had hoped. However, the Kelly version is certainly a step forward in the eventual novel's development. Unlike Francis Melarky, Lew Kelly and Dick Diver are successful, mature men who have families of their own. The story of either Kelly or Diver's collapse is inherently more consequential and thus more involving to the reader than Francis Melarky's. The question, then, of why Fitzgerald abandoned the promising Kelly beginning to return to the Melarky material is vexing indeed. The answer may well be that Fitzgerald simply felt he had already put too much time and effort into Melarky to make continuing with the Kelly version seem worthwhile when he encountered problems there as well.

"The Rough Crossing" lay closer to the heart of the eventual novel, for in important respects Nicole and Dick Diver resemble Eva and Adrian Smith more than they do Nicole and Lew Kelly. Just as Eva felt that "the mere novelty of people did not seem a sufficient reason for eternally offering everything up to them" (p. 14), Nicole warily

The funeral of Dick Diver's father in the novel is drawn from Fitzgerald's own experience, which he examined in a story, "On Your Own," which he apparently wrote soon after Edward Fitzgerald's death in January 1931. Rejected by The Saturday Evening Post *and other magazines, the story was posthumously published in the 30 January 1979 issue of* Esquire.

In "On Your Own" Evelyn Lovejoy, a successful American actress in London, returns to Maryland to bury her father, just as Dick returns to Virginia to bury his. Fitzgerald strips details from Evelyn's train trip south—"her train shambled down into the low-forested clayland," "[s]he saw a star she knew"—that he uses to show Dick "once more identified with his surroundings." The heart of Evelyn's reaction, however, occurs at the graveside in passages that seem to be written to capture Fitzgerald's own feelings:

At the service next day in the Rocktown churchyard, the sense that she was on a stage, that she was being watched, froze Evelyn's grief—then it was over and the country doctor lay among a hundred Lovejoys and Dorseys and Crawshaws. It was very friendly leaving him there with all his relations around him. Then as they turned from the grave-side her eyes fell on George Ives who stood a little apart with his hat in his hand.

When George returns to take her to the station, Evelyn has him take her again to her father's grave:

They stopped once more at the churchyard—she brought a great armful of flowers to leave as a last offering on her father's grave. Leaving him at the gate she went in.

The flowers scattered on the brown unsettled earth. She had no more ties here now and she did not know whether she would come back any more. She knelt down. All these dead, she knew them all, their weather-beaten faces with hard blue flashing eyes, their spare violent bodies, their souls made of new earth in the long forest-heavy darkness of the seventeenth century. Minute by minute the spell grew on her until it was hard to struggle back to the old world where she had dined with kings and princes, where her name in letters two feet high challenged the curiosity of the night. A line of William McFee's surged through her:

> O staunch old heart that toiled so long for me
> I waste my years sailing along the sea.

The words released her—she broke suddenly and sat back on her heels, crying.

How long she was staying she didn't know; the flowers had grown invisible when a voice called her name from the churchyard and she got up and wiped her eyes.

"I'm coming." And then, "Goodbye then Father, all my fathers."

XIX

For an hour, tied up with his profound reaction to his father's death, the magnificent façade of the homeland, the harbor of New York, seemed all sad and glorious to Dick, but once ashore the feeling vanished, nor did he find it again in the streets or the hotels or the trains that bore him first to Buffalo, and then south to Virginia with his father's body. Only as the local train shambled into the low-forested clayland of Westmoreland County, did he feel once more identified with his surroundings; at the station he saw a star he knew, and a cold moon bright over Chesapeake Bay; he heard the rasping wheels of buckboards turning, the lovely fatuous voices, the sound of sluggish primeval rivers flowing softly under soft Indian names.

Next day at the churchyard his father was laid among a hundred Divers, Dorseys, and Hunters. It was very friendly leaving him there with all his relations around him. Flowers were scattered on the brown unsettled earth. Dick had no more ties here now and did not believe he would come back. He knelt on the hard soil. These dead, he knew them all, their weather-beaten faces with blue flashing eyes, the spare violent bodies, the souls made of new earth in the forest-heavy darkness of the seventeenth century.

"Good-by, my father—good-by, all my fathers."

On the long-roofed steamship piers one is in a country that is no longer here and not yet there. The hazy yellow vault is full of echoing shouts. There are the rumble of trucks and the clump of trunks, the strident chatter of cranes, the first

267

The first two pages of chapter 19 of Book II of Tender Is the Night *with stripped passages indicated*

TENDER IS THE NIGHT

salt smell of the sea. One hurries through, even though there's time; the past, the continent, is behind; the future is the glowing mouth in the side of the ship; the dim, turbulent alley is too confusedly the present.

Up the gangplank and the vision of the world adjusts itself, narrows. One is a citizen of a commonwealth smaller than Andorra, no longer sure of anything. The men at the purser's desk are as oddly shaped as the cabins; disdainful are the eyes of voyagers and their friends. Next the loud mournful whistles, the portentous vibration and the boat, the human idea—is in motion. The pier and its faces slide by and for a moment the boat is a piece accidentally split off from them; the faces become remote, voiceless, the pier is one of many blurs along the water front. The harbor flows swiftly toward the sea.

With it flowed Albert McKisco, labelled by the newspapers as its most precious cargo. McKisco was having a vogue. His novels were pastiches of the work of the best people of his time, a feat not to be disparaged, and in addition he possessed a gift for softening and debasing what he borrowed, so that many readers were charmed by the ease with which they could follow him. Success had improved him and humbled him. He was no fool about his capacities—he realized that he possessed more vitality than many men of superior talent, and he was resolved to enjoy the success he had earned. "I've done nothing yet," he would say. "I don't think I've got any real genius. But if I keep trying I may write a good book." Fine dives have been made from flimsier spring-boards. The innumerable snubs of the past were forgotten. Indeed, his success was founded psychologically upon his duel with Tommy Barban, upon the basis of which, as it withered in his memory, he had created, afresh, a new self-respect.

Spotting Dick Diver the second day out, he eyed him tenta-

268

As finally employed in Tender Is the Night, *the passage that originated in "The Rough Crossing" is improved over its appearance in either the story or the Kelly version. Fitzgerald stripped more of the story for the novel than he had for the Kelly version, connecting two places in its opening to create the scene of Dick entering the ship after attending his father's funeral. Fitzgerald's stylistic sense is clear in the first few sentences. Gone is the story's initial staginess—the words "Once" and "ghostly" and the capitalized "Here" and "There." Throughout the passage, Fitzgerald appropriately uses the formal "one" instead of inconsistently using both "one" and "you" as he had in the story. The passage gains by the shift in context and functions as an evocative transition. The reader is aware of Dick Diver's past—the dead father, the crumbling foundation of his identity—and ironically aware, too, that "the past, the continent" he leaves behind is America, the land of hope and promise and his boyhood ideals.*

observes Dick's "extraordinary virtuosity" (p. 35) in attracting others and worries that "there can be too many people" (p. 212). Under strain, both Eva Smith and Nicole Diver lose control and depend upon their husbands. Eva wants Adrian "to put his arms around her and draw her up out of this dizzy lethargy" (p. 14) and becomes hysterical when Adrian deserts her. But both Adrian and Dick also lose control. Although Adrian knows he risks wounding his wife, he is swept away by a young woman he hardly knows:

> Her youth seemed to flow into him, bearing him up into a delicate, romantic ecstasy that transcended passion. He couldn't relinquish it; he had discovered something that he had thought was lost with his own youth forever. As he walked along the passage he knew that he had stopped thinking, no longer dared to think. (p. 70)

Dick, too, is "swayed and driven as an animal" in his pursuit of Rosemary, though he knows it is "out of line with everything that had preceded it—even out of line with what effect he might hope to produce in Rosemary" (p. 119). In the Kelly version, however, Nicole has no evident worry that her husband will distract himself by attracting too many people. Although probably destined to lose control like the Smiths and the Divers had Fitzgerald continued the draft, the Kellys of the fragment are not subject to the same pressures.

Fitzgerald's abandonment of the Kelly version and the subsequent parallels that have been noted between "The Rough Crossing" and *Tender Is the Night* indicate that his work on stories was leading him to reevaluate the novel but that he did not yet feel sure enough of the material he was exploring in his stories to commit to a new approach. Nearly three more years would pass before Fitzgerald began work on the Diver version.

Notes

1. "The Rough Crossing," *The Saturday Evening Post,* 201 (8 June 1929): 12–14, 70, 75, 78. All subsequent story quotations are from this text.

2. "The Kelly version," in *Tender Is the Night: The Melarky and Kelly Versions Part 2,* edited by Matthew J. Bruccoli (New York & London: Garland, 1990), pp. 279–333.

A Preview of the Novel

During the years he was working, or not working, on Tender Is the Night, *Fitzgerald wrote stories that introduced themes and utilized settings that were subsequently developed in the novel. One of these "cluster stories," "One Trip Abroad," written in August 1930 after Zelda Fitzgerald was hospitalized at Les Rives de Pangins in Switzerland, is most closely linked with* Tender. *Both examine the corrupting effects of European residence on American character. Nelson Kelly's deterioration less powerfully anticipates Dick Diver's fall. Fitzgerald did not reprint "One Trip Abroad" in* Taps at Reveille *(1935), his last story collection, because it included too many details and phrases he had incorporated in* Tender.

One Trip Abroad
F. Scott Fitzgerald
The Saturday Evening Post, 203 (11 October 1930): 6–7, 48, 51, 53–54, 56

I

In the afternoon the air became black with locusts, and some of the women shrieked, sinking to the floor of the motorbus and covering their hair with traveling rugs. The locusts were coming north, eating everything in their path, which was not so much in that part of the world; they were flying silently and in straight lines, flakes of black snow. But none struck the windshield or tumbled into the car, and presently humorists began holding out their hands, trying to catch some. After ten minutes the cloud thinned out, passed, and the women emerged from the blankets, disheveled and feeling silly. And everyone talked together.

Everyone talked; it would have been absurd not to talk after having been through a swarm of locusts on the edge of the Sahara. The Smyrna-American talked to the British widow going down to Biskra to have one last fling with an as-yet-unencountered sheik. The member of the San Francisco Stock Exchange talked shyly to the author. "Aren't you an author?" he said. The father and daughter from Wilmington talked to the cockney airman who was going to fly to Timbuctoo. Even the French chauffeur turned

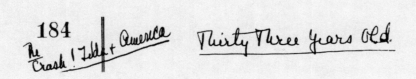

Fitzgerald's summary in his Ledger *of the year from September 1929 to September 1930*

ONE TRIP ABROAD

By F. Scott Fitzgerald

ILLUSTRATED BY HARLEY ENNIS STIVERS

IN THE afternoon the air became black with locusts, and some of the women shrieked, sinking to the floor of the motorbus and covering their hair with traveling rugs. The locusts were coming north, eating everything in their path, which was not so much in that part of the world; they were flying silently and in straight lines, flakes of black snow. But none struck the windshield or tumbled into the car, and presently humorists began holding out their hands, trying to catch some. After ten minutes the cloud thinned out, passed, and the women emerged from the blankets, disheveled and feeling silly. And everyone talked together.

Everyone talked; it would have been absurd not to talk after having been through a swarm of locusts on the edge of the Sahara. The Smyrna-American talked to the British widow going down to Biskra to have one last fling with an as-yet-unencountered sheik. The member of the San Francisco Stock Exchange talked shyly to the author. "Aren't you an author?" he said. The father and daughter from Wilmington talked to the cockney airman who was going to fly to Timbuctoo. Even the French chauffeur turned about and explained in a loud, clear voice: "Bumblebees," which sent the trained nurse from New York into shriek after shriek of hysterical laughter.

Amongst the unsubtle rushing together of the travelers there was one interchange more carefully considered. Mr. and Mrs. Liddell Miles, turning as one person, smiled

worked on business contingent on his recent inheritance of half a million dollars. Also he painted a picture of a smokestack. When one member of the gay crowd in the bar disappeared permanently into the Atlantic just this side of the Azores, the young Kellys were almost glad, for it justified their aloof attitude.

But there was another reason Nicole was sorry they had committed themselves. She spoke to Nelson about it: "I passed that couple in the hall just now."

"Who—the Mileses?"

"No, that young couple—about our age—the ones that were on the other motorbus, that we thought looked so nice, in Bir Rabalou after lunch, in the camel market."

"They did look nice."

"Charming," she said emphatically; "the girl and man, both. I'm almost sure I've met the girl somewhere before."

The couple referred to were sitting across the room at dinner, and Nicole found her eyes drawn irresistibly toward them. They, too, now had companions, and again Nicole, who had not talked to a girl of her own age for two months, felt a faint regret. The Mileses, being formally sophisticated and frankly snobbish, were a different matter. They had been to an alarming number of places and seemed to know all the flashing phantoms of the newspapers.

They dined on the hotel veranda under a sky that was low and full of the presence of a strange and watchful God; around the corners of the hotel the night already stirred with the sounds of which they had

They Loved the Riviera in Full Summer With Many Friends There and the Nights Open and Full of Music

Illustration from the story in which Fitzgerald depicts a young American couple who are corrupted by their experiences in Europe (Bruccoli Collection of Fitzgerald, Thomas Cooper Library, University of South Carolina)

about and explained in a loud, clear voice: "Bumblebees," which sent the trained nurse from New York into shriek after shriek of hysterical laughter.

Amongst the unsubtle rushing together of the travelers there was one interchange more carefully considered. Mr. and Mrs. Liddell Miles, turning as one person, smiled and spoke to the young American couple in the seat behind:

"Didn't catch any in your hair?"

The young couple smiled back politely.

"No. We survived that plague."

They were in their twenties, and there was still a pleasant touch of bride and groom upon them. A handsome couple; the man rather intense and sensitive, the girl arrestingly light of hue in eyes and hair, her face without shadows, its living freshness modulated by a lovely confident calm. Mr. and Mrs. Miles did not fail to notice their air of good breeding, of a specifically "swell" background, expressed both by their unsophistication and by their ingrained reticence that was not stiffness. If they held aloof, it was because they were sufficient to each other, while it must be said that Mr. and Mrs. Miles' aloofness toward the other passengers was a conscious mask, a social attitude, quite as public an affair in its essence as the ubiquitous advances of the Smyrna-American, who was snubbed by all.

The Mileses had, in fact, decided that the young couple were "possible" and, bored with themselves, were frankly approaching them.

"Have you been to Africa before? It's been so utterly fascinating! Are you going on to Tunis?"

The Mileses, if somewhat worn away inside by fifteen years of a particular set in Paris, had undeniable style, even charm, and before the evening arrival at the little oasis town of Bou-Saada they had all four become companionable. They uncovered mutual friends in New York and, meeting for a cocktail in the bar of the Hotel Transatlantique, decided to have dinner together.

As the young Kellys came downstairs later, Nicole was conscious of a certain regret that they had accepted, realizing that now they were probably committed to seeing a certain amount of their new acquaintances as far as Constantine, where their routes diverged.

In the eight months of their marriage she had been so very happy that it seemed like spoiling something. On the Italian liner that had brought them to Gibraltar they had not joined the groups that leaned desperately on one another in the bar; instead, they seriously studied French, and Nelson worked on business contingent on his recent inheritance of half a million dollars. Also he painted a picture of a smokestack. When one member of the gay crowd in the bar disappeared permanently into the Atlantic just this side of the Azores, the young Kellys were almost glad, for it justified their aloof attitude.

But there was another reason Nicole was sorry they had committed themselves. She spoke to Nelson about it: "I passed that couple in the hall just now."

"Who—the Mileses?"

"No, that young couple—about our age—the ones that were on the other motorbus, that we thought looked so nice, in Bir Rabalou after lunch, in the camel market."

"They did look nice."

"Charming," she said emphatically; "the girl and man, both. I'm almost sure I've met the girl somewhere before."

The couple referred to were sitting across the room at dinner, and Nicole found her eyes drawn irresistibly toward them. They, too, now had companions, and again Nicole, who had not talked to a girl of her own age for two months, felt a faint regret. The Mileses, being formally sophisticated and frankly snobbish, were a different matter. They had been to an alarming number of places and seemed to know all the flashing phantoms of the newspapers.

They dined on the hotel veranda under a sky that was low and full of the presence of a strange and watchful God; around the corners of the hotel the night already stirred with the sounds of which they had so often read but that were even so hysterically unfamiliar—drums from Senegal, a native flute, the selfish, effeminate whine of a camel, the Arabs pattering past in shoes made of old automobile tires, the wail of Magian prayer.

At the desk in the hotel, a fellow passenger was arguing monotonously with the clerk about the rate of exchange, and the inappropriateness added to the detachment which had increased steadily as they went south.

Mrs. Miles was the first to break the lingering silence; with a sort of impatience she pulled them with her, in from the night and up to the table.

"We really should have dressed. Dinner's more amusing if people dress, because they feel differently in formal clothes. The English know that."

"Dress here?" her husband objected. "I'd feel like that man in the ragged dress suit we passed today, driving the flock of sheep."

"I always feel like a tourist if I'm not dressed."

"Well, we are, aren't we?" asked Nelson.

"I don't consider myself a tourist. A tourist is somebody who gets up early and goes to cathedrals and talks about scenery."

Nicole and Nelson, having seen all the official sights from Fez to Algiers, and taken reels of moving pictures and felt improved, confessed themselves, but decided that their experiences on the trip would not interest Mrs. Miles.

"Every place is the same," Mrs. Miles continued. "The only thing that matters is who's there. New scenery is fine for half an hour, but after that you want your own kind to see. That's why some places have a certain vogue, and then the vogue changes and the people move on somewhere else. The place itself really never matters."

"But doesn't somebody first decide that the place is nice?" objected Nelson. "The first ones go there because they like the place."

"Where were you going this spring?" Mrs. Miles asked.

"We thought of San Remo, or maybe Sorrento. We've never been to Europe before."

"My children, I know both Sorrento and San Remo, and you won't stand either of them for a week. They're full of the most awful English, reading the Daily Mail and waiting for letters and talking about the most incredibly dull things. You might as well go to Brighton or Bournemouth and buy a white poodle and a sunshade and walk on the pier. How long are you staying in Europe?"

"We don't know; perhaps several years." Nicole hesitated. "Nelson came into a little money, and we wanted a change. When I was young, my father had asthma and I had to live in the most depressing health resorts with him for years; and Nelson was in the fur business in Alaska, and he loathed it; so when we were free we came abroad. Nelson's going to paint and I'm going to study singing." She looked triumphantly at her husband. "So far, it's been absolutely gorgeous."

Mrs. Miles decided, from the evidence of the younger woman's clothes, that it was quite a bit of money, and their enthusiasm was infectious.

"You really must go to Biarritz," she advised them. "Or else come to Monte Carlo."

"They tell me there's a great show here," said Miles, ordering champagne. "The Ouled Nails. The concierge says they're some kind of tribe of girls who come down from the mountains and learn to be dancers, and what not, till they've collected enough gold to go back to their mountains and marry. Well, they give a performance tonight."

Walking over to the Café of the Ouled Nails afterward, Nicole regretted that she and Nelson were not strolling along through the ever-lower, ever-softer, ever-brighter night. Nelson had reciprocated the bottle of champagne at dinner, and neither of them was accustomed to so much. As they drew near the sad flute she didn't want to go inside, but rather to climb to the top of a low hill where a white mosque shone clear as a planet through the night. Life was better than any show; closing in toward Nelson, she pressed his hand.

The little cave of a café was filled with the passengers from the two busses. The girls—light-brown, flat-nosed Berbers with fine, deep-shaded eyes—were already doing each one her solo on the platform. They wore cotton dresses, faintly reminiscent of Southern mammies; under these their bodies writhed in a slow nautch, culminating in a stomach dance, with silver belts bobbing wildly and their strings of real gold coins tinkling on their necks and arms. The flute player was also a comedian; he danced, burlesquing the girls. The drummer, swathed in goatskins like a witch doctor, was a true black from the Sudan.

Through the smoke of cigarettes each girl went in turn through the finger movement, like piano playing in the air—outwardly facile, yet, after a few moments, so obviously exacting—and then through the very simply languid yet equally precise steps of the feet—these were but preparation to the wild sensuality of the culminated dance.

Afterward there was a lull. Though the performance seemed not quite over, most of the audience gradually got up to go, but there was a whispering in the air.

"What is it?" Nicole asked her husband.

"Why I believe—it appears that for a consideration the Ouled Nails dance in more or less—ah—Oriental style—in very little except jewelry."

"Oh."

"We're all staying," Mr. Miles assured her jovially. "After all, we're here to see the real customs and manners of the country; a little prudishness shouldn't stand in our way."

Most of the men remained, and several of the women. Nicole stood up suddenly.

"I'll wait outside," she said.

"Why not stay, Nicole? After all, Mrs. Miles is staying."

The flute player was making preliminary flourishes. Upon the raised dais two pale brown children of perhaps fourteen were taking off their cotton dresses. For an instant Nicole hesitated, torn between repulsion and the desire not to appear to be a prig. Then she saw another young American woman get up quickly and start for the door. Recognizing the attractive young wife from the other bus, her own decision came quickly and she followed.

Nelson hurried after her. "I'm going if you go," he said, but with evident reluctance.

"Please don't bother. I'll wait with the guide outside."

"Well—" The drum was starting. He compromised: "I'll only stay a minute. I want to see what it's like."

Waiting in the fresh night, she found that the incident had hurt her—Nelson's not coming with her at once, giving as an argument the fact that Mrs. Miles was staying. From being hurt, she grew angry and made signs to the guide that she wanted to return to the hotel.

Twenty minutes later, Nelson appeared, angry with the anxiety at finding her gone, as well as to hide his guilt at having left her. Incredulous with themselves, they were suddenly in a quarrel.

Much later, when there were no sounds at all in Bou-Saada and the nomads in the market place were only motionless bundles rolled up in their burnouses, she was asleep upon his shoulder. Life is progressive, no matter what our intentions, but something was harmed, some precedent of possible nonagreement was set. It was a love match, though, and it could stand a great deal. She and Nelson had passed lonely youths, and now they wanted the taste and smell of the living world; for the present they were finding it in each other.

A month later they were in Sorrento, where Nicole took singing lessons and Nelson tried to paint something new into the Bay of Naples. It was the existence they had planned and often read about. But they found, as so many have found, that the charm of idyllic interludes depends upon one person's "giving the party"—which is to say, furnishing the background, the experience, the patience, against which the other seems to enjoy again the spells of pastoral tranquillity recollected from childhood. Nicole and Nelson were at once too old and too young, and too American, to fall into immediate soft agreement with a strange land. Their vitality made them restless, for as yet his painting had no direction and her singing no immediate prospect of becoming serious. They said they were not "getting anywhere"—the evenings were long, so they began to drink a lot of *vin de Capri* at dinner.

The English owned the hotel. They were aged, come South for good wealth and tranquillity; Nelson and Nicole resented the mild tenor of their days. Could people be content to talk eternally about the weather, promenade the same walks, face the same variant of macaroni at dinner month after month? They grew bored, and Americans bored are already in sight of excitement. Things came to a head all in one night.

Over a flask of wine at dinner they decided to go to Paris, settle in an apartment and work seriously. Paris promised metropolitan diversion, friends of their own age, a general intensity that Italy lacked. Eager with new hopes, they strolled into the salon after dinner, when, for the tenth time, Nelson noticed an ancient and enormous mechanical piano and was moved to try it.

Across the salon sat the only English people with whom they had had any connection—Gen. Sir Evelyne Fragelle and Lady Fragelle. The connection had been brief and unpleasant—seeing them walking out of the hotel in peignoirs to swim, she had announced, over quite a few yards of floor space, that it was disgusting and shouldn't be allowed.

But that was nothing compared with her response to the first terrific bursts of sound from the electric piano. As the dust of years trembled off the keyboard at the vibration, she shot galvanically for-

ward with the sort of jerk associated with the electric chair. Somewhat stunned himself by the sudden din of Waiting for the Robert E. Lee, Nelson had scarcely sat down when she projected herself across the room, her train quivering behind her, and, without glancing at the Kellys, turned off the instrument.

It was one of those gestures that are either plainly justified, or else outrageous. For a moment Nelson hesitated uncertainly; then, remembering Lady Fragelle's arrogant remark about his bathing suit, he returned to the instrument in her still-billowing wake and turned it on again.

The incident had become international. The eyes of the entire salon fell eagerly upon the protagonists, watching for the next move. Nicole hurried after Nelson, urging him to let the matter pass, but it was too late. From the outraged English table there arose, joint by joint, Gen. Sir Evelyne Fragelle, faced with perhaps his most crucial situation since the relief of Ladysmith.

"'T'lee outrageous!—'t'lee outrageous!"

"I beg your pardon," said Nelson.

"Here for fifteen years!" screamed Sir Evelyne to himself. "Never heard of anyone doing such a thing before!"

"I gathered that this was put here for the amusement of the guests."

Scorning to answer, Sir Evelyne knelt, reached for the catch, pushed it the wrong way, whereupon the speed and volume of the instrument tripled until they stood in a wild pandemonium of sound; Sir Evelyne livid with military emotions, Nelson on the point of maniacal laughter.

In a moment the firm hand of the hotel manager settled the matter; the instrument gulped and stopped, trembling a little from its unaccustomed outburst, leaving behind it a great silence in which Sir Evelyne turned to the manager.

"Most outrageous affair ever heard of in my life. My wife turned it off once, and he"—this was his first acknowledgment of Nelson's identity as distinct from the instrument—"he put it on again!"

"This is a public room in a hotel," Nelson protested, "The instrument is apparently here to be used."

"Don't get in an argument," Nicole whispered. "They're old."

But Nelson said, "If there's any apology, it's certainly due to me."

Sir Evelyne's eye was fixed menacingly upon the manager, waiting for him to do his duty. The latter thought of Sir Evelyne's fifteen years of residence, and cringed.

"It is not the habitude to play the instrument in the evening. The clients are each one quiet on his or her table."

"American cheek!" snapped Sir Evelyne.

"Very well," Nelson said: "we'll relieve the hotel of our presence tomorrow."

As a reaction from this incident, as a sort of protest against Sir Evelyne Fragelle, they went not to Paris but to Monte Carlo after all. They were through with being alone.

II

A little more than two years after the Kellys' first visit to Monte Carlo, Nicole woke up one morning into what though it bore the same name, had become to her a different place altogether.

In spite of hurried months in Paris or Biarrita, it was not home to them. They had a villa, they had a large acquaintance among the spring and summer crowd—a summer crowd which, naturally, did not include people on charted trips or the shore parties from Mediterranean cruises: these latter had become for them "tourists."

They loved the Riviera in full summer with many friends there and the nights and full of music. Before the maid drew the curtains this morning to shut out the glare, Nicole saw from her window the yacht of T. F. Golding, placid among the swells of the Monacon Bay as if constantly bound on a romantic voyage not dependent upon actual motion.

The yacht had taken the slow tempo of the coast; it had gone no farther than to Cannes and back all summer, though it might have toured the world. The Kellys were dining on board that night.

Nicole spoke excellent French; she had five new evening dresses and four others that would do; she had her husband; she had two men in love with her, and she felt sad for one of them. She had her pretty face. At 10:30 she was meeting a third man, who was just beginning to be in love with her "in a harmless way." At one she was having a dozen charming people to luncheon. All that.

"I'm happy," she brooded toward the bright blinds. "I'm young and good-looking, and my name is often in the paper as having been here and there, but really I don't care about shi-shi. I think it's all awfully silly, but if you do want to see people, you might as well see the chic, amusing ones; and if people call you a snob, it's envy, and they know it and everybody knows it."

She repeated the substance of this to Oscar Dane on the Mont Agel golf course two hours later, and he cursed her quietly.

"Not at all," he said: "You're just getting to be an old snob. Do you call that crowd of drunks you run with amusing people? Why, they're not even very swell. They're so hard that they've shifted down through Europe like nails in a sack of wheat, till they stick out of it a little into the Mediterranean Sea."

Annoyed, Nicole fired a name at him, but he answered: "Class C. A good solid article for beginners."

"The Colbys—anyway, her."

"Third flight."

"Marquis and Marquise de Kalb."

"If she didn't happen to take dope and he didn't have other peculiarities."

"Well, then, where are the amusing people?" she demanded impatiently.

"Off by themselves somewhere. They don't hunt in herds, except occasionally."

"How about you? You'd snap up another invitation from every person I named. I've heard stories about you wilder than any you can make up. There's not a man that's known you six months that would take your check for ten dollars. You're a sponge and a parasite and everything—"

"Shut up for a minute," he interrupted. "I don't want to spoil this drive. . . . I just don't like to see you kid yourself," he continued. "What passes with you for international society is just about as hard to enter nowadays as the public rooms at the Casino; and if I can make my living by sponging off it, I'm still giving twenty times more than I get. We dead beats are about the only people in it with any stuff, and we stay with it because we have to." She laughed, liking him immensely, wondering how angry Nelson would be when he found that Oscar had walked off with his nail scissors and his copy of the New York Herald this morning.

"Anyhow," she thought afterward, as she drove home toward luncheon, "we're getting out of it all soon, and we'll be serious and have a baby. After this last summer."

Stopping for a moment at a florist's, she saw a young woman coming out with an armful of flowers. The young woman glanced at her over the heap of color, and Nicole perceived that she was extremely smart, and then that her face was familiar. It was someone she had known once, but only slightly; the name had escaped her, so she did not nod, and forgot the incident until that afternoon.

They were twelve for luncheon: The Goldings' party from the yacht, Liddell and Cardine Miles, Mr. Dance—seven different nationalities he counted: among them an exquisite young French-woman,

Madame Delauney, whom Nicole referred to lightly as "Nelson's girl." Noel Delauney was perhaps her closest friend: when they made up foursomes for golf or for trips, she paired off with Nelson; but today, as Nicole introduced her to someone as "Nelson's girl," the bantering phrase filled Nicole with distaste.

She said aloud at luncheon: "Nelson and I are going to get away from it all."

Everybody agreed that they, too, were going to get away from it all.

"It's all right for the English," someone said, "because they're doing a sort of dance of death—you know, gayety in the doomed fort, with the Sepoys at the gate. You can see it by their faces when they dance—the intensity. They know it and they want it, and they don't see any future. But you Americans, you're having a rotten time. If you want to wear the green hat or the crushed hat, or whatever it is, you always have to get a little tipsy."

"We're going to get away from it all," Nicole said firmly, but something within her argued: "What a pity—this lovely blue sea, this happy time." What came afterward? Did one just accept a lessening of tension? It was somehow Nelson's business to answer that. His growing discontent that he wasn't getting anywhere ought to explode into a new life for both of them, or rather a new hope and content with life. That secret should be his masculine contribution.

"Well, children, good-bye."

"It was a great luncheon."

"Don't forget about getting away from it all."

"See you when—"

The guests walked down the path toward their cars. Only Oscar, just faintly flushed on liqueurs, stood with Nicole on the veranda, talking on and on about the girl he had invited up to see his stamp collection. Momentarily tired of people, impatient to be alone, Nicole listened for a moment and then, taking a glass vase of flowers from the luncheon table, went through the French windows into the dark, shadowy villa, his voice following her, as he talked on and on out there.

It was when she crossed the first salon, still hearing Oscar's monologue on the veranda, that she began to hear another voice in the next room, cutting sharply across Oscar's voice.

"Ah, but kiss me again," it said, stopped: Nicole stopped too, rigid in the silence, now broken only by the voice on the porch.

"Be careful," Nicole recognized the faint French accent of Noel Delauney.

"I'm tired of being careful. Anyhow, they're on the veranda."

"No, better, the usual place."

"Darling, sweet darling."

The voice of Oscar Dane on the veranda grew weary and stopped and, as if thereby released from her paralysis, Nicole took a step—forward or backward, she did not know which. At the sound of her heel on the floor, she heard the two people in the next room breaking swiftly apart.

Then she went in. Nelson was lighting a cigarette; Noel, with her back turned, was apparently hunting for hat or purse on a chair. With blind horror rather than anger, Nicole threw, or rather pushed away from her, the glass vase which she carried. If at anyone, it was at Nelson she threw it, but the force of her feeling had entered the inanimate thing; it flew past him, and Noel Delauney, just turning about, was struck full on the side of her head and face.

"Say there!" Nelson cried. Noel sank slowly into the chair before which she stood, her hand slowly rising to cover the side of her face. The jar rolled unbroken on the thick carpet, scattering its flowers.

"You look out!" Nelson was at Noel's side, trying to take the hand away to see what happened.

"C'est liquide," gasped Noel in a whisper, "Est-ce que c'est le sang?"

He forced her hand away, and cried breathlessly, "No, it's just water!" and then, to Oscar, who had appeared in the doorway: "Get some cognac!" and to Nicole: "You fool, you must be crazy!"

Nicole, breathing hard, said nothing. When the brandy arrived, there was a continuing silence, like that of people watching an operation, while Nelson poured a glass down Noel's throat. Nicole signaled to Oscar for a drink, and, as if afraid to break the silence without it, they all had a brandy. Then Noel and Nelson spoke at once:

"If you can find my hat—"

"This is the silliest—"

"—I shall go immediately."

"—thing I ever saw; I—"

They all looked at Nicole, who said: "Have her car drive right up to the door." Oscar departed quickly.

"Are you sure you don't want to see a doctor?" asked Nelson anxiously.

"I want to go."

A minute later, when the car had driven away, Nelson came in and poured himself another drink of brandy. A wave of subsiding tension flowed over him, showing in his face: Nicole saw it, and saw also his gathering will to make the best he could of it.

"I want to know just why you did that," he demanded. "No, don't go, Oscar." He saw the story starting out into the world.

"What possible reason—"

"Oh, shut up!" snapped Nicole.

"If I kissed Noel, there's nothing so terrible about it. It's of absolutely no significance."

She made a contemptuous sound. "I heard what you said to her."

"You're crazy."

He said it as if she were crazy, and wild rage filled her.

"You liar! All this time pretending to be so square, and so particular what I did, and all the time behind my back you've been playing around with that little—"

She used a serious word, and as if maddened with the sound of it, she sprang toward his chair. In protection against this sudden attack, he flung up his arm quickly, and the knuckles of his open hand struck across the socket of her eye. Covering her face with her hand as Noel had done ten minutes previously, she fell sobbing to the floor.

"Hasn't this gone far enough?" Oscar cried.

"Yes," admitted Nelson, "I guess it has."

"You go out on the veranda and cool off."

He got Nicole to a couch and sat beside her, holding her hand.

"Brace up—brace up, baby," he said, over and over. "What are you—Jack Dempsey? You can't go around hitting French women; they'll sue you."

"He told her he loved her," she gasped hysterically. "She said she'd meet him at the same place. . . . Has he gone there now?"

"He's out on the porch, walking up and down, sorry as the devil that he accidentally hit you, and sorry he ever saw Noel Delauney."

"Oh yes!"

"You might have heard wrong, and it doesn't prove a thing, anyhow."

After twenty minutes, Nelson came in suddenly and sank down on his knees by the side of his wife. Mr. Oscar Dane, reinforced in his idea that he gave much more than he got, backed discreetly and far from unwillingly to the door.

In another hour, Nelson and Nicole, arm in arm, emerged from their villa and walked slowly down to the Café de Paris. They walked instead of driving, as if trying to return to the simplicity they had once possessed, as if they were trying to unwind something that had become visibly tangled. Nicole accepted his explanations, not because they were credible, but because she wanted passionately to believe them. They were both very quiet and sorry.

The Café de Paris was pleasant at that hour, with sunset drooping through the yellow awnings and the red parasols as through stained glass. Glancing about, Nicole saw the young woman she had encountered that morning. She was with a man now. And Nelson placed them immediately as the young couple they had seen in Algeria, almost three years ago.

"They've changed," he commented. "I suppose we have, too, but not so much. They're harder-looking and he looks dissipated. Dissipation always shows in light eyes rather than in dark ones. The girl is *tout ce qu'il y a de chic,* as they say, but there's a hard look in her face too."

"I like her."

"Do you want me to go and ask them if they are that same couple?"

"No! That'd be like lonesome tourists do. They have their own friends."

At that moment people were joining them at their table.

"Nelson, how about tonight?" Nicole asked a little later. "Do you think we can appear at the Goldings' after what's happened?"

"We not only can but we've got to. If the story's around and we're not there, we'll just be handing them a nice juicy subject of conversation. . . . Hello! What on earth—"

Something strident and violent had happened across the café: a woman screamed and the people at one table were all on their feet, surging back and forth like one person. Then the people at the other tables were standing and crowding forward; for just a moment the Kellys saw the face of the girl they had been watching, pale now, and distorted with anger. Panic-stricken, Nicole plucked at Nelson's sleeve.

"I want to get out, I can't stand any more today. Take me home. Is everybody going crazy?"

On the way home, Nelson glanced at Nicole's face and perceived with a start that they were not going to dinner on the Goldings' yacht after all. For Nicole had the beginnings of a well-defined and unmistakable black eye—an eye that by eleven o'clock would be beyond the aid of all the cosmetics in the principality. His heart sank and he decided to say nothing about it until they reached home.

III

THERE is some wise advice in the catechism about avoiding the occasions of sin, and when the Kellys went up to Paris a month later they made a consci-

"Ah, But Kiss Me Again," it Said, Stopped; Nicole Stopped, Too, Rigid in the Silence

Illustration for "One Trip Abroad" in The Saturday Evening Post *(Bruccoli Collection of Fitzgerald, Thomas Cooper Library, University of South Carolina)*

entious list of the places they wouldn't visit any more and the people they didn't want to see again. The places included several famous bars, all the night clubs except one or two that were highly decorous, all the early-morning clubs of every description, and all summer resorts that made whoopee for its own sake—whoopee triumphant and unrestrained—the main attraction of the season.

The people they were through with included three-fourths of those with whom they had passed the last two years. They did this not in snobbishness, but for self-preservation, and not without a certain fear in their hearts that they were cutting themselves off from human contacts forever.

But the world is always curious, and people become valuable merely for their inaccessibility. They found that there were others in Paris who were only interested in those who had separated from the many. The first crowd they had known was largely American, salted with Europeans; the second was largely European, peppered with Americans. This latter crowd was "society," and here and there it touched the ultimate *milieu,* made up of individuals of high position, of great fortune, very occasionally of genius, and always of power. Without being intimate with the great, they made new friends of a more conservative type. Moreover, Nelson began to paint again; he had a studio, and they visited the studios of Brancusi and Leger and Deschamps. It seemed that they were more part of something than before, and when certain gaudy rendezvous were mentioned, they felt a contempt for their first two years in Europe, speaking of their former acquaintances as "that crowd" and as "people who waste your time."

So, although they kept their rules, they entertained frequently at home and they went out to the houses of others. They were young and handsome and intelligent; they came to know what did go and what did not go, and adapted themselves accordingly. Moreover, they were naturally generous and willing, within the limits of common sense, to pay.

When one went out one generally drank. This meant little to Nicole, who had a horror of losing her *soigné* air, losing a touch of bloom or a ray of admiration, but Nelson, thwarted somewhere, found himself quite as tempted to drink at these small dinners as in the more frankly rowdy world. He was not a drunk, he did nothing conspicuous or sodden, but he was no longer willing to go out socially without the stimulus of liquor. It was with the idea of bringing him to a serious and responsible attitude that Nicole decided, after a year in Paris, that the time had come to have a baby.

This was coincidental with their meeting Count Chiki Sarolai. He was an attractive relic of the Austrian court, with no fortune or pretense to any, but with solid social and financial connections in France. His sister was married to the Marquis de la Clos d'Hirondelle, who, in addition to being of the ancient noblesse, was a successful banker in Paris. Count Chiki roved here and there, frankly sponging, rather like Oscar Dane, but in a different sphere.

His penchant was Americans; he hung on their words with a pathetic eagerness, as if they would sooner or later let slip their mysterious formula for making money. After a casual meeting, his interest gravitated to the Kellys. During Nicole's months of waiting he was in the house continually, tirelessly interested in anything that concerned American crime, slang, finance or manners. He came in for a luncheon or dinner when he had no other place to go, and with tacit gratitude he persuaded his sister to call on Nicole, who was immensely flattered.

It was arranged that when Nicole went to the hospital he would stay at the *appartement* of which Nicole didn't approve, since they were inclined to drink together. But the day on which it was decided, he arrived with news of one of his brother-in-law's famous canal-boat parties on the Seine, to which the Kellys were to be invited and which, conveniently enough, was to occur three weeks after the arrival of the baby. So, when Nicole moved out to the American Hospital Count Chiki moved in.

The baby was a boy. For a while Nicole forgot all about people and their human status and their value. She even wondered at the fact that she had become such a snob, since everything seemed trivial compared with the new individual that, eight times a day, they carried to her breast.

After two weeks she and the baby went back to the apartment, but Chiki and his valet stayed on. It was understood, with that subtlety the Kellys had

only recently begun to appreciate, that he was merely staying until after his brother-in-law's party, but the apartment was crowded and Nicole wished him gone. But her old idea, that if one had to see people they might as well be the best, was carried out in being invited to the De la Clos d'Hirondelles'.

As she lay in her chaise lounge the day before the event, Chiki explained the arrangements, in which he had evidently aided.

"Everyone who arrives must drink two cocktails in the American style before they can come aboard—as a ticket of admission."

"But I thought that very fashionable French—Faubourg St. Germain and all that—didn't drink cocktails."

"Oh, but my family is very modern. We adopt many American customs."

"Who'll be there?"

"Everyone! Everyone in Paris."

Great names swam before her eyes. Next day she could not resist dragging the affair into conversation with her doctor. But she was rather offended at the look of astonishment and incredulity that came into his eyes.

"Did I understand you aright?" he demanded. "Did I understand you to say that you were going to a ball tomorrow?"

"Why, yes," she faltered. "Why not?"

"My dear lady you are not going to stir out of the house for two more weeks; you are not going to dance or do anything strenuous for two more after that."

"That's ridiculous!" she cried. "It's been three weeks already! Esther Sherman went to America after—"

"Never mind," he interrupted. "Every case is different. There is a complication which makes it positively necessary for you to follow my orders."

"But the idea is that I'll just go for two hours, because of course I'll have to come home to Sonny—"

"You'll not go for two minutes."

She knew, from the seriousness of his tone, that he was right, but, perversely, she did not mention the matter to Nelson. She said, instead, that she was tired, that possibly she might not go, and lay awake that night measuring her disappointment against her fear. She woke up for Sonny's first feeding, thinking to herself: "But if I just take ten steps from a limousine to a chair and just sit half an hour—"

At the last minute the pale green evening dress from Callets, draped across a chair in her bedroom, decided her. She went.

Somewhere, during the shuffle and delay on the gangplank while the guests went aboard and were challenged and drank down their cocktails with attendant gayety, Nicole realized that she had made a mistake. There was, at any rate, no formal receiving line and, after greeting their hosts, Nelson found her a chair on deck, where presently her faintness disappeared.

Then she was glad she had come. The boat was hung with fragile lanterns, which blended with the pastels of the bridges and the reflected stars in the dark Seine, like a child's dream out of the Arabian Nights. A crowd of hungry-eyed spectators were gathered on the banks. Champagne moved past in platoons like a drill of bottles, while the music, instead of being loud and obtrusive, drifted down from the upper deck like frosting dripping over a cake. She became aware presently that they were not the only Americans there—across the deck were the Liddell Mileses. whom she had not seen for several years.

Other people from that crowd were present, and she felt a faint disappointment. What if this was not the marquis' best party? She remembered her mother's second days at home. She asked Chiki, who was at her side, to point out celebrities, but when she inquired about several people whom she associated with that set, he replied vaguely that they were away, or coming later, or could not be there. It seemed to her that she saw across the room the girl who had made the scene in the Café de Paris at Monte Carlo, but she could not be sure, for with the faint almost imperceptible movement of the boat, she realized that she was growing faint again. She sent for Nelson to take her home.

"You can come right back, of course. You needn't wait for me, because I'm going right to bed."

He left her in the hands of the nurse, who helped her upstairs and aided her to undress quickly.

"I'm desperately tired," Nicole said. "Will you put my pearls away?"

"Where?"

"In the jewel box on the dressing table."

"I don't see it," said the nurse after a minute.

"Then it's in a drawer."

There was thorough rummaging of the dressing table, without result.

"But of course it's there." Nicole attempted to rise, but fell back, exhausted. "Look for it, please, again. Everything is in it—all my mother's things and my engagement things."

"I'm sorry, Mrs. Kelly. There's nothing in this room that answers to that description."

"Wake up the maid."

The maid knew nothing; then, after a persistent cross-examination, she did know something. Count Sarolai's valet had gone out, carrying his suitcase, half an hour after madame left the house.

Writhing in sharp and sudden pain, with a hastily summoned doctor at her side, it seemed to Nicole hours before Nelson came home. When he arrived, his face was deathly pale and his eyes were wild. He came directly into her room.

"What do you think?" he said savagely. Then he saw the doctor, "Why, what's the matter?"

"Oh, Nelson, I'm sick as a dog and my jewel box is gone, and Chiki's valet has gone. I've told the police. . . . Perhaps Chiki would know where the man—"

"Chiki will never come in this house again," he said slowly. "Do you know whose party that was? Have you got any idea whose party that was?" He burst into wild laughter. "It was our party—our party, do you understand? We gave it—we didn't know it, but we did."

"*Maintenant, monsieur, il ne faut pas exciter madame—*" the doctor began.

"I thought it was odd when the marquis went home early, but I didn't suspect till the end. They were just guests—Chiki invited all the people. After it was over, the caterers and musicians began to come up and ask me where to send their bills. And that damn Chiki had the nerve to tell me he thought I knew all the time. He said that all he'd promised was that it would be his brother-in-law's sort of party, and that his sister would be there. He said perhaps I was drunk, or perhaps I didn't understand French—as if we'd ever talked anything but English to him."

"Don't pay!" she said. "I wouldn't think of paying."

"So I said, but they're going to sue—the boat people and the others. They want twelve thousand dollars."

She relaxed suddenly. "Oh, go away!" she cried. "I don't care! I've lost my jewels and I'm sick, sick!"

IV

THIS IS THE STORY of a trip abroad, and the geographical element must not be slighted. Having visited North Africa, Italy, the Riviera, Paris and points in between, it was not surprising that eventually the Kellys should go to Switzerland. Switzerland is a country where very few things begin, but many things end.

Though there was an element of choice in their other ports of call, the Kellys went to Switzerland because they had to. They had been married a little more than four years when they arrived one spring day at the lake that is the center of Europe–a placid, smiling spot with pastoral hillsides, a backdrop of mountains and waters of postcard blue, waters that are a little sinister beneath the surface with all the misery that has dragged itself here from every corner of Europe. Weariness to recuperate and death to die. There are schools, too, and young people splashing at the sunny plages; there is Bonivard's dungeon and Calvin's city, and the ghosts of Byron and Shelley still sail the dim shores by night; but the Lake Geneva that Nelson and Nicole came to was the dreary one of sanatoriums and rest hotels.

For, as if by some profound sympathy that had continued to exist beneath the unlucky destiny that had pursued their affairs, health had failed them both at the same time; Nicole lay on the balcony of a hotel coming slowly back to life after two successive operations; while Nelson fought for life against jaundice in a hospital two miles away. Even after the reserve force of twenty-nine years had pulled him through, there were months ahead during which he must live quietly. Often they wondered why, of all those who sought pleasure over the face of Europe, this misfortune should have come to them.

"There've been too many people in our lives," Nelson said. "We've never been able to resist people. We were so happy the first year when there weren't any people."

Nicole agreed. "If we could ever be alone–really alone–we could make up some kind of life for ourselves. We'll try, won't we, Nelson?"

But there were other days when they both wanted company desperately, concealing it from each other. Days when they eyed the obese, the wasted, the crippled and the broken of all nationalities who filled the hotel, seeking for one who might be amusing. It was a new life for them, turning on the daily visits of their two doctors, the arrival of the mail and newspapers from Paris, the little walk into the hillside village or occasionally the descent by funicular to the pale resort on the lake, with its *Kursaal,* its grass beach, its tennis clubs and sight-seeing busses. They read Tauchnitz editions and yellow-jacketed Edgar Wallaces; at a certain hour each day they watched the baby being given its bath; three nights a week there was a tired and patient orchestra in the lounge after dinner, that was all.

And sometimes there was a booming from the vine-covered hills on the other side of the lake, which meant that cannons were shooting at hail-bearing clouds, to save the vineyard from an approaching storm; it came with a dark, frightening sky and savage filaments of lightning and crashing, world-splitting thunder, while ragged and destroyed clouds fled along before the wind past the hotel. The mountains and the lake disappeared completely; the hotel crouched alone amid tumult and chaos and darkness.

It was during such a storm, when the mere opening of a door admitted a tornado of rain and wind into the hall, that the Kellys for the first time in months saw someone they knew. Sitting downstairs with other victims of frayed nerves, they became aware of two new arrivals–a man and woman whom they recognized as the couple, first seen in Algiers, who had crossed their path several times since. A single unexpressed thought flashed through Nelson and Nicole. It seemed like destiny that at last here in this desolate place they should know them, and watching, they saw other couples eying them in the same tentative way. Yet something held the Kellys back. Had they not just been complaining that there were too many people in their lives?

Later, when the storm had dozed off into a quiet rain, Nicole found herself near the girl on the glass veranda. Under cover of reading a book, she inspected the face closely. It was an inquisitive face, she saw at once, possible calculating; the eyes, intelligent enough, but with no peace in them, swept over people in a single quick glance as though estimating their value. "Terrible egoist," Nicole thought, with a certain distaste. For the rest, the cheeks were wan, and there were little pouches of ill health under the eyes; these combining with a certain flabbiness of arms and legs to give an impression of unwholesomeness. She was dressed expensively, but with a hint of slovenliness, as if she did not consider the people of the hotel important.

On the whole, Nicole decided she did not like her; she was glad that they had not spoken, but she was rather surprised that she had not noticed these things when the girl crossed her path before.

Telling Nelson her impression at dinner, he agreed with her.

"I ran into the man in the bar, and I noticed we both took nothing but mineral water, so I started to say something. But I got a good look at his face in the mirror and I decided not to. His face is so weak and self-indulgent that it's almost mean–the kind of face that needs half a dozen drinks really to open the eyes and stiffen the mouth up to normal."

After dinner the rain stopped and the night was fine outside. Eager for the air, the Kellys wandered down into the dark garden; on their way they passed the subjects of their late discussion, who withdrew abruptly down a side path.

"I don't think they want to know us any more than we do them," Nicole laughed.

They loitered among the wild rosebushes and the beds of damp-sweet, indistinguishable flowers. Below the hotel, where the terrace fell a thousand feet to the lake, stretched a necklace of lights that was Montreux and Vevey, and then, in a dim pendant, Lausanne; a blurred twinkling across the lake was Evian and France. From somewhere below—probably the *Kursall*—came the sound of full-bodied dance music—American, they guessed, though now they heard American tunes months late, mere distant echoes of what was happening far away.

Over the Dent du Midi, over a black bank of clouds that was the rearguard of the receding storm, the moon lifted itself and the lake brightened; the music and the far-away lights were like hope, like the enchanted distance from which children see things. In their separate hearts Nelson and Nicole gazed backward to a time when life was all like this. Her arm went through his quietly and drew him close.

"We can have it all again," she whispered. "Can't we try, Nelson?"

She paused as two dark forms came into the shadows nearby and stood looking down at the lake below.

Nelson put his arm around Nicole and pulled her closer.

"It's just that we don't understand what's the matter," she said. "Why did we lose peace and love and health, one after the other? If we knew, if there was anybody to tell us, I believe we could try. I'd try so hard."

The last clouds were lifting themselves over the Bernese Alps. Suddenly, with a final intensity, the west flared with pale white lightning. Nelson and Nicole turned, and simultaneously the other couple turned, while for an instant the night was as bright

as day. Then darkness and a last low peal of thunder, and from Nicole a sharp, terrified cry. She flung herself against Nelson; even in the darkness she saw that his face was as white and strained as her own.

"Did you see?" she cried in a whisper. "Did you see them?"

"Yes!"

"They're us! They're us! Don't you see?"

Trembling, they clung together. The clouds merged into the dark mass of mountains; looking around after a moment, Nelson and Nicole saw that they were alone together in the tranquil moonlight.

Planning the Diver Version

The 610-word character sketch for Diver *begins: "The novel should do this. Show a man who is a natural idealist, a spoiled priest, giving in for various causes to the ideas of the haute Burgeoise, and in his rise to the top of the social world losing his idealism, his talent and turning to drink and dissipation. Background one in which the leisure class is at their truly most brilliant + glamorous such as Murphys." During the process of composition Fitzgerald departed from his preliminary plan by omitting Nicole's homicidal mania that results in a murder and by deleting Diver's "communist-liberal-idealist" allegiances. The projected ending would have reinforced the political message: "He sends his neglected son into Soviet Russia to educate him and comes back to America to be a quack thus having accomplished both his burgeoise sentimental idea in the case of his wife and his ideals in the case of his son, + now being himself only a shell to which nothing matters but survival as long as possible with the old order." It is intriguing to speculate whether retention of the political message would have influenced the 1934 reception of* Tender Is the Night.

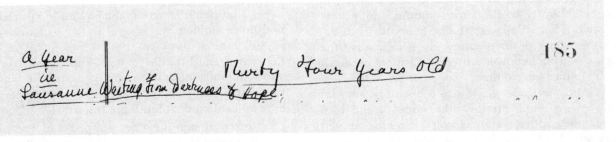

Fitzgerald's summary in his Ledger *of the year from September 1930 to September 1931*

① Sketch

The novel should do this. Show a man who
is a natural idealist, *a spoiled priest,* giving in for various
causes to the ideas of the haute Burgoise,
and in his rise to the top of the social
world losing his idealism, his talent
and turning to drink and dissipation.
Background one in which the leisure class
is at their truly most brilliant +
glamorous such as Murphys.

The hero, *born in 1891,* is a man like myself brought
up in a family sunk from haute burgoise
to petit burgoisie, ~~and~~ yet expensively
educated. He has all the gifts, ~~and at~~ and
~~twenty three he seems to have~~ goes through Yale
almost succeeding but not quite but getting
a Rhodes scholarship which he caps with
a degree from Hopkins, + with a legacy
goes abroad to study *psychology* in Zurich. At the
age of 26 all seems bright. Then he falls
in love with one of his patients who has
a curious homicidal mania toward men
caused by an event of her youth. Aside from
This she is the legendary <u>promiscuous</u>

Plan for the third version of Tender Is the Night, *with the working title "The Drunkard's Holiday"*
(Princeton University Library)

② *[marginal note: in love with him + entirely conscious to completing the cure]*

woman. He "transfers" to himself + she falls in love with him, a love he returns.

After a year of non-active service in the war he returns and marries her *[insert: + is madly]*. She is an aristocrat of half American, half European parentage, young, mysterious + lovely, a new character. He has cured her by pretending to a stability + belief in the current order which he does not have, being in fact a communist - liberal - idealist, *[insert: a moralist in revolt]* But the years ~~have~~ of living under patronage ect. + among the burgeoise have seriously spoiled him and he takes up the marriage as a man divided ~~in~~ himself. During the war he has taken to drink a little + it continues as secret drinking after his marriage. The difficulty of taking care of her is more than he has imagined and he goes more and more to pieces, always keeping up a wonderful face.

At the point when he is socially the most charming and inwardly ~~the most~~ corrupt he meets a young actress on the

144

③ during which he is in Rome with the actress having a disappointing love affair too late he is beaten up by the police He returns to find that instead of taking great care she has

Riviera who falls in love with him, with considerable difficulty he contains himself out of fear of all it would entail since his formal goodness is all that is holding his disintegration together. He knows too that he does not love her as he has loved his wife. Nevertheless the effect of the repression is to throw him toward all women during his secret drinking when he has another life of his own which his wife does not suspect, or at least he thinks she doesn't. On one of his absences he committed a murder and in a revulsion of spirit he tries to conceal it and succeeds. It shows him however that the game is almost up and he will have to perform some violent + Byronic act to save her for he is losing his hold on her + himself.

He has known slightly for some time a very strong + magnetic man and now he deliberately brings them together. When he finds under circumstances of jealous

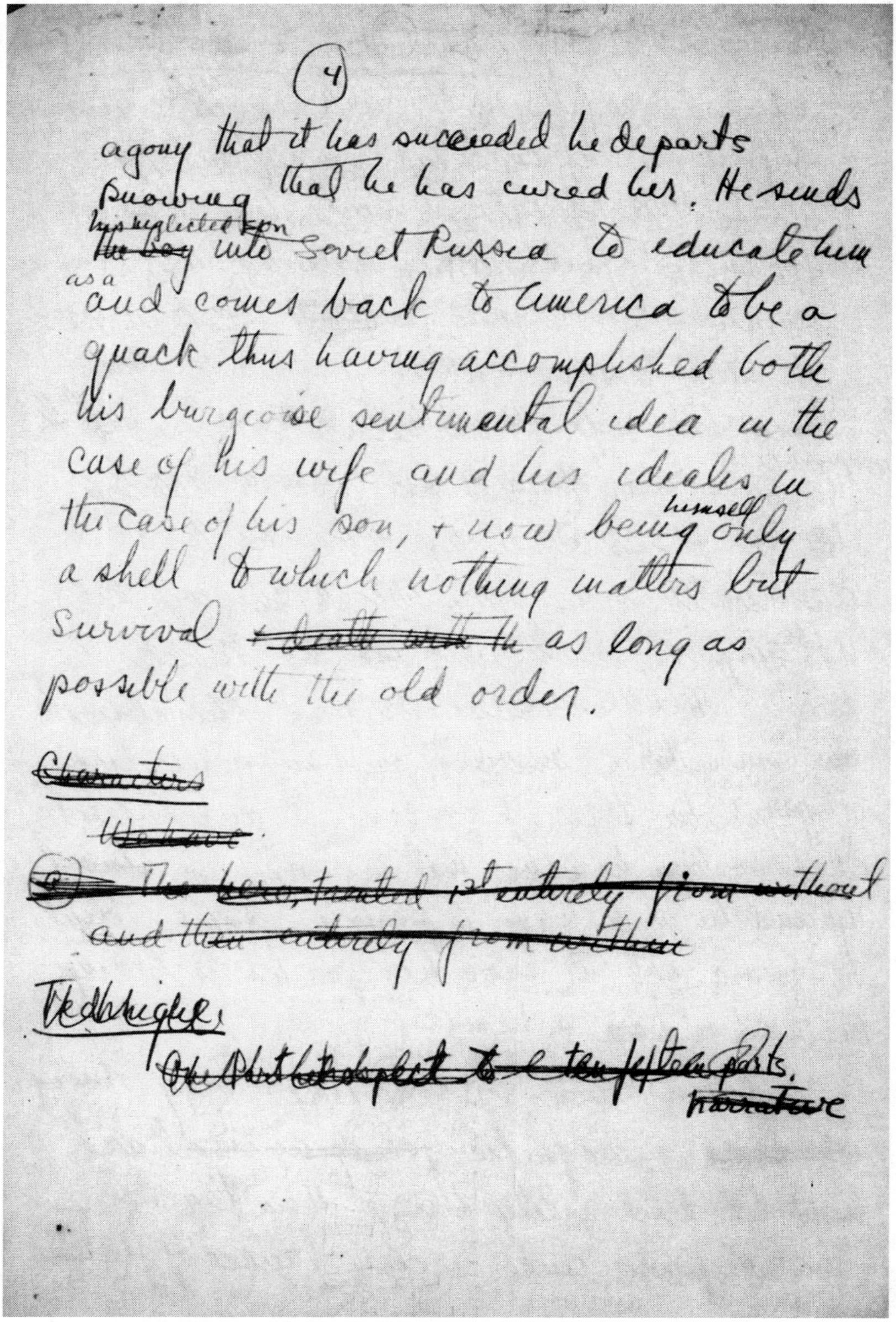

(4)

agony that it has succeeded he departs
knowing that he has cured her. He sends
his neglected son
the boy into Soviet Russia to educate him
as a
"and" comes back to America to be a
quack thus having accomplished both
his bourgeoise sentimental idea in the
case of his wife and his ideals in
the case of his son, + now being himself only
a shell to which nothing matters but
survival ~~death with th~~ as long as
possible with the old order.

~~Characters~~

~~We have~~

~~The hero, treated, 1st entirely from without
and then entirely from within~~

~~Technique.~~

~~The Plot broken into ten fifteen parts.~~
narrative

(*further sketch*)   5.   Approach

The Drunkard's Holiday will be a novel
of our time showing the break up of a
fine personality. Unlike The Beautiful
and Damned the break-up will be
caused not by flabbiness but really
tragic forces such as the inner conflicts
of the idealist and ~~the~~ the compromises
forced upon him by circumstances.

The novel will be a little over
a hundred thousand words long, composed
of fourteen chapters, each 7,500 words long,
five chapters each in the first and
second part four in the third — one
chapter or its equivalent to be composed
of retrospect

(9) most actresses by being

The actress was born in 1908. Her career is like hers or Mary Hay — that is, she ~~is~~ *differs from* a lady, simply seeking of vitality, health, sensuality. Rather gross as compared to the heroine, or rather will be gross for at present her youth covers it. Mimi — Lupe Veley.

We see her first at the very beginning of her career She's already made one big picture.

We follow her from age 17 to age 22

Character sketch for Rosemary (Princeton University Library)

(10)

The friend was born in 1896. He is a wild man. He looks like Tunti and like that dark communist at the meeting. He is half Italian ^or French^, + half American. He is a type who hates all sham + pretense. (See the lunq type who was like Foss Wilson) He is one who would lead tribesmen or communists — utterly aristocratic ^rainbow goose^ King or nothing. He fought three years ~~again~~ in the French foreign legion in the war and then painted a little and then fought the Riff. He's just back from there on his first appearance in the novel and seeking a new outlet. He has money + this French training — otherwise ^he^ would be a revolutionist. He is a fine type, useful or destructive but his mind is not quite as good as the hero's. Touch of Percy Pyne, Denny Holden also

We see him from age 28 to age 33

Character sketch for Tommy Barban (Princeton University Library)

11,000

Summary of Part III (1st half.)

The Divers, as a marriage are at the end of their resources. Medically Nicole is <u>nearly</u> cured but Dick has given out + is sinking toward alcoholism and discouragement. It seems as if the completion of his ruination will be the fact that cures her — almost mystically. However this is merely hinted at. Dick is still in control of the situation and master of the matter practically. They must separate for both their sakes. In wild bitterness he thinks of one tragic idea but controls himself and manages a saner one instead.

His will is broken, the transference is broken. He goes away. He has been used by the rich family and cast aside.

Part III is as much as possible seen through Nicole's eyes. All Dick's stories such as are <u>absolutely nessessary</u>: Edwardo, father, auto catastrophe (child's eyes perhaps), strippen quarrel?, girls on Riviera, must be told without getting in his reactions or feelings. From now on he is mystery man, at least to Nicole with her guessing at the mystery.

Notes for the conclusion of the novel (Princeton University Library)

W Dick

The hero was born in 1891. He is a well formed rather athletic and fine, looking fellow. Also he is very intelligent, widely read — in fact he has all the talents, including especially great personal charm. This is all planted in the beginning. He is a superman in possibilities, that is, he appears to be at first sight from a burgeoise point of view. However he lacks that tensile strength — none of the ruggedness of Brancusi, Leger, Picasso. For his external qualities use anything of Gerald, Ernest, Ben Finny, Archie McLiesh, Charley McArthur or myself. He looks, though, like me.

The faults — the weakness such as the social-climbing, the drinking, the desperate clinging to one woman, finally the neurosis, only come out gradually. We follow him from age 34 to age 39

Character sketch for Dick Diver (Princeton University Library)

Actual Age of the People

DICK

September 1891 Born

"   1908 Entered Yale

June   1912 Graduated Yale aged 20

June   1916 Graduated Hopkins. Left for Vienna (8 mo. there)

June   1917 Was in Zurich after 1 year and other work. Age 26

June   1918 Degree at Zurich. Aged 26

June   1919 Back in Zurich. Aged 27

September 1919 Married--aged 28 (after his refusing fellowship at University in neurology and *xxxx* pathologist to the clinic. Or does he accept?

July   1925 After 5 years and 10 months of marriage is aged almost 34

Story starts

July 1929   After 9 years and 10 months of marriage is aged almost 38.

Chronologies for the Divers: *July 1929 is twice stipulated for the end of their marriage (Princeton University Library).*

Nicole's Age

Always one year younger than century.

Born July 1901

    courtship for two and one half years before that, since she
was 13.

Catastrophe   June 1917   Age almost 16

Clinic.   Feb. 1918   Age 17

                   To middle October bad period
                   After armistice good period

                   He returns in April or May 1919

                   She discharged in June 1, 1919. Almost 18

                   Married September 1919. Aged 18

Child born August 1920

Child born June   1922

    2nd Pousse almost immediately to October 1922 and thereafter

    Frenchman (or what have you in summer of 1923 after almost
            4 years of marriage.

In July 1925 when the story opens she is just 24

    (One child almost 5 (Scotty in Juan les Pins)

    One child 3 (Scotty in Pincio)

In July 1929 when the story ends she is just 28

Gregor

The heroine was born in 1901.   She is beautiful on the order
of Marlene Dietrich or better still the Norah--Kiki Allen girl with
those peculiar eyes. She is American with a streak of some foreign
blood. At fifteen she was raped by her own father under peculiar
circumstances--work out. She collapses, goes to the clinic and there
at sixteen meets the young doctor hero who is ten years older. Only
her transference to him saves her--when it is not working she reverts
to homicidal mania and tries to kill ~~herself~~ men. She is an innocent,
widely read but with no experience and no orientation except what he
supplies her. Portrait of Zelda--that is, a part of Zelda.

We follow her from age 24 to age 29

<u>Method of Dealing with Sickness Material</u>
(1) Read books and decide the general type of case
(2) Prepare a clinical report covering the years 1916-1920
(3) Now examine the different classes of material selecting not too
many things for copying.
      (1) From the sort of letter under E
      (2)   "   "   "   "   "   " F
          (In this case using no factual stuff)
      (3) From the other headings for atmosphere, accuracy and
          material being careful not to reveal basic ignorance
          of psychiatric and medical training yet not being glib.
          Only suggest from the most remote facts. <u>Not</u> like doctor's
          stories.

Must avoid Faulkner attitude and not end with a novelized Kraft-
Ebing--better Ophelia and her flowers.

<u>Classification of the Material on Sickness</u>

A. Accounts

B. Baltimore

C. Clinics and clipping

D. Dancing and 1st Diagnoses

E. Early Prangins--to February 1931

F. From Forel (include Bleuler Consultation)

H. Hollywood

L. Late Prangins

M. My own letters and comments

R. Rosalind and Sayre Family

S. Squires and Schedule

V. Varia

*Fitzgerald's notes on organizing his material for the novel, in which he describes William Faulkner's technique
in* Sanctuary *(1931) as "novelized Krafft-Ebing" (Princeton University Library)*

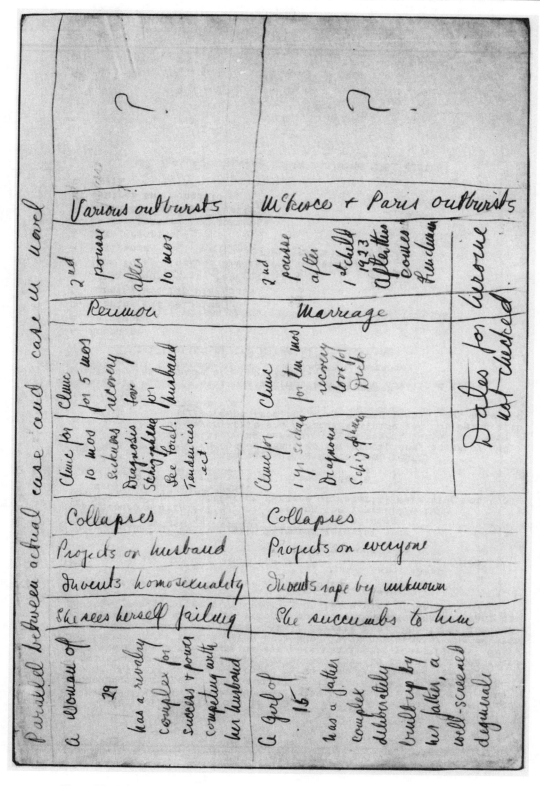

Fitzgerald's chart comparing the case histories of his wife and Nicole (Princeton University Library)

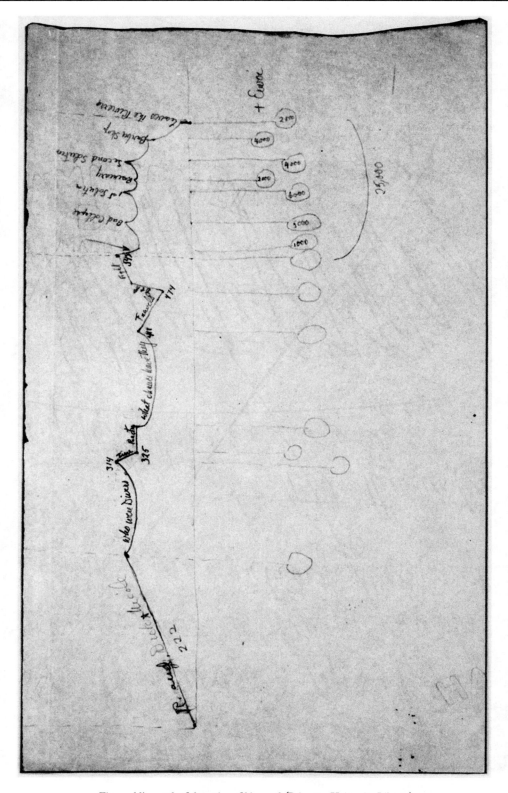

Fitzgerald's graph of the action of his novel (Princeton University Library)

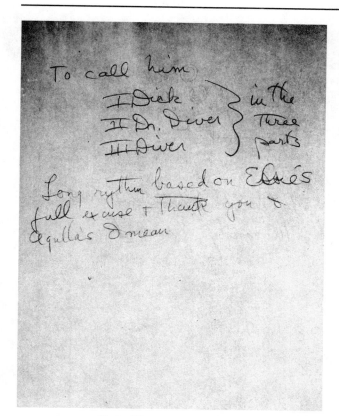
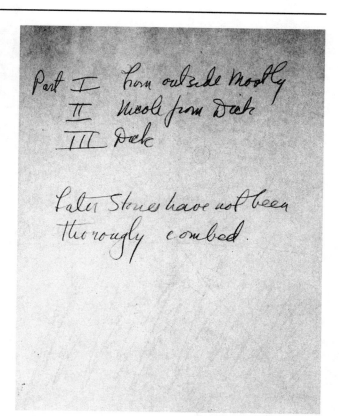

Fitzgerald's notes on narrative strategies for the three-book organization of his novel (Princeton University Library)

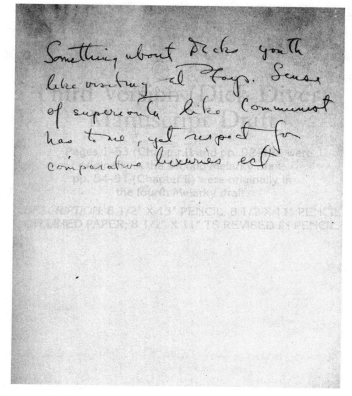

A note on the development of Dick Diver's character (Princeton University Library)

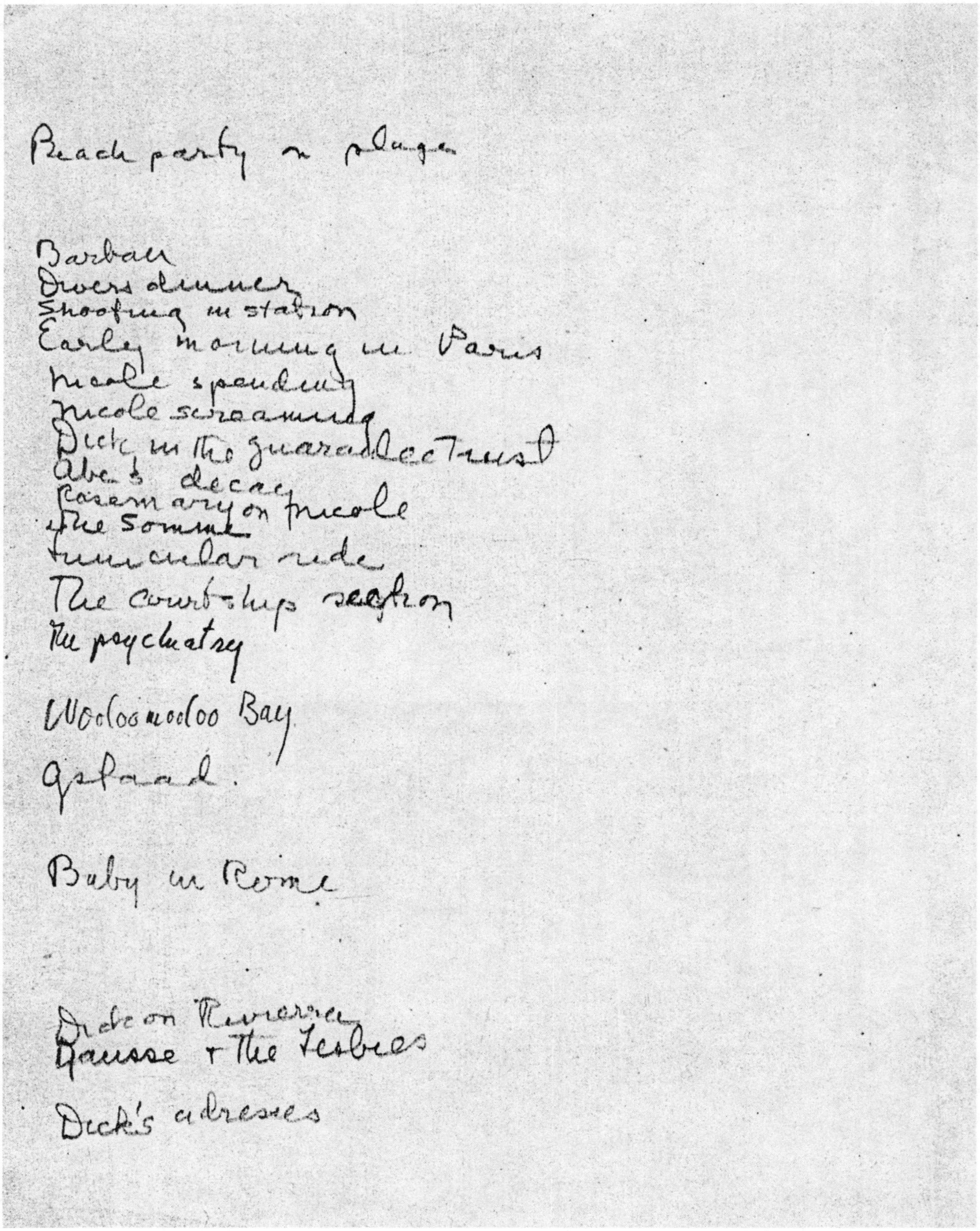

Beach party on plage

Barban
Divers dinner
Shooting in station
Early morning in Paris
Nicole spending
Nicole screaming
Dick in the guaranty Trust
Abe's decay
Rosemary on Nicole
The Somme
tunicular ride
The courtship section
The psychiatry

Woolloomooloo Bay

Gstaad.

Baby in Rome

Dick on Riviera
Rousse + the Lesbies

Dick's adresses

Fitzgerald's note on key events and episodes in Tender Is the Night *(Bruccoli Collection of Fitzgerald, Thomas Cooper Library, University of South Carolina)*

Correspondence, Winter 1932 to Fall 1933

Fitzgerald went to Hollywood during November–December 1931 to write a rejected screenplay for Red-Headed Woman; *he was paid $6,000. Zelda Fitzgerald suffered a relapse in February 1932. She was treated at Johns Hopkins Hospital in Baltimore, and Fitzgerald moved to La Paix to be near her. In August 1932 he wrote in his* Ledger: *"The novel now plotted + planned, never more to be permanently interrupted."*

**Fitzgerald to Perkins, circa 15 January 1932
St. Petersburg, Florida**

At last for the first time in two years + ½ I am going to spend five consecutive months on my novel. I am actually six thousand dollars ahead Am replanning it to include what's good in what I have, adding 41,000 new words + publishing. Don't tell Ernest or anyone—let them think what they want—you're the only one whose ever consistently felt faith in me anyhow.

—*F. Scott Fitzgerald: A Life in Letters,* p. 208

* * *

Perkins to Fitzgerald, 4 August 1933

You have had a mighty hard pull, but it may end rightly. Whenever any of these new writers come up who are brilliant, I always realize that you have more talent and more skill than any of them; —but circumstances have prevented you from realizing upon the fact for a long time.

—*Dear Scott/Dear Max,* p. 180

* * *

Fitzgerald's identification card issued when he was hired to write a screenplay based on Katherine Brush's novel Red-Headed Woman *(Bruccoli Collection of Fitzgerald, Thomas Cooper Library, University of South Carolina)*

**Fitzgerald to Perkins, 25 September 1933
"La Paix," Rodgers' Forge, Towson, Maryland**

The novel has gone ahead faster than I thought. There was a little set back when I went to the hospital for four days but since then things have gone ahead of my schedule, which you will remember, promised you the whole manuscript for reading November 1, with the first one-fourth ready to shoot into the magazine (in case you can use it) and the other three-fourths to undergo further revision. I now figure that this can be achieved by about the 25th of October. I will appear in person carrying the manuscript and wearing a spiked helmet.

There are several points and I wish you would answer them categorically.

1. Did you mean that you could get the first fourth of the story into the copy of the magazine appearing late in December and therefore that the book could appear early in April? I gathered that on the phone but want to be sure. I don't know what the ocean travel statistics promise for the spring but it

Fitzgerald's summary in his Ledger *of the year from September 1931 to September 1932*

La Paix (Bruccoli Collection of Fitzgerald, Thomas Cooper Library, University of South Carolina)

seems to me that a May publication would be too late if there was a great exodus and I should miss being a proper gift book for it. The story, as you know, is laid entirely in Europe—I wish I could have gotten as far as China but Europe was the best I could do, Max (to get into Ernest's rhythm).

2. I would not want a magazine proof of the first part, though of course I would expect your own proof readers to check up on blatant errors, but would want to talk over with you any small changes that would have to be made for magazine publication—in any case, to make them myself.

3. Will publication with you absolutely preclude that the book will be chosen by the Literary Guild or the Book of the Month? Whatever the answer the serial will serve the purpose of bringing my book to the memory and attention of my old public and of getting straight financially with

you. On the other hand, it is to both our advantages to capitalize if possible such facts as that the editors of those book leagues might take a fancy to such a curious idea that the author, Fitzgerald, actually wrote a book after all these years (this is all said with the reservation that the book is good.) Please answer this as it is of importance to me to know whether I must expect my big returns from serial and possibly theatrical and picture rights or whether I have as good a chance at a book sale, launched by one of those organizations, as any other best seller.

Ober is advancing me the money to go through with it (it will probably not need any more than $2,000 though he has promised to go as far as $4,000) and in return I am giving him 10% of the serial rights.

. . . .

You are the only person who knows how near the novel is to being finished, <u>please don't say a word to anyone.</u>

. . . .

You can imagine the pride with which I will enter your office a month from now. <u>Please do not have a band as I do not care for music.</u>

                              —*F. Scott Fitzgerald: A Life in Letters*, pp. 235–237

La Paix

In May 1932 Fitzgerald rented La Paix at Rodgers' Forge, Towson, Maryland, to be near his wife while she was at Johns Hopkins Hospital and at the Phipps Clinic. The fifteen-room house was on the Turnbull estate. Fitzgerald completed Tender Is the Night *there before moving to Baltimore in November 1933.*

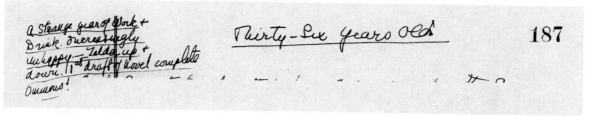

Fitzgerald's summary in his Ledger *of the year from September 1932 to September 1933*

Fitzgerald's Ledger *record of income for the year he completed* Tender Is the Night, *when his total book royalties were $30*

Financing Fitzgerald

The completion of Tender Is the Night was financed by Scribners and Ober. Fitzgerald's accounting system is puzzling, but between 1927 and 1933 he received some $16,000 in advances from Scribners and borrowed from Ober against the anticipated serial rights sale. Liberty had asked for first refusal on the serial in 1926, and Fitzgerald expected between $30,000 and $40,000 for these rights. When Scribner's Magazine offered $10,000, Fitzgerald accepted it because he thought serialization in a quality magazine would be better for the novel. Six thousand dollars of the serial fee was credited against the Scribners advances; $4,000 was paid to Ober, who turned it over to Fitzgerald as needed. Scribners lent Fitzgerald an additional $2,000 at 5 percent interest, and there were other borrowings from Ober. The collateral for these loans was the anticipated sale of movie rights for the novel.

(11)

all the magazines with a little short
change conversation. He was neither a
gent, nor much of a person and then.
on with a short Dr. Diver wondered
if he would have made such a good like decision seven
years ago. Then he believed in himself
and then in all men — now he doubted
himself + then all men. He
didn't like to think how he looked forward
to whole healthy European suspicion of all
men which was very different from either
and which he would find embodied
in Tommy Costello tomorrow.

(Now cheerful cafe scene
but remember to avoid Hemmingway. then
on green felt table cloths, Swiss memories

Page from the Diver manuscript with Fitzgerald's self-warning to resist imitating understated or choppy Hemingwayesque dialogue (Princeton University Library)

CHAPTER I.

On the pleasant shore of the French Riviera, about half way

between Marseilles and the Italian border, stands a large, proud, rose-

colored hotel. ~~Its~~ The style is Second Empire, with a beam of the cres-

cent; deferential palms cool its flushed facade, and before it, like a

prayer rug, stretches a short dazzling beach. ~~This summer many~~ *Insert (1)* new

little ~~houses, b~~ ~~People with nothing to conceal, cluster about it, but~~

~~six years ago at the time of the McIarty case~~, only the cupolas of a

dozen old villas nodded, like rotting water-lilies, from the massed

pines between <u>Gauss' Hotel des Etrangers</u> and Cannes, five miles away.

The hotel opened out to the beach where the sun thundered

down in summer and sea-planes bound for Corsica roared overhead. In

the early morning the image of Cannes, the pink and cream of old forti-

fications, the purple Alp that bounded Italy, were cast across the

water and lay wavering with the ripples and rings sent up by sea-

plants through the clear shallows. Before eight a man came down to the

beach in a blue bath-robe and with much preliminary application to his

person of the chilly water, and *much* ~~some~~ grunting and loud breathing, floun-

dered for a minute in the sea. When he had gone, beach and open bay

First page of the Diver typescript (Princeton University Library)

A Beautiful Veneer

Maxwell Perkins to Ann Chidester, 6 January 1947

When Scott was writing "Tender Is the Night"—he didn't think he ought to talk about the books he was doing, and so put it this way—he said that the whole motif was taken from Ludendorf's memoirs. They were moving up the guns for the great Spring offensive in 1918, and Ludendorf said, "The song of the frogs on the river drowned the rumble of our artillery," when he told me this, it puzzled me, but when I read the book I realized that there was all this beautiful veneer, and rottenness and horror underneath.

Eric von Ludendorf was a German field marshal in World War I.

A Fable's End

Fitzgerald admired the conclusion of David Garnett's first novel, Lady into Fox *(1922), the story of a young wife transformed into a vixen.*

His vixen had at once sprung into Mr. Tebrick's arms, and before he could turn back the hounds were upon them and had pulled them down. Then at that moment there was a scream of despair heard by all the field that had come up, which they declared afterwards was more like a woman's voice than a man's. But yet there was no clear proof whether it was Mr. Tebrick or his wife who had suddenly regained her voice. When the huntsman who had leapt the wall got to them and had whipped off the hounds Mr. Tebrick had been terribly mauled and was bleeding from twenty wounds. As for his vixen she was dead, though he was still clasping her dead body in his arms.

Mr. Tebrick was carried into the house at once and assistance sent for, but there was no doubt now about his neighbours being in the right when they called him mad.

For a long while his life was despaired of, but at last he rallied, and in the end he recovered his reason and lived to be a great age, for that matter he is still alive.

Inscription to David Garnett, who was surprised that Fitzgerald found the conclusion of Lady into Fox *so useful: "the only resemblance between the endings . . . is that the hero survives a great shock and goes on living—not unusual in real life" (McFarlin Library, University of Tulsa)*

Fitzgerald's Stories and the Diver Version

With his decision to abandon the Melarky version finally made, probably in the late spring of 1932, Fitzgerald in the space of a few months conceived his novel anew and planned the Diver version by August. When he turned to the Diver version, Fitzgerald also turned to his stories, which became a portfolio he drew on as he wrote his novel. Eventually Fitzgerald stripped and used phrases and passages from forty-one stories in Tender Is the Night.

The Stories as Portfolio: Fitzgerald's Use of Zola's Method
George Parker Anderson

Fitzgerald's decision to set off so determinedly on a new tack after a seven-year struggle with refractory material is remarkable, and the vigor of his new approach undoubtedly owes much to the inspiration provided by the working method of the French novelist Emile Zola as described in Matthew Josephson's *Zola and His Time* (1929).[1] In the inscribed copy of *Tender Is the Night* Fitzgerald sent to Josephson, Fitzgerald claims that without the reproduction of "the swell organization of 'Zola'" he would not have been able to bring his novel to print.

Among his preparatory papers, Fitzgerald's thesis statement has been regarded by critics as a keystone for understanding *Tender Is the Night*:

> The novel should do this. Show a man who is a natural idealist, a spoiled priest, giving in for various causes to the ideas of the haute Burgeoise, and in his rise to the top of the social world losing his idealism, his talent and turning to drink and dissipation.

The phrasing of this intention is plainly an imitation of Zola's ruling thought for *L'Assommoir*, translated by Josephson in his appendix:

> The novel should do this: show the poor people's quarter and explain through their milieu the customs of the poor. . . .

In Fitzgerald's process of conceiving the Diver version, however, the formulation of his thesis according to Zola's phrasing–as well as other similarly obvious instances of modeling in his character sketches–is less meaningful than is his decision to apply Zola's methodical approach to the stories he had first written primarily to make money, with little or no ulterior intention toward his novel.

In the appendix for *Zola and His Time* Josephson describes Zola's four-stage method of writing a novel. Beginning with only a general idea as to his subject, Zola in his first stage "would surround himself with all documents capable of informing him or suggesting

Fitzgerald's inscription to Matthew Josephson, whose appendix in Zola and His Time *describing Zola's documentary method provided a model for Fitzgerald in planning* Tender Is the Night *(The Edward and Catherine O'Donnell Collection of Modern American Literature, Fall 1979, University of Rochester Library)*

ideas" (p. 538), cataloguing notes in a "portfolio" from general and specific reading and from direct observation and investigation. In the second stage Zola began to write *about* his novel, creating a "Sketch," in which he "puts down everything as it goes through his head, without art or orthography," indicating "the general idea which must govern the novel" (p. 539) and then proceeding to his characters. In his third stage Zola makes a detailed "plan of his book, chapter by chapter" and in his fourth carries out his plans, producing "four manuscript pages every day, almost without crossing out a word" (p. 540).

In the second part of his appendix, Josephson discusses with examples the particular case of *L'Assommoir*–a novel that shows the devastating effect of alcohol on the poor. Before specifically discussing the plans for *L'Assommoir,* however, Josephson pro-

BABYLON REVISITED

"Here for long, Mr. Wales?"

"I'm here for four or five days to see my little girl."

"Oh-h! You have a little girl?"

~~Outside, the fire-red, gas-blue, ghost-green signs shone smokily through the tranquil rain. It was late afternoon and the streets were in movement; the *bistros* gleamed. At the corner of the Boulevard des Capucines he took a taxi. The Place de la Concorde moved by in pink majesty; they crossed the logical Seine, and Charlie felt the sudden provincial quality of the left bank.~~

Used in Tender

Charlie directed his taxi to the Avenue de l'Opera, which was out of his way. But he wanted to see the blue hour spread over the magnificent façade, and imagine that the cab horns, playing endlessly the first few bars of *Le Plus qu Lent,* were the trumpets of the Second Empire. They were closing the iron grill in front of Brentano's Book-store, and people were already at dinner behind the trim little bourgeois hedge of Duval's. He had never eaten at a really cheap restaurant in Paris. Five-course dinner, four francs fifty, eighteen cents, wine included. For some odd reason he wished that he had.

Page from Fitzgerald's copy of Taps at Reveille, *the story collection he published in 1935, in which the author has identified and deleted a passage from "Babylon Revisited" that had been used in his novel. Fitzgerald insisted on including a note of apology with "A Short Trip Home," another story in the volume: "In a moment of hasty misjudgement a whole paragraph of description was lifted out of this tale where it originated, and properly belongs, and applied to quite a different character in a novel of mine. I have ventured none the less to leave it here, even at the risk of seeming to serve warmed-over fare" (Bruccoli Collection of Fitzgerald, Thomas Cooper Library, University of South Carolina).*

vides a table of contents to Zola's 239-page portfolio to give his reader a sense of proportion regarding Zola's preparation:

(1) A general summary plan (pp. 1–3).

(2) Detailed plan (4–92).

(3) Notes on alcoholism (93–99).

(4) The quarters, streets, cabarets, dance-halls (plans and notes, 99–116).

(5) The Characters (117–138).

(6) Notes taken from Denis Poulot's *Le Sublime* (140–155).

(7) The Sketch (156–174).

(8) Notes on public laundries, laundresses, workers, coopers, goldsmiths (175–190).

(9) Diverse information–Newspaper clipping–Slang (191–239).

Josephson then presents selected passages from Zola's portfolio, including the novel's "ruling thought" (p. 542) and an example of a preliminary character sketch, both of which Fitzgerald carefully imitated, though with his own material.

Despite the obvious similarities between Zola's preparation and Fitzgerald's, the evidence of Fitzgerald's surviving notes is not, on its face, enough to even begin to explain the author's assertion that without Josephson's work *Tender Is the Night* would never have been published. In regard to the four stages of Zola's creative process Josephson describes, Fitzgerald's indebtedness could only concern the first two that deal with the conception of the novel, for there is no evidence to suggest that Fitzgerald made detailed chapter-by-chapter plans. Similarly, it is certain that he did not compose as methodically as did Zola. Beyond Fitzgerald's general sketch and character profiles—both of which are brief compared to Zola's—his surviving notes are few indeed when compared to Zola's one hundred pages in categories 3, 4, 6, 8, and 9. Even Fitzgerald's imitation of Zola's phrasing ultimately seems a matter of little consequence, for it is difficult to imagine that the phrasing and structure of preliminary notes alone would have given the author new momentum.

As explained by Josephson, the signal aspect of Zola's preparation is the integral, interactive role of the author's documentation in the conception of his novel, but it is precisely this point that Fitzgerald's meager notes seem to belie. At first, Zola's note taking suggests ideas for the novel; in the second stage, as Josephson's description shows, the interactive role of Zola's portfolio becomes clear:

> The plan of the novel remains open in the meantime. And the portfolio grows in size, amassing through its new turns or requirements, ever more material, more excursions even, further references to field notes, already taken, which are now seen from the angle of the characters and the action he roughly proposes to treat with. His labor has become more selective; but by now he has "a whole mass of data carefully classified," and often two or three times the size of his long two-volume novels. (p. 540)

Zola evidently continually referred to his notes for inspiration, realizing and fulfilling his need for further documentation as his work progressed, and constantly using his notes to refine his plans. Zola's note taking, then, is the foundation on which *L'Assommoir* stands; without this core, Zola would have felt that his novel had no substance.

Although Fitzgerald did not rely on notes amassed from research, his stories and his process of stripping the stories played the same interactive role in his conceiving and writing *Tender Is the Night* as Zola's note taking did in his conception of *L'Assommoir*. Like Zola's notes, Fitzgerald's stories were a source of inspiration that, as the need arose, the author returned to again and again; it is quite possible that for Fitzgerald, as for Zola, the process of recurring to a mass of material gave him the necessary confidence to proceed. Of course, Fitzgerald's method differed from Zola's in that he was not generating or collecting new material in order to document his thesis; instead, Fitzgerald in culling through his old stories for his documentation was allowing his old writing to influence his new. Because of the nature of the strippings as opposed to Zola's documentation—the fact that Zola's notes were recorded "without art" while Fitzgerald's strippings were already honed for their places in his stories—Fitzgerald's strippings necessarily had an even more particular influ-

ence on the texture of the developing novel than did Zola's documentation.

As he reconceived his novel, Fitzgerald carefully reviewed many of his uncollected stories for phrases that he thought he might find useful in his novel. The Distribution of Strippings table lists all the stories that have been identified as stripped for any of the three versions of *Tender Is the Night* or for Fitzgerald's notebooks through 12 April 1934, the date of publication of the novel. It does not include the twenty-three stories that Fitzgerald published in his three story collections prior to 1932, because, apparently, the author decided from the beginning that he would not republish any of the material that had previously appeared in a collection. Evidently, Fitzgerald also decided that some of his uncollected stories did not contain any material that he would find useful, for seventeen of the sixty-six uncollected stories Fitzgerald wrote and published before the publication of *Tender Is the Night* have not been found to have been stripped. Of course, Fitzgerald might have reviewed all of his unpublished work as well as his eighty-nine published stories *before and as* he proceeded on the Diver version, but since he eventually culled phrases from only selected stories, it is likely that he limited the scope of his review.

The table graphically shows the change in Fitzgerald's use of his stories from the Melarky to the Kelly to the Diver version. Fitzgerald adapted a total of fifteen strippings from ten stories in his work on the Melarky and Kelly versions. Up to the writing of the Diver manuscript, then, Fitzgerald's reliance on his stories, though crucial in the Kelly version, may be characterized as occasional, and suggests the author's blindness to the value of his stories as a resource for his novel or, at least, his reluctance to use his stories too much. Fitzgerald's new reliance on his stories is shown dramatically by the more than one hundred strippings he chose from thirty-four stories for the Diver manuscript that was written in little more than a year's time, between August 1932 and September 1933. Instead of only occasionally using strippings from stories he had recently written, Fitzgerald searched back to stories that he had written as early as 1920 as well as incorporating strippings from stories—"One Interne," "On Schedule," and "More Than Just a House"—he wrote during the composition of the manuscript. After the Diver manuscript was written, Fitzgerald continued to recur to his stories. He newly stripped six more stories—"The Adolescent Marriage," "The Bridal Party," "Emotional Bankruptcy," "Diagnosis," "More Than Just a House," and "I Got Shoes"—and returned to already-stripped stories, adding forty-four more strippings as he refined his novel between the completion of the Diver manuscript and its publication.

An examination of Fitzgerald's tear sheets reveals that he used six distinct methods in marking passages.

Fitzgerald's stripped stories	Year of Publication	Melarky Drafts	Number of Strippings Kelly Drafts	Diver Manuscript	*Tender Is the Night*
The Popular Girl	1922			1	2
The Third Casket	1924			1	1
Love in the Night	1925	2		2	3
A Penny Spent	1925	2		3	4
Not in the Guidebook	1925			1	1
The Adolescent Marriage	1926				1
Jacob's Ladder	1927		1	16	17
The Love Boat	1927	1		1	1
A Short Trip Home	1927	2	2	7	7
The Bowl	1928			2	2
Magnetism	1928	1		7	8
The Scandal Detectives	1928	1		1	1
A Night at the Fair	1928			1	2
Basil and Cleopatra	1929			1	1
The Rough Crossing	1929		2	4	4
Majesty	1929		1	1	1
At Your Age	1929			2	3
The Swimmers	1929			4	4
Two Wrongs	1930			1	3
First Blood	1930			2	3

Distribution of passages stripped from stories for the Melarky and Kelly versions,
the Diver manuscript, and Tender Is the Night

Fitzgerald's stripped stories	Year of Publication	Melarky Drafts	Kelly Drafts	Number of Strippings Diver Manuscript	*Tender Is the Night*
A Nice Quiet Place	1930			2	2
The Bridal Party	1930				2
A Woman With a Past	1930			2	2
One Trip Abroad	1930	1		10	10
A Snobbish Story	1930			1	3
The Hotel Child	1931			4	11
Babylon Revisited	1931			2	5
Indecision	1931			11	12
A New Leaf	1931			2	3
Emotional Bankruptcy	1931				3
On Your Own	1979			8	10
Diagnosis	1932				1
Flight and Pursuit	1932			3	3
The Rubber Check	1932			4	9
What a Handsome Pair!	1932			1	2
Crazy Sunday	1932			1	2
One Interne	1932			2	4
On Schedule	1933			2	2
More Than Just a House	1933				1
I Got Shoes	1933				1
Totals		**10**	**6**	**113**	**157**

The fact of the different methods of marking passages strongly supports the idea that his stories played the same interactive role in the composition of *Tender* that Zola's portfolio did in *L'Assommoir*. Clearly, Fitzgerald did not mark all these stories at one time; instead, the various methods of marking were the result of his returning to these stories at different times during his composition of the novel. It is, of course, impossible to gauge the type and extent of the influence Fitzgerald's reconsideration of his stories had upon his plan for the Diver version. However, given Fitzgerald's demonstrable recurrence to his short stories during his composition of the Diver manuscript, it is all but certain that the author's review of his stories contributed significantly to his conception of the characters and their relationships, the settings, and the plot elements of his novel, just as Zola's note taking was crucial to his developing the detailed chapter-by-chapter plans of *L'Assommoir*.

The thematic relevance of many of Fitzgerald's stories to the Diver manuscript is clear to anyone familiar with the stories and the novel. Fitzgerald had already stripped three stories for the Melarky and Kelly versions—"Jacob's Ladder," "Magnetism," and "The Rough Crossing"—that in retrospect could have suggested to the author the Dick-Nicole-Rosemary triangle. In addition, such stories as "The Swimmers," "Two Wrongs," "One Trip Abroad," and "What a Handsome Pair!"—which examine issues of infidelity and competition within marriage—probably contributed to Fitzgerald's thinking on the factors that undermine the Divers. The creation of Dick Diver's character and his intricate destiny may in fact owe as much or more to the author remembering the themes and characters he had already realized in his stories—the aspiration of Basil Duke Lee and the emotional bankruptcy of Josephine Perry, the alcoholism that destroys Dick Ragland in "A New Leaf," and the regret of Charlie Wales for his own dissipation in "Babylon Revisited"—than to the actual men Fitzgerald ostensibly used to assemble his composite. Such connections strongly suggest that Fitzgerald's stories may in large measure have shaped his conception of the Diver version as well as affected its texture.

While the thematic influence of particular stories is surely important, the concrete effect of the stories on the novel is manifest through the strippings. Although strippings occur in all three books of *Tender Is the Night*, they are not distributed uniformly throughout. Fitzgerald uses strippings most frequently in Book Two, less frequently in Book One, and least frequently in Book Three. Twenty of the sixty-one chapters of the novel have no strippings at all, and an additional twenty chapters have only one or two strippings; thus, for nearly two-thirds of the chapters of the novel, Fitzgerald's use of strippings is quite limited. On the other hand, for a third of his chapters, Fitzgerald used three or more strippings and in fifteen of these he

incorporated five or more strippings. As these numbers suggest, certain chapters treat situations or episodes that led Fitzgerald to search his stories for strippings, either because he originally had scenes from a story or stories in mind as he conceived the episode or because something in the episode he was working on suggested a story or stories to him.

When one follows Fitzgerald's progress as he inserts strippings into his manuscript, one finds that the strippings are routinely integrated so smoothly that there is no physical evidence to suggest they originated in another text. Several times Fitzgerald makes parenthetical notes to himself as he writes, but only in a few instances is there enough evidence of his thought process on paper to permit worthwhile speculation into the importance of particular stories in Fitzgerald's structuring of his novel. Nevertheless, it is important to recognize that in most instances an author's thinking weaves a serendipitous path that does not appear on paper and cannot be traced. Like the pebble that started an avalanche and later is lost in the heap, a stripped phrase, even one that seems to have been included as an afterthought, might once have been key in the mysterious process of creation.

Note

1. Matthew Josephson, *Zola and His Times* (New York: Macaulay, 1928).

The Tear Sheets and Fitzgerald's Notebooks

Generally, Fitzgerald employed a two-step approach in marking the tear sheets of his stories, initially marking those strippings he thought he might use in his novel and then later marking the strippings he had decided to have typed for his notebooks. Fitzgerald's notebooks, therefore, were largely a by-product of his stripping process for Tender Is the Night. *The notebooks contain material Fitzgerald decided not to use in his novel but that he collected to serve as a stockpile for writing projects after the novel had been published.*

In introducing The Notebooks of F. Scott Fitzgerald, *Bruccoli states that it "is not known when Fitzgerald began assembling" them, but suggests that "it was after May 1932" (viii) because one of the binders was purchased after Fitzgerald moved to La Paix, outside of Baltimore, where Fitzgerald hired his first secretary. Fitzgerald was methodical about adding to his notebooks during the composition of* Tender Is the Night, *but he was not as thorough in his stripping of his stories for them after the novel was completed. Of the more than forty stories he wrote after the novel, only a dozen were stripped for his notebooks.*

A Short Trip Home

She had magic suddenly in her pink palms

A Short Trip Home

She had one of those exquisite rose skins frequent in our part of the country, and beautiful until the little veins begin to break at about forty, and the cold had lit it to a lovely flame, like the thrilling flush of children after their cold baths in the evening.

The Hotel Child

Fifi Schwartz. An exquisitely, radiantly beautiful Jewess whose fine, high forehead sloped gently up to where her hair, bordering it like an armorial shield, burst into lovelocks and waves and curlicues of soft dark red. Her eyes were bright, big, clear, wet and shining; the color of her cheeks and lips was real, breaking close to the surface from the strong young pump of her heart.

The Adolescent Marriage

Wharton and his wife were gone and a slender, dark-haired girl whose body hovered delicately on the last edge of childhood had come quietly into the room.

A Short Trip Home

She was nearly complete, yet the dew was still on her.

TENDER IS THE NIGHT

had gone, beach and bay were quiet for an hour. Merchantmen crawled westward on the horizon; bus boys shouted in the hotel court; the dew dried upon the pines. In another hour the horns of motors began to blow down from the winding road along the low range of the Maures, which separates the littoral from true Provençal France.

A mile from the sea, where pines give way to dusty poplars, is an isolated railroad stop, whence one June morning in 1925 a victoria brought a woman and her daughter down to Gausse's Hotel. The mother's face was of a fading prettiness that would soon be patted with broken veins; her expression was both tranquil and aware in a pleasant way. However, one's eyes moved on quickly to her daughter, who had magic in her pink palms and her cheeks lit to a lovely flame, like the thrilling flush of children after their cold baths in the evening. Her fine high forehead sloped gently up to where her hair, bordering it like an armorial shield, burst into lovelocks and waves and curlicues of ash blonde and gold. Her eyes were bright, big, clear, wet, and shining, the color of her cheeks was real, breaking close to the surface from the strong young pump of her heart. Her body hovered delicately on the last edge of childhood—she was almost eighteen, nearly complete, but the dew was still on her.

As sea and sky appeared below them in a thin, hot line the mother said:

"Something tells me we're not going to like this place."

"I want to go home anyhow," the girl answered.

They both spoke cheerfully but were obviously without direction and bored by the fact—moreover, just any direction would not do. They wanted high excitement, not from the necessity of stimulating jaded nerves but with the avidity of prize-winning schoolchildren who deserved their vacations.

"We'll stay three days and then go home. I'll wire right away for steamer tickets."

4

Page from the novel in which Fitzgerald uses five strippings from three stories to describe Rosemary Hoyt

XV

"WHAT is it you are giving up?" demanded Rosemary, facing Dick earnestly in the taxi.

"Nothing of importance."

"Are you a scientist?"

"I'm a doctor of medicine."

"Oh-h!" She smiled delightedly. "My father was a doctor too. Then why don't you—" she stopped.

"There's no mystery. I didn't disgrace myself at the height of my career, and hide away on the Riviera. I'm just not practising. You can't tell, I'll probably practise again some day."

Rosemary put up her face quietly to be kissed. He looked at her for a moment as if he didn't understand. Then holding her in the hollow of his arm he rubbed his cheek against her cheek's softness, and then looked down at her for another long moment.

"Such a lovely child," he said gravely.

She smiled up at him; her hands playing conventionally with the lapels of his coat. "I'm in love with you and Nicole. Actually that's my secret—I can't even talk about you to anybody because I don't want any more people to know how wonderful you are. Honestly—I love you and Nicole—I do."

—So many times he had heard this—even the formula was the same.

Suddenly she came toward him, her youth vanishing as she passed inside the focus of his eyes and he had kissed her breathlessly as if she were any age at all. Then she lay back against his arm and sighed.

83

Jacob's Ladder

Driving homeward through the soft night, she put up her face quietly to be kissed. Holding her in the hollow of his arm, Jacob rubbed his cheek against her cheek's softness and then looked down at her for a long moment.

"Such a lovely child," he said gravely.

She smiled back at him; her hands played conventionally with the lapels of his coat.

First Blood

He saw all this and relaxed for a moment to pat her hand, and suddenly she came toward him, her youth vanishing as she passed inside the focus of his eyes, and he had kissed her breathlessly, as if she were thirty. She lay back against his arm.

"I've decided to give you up," she said astonishingly.

He started. For a moment he wondered if he had forgotten something—something he had said to her before—had he ever talked to her more than casually? Had he committed himself to be in some way possessed?

"But that's very mean," he managed to say lightly, "just when I was getting interested."

Pages from the novel in which Dick and Rosemary first kiss. "First Blood" was the initial story of Fitzgerald's Josephine Perry series, which culminates in the emotional bankruptcy of the heroine.

Jacob's Ladder

"Not only are you beautiful," continued Jacob, "but you are somehow on the grand scale. Everything you do—yes, like reaching for that glass, or pretending to be self-conscious, or pretending to despair of me—gets across.

. . . .

Afterward, in the dark cave of the taxi cab, fragrant with the perfume he had bought for her that day, Jenny came close to him, clung to him. He kissed her, without enjoying it. There was no shadow of passion in her eyes or on her mouth; there was a faint spray of champagne on her breath. She clung nearer, desperately.

. . . .

Hesitating tentatively, he kissed her and again he was chilled by the innocence of her kiss, the eyes that at the moment of contact looked beyond him out into the darkness of the night, the darkness of the world. She did not know yet that splendor was something in the heart; at the moment when she should realize that and melt into the passion of the universe he could take her without question or regret.

TENDER IS THE NIGHT

"I've decided to give you up," she said.

Dick started—had he said anything to imply that she possessed any part of him?

"But that's very mean," he managed to say lightly, "just when I was getting interested."

"I've loved you so—" As if it had been for years. She was weeping a little now. "I've loved you so-o-o."

Then he should have laughed, but he heard himself saying, "Not only are you beautiful but you are somehow on the grand scale. Everything you do, like pretending to be in love or pretending to be shy gets across."

In the dark cave of the taxi, fragrant with the perfume Rosemary had bought with Nicole, she came close again, clinging to him. He kissed her without enjoying it. He knew that there was passion there, but there was no shadow of it in her eyes or on her mouth; there was a faint spray of champagne on her breath. She clung nearer desperately and once more he kissed her and was chilled by the innocence of her kiss, by the glance that at the moment of contact looked beyond him out into the darkness of the night, the darkness of the world. She did not know yet that splendor is something in the heart; at the moment when she realized that and melted into the passion of the universe he could take her without question or regret.

Her room in the hotel was diagonally across from theirs and nearer the elevator. When they reached the door she said suddenly:

"I know you don't love me—I don't expect it. But you said I should have told you about my birthday. Well, I did, and now for my birthday present I want you to come into my room a minute while I tell you something. Just one minute."

They went in and he closed the door, and Rosemary stood close to him, not touching him. The night had drawn the

84

At Your Age

Her beauty sparkled bright against his strong, tall form, and they floated hoveringly, delicately, like two people in a nice, amusing dream.

A Penny Spent

She was surprised to find how well he danced, as all tall, slender men should with such a delicacy of suggestion that she felt as though she were being turned here and there as a bright bouquet or a piece of precious cloth before five hundred eyes.

The Bridal Party

For a second as he said this, in a voice that seemed to have come up from his shoes, they were not dancing; they were simply clinging together.

The Rubber Check

Sometime in the early morning they were alone and her damp, powdery young body came up close to him in a crush of tired cloth, and he kissed her, trying not to think of the gap between them.

. . . .

The idea was in both their minds, and in the mind of Mercia Templeton as she passed the door of the cloak room and saw them there crushed against a background of other people's hats and wraps, clinging together.

TENDER IS THE NIGHT

But always there was Dick. Rosemary assured the image of her mother, ever carried with her, that never, never had she known any one so nice, so thoroughly nice as Dick was that night. She compared him with the two Englishmen, whom Abe addressed conscientiously as "Major Hengest and Mr. Horsa," and with the heir to a Scandinavian throne and the novelist just back from Russia, and with Abe, who was desperate and witty, and with Collis Clay, who joined them somewhere and stayed along—and felt there was no comparison. The enthusiasm, the selflessness behind the whole performance ravished her, the technic of moving many varied types, each as immobile, as dependent on supplies of attention as an infantry battalion is dependent on rations, appeared so effortless that he still had pieces of his own most personal self for everyone.

—Afterward she remembered the times when she had felt the happiest. The first time was when she and Dick danced together and she felt her beauty sparkling bright against his tall, strong form as they floated, hovering like people in an amusing dream—he turned her here and there with such a delicacy of suggestion that she was like a bright bouquet, a piece of precious cloth being displayed before fifty eyes. There was a moment when they were not dancing at all, simply clinging together. Some time in the early morning they were alone, and her damp powdery young body came up close to him in a crush of tired cloth, and stayed there, crushed against a background of other people's hats and wraps. . . .

The time she laughed most was later, when six of them, the best of them, noblest relics of the evening, stood in the dusky front lobby of the Ritz telling the night concierge that General Pershing was outside and wanted caviare and champagne. "He brooks no delay. Every man, every gun is at his service." Frantic waiters emerged from nowhere, a table

102

Page from the novel in which Fitzgerald uses five strippings from four stories to describe Rosemary's memory of dancing with Dick

Pulling Down the Curtain in "Basil and Cleopatra"

Chapter 20 of Book I provides the first sure evidence of Dick's weakness and vulnerability. Left alone with Collis Clay, Dick pays him little heed until Collis relates an anecdote concerning Rosemary:

Suddenly his blood ran cold as he realized the content of Collis's confidential monologue.

"—she's not so cold as you'd probably think. I admit I thought she was cold for a long time. But she got into a jam with a friend of mine going from New York to Chicago at Easter—a boy named Hillis she thought was pretty nutsey at New Haven—she had a compartment with a cousin of mine but she and Hillis wanted to be alone, so in the afternoon my cousin came and played cards in our compartment. Well, after about two hours we went back and there was Rosemary and Bill Hillis standing in the vestibule arguing with the conductor—Rosemary white as a sheet. Seems they locked the door and pulled down the blinds and I guess there was some heavy stuff going on when the conductor came for the tickets and knocked on the door. They thought it was us kidding them and wouldn't let him in at first, and when they did, he was plenty sore. He asked Hillis if that was his compartment and whether he and Rosemary were married that they locked the door, and Hillis lost his temper trying to explain there was nothing wrong. He said the conductor had insulted Rosemary and he wanted him to fight, but that conductor could have made trouble—and believe me I had an awful time smoothing it over."

With every detail imagined, with even envy for the pair's community of misfortune in the vestibule, Dick felt a change taking place within him. (pp. 115–116)

This passage, stripped from "Basil and Cleopatra," was a key but not an all-important passage in the story. It functions there to undergird young Basil Duke Lee's dawning suspicions of his "Cleopatra," Minnie Bibble. At the end of the story, Basil, who must force himself to decide that he "had made all his mistakes for this time" (p. 173), is finally able to resist Minnie's wiles.

In Tender Is the Night, *however, the anecdote assumes a far greater importance, for it serves to reveal Dick's uneasiness in the world he has created for himself and to provide a motif that echoes symbolically in chapters 20, 21, and 22 of Book I, and chapter 11 of Book II. At the end of chapter 22, after Dick has regained at least the illusion of control, the question comes to represent Dick's growing estrangement and disillusionment with his life. While dining with Rosemary and Nicole, Dick is moved by the presence of "the gold-star muzzers" at the next table:*

Over the wine Dick looked at them again; in their happy faces, the dignity that surrounded and pervaded the party, he perceived all the maturity of an older America. For a while the sobered women who had come to mourn for their dead, for something they could not repair, made the room beautiful. Momentarily, he sat again on his father's knee, riding with Moseby while the old loyalties and devotions fought on around him. Almost with an effort he turned back to his two women at the table and faced the whole new world in which he believed.

—Do you mind if I pull down the curtain? (pp. 130–131)

Dick stands on the outside alone, separated, unable to truly share "the inviolable secret warmth within" with either Rosemary or Nicole, unable to recapture his father's "old loyalties and devotions," and also unable wholly to believe in the "new world" he has in part created yet will soon fail to sustain.

—George Parker Anderson

For a Moment He Glanced Around as if Blinded; Then His Glance Fell on Minnie Bibble and an Unmistakable Love Light Came Into His Face

The Saturday Evening Post *illustration for Fitzgerald's story "Basil and Cleopatra," 27 April 1929
(Bruccoli Collection of Fitzgerald, Thomas Cooper Library, University of South Carolina)*

One Trip Abroad

Below the hotel, where the terrace fell a thousand feet to the lake, stretched a necklace of lights that was Montreux and Vevey, and then, in a dim pendant, Lausanne; a blurred twinkling across the lake was Evian and France. From somewhere below—probably *Kursaal*—came the sound of full-bodied dance music—American, they guessed, though now they heard American tunes months late, mere distant echoes of what was happening far away.

Flight and Pursuit

"No. I even have to think before I can really remember how I stood waiting for you in the garden that night, holding all my dreams and hopes in my arms like a lot of flowers—they were that to me, anyhow. I thought I was pretty sweet. I'd saved myself up for that—all ready to hand it all to you. And then you came up to me and kicked me."

One Trip Abroad

And sometimes there was a booming from the vine-covered hills on the other side of the lake, which meant that cannons were shooting at hail-bearing clouds, to save the vineyards from an approaching storm; it came swiftly, first falling from the heavens and then falling again in torrents from the mountains, washing loudly down the roads and stone ditches; it came with a dark, frightening sky and savage filaments of lightning and crashing, world-splitting thunder, while ragged and destroyed clouds fled along before the wind past the hotel. The mountains and the lake disappeared completely; the hotel crouched alone amid tumult and chaos and darkness.

TENDER IS THE NIGHT

getting drunk after battle. But she was still afraid of Dick, who stood near her, leaning, characteristically, against the iron fence that rimmed the horseshoe; and this prompted her to say: "I can remember how I stood waiting for you in the garden—holding all my self in my arms like a basket of flowers. It was that to me anyhow—I thought I was sweet— waiting to hand that basket to you."

He breathed over her shoulder and turned her insistently about; she kissed him several times, her face getting big every time she came close, her hands holding him by the shoulders. "It's raining hard."

Suddenly there was a booming from the wine slopes across the lake; cannons were shooting at hail-bearing clouds in order to break them. The lights of the promenade went off, went on again. Then the storm came swiftly, first falling from the heavens, then doubly falling in torrents from the mountains and washing loud down the roads and stone ditches; with it came a dark, frightening sky and savage filaments of lightning and world-splitting thunder, while ragged, destroying clouds fled along past the hotel. Mountains and lake disappeared— the hotel crouched amid tumult, chaos and darkness.

By this time Dick and Nicole had reached the vestibule, where Baby Warren and the three Marmoras were anxiously awaiting them. It was exciting coming out of the wet fog— with the doors banging, to stand and laugh and quiver with emotion, wind in their ears and rain on their clothes. Now in the ballroom the orchestra was playing a Strauss waltz, high and confusing.

. . . For Doctor Diver to marry a mental patient? How did it happen? Where did it begin?

"Won't you come back after you've changed?" Baby Warren asked after a close scrutiny.

"I haven't got any change, except some shorts."

204

Page from chapter 9 of Book II, in which Dick commits himself to Nicole

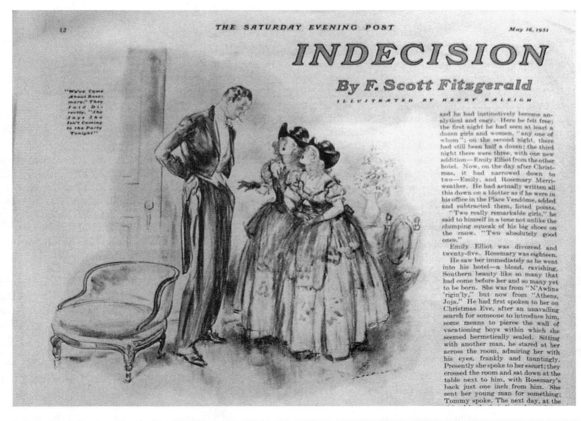

Illustrations from a story that Fitzgerald referred to in writing chapter 13 of Book II (Bruccoli Collection of Fitzgerald, Thomas Cooper Library, University of South Carolina)

"Indecision" and the Diver Manuscript

Written in the first two months of 1931 when Fitzgerald was still committed to the Melarky version, "Indecision" is a story that the author may initially have composed with Francis Melarky's deterioration in mind, for it depicts a shallow, self-obsessed male protagonist. A general similarity in the situation of the story's protagonist and that of Dick Diver is clear. Like Dick, Tommy McLane, a twenty-seven-year-old successful banker on Christmas vacation in the Swiss Alps, is torn between a mature woman, Emily Elliot, and an ingenue, Rosemary Merriweather. The mood of "Indecision," however, is comic rather than tragic. Vacillating between Emily and Rosemary, always keeping his ambivalence hidden from the woman he is with while secretly longing for the other, Tommy eventually proposes to Rosemary, thus neatly resolving his dilemma and setting up the tidy ending: "With the sound of his own voice the other image faded from his mind forever" (p. 62).

Tommy McLane's limitations make it seem likely that Fitzgerald used him as a model first for the degraded Francis and later for the dissipated Dick. Certainly, no character could seem further from the promising young Doctor Diver at a similar age, for Tommy is hardly aware of a world outside of himself. He lives vaguely, aware only that "because the world was round, or for some such reason, there was rosy light still on that big mountain, the Dent de Something" (p. 12). Tommy has no awareness of and no checks upon his childish need to be loved and feels it is "an outrage" that he can not have both women (p. 56). He acts altruistically only when he is "Conscious of Rosemary's eyes staring at him" (p. 56) and may choose to "sulk proudly" when he feels unappreciated. Although he deceitfully plans to "dovetail the affairs with skill and thought" (p. 59), he lacks the ability to manage himself or anyone else. In sum, Tommy seems to be the antithesis of a healthy Dick Diver.

Whatever part "Indecision" might have played in Fitzgerald's planning for his novel, the evidence is undeniable that the author used the story to structure what became chapter 13 of Book II, the chapter in which Dick accepts Franz Gregorovius's proposal to become partners in a clinic. Both story and novel are set at Christmas in a Swiss ski resort, the Gstaad of the novel. Eleven strippings from the story are used in the chapter, the first occurring in the novel's first sentence, where Dick, like Tommy, slaps the snow from his ski suit. In the novel as in the story, Fitzgerald then references popular songs to establish the festive activity of the resort and immediately contrasts two women—Emily and Rosemary in the story, Nicole and Baby in the novel. The events of the novel continue to follow those of the story with the descriptions of the party at the "old-fashioned Swiss taproom," the sleigh ride to the municipal dance, the cigarette points shining in the darkness of the hotel grill, and the passing sound of the Wiener waltzes as both story and chapter end with train departures. The novel follows the story as well in depicting Dick Diver's divided attentions, for like Tommy vacillating between Emily and Rosemary, Dick keeps one eye out for a "special girl" (p. 228)—referenced six times during the chapter—even as he discusses business with Nicole, Baby, and Franz.

Fitzgerald's use of "Indecision" to structure his chapter seems all the more significant when one realizes the crucial role of this episode as it was first conceived in the Diver manuscript. Coming as it does in the manuscript after Nicole's attempt to wreck the car and kill not only herself and Dick but their children as well, the Gstaad vacation marks the turning point in Dick's character. Unlike the chapter as revised for the novel that shows Dick slipping slightly, the episode in the manuscript depicts a Dick Diver who completely disintegrates. "Something's happening in me," Dick confesses at one point, "I don't know what it is and where it'll lead." Although Fitzgerald later toned down the Gstaad episode to make it only a step downward for Dick rather than a cliff, the initial importance of the episode as a structural focus for the novel is manifest from these quoted passages in the manuscript that he later excised.

While the influence of a particular story upon Fitzgerald's conception of the Diver version must always remain largely a matter of speculation, "Indecision" shows that Fitzgerald did not review his stories just for the phrases or passages they might supply; instead, he also clearly considered them, at times at least, in whole or in part as structural entities—"Indecision" being a significant example of a story's structure affecting the novel's. But the case of "Indecision" perhaps reveals something more of the author's imagination in regard to his review of his stories. The fact that a story titled "Indecision" provided a *decisive turning point* in the Diver manuscript suggests that Fitzgerald may have viewed his stories not merely as means to structure his novel but also as *ideas* that he would sometimes turn over in his mind and that in a direct or ironic manner would shape his approach to a scene or episode in his novel. Surely, as he wrote the Gstaad episode, Fitzgerald was fully aware of the connection between Tommy McLane and Dick Diver and aware, too, of the irony of transfiguring a story the *Post* had almost turned down into an integral part of his developing novel. Despite his talk of his popular stories being "trash," Fitzgerald in his review of his stories was alive to all of their qualities—phrasing, characters, settings, plots, symbols, themes—and was determined to waste nothing of value from them as he turned with renewed determination to his novel.

—George Parker Anderson

Charlie Wales and the Ending of *Tender Is the Night*

In the quarrel that precedes the Divers' final break, Dick tells Nicole that he can do no more for her and must try to save himself (p. 389). But having abandoned his serious aspirations, as well as his relationships with Rosemary and Nicole, Dick finds that he has little with which to face his future. In the last paragraph of "Babylon Revisited," Charlie Wales, who at least for the time being has lost custody of Honoria, his only child, invokes his dead wife in the final sentence as a means of giving himself courage:

He would come back some day; they couldn't make him pay forever. But he wanted his child, and nothing was much good now, beside that fact. He wasn't young any more, with a lot of nice thoughts and dreams to have by himself. He was absolutely sure Helen wouldn't have wanted him to be so alone.

By his interlinear insertion of the phrase "He was not young any more with a lot of nice thoughts and dreams to have about himself" in the Diver typescript, Fitzgerald links Charlie Wales and Dick Diver in what would become the penultimate chapter of *Tender Is the Night*.

Both Charlie and Dick have destroyed their own dreams, but Charlie still has a measure of hope and determination. Though Charlie is unwilling to dream by himself, if he recovers Honoria, he may be able to dream again. But Dick has no aspirations. In New York he becomes "entangled with a girl who worked in a grocery store" (p. 407) and involved in a lawsuit: "After that he didn't ask for the children to be sent to America" (p. 408). Dick is alone and will remain alone even if, as Nicole likes to imagine, he settles down "with some one to keep house for him" (p. 408).

–George Parker Anderson

Illustration in The Saturday Evening Post, *21 February 1931, from Fitzgerald's story "Babylon Revisited"*
(Bruccoli Collection of Fitzgerald, Thomas Cooper Library, University of South Carolina)

687
~~698~~

~~As he~~ nodded again and walked off toward the ~~hotel in the~~ *hotel and*

~~dwindling crowd~~ Nicole *whitest* eyes followed him.

"~~He~~ was fair enough," Tommy conceeded, "Darling, ~~my dear~~ *will*

~~love, I love you.~~ ~~Will~~ we be together tonight?"

"I suppose so." ¶Then it had happened--she felt a little

cheated that there had been ~~so little~~ *such a minimum of* drama; she felt ~~a little hurt~~ at *outguessed*

realizing that from the ~~moment~~ *episode* of the ~~jar of~~ camphor-rub Dick had ~~planned~~ *anticipated*

~~out~~ everything ~~completely to this point,~~ But she felt happy and excited *-also*

and the odd little wish that she could tell Dick about it faded quickly. *all*

Yet ~~she~~ *her eyes* followed ~~his still~~ *the* handsome figure ~~with her eyes~~ until it be-

came a dot and mingled with the other dots in the crowd.

He wasn't young any more with a lot of nice thoughts and dreams to have about himself, as he wanted to remember them well. The children

The day before Dr. Diver left the Riviera he spent ~~all~~ the

time with his children. ~~They~~ had been told that this winter they would

be with their aunt in London and that/they were going to come and see *soon*

him in America. The Fraulien who looked after them was not to be dis-

charged without his consent.

Dick was glad he had given much to the little girl, ~~Topsy~~--

~~as for Lanier he had never been~~ *but for the boy he was more* certain ~~what to tell him or teach him.~~ *he had ~~never been~~ always been*

uneasy about the what he had to give to the always ~~to go~~ climbing,
~~ever-climbing~~, breast-searching young. maybe no milk today,
baby, maybe no milk. ¶ *But next*

Page from the revised Diver typescript in which Fitzgerald inserts a phrase from "Babylon Revisited"
(Princeton University Library)

Publication and Reception

Serialization in *Scribner's Magazine*

In October 1933 Fitzgerald delivered the Tender Is the Night *manuscript to Maxwell Perkins at Scribners. The first of four serial installments appeared in the January 1934 issue of* Scribner's Magazine; *Fitzgerald's portrait appeared on the cover.*

At that time magazine prepublication serialization of novels was popular because it provided extra income for the author and generated reader interest in the forthcoming book. Fitzgerald's publisher owned a respected magazine in which they serialized or excerpted forthcoming books by their authors, including Ernest Hemingway and Thomas Wolfe.

The finances for Tender Is the Night *are obscure. Although Fitzgerald kept a detailed ledger, some of the entries reflect his personal interpretations of advances. A 1930 entry reads: "Further advances (Serial new Novel + 1583.06 against bk. $3701.97." But these figures probably represent borrowings from Scribners during 1930 that Fitzgerald regarded as advances to be paid back from the earnings of his new novel. On 25 September 1933 Fitzgerald informed Maxwell Perkins: "Ober is advancing me the money to go through with it (it will probably not need more than $2,000 though he has promised to go as far as $4,000) and in return I am giving him 10% of the serial rights." Perkins outlined terms for the serialization to Fitzgerald on 18 October 1933.* Scribner's Magazine *paid Fitzgerald $10,000—of which $6,000 was applied to his Scribners debt. The $4,000 balance was paid in installments to Ober, who turned it over to Fitzgerald as needed. A release was obtained from* Liberty, *which had contracted for serial rights; but it is not clear whether their 1927–1928 advances were repaid.*

The serial text has twelve long chapters, which had been Fitzgerald's plan in 1932. (The book text is divided into three sections comprising sixty-one chapters.) The first magazine installment included what became the first eighteen chapters of Book I of the novel—through Abe North's departure from Paris. The February installment completed Book I and included the first nine chapters of the flashback section in Book II of the novel—up to Dick's decision to marry Nicole. The March installment completed the flashback and concluded Book II with Dick's beating in Rome. The April installment comprised all of Book III.

Fitzgerald and Scribners anticipated that serialization would generate effective visibility and promote book sales, but serialization may have damaged the initial reception of Tender Is the Night. *The structure of the novel, with its break in chronology and shift in* point of view between Books I and II, was blurred by the thirty-day intervals. Fitzgerald suspected that some of the critics reviewed his novel from the serial and urged his friends to reread it in book form.

The serial version included six short scenes that were dropped from the book: two sequences describing Abe North in the Ritz Bar (Book I); Dick's involvement with a woman at Innsbruck (Book II); and three sequences on the ship during Dick's return to Europe after his father's funeral (Book II). Fitzgerald cut from the typescript *before serialization the account of Tommy and Nicole's visit to an American gangster in Book III. The only passages restored to the book dealt with the sexual material that was unpublishable in the magazine—notably an expansion of Warren's confession of his incestuous relationship with Nicole.*

—Matthew J. Bruccoli

The Fifth Avenue building of Charles Scribner's Sons, Fitzgerald's only publisher for his novels and short-story collections

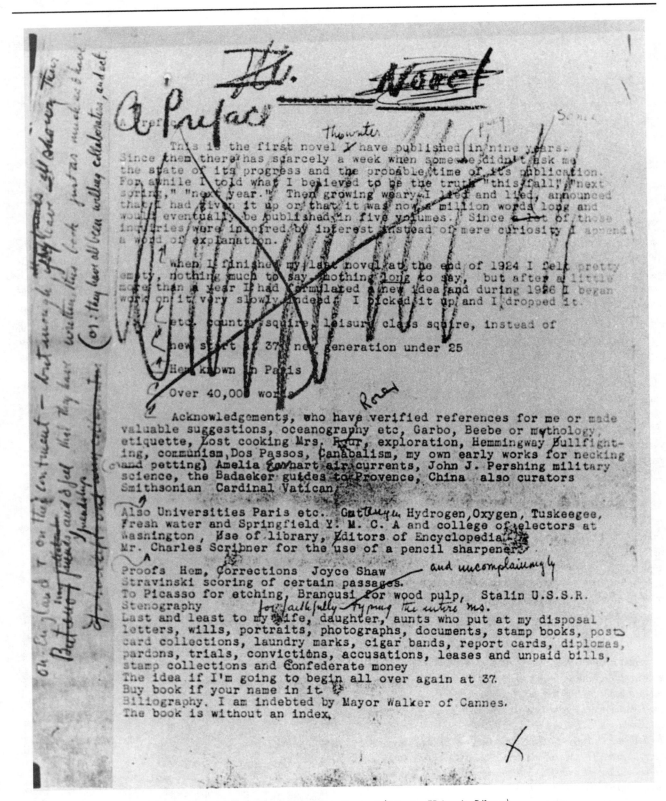

Fitzgerald's unused parody preface to the novel (Princeton University Library)

Correspondence, Fall 1933 to Spring 1934

Fitzgerald to Maxwell Perkins, 19 October 1933
"La Paix," Rodgers' Forge, Towson, Maryland

All goes well here. The first two chapters are in shape and am starting the third one this afternoon. So the first section comprising about 26,000 words will be mailed to you Friday night or Saturday morning.

Naturally, I was delighted by your gesture of coming up two thousand. I hope to God results will show in the circulation of the magazine and I have an idea they will. Negotiations with Cosmopolitan were of course stopped and Ober is sure that getting the release from Liberty is merely a matter of form which he is attending to. I think I will need the money a little quicker than by the month, say $1000 on delivery of the first section and then the other 3 $1000s every fortnight after that. This may not be necessary but the first $2000 will. As you know, I now owe Ober two or three thousand and he should be reimbursed so he can advance me more to carry me through the second section and a Post story. Naturally, payments on the serial should be made to him.

I am saying this now and will remind you later. My idea is that the book form of the novel should be set up from the corrected proof of the serial,–in that I will reinsert the excisions which I am making for the serial.

If you have any way of getting French or Swiss railroad posters it would be well for you to try to. Now as to the blurbs: I think there should not be too many; I am sending you nine.

. . . .

I should say to be careful in saying it's my first book in seven years not to imply that it contains seven years work. People would expect too much in bulk + scope.

This novel, my 4th, completes my story of the boom years. It might be wise to accentuate the fact that it does not deal with the depression. Don't accentuate that it deals with Americans abroad–there's been too much trash under that banner.

No exclamatory "At last, the long awaited ect." That merely creates the "Oh yeah" mood in people.

–*F. Scott Fitzgerald: A Life in Letters*, pp. 239–241

* * *

Fitzgerald to Perkins, 20 October 1933
La Paix

How is this for an advertising approach:

"For several years the impression has prevailed that Scott Fitzgerald had abandoned the writing of novels and in the future would continue to write only popular short stories. His publishers knew different and they are very glad now to be able to present a book which is in line with his three other highly successful and highly esteemed novels, thus demonstrating that Scott Fitzgerald is anything but through as a serious novelist."

I don't mean necessarily these exact words but something on that general line, I mean something politic enough not to disparage the Post stories but saying quite definitely that this is a horse of another color.

–*F. Scott Fitzgerald: A Life in Letters*, p. 241

* * *

Alfred Dashiell was the editor of Scribner's Magazine.

Fitzgerald to Alfred Dashiell, 29 October 1933
La Paix

I cannot come to a decision about the title before Monday or Tuesday. It is, naturally, to me a tremendously important question. My reasons against the lyrical title I've already told you, my reasons against the title which used the word "Doctor" I've already told you, I can also see reasons against "Dick and Nicole Diver"; so I think that I will simply have to dope over the whole thing again; but remember, if I come to no conclusion (no new conclusion) that "Richard Diver" will be the title.

The second section will reach you about the 12th of November. If there is any special reason for wanting it sooner I could probably manage it but I would prefer to have that much time at it.

About the other two installments: I had already talked to Max–after finishing the second installment, I am practically compelled to do a Post story. So the third installment may be delayed five weeks beyond the second, then the fourth will follow in three weeks more.

–*Correspondence of F. Scott Fitzgerald*, pp. 318–319

* * *

Fitzgerald to Dashiell

Towson MD   109P   1933 OCT 31   PM 1 24
HAVENT YET BEEN ABLE TO THINK UP A THING THAT I CONSIDER SATISFACTORY FOR A TITLE WHY DOES A TITLE HAVE TO BE PUBLISHED IN A PREVIEW ANY HOW I'VE ALWAYS BEEN AGAINST IT THE IMPORTANT THING IS THAT A NOVEL BY ME IS APPEARING NO ONE WOULD REMEMBER THE TITLE OVER A WHOLE MONTH AND THIS IS NOT THE ANNOUNCEMENT OF A SPECIAL VOLUME BUT SIMPLY THAT A BOOK WILL APPEAR IN SCRIBNERS IN ANY CASE THIS IS BETTER THAN HAVING AN UNSATISFACTORY TITLE PLEASE ANSWER
    F SCOTT FITZGERALD

–*Correspondence of F. Scott Fitzgerald*, p. 319

* * *

RICHARD DIVER · *A Romance*
By F. SCOTT FITZGERALD
To be published complete in four numbers

The editors of Scribner's Magazine announce the acquisition of the serial rights of F. Scott Fitzgerald's new novel, a literary event of outstanding importance. The only exceptions to our policy of publishing short novels complete in one number in the past have been in the cases of the novels of John Galsworthy, S. S. Van Dine, and Ernest Hemingway. "Richard Diver" is from every standpoint a logical companion for these distinguished novels.

This is Mr. Fitzgerald's first novel since "The Great Gatsby." To the generation that was in youth fourteen years ago when "This Side of Paradise" came out, the name Fitzgerald is associated with the Jazz Age to which he gave the name in his "Tales of a Jazz Age." The author was then twenty-two. He had attained to maturity when he wrote "The Great Gatsby."

Not until long after its success as a story, and then as a play, were its implications fully realized, except by the most discerning. Mr. Fitzgerald's new novel fulfills the promise of that remarkable work.

"Richard Diver" has for its leading character a doctor of medicine, and a problem of his profession springing out of a set of curious human relationships is the basis of its plot. Everything about it—characters, scene, and plot—is fresh and new and exciting.

To Begin in the JANUARY
Scribner's
Magazine

Advertisement with the rejected title

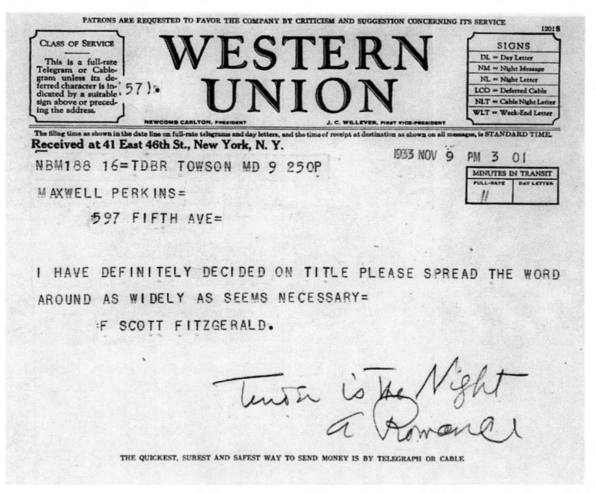

Fitzgerald's telegram confirming the title for his fourth novel. The handwriting is that of Maxwell Perkins (Princeton University Library).

Fitzgerald's Subtitle

Fitzgerald's choice of the subtitle, 'A Romance,' expresses his development beyond the tightly written novel to the emotional and sensory qualities of the romance genre. Tender Is the Night *is a realistic work of fiction—indeed, a source for social history—but it is also an evocation of enchantment, atmosphere, mood, color, and disillusionment. Ultimately, 'Romance' applies to the stylistic richness. Like the Keats ode that provides the title, Fitzgerald's fiction is romantic in the emotional, not the love-story, sense of the term. Moreover, the subtitle is ironic.* Tender Is the Night *is finally about the failure of romance: the impossibility of sustaining emotional commitment as well as the failure of ideals and aspiration.*

Fitzgerald to Perkins, 13 November 1933
La Paix

I was too sanguine in estimating the natural divisions of the novel. As it turns out in the reworking the line up is as follows:

    I. The first triangle story, which you have
                          (26,000 words)
    II. Completion of that story, plus the throw-back to courtship of doctor and his wife (19,000 words)
    III. The doctor's struggle with his problem, concluding with his debacle in Rome.
    IV. The doctor's decline after he has given up.

    These two last parts are going to be <u>long as hell</u>, especially IV, Section III, as you may remember, includes the part about his journeying around Europe, which we agreed could be considerably cut, but Section IV could not be cut much without omission of such key incidents as would cripple the timing of the whole plan. That Section is liable to amount to as much as forty thousand words–could you handle it? Or must I divide it, and lose a month on spring publication?

By that time reader interest in the serial will be thoroughly aroused (or thoroughly killed) so I think the idea of the book publication should be paramount if you can arrange the material factor of such a long installment.

Ever yours,
Scott Fitz—

P.S. By the way: where in hell is the proof? And will you have two struck off? This is important for Section II where the medical part begins, but how can I ask a doctor to judge fairly upon Section II unless he can read Section I?

—*F. Scott Fitzgerald: A Life in Letters,* pp. 242–243

* * *

Illustrating *Tender Is the Night*

Edward Shenton (1895–1977) illustrated nearly one hundred books, including Hemingway's Green Hills of Africa *(1935), Faulkner's* The Unvanquished *(1938), and Marjorie Kinnan Rawlings's* The Yearling *(1938). He was also a muralist and the author of ten books. His "line technique" pen-and-ink illustrations for the* Scribner's Magazine *serial were so effective that it was decided to include them in the book: they are called "decorations." Shenton wrote Fitzgerald in the late fall of 1933.*

I just finished reading the final installment and will start the drawings this week. I wish I could tell you precisely how your novel affected me. Nothing comes readily to hand, except the kind of glib phrases, reviewers use. The pattern of disintegration you've created, is so subtle, adroit, so techinically proficient–and so completely moving–that the book seems to have a new form; something entirely it's own.–That's not what I mean, at least only partially. It's a swell job! Any writer would give his right arm and both legs to have done it. It's the best thing that's been written since "The Great Gatsby"–(This is going to become a "fan-letter" if I don't curb it).

—*Correspondence of F. Scott Fitzgerald,* p. 319

Here begins the new novel by the author of *The Great Gatsby* and *This Side of Paradise.* It will be completed in four numbers of SCRIBNER'S MAGAZINE

Cover and first page for serialization (Bruccoli Collection of Fitzgerald, Thomas Cooper Library, University of South Carolina)

Decoration by Edward Shenton that appeared in the magazine but was not used in the novel (Bruccoli Collection of Fitzgerald, Thomas Cooper Library, University of South Carolina)

Poet and critic John Peale Bishop was Fitzgerald's class-mate at Princeton.

John Peale Bishop to Fitzgerald, December 1933/ January 1934

The first installment of the novel confirms what I have long thought, that your gifts as a novelist surpass those of any of us. It is so skilful, so subtle, so right that I have only praise for it. You get the whole romance of that period, which is now like history.

—*Correspondence of F. Scott Fitzgerald,* p. 321

* * *

Harold Ober to Fitzgerald, 5 January 1934

I tried to write you yesterday afternoon but had a busy day and didn't have a minute.

As I told you, I talked first with Maxwell Perkins and then with Charles Scribner and Max. They were both very enthusiastic about your novel and they showed me the jacket which I think is extremely attractive.

I told them your situation as you outlined it to me, and they were both very sympathetic. Charles Scribner talked at some length about the way book sales had fallen off, especially with their subscription books, from which they usually make a good deal of their income. He said the Galsworthy book had also been a disappointment in sales. I was at Scribner's altogether for a couple of hours, I think. After several conferences Charles Scribner said that they would give me a check today for $2000. which would be returned to them out of any sale that is made of the moving picture rights. He also proposed that you pay 5% interest on this loan. He said he wanted to do this to distinguish it from advances they had made against book royalties. I didn't go into this over the telephone yesterday as I was afraid it would make the cost of the telephone call too high.

I made at first the proposal that you made to me that they buy a share of the picture rights but both Max and Charles Scribner said they didn't want to make such an arrangement. They were against such arrangements in principle and they felt you ought to have all the money that you could get out of the dramatic rights and picture rights. I am sure that they were sincere in their reasons for not wanting to make this arrangement.

I realize that this solves our difficulties only temporarily but if you can finish rewriting the fourth section of the story in eight or ten days and then take a little rest, I think it would probably be much easier for you to do a short story and I am sure we can survive some way until that is done.

I think you are entirely right in not trying to do any short stories until the novel is entirely off your mind.

Maxwell Perkins just called up to say that the check will be ready at two o'clock this afternoon and, as we arranged yesterday, I'll deposit $1000. for you and wire you when it is done. I expect some money next week so, as we arranged, I'll keep the other $1000. in my bank and give it to you as soon as I can next week, but not later than Thursday or Friday.

I hope you and Zelda are well. You must be glad to be so near the end of your work on the novel. You might let me know when you deliver the last installment so that I can keep after Scribner and get complete proofs of the story.

—*As Ever, Scott Fitz–*, pp. 201–202

* * *

Fitzgerald to Perkins, 13 January 1934
Baltimore

What do you think of the idea of using twenty-four of those wood-cuts, which illustrate the serial, as head and tail pieces for chapters in the book or, alternatively, interspersing them through the novel? I think it is comparatively an innovation in recent fiction and might give the book a certain distinction. I've gotten very fond of the illustrations. Who the hell is the illustrator? If it is too expensive a process let me know, but since the cuts are already made I thought it might not be.

. . . .

I did not thank you over the phone for the further advance, which does not mean that I did not appreciate it, but only that I have so much to thank you for.

Tell Dashiell that I cannot promise not to make changes in Section III, but under no conditions will it be lengthened. Section IV is taking longer than I thought and it may be the middle of next week before you get it.

. . . .

P.S. 2. Don't forget my suggestion that the jacket flap should carry an implication that though the book starts in a lyrical way, heavy drama will presently develop.

—*F. Scott Fitzgerald: A Life in Letters*, p. 244

* * *

Perkins to Fitzgerald, 15 January 1934

I know that you are having a hell of a time jumping from iron to iron to keep them all at the right temperature, but I think you might consider (I say it with much hesitation and doubt) the possibility of reducing in length what was in the first installment and the first part of the second. It is probably impossible, and perhaps unwise anyhow. I thought

Shenton decoration, on p. 28 of the first edition (Bruccoli Collection of Fitzgerald, Thomas Cooper Library, University of South Carolina)

Shenton decoration, on p. 61 of the first edition (Bruccoli Collection of Fitzgerald, Thomas Cooper Library, University of South Carolina)

you might conceivably cut out the shooting in the station. The purpose would be only that as soon as people get to Dick Diver their interest in the book, and their perception of its importance increases some thirty to forty percent. People do read a book differently from a serial though. I merely suggest the idea in order that your subconscious mind may work upon it a little without distracting you at all from anything else. — To be considered if at all, only when you come to the book proof.

—*Dear Scott/Dear Max*, p. 190

* * *

Fitzgerald to Perkins, 18 January 1934 Baltimore

Much as I value your advice, by which I profited in the revision of Gatsby, I can't see cutting out the "shooting at the train-side." It serves all sorts of subtle purposes and since I have decided that the plan of the book is best as originally conceived, the small

paring away would be very little help and I think would do more harm than good. I intend to think over this question once more but at the moment I am satisfied with the book as it stands, as well as being pretty dead on it. I want to hear some reactions on Section II, but I like the slow approach, which I think has a psychological significance affecting not only the work in question, but also having a bearing on my career in general. Is that too damn egotistical an association?

—*F. Scott Fitzgerald: A Life in Letters*, pp. 245–246

* * *

Cameron Rogers later reviewed Tender Is the Night *in the* San Francisco Chronicle.

Fitzgerald to Cameron Rogers, 24 January 1934 Baltimore

It is sometimes surprising to have a novel give an effect which was not exactly intended in the plan. Obviously Nicole is going to steal the book when it was intended as Dick Diver's story, and Nicole was to be scarcely more important than Rosemary.

—*Correspondence of F. Scott Fitzgerald*, p. 322

* * *

Fitzgerald to Perkins, 1 February 1934 Baltimore

Confirming my telegram I wish to God I had thought of this a week ago, but having put the proof aside to do my story it didn't occur to me. Now you know what my galleys look like. To transfer twenty-eight pages of those corrections from one kind of galley proof to another kind of galley proof will be a matter, to me, of many days work and it will obscure all the advantage of doing my final revision on clean galleys. My idea was originally to use the benefit of the magazine galleys as an extra chance at corrections. As I said in my wire the reinsertion of the cut scenes is the work of only an afternoon.

Of course if you have gone ahead with Section IV from the manuscript I suppose there is nothing to be done except strike off another galley for me when I have done all that spade work over again, altogether, probably a more expensive process, if Section IV is not already completely set up for the book. This is an awful mess. The ideal way would be, if you haven't already set up a whole block of Section IV, to wait for corrected magazine proof of

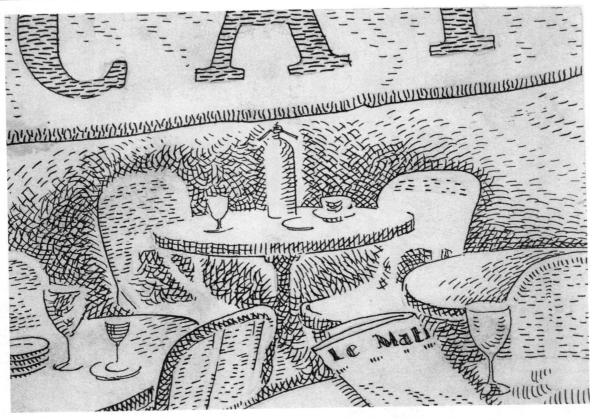

Shenton decoration, on p. 67 and p. 135 of the first edition (Bruccoli Collection of Fitzgerald,
Thomas Cooper Library, University of South Carolina)

Shenton decoration, on p. 156 of the first edition (Bruccoli Collection of Fitzgerald,
Thomas Cooper Library, University of South Carolina)

IV and have some editor roughly dub in the two big cuts, the scene of the fairies and the scene of the Lesbians, and send that to me with my own typescript containing the minor blue underlined magazine cuts. In that way I can work swiftly and efficiently. Meanwhile you could show the Book of the Month Club magazine galley of IV supplemented, just to be honest, with my typescript of the Lesbian scene if The Book of Mo. can get it back to you in time to insert it in my book galley for Section IV. From what you said to me on the phone last night about Wallace Myers' accuracy, perhaps he could handle it.

This is all the result of haste and nobody's fault except mine, but I worried about it all last night and it is essential that it be straightened up. I wish you would wire me immediately. Accept your decision about the jacket but be sure and do your best about that yellow as well as the red. I think every bit of yellow could be changed to white. Maybe somebody who knows about color printing could think of some way of introducing a little of that crimson-purple, as in the last poster I sent you, into the mountains. Oh God, it's hell to bother you about all this but of course the book is my whole life now and I can't help this perfectionist attitude.

You'll see Section I will come out all right.

—Correspondence of F. Scott Fitzgerald,
pp. 326–327

* * *

Thomas Wolfe

In a 1 February 1934 letter to Marjorie Kinnan Rawlings, Maxwell Perkins commented on his work with Thomas Wolfe on Of Time and the River, *which was published in 1935, and on his expectations for* Tender Is the Night, *which was then being serialized.*

I am struggling with Tom Wolfe for a couple of hours every night now, and he is going to get his book done for the fall. But it is the most difficult work I was ever engaged in. I feel that Scott having got his done is a good omen, for that seemed perfectly hopeless many times. Now he has done it, and it is a very fine thing, and will restore him to the position he held after "The Great Gatsby," if not put him in a higher one.

—Editor to Author, p. 88

Fitzgerald to Alfred Dashiell, 2 February 1934 Baltimore

A woman named Pauline Reinsch, 1904 Kendall Avenue, Madison, Wisconsin, has read the book and been interested enough to send me a rather thorough list of errors in French and German for Sections I and II. In spite of everything there were a hell of a lot of them. I wish you would make a special note to send her page proofs of Sections III and IV the minute they are available, otherwise I am going to get one of those terrible bawlings out like Zelda did. There is a certain sort of critic, who, when he is over his head, takes refuge in school marm quibbling, and another type of reader who is legitimately annoyed by inaccuracy.

—Correspondence of F. Scott Fitzgerald, p. 328

* * *

Shenton decoration, on p. 221 of the first edition (Bruccoli Collection of Fitzgerald, Thomas Cooper Library, University of South Carolina)

In a typed, signed letter, dated 3 February 1934, Fitzgerald replied to Pauline Reinsch, a French student at the University of Wisconsin, Madison, who had written to him offering to provide corrections for the French words in Tender Is the Night. *The extent of her help is unknown, but the novel was published with misspelled French and Italian words.*

I am tremendously obligded to you for your letter of January 21. Though I lived in France for many years and studied French, and previous to that had studied French in America for 8 years, I have never been able to speak anything but pigeon-French, having absolutely no capacity as a linguist save in my own language. Even there I am an erratic speller and often misuse words. I shall, of course, incorporate your corrections in the proof and I am further emboldened by your interest to have advance copies mailed to you of the other two installments of my book, in hope that you might be good enough to note any more terrible errors that you might come across. So as not to trespass too much on your time and patience I am enclosing two self addressed envelopes. I am glad you liked the story and am sorry it is marred for you by these inaccuracies. Of course even after leaving me it goes through the hands of a typist and a printer, who do not speak French, so I do not take complete blame for every mislaid 'e.' However, that can't be explained to the public and the guilt will fall on me.

—Robert F. Batchelder, Catalog 58, Item 179

Shenton decoration, on p. 342 of the first edition (Bruccoli Collection of Fitzgerald,
Thomas Cooper Library, University of South Carolina)

In the following two telegrams and letter, all written on 5 February, Fitzgerald responds to a telegram in which Perkins suggested condensing the scene of the arrest in Cannes to eight hundred words for the magazine installment.

Fitzgerald to Perkins

BALTIMORE MD   1934 FEB 5   AM 1 28
FEEL CANNES JAIL SCENE SHOULD GO INTO SERIAL OPIN-IONS INDICATE SAME OTHERWISE DICKS CHARACTER WEAKENS AND NOVEL FORSHOTENS TOWARD END IT IS NEEDED AND WAS WRITTEN TO BOLSTER HIM UP IN INEVITABLY UNDIGNIFIED CUCKOLD SITUATION STOP PLEASE PERMIT WILL TREAT TACTFULLY WIRE
    FITZGERALD.
            —*Correspondence of F. Scott Fitzgerald*, p. 329
                        * * *

Fitzgerald to Perkins

BALTIMORE MD   1248P   1934 FEB 5   PM 1 29
FEEL DOWNRIGHT ESSENTIAL FOR READER TO GET GLIMPSE OF DICK THROUGH IMPERSONAL EYES NOT TOMMYS AND NICOLES TO SUSTAIN HIM AT THE END OTHERWISE FINAL TRIAL OFF INSPIRES SCORN INSTEAD OF PATHOS CANT REPEAT MISTAKE OF BEAUTIFUL DAMNED STOP SCENE IS FOURTEEN HUNDRED WORDS BUT CANT YOU ARRANGE IT SOMEHOW
    SCOTT.
            —*Correspondence of F. Scott Fitzgerald*, p. 329
                        * * *

Fitzgerald to Perkins, 5 February 1934
Baltimore

Isn't there any mechanical means by which you can arrange to include the 1400 words of the arrest in Cannes? The more I think of it the more I think that it is absolutely necessary for the unity of the book and the effectiveness of the finale to show Dick in the dignified and responsible aspect toward the world and his neighbors that was implied so strongly in the first half of the book. It is all very well to say that this can be remedied in book publication but it has transpired that at least two dozen important writers and newspaper men are reading the book in the serial and will form their impressions from that. I have made cuts in Section IV – a good bit of the last scene between Dick and Tommy but also the proof has swollen somewhat in revision which counteracts that, nor can I reduce the 1250 words of that scene to 800. I am saying 1400 because I know there will be a slight expansion. Couldn't you take out some short piece from the number? Surely it hasn't crystallized at this early date. Even with this addition the installment is shorter than the others, as I promised Fritz.

If I do not hold these two characters to the end of the book it might as well never have been written. It is legitimate to ruin Dick but it is by no means legitimate to make him an ineffectual. In the proof I am pointing up the fact that his intention dominated all this last part but it is not enough and the foreshortening without the use of this scene, which was a part of the book structure from the first, does not contain enough of him for the reader to reconstruct his whole personality as viewed as a unit throughout – and the reason for this is my attempt to tell the last part entirely through Nicole's eyes. I was even going to have her in on the Cannes episode but decided against it because of the necessity of seeing Dick alone.

My feeling about this was precipitated by the remarks of the young psychiatrist who is the only person who had read all the magazine proof and only the magazine proof. He felt a sharp lesion at the end which those who had read the whole novel did not feel.

While I am writing you I may as well cover some other points:

1. Please don't forget the indentation of title and author on the front cover as in previous books. There are other Fitzgeralds writing and I would like my whole name on the outside of the book, and also I would prefer uniformity.

2. Would you please strike off at least three book proofs for me, all to be used for revisions such as medical, linguistic, etc.? Also, I would like an extra galley of book proof Section IV when you have it, for Ober to pass on to Davis in order to supply the missing material.

3. In advertising the book some important points are: Please do not use the phrase 'Riviera' or 'gay resorts.' Not only does it sound like the triviality of which I am so often accused, but also the Riviera has been thoroughly exploited by E. Phillips Oppenheim and a whole generation of writers and its very mention invokes a feeling of unreality and unsubstantiality. So I think it would be best to watch this and reduce it only to the statement that the scenes of the book are laid in Europe. If it could be done, a suggestion that, after a romantic start, a serious story unfolds, would not be amiss; also it might be mentionable that for exigencies of serialization, a scene or two was cut. In general, as you know, I don't approve of great ballyhoo advertisements, even of much quoted praise. The public is very, very, very weary of being sold bogus goods and this inevitably reacts on solider manufactures.

I find that revising in this case is pulling up the weakest section of the book and then the next weakest, etc. First, Section III was the weakest and Section IV the strongest, so I bucked up III, then IV was the weakest and is still but when I have fixed that Section I will be the weakest. The section that has best held up is Section II.

. . . .

Please wire about the inclusion of the Cannes episode, and <u>don't</u> sidetrack these advertising points.
—*F. Scott Fitzgerald: A Life in Letters*, pp. 246–247

* * *

As Tender Is the Night *neared publication in book form, Perkins wrote of his hopes for the novel in a 7 February 1934 letter to Hemingway.*

I believe that Scott will be completely reinstated, if not more, by his "Tender Is the Night". He has improved it immensely by his revision—it was chaotic almost when I read it—and he has made it into a really most extraordinary piece of work.- And I believe when he gets through with revising the first quarter for the book, he will have a genuine masterpiece in its kind.

—*The Only Thing That Counts*, p. 207

Shenton decoration, on p. 361 of the first edition (Bruccoli Collection of Fitzgerald, Thomas Cooper Library, University of South Carolina)

Memorandum of Agreement, *made this*   eighth   *day of*   February   *19*34

between   F. SCOTT FITZGERALD

of Baltimore, Maryland,   -   -   -   -   *hereinafter called "the* AUTHOR*,"*
and CHARLES SCRIBNER'S SONS, *of* New York City, N. Y., *hereinafter called "the*
PUBLISHERS*." Said* -   -   - F. Scott Fitzgerald   -   -   *being the* AUTHOR
and PROPRIETOR   *of a work entitled:*

————————— TENDER IS THE NIGHT —————————

in consideration of the covenants and stipulations hereinafter contained, and agreed to be per-
formed by the PUBLISHERS*, grants and guarantees to said* PUBLISHERS *and their successors the*
exclusive right to publish the said work in all forms during the terms of copyright and renewals
thereof, hereby covenanting with said PUBLISHERS *that he is the sole* AUTHOR *and*
PROPRIETOR *of said work.*

Said AUTHOR   *hereby authorizes said* PUBLISHERS *to take out the copyright on said*
work, and further guarantees to said PUBLISHERS *that the said work is in no way whatever a*
violation of any copyright belonging to any other party, and that it contains nothing of a scandal-
ous or libelous character; and that   he   and his   legal representatives shall and will hold
harmless the said PUBLISHERS *from all suits, and all manner of claims and proceedings which*
may be taken on the ground that said work is such violation or contains anything scandalous or
libelous; and   he   further hereby authorizes said PUBLISHERS *to defend at law any and all*
suits and proceedings which may be taken or had against them for infringement of any other copy-
right or for libel, scandal, or any other injurious or hurtful matter or thing contained in or
alleged or claimed to be contained in or caused by said work, and pay to said PUBLISHERS *such*
reasonable costs, disbursements, expenses, and counsel fees as they may incur in such defense.

Said PUBLISHERS*, in consideration of the right herein granted and of the guarantees*
aforesaid, agree to publish said work at their own expense, in such style and manner as they
shall deem most expedient, and to pay said AUTHOR*,   or his   legal representatives,*
FIFTEEN (15) ————————— *per cent. on their Trade-List (retail) price, cloth style, for*
the first twenty thousand (20,000) copies of said work sold by them in the United
States, SEVENTEEN & ONE-HALF (17½) per cent. for all copies sold thereafter up to forty
thousand(40,000), and TWENTY(20)per cent. for all copies sold beyond forty thousand.

Provided, nevertheless, that one-half the above named royalty shall be paid on all copies sold out-
side the United States; and provided that no percentage whatever shall be paid on any copies
destroyed by fire or water, or sold at or below cost, or given away for the purpose of aiding the
sale of said work.

It is further agreed that the profits arising from any publication of said work, during
the period covered by this agreement, in other than book form shall be divided equally between said
PUBLISHERS *and said* AUTHOR*.*

The contract for Fitzgerald's fourth novel. It was priced at $2.50 a copy; Fitzgerald received a 15 percent royalty,
or 37½¢ for each copy sold. The novel earned $5,104.65 for Fitzgerald in 1934—less than the $6,600
he had been advanced (Princeton University Library).

Expenses incurred for alterations in type or plates, exceeding twenty per cent. of the cost of composition and electrotyping said work, are to be charged to the AUTHOR's account.

The first statement shall not be rendered until six months after date of publication; and thereafter statements shall be rendered semi-annually, on the AUTHOR's application therefor, in the months of February and August; settlements to be made in cash, four months after date of statement.

If, on the expiration of five *years from date of publication, or at any time thereafter, the demand for said work should not, in the opinion of said PUBLISHERS, be sufficient to render its publication profitable, then, upon written notice by said PUBLISHERS to said AUTHOR, this contract shall cease and determine; and thereupon said AUTHOR shall have the right, at* his *option, to take from said PUBLISHERS, at* c *whatever copies of said work they may then have on hand; or, failing to take said copies at cost, then said PUBLISHERS shall have the right to dispose of the copies on hand as they may see fit, free from any percentage or royalty, and to cancel this contract.*

Provided, also, that if, at any time during the continuance of this agreement, said work shall become unsalable in the ordinary channels of trade, said PUBLISHERS shall have the right to dispose of any copies on hand paying to said AUTHOR twenty (20) *per cent. of the net amount received therefor, in lieu of the percentage hereinbefore prescribed.*

Said Publishers shall pay to said Author the sum of Sixty-six Hundred Dollars ($6,600.00), the receipt of which is hereby acknowledged, as an advance payment on royalty account, said amount to be reimbursed to said Publishers from the first moneys accruing under said royalties.

~~All moneys due under this contract shall be paid to Harold Ober, 40 West 49th Street, New York City, as representative of said author, and his receipt shall be a valid discharge for all said moneys.~~

In consideration of the mutuality of this contract, the aforesaid parties agree to all its provisions, and in testimony thereof affix their signatures and seals.

Witness to signature of
F. Scott Fitzgerald

F Scott Fitzgerald

Witness to signature of
Charles Scribner's Sons

[L. S.]

Perkins to Fitzgerald, 14 February 1934

Here are comments from Marjorie Rawlings: "I hear much talk already of 'Tender Is the Night'. I thought, beginning to read it after I had written you, that Fitzgerald had filled the contract I was setting up for myself – a book disturbing, bitter and beautiful. I am totally unable to analyze the almost overpowering effect that some of his passages create – some of them about quite trivial people and dealing with trivial situations. There is something terrifying about it when it happens, and the closest I can come to understanding it is to think that he does, successfully at such times, what I want to do – that is, visualizes the people not in their immediate setting, from the human point of view – but in time and space – almost, you might say, with the divine detachment. The effect is very weird when he does it with unimportant people moving in a superficial and sophisticated setting. I shouldn't put it that way, for of course importance and un-importance are relative – if they exist at all."

–Dear Scott/Dear Max, p. 193

* * *

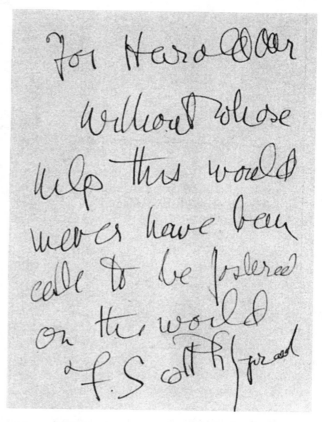

Fitzgerald's inscription to his agent. This inscribed copy of the novel was offered for sale for $85,000 by a dealer in 2001 (from As Ever, Scott Fitz–, *1972).*

On 12 February 1934 Zelda reentered Phipps after her third breakdown. In March she was transferred to Craig House, a sanitarium in Beacon, New York.

Fitzgerald to Ober, 21 February 1934

WANT TO DECIDE NOW HOW TO RAISE MONEY TO TIDE ME OVER THE MONTH BEFORE FINISHING FINAL BOOK REVISION WITHOUT CONSULTING MAX CAN YOU GET OPINION OF ONE PROMINENT PLAYWRIGHT ABOUT POSSIBILITIES OF DRAMATIZATION OTHERWISE I WOULD RATHER SHOOT THE WORKS AND SELL TO THE PICTURES TO GET OUT OF THIS FINANCIAL HOLE IT MUST BE DECIDED IMMEDIATELY LUNCHING WITH CLARK GABLE TOMORROW AND WANT TO KNOW PRESENT STATUS OF GATSDY AS HE WOULD LIKE TO PLAY IT PLEASE WIRE IMMEDIATELY

F SCOTT FITZGERALD

–F. Scott Fitzgerald: A Life in Letters, p. 248

Harold Ober, Fitzgerald's agent (Bruccoli Collection of Fitzgerald, Thomas Cooper Library, University of South Carolina)

Fitzgerald to Edmund Wilson, circa 12 March 1934 Baltimore

Despite your intention of mild criticism in our conversation, I felt more elated than otherwise—if the characters got real enough so that you disagreed with what I chose for their manifest destiny the main purpose was accomplished. (By the way, your notion that Dick should have faded out as a shyster alienist was in my original design, but I thought of him, in reconsideration, as an 'homme épuisé,' not only an 'homme manqué.' I thought that, since his choice of a profession had accidentally wrecked him, he might plausibly have walked out on the profession itself.)

Any attempt by an author to explain away a partial failure in a work is of course doomed to absurdity—yet I could wish that you, and others, had read the book version rather than the magazine version which in spots was hastily put together. The last half for example has a <u>much</u> more polished facade now. Oddly enough several people have felt that the surface of the first chapters was <u>too</u> ornate. One man even advised me to 'coarsen the texture,' as being remote from the speed of the main narrative!

In any case when it appears I hope you'll find time to look it over again. Such irrelevancies as Morton Hoyt's nose-dive and Dick's affair in Inns-

---

Fitzgerald's Revisions of the Serial

In his letter to Wilson, Fitzgerald provides a helpful but inaccurate explanation of his purpose in revising the serial. The most densely revised section of the novel is Book I; and within it the first eighteen chapters, which correspond to the first serial installment, have an even greater concentration of revisions. The first installment had been the one least revised in serial galley proof; yet, Fitzgerald felt that it had not achieved the same state of finish as the others and took the opportunity to claim that "the last half . . . has a much more polished facade now." Fitzgerald did comparatively little polishing in the later sections of the book. He did omit four scenes from Book II, but this is not the same as revising. It may be, as his reference to the Beaulieu scene indicates, that Fitzgerald forgot he had made his heavy revisions of the last half before serial publication.

---

bruck are out, together with the scene of calling on the retired bootlegger at Beaulieu, and innumerable minor details. I have driven the Scribner proofreaders half nuts but I think I've made it incomparably smoother.

—*F. Scott Fitzgerald: A Life in Letters,* p. 250

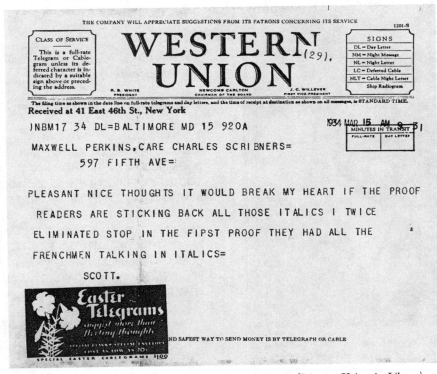

Fitzgerald was concerned about editorial tampering with his text (Princeton University Library).

Dear Scott:

Thanks for your note. It's good to hear from you again. I'll be delighted to visit Zelda's exhibition when I'm in town. I live in Brooklyn now and it's sometimes hard to get over to Manhattan in daytime, but I should like to see her painting before the exhibition is over.

Scott, I want to tell you how glad I am that your book is being published next month, and also what a fine book it is. I read it as it came out in <u>Scribner's Magazine</u> and even read the proofs of the last two installments. I tell you this because I got the jump on most readers in this way. I thought you'd be interested to know that the people in the book are even more real and living now than they were at the time I read it. It seems to me you've gone deeper in this book than in anything you ever wrote. I don't pretend to know anything about the book business and have no idea whether it will have a big sale or not, but I do know that other people are going to feel about it as I do. I think it's the best work you've done so far, and I know you'll understand what I mean and won't mind if I get a kind of selfish hope and joy out of your own success. I have sweated blood these last four years on an enormous manuscript of my own, and the knowledge that you have now come through with this fine book makes me want to cheer. I felt a personal interest in parts of the book where you described places we had been together, particularly Glion and Caux and that funicular that goes up the mountain. I don't think anyone will know just how good that piece of writing is unless he has been there.

This is all for the present. I am still working like hell but I'd like to see you if you come up here. Meanwhile, I am wishing for the best kind of success in every way for your book when it is published.

Yours,

A March 1934 letter from Wolfe (from The Romantic Egoists*)*

*Shenton decoration, on p. 385 of the first edition (Bruccoli Collection,
Thomas Cooper Library, University of South Carolina)*

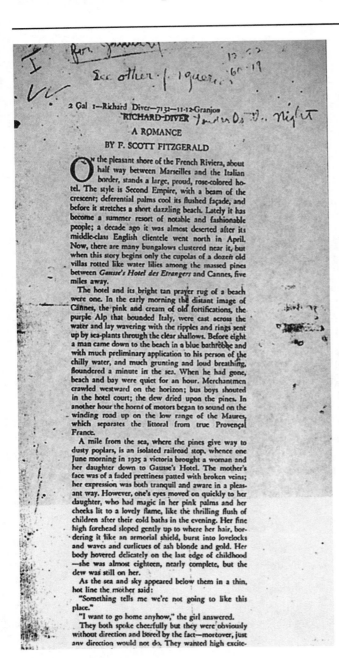

First page of galley with the title alteration from the serialization in Scribner's Magazine *(Bruccoli Collection of Fitzgerald, Thomas Cooper Library, University of South Carolina)*

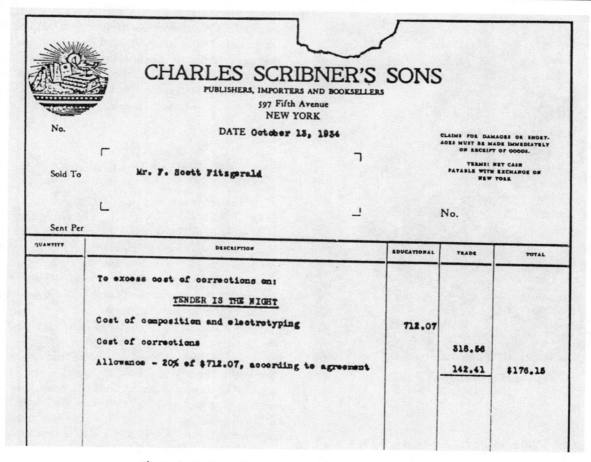

The invoice for Fitzgerald's proof revisions (Princeton University Library)

**Fitzgerald to John Peale Bishop, 2 April 1934
Baltimore**

Two things I forgot to say—

1. There's a deliberate choice in my avoidance of a dramatic ending—I deliberately did not want it.

2. Without making apologies, I'd prefer to <u>fade off</u> my book, like the last of <u>The Brothers Karanzoff</u>, or <u>Time Regained</u>, and let the belly carry my story, than to resort the arbitrary blood-letting of Flaubert, Stendahl and the Elizabethans.

You see we must talk—no room in a letter.

F. S. F.

—*F. Scott Fitzgerald: A Life in Letters,* p. 253

* * *

John Peale Bishop to Fitzgerald, 3 April 1934

I come fresh from reading *Tender Is the Night* and am overcome with the magnificence of it. It surpasses *The Great Gatsby.* You have shown us, what we have wanted so long and impatiently to see, that you are a true, a beautiful and a tragic novelist. I have only praise for its understanding, its characterization and its deep tenderness. I write you much enthusiasm.

—*Correspondence of F. Scott Fitzgerald,* p. 339

* * *

Bishop received Fitzgerald's 2 April 1934 letter after he had mailed his first letter about the novel.

John Peale Bishop to Fitzgerald, 4 April 1934

It is true that the tone of the first section bothered me when I read it in Scribner's. But I know now that it was right—to see the Drivers through Rosemary's romantic and naive eyes. And as for the end of your novel, I don't see how it could be bettered. It moved me profoundly.

—*Correspondence of F. Scott Fitzgerald,* p. 340

* * *

*Zelda and F. Scott Fitzgerald in a publicity
photo taken for the novel*

Fitzgerald to John Peale Bishop, 7 April 1934 Baltimore

On receiving your first letter with its' handsome tribute and generous praise I realized that I had been hasty in crediting that you would make such a criticism as "this book is no advance on <u>Gatsby.</u>" You would be the first to feel that the intention in the two books was entirely different, that (to promote myself momentarily) <u>Gatsby</u> was shooting at something like <u>Henry Esmond</u> while this was shooting at something like <u>Vanity Fair.</u> The dramatic novel has cannons quite different from the philosophical, now called psychological novel. One is a kind of <u>tour de force</u> and the other a confession of faith. It would be like comparing a sonnet sequence with an epic.

The point of my letter which survives is that there were moments all through the book where I could have pointed up dramatic scenes, and I <u>deliberately</u> refrained from doing so because the material itself was so harrowing and highly charged that I did not want to subject the reader to a series of nervous shocks in a novel that was inevitably close to whoever read it in my generation.

—contrariwise, in dealing with figures as remote as are a bootlegger-crook to most of us, I was not afraid of heightening and melodramatizing any scenes; and I was thinking that in your novel I would like to pass on

this theory to you for what it is worth. Such advice from fellow-craftsmen has been a great help to me in the past, indeed, I believe it was Ernest Hemingway who developed to me, in conversation, that the dying fall was preferable to the dramatic ending under certain conditions, and I think we both got the germ of the idea from Conrad.

—*F. Scott Fitzgerald: A Life in Letters,* p. 255

Book Publication

Tender Is the Night *was published on 12 April 1934 at $2.50. It had been nine years since* The Great Gatsby. *One of the myths about Fitzgerald is that the novel was a failure when it was published. It was a failure in terms of Fitzgerald's expectations; otherwise, it had a respectable sale for a Depression-year novel. The first printing of 7,600 copies sold out promptly, and in the spring there were two more printings of 5,075 and 2,520 copies.* Tender Is the Night *was tenth on the* Publishers' Weekly *best-seller lists for April and May. Even so, the royalties did not pay off Fitzgerald's advances.*

John O'Hara *endorsed the generally held view that* Tender Is the Night *was a victim of the Depression: "The book came out at precisely the wrong time in the national history. No matter how good it was, it was about the Bad People, the well fed, well housed, well educated, well born—the villains of the depression. It was a time for Odets and the imitators of Odets, and of Steinbeck and the imitators of Steinbeck . . . I am proud to say I did not go along with the gutless thinking that all but destroyed TENDER IS THE NIGHT and without a doubt broke Fitzgerald's heart" (*Selected Letters of John O'Hara, *p. 266).*

A Bibliographic Description of the First Edition

The following description is adapted from the revised edition of F. Scott Fitzgerald: A Descriptive Bibliography, *by Matthew J. Bruccoli, published in 1987 by the University of Pittsburgh Press.*

A15.1.a
First edition, first printing (1934)
7 3/8" x 5 1/8"

[i–x] [1–2] 3–148 [149–150] 151–306 [307–308] 309–408 [409–410]
[1–25]⁸ [26]¹⁰

Contents: pp. i–iii: blank; p. iv: 'BY F. SCOTT FITZGERALD | [eight titles]'; p. v: half title; p. vi:

epigraph from "Ode to a Nightingale"; p. vii: title; p. viii: copyright; p. ix: 'TO | GERALD AND SARA | MANY FÊTES'; p. x: blank; p. 1: 'TENDER IS THE NIGHT | BOOK ONE'; p. 2: blank; pp. 3–408: text; p. 149: 'BOOK II'; p. 307: 'BOOK III'; pp. 409–410: blank.

Typography and paper: 10½ point on 11½, Old Style. Pen and ink drawings by Edward Shenton. 5½" (6") x 3 11/16"; thirty-three lines per page. Running heads: rectos and versos, 'TENDER IS THE NIGHT'. Wove paper.

Binding: Dark bluish green (#165) B cloth (linen-like grain) or T cloth (vertical lines). Front has blind-stamped single-rule frame. Spine goldstamped: 'TEN-DER | IS THE | NIGHT | [rule] | Fitzgerald | SCRIBNERS'. White wove endpapers of coated stock. Top and bottom edges trimmed.

Dust jacket: Front has drawing of Riviera scene: '[yellow] F. SCOTT FITZGERALD | [white rule] | [red] TENDER IS | THE NIGHT'. Spine: '[red] TENDER | IS THE | NIGHT | [yellow] F. SCOTT | FITZGERALD | [red] SCRIBNERS'. Back has profile drawings of Fitzgerald and blurb for *TITN*. Front flap has blurbs by T. S. Eliot, H. L. Mencken, and Paul Rosenfeld; back flap lists books by Fitzgerald. A later jacket exists with blurbs by Padraic Colum, Gilbert Seldes, and Marjorie Kinnan Rawlings on front flap.

Publication: 7,600 copies of the front printing. Published 12 April 1934. $2.50. Copyright #A72045.

Printing: Printed by the Scribner Press from plates made and typeset by Brown Bros. Linotypers. Bound by the Scribner Press. (The cost of composition and electrotyping was $712.07; the cost of corrections was $318.56.)

Locations: LC (APR 14 1934–B cloth); Lilly (B cloth, dj); MJB (B cloth and T cloth, both with dj); PSt (B cloth).

Review copy
Bound in wrappers made from the dust jacket. The Scribners records indicate that 500 copies in wrappers were ordered. Locations: C. Burden; MJB; ViU.

A15.1.b.
Second printing: New York: Scribners, 1934. Not differentiated on copyright page, except that the 'A' is removed. April 1934. 5,075 copies.

A15.1.c
Third printing: New York: Scribners, 1934. Not differentiated on copyright page. May 1934. 2,520 copies.

There is one plate alteration between the second and third printings:

  320.17 Charles [Devereux

Location: NjP (Fitzgerald's marked copy).

A15.1.d
Fourth printing: New York: Scribners, 1951. Omits illustrations. The following plate alterations were made in this printing:

vii FÊTES [FÉTES *[possibly batter]*
344.7 Saland [Salaud

A15.1.e
First edition, fifth printing (1995)

F. Scott Fitzgerald | TENDER IS THE NIGHT | A Romance | Text established by Matthew J. Bruccoli | London: Samuel Johnson, 1995
'This volume reproduces the editor's marked copy of the first printing of *Tender Is the Night,* providing the emendations required for a critical edition.' See Matthew J. Bruccoli and Judith S. Baughman, *Reader's Companion to F. Scott Fitzgerald's* Tender Is the Night (Columbia: University of South Carolina Press, 1996).

Note one: See Bruccoli, *The Composition of* Tender Is the Night (Pittsburgh, Pa.: University of Pittsburgh Press, 1963) and "Material for a Centenary Edition of *Tender Is the Night,*" *Studies in Bibliography,* 17 (1964), 177–193.

Note two: *TITN* was serialized in four installments of *Scribner's Magazine,* 95 (January–April 1934). The text was slightly bowdlerized.

Note three: *TITN* was a Literary Guild alternate in June 1934.

Note four: See Malcolm Lowry and Margerie Bonner Lowry, *Notes on a Screenplay for F. Scott Fitzgerald's* Tender Is the Night (Bloomfield Hills, Mich. & Columbia, S.C.: Bruccoli Clark, 1976). Introduction by Paul Tiessen.

Note five: A facsimile of the first printing was produced by Collector's Reprints (Shelton, Conn.) in 1991. The volume is identified as a facsimile on the copyright page; the dust jacket is identified by 'F•E•L' on the back flap. Slipcase with facsimiles of front and back dust jacket.

Dust jacket for Fitzgerald's fourth novel (Bruccoli Collection of Fitzgerald, Thomas Cooper Library, University of South Carolina)

Tender Is the Night

A Romance *by*

F. SCOTT FITZGERALD

To the generation that was young when "This Side of Paradise" came out, the name Fitzgerald is still perhaps associated with adolescence, and with the Jazz Age to which he gave the name in his "Tales of the Jazz Age." The author was twenty-two when he wrote "This Side of Paradise." He had attained to full maturity when he wrote "The Great Gatsby." The estimates of his present position and promise are suggested by these more recent opinions:

T. S. Eliot: "I have been waiting impatiently for another book by Mr. Scott Fitzgerald; with more eagerness and curiosity than I should feel towards the work of any of his contemporaries, except that of Mr. Ernest Hemingway."

H. L. Mencken: "His whole attitude has changed from that of a brilliant improvisateur to that of a painstaking and conscientious artist."

Paul Rosenfeld: "Not a contemporary American senses as thoroughly in every fiber the tempo of privileged post-adolescent America."

All who truly care about the future of American letters have awaited Mr. Fitzgerald's new novel with great expectations. Here these expectations are fulfilled.

A description of "Tender Is the Night" appears on the back of this jacket.

Earliest front flap

Tender Is the Night

A Romance *by*

F. SCOTT FITZGERALD

"This book shows its author's distinctive gifts—a romantic imagination, a style that is often brilliant, a swiftness of movement, and a sense of enchantment in people and places, all of which combine to give his books the great merit of being always entertaining."
—MARY COLUM in *The Forum*.

"The consummation of all Scott Fitzgerald's works, the novel which every one who understood 'The Great Gatsby' was sure he would have to write. It shows again his prodigious talent; his skill in inventing action and his brilliance in realizing characters were never at a higher point. With "Tender Is the Night" Fitzgerald moves confidently forward to his natural place at the head of the American novelists of our time." —GILBERT SELDES.

"Disturbing, bitter, and beautiful. I am totally unable to analyze the almost overpowering effect that some of his passages create. There is something terrifying about it, and the closest I can come to understanding it is to think that he visualizes people not in their immediate setting, from the human point of view—but in time and space—almost, you might say, with the divine detachment."
—MARJORIE KINNAN RAWLINGS.

Later front flap

Fitzgerald asked to have the Eliot statement on the dust jacket replaced because it had been printed without Eliot's permission. It is not known why the quotations from H. L. Mencken and Paul Rosenfeld were replaced (Bruccoli Collection of Fitzgerald, Thomas Cooper Library, University of South Carolina).

Reception of *Tender Is the Night*

An Overview
Matthew J. Bruccoli

Despite the expectations that had been aroused during the nine-year interval after *The Great Gatsby,* the reviews of *Tender Is the Night* were restrained. In the June number of the *North American Review,* Herschel Brickell mentioned "the kind of violent arguments that have been going on about *Tender Is the Night";*[1] since there was no controversy in print—only disagreement— the "violent argument" presumably raged orally among readers. Disagreement about the merits of the novel has continued since 1934.

Discussions of the novel habitually return to the initial reception of *Tender,* a topic which provides its own controversy. One of the commonplaces of Fitzgerald criticism is that *Tender* failed in 1934 because the critics ganged up on it and dismissed the novel as politically irrelevant. As Cowley explained in his 1951 introduction to "The Author's Final Version," "It dealt with fashionable life in the 1920s at a time when most readers wanted to forget that they had ever been concerned with frivolities; the new fashion was for novels about destitution and revolt. . . . most reviewers implied that it belonged to the bad old days before the crash. . . . "[2] Fitzgerald's friends Budd Schulberg and John O'Hara supported Cowley's conclusion. O'Hara wrote in 1968:

> . . . after *The Great Gatsby* he had toiled and sweated over *Tender Is the Night,* which I considered far and away his best novel. As a favor to Fitzgerald I had read proof on *Tender Is the Night,* galleys and page proofs, and I was shocked and probably frightened by what the critics and the public had done to it and to him. People from whom he had the right to expect respectful treatment were condescending or worse. . . .[3]

According to this influential interpretation the critics compounded their socio-political prejudice with obtuseness by claiming to find difficulty with the simple flashback structure. The reviewers were allegedly abetted by the reading public, which rejected Fitzgerald in favor of social tracts. Depending upon whether one is listening to a revisionist or anti-revisionist, the accord between the opinion makers and readers either revealed to Fitzgerald what was wrong with the structure of *Tender,* or their response so befuddled his critical judgement so that he subsequently attempted to restructure *Tender* in straight chronology.

Like many biographical-critical explanations of Fitzgerald's literary conduct, these alternatives combine fact with romantic invention. Fitzgerald's most ambitious novel sold disappointingly in its own time; yet,

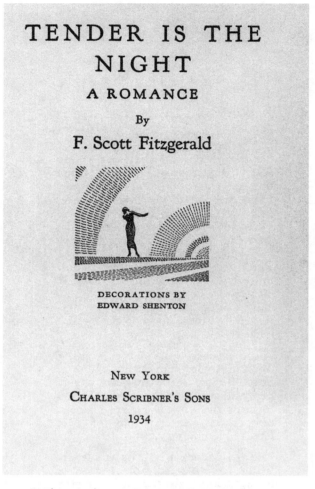

Title page (Bruccoli Collection of Fitzgerald, Thomas Cooper Library, University of South Carolina)

three printings totaling 14,595 copies was not a catastrophic sale in 1934. The reception hurt and puzzled Fitzgerald, but it is not demonstrable that he was the victim of a critical conspiracy. The notices were mainly favorable, and there was little complaint about the setting or the flashback. Some of the mainly favorable reviews patronized Fitzgerald, but critics had patronized him in the Twenties.

Examination of the best-selling novels of 1934 provides no support for the notion that readers of the Depression rejected *Tender* because they preferred proletarian fiction: Hervey Allen's *Anthony Adverse,* Caroline Miller's *Lamb in His Bosom* (Pulitzer Prize), Stark Young's *So Red the Rose,* James Hilton's *Good-bye, Mr. Chips,* Margaret Ayers Barne's *Within This Present,* Sinclair Lewis's *Work of Art,* Phyllis Bottome's *Private Worlds,* Mary Ellen Chase's *Mary Peters,* Alice Tisdale Hobart's *Oil for the Lamps of China,* and Isak Dinesen's *Seven Gothic Tales.* The three top sellers of the year were

C. Hartley Grattan and Edward Weeks, reviewers who commented on the flashback structure of Tender Is the Night

historical novels, and the number-four was Hilton's sentimental story about a schoolmaster.

People who lament the commercial failure of *Tender* usually ignore the circumstance that Fitzgerald had never written a prodigious seller: *This Side of Paradise* sold about 41,000 copies in 1920; *The Beautiful and Damned* sold about 50,000 copies in 1922; and *The Great Gatsby* about 23,000 copies in 1925. During his lifetime Fitzgerald was much better known as a magazine story writer than as a novelist.

Four days after publication, John Chamberlain commented in *The New York Times* on the responses of his fellow reviewers:

> The critical reception of F. Scott Fitzgerald's "Tender Is the Night" might serve as the basis for one of those cartoons on "Why Men Go Mad." No two reviews were alike; no two had the same tone.[4]

Of twenty-four reviews by influential critics or by critics appearing in influential American periodicals, nine were favorable, six were unfavorable, and nine were mixed. Gilbert Seldes, who was Fitzgerald's

friend, recognized *Tender* as "a great novel": "He has gone behind generations, old or new, and created his own image of human beings. And in doing so has stepped again to his natural place at the head of the American writers of our time."

Three reviews commented on the flashback:

> C. Harley Grattan, "The integral significance of the opening pages of the book has been missed by most reviewers."[5]

> Edward Weeks, "Don't make up your mind until you have read past page 151!"[6]

> John Chamberlain, "At this point one could almost guarantee that "Tender Is the Night" is going to be a failure. But, as a matter of fact, the novel does not really begin until Rosemary is more or less out of the way."[7]

Cowley's *New Republic* review analyzed Fitzgerald's apparent indecision between writing a psychological or a social novel. Fitzgerald thought of it as a dramatic novel. Then Cowley offered a theory that

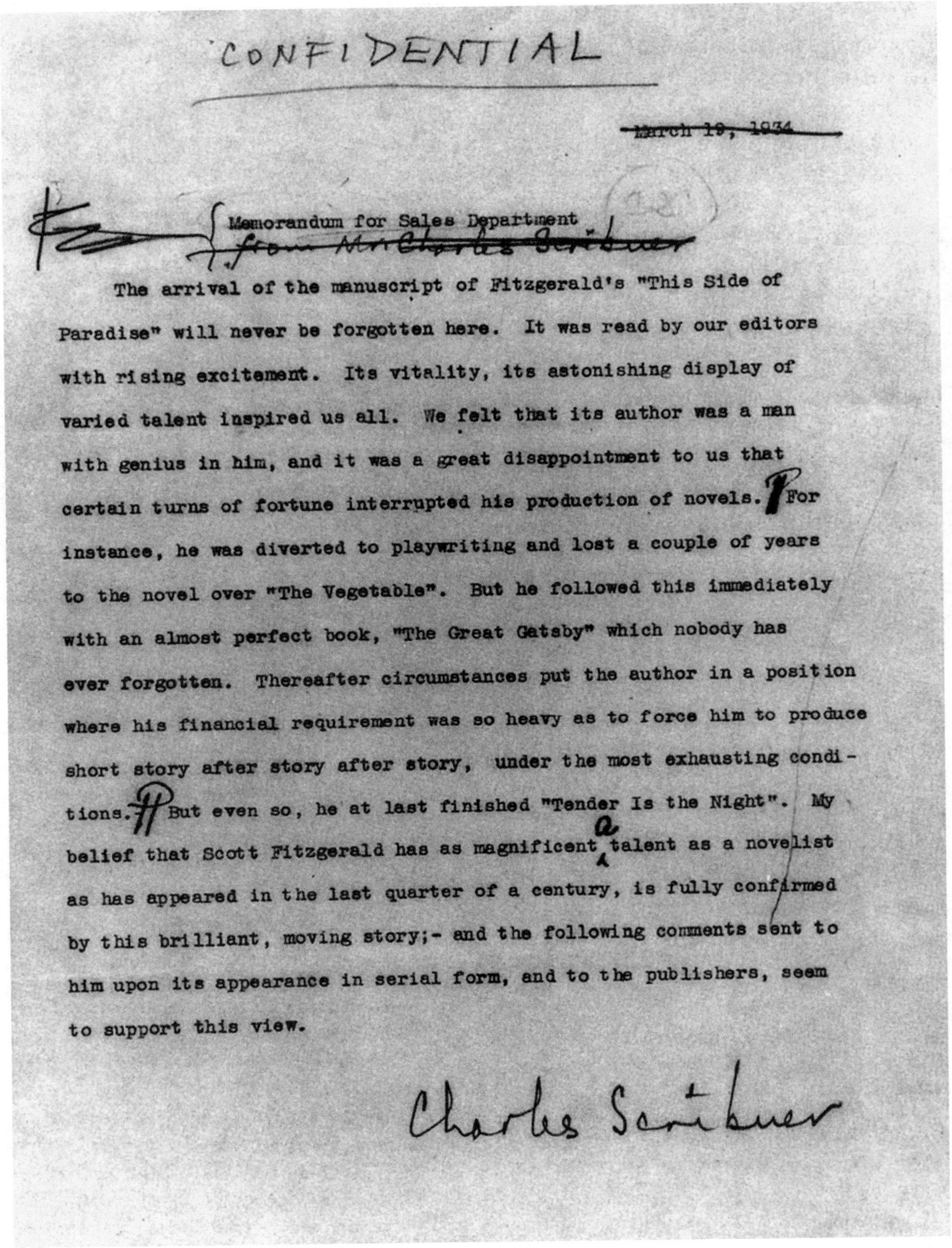

CONFIDENTIAL

March 19, 1934

Memorandum for Sales Department
from Mr Charles Scribner

The arrival of the manuscript of Fitzgerald's "This Side of Paradise" will never be forgotten here. It was read by our editors with rising excitement. Its vitality, its astonishing display of varied talent inspired us all. We felt that its author was a man with genius in him, and it was a great disappointment to us that certain turns of fortune interrupted his production of novels. For instance, he was diverted to playwriting and lost a couple of years to the novel over "The Vegetable". But he followed this immediately with an almost perfect book, "The Great Gatsby" which nobody has ever forgotten. Thereafter circumstances put the author in a position where his financial requirement was so heavy as to force him to produce short story after story after story, under the most exhausting conditions. But even so, he at last finished "Tender Is the Night". My belief that Scott Fitzgerald has as magnificent a talent as a novelist as has appeared in the last quarter of a century, is fully confirmed by this brilliant, moving story;- and the following comments sent to him upon its appearance in serial form, and to the publishers, seem to support this view.

Charles Scribner

Statement of Charles Scribner III expressing the pride his company took in publishing
Fitzgerald's work (Princeton University Library)

Zelda Fitzgerald wrote to her husband in April 1934 from Craig House, Beacon, New York.

Dear—The book is grand. The emotional lift sustained by the force of a fine poetic prose and the characters *subserviated* to forces stronger than their interpretations of life is very moving. It is tear-evoking to witness individual belief in individual volition succumbing to the purpose of a changing world. That is the purpose of a good book and you have written it— Those people are helpless before themselves and the prose is beautiful and there is manifest an integrity in the belief of both those expressions. It is a reverential and very fine book and the first literary contribution to what writers will be concerning themselves with some years from now.

—*Correspondence of F. Scott Fitzgerald,* p. 341

---

acquired currency: that as the novel developed through its several versions during the years of writing, the early sections crystallized so that Fitzgerald was unable to unify them with the later sections.[8]

Two reviews complained about the expatriate material from the Twenties. The unsigned *News-Week* review was headlined "A Sinful, Ginful Tale" and noted that "it is a long time since the decay of American expatriates on the Riviera was hot news."[9] In *The Daily Worker,* the journal of the American Communist Party, Philip Rahv admonished: "Dear Mr. Fitzgerald, you can't hide from a hurricane under a beach umbrella."[10]

Seven reviewers (Mary Colum, Henry Seidel Canby, Clifton Fadiman, J. Donald Adams, Horace Gregory, William Troy, and Edith Walton) expressed reservations about the credibility of Dick Diver and his crack-up. In *The New Yorker* Clifton Fadiman cited the absence of a psychoanalytic approach to Diver:

Dick's rapid acceptance of his failure, for instance, is not convincing; there must have been some fundamental weakness in his early youth to account for his defeatism. . . . The events of the narrative, tragic as they are, are insufficient to motivate his downfall. It is the failure to reach far, far back into his characters' lives that helps prevent this novel from being the first-rate work of fiction we have been expecting from F. Scott Fitzgerald.[11]

Fadiman also complained about the sloppy copyediting and listed thirteen errors. Henry Seidel Canby in *The Saturday Review of Literature* also criticized Fitzgerald for inadequate or unclear causality:

What begins as a study of a subtle relationship ends as the accelerating decline into nothingness of Dr. Driver (sic)—not for no reason, but for too many reasons, no one of which is dominant. This book may be life with its veil over causality, but it is not art which should pierce that veil.[12]

J. Donald Adams's review in the Sunday *New York Times Book Review* charged that Nicole and Rosemary were unconvincing and that Dick's collapse was contrived. The following day Chamberlain interrupted his *Times* review of Faulkner's *Dr. Martino* to defend the effectiveness of Diver's characterization.

The question about the hero's deterioration and collapse were the most serious challenges to the achievement of *Tender*. The flashback structure was meant to reinforce the terror of Dick's destruction. If Fitzgerald believed that the critics were right about Dick Diver, he had to blame the structure. They weren't right.

The two reviews in the papers in Fitzgerald's hometown, St. Paul, Minnesota, were strongly negative.[13] Both James Gray ("This is a big, sprawling, undisciplined, badly coordinated book") and H. A. MacMillan ("the obscure manner in which the narrative is developed") denounced the structure. The unsigned review in *The Princeton Alumni Weekly* commented on the structural disagreements engendered by the novel: "*Tender Is the Night* lacks unity in the ordinary sense of the word; the debate of the reviewers is concerned with whether or not Mr. Fitzgerald has achieved a unity less conventional but not less servicable."[14] The most thorough defense of Fitzgerald's structure appeared in *The Modern Monthly,* a Marxist journal, some three months after publication of *Tender.* C. Hartley Grattan observed:

The integral significance of the opening pages of the book has been missed by most reviewers. Almost to a man they have complained that the stress laid upon Rosemary, the beautiful cinema star, is unjustified by the future action of the story, that the pages devoted to building her up are really wasted effort, and that they "throw the reader off." Rather I should say that in these pages Fitzgerald is presenting the type of girl who, in the past, has always been foreordained to absorption into the world of his characters. . . . Seen through his eyes, however, what glamour remains can legitimately be exploited and by the same token, the tragedy of its actuality can be all the more accentuated.

After quoting Fitzgerald's explication of Nicole's spending habits ("For her sake trains began their run at Chicago. . . ."), Grattan concluded his review:

This is perceptive writing and I should like to stress for the benefit of those austere individuals who see in the bourgeois world nothing but filth and corruption the significance of the words "feverish bloom" and "grace." Only a person utterly insensitive to the grace and beauty of the way of life open to the leisured will fail to see that even in decay these people are infinitely charming, insidiously beguiling to all but seagreen incorruptibles.[15]

The attacks on the verisimilitude of Diver's decline probably troubled Fitzgerald more than anything else the critics wrote. On 23 April he sent H. L. Mencken—who had not reviewed *Tender*—an eloquent defense of the novel's construction:

. . . . I would like to say in regard to my book that there was a deliberate intention in every part of it except the first. The first part, the romantic introduction, was too long and too elaborated, largely because of the fact that it had been written over a series of years with varying plans, but everything else in the book conformed to a *definite intention* and if I had to start to write it again tomorrow I would adopt the same plan, irrespective of the fact of whether I had, in this case, brought it off or not brought it off. That is what most of the critics fail to understand (outside of the fact that they fail to recognize and identify anything in the book) that the motif of the "dying fall" was absolutely deliberate and did not come from any diminution of vitality, but from a definite plan.

That particular trick is one that Ernest Hemmingway and I worked out—probably from Conrad's preface to "The Nigger"—and it has been the greatest "credo" in my life, ever since I decided that I would rather be an artist than a careerist. I would rather impress my image (even though an image the size of a nickel) upon the soul of a people than be known, except in so far as I have my natural obligation to my family—to provide for them. I would as soon be anonymous as Rimbaud, if I could feel that I had accomplished that purpose—and that is no sentimental yapping about being disinterested. It is simply that having once found the intensity of art, nothing else that can happen in life can ever again seem as important as the creative process.[16]

This statement indicates that Fitzgerald's subsequent attempt to reorganize the novel resulted from his desire to reinforce the documentation of Diver's decline by putting together all the information about him—not from his decision that the flashback structure was confusing.

Fitzgerald took satisfaction from the anonymous 1935 review in the *Journal of Nervous and Mental Disease,* which concluded: "an achievement which no student of the psychobiological sources of human

---

Fitzgerald kept this 11 April 1934 letter from James Branch Cabell in his scrapbook.

Dear Scott Fitzgerald:
    Completely, admiringly, and a bit enviously, have I relished each page of Tender Is the Night. I think it a superb piece of writing—solid (in the word's best sense), urbane, true, and unfailingly picturesque. To call it your best book were mere idle understatement: it is immeasurably your best book.
    All luck to it and you. And all my thanks for remembering me thus handsomely, in a fashion so pleasure giving.

                    —*Correspondence of F. Scott Fitzgerald,* p. 342

---

behavior, and of its particular social correlates extant today, can afford not to read.[17]

Tender Is the Night was published in England in September 1934, and the located reviews[18] resembled the American reception. D. W. Harding asserted in *Scrutiny* that Fitzgerald had not supplied any cause for Diver's crack-up; yet he admits that he had been moved against his will by Diver's fate, and he concludes by echoing Fitzgerald's style: ". . . I am prepared to be told that this attempt at analysis is itself childish—an attempt to assure myself that the magician didn't really cut the lady's head off, did he? I still believe there was a trick in it."[19] The trick usually goes under the name of genius.

Reviewers who questioned the convincingness of Diver's crack-up may really have been troubled by the chronological flaws in *Tender*. It is difficult for the reader to gauge the velocity of the hero's deterioration because the time signals are inadequate and contradictory. For example, it is unclear whether the novel ends in summer 1929 or summer 1930—before or after the Wall Street Crash—a meaningful matter in a novel about the effects of many on character.

The reception and subsequent reputation of *Tender Is the Night* were damaged by its many errors of fact and spelling. The text requires some substantive emendation including time-scheme adjustments. Fitzgerald was a social historian who used details purposefully but nonetheless got them wrong. The attentive reader who knows the things Fitzgerald wrote about and understands how the meaning of fiction and its verisimilitude are reinforced by accurate data is distracted—or worse—by authorial errors. There is no alibi or defense for Fitzgerald's lapses.

Notes

1. 237, pp. 569–570.

2. Introduction, *Tender Is the Night: With the Author's Final Revisions* (New York: Scribners, 1951), p. x.

3. "Hello Hollywood Good-Bye," *Holiday,* 43 (May 1968), 54–55, 125–126, 128–129.

4. "Books of the Times" (16 April 1934), 15.

5. C. Hartley Grattan, *Modern Monthly,* 8 (July 1934), 375–377.

6. Edward Weeks, *Atlantic Monthly,* 153 (April 1934), 17.

7. John Chamberlain, *New York Times* (13 April 1934), 17.

8. Malcolm Cowley, *New Republic,* 79 (6 June 1934), 105–106.

9. *News-Week,* 3 (14 April 1934), 39–40.

10. Philip Rahv, *Daily Worker* (5 May 1934), 7.

11. Clifton Fadiman, *New Yorker,* 10 (14 April 1934), 112–115.

12. Henry Seidel Canby, *Saturday Review of Literature,* 10 (14 April 1934), 630–631.

13. Gray, *St. Paul Daily News* (12 April 1934), I, 8; Mac-Millan, *St. Paul Daily News* (22 April 1934), magazine section, 4.

14. 34 (4 May 1934), 665.

15. Grattan, *Modern Monthly,* 8 (July 1934), 375–377.

16. *A Life in Letters,* pp. 255–256.

17. 82 (July 1935), 115–117.

18. Peter Quennell, *New Statesman & Nation,* 7 (28 April 1934), 642; E. B. C. Jones, *New Statesman & Nation,* 8 (22 September 1934), 364–366.

19. D. W. Harding, *Scrutiny,* 3 (December 1934), 316–319.

Fitzgerald's inscription in The Great Gatsby *to a newspaper book reviewer (courtesy of Glenn Horowitz)*

American Reviews

*Gilbert Seldes, critic, editor, and cultural historian (*The Seven Lively Arts*), was probably the first critic to identify Fitzgerald's high stature. His review of* The Great Gatsby *stated that "Fitzgerald has more than matured; he has mastered his talents and gone soaring on a beautiful flight, leaving behind him everything dubious and tricky in his earlier work, and leaving further behind all the men of his own generation and most of his elders" (*The Dial, *August 1925).*

True to Type—Scott Fitzgerald Writes Superb Tragic Novel

Gilbert Seldes

New York Evening Journal, 12 April 1934, p. 23

About ten years ago I met Scott Fitzgerald because he wanted to meet anyone who thought as little of his work as I did. It was the time when we were getting up lists of people and marking them plus and minus.

Fitzgerald had published "This Side of Paradise" and "The Beautiful and Damned" and one of two volumes of short stories and was generally the top boy of young American letters—and I gave him minus 90 per cent.

No explanations went with the ratings, but in my own mind I said that he had more talent—more positive genius—than anyone else writing in America and was throwing it away on everything trivial and insignificant.

Three years or so later Fitzgerald wrote "The Great Gatsby," the turning point in his career, the first novel which indicated that he could control all his powers and would eventually write a great novel.

Now he has written the great novel: "Tender Is the Night."

The publishers, Scribners, sent me an advance copy about two weeks ago and I read this beautiful and profoundly tragic story at once. It has been in my mind ever since. You feel, as you read it, that you will never forget it.

This is exactly the reverse of the feeling made famous by reviewers, that you "cannot lay the book down." I haven't met many of these and don't care if I never do again.

The great books are the ones you have to put down because they bring life to you so intensely that you are compelled to stop, to think and to feel. Reading "Tender Is the Night" was for me the satisfaction of an appetite; a long, deep satisfaction.

Gilbert Seldes

The book begins with a group of people on the French Riviera seen through the innocent eyes of a young American girl, a movie actress, as it happens. They seem to her the most attractive human beings in the world.

All Fitzgerald's romantic talent is expended on this overture to his dark tragedy. Bizarre, absurd, half desperate events occur: quarrels, drunkenness, a duel, a murder which accidentally touches the lives of the principal people. Then the book takes hold of its principal theme.

Below the surface of the lives of Richard and Nicole Diver lies the tragedy of Nicole's recurrent madness. How the madness came, how Doctor Diver met and married Nicole, how their lives went on, and how their lives separated, form the material of the book.

Fitzgerald's triumph is that without a trace of symbolism or allegory, he makes this special story universally interesting. The emotions are not special; they are devotion, exasperation, love, hatred, despair. The people are men and women, of tremendous passions, doing fine things and ignoble things; living.

Gertrude Stein said that Fitzgerald "really created for the public the new generation." It is easy to say that in his new book he has shown to what that generation tended. But I think he has done more. He has gone behind generations, old or new, and created his own image of human beings. And in doing so has stepped again to his natural place at the head of the American writers of our time.

Books of The Times

John Chamberlain

The New York Times, 13 April 1934, p. 17

As one who would rather have written "The Great Gatsby" than any other American novel published in the Twenties, we approached F. Scott Fitzgerald's "Tender Is the Night" with anticipation and trepidation. "The Great Gatsby" was so perfect in its feeling and its symbolism, such a magnificent evocation of the spirit of a whole decade, so great an improvement over Mr. Fitzgerald's second novel, "The Beautiful and Damned" (which might have been, as Jerome Hill once called it, "an American 'Madame Bovary,'" were it not for its diffuse quality), that one could hardly see Mr. Fitzgerald striking the same high level twice in succession. As the years went by, recurrent surges of gossip had it that Mr. Fitzgerald was unable to bring his unfinished post-"Gatsby" novel to any satisfactory conclusion. He had been a child of boom America; had the lean years after 1929 sapped his artistic vitality by stealing from him his field of reference?

After having read "Tender Is the Night," we now know that the gossip was—just gossip. Mr. Fitzgerald has not forgotten his craftsmanship, his marvelous sense of what might be called social climate, his sheer writing ability. Judged purely as prose, "Tender Is the Night" is a continually pleasurable performance. From a technical point of view, it is not as perfect a novel as "The Great Gatsby," but once the reader has gotten past the single barrier to complete appreciation of the book, it proves to be an exciting and psychologically apt study in the disintegration of a marriage.

Seemingly, Mr. Fitzgerald begins well. He introduces us to a fledgling film actress, Rosemary Hoyt, a girl with the dew still on her, who is taken up by Richard and Nicole Diver during a summer stay at the Riviera. For some eighty pages or more we constantly

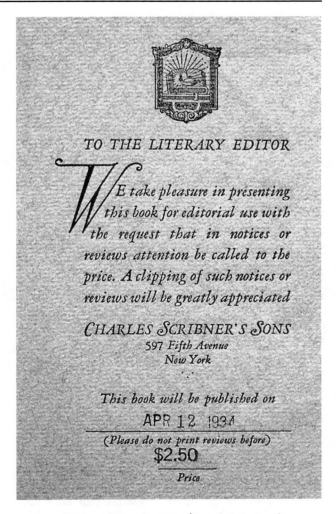

Slip inserted in review copies (Bruccoli Collection of Fitzgerald, Thomas Cooper Library, University of South Carolina)

expect Rosemary to develop, to become more and more important in the story. And then suddenly, we realize that this innocent and as yet entirely plastic girl is introduced merely as a catalytic agent. When Dick Diver, who is a psychiatrist without a practice, falls in love with Rosemary, his marriage to Nicole commences to founder. But, Rosemary, having started a chain of developments, is dismissed almost completely from the novel, and the reader pauses, at page 100, in rueful bewilderment.

In the critical terminology of Kenneth Burke, Mr. Fitzgerald has violated a "categorical expectancy." He has caused the arrows of attention to point toward Rosemary. Then, like a broken field runner reversing his field, he shifts suddenly, and those who have been chasing him fall figuratively on their noses as Mr. Fitzgerald is off on a new tack.

At this point one could almost guarantee that "Tender Is the Night" is going to be a failure. But, as a matter of fact, the novel does not really begin until Rosemary is more or less out of the way. What follows is a study of a love affair and a marriage between doctor and mental patient that is as successful a bit of writing as it must have been difficult to create in dramatic terms. Mr. Fitzgerald set himself an incredibly confused problem, but he draws the lines clearly as he works the problem out in terms of two human beings.

"Tender Is the Night" is not, as might be thought, a story of post-war degeneracy. The story has nothing much to do with the famous "lost generation," although many playboy Americans figure on the periphery as Mr. Fitzgerald's drama moves through Europe, from the Riviera to Paris, and thence to Switzerland and Rome. Nicole Warren could have been psychologically violated by the attack by her father in any decade. She might not have found psychiatrists to take her case before Jung commenced practicing and before Freud commenced writing, but that is not germane to the "lost generation." Dick Diver himself is a brilliant young man; Nicole saves herself by transferring her outraged affection for her father to the young psychiatrist with his "cat's face" and his air of being a good, solid bulwark for distress.

What follows is dimly prefigured in the first hundred pages of the book, when Rosemary is seemingly the star attraction. We know that some horror lurks behind the facade of happiness that Dick and Nicole present to the world. But it is not until Mr. Fitzgerald suddenly cuts back to Nicole's years at the Swiss neurological hospital that we know much about the circumstances. And, given the circumstances, it is a foregone conclusion that Nicole will remain in love with Dr. Diver only so long as she needs him. The fact that she is in love with him is predicated on sickness; when she ultimately comes to feel that she can stand by herself, her love for him collapses. Mr. Fitzgerald, in nervous scenes of great skill, traces the forces leading to this collapse. And Dr. Diver is ruined in the process. We see him, at the end, pursuing a meaningless career as a general practitioner in upper New York State, where he had lived as a boy. Any love he may have had for Rosemary, the precipitant of the solution, has been smothered by events. And when he ceased to be Nicole's physician, he ceased also to be her lover. He has been mentally corrupted, too, by living for many years on Nicole's money, and by absence from active work as a psychiatrist taking many and all cases.

Beyond the story, there is Mr. Fitzgerald's ability to catch the "essence of a continent," the flavor of a period, the fragrance of a night and a snatch of old song, in a phrase. A comparison of "Tender Is the Night" as it ran in Scribner's Magazine and as it appears in book form gives a measure of the author's artistic conscience. He has made many deft excisions, many sound reallocations of conversation. If, with Rosemary, he presents nothing much beyond an unformed girl, that must lie within the conception of his novel. Rosemary was evidently intended to be meaningless in herself, an unknown quantity projecting itself into a situation that merely required leverage, any leverage, to start its development toward a predictable end. The story is the story of the Divers, husband and wife, how they came together, and how they parted. As such it is a skillfully done dramatic sequence. By the time the end is reached, the false start is forgotten.

BOOKS

F. Scott Fitzgerald

IN Mr. Fitzgerald's case, at any rate, money is the root of all novels. In "This Side of Paradise," the world of super-wealth was viewed through the glass of undergraduate gaiety, sentiment, and satire. With "The Great Gatsby," the good-time note was dropped, to be replaced by a darker accent of tragic questioning. The questions have become sharper, bitterer in "Tender Is the Night," but the world of luxurious living remains his only world. It has even become a trifle narrower—a Fitzgerald contraction, so to speak. This universe he both loves and despises; he sees through it and is confused by it. It is the contradictoriness of this emotional attitude that gives his novels their special quality, and is also in part responsible for some of their weaknesses.

A clipping from Clifton Fadiman's review in the 14 April 1934 issue of The New Yorker *that Fitzgerald saved for his scrapbook*

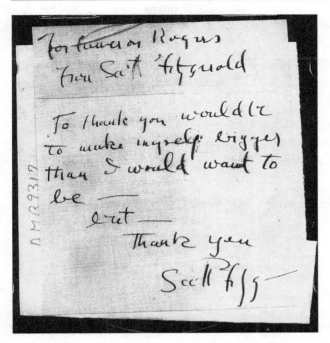

Inscription to Cameron Rogers (Bruccoli Collection of Fitzgerald, Thomas Cooper Library, University of South Carolina)

Fitzgerald's Novel a Masterpiece
Cameron Rogers
San Francisco Chronicle, 15 April 1934, p. 4D

A novel from F. Scott Fitzgerald, silent since 1925 save for short stories of a variety acceptable to the better popular magazines, is a major event in contemporary American letters. Fitzgerald placed his talent before an international reading public at so early an age (he was 24 when "This Side of Paradise" held spellbound a whole generation now not so young) and display so rapid a mastery of his profession that for the past nine years his readers might have likened him to a rocket which imperiously soared to a point defined by the publication in 1925 of "The Great Gatsby," but which then exploded into stars and streamers of brilliance too delicate to survive. For while everything he has written in, say, the Saturday Evening Post, has been informed by his talent, in it the sinews of his greater powers have been lacking.

We have waited for almost a decade, but "Tender Is the Night" is so well worth it that Fitzgerald's silence during that time seems natural and explicable. For in the characterization in this story of a few Americans forming a shifting, dissolving and reassembling group in Europe in the years following the war, there is so much beauty, so much compassion and so much understanding that it seems as though it could only have

sprung from a mind left wisely fallow. Fitzgerald's style was always admirable; deft, delicate, flexible and essentially his own. Wedded in "Tender Is the Night" to those other qualities of mind, it achieves a final significance as a medium of expression in English which hereafter should be difficult to overestimate.

To a very definite degree a psychopathic novel, an amazingly competent study of schizophrenia, the term applied by Bleuler to cases of split personality, "Tender Is the Night" owes to the description and cure of this mental disease in the girl, Nicole, many of its most beautiful and touching passages. Daughter of one of those fabulously rich Americans, Nicole, apparently doomed by what seems to have been an incestuous attack, to a swift decline into hopeless dementia, falls in love with Dr. Diver, a young American completing in Europe at the conclusion of the war his studies in psychopathia. Diver, unwillingly at first, succumbs to a helplessness and a beauty memorably described and for some ten years devotes his life to the cure of Nicole, who becomes his wife. It's about these two figures that the action develops to Paris, and from Switzerland to Italy and back again to the Cote d'Azur.

Such in the barest outline, is the story of "Tender Is the Night." Of the unforgettable balance of the dramatis personae there is no space here to speak, but each is developed with a skill in observation and description which is notable and their reactions to each other and to the circumstances of their lives when together or when alone read so convincingly as to remind one of the explanation of an exact science.

"Tender Is the Night" is a profoundly moving, beautifully written story, and it should assure Fitzgerald's stature as an American author when the brutal improvisations on police blotter themes of currently better known writers are forgotten.

Chamberlain initially reviewed the novel four days earlier, on 13 April 1934. In this second review, which appeared in a column with his review of William Faulkner's Dr. Martino, he responded to critics who found Dick Diver's collapse unconvincing.

Books of The Times
John Chamberlain
The New York Times, 16 April 1934, p. 15

The critical reception of F. Scott Fitzgerald's "Tender Is the Night" might serve as the basis for one of those cartoons on "Why Men Go Mad." No two reviews were alike; no two had the same tone. Some seemed to think that Mr. Fitzgerald was writ-

TENDER IS THE NIGHT

■ Another Fitzgerald sensation greeted with the same storm of praise and sales producing discussion that greeted "This Side of Paradise," and "The Great Gatsby."

Read what the first-string critics say about it:

"It has been months since anything by an American writer has given me such good reading as this."
—*Harry Hansen in The New York World Telegram.*

■ ■ ■

"Exciting . . . moving. . . . Once again he has issued a promise that is more exciting than most of his contemporaries' achievements."
—*Time Magazine.*

■ ■ ■

"You feel as you read it, that you will never forget it . . . universally interesting. . . . The people are men and women of tremendous passions, doing fine things and ignoble things. . . . He has stepped again to his natural place at the head of American writers of our time."
—*Gilbert Seldes.*

■ ■ ■

"As a picture of slow moral decay and of the steady growth of a parasite which eventually chokes the parent plan, 'Tender Is the Night' is wholly successful. It cuts through sham and pretense magnificently."
—*Hal Borland in The Philadelphia Ledger.*

"A continually pleasurable performance. . . . An exciting and psychologically apt study in the disintegration of a marriage."
—*John Chamberlain in The New York Times.*

■ ■ ■

"A major event in contemporary American letters. . . . A profoundly moving, beautifully written story."
—*Cameron Rogers in The San Francisco Chronicle.*

■ ■ ■

"Its haunting tragedy has not let me alone for a moment since I read it. . . . A brilliant novel, and a novel that deserves to be read. . . . It ranks high in readability, both because Mr. Fitzgerald is a story-teller and because he writes with color, wit, and penetration."
—*Herschel Brickell in The New York Evening Post.*

■ ■ ■

"The depths of his probing into character, mood, and emotion is, I think, unmatched in our country . . . by all odds the finest novel to have come my way in ten years.
—*Michael March in The Brooklyn Citizen.*

"The book is a grand affair."—Horace Gregory in The New York Herald Tribune.

■ "The critical reception of 'Tender Is the Night' might serve as the basis for one of those cartoons on 'Why Men Go Mad.' No two reviews are alike; no two had the same tone," wrote *John Chamberlain* in *The New York Times* in his *second* column within four days that featured the Fitzgerald book (an attention conspicuously rare in *The Times*). But even the most critical agree on one thing —it's a novel that MUST be read. Months ago we said this would be the "most talked about novel of the year." The talk has started. Talk that SELLS. It will increase— and so will sales.

$2.50   **CHARLES SCRIBNER'S SONS**

F. SCOTT FITZGERALD

Promotional piece in which the publisher anticipates that the critical debate about the novel will boost sales

ing about his usual jazz age boys and girls; others that he had a "timeless" problem on his hands. And some seemed to think that Doctor Diver's collapse was insufficiently documented.

With this we can't agree. It seemed to us that Mr. Fitzgerald proceeded accurately, step by step, with just enough documentation to keep the drama from being misty, but without destroying the suggestiveness that added to the horror lurking behind the surface. Consider Doctor Diver's predicament in being married to a woman with a "split personality" deriving from a brutal misadventure in adolescence. He had married Nicole against his better judgment, partially because she brought him memories of home after years spent abroad. He was drawn into accepting her money, for reasons that living up to a certain income and "cushioning" existence were bound up with the cure. His husband-physician relationship to Nicole, involving constant companionship, cut him off from his practice, and he thought wistfully at times of how the German psychiatrists were getting ahead of him.

With all these factors preparing the ground, it would merely take the sight of an uncomplicated girl (Rosemary) to jar him into active unrest. And when Nicole, subconsciously jealous of Rosemary, comes to a new phase of her disease, and attempts to throw the car off the road when Dick is driving with her and the two children, it is enough to give any one the jitters. Weakness indeed! The wonder to us is

Archibald MacLeish

that Dick didn't collapse long before Mr. Fitzgerald causes him to break down. And when he does collapse, his youth is gone, it is too late to catch up with the Germans who have been studying new cases for years. This seems to us to be a sufficient exercise in cause-and-effect. Compared to the motivation in Faulkner, it is logic personified.

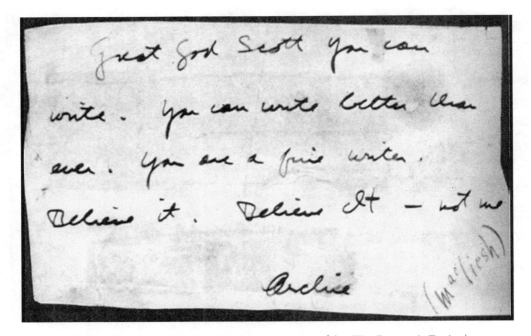

Note from MacLeish that Fitzgerald saved in his scrapbook (from The Romantic Egoists*)*

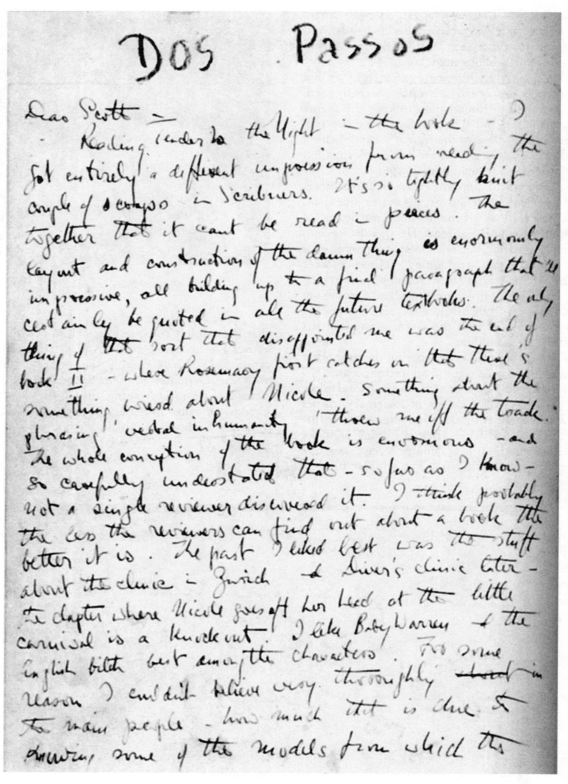

*First page of a congratulatory letter from Dos Passos that Fitzgerald preserved
in his scrapbook (Princeton University Library)*

John Dos Passos

The Psychopathic Novel
Mary M. Colum
Forum and Century, 91(April 1934): 219–223

. . . At least three of the writers whose new books are before me—Scott Fitzgerald, Morley Callaghan, and William March—are approaching their forties, and it is well to consider how their minds and brains burn, and how their futures appear. The restlessness and originality in their minds is seen in their choice of material; all three take a plunge into that latest of literary interests, the study of the psychopathic personality, the personality which is either on the borderland of insanity, or which some happening in life can drive over that borderland.

Judging by his present book, *Such Is My Beloved,* the one of these writers who has the greatest depth of emotion and widest range of sympathy, as well as a real power of meditating on life, is Morley Callaghan. Therefore one can foresee for him a continual growth, unless he does something to atrophy his faculties or ceases giving to them nutriment. For minds, like bodies, have to be continually nourished or they will become anemic and unproductive.

William March, in *Come in at the Door,* has developed further the tragic sense of life which showed its beginning in his first book, *Company K.* But it has not yet reached its full intensity, and he is as yet more remarkable for his potentialities than for his achievement.

Scott Fitzgerald has been longer before the public than either of these writers. He has a far more varied talent and a brilliance that has not dimmed. It simply has not grown more profound nor does it seem to have drawn any fresh sustenance from life. More complex excitements than were rife in his previous books are found in *Tender Is the Night,* but all of them are on too shallow a level of experience, and his mental nutriment seems to have been a trifle too jazzy and lacking in some of those more solid vitamins which give a writer sympathy with the characters he is creating. . . .

In the three novels previously mentioned the most remarkable psychologic study is certainly that of Morley Callaghan's Father Dowling, whose character is drawn with such subtlety and insight that it is powerfully convincing to readers, whether or not they have any special knowledge. It is the study of a type whose outstanding characteristics are goodness, benevolence, and self-sacrifice, beginning at a certain point of eccentricity which, like the initial mistake of a single figure in a long calculation, finally throws out the total. The case of Father Dowling would, I think, seem authentic to any psychiatrist, and it never becomes merely distressing, as does the bathroom scene in Scott Fitzgerald's story, where the breakdown is not sufficiently prepared for. Father Dowling remains an attractive person, lovable and pathetic in everything he does; his gradual sinking into mental confusion, after an emotional upset and bewilderment at the injustice of the world, is done with such beauty and reality that the man remains as he was at the beginning, a kind of saint without weakness or milksoppery.

On the other hand, Scott Fitzgerald's chief woman character, Nicole, in her insane passages seems more like a case history from a textbook than a novelist's study of a real character. It is, indeed, a study of the disease rather than a study of that type of personality which may be subject to the disease. Considerable knowledge of psychiatry and its history is shown, and psychiatric terms are scattered lavishly through the pages, along with the names of great mental experts like Kraepelin and Bleuler. There is far too much external documentation and too little of the novelist's intuitive knowledge of the character he is creating. The heroine, Nicole, can pass for long periods as a normal wife and mother and as an entertaining member of a social set. But she is a psychopath, afflicted with that baffling mental disease which, because it often begins between the ages of fifteen and twenty-five, used to be called dementia præcox. It also breaks out in people up to the age of fifty and is often unaccompanied by dementia, and for this reason Bleuler found the term inexact; he named it schizophrenia, or split personality, thereby indicating that

Inscription in Tender Is the Night *to Carl Van Vechten, who had written the Fitzgeralds into his 1930 novel* Parties *(Yale University)*

the disease destroys the cohesion of the personality, causes the will to deteriorate and the affective power to diminish so that ideas of death or love or liberty lose all meaning. In such cases, the previous attachments of patients are changed into hatreds when they do not sink into indifference, living in a dream detached from all reality.

A number of these traits in some form can be observed in people we consort with every day who we think are normal—people who have no feeling or who feel only in patches or people who live forever in a sort of dream, who have what is called shut-in personalities. There are others, apparently living a normal life, who have achieved hardly as much consciousness as an intelligent animal. Most authorities on the subject say that the disease in a simple form is widespread, but that many touched by it are capable of living a moderately normal life. But how disastrous they can be for the people they live with!

In the old classic novel the character was always depicted as the normal integrated human being, able to impose a unity on himself and his actions and actuated on the whole, if he was the hero, by distinguished principles. Now there is coming into literature this other type which may, after all, be as common—the people who are unreliable, lying, subject to fears; who are treacherous; who cannot keep a secret; who, if they have any affections at all, have them for one person; who are full of jealousies and terrors; and who, above all, are alone and lonely.

The chief character, Chester, in William March's *Come in at the Door,* is a man who had received in childhood what psychologists call a trauma, in this instance a result of witnessing the hanging of a negro whom he himself had treacherously betrayed. Though he is highly intelligent, Chester is almost completely lacking in affectivity and experiences just enough positive emotion to fall in love a little and to marry. But this transient feeling does not last long, and we are left contemplating a character who loses everything that attaches him to the world. In the last chapter, after the funeral of his estranged and eccentric father, there flashes back to his consciousness the memory of the hanging, and we see his mind suddenly break as he runs and runs as madmen run. "His face was twisted with pain and his hands pressed together in agony. 'I'm very amusing,' he shouted over and over, 'I'm essentially a comic character,' but his words were lost to the larger sound of the world's fury."

There is a deeply intuitive quality about the revelation of this character that may elude the general reader. It is, as is Scott Fitzgerald's Nicole, the study of the schizophrenic personality, and there are therefore certain points in common between the two characters to which it is necessary to draw attention. Both have suffered a psychic injury in childhood, the effect of which eventually causes the breakdown of their minds—Chester, because he witnessed the hanging, Nicole because of what seems to be an incestuous attack, though this has the air of an incident tacked on to the character by the author, rather than a happening woven into her subconsciousness, as the psychic injury to Chester is woven into his subconscious.

There is in both books a wild running scene, but the one in Fitzgerald's is the more dramatic, authentic, and memorable. The heroine, feeling an attack coming on, begins to run suddenly and madly through the

Photo of H. L. Mencken taken by Fitzgerald at La Paix in 1932 (courtesy of the Enoch Pratt Free Library)

H. L. Mencken responded to Fitzgerald's complaint that reviewers had mistaken the "dying fall" conclusion of his novel for a "diminution of vitality."

H. L Mencken to Fitzgerald, 26 April 1934

I hope you don't let yourself be upset by a few silly notices. The quality of book reviewing in the American newspapers is really appalling. Reviews are printed by imbeciles who know nothing whatever about the process of writing, and hence usually miss the author's intentions completely. I think your own scheme is a capital cone, and that you have carried it out very effectively in the book.

—*Letters of H. L. Mencken* (1961), p. 375

crowd at the fair, eluding her husband. She is eventually found, revolving in a boat on a Ferris wheel and laughing hysterically as the astonished bystanders gaze at her. This episode is beautifully and revealingly done, and could have been written only by a man of high gifts. But always the personality is revealed from the outside, whereas William March, with a less brilliant mind than Fitzgerald's, reveals his hero from the inside and from the character he has created. We get the sensation that we have met a man so constructed by nature and inheritance that under the buffets of fate his mind must break.

How, it may be asked, can a sane and normal person depict the personality of one who is abnormal? Nearly everybody under some strain in life has felt sufficiently near breaking to understand how a neurotic can lose his balance. But even the inventive mind of the novelist needs some first-hand observation of a broken mind before he can begin to create one. At that, no matter how realistic his data may be, he must have that power, which all the great creators of characters had, whether they were creating beggar, king, pimp, or madman, of first discovering the beggar, king, pimp, or madman in themselves. This is the quality in which Scott Fitzgerald's creation of Nicole is inferior to March's Chester and to Callaghan's Father Dowling. Among the multiple crea-

tures that people every novelist's mind Morley Callaghan was able to discover, not only the lovable and eccentric priest, who ascetically loved the two prostitutes, but also the prostitutes themselves, the bishop, and the respectable parishioners. And William March was able to find in the creatures of his mind, not only the Chester who betrayed Baptiste, but also Baptiste himself and the negro woman Matty.

The only character in *Tender Is the Night* who has life like these is Dick Diver, Nicole's husband. Fitzgerald, however, in sheer writing power is superior to both Callaghan and March, and this book, despite the impression it gives of being slung together, rather than constructed, shows its author's distinctive gifts—a romantic imagination, a style that is often brilliant, a swiftness of movement, and a sense of enchantment in people and places, all of which combine to give his books the great merit of being always entertaining. Nevertheless, nearly all his early faults remain: his male characters are still as they were over a decade ago, prankish sophomores; his female characters are bright, brittle, and young, with all the material sophistications, and those of the social sophistications understood, in a jazzy and superficially cultivated society. He can summon up terror and pathos, but what pity and tragedy are he does not know, for he has never really meditated on life. Yet he has expressed very well indeed a section of the life of his time, a section that may perhaps seem totally crazy to our descendants. And because he is its chronicler and because there is that sort of personality in his writing that there is in the memoir writers, he may last a trifle longer than his superiors in profundity—than, for example, Callaghan, who is a profounder writer, but a less interesting one, and who has a style which is too often queerly pedestrian. . . .

Dear John:

May we meet soon in equally Celtic but more communicable condition

Scott Fitz

Fitzgerald's Tender Is the Night *inscription to John O'Hara*
(from Fitzgerald/ Hemingway Annual 1973)

Fitzgerald and O'Hara

John O'Hara met Fitzgerald when he was writing Appointment in Samarra, *published the same year as* Tender Is the Night. *He remained unshaken in his admiration for Fitzgerald's genius during the years when Fitzgerald's work was unfashionable. O'Hara's 1945 introduction to the* Portable Fitzgerald—*which included* Tender—*stated: "All he was was our best novelist, one of our best novella-ists and one of our finest writers of short stories." O'Hara told John Steinbeck that "Scott Fitzgerald was a better writer than all of us put together. Just words writing."*

Fitzgerald and O'Hara, Encino, California, 1940 (photograph by Belle O'Hara; Bruccoli Collection, Thomas Cooper Library, University of South Carolina)

Dust jacket for O'Hara's first novel, published in the same year as was Tender Is the Night *(Bruccoli Collection, Kent State University Libraries)*

Dear Scott:

Thank you, for myself and my bibliophile grandchildren, for the inscribed copy of Tender Is the Night. The little bastards will have to be satisfied with cut leaves, because I am reading the novel once again, having read it in the magazine, in galley proof, and now. I will say now that Tender Is the Night is in the early stages of being my favorite book, even more than This Side of Paradise. As I told you once before, I don't read many books, but the same ones over again. Right now I can't think of any other book clearly enough to make a comparison between it and Tender Is the Night, and I guess in its way that is the most important thing I've ever said about anybook.

You helped me finish my novel. I finished it yesterday. The little we talked when you were in New York did it. I reasoned that the best parts of my novel will be said to derive from Fitzgerald, and I think I have muffed my story, but I became reconciled to having done that after talking to you and reading Tender Is the Night in proof. No one else can write that like that, and I haven't tried, but the best parts of my novel are facile pupils of The Beautiful and Damned and The Great Gatsby. I was bushed, as Dottie says, and the fact that I need money terribly was enough to make me say the hell with my boook until you talked to me and seemed to accept me. So then I went ahead and finished my second-rate novel in peace. My message to the world is Fuck it! I know this is not the right, the classical (as Hergesheimer would punctuate it), attitude, but I can write better than Louis Bromfield, Tiffany Thayer, Kathleen Norris, Erskine Caldwell or Mike Gold, so I am not the worst writer there is. I neverwon anything, except a German helmet for writing an essay on Our Flag, and a couple of Father Lasance's My Prayer Book's for spelling bees.

Please look me up when you come to New York, and thank you for the book.

John O'Hara

Fitzgerald kept this April 1934 letter from John O'Hara in his scrapbook.

Writing to movie producer David Brown, John O'Hara stated his conviction that the hostile reception and reputation of Tender Is the Night *had been determined by the politics of the Depression Left. The reference at the end of the letter to "Pep West" is to Nathanael West, author of* The Day of The Locust *(1939).*

John O'Hara to David Brown, 12 August 1957

I may have told you this before, but if not, I tell you now that as a personal favor to Fitzgerald, I read page proofs and galley proofs on that book. At the time of publication, just before and just after, I was quite possibly the only writer who *loved* the book. Dottie Parker also had proofs and I telephoned her late the first night and told her how much I liked it; she said she had been unable to stay with it, and I urged her to go beyond the very early spot where she had given up. As a result she telephoned me to thank me. Dottie's first judgment was typical, not so much of her as of the professional and non-professional judgment. The book came out at precisely the wrong time in the national history. No matter how good it was, it was about the Bad People, the well fed, well housed, well educated, well born—the villains of the depression. It was a time for Odets and the imitators of Odets, and of Steinbeck and the imitators of Steinbeck. I am, as you know, an Odets man and a Steinbeck man, but I did not feel compelled to hang Fitzgerald and Phil Barry as counter-revolutionists, and I am proud to say I did not go along with the gutless thinking that all but destroyed TENDER IS THE NIGHT and without a doubt broke Fitzgerald's heart. One group, which I shall disguise under the heading of Hammett-Hellman-Perelman-Kober group, had no time for Fitzgerald (or, later, me), and I note with some sardonic pleasure that they are now having trouble convincing the people that Pep West was better than Fitzgerald *and* Jonathan Swift. He *was* better than Cornell Woolrich, but that's as far as I'll go.

—Selected Letters of John O'Hara (1978), p. 266

*Robert Benchley, drama critic,
humorist, and actor*

ROBERT BENCHLEY
44 WEST 44TH STREET
NEW YORK CITY

April 29th, 1934

Dear Scott:

It was damned nice of you to write
in your book for me. I don't remember ever having said anything that appears on page 25,or on
any other page,but I would have given my two
expensivly-filled eye-teeth to have written just
one page of the book.

Honestly,Scott,I think that it is a
beautiful piece of work,not only technically,but
emotionally. I haven't had a book get hold of me
like that for years. As a journeyman writer,I
can not even conceive of anyone's being able to
do that scene in the Guaranty Trust,just from the
point of view of sheer manipulation ff words,to
say nothing of the observation contained in it.
And the feeling of the whole book is so strong
upon me,even now,that I am oppressed by a not-
quite-vague-enough fear that several people I
am fond of are very unhappy.

I hope that you,yourself,are not any
unhappier than is called for in the general blue-
print specifications for Living. Please don't be.
Anyone who gets down on his stomach and crawls
all afternoon around a yard playing tin-soldiers
with a lot of kids,shouldn't be made too unhappy.
I cry a little every time I think of you that
afternoon in Antibes.

Thanks again for thinking of me,and look
me up the next time you come to town. My number
is Vanderbilt 3-6498.

Gratefully,

Bob.

*In his unlocated inscription to Benchley, Fitzgerald evidently alluded to a particular
passage in* Tender Is the Night *(Princeton University Library).*

The Daily Worker *(1924–1957) was the organ for the American Communist Party.*

You Can't Duck Hurricane Under a Beach Umbrella
Philip Rahv
Daily Worker, 5 May 1934, p. 7

F. Scott Fitzgerald made a name for himself in the literature of the past decade as the voice and chronicler of the jazz age. This, in a sense, was his strength, as he showed himself capable of quickly responding to features of American life that other writers assimilated rather slowly; but it also proved to be his greatest defect, since he failed to place what he saw in its social setting. He himself was swept away by the waste and extravagance of the people he described, and he identified himself with them. Hence the critics who, at his appearance on the literary scene, saw in him a major talent in post-war American literature, soon realized that here was another creative promise petering out. The fever of the boom days settled in his bones. In the end he surrendered to the standards of the *Saturday Evening Post.*

In these days, however, even Fitzgerald cannot escape realizing how near the collapse of his class really is. In this new work he no longer writes of expensive blondes and yachting parties, lavish surroundings and insane love-affairs from the same angle of vision as in the past. These things are still there, but the author's enthusiasm for them has faded, giving way to the sweat of exhaustion. The rich expatriates who trail their weary lives across the pages of the novel breathe the thin air of a crazy last autumn. The author is still in love with his characters, but he no longer

In April 1934, Zelda Fitzgerald responded to a letter from her husband with more of her reaction to his novel.

Thanks for your long sweet letter: I have just finished part I of your book again. It is the most beautiful prose, without a wasted or irrelevant word. It is also very moving and a fine presentation of those sun lit places, which its bright glare finally faded and streaked–perhaps to dimmer nuances. In fact, Do Do, it's a swell book and well imbued with that sense of impersonal tragedy, as good books should be: of individual happiness drained to fill out the schemas for momentary pleasure-theories. Also, you have kept beautifully intact the personalities against so vivid a mise en-scene that any lesser creations would have been submerged in the glitter. It is a beautiful book.

You seem afraid that it will make me recapitulate the past: remember, that at that time, I was immersed in something else–and I guess most of life is a re-hashing of the tragedies and happinesses of which it consisted in days before we started to promulgate reasons for their being so. Of cource, it is a haunting book–everything good is haunting because it calls to light something new in our consciousness

–*Correspondence of F. Scott Fitzgerald,* p. 357

entertains any illusions concerning their survival. Morally, spiritually, and even physically they are dying in hospitals for the mentally diseased, in swanky Paris hotels and on the Riviera beaches. Yet, having immersed himself in the atmosphere of corruption, Fitzgerald's eye discerns a cer-

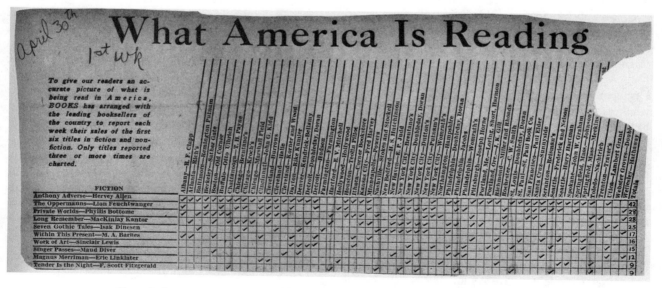

Chart plotting popular reading in America from the New York Herald Tribune, *29 April 1934*

Congratulatory letter from Shane Leslie, the Anglo-Irish man of letters who had encouraged Fitzgerald's schoolboy literary ambitions (from The Romantic Egoists*)*

tain grace even in their last contortions. The morbid romance of death sways his mind, and signs are not wanting that instead of severing the cords that bind him to their degradation, he prefers to stick out with them to the end. Even while perceiving their doom, he still continues to console and caress them with soft words uttered in the furry voice of a family doctor pledged to keep the fatal diagnosis from his patients.

A number of things happen in *Tender is the Night*. First, let us introduce Mr. Warren, a Chicago millionaire who rapes his sixteen-year-old daughter Nicole. This non-plebeian act drives the girl out of her mind, and she is sent to a sanatorium in Switzerland, where she is partially cured and where she meets Dick Diver, a young American psychologist who marries her. Nicole is extremely wealthy and the Divers lead a model parasitic life, flitting from one European high spot to another, accompanied by a varied assortment of neurotics and alcoholics. Wherever they go they are intent on smashing things up. Dick Diver's strength and charm fall apart in the insufferable atmosphere of sophisticated brutality. In the course of time he realizes his role as a live commodity bought by the Warren family to act as husband-doctor to their crazy daughter. And Nicole, sensing Dick's growing despair,

flies from him to the arms of Tommy Barban, the stylized young barbarian who is potentially an ideal leader of a Nazi storm-troop.

When the plot is thus bluntly stated, stripped of its delicate introspective wording, of its tortuous style that varnishes rather than reveals the essential facts, we can easily see that the book is a fearful indictment of the moneyed aristocracy. But Fitzgerald's form blunts the essence, transforming it into a mere opportunity for endless psychologizing. And on account of it many a reader will let himself float on the novel's tender surface, without gauging the horror underneath.

The reviewer is inclined to think that in creating the figure of Dick Diver, Fitzgerald has created—perhaps unconsciously—the image of a life closely corresponding to his own. The truth is that Nicole can be understood as a symbol of the entire crazy social system to which Fitzgerald has long been playing Dick Diver.

And lastly, a not too private postscript to the author. Dear Mr. Fitzgerald, you can't hide from a hurricane under a beach umbrella.

Mabel Dodge Luhan in 1930

Born to a socially prominent family in Buffalo, New York, Mabel Dodge Luhan (1876–1962) became a liberal leader in the arts. In 1918 she moved to Taos, New Mexico, where her home on the outer edge of Pueblo land attracted celebrated artists, writers, and thinkers of the day.

Scott Fitzgerald a Modern Orpheus

Mabel Dodge Luhan
New York Herald Tribune Books, 6 May 1934, p. 21

To the Editor of BOOKS:

Here are some thoughts about "Tender Is the Night." Max Eastman says I don't know how to think and maybe that is true, so perhaps these will not be thoughts, really, so much as approximations of my impressions, perceptions of a manly performance, set down with great respect.

When Orpheus first went down into the underworld to bring back Eurydice it was not so risky an excursion as in these days we live in. It took then, apparently, rather a simple courage and it was more cut and dried for there was a stout surface to his world and a more definite descent and emergence. He went down and he returned.

But now the whole surface is worn thin. Every-where the social tissue is giving way, ominous cracks appear upon the pleasant rink of our conscious life where we skim to and fro upon the thin thin ice.

Once in a while, quite frequently, as compared with Orpheus's day, some one sinks under and disappears and Orpheus is not there to save. Neither love nor courage is available to many and for the few there is only the cold sport of science frisking delicately in the dangerous stream, trying to hook these fish.

The greater number, then, disappear with the vast undifferentiated gray underworld and are seen no more. They are engulfed in the ancient reservoir where good and evil are all one and nothing matters yet, but

---

Fitzgerald responded to Mabel Dodge Luhan's published letter on 10 May 1934.

Dear Mrs. Luhan:

I was tremendously pleased and touched by your letter and by your communication to the Tribune. It always strikes me as very strange when I find new people in the world, because I always crystallize any immediate group in which I move as being an all-sufficient, all-inclusive cross-section of the world, at the time I know it (the group)—this all the more because a man with the mobility of the writing profession and a certain notoriety thinks that he has a good deal of choice as to whom he will know. That from the outer bleakness, where you were only a name to me, you should have felt a necessity of communicating an emotion felt about a stranger, gave me again the feeling that Conrad expresses as "the solidarity of innumerable human hearts," at times a pretty good feeling, and your letter came to me at one of those times. Having been compared to Homer and Harold Bell Wright for fifteen years, I get a pretty highly developed delirium tremens at the professional reviewers: the light men who bubble at the mouth with enthusiasm because they see other bubbles floating around, the dumb men who regularly mistake your worst stuff for your best and your best for your worst, and, most of all, the cowards who straddle and the leeches who review your books in terms that they have cribbed out of the book itself, like scholars under some extraordinary dispensation which allows them to heckle the teacher. With every book I have ever published there have always been two or three people, as often as not strangers, who have seen the intention, appreciated it, and allowed me whatever percentage I rated on the achievement of that intention. In the case of this book your appreciation has given me more pleasure than any other, not excepting Gilbert Seldes who seemed to think that I had done completely what I started out to do and that it was worth doing.

—Correspondence of F. Scott Fitzgerald, p. 258

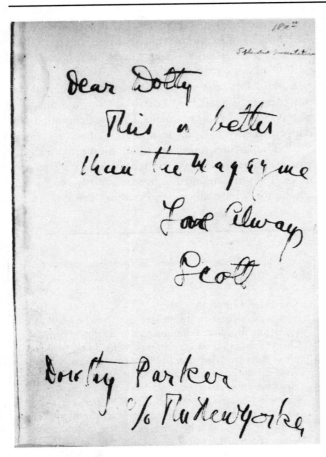

Inscription to Dorothy Parker, which shows that Fitzgerald was concerned about misjudgment of his novel in its serialization (from Inscriptions)

where the eager unnamed elements wait for a chance to rise and be; for while the children of this world are sinking through these terrible exits, the powers of the undisclosed world make their entrances.

Now, it seems to me, Scott Fitzgerald is a man who knows about all this—and what realizations has he gazed at and accepted before he could tell of it? In the wrack and ruin of his environment he ponders and smiles. Even while the waters close over him he smiles and tells of life as it has come to him, tells about his experience that was the experience of Orpheus, with this vast difference between them, that Orpheus didn't know what he was doing nor what happened to him. Some one else had to tell about him while here is one who can and does tell his own story. This makes people murmur about "taste." Is it "taste"? Well, has life taste? Because this writing is as actual as talking, the critics are confused. They are habituated to art forms and here is something that does not fit into them. Here is something real and confused and no more a novel than life is. Yet readers talk about it "as a novel" and compare it with "The Great Gatsby," and

they debate whether or no the author has fulfilled his earlier promise. Why can't they see that this is stern stuff and not to be mixed up with just books? But no—they are disappointed and they cover that up as best they can by calling it "brilliant"—which is their way of condoning it for its lack of this and that!

Do they realize, I wonder, that here is a book that is very close to being a live, organic resume of present reality and that that is something rare? I don't believe they do or they would drop their little measures and realize that something important, more important than a novel, has happened.

Here is an objective grasp of the conditioned, mechanical activity of oneself, the picture taken of oneself upon a journey, the lens directed and the shutter clicked at the moment of submersion, at the opening of the waters.

In these days it is Orpheus who must be saved. The roles are reversed but Eurydice is not aware yet of her predestined importance for still she is not strong enough to endure. She is still unstable although he has brought her through. Again and again she sinks into those grey depths where the amorphous things wait for birth. Each time she rises they come too, clinging about her unseen. She is, all unbeknownst, a carrier of forces that are evil when set loose—she is, as Gilbert Seldes said, a kind of "Typhoid Mary," and where she passes in her pleasant places, things happen. Her neighborhood is lively with potential battle, murder and sudden death. The gulf is open beneath her and ghastly eventualities attend her. Yet she is saved herself because Orpheus has taken over her account. With ignorance and loving blindness he will atone for an old, old mistake: that of touching with love those who are lost. He has not learned to save by the cold and scientific methods of modern salvation. Sacrifice is all he knows—that and knowing himself. He is the child of transition wandering in no man's land, between two worlds, one dead, the other not yet born. But he creates the future for us. He is not inactively resigned, nor passively submissive. With dreadful endurance and clarity he attempts to tell us—"this is how it is"—and by adding his portion to consciousness he changes the present.

I am afraid I have been clumsy and inadequate in trying to show how much I admire this mature act. The book doesn't need defense or interpretation. Of its own vitality it will make its own way, and gathering momentum it will cover long spaces and I hope I may be excused for seeming to think it needs any one to defend it.

MABEL DODGE LUHAN.

New York.

Novelist Joseph Hergesheimer, circa 1920
(photograph by Robert Hobart Davis)

Dear Joe :

You talked to someone who didn't
like this book — I don't know who, or
why they didn't. But I could tell in the
Stafford Bar that afternoon when you
said that it was "almost impossible to
write a book about an actress" that you
hadn't read it thru because the actress
fades out of it in the first third +
is only a catalytic agent.

Sometime will you open it at
the middle, perhaps at page 155
+ read on for five or ten minutes —?
If it were not for my sincere admiration for your judgment I would
forego this plea. You were not the
only one repelled by the apparent
triviality of the opening — I would like
this favorite among my books to have
another chance in the chrystal light
of your taste
                                    Ever yrs
                              F Scott Fitzgerald

Page 155 — _et seq_.

Fitzgerald inscription to Hergesheimer in Tender Is the Night *(University of Virginia)*

Malcolm Cowley

*Inscription to Cowley (Sotheby-Parke Bernet catalogue
3966 [1977], #114)*

Malcolm Cowley was book critic for The New Republic, *a liberal weekly. Although Fitzgerald did not share Cowley's
hard-line leftism, Cowley advanced Fitzgerald's work and played
a major role in the revival of the author's career. The following
review developed what became an influential critical approach to
Fitzgerald's work: "double vision"—Fitzgerald's capacity to be
participant and observer at the same time.*

Breakdown
Malcolm Cowley
New Republic, 79 (6 June 1934): 105–106

"Tender Is the Night" is a good novel that puz-
zles you and ends by making you a little angry
because it isn't a great novel also. It doesn't give the
feeling of being complete in itself.

The theme of it is stated in a conversation
among the three principal characters. "What did this
to him?" Rosemary asks. They are talking about
Abe North, an American composer who became
prominent shortly after the War. He was shy and
very talented; often he came to stay with Dick and

Nicole Diver in their villa near the Cape d'Antibes
and they scarcely knew he was there—"sometimes
he'd be in the library with a muted piano, making
love to it by the hour." But for years now he hadn't
been working; his eyes had a hurt look; he got
drunk every day as if trying to escape from nobody
knew what. And Rosemary wondered, "Why does
he have to drink?"

Nicole shook her head right and left, disclaiming
responsibility for the matter: "So many smart men
go to pieces nowadays."
"And when haven't they?" Dick asked. "Smart
men play close to the line because they have to—
some of them can't stand it, so they quit."
"It must lie deeper than that. . . . Artists like—
well, like Fernand don't seem to have to wallow in
alcohol. Why is it just Americans who dissipate?"
There were so many answers to this question
that Dick decided to leave it in the air, to buzz victoriously in Nicole's ears.

The question remains victoriously buzzing in
the reader's ears long after the story has ended.

In May 1934, Malcolm Cowley sent a letter to Fitzgerald along with his review.

Here is the review. I'm not especially proud of it. After waiting all this time, and writing it against your wishes, I should have given you something better. I wanted to write you a long letter about the book, which I liked more and was more deeply impressed by than the review seems to say.—Outside of all I said here, I think the double introduction interfered with the novel more than anything else—I mean the presenting of all the characters through Rosemary's eyes and then the going back to tell the story from 1919 to 1924; there is confusion of time here that bothers most of the readers with whom I have talked. Wouldn't it have been better to have the story develop directly into Rosemary's meeting with the Divers? As soon as Dick fell in love with Rosemary his first instinct would be to tell her all about himself, even at the risk of a spiritual infidelity to his wife—that would have obviated the second introduction. You were certainly right in saying that the sideshows were fine—some of them are unforgettable.

—*Correspondence of F. Scott Fitzgerald,* p. 366

Fitzgerald tries to answer it, but obliquely. He tells us why Dr. Richard Diver went to pieces—because he married a rich woman and became so dependent on her money that his own work seemed unimportant and he no longer had a purpose in living; that is the principal reason, although he is also shaken by his love for Rosemary and by Nicole's recurrent fits of insanity, during one of which she came near killing not only her husband and herself but also their two children. Dick's case seems clear enough—but what about Abe North, whose wife was poor and sane and devoted? What about the other nice people who ended as lunatics or drunkards? Fitzgerald is continually suggesting and reiterating these questions that he leaves in the air.

The Divers and their friends are, in reality, the characters he has always written about, and written well. They are the richer members of his own generation, the young women who learned to smoke and pet in 1917 and the Yale and Princeton men who attended their coming-out parties in new uniforms. In his early books, especially in "This Side of Paradise," he celebrated the youth of these people in a tone of unmixed pride—"Here we are," he seemed to be saying, "the children of the conquerors, the free and beautiful and very wicked youngsters who are setting the standards for a nation." Later, when he described their business careers and their life in great country houses on the north shore of Long Island, his admiration began to be mixed with irony and disillusionment. In the present novel, which chronicles their years of exile, the admiration has almost completely vanished; the prevailing tone is one of disillusionment mixed with nostalgia. "We had good times together," Fitzgerald seems to say, "but that was a long time ago." Dick Diver is now an unsuccessful drunken country doctor, divorced and living somewhere in central New York State. Rosemary is an empty and selfish movie star; Abe North is dead, killed brawling in a speakeasy—all the kind and sensitive people of their circle have gone to pieces, and there remain only the "wooden and onanistic" women like Nicole's sister, only the *arrivistes* like Albert McKisco and the cultivated savages like Tommy Barban. A whole class has flourished and decayed and suddenly broken into fragments.

Here is a magnificent subject for a novel. The trouble is that Fitzgerald has never completely decided what kind of novel he wanted to write—whether it should center round a single hero or deal with a whole group. Both types of approach are present, the individual and the collective, and they interfere with each other. We are conscious of a divided purpose that perhaps goes back to a division in the author himself.

Fitzgerald has always been the poet of the American upper bourgeoisie; he has been the only writer able to invest their lives with glamour. Yet he has never been sure that he owed his loyalty to the class about which he was writing. It is as if he had a double personality. Part of him is a guest at the ball given by the people in the big house; part of him has been a little boy peeping in through the window and being thrilled by the music and the beautifully dressed women—a romantic but hard-headed little boy who stops every once in a while to wonder how much it all cost and where the money came from. (Fitzgerald says, "There is a streak of vulgarity in me that I try to cultivate.") In his early books, this divided personality was wholly an advantage: it enabled him to portray American society from the inside, and yet at the same time to surround it with an atmosphere of magic and romance that exists only in the eyes of people watching at the carriage entrance as the guests arrive in limousines. Since those days, however, the division has been emphasized and has become a liability. The little boy outside the window has grown mature and cold-eyed; from an enraptured spectator he has developed into a social historian. At the same time, part of Fitzgerald remains inside, among the dancers. And now

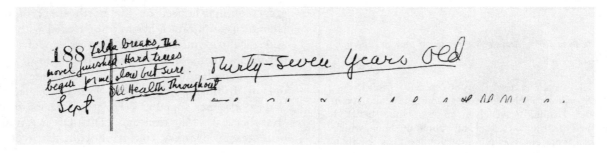

Fitzgerald's summary in his Ledger *of the year from September 1933 to September 1934*

that the ball is ending in tragedy, he doesn't know how to describe it—whether as a guest, a participant, in which case he will be writing a purely psychological novel; or whether from the detached point of view of a social historian.

There is another reason, too, for the technical faults of "Tender Is the Night." Fitzgerald has been working on it at intervals for the last nine years, ever since he published "The Great Gatsby" in 1925. During these years his attitude has inevitably changed, as has that of every other sensitive writer. Yet no matter how much he revised his early chapters, he could not make them wholly agree with those written later—for once a chapter has assumed what seems to be a final shape, it undergoes a process of crystallization: it can no longer be remolded. The result is that several of his characters are self-contradictory; they don't merely change as living creatures change: they transform themselves into different people.

If I didn't like the book so much, I wouldn't have spoken at such length about its shortcomings. It has virtues that deserve more space than I can give them here. Especially it has a richness of meaning and emotion—one feels that every scene is selected among many possible scenes and that every event has pressure behind it. There is nothing false or borrowed in the book: everything is observed at first hand. Some of the minor figures—especially Gausse, the hotel keeper who was once a bus boy in London, and Lady Caroline Sibley-Biers, who carries her English bad manners to the point of viciousness—are more vivid than Rosemary or Dick; and the encounter between Gausse and Lady Caroline is one of those enormous episodes in which two social castes are depicted melodramatically, farcically and yet convincingly in a brief conversation and one gesture.

Fitzgerald says that this book is his farewell to the members of his own generation; I hope he changes his mind. He has in him at least one great novel about them, and it is a novel that I want to read.

Review of *Tender Is the Night*
Journal of Nervous and Mental Disease, 82 (July 1935): 115–117

In *Tender is the Night* Mr. Fitzgerald draws a detailed and fascinating picture of the circumstantial and effective involvements attending inner dynamic developments in the lives of a young American couple living abroad. As one grasps fully the scope of the author's aim, and his discernment in face of the balance of psychotic cause and effect, the rich endowment of the book in regard to conscious mastery of authentic experience and exceptional descriptive powers becomes increasingly evident.

For the psychiatrist and psychoanalyst the book is of special value as a probing story of some of the major dynamic interlockings in marriage which, conditioned by set economic and psychobiological situations, have their innumerable counterparts in differences of degree rather than of kind. After her mother's death Nicole Warren suffers intercourse with the father. The psychotic effects, accruing during adolescence and early maturity, develop into a severe schizophrenia. The father, a capitalist "builder" of the middle west, presents the customary ignorance and adaptative weakness before demands of natural knowledge and discipline common to persons recapitulating psychobiological end-results derived from repeated conditionings of anal and acquisitive ingoing trends. Anxious to be rid of responsibility for the daughter, and afraid of knowledge of the consequences of his act, Warren leaves her in a Zurich psychiatric hospital.

Richard Diver, an American physician studying psychiatry abroad, makes the girl's acquaintance through correspondence during the war. She improves greatly by means of this affective outlet; and after their meeting later they marry—Diver being, at the time he makes the step, both cognizant of the unconscious implications of the transference and pre-

FITZGERALD, F. Scott   TENDER IS THE NIGHT

APR 12 1934

Feb. 25	Publishers Weekly	73.00
April	Atlantic Monthly	32.50
April	Harper's Magazine	31.00
April	Books of the Month	18.00
March 3	Publishers Weekly	68.00
April	Scribner's Magazine	30.00
May	Latest Books	12.00
Mar. 24	Publishers Weekly	36.00
May	Bowker - What to Read in Books	10.00
May	Books of the Month	62.50
May	Atlantic Monthly	90.00
May	Scribner's Magazine	80.00
April 17	N. Y. Times	70.95
April 17	N. Y. World Telegram	43.40
April 13	N. Y. Sun	
April 12	N. Y. Herald Tribune	96.74
April 12	N. Y. Times	96.75
April 12	N. Y. World Telegram	40.92
April 18	Chicago News	33.70
April 14	Chicago Tribune	47.10
April 14	Phila. Inquirer	31.96
April 15	N. Y. Herald Tribune	147.17
April 14	Saturday Review of Literature	71.80
April 15	N. Y. Times	882.98
Apr. 22	N. Y. Times	200.79
April 14	Boston Transcript	25.20
May	Book of Books	3.00
April 19	N. Y. Times	35.48
June	Latest Books	12.00
April 29	N. Y. Times	175.00 — 2596.2?
May 5	Saturday Review of Literature	31.50
June	Scribner's Magazine	42.00
May 13	N. Y. Herald Tribune	300.00
May 6	N. Y. Times	450.00
June	Womrath - Book of Books	3.00
May 27	N. Y. Times	119.60
May 26	Publishers Weekly	22.50
July	Latest Books	12.00
May 20	N. Y. Herald Tribune	80.00
May 20	N. Y. Times	450.00 — 4106.8?
June 10	N. Y. Times	230.38
June 3	N. Y. Herald Tribune	147.40
June 3	N. Y. Times	300.00
July	Scribner's Magazine	18.00 — 4802.?
July 15	Princeton Alumni Weekly	25.00
August	Scribner's Magazine	33.00
July	Bowker - What to Read in Books	10.00
June 30	Saturday Review of Literature	24.90
July 1	N. Y. Times	89.60
July 1	N. Y. Herald Tribune	61.09 — 5?65.

(over

FITZGERALD, F. Scott   TENDER IS THE NIGHT

August 4	Saturday Review of Literature	5.00
August 5	N. Y. Herald Tribune	10.00
August 5	N. Y. Times	15.00 — 5075 1?
September	Scribner's Magazine	8.00 — 5083.1?

List of dates, publications, and costs of advertisements Scribners placed for Tender Is the Night. *The publisher continued to promote the novel throughout the summer of 1934 (Princeton University Library).*

pared to fully incorporate in his creative energic organization the demands of her further cure with the work already planned for himself. In the following years there are two children, and, settled in a secluded spot on the Riviera, Diver's chief efforts are devoted to strengthening Nicole against the psychotic relapses of her illness. As, through Diver's care and constant attendance, she gains gradually to a firmer hold on reality, Diver himself slowly begins to slip: it would appear in the time scale of the novel that in proportion as Nicole's improvement becomes more definite and complete, Diver, superficially at first, but later more deeply and pragmatically, is aware of the accruing effects on his own disintegration.

The slipping of his own hold on the exigencies of creative advancement is increasingly manifest in various ways: his work, laid out definitely at first, is now sporadic, becoming more and more elusive; his partnership with a friend in a clinic, begun earnestly at first, falls through; and, concomitant with an extra-marital affair, there is a gradual emergence of destructive attitudes in all his contacts and orientations. As the story unfolds to the point where they separate finally several factors are clearly drawn as of important bearing on these new dynamic patternings. There is the extent of his wife's wealth and the proprietary attitude of her narcissistic sister. Both facts, seemingly inconsequential at first, are shown clearly to have deep psychological cumulative effects, projecting their roots beneath all his plans and activities. At another level, his wife, aware of her husband's slow disintegration, realizes at the same time her increasing freedom from affective dependence on him; a situation which as described here clearly evidences the progressive comparative values in ego development between them.

Around the figures of Diver and his wife are grouped certain other characters, all of which in some degree have a bearing on the emotional relations between them. There is the old friend, the defeated composer North, whose dissolution is marked by the progressions of an acute alcoholism; Rosemary Hoyt, the young movie star through whom the first perspective of the Divers is cast and whose affair with Diver is one of the first objective signs of his disintegration; Barban, the Don Juanesque type who goes back and forth waiting for the couple's separation, casting himself as Nicole's second protector; and Franz, the one-time fellow-worker whose undeviating activity somehow stands as a symbol for a way of life opposite to that which

may be abstracted from the histories here mainly described. These characters, round whom component parts of the history center, are in each instance deeply realized and completely drawn. They present a compact handling of detail making for very clear impressions of the post-war decade with all its aspects of manners, disintegration, and individual loss. Mr. Fitzgerald has written a book which is extremely valuable both as an understanding and sensitive record of human life, and as an accurate and fully prepared chronicle of European life *circa* 1917–1930. Its content and fine treatment in these respects, as in many others which present space limitations make it impossible to discuss fully, together with the author's insight and skill, constitute an achievement which no student of the psychobiological sources of human behavior, and of its particular social correlates extant today, can afford not to read.

The First English Edition

The following description is taken from the revised edition of F. Scott Fitzgerald: A Descriptive Bibliography, *edited by Matthew J. Bruccoli, published in 1987 by the University of Pittsburgh Press.*

A15.2.a
First English edition, first printing (1934)
7 3/8" x 4 7/8"
Copyright page: 'PRINTED IN GREAT BRITAIN | ALL RIGHTS RESERVED'.

[i–viii] [1–2] 3–148 [149–150] 151–306 [307–308] 309–408

[A]⁴ B–I⁸ K–U⁸ X–Z⁸, AA–CC⁸, DD⁴; four-page gathering of ads, beginning with *Brave New World* and ending with *None So Pretty,* inserted at rear.

Contents: p. i: half title; p. ii: blank; p. iii: title; p. iv: copyright; p. v: dedication; p. vi: blank; p. vii: epigraph; p. viii: blank; p. 1: 'BOOK I'; p. 2: blank; pp. 3–408: text, headed 'I'.

Typography and paper: 5¼" (5 9/16") x 3 1/2"; thirty-five lines per page. Running heads: rectos, book and chapter; versos, 'TENDER IS THE NIGHT'. Laid paper, vertical chainmarks 15/16" apart.

Binding: Medium blue (#182) V cloth (fine linen-like grain). Spine yellowstamped: 'TENDER | IS THE | NIGHT | [star] | F. SCOTT | FITZGERALD | CHATTO & WINDUS'. White wove endpapers. Top and front edges trimmed.

Dust jacket: Front has drawing of man and woman in bathing suits against blue background with yellow stars, signed by THÉA: '[white] TENDER | IS THE | NIGHT | [red] BY F. SCOTT FITZGERALD'. Spine: '[red] TENDER | IS | THE | NIGHT | [woman's head in a star] | BY | F. SCOTT | FITZGERALD | [blue] CHATTO & | WINDUS'. Back: 'NEW FICTION | [nine titles]'. Front flap has blurb for *TITN;* back flap blank.

Publication: Unknown number of copies of the first printing. Published September 1934. 7/6.

Printing: P. 408: 'Printed in Great Britain by Butler & Tanner Ltd., Frome and London'.

Locations: BL (12 SEP 34); Bod (SEP 18 1934); Cam (17 SP 1934); MJB (dj); NjP; NLW (OC 1 34-dj); ViU.
Note: The first Chatto & Windus printing of *TITN* varies from the first Scribners printing in some 860 readings, of which 6 are substantive:

61.10 words [61.10 worlds
133.4–5 this name [133.3 his name
169.17 may I add [168.9 may add
347.3 lay own [346.31 lay, down
362.2 with insincerity [361.24 within sincerity
396.9 her raging [395.16 her, raging

The authority for these alterations is unknown.

Proof Copy: Printed on thin wove paper and bound in brown paper wrappers. White label printed in black on front wrapper: 'TENDER IS THE | NIGHT | F. SCOTT FITZGERALD | [decoration] | CHATTO & WINDUS | [rule] | Butler & Tanner Ltd., Frome and London'. Possibly used as a review copy. Location: MJB.

A15.2.a†
Butler & Tanner Ltd. prepared a Chatto & Windus "cheap edition" from remainder copies in September 1936 by pasting a printed label '2/6' on the spine of the dust jacket; ads omitted. Location: MJB (publisher's office copy, dj). 250 sets of sheets were bound in a cheaper binding—not seen.

English Reviews

New Novels

Peter Quennell

New Statesman and Nation, new series 7 (28 April 1934): 642

Mr. Scott Fitzgerald is wildly uneven. After *The Great Gatsby,* a book which, when it was published several years ago, aroused an intellectual furore and was acclaimed by critics as diverse as Mencken, T. S. Eliot and Gertrude Stein, Mr. Fitzgerald's new novel seems wordy and shapeless. It is very long and its narrative method is far from direct. A hundred and fifty pages are occupied by Mr. Fitzgerald in his description of a Mediterranean beach, and of the smart Europeanised Americans who congregate there, as observed through the personality of a famous but innocent film actress, Rosemary Hoyt; and it is not until the hundred-and-forty-eighth page that the novelist supplies us with a key to some of the less easily explicable aspects of the foregoing chapters, letting it appear—quite abruptly—that Nicole, the wife of the engaging young student of mental disorders with whom Rosemary has fallen in love, is herself on the borderline of madness and that behind the calm façade of their affluent household lurked a secret and atrocious preoccupation.

The second half of the book is vivid and memorable. Elsewhere, the delicacy and acuteness that, in *The Great Gatsby,* distinguished Mr. Fitzgerald's choice of epithets and informed his delineation of contemporary characters have degenerated into a rather irritating type of *chic.* His imagery is elaborate and euphuistic; in his former novel he scored bull's-eyes with the accuracy of a crack marksman in the booth at a country fair, and in his present novel he hits everything except his objective, drilling holes just as it pleases him, making the splinters fly, but very seldom getting down to the main business. His incidental commentary is often shrewd. Mr. Fitzgerald knows his modern Americans; he has a firm grasp of their foibles and their slang; he is the prophet of a generation which, though it has passed away, has left a distinct mark on contemporary American literature.

EIGHT years have gone by since the appearance in England of *The Great Gatsby*, a book which Mr. T. S. Eliot called "the first step forward in the American novel since Henry James." He has said further: "I have been waiting impatiently for another book by Mr. Scott Fitzgerald with more eagerness and curiosity than I should feel towards the work of any of his contemporaries, except that of Mr. Ernest Hemingway."

After this long silence Mr. Fitzgerald resumes his place among the leading novelists of the day, whether British or American. In his new book the principal characters are Richard Diver, a young American mental specialist, his rich and beautiful wife, Nicole, and Rosemary Hoyt, a young film star. The first part of the book is all glitter and glamour, a brilliant picture of the life of rich American "intellectuals" in France. But the reader soon perceives that lurking beneath these gaily-coloured scenes are horror and brutality, and the author savagely reveals the pseudo-sophistication and barbarism of the idle and luxurious life led by his characters. Gradually the story centres round the slow disintegration of Dick Diver, whose promising career has been thwarted through his marriage, partly through pity, partly through self-interest, to Nicole, the child of a raw middle-western family.

This is a book of intense psychological interest, varied by scenes of astonishing descriptive power and bitter humour.

Dust jacket and front flap for the first English edition (Bruccoli Collection of Fitzgerald, Thomas Cooper Library, University of South Carolina)

The reviewer for The Spectator *(London) compares* Tender Is the Night *(Chatto and Windus. 7s. 6d.) to Julian Green's* The Dreamer *(Heinemann. 7s. 6d.).*

The Psychological Novel
The Spectator, 153 (21 September 1934): 410

THERE is a sense in which any novel is psychological, but one uses the term here in the loose modern sense to indicate the influence of the psycho-analytical theories of Freud. Their importance to the novelist can be exaggerated; psycho-analysis is only a therapeutic method and dream symbolism is of doubtful value in establishing a fictional character. The symbols are usually common ones; it is only in his personal associations to those symbols that the individual character is revealed.

This is why one feels that Mr. Fitzgerald has used psycho-analysis more legitimately than M. Green. Richard Diver, a psycho-therapist, has married a rich young American, the balance of whose mind he has helped precariously to restore. The curious double relationship of doctor and husband, the double responsibility, ruins him. His love is normal; her love is a transference of her sense of affection and trust from her father after the shock which had shaken her sanity. When he is momentarily unfaithful to her the transference takes place again. She is cured of her dependence: the unbalanced mind has a freedom denied to the normal mind with its prejudices and moralities. It is the normal mind which cannot adjust itself, the sane man who is broken. Psycho-analytical theory is here part of the material of the story, not of the method of narration. This is legitimate, but because a novel's force lies, as a rule, in its width of reference, there is a weakness in the abnormality of Mr. Fitzgerald's subject matter. This reservation made, the imagination capitulates before the subtlety of Mr. Fitzgerald's style, the accurate irony of the climax:

"While he did not answer she began to feel the old hypnotism of his intelligence, sometimes exercised without power but always with substrata of truth under truth which she could not break or even crack. Again she struggled with it, fighting him with her small, fine eyes, with the plush arrogance of a top dog, with her nascent transference to another man, with the accumulated resentment of years; she fought him with her money and her faith that her sister disliked him and was behind her now; with the thought of the new enemies he was making with his bitterness, with her quick guile against his wineing and dine-ing slowness, her health and beauty against his physical deterioration, her unscrupulousness against his moralities for this inner battle she used even her weaknesses fighting bravely and courageously with the old cans and crockery and bot-

TENDER IS THE NIGHT
A ROMANCE

By

F. Scott Fitzgerald

1934
CHATTO & WINDUS
LONDON

Title page (Bruccoli Collection of Fitzgerald, Thomas Cooper Library, University of South Carolina)

tles, empty receptacles of her expiated sins, outrages, mistakes. And suddenly, in the space of two minutes she achieved her victory and justified herself to herself without lie or subterfuge, cut the cord for ever. . . . The case was finished. Doctor Diver was at liberty."

The mournful echoing cadences of the style remind one of a great badly lit railway station, where many people are saying goodbye. In its voluptuous sentiment, its rich obscurity, its sense of *chic* it is definitely post-War. But Mr. Fitzgerald now begins where the author of *Tales of the Jazz Age* used to leave off; his style has lost none of its glittering contemporaneity, but one is suddenly presented with an unsuspected brutality, a background of corruption which lends to the sad wit and the wistful haphazard poetry of departure the lost gas-lamp urban note which our generation has rediscovered in the poetry of Baudelaire and Laforgue.

M. Green uses psycho-analytic theory less legitimately. . . .

New Novels

E. B. C. Jones

New Statesman and Nation, new series 8 (22 September 1934): 366

We have grown so used to skilful stage-management in fiction—the standard of technical accomplishment is now so high—that it is surprising to find Mr. Scott Fitzgerald muddling us by the introduction of too many persons in his opening scene. But this minor fault is readily overlooked when it becomes clear what a feast of interesting situation and complex character is spread before us—and of ideas expressing themselves through situation and character. Unlike technical accomplishment, ideas are not common in fiction, and when present seldom coalesce with the "story"; more often than not poverty of ideas lies behind the careful prose, the subtle epithet. The richness of *Tender is the Night* resides in the author's conception of life and personality. Incidentally, he evokes the Mediterranean coast in June, so that it is with a shock that the reader, coming to, finds himself surrounded by an English autumn; but his chief concern is to reveal the intricacy of Dick Diver's relation to his rich and beautiful young wife Nicole, and the way in which, in the space of five years, her extreme dependence on him was changed into emancipation, and how this very process entailed his deterioration from a brilliant young psychiatrist to an obscure, tippling doctor.

We meet the Divers in 1925, on the beach which their "discovery" is making fashionable, and see them first through the eyes of the very young film-star Rosemary Hoyt. They are all American. Rosemary falls in love with Dick (in an amusing passage, he wearily registers the familiarity of her gambit, "I'm in love with you *and Nicole*") and he less quickly with her, but he rejects her on the grounds of his love for his wife, without informing her or us what the explanation of the slight mystery surrounding Nicole is. They are happy together: "Later she remembered all the hours of the afternoon as happy—one of those uneventful times that seem at the moment only a link between past and future pleasure, but turn out to have been the pleasure itself." But they separate, and in a throw-back we are shown how Dick and Nicole met, and the earlier stages of Nicole's recurrent mental disorder. Rosemary is but one nail in the coffin of the Divers' love, and I am not convinced that the method of the initial mystery and the subsequent throw-back are here justified. Rosemary is thereby given an importance at the start which is not sustained; for later in the book, after she has become Dick's mistress, she

is casually dismissed by him as "never having grown up" without the author bothering to confirm the verdict. The book, that is to say, is not as shapely as it might have been; and the introduction of various violent incidents owes more to Faulkner, Dashiel Hamnet and Hemingway than to the authentic Mr. Scott Fitzgerald; but the main situation is handled with delicacy and force, and makes *Tender is the Night* one of those rare novels which one can with enthusiasm and a clear conscience recommend.

TENDER IS THE NIGHT

Times Literary Supplement, 27 September 1934, p. 652

The literary career of Mr. F. Scott Fitzgerald has been a curious one. Having achieved a considerable popularity with his two earliest novels, "This Side of Paradise" and "The Beautiful and Damned," brilliant, almost garish, studies in American post-War disillusion: his subsequent volumes proved disappointing until the appearance of his best book, "The Great Gatsby," in 1926. But consequent expectation was not fulfilled as one had hoped. TENDER IS THE NIGHT (Chatto and Windus, 7s. 6d. net) is his first work to break, at least in this country, the silence of eight years. It is, in its way, and particularly to follow such a gap, an impressive and yet a depressing achievement. It displays, with all its skill, with all its maturer understanding and abiding sympathy, the mood of disillusion still. This world of wealthy Americans in Europe is only too far this side of paradise: the beautiful, in body and soul, are still the damned: greatness is found nowhere, not even as an aspiration. The very title is ominous: "tender is the night . . . But here there is no light," and the narrative is a panorama of wasted or shattered lives, alike in its central and its minor figures. It is almost all of it tragedy without nobility, and therefore the less tragedy. If fineness is glimpsed, it is in the principal character, Richard Diver, an American mental specialist who is partner in a psychopathic clinic in Switzerland, and in his wife Nicole, an ex-patient and a lovely flower with a worm at its root. But even they seem to float rudderless upon the stream of circumstance. In one sense she has never ceased to be his patient. He is continually aware of the dangers of relapse, not always to be evaded, and of her dependence upon him: and he knows when he falls in love with the spring freshness of Rosemary Hoyt, an eighteen-year-old film star, that there is nothing to be done about it. Besides, he is himself still deeply in love with Nicole, for whose mending, it gradually appears, he has given up all. Yet it proves but another in a complicated series of factors making for his final disintegration, and, one feels, for Nicole's, despite her apparent cure. Grouped about this central inutile progress are any number of minor persons and incidents, the latter often fantastic or brutal, farcical or distressing. The setting of a Riviera and Paris peopled principally by Americans who drink, swim, sun-bathe, gossip, quarrel, and tumble in and out of each other's beds has been drawn before by not a few writers: and, well done as it is here, one would be less inclined to regard Mr. Scott Fitzgerald's novel seriously were it not for the real tenderness informing his portrayal of the relationship between Richard and Nicole, and for a persistent and inescapable note of despair underlying its lightest pages.

"Daring" in Novels—Old Style and New
G. B. Stern
Daily Telegraph (London), 19 Oct 1934, p. 6

Contrasts in "Courage"

I believe very few books nowadays are forbidden to the young. Once upon a time there was a whole school of fiction that had to be read with throbbing hearts and flaming cheeks, in moist secluded places under seaside piers: "Jane Eyre" and Ouida; and then "Comin' through the Rye," "Cometh up as a Flower" and "Three Weeks"; also "Six Nights" (or was it "Seven Women"!), and "Anna Lombard" and "Life's Shop Window." The author of these last, Victoria Cross, used to have sales that ran into millions; and, for all we know, her postman still rings twice.

They were called "courageous"; the word nowadays is "brutal." Not unnaturally, when I recently saw a novel advertised called "THE GIRL IN THE STUDIO: The Story of Her Strange New Way of Loving," by Victoria Cross, I had to see if the "strange new way" had become brutal, or was still courageous in the old pure shining way of a recent advertisement which describes another best seller: "The love of an Englishwoman and of an Englishman who became a monk by mischance!" ("Mischance" is a most awe-inspiring selection of le mot juste). "Love leads these two up and up until they reach the heights where peace reigns."

But, on the other hand, there is a new novel, after many years, by Scott Fitzgerald, called "TEN-

British novelist Gladys Bertha Stern (1890–1973)

DER IS THE NIGHT," where love does no such thing. Scott Fitzgerald wrote "The Great Gatsby," and is one of the best living American writers of what is known as "the advanced school"; though unlike some of his popular contemporaries, he does not appear obsessed by the continual necessity for letting his hero strike his heroine. This is an appropriate entrance for a quotation, from "The Girl in the Studio," with which, as an example of the older type of "advanced" fiction, it is our pleasure to compare "Tender is the Night":

> "A kiss in itself is a free, joyous, innocent, pleasure-giving thing. Why necessarily harness it to other far more serious, complicated and often dangerous matters? But in her kisses Augusta kept her lips closed. She preferred it so."

Demand for the Wholesome

A sudden campaign has arisen in England and America clamouring for the Wholesome in plays, books and films. "Wholesome" as applied to cereals is an adequate and well-meaning word; we feel it should never be applied to heroines. Yet probably if you asked this school of readers (for there are Schools of readers as well as of porpoises and writers) what they meant by "wholesome," or what they did not like in, for instance, "A Handful of Dust" or "Tender is the Night," they would reply; "We meet enough unpleasant people in real life. We don't want to meet them in books."

You might then argue that "wholesome" people in fiction are probably identical with the "unpleasant" people they complain of in real life; that is, prurient complacent people who have kept reality at arm's length. An old-fashioned type of best-seller was almost bound to contain a heroine of this excessive purity; so pure that she could succeed in detaching herself, white as driven snow, from passions black as driven men. Augusta in "The Girl in the Studio," is no exception, proving, to our astonishment, that this sort of heroine (the old girl wears wonderfully well) is still going on and in demand. She loves, indeed; ah, but what she loves is the nobility in music, nature, sculpture, horses, boar-hounds, and the North wind, and the chaste pleasures of intelligent conversations with her men friends. One cannot help suspecting that Miss Stella Gibbons solved the problem of these heroines when she wrote "Cold Comfort Farm," and that once upon a time they had seen something nasty in the woodshed.

"Well," the discipline of the Wholesome School would finally assert, "we don't want to read about worthless people with nothing to *do* all day long but fritter away their time."

And now we are down to it. Certainly the characters in "Tender is the Night" have, during the first half of their story, very little to do all day long. It is a general though surprising assumption that however dull and poor a book about people who labour in factories or offices, it will yet be adjudged admirable and worth-while as solvency. But "Tender is the Night," on the contrary, lightly introduces us to a totally "worthless" group of young, not too young, super-modern Americans frittering away their time on the Riviera and Paris.

They are enchanting, witty personalities, sophisticated and unprincipled; a careless over-tolerance their chief fault; frank and flippant, but with that flippancy which is the subtle art of telling the truth in a way to make your hearers believe it to be a lie. You wonder why the author places them in such a concentrated atmosphere, ringed about by a savage unspoken threat. And gradually you become conscious, even before you are told, of why Dick Diver, so ardently in love with his beautiful young wife

Nicole, is not a worker, not a mental specialist any longer, after the powerful promise of his beginnings.

Below the Surface

With the sliding inevitability of Greek drama, you are tilted from enchantment into horror; from horror into wickedness and tragic disintegration. And you are all the more appalled because this book is as true and wry, as bitter and complex as contemporary life can be directly you get below its highly polished surface; beneath the mocking promise of that lovely, soothing title: "Tender is the Night."

Tender? But take the chapter where Dick Diver and his party go to visit the battlefields and trenches near Amiens. . . .

D. W. Harding, a professor of psychology as well as a critic of English literature, was a member of the editorial board (1933–1947) of Scrutiny, *an influential critical journal.*

Mechanisms of Misery
D. W. Harding
Scrutiny, 3 (December 1934): 316–319

Many of the features that go to making *The Great Gatsby* as fine as it is are also present in this latest novel of Scott Fitzgerald's. There is still his power of seeming to lose himself in incident and letting the theme emerge by itself, there is his sensitiveness (occasionally touching sentimentality) and his awareness of the brutalities in civilized people's behaviour, and there is simultaneously his keen appreciation, not entirely ironic, of the superficies of the same people's lives. This last is the feature that is most nearly lost in the new book. Here there is no more gusto, but right from the start an undercurrent of misery which draws away even the superficial vitality of the Euramerican life he depicts.

The story is the acutely unhappy one of a young psychiatrist, brilliant in every way, who gradually deteriorates. In place of plot there is a fine string of carefully graduated incidents to illustrate the stages of the descent. Rather than tragedy, however, the book appears to me to be one variety of the harrowing, if this can be taken to mean that as we read it our feelings are of misery and protest, and that, unlike tragedy, it can give no satisfactions to those who wish to go on living. On the other hand, it is so effectively and sincerely harrowing that its mechanisms deserve close examination.

In the first place the doomed hero is offered as the most admirable kind of modern man we can reasonably ask for, and throughout the novel he is made to stand out as superior to all the other personæ. This being so we look for some explanation of his collapse, and the first mechanism of misery appears in the ambiguity here. Various possible explanations are hinted at but none is allowed to stand. His wife's wealth, with its heavy burden of smart leisure, Dick deals with like a disciplined artist; he shows himself heroically adequate to the strain of her recurrent mental trouble; and he has as full an insight into himself and the strains his work imposes as he has into his patients. Everything that we could hope to do he is shown doing better, and—apparently as a consequence—he cracks up. The gloomy generalization is made by Dick himself in commenting on a man who precedes him to ruin: 'Smart men play close to the line because they have to—some of them can't stand it, so they quit.' But the pessimistic conviction of the book goes deeper than that, and its puritan roots are suggested by Dick's misgivings over his good fortunes and achievements in his heigh-day. He soliloquises: '—And Lucky Dick can't be one of these clever men; he must be less intact, even faintly destroyed. If life won't do it for him, it's not a substitute to get a disease, or a broken heart, or an inferiority complex, though it'd be nice to build out some broken side till it was better than the original structure.' Scott Fitzgerald sees to it that life *will* do it for him.

But in addition to the puritan conviction, there is also present a curious mingling of a childish fantasy with an adult's attempt to correct it, and much of the harrowing effect of the book depends on this. On the one hand, Dick is the tragic fantasy hero who is so great and fine that everyone else expects to go on taking and taking from him and never give back; and so he gets tired, so tired; and he breaks under the strain with no one big enough to help him, and it's terribly pathetic and admirable. The vital point of this childish fantasy is that he should remain admirable and (posthumously) win everyone's remorseful respect. But the story is too obviously sentimental in those terms. To try ruthlessly to tear out the sentimentality, Scott Fitzgerald brings in a much more mature bit of knowledge: that people who disintegrate in the adult world don't at all win our respect and can hardly retain even our pity. He gets his intense painfulness by inviting our hearts to go out to the hero of the childish fantasy and then checking them with the embarrassment which everyone nearest him in the story, especially Nicole his wife, feels for the failure.

The question is whether the situation could in fact occur. Not whether the main events could be paralleled in real life, but whether all the elements of action and feeling could co-exist in the way they are presented here, whether we are not being trapped into incompatible attitudes towards the same events. In short, is an emotional trick being played on us?

Dust jacket for a remaindered copy of the English first edition. The printed label with the price 2 shillings and 6 pence covered the original price, 7/6 (Bruccoli Collection, Thomas Cooper Library, University of South Carolina).

There seem to me to be several tricks, though without extensive quotation they are hard to demonstrate. Chief among them is the social isolation of the hero, isolation in the sense that no one gives him any help and he has no genuinely reciprocal social relationships; he remains the tragic child hero whom no one is great enough to help. Even towards the end he is made to seem superior to the others so that they are inhibited from approaching him with help. That this should be so is made plausible by the continual returns of his old self amongst the wreckage, returns of self-discipline and willingness to shoulder responsibility that amount almost to alternations of personality. He explains it himself: 'The manner remains intact for some time after the morale cracks.' But it seems highly doubtful whether anyone could remain so formidable spiritually during a process of spiritual disintegration, especially to someone who had been as

Fitzgerald's record of income for 1934 from his Ledger. *For the year* Tender Is the Night *was published, his total book royalties were $58.35. He sold three parts of the* Count of Darkness *medieval series, intended to be a serial novel, to* Red Book *and began writing stories for* Esquire *at greatly reduced rates.*

close to him as Nicole had been. But here another trick appears in the interests of plausibility: the patient-physician relationship between the two of them is now emphasized, and Nicole's abandonment of Dick is interpreted as an emergence from fixation, whereas much of the misery of the collapse springs from its wrecking what has earlier been made to seem a genuine and complete marriage.

Once achieved, Dick's isolation permits of the further device of making his suffering dumb. Reading the aquaplane episode in particular is like watching a rabbit in a trap. The story begins to become less harrowing and more like tragedy when, once or twice, Dick is articulate about himself. This happens momentarily when he comments on the manner remaining intact after the morale has cracked; but no other persona is allowed to be big enough to hear more, and

Tax form showing Fitzgerald's income from Scribner in the year Tender Is the Night *was published*
(Bruccoli Collection, Thomas Cooper Library, University of South Carolina)

'"Do you practise on the Riviera?" Rosemary demanded hastily.' At one point the cloud of dumb misery lifts again for a moment, when he thinks he is unobserved and Nicole sees from his face that he is going back over his whole story, and actually feels sympathy for him; but this episode only introduces the final harrowing isolation. His position at the end is the apotheosis of the hurt child saying "Nobody loves me," but the child's self-pity and reproaches against the grown-ups have largely been rooted out and in their place is a fluctuation between self-disgust and a fatalistic conviction that this is bound to happen to the nicest children.

The difficulty of making a convincing analysis of the painful quality of this novel, and the conviction that it was worth while trying to, are evidence of Scott Fitzgerald's skill and effectiveness. Personal peculiarities may of course make one reader react more intensely than another to a book of this kind, and I am prepared to be told that this attempt at analysis is itself childish—an attempt to assure myself that the magician didn't really cut the lady's head off, did he? I still believe there was a trick in it.

A Study in Disillusion
Saturday Review, 158 (8 December 1934): 501

It is eight years since Mr. F. Scott Fitzgerald wrote "The Great Gatsby" which has been accounted his best novel. The long silence of the intervening years has now been broken by the appearance of what he calls a romance entitled "Tender Is the Night" (Chatto and Windus, 7s. 6d.). The rest of the verse from which the title is taken gives some clue to the nature of this book.

. . . . But here there is no light
Save what from heaven is with the breezes blown
Through verdurous glooms and winding mossy ways

It is the story of wealthy Americans in Europe, with all the glitter and glamour and empty lives that lead only to disillusionment and disintegration of character. It is brilliantly written with all the author's gift for description and mordant humour to give it special distinction.

Fitzgerald's 1934 tax return (Bruccoli Collection of Fitzgerald, Thomas Cooper Library, University of South Carolina)

SCHEDULE A—INCOME (OR LOSS) FROM BUSINESS OR PROFESSION (See Instruction 2)

1. Total receipts from business or profession (state kind of business) $29,032 33

COST OF GOODS SOLD

2. Labor .... $
3. Material and supplies ....
4. Merchandise bought for sale ....
5. Other costs (itemize below or on separate sheet) ....
6. Plus inventory at beginning of year ....
7.   TOTAL (Lines 2 to 6) .... $
8. Less inventory at end of year ....
9. NET COST OF GOODS SOLD (Line 7 minus Line 8) .... $

Enter "C", or "C or M", on Lines 6 and 8 to indicate whether inventories are valued at cost, or cost or market, whichever is lower.

OTHER BUSINESS DEDUCTIONS

10. Salaries not included as "Labor" in Line 2 (do not deduct compensation for your services) .... $ 14,851 96
11. Interest on business indebtedness to others 77 22
12. Taxes on business and business property ....
13. Losses (explain in table at foot of page) ....
14. Bad debts arising from sales or services ....
15. Depreciation, obsolescence, and depletion (explain in table provided at foot of page) ....
16. Rent, repairs, and other expenses (itemize below or on separate sheet) 2,694 54
17.   See Slip A   TOTAL (Lines 10 to 16) $4257 72
18. TOTAL DEDUCTIONS (Line 9 plus Line 17) 4257 72
19. NET PROFIT (OR LOSS) (Line 1 minus Line 18) (Enter as Item 2) $15,774 61

Explanation of deductions claimed on Lines 5 and 16 ....

A Movie Treatment for *Tender Is the Night*

There were no immediate movie offers for Tender Is the Night *when the novel was published. Hoping to make the property more attractive to the studios, Fitzgerald prepared a movie treatment in 1934 with Charles Marquis Warren, a young Baltimore writer. Lacking the manuscript, it is impossible to differentiate the collaborators' contributions; but this treatment had Fitzgerald's approval. As such, it shows how Fitzgerald tried to satisfy Hollywood's requirements by providing melodramatic action and the obligatory happy ending. Even so, no studio was willing to buy* Tender Is the Night *at that time. This treatment was first published in* Some Sort of Epic Grandeur.

Prince Paklin Troubetskoi, exiled Russian nobleman and ex-Cossack, has established a fashionable girls' riding school on the shores of Lake Geneva in Switzerland. It is his habit every afternoon to take his pupils, girls from a nearby school, for a short, hilarious gallop through the surrounding countryside. It is on one of these escapades that Nicole Warren, seventeen year old American heiress and Troubetskoi's pet (though Troubetskoi is not cast as the type that would quite appeal to the average man as a son-in-law), loses control of her mount, and despite the valiant efforts of the Russian riding master to save her, is thrown in a nasty fall and dashed against the base of a tree. After having worked frantically to revive the unconscious girl, Troubetskoi dispatches one of his pupils to bring a doctor immediately.

A charity hospital is near the scene of the accident. Richard Diver, Assistant Resident therein, promising young brain surgeon and psychiatrist, is just completing a delicate operation. When word is brought to him of the accident he feels he is too busy to go, but when he is informed that the girl is an American and badly hurt he throws off his preoccupation and taking another horse rides to the scene. While hurriedly examining the injured girl, Dr. Dick Diver finds out what he can from the anxious Russian, Troubetskoi, and the distraught girl pupils. He learns that Nicole evidently suffered a severe blow on the head, and while she is still unconscious he has her removed to the hospital.

Word is sent to Nicole's elder sister, "Baby" Warren, living in Vienna. Two days later Baby arrives. Tall, handsome and distinctly conscious of the prominence of the Warren name in America; she is slightly more irritated than sympathetic over her sister's accident. Although X-rays prove that the skull is not fractured or any obvious damage done Nicole remains in a coma for two days. At Dick's suggestion Baby puts up at a hotel not far from the hospital. Returning to consciousness Nicole shows some disturbing outward signs of mental disorder—nothing violent, but a tendency toward exaggerated elation and exaggerated melancholy, a sort of confusion. At the end of a week Dr. Dick Diver permits Baby to take Nicole to a cottage that she has found not far from the hospital and on the shore, where Nicole will get rest and quiet. At first only the anxious Troubetskoi and Dr. Diver are permitted to visit Nicole—Troubetskoi

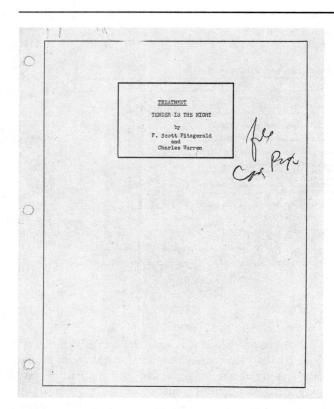

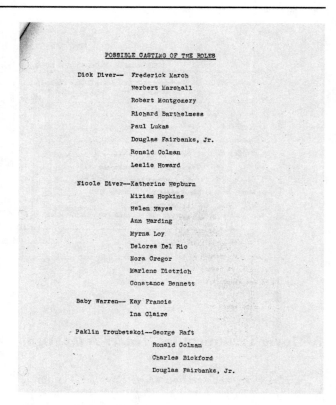

Title page and casting list for the movie treatment on which Fitzgerald collaborated (Princeton University Library)

in the role of a man fast falling in love and Dick Diver purely as a physician. Even then, Dr. Diver calls rarely and only because he has a suspicion that there is some definite physical lesion in Nicole's brain, whether or not caused by the accident–a suspicion, however, that he does not reveal to anyone.

But it is a different case with Nicole. She finds this young doctor fascinating. And in the course of three months she falls in love with him. This has been a monotonous three months for Baby Warren and when she learns of Nicole's attraction to Dick she formulates a plan to "buy" Dick as Nicole's husband, thus insuring her sister's health and taking Nicole off her own hands.

In appreciation for his fine work at the hospital and out of respect for his tired condition, Dick Diver is granted a vacation. He plans to bicycle through Switzerland–and it is evening when he calls on the Warrens to say good-bye. Baby Warren, realizing that her plans to capture Dr. Dick Diver might run aground if she lets him get away, decides to put her proposition before him immediately. She takes Dick aside and in no uncertain terms tells him of the wealth of the Warren family, the sickness of her sister, the need of a medical man to take care of her, and the

decision that, in return for Dick's marriage to Nicole, he will be supplied with the money he needs to continue his work. Dick flatly refuses. The cold indifference of this older sister has stunned him. What about Nicole? Hasn't Baby Warren considered her sister's feelings in this matter? Nicole, though a patient, is still a human being. Baby explains casually that Nicole thinks she is in love with him.

To Dick the entire proposition is preposterous. Nicole is only a child–but quite a lovely child. He leaves Baby Warren but on his way out of the cottage runs into Nicole. The various influences of the evening on the lakeside, of Nicole's beauty, and of her new-found love for him are not to be denied, and though he leaves somewhat abruptly with a few formal instructions for her as a patient, she has registered big on Dick Diver's heart.

Bicycling is not the best thing in the world to take a man's mind off a woman, and Dick finds himself constantly haunted by the girl, who has blossomed forth in his mind as a young woman. So, when by coincidence he meets Baby and Nicole in a funicular making the trip up a mountain for pleasure, his gaiety is somewhat forced. A casual conversation between two of the passengers about the possibilities of the cables that pull the car breaking seems to upset Nicole, and Dick again finds himself concerned about this delicate girl. Something goes wrong with the cable. The car begins to tremble and amid the terror of the passengers, Dick's one thought is for Nicole's safety. The cable splits and the funicular is precipitated down the incline for a horrible moment, then derailed. It crashes over on its side and amid the confusion that follows, Dick clutches Nicole tightly to his heart. Thankful that she is safe, and realizing that this girl and her future mean everything to him, he looks across her still body at Baby Warren, who is slightly shaken up and holding in his arms the girl that he now realizes is his love, indicates to Baby Warren his acquiescence in her proposition that he is to be her husband and private doctor for life.

    This treatment must be broken off for a moment to explain the intention of what comes next. In the book, *Tender Is the Night,* there is much emphasis on the personal charm of the two Divers and of the charming manner in which they're able to live. In the book this was conveyed largely in description, "fine writing", poetic passages, etc. It has occurred to us that a similar effect can be transferred to the spectator by means of music, and to accomplish that we have interpolated in the way shown below a melody written and copyrighted by Charles M. Warren.

    Now go on with the treatment.

There is a view of the frayed end of the split cable, which gradually changes into a thick dangling rope. This rope is suspended over a cliff ledge and falls down to the shore below. At the top of the cliff is "Villa Diana", the luxurious house of the Divers. With the Warren money, Dick and Nicole have literally bought an old mountain village and converted it into the most charming place in Southern France. At the bottom of the cliff two French workmen contemplate the possibilities of using this suspended rope to hoist a giant grand piano to the house above.

"Who lives up there?"

"The Divers, and believe me they tip well."

"They better." (Adjusting rope to piano) "Look at the size of the thing. It ought to be worth plenty to have this baby hauled up to that house." (They look up at the cliff, that mounts like a wide staircase to the "Villa Diana".)

"If the road hadn't been washed away we could a used a truck. What do they want it for now? You said they already had one piano."

"These crazy rich Americans! They're giving a party tonight."

"Well, it's a good piano, anyway."

Perching himself precariously on top of the piano he leans down and fingers the keys.

[music]

"Watch yourself!" comes a sharp caution from his co-worker.

But it is too late. On the top level of the cliff, eight farm horses, harnessed together and driven by a farmer, have begun to pull, and the piano is rising. Against his will the man is carried up with it. His fellow workman runs up a zig-zag staircase, cut on the side of the stone hill, crying in alarm to the driver on top to "Stop the horses!" The driver does so and the piano swings into one of the indentations higher up on the cliff where it is allowed to come gently to rest. The danger over, the frightened workman hops off the piano and with forced bravado says:

"It wasn't anything. See—I'll play the rest of the tune."

He plays with one hand:
[music]

"It doesn't go like that," says the first workman.

"*Sure* it does."

They are interrupted by a woman's voice:

"No, it goes like this."

[music]

It is Nicole, happy and the picture of health. She has played the tune more fully than the workmen, who stand respectfully, listening. Dick joins her and with one arm around Nicole improves on her version of the music. As Nicole diminishes the melody to pianissimo Dick speaks to the workmen:

"Careful with this piano! Don't let it bang now as it goes up!"

"We'll follow it, Monsieur Diver, and see that it won't scrape against the stone, so it'll be in good condition for your party tonight."

Dick turns to Nicole. "Come along, young lady. You have to get some good rest before the party—remember! Papa doesn't consider you entirely strong yet."

As they start trailing upward along the zig-zag walk we hear:

". . . so damn glad to get a few minutes alone with you. We won't have much time when that crowd comes." Upon Nicole's encouragement they sit down and kiss then and there . . .

. . . Throughout this the tinkle of the piano is heard continuing as if by itself. But now there is just the suggestion of an ominous note in its melody as it reaches a still higher level, and swings from side to side and then comes to rest like a pendulum might.

OVER THE HEADS OF:

Baby Warren and her latest "royalty". He is a small pudgy individual, a Prince Somebody from the Balkans—a type with whom Baby is invariably involved, and just as invariably discards.

Due to some difficulty overhead, the piano is temporarily lowered, and, giggling, Baby's boy friend plays a repetition of the previous melody but now comically in the highest octave of the piano. Again there is an ominous note in the score as Baby Warren walks over to his side and finishes the tune in the bass cleff.

[music]

The workmen, impatient to get their job done, signal the man above, who lifts, and so almost snatches the piano from under Baby's hands.

"Crude fellow. Might hurt someone doing that sort of thing."

"That reminds me. As I was telling you—you might say we—well, why not come out with it—you'll understand—we *bought* this doctor, and now it seems—" Their voices fade as they begin climbing—

—And up above, the driver looks over the edge and blusters down to his companions:

"What is this—anyhow? You're hired to help them get the piano to the house 'Villa Diana'?—or do you want 'em to play it on the side of this cliff? Tell those people to lay off this God—" The crack of his whip starting the team of horses behind him and the sound of the horses moving, drown out his description of the piano job.

And our piano, at first lazily spiraling as it moves upwards, begins to twist around and around so quickly that it, and the eccentric music accompanying it in its rise, blend into a whirling blur.

Finally it slows, and as it gently rights itself the keys are seemingly played by an unseen hand. Slowly a figure at the piano emerges and is playing. Blending into the picture is an orchestra surrounding the musician at the piano. *The orchestra is now rendering a full score of the melody that accompanied the piano up the cliff!*

The Divers are giving a dinner. Here all the charm of the menage which the Divers have created is apparent. The atmosphere of luxury and good taste of intimate friends has *not yet* been broken by the underlying sinister threat of cold hard calculating selfishness as personified by Baby Warren.

There is Dick, the compelling and magnetic host; there is Nicole, incomparable hostess and wife supreme; there is Rosemary Hoyt, motion picture star—young and beautiful and obviously infatuated with the enchanting Dick Diver; there is Prince Troubetskoi, with such attractions as women associate with romance, vainly endeavoring to conceal his passion for Nicole; there is Baby Warren, half-comic in her pretended aloofness; there is her little pudgy beau, pal of Troubetskoi and heir to the throne of some other vague Balkan principality, and there is an elderly English doctor from Cannes.

During the past three years of happy married life, the luxury and ample supply of the Warrens' money have caused Dick Diver's charm and ability to stage-manage his parties to overshadow his interest in the medical profession, even to the extent of dropping "Doctor" as a prefix to his name. But inwardly there have been longings and old regrets, even though Dick is too proud to show them, and dreads the effect upon Nicole.

After dinner the men and women separate—the men following Prince Paklin to a series of small tables placed beside the cliff, the women going to the flat Moorish roof of the villa.

Dick and the old English doctor from Cannes remain at table—finishing a glass of champagne—they are naturally less interested in the visits from the cliff. The doctor has begun to take a paternal interest in Dick but his persistent remarks about getting back to work are irritating to Dick.

On the roof directly overhead the women closest to the edge are able to overhear the conversation that ensues. First Baby hears it, then Nicole, then Rosemary and a couple of curious guests.

Down below Dick has exploded.

"Stop it! Do you think I don't know? Do you think *you* are the *only* one who knows? Cooped up for three years! Private *doctor*? Private *nurse*!"

And he leaves the table and walks out on the terrace. Nicole is shocked and hurt. It is the first suspicion she has had that Dick was not entirely satisfied with their easy existence. Young Rosemary Hoyt's exaggerated sympathy for Dick tends to deepen Nicole's hurt. Baby Warren immediately takes possession of the situation. Her suspicions have been further aroused by Dick's outburst of discontent—and by Rosemary's tearing down the stairs to console Dick. Finding that Dick prefers to be alone, Rosemary kisses him lightly. Nicole arrives upon the scene at this moment and falsely interprets it as a love passage between Dick and Rosemary.

Fitzgerald's inscription to Charles Marquis Warren in a copy of Tender Is the Night
(James Cummins Bookseller, catalogue 75 [2001], item 118)

The panic in Nicole's expression is the fade out on this sequence.

We open up on the Divers and their house guests on the beach next morning taking their customary dip in the blue Mediterranean and the inevitable sun bath on the beach. Dick suggests that they take the Divers' speed boat and do some aquaplaning. Nicole, with the jealousy of the previous evening still close to her, interprets Dick's desire to aquaplane as a method of showing off physically before Rosemary's exciting youth.

With Paklin Troubetskoi guiding the smooth little craft, each member of the party takes his turn on the board. When it comes to Dick's turn Nicole finds herself wondering with growing coldness if he will make a spectacle of himself, fumbling through stunts he had once done with ease. She compared him with the romantic figure of the Russian riding master beside her. For the first time Dick suffers from a comparison made by his wife.

Dick is preparing to do his old lifting trick—the object being to straighten all the way up, from a kneeling position, and carry a man on his shoulders. It is noticeable to the people in the boat, watching closely, that he is having difficulties. As the boat gathers momentum and the men on the board get their balance, Dick, with a last wrenching effort, stands upright, but the board slips side-wise simultaneously and they both topple off into the sea. Rosemary is enthused. "Wonderful!

They almost had it!" Baby Warren and Nicole are a little disgusted.

Dick—annoyed and perhaps a little embarrassed—tries again. He is more careful in this second attempt, and almost succeeds; but at the crucial moment his legs suddenly buckle, and both men are throne into the water again.

Dick is angry and asks for another chance, which, though he looks tired, is readily granted. As the speed of the boat increases, Dick rests for a moment, belly-down on the board. Then he crouches beneath the man and his muscles flex as he tries to rise. The passengers in the boat scarcely raise him-and-his-burden two inches from the board and exhausted, he collapses into the water. The boat races back to pick him up and Nicole's anxiety changes to contempt as she finds him floating exhaustedly but safely in the water. On the way in to the shore Baby Warren smiles as she remarks that the huge, well-built riding master beside him could have turned the trick easily "with *three* men on his back!"

It is the last day of the week-end party and every one decides to go to a fair that is being held close to the Divers' home. On the way Dick senses Nicole's attitude towards the episode on the aquaplane that morning and this causes him to show more than ordinary interest in Rosemary. Arriving at the fair, Nicole suddenly opens the door of the car and leaps out. Dick and Baby follow her on the run while the riding master is left with Rosemary.

After bursting through countless tents and zig-zagging through the grounds of the entire fair, Dick finally sees Nicole riding on a ferris-wheel. As the car in which she is riding nears the top Nicole stands up and looks bewilderedly at the ground far below. Dick shouts to the operator of the wheel to stop it immediately. The man at first refuses, but Dick frantically presses money into his hand and the wheel is brought to a stop. Childishly, Nicole is reluctant to leave, scolding Dick and Baby for following her. Dick and Baby realize that the mental disorder, which has been dormant for three years, has cropped up again. Baby accuses Dick.

"It's your fault that this happened. Your attitude towards that little kid, Rosemary—"

Dick and Baby lead Nicole against her will back to the car.

Nicole's mind wanders.

"I won't ride. I never want to see another horse. I had an accident riding a horse. They always frighten me now. Please don't make me ride—I'm afraid of horses." (She sees Paklin Troubetskoi) "But I'm not afraid if he's here. He was my riding master."

Bewildered and uncertain, Nicole sits next to Dick who is driving. It is when Dick has stepped on the accelerator for a short straightaway run that Nicole, laughing hysterically, clutches the steering wheel and swerves the car off the road, down a little incline at the bottom of which it rolls over on its side. Dick's leg, unknown to the others, is pinned agonizingly under the side of the car. Rosemary is thrown against him in such a way that it looks as though he might have crawled over to her. Baby, unhurt, is draped awkwardly over the upright side of the car. Paklin Troubetskoi's first thought has been of Nicole and he scrambles out of the car with Nicole in his arms, holding her until she assures him, still hysterically, that she has not been hurt. Paklin has already hailed a passing car to take them home when the three women discover that Dick is hurt. But his injury doesn't succeed in quieting Nicole or curing the suspicion in Baby's mind that Dick's usefulness as Nicole's husband is over.

At the Divers' home Dick and Nicole are immediately put to bed in separate rooms. Baby Warren, who has been waiting for a chance to get another doctor's opinion on Nicole's case, calls in a physician from Cannes. He turns out to be the same old senile Englishman who aroused Dick Diver's ire during the dinner party. Being a simple country practitioner, it is comparatively easy for Baby to convince him, during the examination, that the sick girl's husband is responsible for her condition.

"He causes her worry over every new face he sees. He's lost all interest in my sister and thinks only of himself. How can we blame Nicole for getting sick when her husband, the man who should take care of her, does nothing but cause her mental anguish?"

Convinced, the small-time doctor prescribes a change of environment and urges that Nicole should be spared even seeing Dick.

This is all that Baby Warren needs and she goes into Dick's room and tells him as a matter of fact that Nicole would be better off without him. It is not in Baby's character to mince matters or situations; and without regard for Dick's injured condition she ends by telling Dick:

"We hired you to take care of my sister—not to make her worse. The doctor and I have decided that it would be better for Nicole to forget you entirely.

Nicole herself will realize that it is the best thing that could possibly happen to her."

Dick, lying in bed with his leg badly crushed–physically and mentally hurt, and weary of Nicole's sickness, gives up. That Baby should come to him at a time like this and tell him flatly that they no longer require his service is more than he can stand. He murmurs:

"Do you think I could have stood a moment with Nicole if I hadn't loved her? Would I have locked myself away from everything for three years if I hadn't cared? All right–I'm through. If you think Nicole can get along better without me–I'll leave. Perhaps I won't make such a mess of things alone."

Impulsively, he topples out of bed and hobbles painfully to the door. The car is called and he leaves them. There is no restraining hand–they are glad to see him go. Baby and the doctor and Prince Paklin Troubetskoi watch the receding lights of his car as it threads its way down the steep descent to the road which leads away from the "Villa Diana". The case is finished. Doctor Diver is at liberty.

Now the flowers and foliage of the gardens and terraces which surround the "Villa Diana" with their loveliness of spring have bared themselves in the lonely bleakness of winter. An atmosphere of restlessness prevails in the Divers' household. In particular, Baby Warren, a guest, cannot suppress her restless desire to leave the "Villa Diana". She intimates as much to the senile old English doctor from Cannes, who has been a regular visitor attending Nicole.

"I feel as though I'm shut off from the rest of the world–as though I'm a prisoner up here on this cliff."

"That is what her husband said as he left," says the doctor.

"This is different. I'm thinking of Nicole. She needs a change. The place gets on her nerves."

"The young Russian who visits your sister so often–doesn't he relieve the monotony?"

"He can't change this place. This house is still the same, whether he's here or not. Besides, he thinks she should go away, too."

Nicole is living in confusion. Something is missing. She cannot decide whether it is her condition or the loss of her husband that bewilders her. She had thought of Dick really as an inexhaustible energy, incapable of fatigue and she had forgotten the trouble she had caused him. Sometimes she has felt the old hypnotism of his intelligence, his kindness and patience with her. Yet, this Russian has been kind and undoubtedly patient. And most of all he has loved her for herself–not through the eyes of

Inscription to Lady Florence Willert, a Riviera acquaintance of the Fitzgeralds (Bruccoli Collection of Fitzgerald, Thomas Cooper Library, University of South Carolina)

a professional man seeing only the work he revers so much.

Paklin enters even as Baby and the doctor are talking and goes into the next room to see Nicole. He comes right to the point.

"You've been keeping me waiting here for six months. Can't we go away? Your sister says you need the change."

Comparative pictures of Dick and Paklin flash before Nicole's eyes. Doctor Diver–working, play-

---

Lady Florence Willert to Fizgerald, October 1934

I have just this minute finished y. book. It is a living thing–it is a miracle. It is writing + painting in one– + instantaneous photography too! You have somehow got it all down–transmuted into the highest art–outsider + insider: people + their surroundings to the last fleeting expression of a finger: clothes, houses, rooms + furniture: colour, weather, food–all that makes life.

ing, knowing all. Paklin Troubetskoi—handsome, romantic, loving her because she is the rich Nicole Warren.

Baby Warren and the doctor enter. Baby explains that Nicole must leave "Villa Diana" for her own good.

"The Doctor and I have decided that a change—"
There follows a week of quiet, but thorough levity. The music, the dancing, and the gay nights are a tonic to Baby Warren's pent up nerves and incidentally serve as a change of environment for her sister. Back in circulation again, Baby nails one of her many admirers (the one who happened to attend the Divers' week-end party) and he invites them to his principality. Nicole and Paklin enjoy this rough little Balkan sea-side town (planted to be like Corfu or Ragusa) but Baby tires quickly and leaving the two alone, takes her Prince and goes to Vienna.

Meanwhile Doctor Diver has resumed his studies in Vienna, and has been practising brain surgery. He is badly in need of money. On his way home from one of the hospitals he sees Baby Warren sweeping grandly into the finest hotel, where she is staying. He enters and follows her into her suite in order to inquire after Nicole. Baby politely but coldly tells him that her sister is doing very well. A telephone call comes through at the moment from Nicole who is in trouble.

Upon Baby Warren's departure from the little Balkan resort Nicole and Paklin were elated to find themselves just as completely alone as though they had been stranded in mid-ocean. Nicole wanted an "affair"—she did not want any vague spiritual romance; she wanted a change. And this Russian was making her thrill with delight in thinking of herself in a new way.

Driving through the pleasant countryside Nicole does not object when Paklin turns the car into a drive that leads to a small mountain hotel. She hovers, outwardly tranquil, as Paklin fills out the police blanks and registers the names—his real, hers false. Their room is simple, almost ascetic. Paklin orders brandy and when the waiter has brought it and left—they suddenly move together and meet standing up. Then he is kissing her as they sit on the bed.

Suddenly Nicole is conscious of that nameless fear that precedes all emotions, joyous or sorrowful, inevitably as a hum of thunder precedes a storm.

In spring 1934 Fitzgerald wrote a letter of introduction for Charles Marquis Warren to Samuel Marx, head of the M-G-M script department. This letter was typed and sent from Baltimore.

Apropos of a proposed treatment of my book (Tender Is the Night) which went to you (by the way Publishers Weekly lists it third best seller this week) you will remember that I collaborated on that first treatment with a kid named Charles Warren who has shown a remarkable talent for the theatre in writing, composing and directing two shows which have packed them in and had repeat weeks here in Baltimore and in Princeton. My intention, if Tender Is the Night was sold immediately, was to back him in going out there and seeing if he could help round it into shape. So far the offers have been unsatisfactory considering the work put on it—nevertheless Warren has planned to brave Hollywood even without the permit to enter which a definite connection would be to him. He will be without acquaintance there save for such letters as I can give him. I would be much in your debt if you will see him, give him what advice you can about finding an opening. His talents are amazingly varied—he writes, composes, draws and has this aforesaid general gift for the theatre—and I have a feeling that he should fit in there somewhere within a short time and should go close to the top, in fact I haven't believed in anybody so strongly since Ernest Hemingway. Incidentally, he is not a highbrow, his instincts are toward practical showmanship which is why I engaged him, as a sort of complement to me. Perhaps you could arrange to let him look around the lot for a few hours, lend him a few sample treatments that he could take back to his hotel and study and also some story that he could work on without salary . . . Ever your friend, Scott Fitzgerald.

—Jack Potter Catalogue, *Modern Rare Books and First Editions,* Autumn 1952, Item 50

Moment by moment all that Dick has taught her, all that he has grown to mean to her comes back. Realizing that she cannot go through with her "affair", she tells Paklin so, as gently as she can. Paklin is astounded and at first does not believe her. When he is convinced that she means what she says, his hurt and disappointment turn to anger. He accuses her of being afraid of Dick, of being mentally still attuned to her doctor husband—unable to break away from his professional grip on her. But Nicole's mind is made up. She knows now that Dick matters more to her than anything else.

Paklin, who has drunk the remainder of the brandy, becomes defiant and drives Nicole back to town, telling her furiously that he will break this hold that Dick has on her.

"You don't know what a really good time is. You've never had one. You couldn't be gay—really gay, with a psychiatrist nagging you all the time. Now you're throwing over what could be the happiest part of your life—"

"Because I love Dick."

"You don't love him. You didn't love him an hour ago. It's because you're always afraid of him. Well, tonight I'm going to get rid of that fear. You'll be gay tonight if it's the last thing you do."

Frightened, Nicole is taken by Paklin to various bars and cafes. The Russian's method of showing her a gay time merely serves to disgust and frighten Nicole, and to make an objectionable drunk out of himself.

At last they reach a cabaret where a listless band is playing and a dozen couples cover the wide floor. Paklin has become somewhat noisy. With apparently no reason he picks a fight with one of the waiters. When they see that the big man is easily beating their co-worker, the other waiters join in the fight and before Nicole's horrified eyes Paklin is beaten brutally to the floor. The police come in and take Paklin to the police station. Nicole is left in the cabaret with Paklin's drunken shouts for her to "do something" still ringing in her ears. "Go to the American Ministry! Go to the Consulate! Go *somewhere* and get me out of this filthy mess!"

In a daze Nicole goes to the Ministry to get help. It is late at night and everyone there is asleep. She goes almost automatically through the torture of shouting to half asleep men in their night shirts, explaining to them why she is there, what has happened and what is needed. But she runs up against a stone wall. They refuse to help her saying it is impossible to assist a man who has started a street brawl and resisted the police.

Nicole is frantic. The day and night has progressed at a staccato rate and she is not habituated to such strains. She feels the old mental reaction coming on and the need of her husband's steadying hand. Hurrying to the last resource, the Consulate, she finally succeeds in awakening the Consul and almost hysterically with her impotence to get results, repeats her story. The Consul is galvanized into activity and sends the vice-Consul with Nicole to rescue Paklin.

They find Paklin, under guard, slumped in a solitary chair in a cell. His face is bruised and cut, his hair matted with blood. The vice-Consul asks Nicole to call for a doctor. She does so, and then, thoroughly exhausted, phones to her sister in the hotel in Vienna—

—where Baby Warren and Dick are talking. Nicole is at the breaking point. At intervals a stupid central cuts in on the frantic conversation—this serving further to upset Nicole.

"Baby—Baby! Come quickly. We're here—police station. It's Paklin. He's—He's—" Hilarious hysterical laughter as Nicole sinks to the floor still grasping the phone and her voice continuing: "Where's Dick? Find him, bring him with you—I want him. Please find Dick—" Nicole drops the phone as she slips into unconsciousness. At the other end of the line Baby is confused and worried. Dick senses that it is Nicole who has phoned.

"What's the matter?"

"She's in trouble. Something wrong with Paklin, too. I'm going to her."

"I'm coming with you."

"No. They don't need you."

"Coming anyway."

By the time Baby and Dick arrive, Nicole has been taken to a hospital. Doctors there consider her condition very serious and are at a loss as to the origin of it. When they hear that Dr. Diver has arrived they consult him on what to do. The implication is that it is a mysterious organic disease of the brain, something new to medical science. To operate calls for the skill of the best of brain surgeons and Dick is called upon to operate on his wife.

Whether he is operating on Nicole to save her for Paklin, Dick doesn't know, but he is making the attempt regardless.

In the quiet, mechanical smoothness of the operating room, in the midst of his delicate work—with the newness and mystery of this particular operation—and the burning sensation that he is trying to save Nicole for another man, Dick's nerve fails.

But Nicole, deep in the oblivion of the anesthetic murmurs once "Dick" and his hand does not falter after that.

It takes weeks for Nicole to be able to sit up, but with her peace of mind and Dick's nearness it is made possible.

Finally when Baby Warren brings in Prince Paklin (whose face still shows the disfiguration of his battle with the police) to say goodbye before she (Baby) and Prince Paklin start on their newly planned love trip, both Nicole and Dick are happily content to look towards a future that promises brighter than it ever has before.

—F. Scott Fitzgerald Papers,
Princeton University Library

The Wages of Friendship:
Ernest Hemingway's Response to *Tender*

Hemingway attacked Fitzgerald's novel in a 30 April 1934 letter to Perkins.

Now about Scott's book. I finished it and it has all the brilliance and most of the defects he always has. In spite of marvellous places there is something wrong with it and, as a writer, this is what I believe is wrong. He starts with two people Gerald and Sara Murphy. He has the accent of their voices, their home, their looks marvellously. But he knows nothing about them. Sara Murphy is a lovely and a marvellously strong woman. Gerald is a man of great charm but very complicated emotionally and Scott depicts his charm very well at various times. He knows <u>nothing</u> about him emotionally.

But he takes these people who are formed by certain things, suffer from certain faults, which he knows nothing of because when he was with them he was busy making them into romantic figures instead of knowing what they were about (you do not learn about people by asking them questions), creating these romantic figures and then asking them concrete questions such as 'did you sleep with your wife before you married her?' in order to obtain "facts" to insert in the plasticine of his figures to try to make them seem true—it's awfully silly.

But anyway he takes a strong woman like Sara, a regular pioneer mother, and first arbitrarily makes her into a psychopathic case and then makes her into Zelda, then back into Sara, and then finally into nothing. It's bloody hopeless.

Gerald is Gerald for a while, then made-up, the made-up part is good, then becomes Scott and has things happen to him that could never happen to Gerald. The beating up by the Carabiniere in Rome etc. So you are never convinced about him going to pieces.

He has taken a series of incidents, good incidents from his life and used them quite arbitrarily, made the story conform to the few wows he had saved up out of his life.

It isn't the way prose is written when the prose is any damned good—but then by Jesus he has so lousy much talent and he has suffered so without knowing why, has destroyed himself so and destroyed Zelda, though never as much as she has tried to destroy him, that out of this little children's, immature, misunderstood, whining for lost youth death-dance that they have been dragging into and out of insanity to the tune of, the guy all but makes a fine book, all but makes a splendid book.

But the hell of it is that you can't write Prose after you are thirty five unless you can think straight. And it is the flashes where he <u>does</u> think straight that carry this book in spite of all the worn christmas tree ornaments that are Scott's idea of literature.

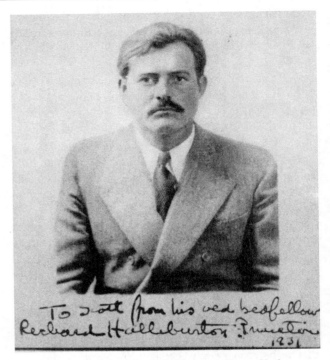

Ernest Hemingway inscribed this photo to Fitzgerald; they first met in Paris, spring 1925 (Bruccoli Collection, Thomas Cooper Library, University of South Carolina).

The trouble is that he wouldn't learn his trade and he won't be honest. He is always the brilliant young gentleman writer, fallen gentleman writer, gent in the gutter, gent ruined, but never a man. If he is writing about a woman going crazy he has to take a woman who has gone crazy. He can't take one woman who would never go crazy and make her go. In life she wouldn't go crazy. Thats what makes it false. If he is writing about himself going to hell as a man and a writer he has to accept that and write about that. He can make it all up and imagine it all but he must imagine it truly. That is. If he wants it to be literature. You can make up every word, thought, and action. But you must make them up truly. Not fake them to suit your convenience or to fit some remembered actions. And you must know what things are about. He misunderstands everything. But he has this marvellous talent, this readability, and if he would write a good one now, making it all up, he could do it. But using actual stuff is the most difficult writing in the world to have good. Making it all up is the easiest and the best. But you have to know what things are about before you start and you have to have confidence. It is like navigating once you have dropped the shore out of sight astern. If you have confidence you are all right. But to have confidence you have to know your stuff.

—*The Only Thing That Counts*, pp. 208–210

* * *

Fitzgerald wrote to Hemingway on 10 May 1934.

Dear Ernest:

Did you like the book? For God's sake drop me a line and tell me one way or another. You can't hurt my feelings. I just want to get a few intelligent slants at it to get some of the reviewers jargon out of my head.

Ever Your Friend
Scott

—*F. Scott Fitzgerald: A Life in Letters,* p. 259

On 28 May, Hemingway sent Fitzgerald a three-page typed letter saying that even though the writing was brilliant, Tender *was untrue because it distorted the Murphys.*

Goddamn it you took liberties with peoples' pasts and futures that produced not people but damned marvellously faked case histories. You, who can write better than anybody can, who are so lousy with talent that you have to—the hell with it. Scott for gods sake write and write truly no matter who or what it hurts but do not make these silly compromises. You could write a fine book about Gerald and Sara for instance if you knew enough about them and they would not have any feeling, except passing, if it were true.

There were wonderful places and nobody else nor none of the boys can write a good one half as good reading as one that doesn't come out by you, but you cheated too damned much in this one. And you don't need to.

In the first place I've always claimed that you can't think. All right, we'll admit you can think. But say you couldn't think; then you ought to write, invent, out of what you know and keep the people's antecedants straight. Second place, a long time ago you stopped listening except to the answers to your own questions. You had good stuff in too that it didn't need. That's what dries a writer up (we all dry up. That's no insult to you in person) not listening. That is where it all comes from. Seeing, listening. You see well enough. But you stop listening.

. . . .

Forget your personal tragedy. We are all bitched from the start and you especially have to be hurt like hell before you can write seriously. But when you get the damned hurt use it—don't cheat with it.

. . . .

You see, Bo, you're not a tragic character. Neither am I. All we are is writers and what we should do is write. Of all people on earth you needed discipline in your work and instead you marry someone who is jealous of your work, wants to compete with you and ruins you. It's not as simple as that and I thought Zelda was crazy the first time I met her and you complicated it even more by being in love with her and, of course you're a rummy. But you're no more of a rummy than Joyce is and most good writers are. But Scott, good writers always come back. Always. You are twice as good now as you were at the time you think you were so marvellous. You know I never thought so much of Gatsby at the time. You can write twice as well now as you ever could. All you need to do is write truly and not care about what the fate of it is.

—*Ernest Hemingway: Selected Letters, 1917–1961,*
pp. 407, 408

* * *

Hemingway added on the envelope that he had not commented on the good parts of Tender *but Fitzgerald knew what they were. Fitzgerald wrote a restrained six-page typed reply on 1 June 1934.*

Next to go to the mat with you on a couple of technical points. The reason I had written you a letter was that Dos dropped in in passing through and said you had brought up about my book what we talked about once in a cafe on the Avenue de Neuilly about composite characters. Now, I don't entirely dissent from the theory but I don't believe you can try to prove your point on such a case as Bunny using his own father as the sire of John Dos Passos, or in the case of this book that covers ground that you personally paced off about the same time I was doing it. In either of those cases how could you trust your own detach-

Perkins replied to Hemingway in a 23 May 1934 letter.

If ever I get down to Key West I would like to talk about Scott's book. Anyhow it was a mighty notable book, and is quite furiously discussed. I know of course, that there is that conflict in Scott's character, and a kind of basic illusion which causes a defect in the book and did not cause one in "The Great Gatsby" which was completely fitted to the illusion and the conflict. The other difficulty came very largely from the fact that Scott was too, too long in getting the book written, and he could not bear to exclude all of the superfluous material which he had gathered up in those years. He did exclude a good deal that was in the first manuscript, but he could not—though he prides himself in his relentlessness in this regard—bring himself to exclude a good deal more that should have been left out.

—*The Only Thing That Counts,* p. 211

ment? If you had never met any of the originals then your opinion would be more convincing.

Following this out a little farther, when does the proper and logical combination of events, cause and effect, etc. end and the field of imagination begin? Again you may be entirely right because I suppose you were applying the idea particularly to the handling of the creative faculty in one's mind rather than to the effect upon the stranger reading it. Nevertheless, I am not sold on the subject, and especially to account for the big flaws of Tender on that ground doesn't convince me. Think of the case of the Renaissance artists, and of the Elizabethan dramatists, the first having to superimpose a medieval conception of science and archeology, etc. upon the bible story, and in the second, of Shakespeare's trying to interpret the results of his own observation of the life around him on the basis of Plutarch's Lives and Hollinshed's Chronicles. There you must admit that the feat of building a monument out of three kinds of marble was brought off. You can accuse me justly of not having the power to bring it off, but a theory that it can't be done is highly questionable. I make this point with such persistence because such a conception, if you stick to it, might limit your own choice of materials. The idea can be reduced simply to: you can't say accurately that composite characterization hurt my book, but that it only hurt it for you.

To take a case specifically, that of Gerald and Sara. I don't know how much you think you know about my relations with them over a long time, but from certain remarks that you let drop, such as one "Gerald threw you over," I guess that you didn't even know the beginning of our relations. In that case you hit on the exact opposite of the truth.

I think it is obvious that my respect for your artistic life is absolutely unqualified, that save for a few of the dead or dying old men you are the only man writing fiction in America that I look up to very much. There are pieces and paragraphs of your work that I read over and over—in fact, I stopped myself doing it for a year and a half because I was afraid that your particular rhythms were going to creep in on mine by process of infiltration. Perhaps you will recognize some of your remarks in Tender, but I did every damn thing I could to avoid that.

. . . .

To go back to my theme song, the second technical point that might be of interest to you concerns direct steals from an idea of yours, an idea of Conrad's and a few lines out of David-into-Fox-Garnett. The theory back of it I got from Conrad's preface to The Nigger, that the purpose of a work of fiction is to appeal to the lingering after-effects in the reader's mind as differing from, say, the purpose of oratory or philosophy which leave respectively leave people in a fighting or thoughtful mood. The second contribution to the burglary was your trying to work out some such theory in your troubles with the very end of A Fare-

Conrad's Preface

In his 23 April 1934 letter to H. L. Mencken, Fitzgerald refers to Joseph Conrad's preface to The Nigger of the Narcissus *(1897) as "the greatest 'credo' in my life." Conrad begins his essay by defining "the condition of art."*

A work that aspires, however humbly, to the condition of art should carry its justification in every line. And art itself may be defined as a single-minded attempt to render the highest kind of justice to the visible universe, by bringing to light the truth, manifold and one, underlying its every aspect. It is an attempt to find in its forms, in its colors, in its light, in its shadows, in the aspects of matter and in the facts of life, what of each is fundamental, what is enduring and essential—their one illuminating and convincing quality—the very truth of their existence. The artist, then, like the thinker or the scientist, seeks the truth and makes his appeal.

. . . .

Conrad briefly discusses the thinker, who "plunges into ideas," and the scientist, who is interested in "facts," before turning to the role of the artist.

It is otherwise with the artist.

Confronted by the same enigmatical spectacle the artist descends within himself, and in that lonely region of stress and strife, if he be deserving and fortunate, he finds the terms of his appeal. His appeal is made to our less obvious capacities: to that part of our nature which, because of the warlike conditions of existence, is necessarily kept out of sight within the more resisting and hard qualities—like the vulnerable body within a steel armor. His appeal is less loud, more profound, less distinct, more stirring—and sooner forgotten. Yet its effect endures forever. The changing wisdom of successive generations discards ideas, questions facts, demolishes theories. But the artist appeals to that part of our being which is not dependent on wisdom: to that in us which is a gift and not an acquisition—and, therefore, more permanently enduring. He speaks to our capacity for delight and wonder, to the sense of mystery surrounding our lives; to our sense of pity, and beauty, and pain; to the latent feeling of fellowship with all creation—to the subtle but invincible conviction of solidarity that knits together the loneliness of innumerable hearts, to the solidarity in dreams, in joy, in sorrow, in aspirations, in illusions, in hope, in fear, which binds men to each other, which binds together all humanity—the dead to the living and the living to the unborn.

well to Arms. I remember that your first draft—or at least the first one I saw—gave a sort of old-fashioned Alger book summary of the future lives of the characters: "The priest became a priest under Fascism," etc., and you may remember my suggestion to take a burst of eloquence from anywhere in the book that you could find it and tag off with that; you were against this idea because you felt that the true line of a work of fiction was to take a reader up to a

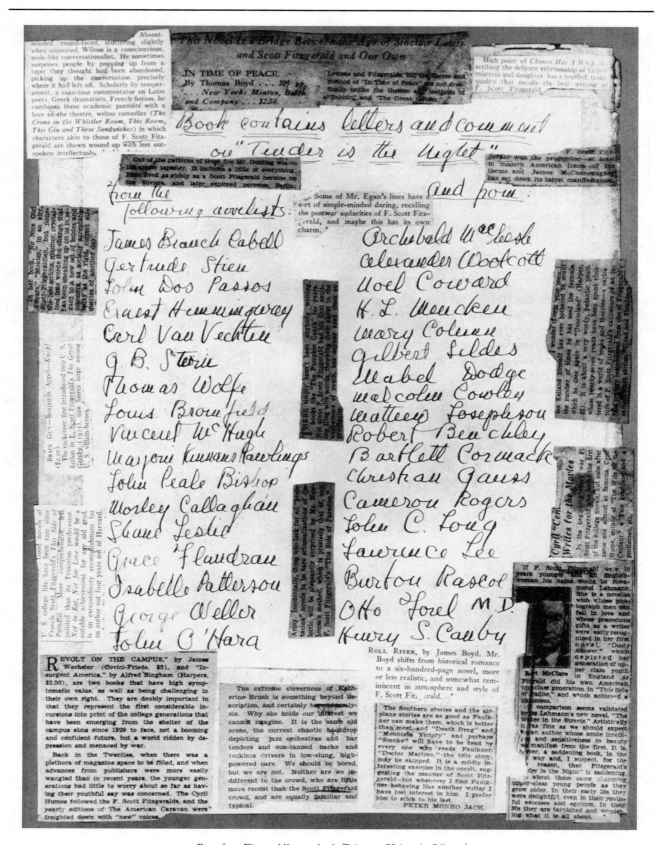

Page from Fitzgerald's scrapbook (Princeton University Library)

> *Gerald Murphy wrote to Fitzgerald on 31 December 1935, a year in which one of his sons, Baoth, had died and his other son, Patrick, had contracted tuberculosis.*
>
> Of all our friends, it seems to me that you alone knew how we felt these days,—still feel. You are the only person to whom I can ever tell the bleak truth of what I feel. Sara's courage and the amazing job which she is doing for Patrick make unbearably poignant the tragedy of what has happened—what life has tried to do to her. I know now that what you said in "Tender is the Night" is true. Only the invented part of our life,—the unreal part—has had any scheme any beauty. Life itself has stepped in now and blundered, scarred and destroyed.
>
> *—Correspondence of F. Scott Fitzgerald, p. 425*

high emotional pitch but then let him down or ease him off. You gave no aesthetic reason for this—nevertheless, you convinced me. The third piece of burglary contributing to this symposing was my admiration of the dying fall in the aforesaid Garnett's book and I imitated it as accurately as it is humanly decent in my own ending of Tender, telling the reader in the last pages that, after all, this is just a casual event, and trying to let him come to bat for me rather than going out to shake his nerves, whoop him up, then leaving him rather in a condition of a frustrated woman in bed. (Did that ever happen to you in your days with MacCallagan or McKisco, Sweetie?)

—F. Scott Fitzgerald: A Life in Letters, pp. 262–264

* * *

Sara Murphy shared Hemingway's view that Fitzgerald did not understand people: "I have always told you you haven't the faintest idea what anybody else but yourself is like. . . ." Fitzgerald regarded her view as a dismissal of his career, and in August 1935 he tried to convince Sara that he had captured the essence of her personality in Tender:

In my theory, utterly opposite to Ernest's, about fiction i.e. that it takes half a dozen people to make a synthesis strong enough to create a fiction character—in that theory, or rather in despite of it, I used you again + again in Tender:

> "Her face was hard + lovely + pitiful"
>
> and again
>
> "He had been heavy, belly-frightened with love of her for years"

—in those and in a hundred other places I tried to evoke not you but the effect that you produce on men—the echoes and reverberations—a poor return for what you have given by your living presence, but nevertheless an artist's (what a word!) sincere attempt to preserve a true fragment rather than a "portrait" by Mr. Sargent. And someday in spite of all the affectionate skepticism you felt toward the brash young man you met on the Riviera eleven years ago, you'll let me have my little corner of you where I know you better than anybody—yes, even better than Gerald.

—F. Scott Fitzgerald: A Life in Letters, p. 288

Reputation

Fitzgerald's Death

In the often condescending obituaries and editorials on his death, Fitzgerald was treated as a writer whose reputation had not survived the Twenties. This Side of Paradise *and* The Great Gatsby *were recalled as his best works;* Tender Is the Night *was often listed without comment.*

Death Takes Fitzgerald, Noted Author
Heart Attack Fatal to Eloquent Voice of
World War Generation
Los Angeles Times, 22 December 1940

All the sad young men—those now grown-up members of the World War generation—had lost their spokesman yesterday.

F. Scott Fitzgerald died of a heart attack in Hollywood at the age of 44.

Immediately after word of the death of the author of "This Side of Paradise" was telegraphed to his wife at Montgomery, Ala., arrangements were made through Pierce Bros. mortuary to send his body to Baltimore, Md., his family home, for burial.

Readers of the 1930's did not know Fitzgerald as did those of the postwar era.

For he was the latters' most articulate voice.

His own early life paralleled that of his recurrent protagonist: the young man, caught in a turbulent age, uncertain, seeking.

The photograph of F. Scott Fitzgerald that ran with his 22 December 1940 obituary in The New York Times, *in which he was described as a writer whose "career began and ended with the Nineteen Twenties"*

Composer's Descendant

Born at St. Paul, Minn., on Sept. 24, 1896, he was christened Francis Scott Key Fitzgerald, after the composer of "The Star Spangled Banner," an ancestor on his mother's side. He was first educated at Hackensack, N.J. Then he attended Princeton.

There he found much of the atmosphere which fills his first books.

It was wartime. In 1917, deserting the university in his senior year, he entered the Army as a second lieutenant in the 45th Infantry. Two years later he left the service. He was 23.

First Novel Hailed

In 1920 "This Side of Paradise" appeared.

Its hero, Amory Blaine, approximated "all the sad young men" of the distracted time. (That phrase was to become the title of a Fitzgerald short-story collection six years later.) Hailed by critics as a great first novel, "This Side of Paradise" was a period piece, a sort of social paper.

At 26, Fitzgerald was in Who's Who. His clubs were listed as Cottage (Princeton) and Sound View Golf. His politics was Socialist. One critic described his works as documentary "in their vivid presentations of adolescent life, its turbulent spirit, swift tempo, charged atmosphere, excesses and boldness, as well as its uncertain psychology and groping to know itself in new and unadjusted conditions."

His books also were milestones of this topsy-turvy epoch.

"The Beautiful and Damned" came in 1922, two years after his first novel and "Flappers and Philosophers." Later he wrote "The Great Gatsby" and "Tender Is the Night." He saw his generation as truly lost. One of his collected volumes was titled "Taps at Reveille."

In recent years Fitzgerald wrote no novels. Instead, he came to Hollywood in 1937. He adapted Gatsby to the screen, then did the scenario for Remarque's "Three Comrades."

Second Attack Fatal

Three weeks ago he had his first heart attack.

Saturday he succumbed to a second.

His life in Hollywood had been quiet. His hobbies were children and water sports. He was a connoisseur of fine wines. Occasionally a Fitzgerald short story would appear in a national magazine. But mostly he worked on his last play for the New York stage. He lived at 1403 N. Laurel Ave.

In 1920 he married Zelda Sayre, daughter of an Alabama Supreme Court justice. They had one daughter, Frances Scott Fitzgerald.

* * *

F. Scott Fitzgerald
New York Herald Tribune, 22 December 1940

It was only twenty years ago that a novel called "This Side of Paradise" was published, and the world became aware of the existence of the author, F. Scott Fitzgerald, a young man of rare talent. The story was deft, romantic, gay, alcoholic and bitter. It was the first year of prohibition. Flaming youth was rampant. People talked of the post-war moral let-down. Raccoon coats were coming in. There were rumors of strange goings-on in the colleges. It was the beginning of a fantastic era (how long ago it seems!), and Fitzgerald, handsome, insouciant and possessing unusual gifts for story telling, instantly became its prophet and its interpreter. Flappers adored him; moreover, the grave gentlemen who sit in judgment on literary products agreed that here, indeed, was one who showed magnificent "promise."

Fitzgerald, who died yesterday at the tragically early age of forty-four, continued to show "promise" all through his tortured career. He turned out many glittering short stories which were commercial successes. His admirers kept hoping for the elusive something which would be called great. In 1925, with a compact and brilliant novel,

"The Great Gatsby," the story of the rise and fall of a Long Island bootlegger, he renewed their faith. As literature it was perhaps the best thing he ever did. Then came long periods when he did little, or nothing. He was ill, troubled, unhappy. In 1934, with "Tender Is the Night," he had another success—but again the critics, while admiring much of it, confessed that they had been expecting something better. Once more he had shown the high promise that somehow always fell just short of fulfillment. And yet, it cannot be taken away from him that he left a substantial literary legacy. He could write prose that was extraordinarily smooth, but it was never soft. It had, as the saying has it, "bones" in it.

The gaudy world of which Fitzgerald wrote—the penthouses, the long week-end drunks, the young people who were always on the brink of madness, the vacuous conversation, the lush intoxication of easy money—has in large measure been swept away. But Fitzgerald understood this world perhaps better than any of his contemporaries. And as a literary craftsman he described it, accurately and sometimes poignantly, in work that deserves respect.

* * *

Trade Winds
P. E. G. Quercus Associates
The Saturday Review of Literature,
   23 (28 December 1940): 22

The year ends with the death of F. Scott Fitzgerald. It is hard to believe that it is a generation since the dashing Fitzgerald came out of Princeton with tales that labeled an era. Harding was president during this Jazz Age: girls were wearing knee-length skirts, men bell-bottom trousers; the most-discussed beverage was bath-tub gin. We liked Fitzgerald's books and we liked his reporting. Social historians, in resurrecting the 1920's, will find much truth and accuracy in his earlier novels and short stories of college days, jazz, booze, clothes and prohibitions. F. Scott Fitzgerald was in his early forties when he died.

* * *

Tale of the Jazz Age
The New Republic, 103 (30 December 1940): 885

Nobody else wrote about the American aristocracy of the post-war years as did Scott Fitzgerald. Nobody else could make it seem glamorous while retaining his integrity as a literary craftsman and his clear-sightedness as an observer. The heroes of his early novels and short stories were boys who had gone to the right prep schools and made the right eating clubs at Princeton. The heroines were girls who had won their moral freedom in the excitement of

The Fitzgerald Revival and *Tender Is the Night*

Power without Glory
Times Literary Supplement, 20 January 1950

When Scott Fitzgerald died in 1940 his work, outside a very small circle, was hardly known in this country. By now *The Great Gatsby* might perhaps be said to be slowly establishing a position for itself; but one that still remains infinitely short of that novel's reputation in America, where it is looked upon almost as a classic: certainly a classic of its period, the early 1920s. Indeed, Fitzgerald's habitual connotation in many people's minds with the "jazz age" has sometimes obscured his merits. He is, it is true, a remarkable example of a writer of great gifts striking when the iron was hot–and failing to produce another masterpiece largely on account of the limitations of his time-bound point of view–but he stands apart from most of the American, or English, novelists, among contemporaries who might be considered in his class; and at his best he certainly rises far above recommendation merely as an interesting period piece.

The much simplified life-story, beloved of his countrymen, presents a picture of a talented, ambitious, attractive young man, whose early years were embittered by failure to play football for Princeton (where, like most undergraduates, he could also have done with a larger allowance); and also by the signing of the Armistice after the First World War, an event that precluded military service oversea. Later, in spite of enormous popular success with his first novel, *This Side of Paradise,* there were struggles to earn a living: short stories for the commercial market: *The Great Gatsby:* more drink than was probably wise: and, finally, scenario-writing in Hollywood, where at the time of his death in the middle forties, he had begun to build up something of a new life. Such broad outlines may be gathered from *The Crack-up* (taking its name from the autobiographical piece describing his own nervous collapse), which contains a number of uncollected writings, including Fitzgerald's note-books, selected correspondence, and appreciations of his work by various American writers.

His first two books attempted to impose on the American novel certain alien elements, notably in choice of hero. However, not all characters in novels can be exported without deterioration, and the particular type that Fitzgerald, in the first instance adumbrated (although swallowed whole by the American public) was, it might be thought, quite inappropriate to the circumstances and traditions of American life. *This Side of Paradise* derives from many sources, the chief one *Sinister Street:* Amory Blaine being an American edition of the English dilettante, half-aristocrat, half-bohemian,

wartime, who had learned to smoke and neck and take nips out of pocket flasks, with a general air of glitter and defiance. When they married the heroes, both were launched into that post-war metropolitan world where it was so easy to make money. Fitzgerald himself, about the time that he published his "Tales of the Jazz Age," was telling the readers of The Saturday Evening Post how to live on $50,000 a year. He was earning almost as much by his writing.

All that seems a very long time ago. In the years after 1927, something happened to these people that Fitzgerald found hard to understand. They lost their glamor, they grew soft and middle-aged; they began quarreling among themselves and drinking too much. He tried to tell that story too, in his last novel, "Tender Is the Night," and he wrote with even more than his usual care. But he did not succeed in organizing his material, or in clearly stating his attitude toward it, and the book that he had taken nine years to finish was not even a nine days' success. Shortly afterwards he retired to the well paid anonymity of Hollywood. His death there, for anyone who was young in the 1920's, is like the death of one's own youth. It is like a stone placed over the grave of all the flappers and smoothies, all the glitter and foolishness and wild good humor.

I found Scott's "Tender Is the Night" in Cuba and read it over. It's amazing how <u>excellent</u> much of it is. Much of it is better than anything else he ever wrote. How I wish he would have kept on writing. Is it really all over or will he write again? If you write him give him my great affection. Reading that novel much of it was so good it was frightening.

ERNEST HEMMINGWAY (in letter to Max Perkins)

Postscript from Ernest Hemingway's 25 March 1939 letter to Maxwell Perkins, which Fitzgerald saved for his scrapbook (Princeton University Library)

In a 15 November 1941 letter to Maxwell Perkins, Hemingway gave a final estimation of Tender Is the Night *when he read* The Last Tycoon *(1941), Fitzgerald's unfinished novel that was edited by Edmund Wilson and published after the author's death.*

The best book he ever wrote, I think, is still "Tender Is The Night" with all of its mix-up of who was Scott and Zelda and who was Sara and Gerald Murphy. I read it last year again and it has all the realization of tragedy that Scott ever found. Wonderful atmosphere and magical descriptions and none of the impossible dramatic tricks that he had outlined for the final book.

—The Only Thing That Counts, p. 313

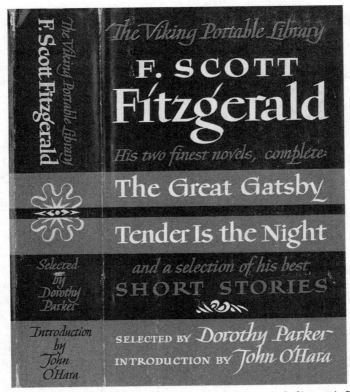

Dust jacket for the 1945 collection, priced at $2, that signaled the revival of interest in Fitzgerald (Bruccoli Collection of Fitzgerald, Thomas Cooper Library, University of South Carolina)

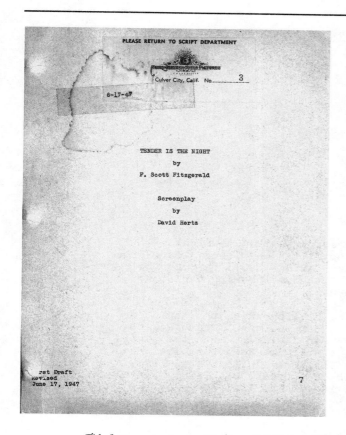

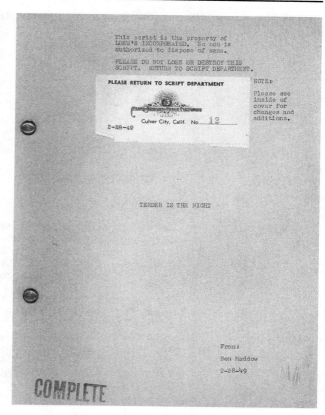

Title for two unproduced scripts (Bruccoli Collection of Fitzgerald, Thomas Cooper Library, University of South Carolina)

lover, scholar, and man-of-the-world, nearing disintegration, after a good run for his money, even in England by 1914. *This Side of Paradise* cannot be called a good book; its successor, *The Beautiful and the Damned* is scarcely, if at all, better; yet even in these shapeless, sentimental pieces of romanticized autobiography flashes of wit and vital force are easily perceptible. Clearly the author's facility is great; and judging from these two novels—and short stories like "The Rich Boy" and "The Diamond as Big as the Ritz"—it might have been supposed that Fitzgerald would turn into a prolific popular novelist, telling the same story over and over again, until all trace of promise had vanished from his pages. Nothing could have been farther from the truth.

In *The Great Gatsby* (1925) worship of the golden calf and a strong tinge of narcissism, hitherto obtrusive, accept a reasonable place. A tendency to write untidily changes to a severe sense of form.

. . . .

Tender is the Night, *Gatsby's* successor, ambitious in the manner in which it was planned, is really a step back, in its retreat from objectivity, and unwillingness to follow up the logical conclusions of the earlier novel. The book falls into three sections: first, the south of France, where Dick Diver,

an American doctor, falls in with an eighteen-year-old film actress, of great beauty and respectable antecedents: secondly, an earlier period when Diver is in Switzerland, treating a rich heiress, Nicole Warren, for madness: thirdly, the scene principally in France, Diver having married Nicole, who, her cure effected, decides that she no longer loves him. The marriage breaks up, and we are led to suppose

---

Screen and Television Versions of *Tender Is the Night*

There has never been a satisfactory movie adaptation of this Fitzgerald novel. Several attempts to write Tender Is the Night *as a movie—including an early proposed treatment by Fitzgerald and Charles Warren and a screenplay by Malcolm and Margorie Lowry—went unproduced. The first television broadcast of the novel was presented in 1955 as a* Front Row Center *production by Fletcher Markle. The novel received a lavish but miscast movie production with a screenplay by Ivan Moffat in 1962. Another made-for-television movie was produced in 1985 with a script by Dennis Potter. It is impossible to photograph F. Scott Fitzgerald's style.*

1

TENDER IS THE NIGHT

FADE IN:

UNDER MAIN TITLES:

1   LONG SHOT - ZURICH STREET - DAY

As a brightly painted streetcar marked "Zurichsee" climbs clanking up a steep hill. On either side of the street are plane trees and CAMERA SHOOTS through their greenery, PANNING SLOWLY with the laboring streetcar until it stops at the corner.

The effect, looking up the hill on which the streetcar runs, to the tall mountain known as the "Krenzegg," is of a city built on the perpendicular. Above the purple steeples of the chalets, the Alpine meadows shine green and rich with cattle and flowers. In the warm, late afternoon sunshine Zurich is a fresh, beautiful, and vertical city. The time is summer, 1921.

2   MED. LONG SHOT - STREETCAR

As the streetcar stops at the corner, a young man jumps from the platform, turns and receives his baggage which the conductor hands down to him. He carries a World War I duffle bag and a large, cheap suitcase. At first glance, we know he is an American. He wears an American imitation of a British tweed, loose and used, but he is the sort of young man who looks well in any clothes. He wears no hat.

With the duffle bag over one shoulder and the suitcase under the other arm, the young man walks with happy energy to the curb and therefore toward the CAMERA.

As the audience examines DICK DIVER, let us describe him to the reader.

He is twenty-six years old. His complexion is ruddy and weather-burnt. There is never any doubt at whom he is looking or talking, and this is a flattering attention - for who looks at us? This is a charming man, expert at being charming, yet honest and effortless in its practice.

CONTINUED:

First pages for two unproduced scripts: left, by David Hertz, and right, by Ben Maddow (Bruccoli Collection of Fitzgerald, Thomas Cooper Library, University of South Carolina)

TENDER IS THE NIGHT

1.

Very close, the head and nude shoulders of Rosemary Hoyt. Her eyes are shut against the brilliance of the sun in the sky and the ocean and reflecting from the sand on which she is resting. Away in the distance, there are two children shouting against one another in piping French. Rosemary opens her eyes, looks around. Pan of the ocean, purest Mediterranean blue, and the narrow beach, the coast, the irregular cliff, and the villas high up, above the town of Antibes, and down again across the beach and the striped umbrellas and the ocean once more.

A man introduces himself to her, suggesting that a newcomer like herself can easily get burnt in the morning sun. He is Dick Diver, the magnetic center of the beach society at the Cap d' Antibes; and through him she is introduced to the others. They already know her face: she's a young actress whose latest film is suddenly very famous. In turn she's interested in the group, in Nicole, Dick's wife, wearing pearls and a dove-gray bathing suit, and copying very calmly and neatly a recipe for Maryland chicken; and in Tommy Barban, an extraordinarily handsome and laconic man, with a puckered scar on his shoulder; in Abe North, already drinking and loquacious, full of a self-destructive irony, a composer whose first piano Concerto was so great a success that it paralyzed his brain; in his friend, Gertrude Stein, on a small chair under an umbrella, a sort of monument in a plain gingham dress, dictating curious letters to her secretary.

MALCOLM LOWRY
MARGERIE BONNER LOWRY

Notes on a Screenplay for
F. Scott Fitzgerald's
TENDER IS THE NIGHT

Introduction by Paul Tiessen

Bruccoli Clark
Bloomfield Hills, Michigan
Columbia, South Carolina
1976

*Novelist Malcolm Lowry and the title page of the book published from the work he and his wife did on a script for
Fitzgerald's novel from July 1949 to April 1950. The unproduced script was 455 pages.*

that Diver sinks into a world of casual love affairs and small-town doctoring.

Fitzgerald is attempting something on a larger scale and, in a sense, in a more serious manner; but this new seriousness seems to have betrayed him. In all his writing we are conscious of a desire, almost comparable to Kipling's, for some form of life that may be held up to admiration. However, in Fitzgerald's case, he never managed to objectify the things he held in respect sufficiently for them to carry the weight of his own admiration; and, while Kipling could, for example, depict the sordid side of Victorian army life and remain a passionate partisan of all the army stood for, Fitzgerald always expects the objects of his admiration to possess outward and visible trappings suitable to their inner enchantment. Thus in *Tender is the Night* attention is concentrated on Diver's skill as a doctor; but the author never seems to strike a happy balance between Diver, the physician, and Diver, the man.

The opening scenes in the south of France are, on the whole, handled satirically and well; and, so far as it goes, the Swiss clinic is convincing, if a trifle heavy going;

but as Diver grows older, although we can sympathize with his troubles in handling the problem of his only partly cured wife, we cannot share the author's attitude towards his hero's general behaviour, which is often ludicrous, if not inexcusable. When, for example, Diver, at the age of forty, before a party, stands on his hands "to limber himself up," and his pince-nez fall out of his breast-pocket, we have an uneasy feeling that Fitzgerald does not think this incident so farcical as does the reader: and Diver's brain-storms in Rome, resulting in brawls and arrest, are presented vividly but with little feeling for the preposterous behaviour of the doctor himself.

The truth is that Fitzgerald has slipped back into subjective autobiography. All the things that happened to Diver did not, of course, happen literally to Fitzgerald, but the breakdown in the conviction that the novel carries is due to some essential lack of appreciation on the author's part of the manner in which normal professional life is lived. He is prepared to romanticize Dr. Diver's work; even to take pains in recording its correct detail; but in the last resort he fails to grasp any reality but that of his own tortured nerves as a writer. The unfolding of *Tender is the Night,* from the point of view of different characters, adds technically to the handicaps under which the novel labours; but in spite of undoubted failings it remains a somewhat magnificent failure, and a book that should certainly be read by those interested in the American novel.

Tender is the Night represents the final important piece of work before the "crack-up": *The Last Tycoon,* the only serious fragment that took shape during the period between that crisis and Fitzgerald's death. To call the latter work a "fragment" is perhaps to insist too much on its unfinished state; because the essential core is there, and although completion might possibly have brought with it many minor good things, tone and general action would have remained the same. It is hard to agree with the many critics who have said that *The Last Tycoon* would have crowned Fitzgerald's achievement. The flaws suggested in *Tender is the Night* are here more than ever apparent; and although the novel has a kind of distinction that clung to Fitzgerald's writing, even in the depths of his least engaging journalism, there is nothing in this final book to compare with *The Great Gatsby.*

. . . .

For the moment, anyway, American novelists have set their faces against the Fitzgerald tradition. They burn incense at other altars: Dreiser's Teutonic mountains of words: Mr. Ernest Hemingway's self-conscious violence: the inward-looking romanticisms and eclectic verbiage of the Deep South: the *minutiae* of political opinion. If a time should come when they turn again to a more English tradition, Scott Fitzgerald would provide a rock on which to build. He deserves better treatment than that accorded to him in this edition, in which the verse by Thomas Parke D'Invilliers (one of the characters in *This Side of Paradise*) is omitted from the title-page of *The Great Gatsby,* also marred by a piece of misplaced dialogue on page 27 making nonsense of several lines. The quotation from Keats has been removed from the beginning of *Tender is the Night;* and Fitzgerald's death is variously described, in the introduction to *The Last Tycoon,* as taking place in 1940, and on all the dust-wrappers as in 1941.

* * *

The following article is indicative of the excitement in the publishing world as the Fitzgerald revival gained momentum. It is interesting to note that the cheap Bantam paperback edition of Tender Is the Night *enjoyed strong sales in the spring of 1951, months before the publication of Malcolm Cowley's re-ordered version of the novel on 12 November 1951.*

Tips for the Bookseller
Publishers' Weekly, 159 (10 February 1951): 879–880

THE CURRENT intense interest in the life and writings of F. Scott Fitzgerald was given another boost by the wide-spread publicity attending the publication on January 31 of Arthur Mizener's biography of Fitzgerald, "The Far Side of Paradise" (*PW,* October 14, January 27). At the height of the demand, however, there was a shortage of Fitzgerald material. Shortly before Christmas, the successful "Viking Portable F. Scott Fitzgerald" went out of print, Viking's time limit on the material leased to them by Scribners having expired. Scribners had not reprinted any of the novels or short stories, many of which had been unavailable for years. "The Crack-up" (*New Directions*) was out of stock last week, and New Directions was holding 427 back orders against the new fifth printing of 3,500 copies which has just been made available. Bantam Books edition of "Tender is the Night," published on January 10, sold out a first printing of 240,000 copies within the month with 62 per cent of the sale in the first ten days. Bantam has reprinted its 35-cent edition of the novel but there has been a delay, caused by the railroad strike, in getting the new printing out.

Scribners has pushed up its publication date for "The Stories of F. Scott Fitzgerald" edited by Malcolm Cowley from March 19 to March 5. On February 19, a new edition of "The Last Tycoon" containing "The Last Tycoon" and "The Great Gatsby" in one volume will be made available. Unlike the previous edition this will not contain any of the short stories. The new edition will be uniform in format with "The Stories of F. Scott Fitzgerald." "Tender is the Night," which has been out of print since 1942, will be reissued on February 23, and about March 1 "This Side of Paradise" will be brought back into print. These two novels will be uniform in format, and both will have new jackets. All these reissues will be included in the advertising for "The Short Stories of F. Scott Fitzgerald."

. . . .

Meanwhile, Budd Shulberg's best-selling novel, "The Disenchanted" (*Random House*), based on the life of Fitzgerald, continues to sell at a very rapid rate. Five thousand copies were sold in January.

* * *

In his retrospective essay on the occasion of the publication of Alfred Kazin's F. Scott Fitzgerald: the Man and his Work *(1951) and Arthur Mizener's* The Far Side of Paradise *(1951), Harding assesses the weakness and poignancy of* Tender Is the Night. *He had previously reviewed the novel for the 8 December 1934 issue of* Scrutiny.

Scott Fitzgerald

D. W. Harding

Scrutiny, 18 (Winter 1951–1952): 172–174

Many writers, including his slightly younger contemporaries, have been at least as intimately personal as Fitzgerald and still retained their literary respectability. The trouble is that he reveals his personal weaknesses and unhappiness without hitting back with any defiance, without using the fact of his misery as evidence of his unusual sensitiveness or the injustice or futility of his environment. His handling of his weakness never contributes indirectly to his greater personal glory. This characteristic shows itself not only when he makes his heroes take the blame for misfortunes they bring on themselves but also when things go miserably wrong without much identifiable fault in the protagonists (as, for instance, in *The Beautiful and Damned,* immature as that is). If Fitzgerald cannot see where the fault lies in himself he does not find relief in protest, whether against society or the nature of things. His people rarely protest, explicitly or covertly; they more often seek relief in the unconvinced sociability and the alcohol that make their plight worse.

But the real limitations of his work also bring one back to his personal life. His lack of insight into himself at crucial points, above all into the addiction to alcohol, has more than biographical significance. It is a clue to the weakness of his most ambitious finished novel, *Tender is the Night,* which, as many of Mr. Kazin's writers complain, leaves the collapse of the hero essentially unexplained. What Fitzgerald could not understand in himself he could not account for in his hero. It is not satisfactory to use biographical material to supply the place of what he failed to put into the novels, and this seems to me the inadequacy of Mr. Mizener's defence of *Tender is the Night.* He tries hard to show that the collapse of the hero can be made intelligible and acceptable by reference to Fitzgerald's theory of 'emotional bankruptcy', the idea that he uses in letters and journals to indicate the psychological condition in which he found himself towards the end of his life. Even if this idea had amounted to an understanding of his condition it would not be enough for Mr. Mizener to show that Fitzgerald had elaborated it privately; if it is not

Writing for a leftist journal in 1951, critic Leslie Fiedler noted that Fitzgerald did not compromise the ending of Tender Is the Night.

There is always the style of the details, the glow and motion of the close of *Gatsby* or the opening of *Tender is the Night,* those wonderful approaches and fadeouts. There is always the naive honesty of reminiscence, the embarrassing rightness of his adolescents. And there is the supreme negative virtue: Fitzgerald's refusal to swap his own lived sentimentalities for the mass sentimentalities of social protest that swamp the later Hemingway. Even the compulsive theme of the *femme fatale,* the All-American banality of woman as destroyer, is capable of subtleties forever beyond the 'proletarian novel'. When Fitzgerald treats social themes he is absurd; surely there appears in the overrated fragment *The Last Tycoon,* the least convincing Communist in American fiction. But he resisted the temptation to end *Tender is the Night* with Dick Diver sending his kids off to the Soviet Union, a close that might well have won him the plaudits he so needed in 1934.

–"Some Notes on F. Scott Fitzgerald," *New Leader,* 34 (9 April 1951): 20–21

effectively expressed in the novel without illumination from biographical research it is not much help. In fact it seems to be only a way of describing the experience of collapse, not understanding it. He simply recorded his conviction–based on his experience–of the inevitability of cracking up; he had no insight into its causes within himself. He knew, it is true, the relevant features of his life which might with re-arrangement have given him a clearer view of his trouble. The very sad quality of *The Crack-Up* comes from the courageous frankness with which he exposes himself and the simultaneous inability to grasp the nature of his central difficulties.

. . . .

Disillusionment was really there, of course. He had some magnificent friends, whose loyalty he must have tested to the utmost; there were others who felt sure of their superiority and gave him good advice; and at times he met with cynical cruelty. With this rather usual sample of human experience he was disappointed. It failed to give the response he wanted to his generous outflowing of feeling. But impulsive friendliness was for him still the norm, and the revulsion he expresses in *The Crack-Up* is a revulsion against the social world he trusted too freely, not a genuine revulsion against his trustful-

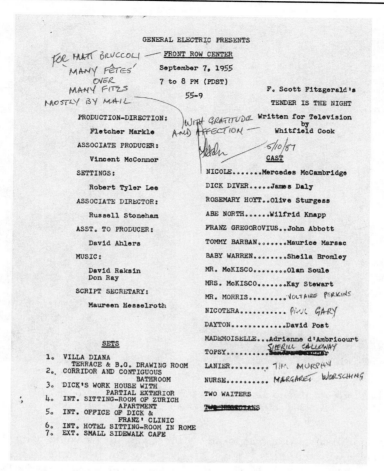

Credit list with comments by Fletcher Markle (Bruccoli Collection of Fitzgerald, Thomas Cooper Library, University of South Carolina)

General Electric Presents

Producer and director Fletcher Markle introduced the first television production of Fitzgerald's novel.

MARKLE

Tonight, you have a seat FRONT ROW CENTER for a television premiere–the first dramatic performance of F. Scott Fitzgerald's unforgettable novel, TENDER IS THE NIGHT. It has been described as "shocking," "disturbingly intimate," "fantastic," and "entirely real."

John O'Hara, a tough-minded friend of Mr. Fitzgerald has even made so bold as to consider it "a work of art." But however you describe it, TENDER IS THE NIGHT is the portrait of a tragic love affair involving a husband and wife who were, also, a doctor and his patient. In Whitfield Cook's present-day version for viewing, Nicole and Dick Diver are as alive and actual as when Scott Fitzgerald first recorded their personal history more than two decades ago. Playing Nicole Diver, our leading lady tonight is an actress for whose remarkable talents I have an admitted prejudice: Miss Mercedes McCambridge. As Dick Diver, Nicole's husband, we are pleased to have with us the very gifted Mr. James Daly. And as Rosemary Hoyt, FRONT ROW CENTER welcomes back the lovely Miss Olive Sturgess.

Featured among others in the cast, you'll be seeing John Abbott, Wilfrid Knapp, Maruice Marsac, Sheila Bromley and Olan Soule.

(SOUND: NIGHTINGALE)

John Keats, appreciating a nightingale, provided Mr. Fitzgerald with his title:

". . . Tender is the Night . . .
. . . But here there is no light,
Save what from heaven is with breezes blown,
Through verdurous glooms and winding mossy ways."

Our astonishing story begins in just one minute.

*James Daly as Dick Diver and Mercedes McCambridge as Nicole Diver in Fletcher Markle's 1955 television production
(Bruccoli Collection of Fitzgerald, Thomas Cooper Library, University of South Carolina)*

ness. Some generous responsiveness that he looked for was missing. How far it was neurotic of him to look for it and how far our culture fails by denying it to such people must be for us, embedded in that culture, a difficult question to answer. It is appropriate that Keats, with his trustful and uncensored outpourings of himself, should have meant so much to Fitzgerald. It was the 'Ode to a Nightingale' from which, in spite of the publisher's objection that it had no connection with the story, Fitzgerald took the title and prefatory quotation for his novel:

Already with thee! tender is the night . . .
. . . But here there is no light,
Save what from heaven is with the breezes blown
Through verdurous glooms and winding mossy ways.

The 'Ode' expresses Keats's longing (and a transient fantasy of its fulfilment) for escape from the problems of ordinary life into acceptance as part of the tender night, ruled over by the Queen-Moon, and richly adequate without any contribution from him. The novel describes the psychological bankruptcy of a man who gave himself more generously than Fitzgerald thought he could afford. That they were linked for Fitzgerald implies that his generous responsiveness and his outpouring of himself

received no welcome commensurate with his great craving for welcome. The impulsive response to what he supposed to be the feelings of others is illustrated in the incident recorded by Mr. Mizener when Fitzgerald and a friend, both Yankees, visited an old Southern house which was of interest in the history of the Civil War. Suddenly Fitzgerald felt that their interest might be painful to their host, a Southerner, and he promptly launched into a fantasy about the press photographers at Appomattox and their mistake which led to the belief that Lee handed his sword to Grant in surrender. Sheer buoyancy and lightness of touch seem to have enabled him to carry it off, but one can see the expense of spirit involved in such efforts, especially if they fell flat, as some always must. No doubt there was ready acceptance of what he had to offer—everyone likes trustful and impulsive friendliness—but there was evidently too seldom the reciprocal flow of feeling that Fitzgerald wanted. Drink gave him a delusive consolation. But nothing could answer his longing for the complete, undemanding acceptance of himself that he found symbolized by Keats in the tenderly enveloping night.

* * *

A critic who maintained that "The obvious truth about Fitzgerald is that he is not a writer of major importance," Lubell writes this essay as a "corrective" to the revival of interest in the author. His comments on Tender Is the Night *are representative of the views of Fitzgerald's detractors.*

The Fitzgerald Revival
Albert J. Lubell
The South Atlantic Quarterly (January 1955): 102–104

Nine years elapsed between the publication of *Gatsby* and *Tender Is the Night.* Although *Gatsby* was superior to anything Fitzgerald had previously done, it did not sell as well as his first two novels. Meantime, in this long period, Fitzgerald broke his silence only once, in 1926, with a volume of short stories entitled *All the Sad Young Men.* The old audience for his novels had time almost to forget him; by the time *Tender Is the Night* was published (1934), he was faced not only with a new audience but also with a different social and intellectual climate. The latter factor is not to be dismissed in attempting to explain the very mixed reception which the novel received from critics and lay readers. By 1934 the audience for serious novels in America was interested in themes different from that of *Tender Is the Night.* Apart from that, Fitzgerald did not succeed in fusing the story's different "layers of experience," in Malcolm Cowley's phrase, into an artistically unified whole. This is particularly true in the original version of the novel, where the first part, in which Rosemary Hoyt occupies the center of the stage and in which we see the other characters from her point of view, fails to prepare the reader for the later sections, when Dick Diver and Nicolle assume the central roles. Critics were not slow to point out that with the disappearance of Rosemary Hoyt from the scene the novel breaks in two. Fitzgerald himself came to realize this serious structural flaw and some years later, having determined upon a revision, rearranged the three sections of his story, putting them into chronological order, thus giving the story of Dick's early life first. Malcolm Cowley, in his introduction to this revised version, published in 1951, argues that, while the rearrangement of the parts of the story sacrifices a brilliant beginning, the novel gains much in unity and clarity of purpose. That the main theme of the novel is thereby brought into sharper focus cannot be denied. But Fitzgerald's instinct as a story teller did not really betray him when he decided to plunge into his story *in medias res.* He was following a technique as old and respectable as that of ancient epic poetry and as new as Hollywood's latest. The point is that even in the new version, while Fitzgerald's intention is made clearer, the novel still suffers from an all but fatal diffuseness, which can be explained only by the author's lack of control over his material. Whatever unity the novel possesses is one of tone and mood, resulting largely from Fitzgerald's style, which in this book is at its richest and best.

Fitzgerald's lack of control over his material can best be seen in his treatment of his central character; hence it may be said that Dick Diver represents for the author a step backward from Gatsby rather than one forward. After presenting Dick Diver as a successful psychiatrist and husband, as a brilliant social luminary around whom certain lesser ones revolved as about a sun, Fitzgerald does not prepare us sufficiently to witness the disintegration of his personality. Malcolm Cowley, on the other hand, thinks that, at the point when his hero's deterioration began, Fitzgerald was right when he "stopped telling the story from Dick's point of view and allowed us merely to guess at the hero's thoughts, so that we are never quite certain of the reason for his decline." But here, it is reasonable to argue, lies the fatal weakness of the novel, namely, the instability on the part of the author to understand his own creation. The reason—or reasons—for the disintegration of a fictional character should grow clearly out of his nature as we learn to know it and out of the circumstances of his life, or, better, out of the interaction between these two forces. If the writer of fiction fails to show us how this has come about, he fails in his basic job, which is to create characters that convince us of their fundamental reality.

The reason for Fitzgerald's failure to understand Dick Diver is not far to seek. Dick Diver is a projection of Fitzgerald himself after, say, 1932. About this time he first became conscious of a failing of his powers, of a general depletion of energy, of an emotional exhaustion, which he later likened to the situation of a person who has been spending money recklessly and suddenly finds himself overdrawn at the bank. Beyond that he could not go in giving a reason for his failing powers. Fitzgerald understood Dick Diver no better than he understood himself. From this point of view, it may be said that Fitzgerald's portrayal was closer to life, since in life too we are often left to guess why this or that person has suffered a breakdown. But this is precisely where the art of fiction, if it is to satisfy us, must be superior to our ordinary knowledge of life. Art cannot stop short at the buzzing confusion of the flux, which is what life about us is most often like. Art must bring illumination, understanding, or it fails. Not that a novelist can spell out the causes of a character's disintegration in the clinical manner of a psychiatrist. But he can, and should, provide us with a key to the understanding of a character, which should show us why the character did what he did or suffered what he suffered. This key to the understanding of Dick Diver, Fitzgerald in the end has failed to give. Thus Fitzgerald's failure in *Tender Is the Night* is fundamentally a failure to objectify his material and to fuse its "layers of experience" into an artistically unified whole. Whether he would have succeeded better in that respect in *The Last Tycoon*—his final heroic effort to realize himself as an artist—surely no one can say.

Malcolm Cowley's Edition of
Tender Is the Night

In his introduction Cowley explains the rationale for bring-
ing out a revised edition of Tender Is the Night *seventeen*
years after it was first published.

Introduction to "The Author's Final Version"
Malcolm Cowley

TO THE END OF his life Fitzgerald was puzzled by the comparative failure of *Tender Is the Night,* after the years he spent on it and his efforts to make it the best American novel of his time. He had started it when he was living on the Riviera in the late summer of 1925. At first he had worked in bursts and had put aside the manuscript for months at a time while he wrote his profitable stories for the *Saturday Evening Post;* but early in 1932 he had found a more ambitious plan for it and had gone into debt to work on it steadily until the last chapters were written and the last deletions made in proof. He had watched it grow from a short dramatic novel like *The Great Gatsby* to a long psychological or philosophical novel on the model of *Vanity Fair,* and then, as he omitted scene after scene, he had watched it diminish again to a medium-length novel, but one in which he was sure that the overtones of the longer book remained. Nine years of his life had gone into the writing and into the story itself. Reading closely one could find in it the bedazzlement of his first summer at the Cap d'Antibes—for he could picture himself as Rosemary Hoyt in the novel, besides playing the part of Dick Diver; then his feelings about money and about the different levels of American society; then his struggle with alcoholism and his worries about becoming an emotional bankrupt; then his wife's illness and everything he learned from the Swiss and American doctors who diagnosed her case; then the bitter wisdom he gained from experience and couldn't put back into it, but only into his stories; then darker things as well, his sense of guilt, his fear of disaster that became a longing for disaster—it was all in the book, in different layers, like the nine buried cities of Troy.

When another writer went to see him at Rodgers Forge, near Baltimore, in the spring of 1933, Fitzgerald took the visitor to his study and showed him a pile of manuscript nearly a foot high. "There's my new novel," he said. "I've written four hundred thousand words and thrown away three-fourths of it. Now I only have fifteen thousand left to write and—" He stood there with a glass in his hand, then suddenly burst out, "It's good, good, good. When it's published people will say that it's good, good, good."

Bennett Cerf, one of the two founders of Random House, had
reprinted The Great Gatsby *in* The Modern Library *in 1934*
with Fitzgerald's new introduction that obliquely commented on
the reception of Tender Is the Night: *". . . I had recently been*
kidded half haywire by critics who felt that my material was such
as to preclude all dealing with mature persons in a mature world.
But, my God! it was my material and it was all I had to deal
with."
Fitzgerald contacted Cerf when he was seeking a publisher
for a revised text of Tender; *but the proposal was declined.*

Fitzgerald to Bennett Cerf, 13 August 1936

The revision job would take the form, to a large extent, of a certain new alignment of the scenes—without changing their order in any case. Some such line as this:

That the parts instead of being one, two, and three (they were one, two, three and four in the magazine serial) would include in several cases sudden stops and part headings which would be to some extent explanatory; certain pages would have to be inserted bearing merely headings. Part two, for example, should say in a terse and graceful way that the scene is now back on the Riviera in the fall after these events have taken place, or that, This brings us up to where Rosemary first encounters the Divers. Those examples are not accurate to my intention nor are they at all couched as I would have them, but that's the general idea. (Do you remember the number of subheads I used in "This Side of Paradise"—at that time a rather novel experiment, the germ of which I borrowed from Bernard Shaw's preface headings to his plays; indeed that was one of the few consciously original things in "This Side of Paradise".)

There would be certain changes but I would supply the equivalent line lengths. I have not my plan with me; it seems to be in Baltimore. But I know how printing costs are. It was evolved to have a very minimum of replacement. There is not more than one complete sentence that I want to eliminate, one that has offended many people and that I admit is out of Dick's character: "I never did go in for making love to dry loins." It is a strong line but definitely offensive. These are all the changes I contemplated with in addition some minor spelling corrections such as would disturb nothing but what was within a printed line. There will be no pushing over of paragraphs or disorganization of the present set-up except in the aforesaid inserted pages. I don't want to change anything in the book but sometimes by a single word change one can throw a new emphasis or give a new value to the exact same scene or setting.

—F. Scott Fitzgerald: A Life in Letters,
pp. 306–307

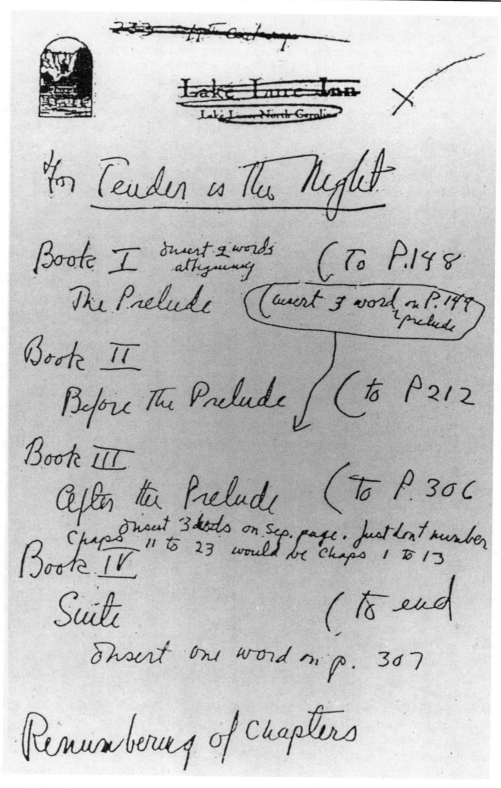

Fitzgerald's plan for reorganizing Tender Is the Night *into four books. Fitzgerald was in North Carolina 1936–1937, the so-called crack-up period, after the disappointing reception of his novel. The published revised edition was based on a five-book organizational plan found in Fizgerald's notebook (Princeton University Library).*

Tender was published in the spring of 1934 and people said nothing of the sort. It dealt with fashionable life in the 1920s at a time when most readers wanted to forget that they had ever been concerned with frivolities; the new fashion was for novels about destitution and revolt. The book had some friendly and even admiring notices, but most reviewers implied that it belonged to the bad old days before the crash; they dismissed it as having a "clever and brilliant surface" without being "wise and mature." Nor was it a popular success as compared with Fitzgerald's first three novels, which had been easier to write; in the first season it sold twelve thousand copies, or less than one-fourth as much as *This Side of Paradise*. In the following seasons the sale dwindled and stopped.

Fitzgerald didn't blame the public or the critics. It was one of the conditions of the game he played with life to accept the rules as they were written; if he lost point and set after playing his hardest, that was due to some mistake in strategy to be corrected in the future. He began looking in a puzzled fashion for the mistake in *Tender Is the Night*. There must have been an error in presentation that had kept his readers from grasping the richness and force of his material; for a time he suspected that it might merely be the lack of something that corresponded to stage directions at the beginning of each scene. In 1936 the book was being considered for republication by the Modern Library. The new edition, if it appeared, would have to be printed from the plates of the first edition in order to reduce the manufacturing costs, but Fitzgerald begged for the privilege of making some minor changes. These, he said in a letter to Bennett Cerf, "would include in several cases sudden stops and part headings which would be to some extent explanatory; certain pages would have to be inserted bearing merely headings. . . .

"I know what printing costs are," he added humbly. "There will be no pushing over of paragraphs or disorganization of the present set-up except in the aforesaid inserted pages. I don't want to change anything in the book but sometimes by a single word change one can throw a new emphasis or give a new value to the exact same scene or setting."

The new edition didn't appear and *Tender* seemed to be forgotten, although it really wasn't; it stayed in people's minds like a regret or an unanswered question. "A strange thing is that in retrospect his *Tender Is the Night* gets better and better," Ernest Hemingway told Maxwell Perkins, of Scribners, who was the editor of both novelists. In scores of midnight arguments that I remember, other writers ended by finding that they had the same feeling about the book. Fitzgerald continued to brood about it. In December 1938, when he was in Hollywood and was drawing near the end of his contract with Metro-Goldwyn-Mayer, he wrote to Perkins suggesting that three of his novels might be reprinted in one volume. *This Side of Paradise* would appear with a glossary that Fitzgerald planned to make of its absurdities and inaccuracies. *Gatsby* would be unchanged except for some corrections in the text. "But I am especially concerned about *Tender*," he added, "—that book is not dead. The *depth* of its appeal exists—I meet people constantly who have the same exclusive attachment to it as others had to *Gatsby* and *Paradise*, people who identified themselves with Dick Diver. Its great fault is that the *true* beginning—the young psychiatrist in Switzerland—is tucked away in the middle of the book."

The first edition of the novel had opened with the visit to the Cap d'Antibes of a young moving-picture actress, Rosemary Hoyt, and her meeting with the circle that surrounded the Richard Divers. It was the summer of 1925 and Antibes was enjoying its days of quiet glory. Rosemary had been entranced with the Divers and their friends, had fallen in love with Dick in a pleasantly hopeless fashion, and had become aware that there was some mystery about his wife. Then, on pages 151–212, the story had gone back to wartime Switzerland in order to explain the mystery by telling about Doctor Diver's courtship and marriage. Fitzgerald now proposed to rearrange the book in chronological order. "If pages 151–212 were taken from their present place and put at the start," he said in his letter to Perkins, "the improvement in appeal would be enormous."

It must have been about the same time that Fitzgerald made an entry in his notebook, outlining the changed order and dividing the novel into five books instead of three. The entry reads:

Analysis of *Tender*:
I   Case History 151–212 61 pps. (change moon) p. 212
II Rosemary's Angle 3–104 101 pps. P. 3
III Casualties 104–148, 213–224 55 pps. (–2) (120 & 121)
IV Escape 225–306 82 pps.
V   The Way Home 306–408 103 pps. (–8) (332–341)

I haven't been able to find the moon that was to be changed in Book I; perhaps Fitzgerald gave some special meaning to the word, and in any case it doesn't occur on 212. That was of course the last page of "Case History" and it had to be revised in order to prepare the reader for 3, which was the first page of Book II and also needed minor revisions. The page numbers in parenthesis—(120 & 121), (332–341)—were passages that the author planned to omit. All these changes were made in Fitzgerald's personal copy of *Tender Is the Night*, which is now in the manuscript room of the Princeton University Library. In that copy the pages are cut loose from the binding and rearranged as suggested in the note-

Fitzgerald letter to Perkins, 24 December 1938
Culver City, California

But I am especially concerned about Tender–that book is not dead. The depth of its appeal exists–I meet people constantly who have the same exclusive attachment to it as others had to Gatsby and Paradise, people who identified themselves with Dick Diver. It's great fault is that the true beginning–the young psychiatrist in Switzerland–is tucked away in the middle of the book. If pages 151–212 were taken from their present place and put at the start the improvement in appeal would be enormous. In fact the mistake was noted and suggested by a dozen reviewers. To shape up the ends of that change would, of course, require changes in half a dozen other pages.

–F. Scott Fitzgerald: A Life in Letters, p. 372

book; but Fitzgerald had some afterthoughts while working over them. Pages 207–212, instead of being the last chapter of Book I, are now the beginning of Book II. The necessary small revisions are made on pages 3 and 212. Book III, the one he thought of as "Casualties," begins on 74, with the Divers' visit to the battlefield of the Somme–and it is a good beginning, too, since it sets the tone for what will follow. There are many small changes and corrections in the text, especially at the beginning of Book I. On the inside front cover Fitzgerald had written in pencil:

"This it the *final version* of the book as I would like it."

The words "final version" are underlined, but they have to be taken as a statement of intention rather than as an accomplished fact. It is clear that Fitzgerald had other changes in mind besides his rearrangement of the narrative and the minor revisions already mentioned: he also planned to correct the text from beginning to end. One can see what he intended to do if one reads the first two chapters of the Princeton copy. There he has caught some of his errors in spelling proper names, has revised the punctuation to make it more logical, has sharpened a number of phrases, and has omitted others. Small as the changes are, they make the style smoother and remove the reader's occasional suspicion that the author had hesitated over a word or had failed to hear a name correctly. Near the end of Chapter II there is a pencilled asterisk and a note in Fitzgerald's handwriting: "This is my mark to say that I have made final corrections up to this point." Beyond the mark are a few other corrections but only of errors that happened to catch his eye.

It is too late now to make the changes in phrasing that, as he said, "can throw a new emphasis or give a new value to the exact same scene or setting." It is not too late, however, to correct the mistakes in spelling and punctuation, and sometimes in grammar and chronology, that disfigure the first edition of Tender. On this mechanical level the book was full of errors; in fact, a combination of circumstances was required to get so many of them into one published volume. Fitzgerald had a fine ear for words, but a weak eye for them; he was possibly the worst speller who ever failed to graduate from Princeton. His punctuation was impulsive and his grammar more instinctive than reasoned. Maxwell Perkins, his editor, was better in all these departments, but had an aristocratic disregard for details so long as a book was right in its feeling for life. Since Fitzgerald was regarded as one of his special authors, the manuscript was never copy-edited by others. The author received the proofs while his wife was critically ill. He worked over them for weeks, making extensive changes and omitting long passages, but he was in no state to notice his own errors of detail. Scores of them slipped into the first edition and, though they were unimportant if taken separately, I suspect that they had a cumulative effect on readers and ended by distracting their attention, like flaws in a window through which they were looking at the countryside. That the novel continued to be read in spite of the flaws was evidence of its lasting emotion and vitality.

Now that it is being reissued with Fitzgerald's changes I have tried to give it the sort of proofreading that the first edition failed to receive. I used dictionaries and Baedekers and consulted several of the author's friends; two or three of them had made their own lists of errors in the text. For a long time I hesitated over the two passages that Fitzgerald had marked for omission. One was the episode of the American newspaper vendor, on pages 120–121 of the first edition, and I ended by feeling that the pages could be dropped without much loss (although the newspaper vendor reappears on page 399 and once again serves as a herald of disaster). A longer omission was the Divers' visit to Mary Minghetti on pages 332–341. That change was not so easy to make, because it would have required an explanation in a later chapter of how the former Mary North had become very rich and a papal countess; besides, the episode is good in itself and that was a further reason for retaining it. Except in this instance I have tried to follow Fitzgerald's wishes at all points and to provide, so far as possible, the permanent text of a book that will continue to be read for a long time.

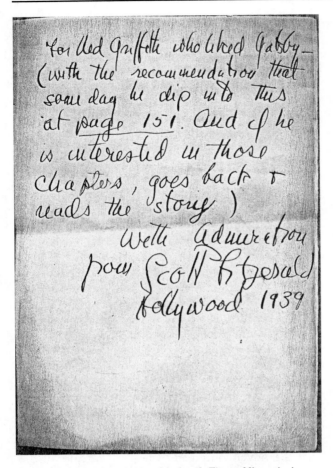

Inscription to a screenwriter that reveals Fitzgerald's continuing
concern about the structure of Tender Is the Night
(Bruccoli Collection of Fitzgerald, Thomas Cooper
Library, University of South Carolina)

The question remains whether the final version as Fitzgerald would like it is also the best version of the novel. I was slow to make up my mind about it, perhaps out of affection for the book in its earlier form. The beginning of the first edition, with the Divers seen and admired through the innocent eyes of Rosemary Hoyt, is effective by any standards. Some of the effectiveness is lost in the new arrangement, where the reader already knows the truth about the Divers before Rosemary meets them. There is a mystery-story element in the earlier draft: something has passed between Nicole Diver and Mrs. McKisco that is shocking enough to cause a duel, and we read on to learn what Nicole has done or said. There is also the suggestion of a psychoanalytical case study: it is as if we were listening behind the analyst's door while his two patients, Nicole and Dick, help him to penetrate slowly beneath their glittering surfaces. But the mystery story ends when

Rosemary discovers—on page 148 of the first edition—what Violet McKisco had seen in the bathroom at Villa Diana. The psychoanalytical case study is finished by page 212, when the reader has all the pertinent information about the past life of the Divers; but meanwhile half of the novel is still to come. The early critics of *Tender* were right when they said that it broke in two after Rosemary left the scene and that the first part failed to prepare us for what would follow. By rearranging the story in chronological order Fitzgerald tied it together. He sacrificed a brilliant beginning and all the element of mystery, but there is no escaping the judgment that he ended with a better constructed and more effective novel.

One fault of the earlier version was its uncertainty of focus. We weren't quite sure in reading it whether the author had intended to write about a whole group of Americans on the Riviera—that is, to make the book a social study with a collective hero—or whether he had intended to write a psychological novel about the glory and decline of Richard Diver as a person. Simply by changing the order of the story and starting with Diver as a young doctor in Zurich, Fitzgerald answered our hesitation. We are certain in reading the final version that the novel is psychological, that it is about Dick Diver, and that its social meanings are obtained by extension or synecdoche. Dick is the part that stands for the whole. He stands for other Americans on the Riviera, he stands for all the smart men who played too close to the line, he even stands for the age that was ending with the Wall Street crash, but first he stands for himself. The other characters are grouped around him in their subordinate roles: Rosemary sets in operation the forces waiting to destroy him, Abe North announces his fate, and Tommy Barban is his stronger and less talented successor. From beginning to end Dick is the center of the novel.

All this corresponds to the plan that Fitzgerald made early in 1932, after working for years on other plans and putting them aside. At first he had intended to write a short novel about a young man named Francis Melarky, a movie technician who visited the Riviera with his possessive mother. He met the Seth Pipers, a couple much like the Divers; he fell in love with the wife, followed them to Paris, went on a round of parties, and lost control of himself. The last chapters of this early draft are missing—if Fitzgerald ever wrote them—but it seems that Melarky was to kill his mother in a fit of rage, run away from the police, and then meet his own death—just how we aren't certain. In later versions of the story Melarky was somewhat less the central figure, while Abe Grant (later Abe North) and Seth Piper moved into the foreground. Then, at the beginning of 1932, Fitzgerald drew up the outline of a more ambitious book. "The novel should do this," he said in a memorandum to himself that was written at the time: "Show a man who is a natural idealist, a spoiled priest, giving in for various causes to the ideas of the haute bourgeoisie, and in his rise to the top of the social world losing his idealism, his talent and turning to drink and dissipation. Background one in which the leisure class is at their truly most brilliant and glamorous. . . ." In finishing the book Fitzgerald changed and deepened and complicated his picture of Dick Diver, but his statement of purpose is still the best short definition of the finished novel. His final revision brings the book even closer to the plan made in 1932.

It has to be said that Fitzgerald could never have revised *Tender* into the perfect novel that existed as an ideal in his mind. He had worked too long over it and his plans for it had changed too often, just as the author himself had changed in the years since his first summer on the Riviera. To make it all of a piece he would have had to start over from the beginning and invent a wholly new series of episodes, instead of trying to salvage as much as possible from the earlier versions. No matter how often he threw his material back into the melting pot, some of it would prove refractory to heat and would keep its former shape when poured into the new mould. The scenes written for Francis Melarky, then reassigned to Rosemary or Dick, would retain some marks of their origin. The whole Rosemary episode, being rewritten from the oldest chapters of the book, would be a little out of key with the story of Dick Diver as witnessed by himself and by his wife. But a novel has to be judged for what it gives us, not for its defects in execution, and *Tender* gives us an honesty of feeling, a complexity of life, that we miss in many books admired for being nearly perfect in form.

Moreover, in Fitzgerald's final revision it has a symmetry that we do not often find in long psychological novels. All the themes introduced in the first book are resolved in the last, and both books are written in the same key. In the first book young Doctor Diver is like Grant in his general store in Galena, waiting "to be called to an intricate destiny"; meanwhile he helps another psychiatrist with the case of Nicole Warren, a beautiful heiress suffering from schizophrenia, and learns that the Warrens have planned to buy a young doctor for her to marry. In the last book he finishes her cure, realizes that the Warrens have indeed purchased and used him—"That's what he was educated for," Nicole's sister

---

Edmund Wilson, Fitzgerald's Princeton classmate, had edited The Last Tycoon *(1941), Fitzgerald's unfinished novel, and* The Crack-Up, *a collection of his essays.*

Edmund Wilson to Malcolm Cowley, 1951

I have always felt that "the weakness of *Tender is the Night* was that Scott, when he wrote the first part, was thinking only about Gerald Murphy and had no idea that Dick Diver was a brilliant psychiatrist. It is hard to believe in him as a scientist—and also, I think, hard to believe that such a man as Scott tries later to imagine should eventually have sunk into obscurity instead of becoming a successful doctor with a fashionable practice in New York or attached to an expensive sanatorium. Except for the movies, Scott never had any kind of organized professional life. It is, of course, a remarkable book just the same.

*—Letters on Literature and Politics,
1912–1972 (1977), pp. 253–254*

---

says—and is left biding his time, "again like Grant in Galena," but with the difference that his one great adventure has ended. The Rosemary section of the novel no longer misleads our expectations; coming in the middle it simply adds fullness and relief to the story.

Although the new beginning is less brilliant than the older one, it prepares us for the end and helps us to appreciate the last section of the novel as we had probably failed to do on our first reading. That is the principal virtue of Fitzgerald's new arrangement. When I read *Tender* in 1934 it seemed to me as to many others that the Rosemary section was the best part of it. The writing there was of a type too seldom encountered in serious American fiction. It was not an attempt to analyze social values, show their falseness, tear them down—that is a necessary attempt at all times when values have become perverted, but it requires no special imaginative vitality and Fitzgerald was doing something more difficult: he was trying to discover and even create values in a society where they had seemed to be lacking. Rosemary with her special type of innocence offered the right point of view from which to reveal the grace and manners and apparent moral superiority of the Diver clan. The high point of her experience—and of the reader's—was the dinner at Villa Diana, when "The table seemed to have risen a little toward the sky like a mechanical dancing platform, giving the people around it a sense of being alone with each other in the

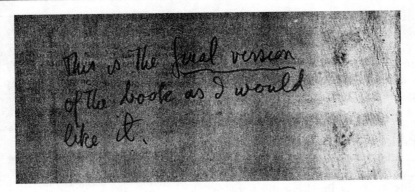

Fitzgerald's note in his re-ordered copy of Tender Is the Night *(Princeton University Library)*

The Order of "The Author's Final Version"

This table shows how Malcolm Cowley reorganized the revised edition of Tender Is the Night. *The chapters of the first edition are given in parentheses.*

Book I:	1	(Book II: 1)		10	(Book I: 22)
	2	(Book II: 2)		11	(Book I: 23)
	3	(Book II: 3)		12	(Book I: 24)
	4	(Book II: 4)		13	(Book I: 25)
	5	(Book II: 5)		14	(Book II: 11)
	6	(Book II: 6)		15	(Book II: 12)
	7	(Book II: 7)			
	8	(Book II: 8)	Book IV:	1	(Book II: 12 and 13)
	9	(Book II: 9)		2	(Book II: 14)
				3	(Book II: 15)
Book II:	1	(Book II: 10)		4	(Book II: 16)
	2	(Book I: 1)		5	(Book II: 17)
	3	(Book I: 2)		6	(Book II: 18)
	4	(Book I: 3)		7	(Book II: 19)
	5	(Book I: 4)		8	(Book II: 20)
	6	(Book I: 5)		9	(Book II: 21)
	7	(Book I: 6)		10	(Book II: 22)
	8	(Book I: 7)		11	(Book II: 23)
	9	(Book I: 8)			
	10	(Book I: 9)	Book V:	1	(Book III: 1)
	11	(Book I: 10)		2	(Book III: 2)
	12	(Book I: 11)		3	(Book III: 3)
	13	(Book I: 12)		4	(Book III: 4)
				5	(Book III: 5)
Book III:	1	(Book I: 13)		6	(Book III: 6)
	2	(Book I: 14)		7	(Book III: 7)
	3	(Book I: 15)		8	(Book III: 8)
	4	(Book I: 16)		9	(Book III: 9)
	5	(Book I: 17)		10	(Book III: 10)
	6	(Book I: 18)		11	(Book III: 11)
	7	(Book I: 19)		12	(Book III: 12)
	8	(Book I: 20)		13	(Book III: 13)
	9	(Book I: 21)			

dark universe, nourished by its only food, warmed by its only lights." Then came the underside of the Divers' little world, as revealed in Abe North's self-destructiveness and in what Violet McKisco had seen in the bathroom at Villa Diana, and everything that followed seemed a long anticlimax or at best the end of a different story.

Coming back to the novel long afterward and reading it in the new arrangement I had a different impression. The Rosemary section had its old charm and something new as well, for it now seemed the evocation of an age first condemned, then forgotten, and finally recalled with pleasure in the midst of harsher events; but the writing seemed to be on a lower level of intensity than the story of the hero's decay as told in the last section of the novel. That becomes the truly memorable passage: not Dick as the "organizer of private gaiety, curator of a richly incrusted happiness"; not Dick creating his group of friends and making them seem incredibly distinguished—"so bright a unit that Rosemary felt an impatient disregard for all who were not at their table"; but another Dick who has lost command of himself and deteriorates before our eyes in a strict progression from scene to scene. At this point Fitzgerald was right when he stopped telling the story from Dick's point of view and allowed us merely to guess at the hero's thoughts. Dick fades like a friend who is withdrawing into a private world or sinking to another level of society and, in spite of knowing so much about him, we are never quite certain of the reasons for his decline. Perhaps, as Fitzgerald first planned, it was the standards of the leisure class that corrupted him; perhaps it was the strain of curing a psychotic wife, who gains strength as he loses it by a mysterious transfer of vitality; perhaps it was a form of emotional exhaustion, a giving of himself so generously that he went beyond his resources, "like a man overdrawing at his bank," as Fitzgerald would later say of his own crack-up; or perhaps it was something far back in his childhood that could only be discovered by deep analysis—we can argue about the causes as we can argue about the decline of a once-intimate friend, without coming to any fixed conclusion; but the point is that we always believe in Dick and in his progress in a circle from obscurity to obscurity. With our last glimpse of him swaying a little as he stands on a high terrace and makes a papal cross over the beach that he had found and peopled and that has now rejected him, his fate is accomplished and the circle closed.

A Bibliographic Description of the Revised Edition of *Tender Is the Night*

A16.1.a$_1$
First revised edition, first printing, first state (1951)

8¼" x 5½"

[i–viii] ix–xviii [xix–xx] [1–2] 3–50 [51–52] 53–114 [115–116] 117–183 [184–186] 187–253 [254–256] 257–356

[1–11]^{16} [12]^{12}

Contents: p. i: half title; p. ii: 'BY F. SCOTT FITZGERALD | [five titles]'; p. iii: title; p. iv: copyright; p. v: dedication; p. vi: blank; p. vii: contents; p. viii: blank; pp. ix–xviii: '*INTRODUCTION*'; p. xix: epigraph; p. xx: blank; p. 1: 'BOOK I | CASE HISTORY | 1917–1919 | [tapered rule]'; p. 2: blank; pp. 3–334: text, headed 'TENDER IS THE NIGHT | CHAPTER I'; p. 51: 'BOOK II | ROSEMARY'S ANGLE | 1919–1925 | [tapered rule]'; p. 115: 'BOOK III | CASUALTIES | 1925 | [tapered rule]'; p. 185: 'BOOK IV | ESCAPE | 1925–1929 | [tapered rule]'; p. 255: 'BOOK V | THE WAY HOME | 1929-1930 | [tapered rule]'; pp. 335–348: 'APPENDIX | [swash] The Manuscripts of "Tender"'; pp. 349–356: '[swash] Notes'.

Typography and paper: 6 3/16" (6 3/8") X 3 7/8"; thirty-eight lines per page. Running heads: rectos and versos, 'TENDER IS THE NIGHT'. Wove paper.

Binding: Dark grayish yellow (#91) V cloth (fine linen-like grain). Spine black-stamped with four red compartments: '[three rules] | TENDER | IS THE | NIGHT | [three rules] | F. SCOTT | FITZGERALD | [three rules] | AUTHOR'S | FINAL | REVISION | [six rules] | SCRIBNERS | [three rules]'. White wove endpapers of different stock from text paper. All edges trimmed. White and black headbands and footbands.

Dust jacket: Tan laid paper. Front has seventeen lines of type in red and black: 'THE AUTHOR'S FINAL VERSION, COMPLETELY | RESET, AND NOW PUBLISHED FOR THE FIRST TIME | F. SCOTT FITZGERALD | [red] *Tender is the Night* | [twelve lines of type printed in black quoting Fitzgerald's 24 December 1938 letter to Perkins and Fitzgerald's note in his own copy of *TITN* | WITH AN INTRODUCTION BY *Malcolm Cowley*'.

$3.50

THE AUTHOR'S FINAL VERSION, COMPLETELY

RESET, AND NOW PUBLISHED FOR THE FIRST TIME

F. SCOTT FITZGERALD

Tender is the Night

ALMOST TO THE END of his life, F. Scott Fitzgerald was puzzled by the comparative failure of *Tender Is The Night*. Nine years of his life, nine years of his best efforts, had gone into the writing. Two years before he died he came to a conclusion. "Its great fault," he wrote then in a letter, "is that the *true* beginning — the young psychiatrist in Switzerland — is tucked away in the middle of the book." In his personal copy of the novel, he cut the pages loose and rearranged them, making also many small revisions and corrections. On the inside front cover he wrote: "This is the *final version* of the book as I would like it."

This new edition provides, in the present editor's words, "the permanent text of a book that will continue to be read for a long time."

WITH AN INTRODUCTION BY *Malcolm Cowley*

Tender is the Night

BY F. SCOTT FITZGERALD

Scott Fitzgerald himself gave the best short definition of *Tender Is the Night* in an outline for the novel which he drew up in 1932. He wanted to "show a man who is a natural idealist . . . giving in for various causes to the ideas of the haute bourgeoisie, and in his rise to the top of the social world losing his idealism, his talent and turning to drink and dissipation."

It is the story of Dick Diver, a young psychiatrist whose career was thwarted and his genius numbed through his marriage to the exquisite and wealthy Nicole Warren. On the outside their life was all glitter and glamour, but beneath the smooth, beautiful surface lay the corroding falseness of their social values and the tragedy of her disturbed mind. Against the opulent background of the Riviera peopled with rich Americans and "intellectuals," Fitzgerald tells of Dick Diver's progress from obscurity to obscurity.

In this revised version, *Tender Is the Night*, always a strangely haunting story, has gained in symmetry, and the plot progresses more directly to its conclusion. The emphasis has subtly changed too. Now our attention is focused on Dick Diver from beginning to end, and, as a result, his dark figure emerges strongly from the gleaming background.

Front cover and front flap of the dust jacket of the novel re-ordered and edited by Malcolm Cowley (Bruccoli Collection of Fitzgerald, Thomas Cooper Library, University of South Carolina)

Spine: '[black script] Tender | is the | Night | [red] F. SCOTT | FITZGERALD | [black] SCRIBNERS'. Back has list of five volumes by Fitzgerald. Front flap has blurb for *TITN*; back flap has blurb for *Stories*.

Publication: 5,075 copies of the first printing. Published 12 November 1951. $3.50. Copyright #A61314.

Printing: Composed and printed from plates by the Scribner Press. Bound by the Scribner Press.

Locations: LC (deposited 21 November 1951); MJB (dj–review copy).

Note one: A mimeographed *Erratum Slip for Reviewers* on Scribner letterhead was inserted in review copies and lists the four errata noted under A.15.1.a$_2$.

Note two: Appendix includes the "Wanda Breasted" episode and first publications of the "Monsieur Irv" episode. "Wanda Breasted" was previously published as "The World's Fair"; see B 44, C 314.

A16.1.a$_2$
First printing, second state

$[1]^{16}(1\pm_{6,7,9})\ [2\text{–}11]^{16}\ [12]^{12}$

Three leaves were canceled in Cowley's introduction to correct four errors:

xi.18   xett [text
xiv.19 tsandards [standards
xviii.23 b each [beach
xviii.24 accompanied [accomplished

Locations: Lilly (dj); MJB (dj); NjP.

LATER PRINTINGS WITHIN THE REVISED TEXT

A16.1.b
New York: Scribners, 1953.

A16.1.c
Modern Standard Authors Three Novels of F. Scott Fitzgerald. New York: Scribners [1953]. See AA 4.

A16.1.d
New York: Scribners, 1956.

A16.1.e
New York: Scribners, [1959]. On copyright page: 'J-9.59 [MH]'.

A16.1.f
New York: Scribners, [1970]. Scribner Library #SL2. On copyright page: '0-5.70[MC]'. The Scribner Library series normally published the original text, but the plates of the revised text were used inadvertently in the Contemporary Classics/Scribner Library O, P, and Q printings.

ENGLISH EDITIONS

A16.2.a
First revised English edition, first printing (1953)

scant 7¼" x 4 13/16"

[i-x] xi-xxii [1-2] 3-55 [56-58] 59-131 [132-134] 135-213 [214-216] 217-297 [298-300] 301-407 [408] 409-418

[A]⁸ B-I⁸ K-Y⁸ AA-CC⁸ DD⁴

Contents: p. 1: half title; p. ii: *'by the same author* | [three titles]'; p. iii: title; p. iv: copyright; p. v: dedication; p. vi: blank; p. vii: epigraph; p. viii: blank; p. ix: contents; p. x: blank; pp. xi-xxii: *'INTRODUCTION'*; p. 1: section title; p. 2: blank; pp. 3-392: text, headed

Title page for the re-ordered novel (Bruccoli Collection of Fitzgerald, Thomas Cooper Library, University of South Carolina)

'I'; pp. 57, 133, 215, 299: section titles; pp. 393-407: *'APPENDIX'*; pp. 409-418: 'Notes'.

Typography and paper: 5 3/4" (5 7/8") X 3 5/8"; thirty-five lines per page. Wove paper.

Binding: Light Brown (#57) V cloth (fine linen-like grain) or light yellowish brown (#76) paper-covered boards. Priority of bindings undermined. Spine gold-stamped: *'TENDER | IS THE | NIGHT | [asterisk] | F. SCOTT | FITZGERALD | GREY | WALLS | PRESS'.* White wove endpapers of different stock from text paper. All edges trimmed.

Dust jacket: City night scene in shades of black, gray, and white on front, spine, and back, signed by PAGRAM. Front: '[white] TENDER IS THE NIGHT | [white] *by* | F. Scott | Fitzgerald | [black] GREY | WALLS | PRESS'. Front flap has blurb for *TITN;*

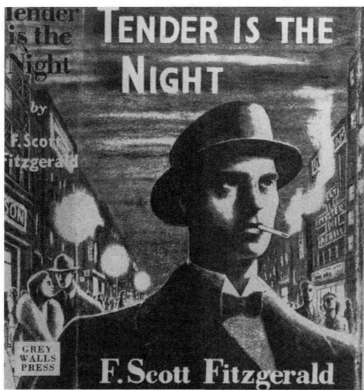

ALMOST to the end of his life, Scott Fitzgerald, was puzzled by the complete failure, at that time, of *Tender is the Night*. In his personal copy of the novel he cut the pages and rearranged them, making many small revisions and corrections. On the inside front cover he wrote, 'this is the final version of the book as I would like it'.

It is the story of a young psychiatrist who falls in love with, and marries, a rich girl who was once his patient, and who for many years remained more or less a mental invalid. To her he devotes his life, gradually allowing his career and his work to drift away, while they wander around Europe seeking pleasure and distraction. Against the opulent background of the Riviera peopled with rich Americans and 'intellectuals', Fitzgerald tells of the young man's progress from obscurity to obscurity.

In this revised version, *Tender is the Night*, always a strangely haunting story, has gained much. The plot progresses more directly towards its conclusion and the emphasis has subtly changed. For now our attention is focused on the young man from beginning to end, and as a result his figure emerges far more strongly from its gleaming background.

Malcolm Cowley, Fitzgerald's friend and contemporary, has written in his introduction 'this edition provides the permanent text of a book that will continue to be read for a very long time.'

Jacket design by Edward Pagram

12s. 6d.

F. SCOTT FITZGERALD

Through the years of the 'twenties, the years of the 'speak-easy', the gangster, the 'flapper' and wood alcohol, Scott Fitzgerald recorded the hectic life of the participants. His books remain as a superbly exact and imaginative testimony of those magnificently carefree years of a nation trying to recover from the hang-over of a war which had claimed a generation.

The novels and stories of
F. SCOTT FITZGERALD

THE BEAUTIFUL AND DAMNED
'This is a superb piece of craftsmanship'. *The Sphere*. 12s. 6d.

THE GREAT GATSBY
'... one of the finest novels thrown up by America between wars.'—*The Evening Standard*. 8s. 6d.

THE LAST TYCOON
'... here is a story that will stand very well as it is. Scott Fitzgerald, uncut, unsharpened, unrevised, can still make most of his colleagues look like amateurs.'—*Spectator*. 8s. 6d.

THIS SIDE OF PARADISE
'... reinforces the impression that this elusive writer has a strong claim to be the most talented member of that "lost generation" to which Gertrude Stein referred. ... It is a beautiful and painful book to read.'—*Irish Times*. 8s. 6d.

If you wish to be placed on our mailing list will you please send a postcard giving your name and address to:

THE FALCON PRESS LTD.,
6-7 CROWN PASSAGE,
PALL MALL, LONDON, S.W.1.

Catalogue No. R.6714.

Dust jacket for the first revised English edition published in 1953 (Bruccoli Collection of Fitzgerald, Thomas Cooper Library, University of South Carolina)

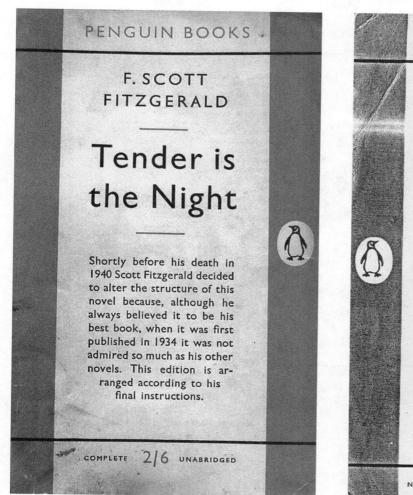
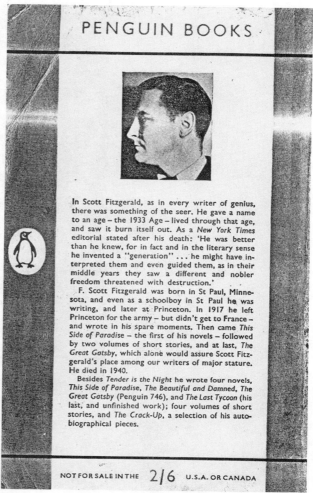

Front and back covers for the Penguin revised edition published in 1955 (Bruccoli Collection of Fitzgerald,
Thomas Cooper Library, University of South Carolina)

back flap lists four other Fitzgerald titles, 'Catalogue No. R.6714.'

Publication: Unknown number of copies of the first printing. Published 30 July 1953. 12/6.

Publication: See copyright page.

Locations: Bod (7 DEC 1953–cloth); Cam (7 DE 1953–cloth); Lilly (cloth–dj); MJB (Both bindings with dj); ViU (cloth–dj).

A16.3
Second English edition

F. SCOTT FITZGERALD | TENDER IS THE NIGHT | A ROMANCE | [double rule] | WITH THE AUTHOR'S FINAL REVISION | PREFACE BY | MALCOLM COWLEY | PENGUIN BOOKS

Harmondsworth, 1955. #906. Wrappers. 2/6. Reprinted 1958, 1961, 1963, 1964, 1966, 1968, 1970, 1971, 1972, 1973, 1974, 1976, 1977, 1978. There are two errors on the copyright page: *TITN* was not first published in 1939, and the revised versison was not published in 1948.

Covers for Penguin revised editions, 1958, 1970, and 1978 (Bruccoli Collection of Fitzgerald,
Thomas Cooper Library, University of South Carolina)

Budd Schulberg (Bruccoli Collection of Fitzgerald, Thomas Cooper Library, University of South Carolina)

The Response to the Revised Edition

Budd Schulberg met Fitzgerald in 1939 when they were teamed on the screenplay for Winter Carnival *and sent to Dartmouth College for location shooting. Fitzgerald went on a bender and was fired in Hanover. They remained friends; and* The Disenchanted, *Schulberg's 1950 novel based on the Dartmouth College debacle, helped to stimulate the Fitzgerald revival.*

Prodded by Pride and Desperation
Budd Schulberg
The New York Times Book Review, 18 November 1951,
pp. 5, 38

The currents of literary success are tricky and perverse. Only the strong of heart can sustain their careers to the sweet or bitter end. One of these was F. Scott Fitzgerald, whose story is now almost too well known—perhaps I mean known for the wrong reasons. His life itself, not without some justification, has become a *succès scandale* of such proportion as to overshadow the substance of his work. Waste or no waste, false values or no false values, he

ranks among the two or three most gifted and most scrupulous, fastidious and craftsmanlike of twentieth-century American novelists.

You ask for evidence. I say here it is again: "Tender Is the Night," Fitzgerald's fourth and last completed novel, first published in 1934 but now printed for the first time in his final version rearranged out of pride and desperation in the late middle Thirties.

The tides of critical and public approval have never moved more quixotically and puzzlingly than they did against "Tender Is The Night." With "The Great Gatsby" in 1925 Fitzgerald was hurried into the inner circle of American writers of first rank. Almost everybody was ready to agree with T. S. Eliot's appraisal of "Gatsby": "The first step that American fiction has taken since Henry James." Critics speculated as to the eventual stature of young Fitzgerald if his next book were to mark as great an advance over "Gatsby" as "Gatsby" had been over "This Side of Paradise" and "The Beautiful and Damned." But year after year there was no next book. With the Thir-

Dust jacket for Schulberg's 1950 novel in which the protagonist is modeled on Fitzgerald (Bruccoli Collection of Fitzgerald, Thomas Cooper Library, University of South Carolina)

*Review slip sent with Cowley's revised version of the novel
(Bruccoli Collection of Fitzgerald, Thomas Cooper
Library, University of South Carolina)*

I happened to read the book some fifteen years ago when my favorites were supposed to be (and to some extent were) Steinbeck and Farrell. I read the stately opening paragraph and thought it could not be improved (I was wrong: with a word out here, a word changed there, Fitzgerald brought it to perfection for this edition). I knew I was in the hands of a master story-teller, and that rare exception to the run of crude, powerful, American sluggers, a master stylist. There *are* books you cannot put down. But here was a book with lines, images, shafts of wit, moments of revelation and some pure and impure magic I could not put out of my mind; and these dazzling fragments were held together by a plan of exacting moral and artistic discipline.

If "Tender Is the Night" did not quite have the courage of its conviction, it had the courage of its sensibilities. Fitzgerald had gone down into himself for this book in a way he had never been able to do before, articulating and using for literary entertainment of high order his inmost

ties, the depression, the proletarianization of literature, the critics no longer speculated about this brilliant young man on the high bars. They had moved on to other gods.

By the time "Tender Is the Night" appeared, in 1934, after being on the fire nine years long, Fitzgerald already was relegated to the scrapheap of the bankrupt Twenties. That he *had* surpassed himself, that he had written a delicate and difficult novel superbly, that he had deepened if not broadened, that what he had written was not a frivolous but a serious novel of character and manners; yes, and of social significance that would outlast and eventually eclipse the Big-S socially significant tracts then passing for literature—this was overlooked by most of the reading public and all but a few of the critics.

So "Tender Is the Night" "failed." It sold around 12,000 copies; got lambasted by righteous Leftish critics who wondered how Fitzgerald could still concern himself with the idle rich on the Riviera when Reality and Humanity and Truth were to be found on the home front, in factories, Hoovervilles and on the picket line; got damned with faint praise by critics who applauded his "surface brilliance" while deploring his subject-matter, his emotional confusion, his false values.

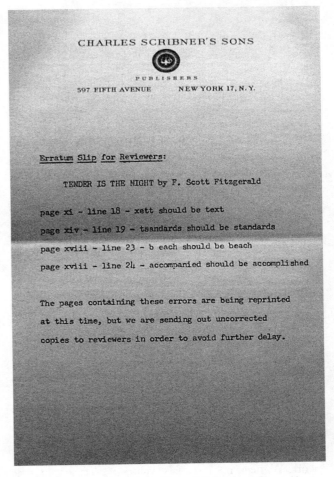

Slip inserted in review copies (Bruccoli Collection of Fitzgerald, Thomas Cooper Library, University of South Carolina)

experience, his woe, his insecurity, his anxiety, his frustration, his self-doubt, self-knowledge and his love.

After years of hard, frustrating work (shown by the bulk of penciled manuscripts in the Princeton Library) along various plot-lines related to his eventual plan, Fitzgerald began to see, in 1932, the theme he had been groping toward since 1925. In one of those memoranda that project his ambition and the seriousness of purpose that never failed him, he wrote: "The novel should do this: Show a man who is a natural idealist, a spoiled priest, giving in for various causes to the ideas of the haute bourgeoisie, and in his rise to the top of the social world losing his idealism, his talent and turning to drink and dissipation. Background one in which the leisure class is at their truly most brilliant and glamorous * * *."

"Tender Is the Night" failed to do what its author had prayed and worked for and counted on. It restored neither his fame nor his fortune. He brooded over this. The favorite criticism of "Tender Is the Night" was that its structure was awry.

The theme is classic: Young psychiatrist with brilliant future (Dick Diver) is encouraged to correspond with beautiful heiress (Nicole Warren) suffering mental breakdown as result of early incestuous experience with father. Dick falls in love with Nicole and this love restores to her the power to return love and to go back into the world again. The book opened on the Divers at the Riviera six years after Nicole had left the sanitarium with Dick. They are first seen through the eyes of a naive Hollywood starlet, Rosemary Hoyt, for whom the gates of womanhood are just beginning to swing open. Her infatuation with the Divers as a couple and gradually with Dick as the most enchanting man she has ever known, and Fitzgerald's ability to create a vibrant young girl of persuasive charm, led many readers to the mistaken idea that she was to be a key figure. When she is ditched and the narrative switches back seven years to the sanitarium and the courtship (and what a delight that is!) of Nicole and Dick, these readers felt cheated and confused.

Fitzgerald reconsidered. He pulled the sanitarium section (1917–1919) from the middle and placed it at the beginning. Then Rosemary came in fifty pages later, in 1925, where she belonged both chronologically and in terms of dramatic logic. Now the book begins and ends with Dick Diver and he is quickly identified as the central figure. Fitzgerald hoped the Modern Library would publish his revised version. Or perhaps that Scribners would include it in a new one-volume Fitzgerald. Whether his publishers saw it or not, it was no sale. It was not his time. Fifteen years would have to pass before Fitzgerald's hope would be realized. Malcolm Cowley, a critic of stature and a man who knows and serves Fitzgerald well, says in his good, businesslike introduction that by rearranging the story in chronological order Fitzgerald had a more effective novel, with a "symmetry that we do not often find in long psychological novels."

Well, maybe a reader gets set in his ways after reading a novel innumerable times, for I remain unconvinced. There was nice irony in the way we met the Divers for the first time with Rosemary; through her innocent and romantic eyes we saw them on the crest and apparently intact. That way the tension grew, the mystery gathered. I find it more artful. The new opening disconcerts me as one that Fitzgerald would not have written if he were doing his book from scratch. It is too clinical, and what is known in Hollywood as *head-on*.

We learn so much about Nicole's mental condition and her pitiful dependence on Dick that the subsequent Riviera scenes and the Divers' relationship with Rosemary suffer for the cloud of horror we now know to hang over them. Logic and clarity have been gained, but at the cost of irony, beauty and a dramatic suspense that always added to the book for me. I can't help wishing the false lead of Rosemary's predominance in the first section could have been corrected in some less dramatic way. I believe that Fitzgerald's first esthetic instincts were sound, as usual, and that he was panicked by failure and disappointment.

I don't think that Fitzgerald's main trouble in 1934 was either the chronology or the more valid complaint that the reason for Dick's collapse might have been more clearly defined. No, I think Fitzgerald's main trouble was 1934 itself. It wasn't his talent, just his luck that had run out. In 1934 this book, its people, its world, its poetry were out of style. But read it now or read it again and I think you may agree that what F. Scott Fitzgerald had to say was good and timeless, and how he says it rarely has been equaled in American prose fiction.

Ernest Hemingway to Edmund Wilson, 28 November 1951

What [do] you think of the business of putting *Tender is the Night* into chronological order rather than the way it was published. I read it all through and it seemed to take the magic out of it. Nothing came as a surprise and the mystery had all been removed. I think it was one of those ideas Scott had sometimes, like his titles that Max Perkins kept him from using, which was not too good.

—Ernest Hemingway:
Selected Letters, 1917–1961 (1981), p. 743

Interview with Budd Schulberg
29 May 2002

DLB: Talk to me about how *Tender Is the Night* was received. There's John O'Hara's explanation—which is more-or-less the official explanation—that the concerned intellectuals damned it during the Depression because it failed to express the appropriate proletarian concerns. O'Hara indicates that Fitzgerald became a kind of sacrificial figure during the Thirties. Can you respond to that, Budd?

BS: I can pin a seconding motion on it. That was the feeling in the Party, in the Communist Party, and it's amazing what an influence it seemed to have. Most of the critics—I would say almost 90 percent it seemed—were very Left-leaning. To them the subject matter of *Tender Is the Night* seemed like a fallback to the concerns of the Twenties. The key word for it was *decadent*. That was also used about Faulkner. When I was still in the Party, there was a split between most of the people thinking that any work that was decadent was no good, was second-rate or out of date, reactionary, etcetera, etcetera. There was a minority, including me and a few, who saw the work itself as a piece of literature that had to be recognized and admired. Just as it went for Faulkner. Faulkner was also damned by many in the Party, or I would say Party-influenced. The whole atmosphere was against the subject matter of a book like *Tender Is the Night.*

DLB: Do you remember when you read it? In 1934 when it first came out or later?

BS: I read it early. I don't think in college, but right after. I read it around 1936. And I was very, very impressed with it, as I had been by Scott's work. So that it further set me apart. But there were writers out there, Dorothy Parker, Nathanael West, many of the more literary people out there, who did not go along with the Party line on the book. And that extended way, way beyond the Party, as you've probably seen from reading the reviews.

DLB: The best reviews were by John Chamberlain, who reviewed it twice. After he first reviewed it, he reviewed it again a couple of days later to argue with the other reviewers. That was a heroic moment in American book reviewing. And Gilbert Seldes, who was always right about Fitzgerald. The other reviews never said "decadent." They complained that Dick Diver is unconvincing. They managed to convince Fitzgerald that they were right, and that led to the so-called "Author's Final Version." Did he ever talk to you about that?

BS: Yes, I did talk to him about it. What he was really trying to do was puzzle out why *Tender* didn't do better. Maybe it's because it's confusing, he thought; maybe if it started chronologically it wouldn't have confused the reader, and so forth. I think he was fumbling around trying to get the answer to why it had not done as well as he hoped.

DLB: When Malcolm Cowley published the revised version in 1951, you reviewed it. What your review in effect said is, "It's different, but it's not better."

BS: Yes, that's correct. Didn't I say that I preferred the original? What I wrote is very much what I told Scott. But I felt he was groping, in a way. Groping for an answer to why that book had not succeeded.

DLB: During '35, '36, '37, '38 were people aware of it or was it just forgotten and buried?

BS: Very much. Very forgotten and buried. Very. Very. It's a shocking thing, but it was true. It really was. I truly think he was shaken by the failure and trying to fix it. I didn't think it needed to be fixed.

DLB: But before the Viking *Portable Fitzgerald* I never saw a copy of *Tender.* I never heard anybody talk about it.

BS: Really. I have to read that O'Hara introduction again; I haven't read it in many years.

DLB: The great sentence: "All he was was our best novelist, one of our best novella-ists, and one of our finest writers of short stories."

BS: Well, he was a real champion, John was. He was.

Correcting a Fault

In The Rhetoric of Fiction *(1961), Wayne Booth argues that Fitzgerald was initially mistaken in deciding on the flashback structure.*

The achievement of the revision is, in short, to correct a fault of over-distancing, a fault that springs from a method appropriate to other works at other times but not to the tragedy Fitzgerald wanted to write. His true effect could be obtained only by repudiating much of what was being said by important critics of fiction about point of view and developing a clean, direct, old-fashioned presentation of his hero's initial pre-eminence and gradual decline.

                                                                    –p. 195

DLB: You've confirmed what I didn't want to hear confirmed. That during the Thirties, into the Forties, *Tender Is the Night* didn't exist. I hate like hell to use the word "suppressed," because "suppressed" carries the meaning of enemy action. I don't think it was active, was it?

BS: No, it was not active.

DLB: People didn't bother damning it. They just ignored it.

BS: That's right. Subconsciously suppressed it, in a sense. I knew people who—young radicals that were part of the whole movement that I was in—if anything was said of the book, they thought, "What is anyone doing wasting their time writing about these useless social parasites?" But you could say the same thing about *The Sun Also Rises*.

DLB: Except they were afraid of Hemingway. They were never afraid of Fitzgerald. Fitzgerald was a punching bag.

BS: Also a book like *To Have and Have Not* to the—you shouldn't even say radicals, because you don't need to say radicals—the literary tide was going that way, and a book like *To Have and Have Not* was read as sort of a faltering move to the Left, you see. But even that fumbling at the end in which Harry Morgan is realizing that no one man can do it alone, that helped Hemingway. It sounds funny now, maybe, but the literary world was so politicized by the Left in those days, that I really think that book helped him. And because of his involvement in the Spanish Civil War, so forth, he was accepted.

DLB: In the notes for *Tender*, Fitzgerald played with the idea of Diver sending his son to Russia to be educated. If *Tender Is the Night* had ended that way, what would have happened? Would it have been hailed as a masterpiece?

BS: I think it might have been, yes. It would have made a big difference, a major difference, I think, yes, absolutely. Everything was judged, everybody was judged that way. The irony, of course, is that when I got to know Scott, he was very, very liberal, Left, really.

DLB: How Left? Further Left than the New Deal?

BS: Well, New Deal Left. Curious about the cause, I would say. Not having embraced them on it, but curious about it. Opened-minded about it. That's what I found.

Chamberlain had twice reviewed Tender Is the Night *when it was first published, defending the novel against critics who found Dick Diver's decline unconvincing.*

A Reviewer's Notebook
John Chamberlain
Freeman, no. 2 (19 November 1951): 121–122

The destiny of man in our barren epoch seems to be almost inextricably bound up with politics. Yet politics is the least satisfying, the least rewarding, of human preoccupations. The more we intensify our political activities, the less time we have to spend on personal development, or the arts, or creativity in general. It is some such realization, I think, that is at the bottom of all the recent refurbishing and evaluation of the decade of the nineteen twenties. Few of our "intellectuals" loved the American twenties when they were living through them: that was the decade when the superior children of the arts were saying "Good-bye, Wisconsin" (or Kansas, or wherever), when Main Street was considered a hopelessly benighted place, when our "business civilization" was being damned from hell to breakfast by reengage businessmen turned writers. But in the twenties no one had to enlist for self-protection, or for the protection of a way of life, in murderously serious political wars. Life had (or at least it seemed to have) a margin, an area of velvet; the human being had time to love, to create, to play.

He also had time to make a damned fool of himself, which is what lots of people did. During the nineteen thirties all that could be seen in retrospect was the foolishness and the wantonness of the period. In their rush to hail the new bottomside mobility of the proletarian cult, our critics tended to dismiss all the salient figures of the twenties. Two particularly representative luminaries, F. Scott Fitzgerald and Edna St. Vincent Millay, sold off in the literary market just about as disastrously as Radio Corporation sold off on the Big Board. Fitzgerald was remembered, if at all, as the man who tried to make Princeton University into a country club; Edna Millay was typed as the girl who had lost her spontaneity when she turned from flapper defiance of the conventions to more sober and classic themes. What the new critics of the thirties failed to perceive was that both Fitzgerald and Millay loved the more solid and lasting boons of life as well as the froth. Hanging grimly to a pendulum that was gathering momentum in its swing toward Moscow, our critics, who are always more fashionable than free, forgot that the first duty of an intellectual is to grasp and analyze a phenomenon in its entirety.

Now the penitents are coming back.

. . . .

I hope, too, that Malcolm Cowley and Alfred Kazin, two critics who spent a good deal of their time in the nineteen thirties cultivating the illusion that the way to free man was to put his energies under the control of Socialist politicians, have turned for good to other themes. Malcolm Cowley has just finished rearranging F. Scott Fitzgerald's "Tender is the Night" (Scribner's, $3.50) in accordance with an outline left by Fitzgerald himself in his notebook. The reshuffling of the components of "Tender is the Night" into more strictly chronological order does improve the novel. Edward Dahlberg, who thinks Fitzgerald an overrated man, sent me to reading the new Cowley-Fitzgerald version of "Tender is the Night" with trepidation; I was afraid that I would discover Fitzgerald had become a diminished figure. But I found that the writing in "Tender is the Night" is just as good as I thought it was in 1934, when I first read it. There is a shoddy strain in some of Fitzgerald's work, and Mr. Dahlberg is quite right to feel angry at the general American habit of periodically overpraising what has been neglected and underpraised before. But Fitzgerald had purified both his style and his attitude for the writing of "Tender is the Night."

Mr. Kazin's "F. Scott Fitzgerald: The Man and His Work" (World, $3) is a collection of criticisms and appreciations of Fitzgerald that span a full thirty years of time. The collection makes for some interesting reading. One of the things which it proves, inadvertently, is that our off-the-cuff reviewing has been considerably better than our more pretentious criticism. When a single critic feels he has to drag in the names of Racine, André Gide, Goethe, John Milton, Proust, Yeats, Shakespeare, Dickens, Voltaire, Balzac, Henry James, George Moore, Æ, Stendhal, St. John of the Cross, Wordsworth, Keats, Shelley, Dostoevski, Byron, Shaw and Samuel Butler to explain Fitzgerald, the traffic becomes a trifle overburdened, to say the least.

In F. Scott Fitzgerald: The Last Loacoön *(1967), Robert Sklar finds fault with both the original and the revised editions of* Tender Is the Night.

Tender is the Night ends thus without the promise of a new beginning, slips quietly back into the unrecoverable past. Into the novel which occupied nine years of his life, Fitzgerald poured a profusion of themes and images, poured all the passion of his social discontent and his historical understanding. *Tender is the Night* is most of all a novel of emotion, of beautiful and sad and sometimes artistically uncontrolled emotion. Through the carelessness of his publisher it was—and still is—a novel of incongruous and distracting imperfections, misspellings, repetitions, wrong words; but through Fitzgerald's own lack of artistic detachment it is also a novel of imperfect form, a novel whose dramatic structure is continually broken by the author's effort to insert a wider social perspective that he felt he had not fully made clear. It was this flaw in the novel's form that led Fitzgerald to plan a structural revision. But when the revised version was posthumously prepared and published it lost the dramatic energy of the novel without gaining the formal clarity that only a textual revision could have attained.

–p. 291

Advertisement in the 18 November 1951 issue of The New York Times

Editing *Tender Is the Night*

The following time scheme for Tender Is the Night *was prepared for the 1996 Everyman Centennial Edition of the novel.*

Time Scheme
Arlyn Bruccoli

The clear understanding of the chronology of events and the passage of time in *Tender Is the Night* is essential to the reader's proper response to the novel. The 1925–1917–1925 flashback has generated debate; but the structural flaw in *Tender* is the blurred time scheme from summer 1925 to summer 1929. Reviewers who challenged the credibility of Dick Diver's dive were in part reacting to inadequate or contradictory time signals in the novel. The progress of Dr. Diver's decline from brilliantly promising psychiatrist to alcoholic failure is difficult to trace because the reader is not always certain when an episode is occurring. How much time elapses between the Gstaad trip at Christmas 1925 and the next chapter at the clinic? *Nineteen or twenty months.* How much time elapses between Nicole's breakdown at the fair and Diver's arrival in Rome? *About eight months.* How much time elapses between the Divers' departure from the clinic and their return to the Villa Diana? *About nine months.* Does Diver depart from the Riviera in 1929 or 1930? *1929.* What is the time span of the novel from Book I, chapter 1 to Book III, chapter 12? *Four years: summer 1925–summer 1929.*

The key time signals are at 236.18 ("this past year and a half on the Zugersee") and 283.3–4 ("For eighteen months now he had lived at the clinic."). Eighteen months after Christmas 1925 in the previous chapter places the time of Book II, chapter 14 in summer 1927, allowing a month or two for the Divers' move to Switzerland. This calculation fits the 1928 date (276.13) that Fitzgerald stipulates in the Rome chapters.

The chronology difficulties can be attributed to the conditions of writing, editing, and publication. Fitzgerald was revising or rewriting the serial and book texts at the same time; the production schedules made it impossible for Scribners to give *Tender* the scrupulous line-editing it required—even if the publisher had been prepared to invest the time.

The chronology in the first edition is unworkable, but Fitzgerald meant it to be accurate. He prepared preliminary character chronologies—though they have internal contractions and he did not strictly adhere to them. It is improper for an editor to insert dates or other time signals into the text of *Tender,* but a critical edition must emend the misleading time references that are in the first edition.

The editor of *Tender* has two choices: to retain the years that Fitzgerald stipulates (1925 and 1928) in the first edition, emending the intervening elapsed time, or to emend the year 1928. The former option requires that Diver's departure from the Riviera in Book III, chapter 12 take place in summer 1929; the latter option extends the time-span to summer 1930. There is more involved in this decision than arithmetic. Whether Diver's departure occurs before or after the October 1929 stock-market crash shapes the concluding moods of the novel. If, as the editor of this text contends, the final Riviera episodes take place before the crash, there is the dramatic irony of impending catastrophe—a sense that the rich who have corrupted Diver and his Riviera protectorate are unknowingly living on borrowed time. A post-crash ending conveys the different irony that the very rich are still rich but that Diver has been ruined by them.

The compelling reason for preferring the pre-crash ending is that the crash is not mentioned in the novel. The financial data in the closing chapters are all related to the boom: aboard "The Margin" Barban states that he has "good stocks in the hands of friends who are holding it for me. All goes well"; and Nicole replies that "Dick's getting rich" (353.15–17). The assertion that Fitzgerald was unaware of the crash or indifferent to its consequences is unconvincing. He had written brilliantly about the effects of the crash on American expatriates in "Babylon Revisited" (published in February 1931). The preliminary age tables for Diver and Nicole both stipulate that the story ends in July 1929.

The only piece of documentary evidence supporting the post-crash ending is an inscription in a copy of the novel: "F Scott Fitzgerald requests the pleasure of Laura Guthrie's Company in Europe 1917–1930."[1] This inscription was written in 1936 or 1937. Malcolm Cowley, who supported the 1925–1930 time span, claimed that 1930 "was the year when, in spite of the crash, there were more rich Americans in Europe than ever before and when the summer season on the Riviera was the biggest and maddest."[2] He was not in France at that time. Cowley argues that "the chronology of the novel requires thirty months, not eighteen, between the Christmas holidays at Gstaad and Dick's working at the clinic. One can assume that the Divers spent another year on the Riviera while the clinic was being remodelled, and then eighteen months on the Zugersee."[3] This assumption creates a hole in the novel.

The chronology for this edited text of *Tender Is the Night* provides an emended scheme for the 1925, 1917–1925, 1925–1929 structure.

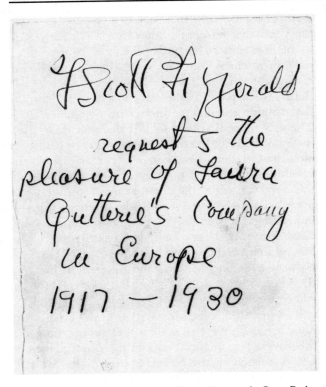

Inscription to Laura Guthrie, whom Fitzgerald met at the Grove Park Inn, Asheville, North Carolina, in 1936. The "1930" ending is problematic as most time cues indicate that the story comes to an end in 1929. Twice in the preliminary notes Fitzgerald stipulates 1929 as the year the Divers' marriage ends (Bruccoli Collection of Fitzgerald, Thomas Cooper Library, University of South Carolina).

Notes

1. Bruccoli, "Inscribed TITN," *Fitzgerald Newsletter* (Washington, D.C.: NCR Microcard Editions, 1969), 202. See also *F. Scott Fitzgerald: Inscriptions* (Columbia, S.C., 1988), Item 27.
2. *Tender Is the Night,* "With the Author's Final Revisions," ed. Malcolm Cowley (New York: Scribners, 1951), p. 355.
3. p. 352.

Chronology

The *Tender Is the Night* readings cited in this chronology are from the emended text.

April 1889 Birth of Richard Diver.

Mid-1896 Birth of Baby Warren. At Christmas 1925 she is "almost thirty" (*Tender,* 226.5).

Mid-1900 Birth of Nicole Warren. In June 1929 she is described as "a woman of twenty-nine" (*Tender,* 376.7, 14, 20).

July 1907 Birth of Rosemary Hoyt. In July 1925 she celebrates her birthday with the Divers and the Norths: "yesterday was my birthday—I was eighteen" (*Tender,* 81.1–2).

Fall 1907 Diver enters Yale; he is about eighteen and one-half years old.

Spring 1911 Diver graduates from Yale.

Fall 1911 Diver enters Johns Hopkins School of Medicine.

1914 "Nicole's mother died when she was fourteen" (see "Explanatory Notes," 167.7).

1914–15 Diver attends Oxford University: "he was an Oxford Rhodes Scholar from Connecticut in 1914."

1915–16 Diver completes medical school: "He returned home for a final year at Johns Hopkins, and took his degree."

1916–early 1917 Diver is in Vienna where he writes pamphlets and studies at the university: "In 1916 he managed to get to Vienna" (*Tender,* 152.14); "At the beginning of 1917 . . ." (*Tender,* 152.32–154.25).

Early 1917 Following incestuous episode, Nicole Warren shows signs of mental illness: "'About eight months ago, or maybe it was six months ago or maybe ten'" (*Tender,* 167.26–27). She is not yet seventeen years old.

Spring 1917 Diver goes to Zurich where he studies at the university: "In the spring of 1917, when Doctor Richard Diver first arrived in Zurich, he was twenty-seven" (see "Explanatory Notes," 151.2).

Late 1917 "About a year and a half before" (*Tender,* 166.1) Diver's second visit to the clinic in April 1919, Devereux Warren brings Nicole to Dr. Dohmler's clinic in Zurich; she is "a girl of seventeen."

1918 Diver receives post-MD degree from the University of Zurich and is commissioned in the American army: "After he took his degree, he received his orders to join a neurological unit forming in Bar-sur-Aube" (*Tender,* 154.30–32).

1918 At Dohmler's clinic Diver meets Nicole Warren for the first time: "'I only saw her one time. . . . It was the first time I put on my uniform'" (*Tender*, 158.1–4).

Spring 1919 Diver is discharged from the army: "He returned to Zurich in the spring of 1919 discharged" (*Tender*, 155.3).

April 1919 Diver sees Nicole for the second time at Dohmler's clinic: "It was a damp April day" (*Tender*, 156.1).

May 1919 Dick lunches with Nicole in a Zurich restaurant: "It was May when he next found her" (*Tender*, 181.1).

June 1919 "The first week of summer found Dick reestablished in Zurich" (*Tender*, 181.24–25).

July 1919 Diver bicycles from Zurich to Montreux: "'By August, if not in July?'"; he encounters Nicole on the Glion funicular (*Tender*, 195.22–23).

July 1919 Diver escorts Nicole back to the clinic and commits himself to her care: "he knew her problem was one they had together for good now" (*Tender*, 206.31–32).

September 1919 The marriage is agreed upon and may take place the same month: "In Zurich in September Doctor Diver had tea with Baby Warren" (*Tender*, 207.1–2).

Fall 1919 Marriage and honeymoon: "How do you do, lawyer. We're going to Como tomorrow for a week and then back to Zurich" (*Tender*, 208.24–25).

1920 Birth of Lanier: "–I'm afraid of falling, I'm so heavy and clumsy–" (*Tender*, 209.14).

1920–21 After birth of Lanier, Nicole has relapse: ". . . We travelled a lot that year" (*Tender*, 210.24); "But I was gone again by that time. . . . That was why he took me travelling" (*Tender*, 210.32–211.1).

1922 Following the birth of Topsy in 1922, Nicole has a more serious relapse: "after my second child, my little girl, Topsy, was born everything got dark again" (*Tender*, 211.1–3).

1923 Rosemary Hoyt is hired by a film producer "when she blossomed out at sixteen" (*Tender*, 52.7–8).

Fall 1924 Rosemary attends the Yale prom with Collis Clay: "the boy who had taken her to the Yale prom last fall" (*Tender*, 88.4–5).

Jan.–June 1925 Rosemary contracts pneumonia and convalesces while traveling in Europe with her mother: "'–we landed in Sicily in March. . . . I got pneumonia making a picture last January'?" (*Tender*, 21.22–24).

June 1925 Rosemary arrives on the Riviera beach where she first meets the Divers: "one June morning in 1925" (*Tender*, 4.8–9); "very fashionable for June."

July 1925 Rosemary celebrates her eighteenth birthday in Paris. Diver is thirty-six: "Eighteen might look at thirty-six through a rising mist of adolescence."

August 1925 Diver tries to resume work after his return from Paris to the Riviera: "Doctor Richard Diver and Mrs. Elsie Speers sat in the Café des Allées in August" (*Tender*, 213.1–2).

August 1925 The Divers have been married almost six years; Dick tries unsuccessfully to conceal from Nicole his growing sense of estrangement: "this pretense became more arduous in this effortless immobility, in which he was inevitably subject to microscopic examination" (*Tender*, 223.18–20).

Dec. 1925 Franz Gregorovious joins Diver in Gstaad with proposal for partnership in a psychiatric clinic: "they went to the Swiss Alps for the Christmas holidays" (*Tender*, 224.6–7).

Summer 1927 Allowing time for the Divers' move from the Riviera to the clinic on the Zugersee after Christmas 1925, summer 1927 is the earliest possible date for Nicole's relapse at the Ageri Fair: "Even this past year and a half on the Zugersee" (*Tender*, 236.18); "For eighteen months now he had lived at the clinic" (*Tender*, 238.3); "He was thirty-eight" (*Tender*, 238.1). It has been roughly six years since Nicole's collapse and recovery following Lanier's birth: "In these six years she had several times carried him over the line with her" (*Tender*, 246.22–23). The summer dating for the Ageri fair episode is further supported by the open car ("they all stuck out of it" [*Tender*, 245.23–24]) and the "hot afternoon" (*Tender*, 247.8).

Early 1928 "For three months she had been all right" (*Tender*, 253.11): After Nicole's recovery from her summer breakdown, Diver goes to Munich where he learns of Abe North's death.

Early 1928 "'I've wasted eight years teaching the rich the A B C's of human decency'" (*Tender*, 263.9–10): The Divers have been married about eight and one-half years when Dick, in Innsbruck, learns of his father's death.

March 1928 Returning from America after his father's burial, Diver encounters Rosemary in Rome. Spring has not yet arrived: "She plucked a twig and broke it, but she found no spring in it" (*Tender*, 276.32–33). In March 1928, Rosemary is approaching her twenty-first birthday, and Diver is just short of his thirty-ninth. The coming June will mark the third anniversary of their initial meeting on the Riviera: "He guessed that she had had lovers and had loved them during the last three years. . . . He tried to collect all that might attract her—it was less than it had been three years ago. Eighteen might look at thirty-six through a rising mist of adolescence; but twenty-one would see thirty-nine with discerning clarity." Fitzgerald stipulates that the Rome encounter between Diver and Rosemary occurs in 1928: "'living in the year nineteen twenty-eight'" (*Tender*, 276.13). Since this is the latest date provided by the novel, it provides crucial evidence for working out the time scheme after 1925.

May 1928 After Diver returns to the clinic following the Rome beating, Gregorovious loses respect for him: "Yet it was May before Franz found an opportunity to insert the first wedge" (*Tender*, 313.18–19). In May of 1928 Diver is not yet forty but has begun his fortieth year; thus, he can appropriately meditate that "life in the forties seemed capable of being observed only in segments" (*Tender*, 317.2–4). During this month Diver goes to Lausanne and encounters Devereux Warren.

May/June 1928 Following Diver's row with the Morris family, Gregorovious eases him out of the clinic partnership: "One morning a week later" (*Tender*, 326.1).

Summer 1928 The Divers travel "between German spas and French cathedral towns" (*Tender*, 331.3–4) until they can return to their home on the Riviera: "The Villa Diana had been rented again for the summer" (*Tender*, 331.2–3).

Fall? 1928 The Divers pay a truncated visit to Bozen: "Their hostess was the Contessa di Minghetti, lately Mary North" (*Tender*, 333.26–27).

February 1929 The Divers "return to the Villa Diana in February" (*Tender*, 342.6).

April 1929 Diver's altercation with the cook, as "the April sun shone pink" (*Tender*, 342.3), is immediately followed by the Golding yacht episode (*Tender*, 345.22–354.15), which reunites Nicole and Tommy Barban for the first time since June 1925, not quite "Four years" before.

June 1929 During "the first hot blast of June" (*Tender*, 359.30), Barban writes to the Divers from Nice, and Rosemary wires them (*Tender*, 360.4–6) of her impending return to the Riviera. Dick and Rosemary's behavior on the beach recalls, three times, their first beach encounter in June 1925: "four years ago." Later in June Nicole sleeps with Tommy Barban; she has just passed her twenty-ninth birthday (*Tender*, 376.7, 14, 20).

15 July 1929 Barban and Diver have their confrontation over Nicole on the day that the Tour de France arrives in Cannes.

Late July 1929 Nicole tells Baby Warren, "'Dick was a good husband to me for six years'" (*Tender*, 403.29). The marriage endured for nine years and eight months to the time of Nicole's infidelity, but she recognizes that Diver's full emotional commitment to her terminated during the summer of Rosemary's first intrusion in 1925—in the sixth year of the Divers' marriage, four years before the July 1929 conclusion of the novel.

* * *

Fredson Bowers drafted this editorial rationale when he and Matthew J. Bruccoli were working on their terminated edition of Tender Is the Night *for Cambridge University Press. It provides the case for rejecting the "Author's Final Version" as argued by the greatest textual theorist and scholarly editor of his time. The term "copy-text" identifies the text of a work that provides the basis for a critical edition.*

Choosing the Copy-Text for *Tender Is the Night*
Fredson Bowers

It seems clear, on the other hand, that on his own Fitzgerald would never have considered restructuring the novel. The flashback had been present from the earliest of the Diver versions of the story and had not been tinkered with in any of the revisory stages. But it had become something of a focus of the reviewers' reception of the novel and had been severely criticized as a serious flaw. Fitzgerald must have been stunned by the cold reception of what he considered to be his masterpiece, the result of nine years of labour. He certainly wanted it to be better received, as his letters urging friends to reread the book and not trust to the serial version indicates, as well as his abortive efforts to make some clarifying changes of other matters in the Modern Library edition. It would seem that in his overwhelming desire to have the book accepted for what he thought it was he was willing to let its critical reception—and one of the major sources of disapproval in the emphasis on the flashback—influence his own original and continued structural vision of the best way to introduce the fall of Dick Diver. In whatever posterity he may have imagined his revised marked copy (of which the structural rearrangement was only a part) might influence the book's reception for the better—if the critical disapproval of the flashback was no indication of future reaction—it would seem that he was prepared to defer if that would ensure future approval. This situation, then, is basically different from the other major structural changes in the marked copy by which two cuts were ordered. These, it is clear, were self-induced, his own literary critical instincts operating to continue a characteristic process already begun at an earlier stage in the text's transmission. On the contrary, the forces that operated on him in the matter of the flashback were external. To repeat, no evidence exists that at any point prior to the reviewers' attack had Fitzgerald ever questioned the essential flashback. When he

Fredson Bowers

wrote to Perkins in December of 1938 about a proposal to reissue three of his novels in one volume, he showed the depth of his concern by singling *Tender* for special revision: 'I am especially concerned about *Tender*,' he added, '—that book is not dead. The *depth* of its appeal exists—I meet people constantly who have the same exclusive attachment to it as others had to *Gatsby* and *Paradise,* people who identified themselves with Dick Diver. Its great fault is that the *true* beginning—the young psychiatrist in Switzerland—is tucked away in the middle of the book.' It is not unreasonable to take it that this sentence would never have been written had *Tender* been a critical success and the flashback technique accepted.

Literary history has other instances of authors being influenced by outside opinion to change their original conceptions of the presentation or content of a work. It is interesting that not one of these has gone unchallenged by posterity. Self-censorship is sometimes a prominent reason for a change in authorial expression, but closely related to this is the influence of outside opinion that has succeeded in convincing an author, however reluctantly, that if his book is to succeed to his hopes it must undergo some major alteration. An author's reliance on such outside opinion as to a book's reception instead of his own creative force that produced the version under criticism has not always been found—as remarked—to be in his ultimate best interest. Most authors are right in the end when they trust to their instincts and their original creative plan. We may take this as applying with particular weight to Fitzgerald's acceptance of what the critics believed to be a serious flaw. The depth of his acceptance of the flashback as 'a serious fault' cannot be estimated—how much he convinced himself in his desire for a reversal of the book's initial reception remains unknown. What is of textual importance to an editor is the distinction between the internal forces that generated Fitzgerald's recognition of the desirability of removing the lengthy incident of the governess at Innsbruck and the external forces that (post-creation) led him to want to ensure the future success of the novel by convincing himself that the critics' view of the flashback was correct.

In fact, it is the present editors' opinion that the critics were wrong. Fitzgerald's reason for agreement—that the true beginning was tucked away in the middle of the book—is an ambiguous one, for not every true beginning must actually come at the start of a narrative, as Greek tragedy shows us. In short, conventional chronological structure is not always the best. As exemplified in *The Last Tycoon*, in his best work Fitzgerald had a strong sense that the past is always an integral part of the present, and the present of the past. This sense is strongly pointed by the use of the flashback in *Tender*. It is of importance, of course, that its beginning in medias res on the beach and the subsequent part, with the reader led by Rosemary's dazzled reactions, produces a brilliant start that, with its accompanying mystery, draws the reader instantly into these people's affairs. But it is more important that the insight and coloration of this immensely successful opening has an important role in causing a reader to understand and to estimate at their true value the anterior events that are later to be introduced in Switzerland. In turn, these initial episodes lead to a retrospective understanding of the hinted but never explicit mysteries and nuances of the opening, so that once the flashback has concluded in Switzerland and we are brought back to the present it is

with a greater understanding, a jelling one might say, of the central situation of the book in Diver's dilemma and the failure to solve it.

One other consideration is appropriate. When a narrative has been structured in a particular way, the balance of the treatment rests on it accordingly. The account of the earlier events in Switzerland and of the ironic consequences up to the opening on the beach is written with the technique of a catching-up of the narrative. Merely to rearrange the sequence of events to a chronological order does violence to the balance of the opening and then in a sense réprise in the original book. There can be little question that if Fitzgerald had reordered the events at some stage in the composition, even so late as the book's galley proofs, the early events would have been differently narrated, since there could be no reliance on the reader's understanding of them resulting from his view of the Divers in their introduction on the Riviera. *Tender* is not so mechanically conceived and executed as to yield to post-creation restructuring in such an important matter that has dictated the treatment both of start and of middle. In the sense of 'might-have-been' we can envisage a novel that Fitzgerald himself had composed, or revised, to read in chronological order, but it would be a fundamentally different novel from what results in the Cowley edition when the middle is bodily transferred to the beginning without the necessary reworking. This is no doubt special pleading, but the concept is true. Scribners exhibited the right attitude when the firm re-issued in paperback the originally conceived (and in fact the only published) version as a substitute for Cowley's extrapolation of Fitzgerald's letter to Perkins and his note in his private copy. This is one instance where an author's own version must be respected despite his after-the-event wishes. To choose the Cowley ordering as the base-text for a critical edition would be an act of violence to the inner coherence of authorial conception and execution. The pressure that Fitzgerald felt to popularize his novel was illegitimate. His capitulation to what he conceived of as public opinion, no matter how rationalized, should not be permitted to tear apart the living fabric of the novel as he wrote it.

Later Editions and Reprints
of *Tender Is the Night*

A15.3

Second American edition

The Portable F. Scott Fitzgerald, selected by Dorothy Parker and with an introduction by John O'Hara. New York: Viking, 1945. See AA 1.

A15.4

Second English edition

TENDER | IS THE NIGHT | [tapered rule] | by | F. SCOTT FITZGERALD | THE GREY WALLS PRESS LTD. | Crown Passage, Pall Mall | London 1948.

A15.5

Third American edition

[two-page title] [script] Tender is the Night | [wavy rule] | [roman] by | F. Scott Fitzgerald | [wavy rule] | [rooster] | BANTAM BOOKS · New York

1951. #A867. Wrappers. 35¢. reprinted February and April 1951.

A15.6.a

F. SCOTT FITZGERALD | *Tender is the Night* | [four lines in italic type] | – ODE TO A NIGHTINGALE [decorations] | NEW YORK | *CHARLES SCRIBNER'S SONS* 1960. Scribner Library #SL2. Wrappers. $1.45. On copyright page: 'A-1.60 [C]'. Reprints noted: 'E-8.61 [C]'; 'H-10.63 [Col]'; 'I-9.64 [Col]'; 'L-2.67 [Col]'; 'N-5.69 [C]'; 'P-6.71 [C]'; 'R-2.72 (C)'. Latest reprint noted: '29 Y/P 30 28'.

A15.6.b

New York: Scribners, [1977]. Hudson River Editions. ISBN #0-684-15151-0. On copyright page of first print: 'I [. . .] 19 B/c 20 [. . .] 2'.

A15.7

TENDER | IS THE | NIGHT | F. SCOTT | FITZGERALD | [four lines of italic type] | *ODE TO A*

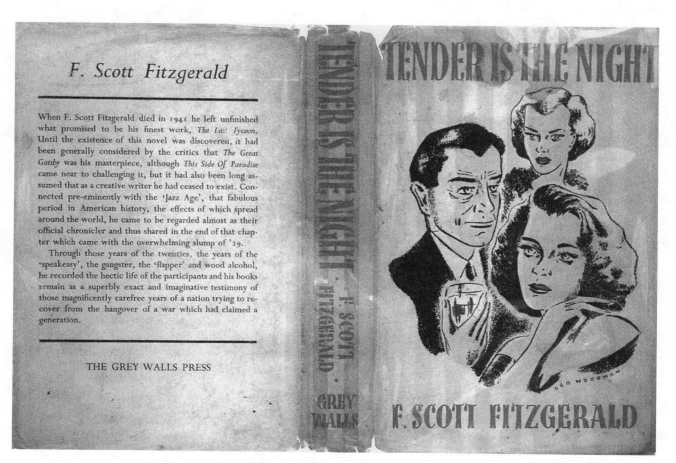

Dust jacket for the 1948 English edition of the original version (Bruccoli Collection of Fitzgerald, Thomas Cooper Library, University of South Carolina)

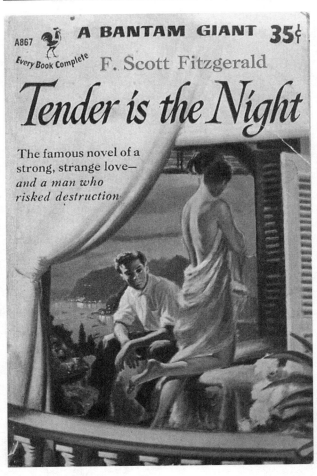 

Covers for the 1951 and 1962 mass-market paperback editions (Bruccoli Collection of Fitzgerald, Thomas Cooper Library, University of South Carolina)

NIGHTINGALE | BANTAM BOOKS [rooster] NEW YORK
1962. #S2385/5. Wrappers. 75¢. Reprinted four times.

A15.8.a
TENDER | IS THE NIGHT | BY | F. SCOTT FITZGERALD | [four lines of italic type] | —ODE TO A NIGHTINGALE | CHARLES SCRIBNER'S SONS *New York*
1970. Part of a four-volume set (with *TSOP, GG, LT*) distributed by The Literary Guild of America and its associated book clubs. See AA 15.

A15.8.b
Garden City, N.Y.: International Collectors Library, [   ].

A15.9.a
New York: Scribners, [1982]. Scribner Classics. Wrappers (rack size). $3.95. ISBN #0-684-17817-6. Latest printing noted: '5 [. . .] 19 K/P 20 [. . .] 6'.

A15.9.b
New York: Scribners, [1985]. Scribner Classics. Wrappers (rack size). $4.95. TV tie-in edition. ISBN #0-684-18611-X. On copyright page of first printing: '1 [. . .] 19 K/P 20 [. . .] 2'.

A15.10
F. SCOTT FITZGERALD | [aqua] TENDER | [black] IS | THE | NIGHT | [aqua] WITH AN INTRODUCTION BY | [black] CHARLES SCRIBNER III | [aqua] AND ILLUSTRATIONS BY | [black] FRED MEYER | [aqua] PRINTED FOR THE MEMBERS OF | [black] THE LIMITED EDITIONS CLUB

1982. 2,000 numbered copies signed by Meyer and initialed by Scribner.

A15.11
F. SCOTT FITZGERALD | TENDER IS THE NIGHT | A ROMANCE | PENGUIN BOOKS

Cover and title page for the 1983 edition of the novel published with a Russian introduction (Bruccoli Collection of Fitzgerald, Thomas Cooper Library, University of South Carolina)

Harmondsworth, 1982. ISBN #0 14 00.56 16 5. Wrappers. £1.95. Emendations and editorial apparatus by Arnold Goldman. Reprinted 1983 (twice), 1984.

A15.12
TENDER | IS THE | NIGHT | by | Francis | Scott Fitzgerald | [circular tan illustration] | Moscow | RADUGA PUBLISHERS | 1983
With Russian introduction, explanatory notes, and bibliography.

A15.13
F. SCOTT FITZGERALD | TENDER IS THE NIGHT | A ROMANCE | [penguin] | PENGUIN BOOKS
Harmondsworth, 1985. Wrappers. £3.95. ISBN #0-14-008273-5. TV tie-in edition. Edited by Arnold Goldman.

A15.13a
F. SCOTT FITZGERALD | TENDER IS THE NIGHT | A ROMANCE | [star] | Introduction by Dennis Potter | Lithographs by Glynn Boyd Harte |

[star] | [4 lines of italic type] | ODE TO A NIGHTINGALE | LONDON | FOLIO SOCIETY | 1987

A15.14.
F. Scott Fitzgerald | TENDER IS THE NIGHT | A ROMANCE | [rule] | *Text established by* | MATTHEW J. BRUCCOLI | *University of South Carolina* | [seal] | [rule] | EVERYMAN | J. M. DENT LONDON | CHARLES E. TUTTLE | VERMONT
1996. ISBN 0 460 87791 7. UK £3.99; Canada $6.99.

EXCERPTS FROM *TITN*
Reading Writing and Rewriting, ed. W. T. Moynihan, et al. Philadelphia & New York: Lippincott, [1964], p. 180.

Fitzgerald and the Jazz Age, ed. Malcolm and Robert Cowley. New York: Scribners, [1966], pp. 36–38.

Cole, ed. Robert Kimball and Brendan Gill. New York: Chicago & San Francisco: Holt, Rinehart & Winston, [1971], p. 53.

The Novel, ed. Richard Freedman. New York: Newsweek Books, [1975], pp. 176–177.

*Cover for the emended edition published in England to mark
the one-hundredth anniversary of Fitzgerald's birth
(Bruccoli Collection of Fitzgerald, Thomas Cooper
Library, University of South Carolina)*

Critical Views, 1950s–1970s

*Sir Victor Swadon Pritchett (1900–1997) was a
respected British fiction writer and critic.*

Scott Fitzgerald
V. S. Pritchett,
New Statesman, 11 October 1958

A few lines about people seen from a bus out of
Scott Fitzgerald's short piece, *Afternoon of an Author,* a
sad non-death in the afternoon, published in *Esquire*
in 1936:

> The street narrowed as the business section began
> and there were suddenly brightly dressed girls, all
> very beautiful—he thought he had never seen such
> beautiful girls. There were men too, but they all
> looked rather silly, like himself in the mirror, and
> there were old undecorative women, and presently,
> too, there were plain and unpleasant faces among the
> girls; but in general they were lovely, dressed in real
> colours all the way from six to thirty, no plans or
> struggles in their faces, only a state of sweet suspen-
> sion, provocative and serene. He loved life terribly
> for a minute, not wanting to give it up at all.

By the Numbers: Sales of *Tender Is the Night*

F. Scott Fitzgerald inscribed a copy of *Tender Is the Night*
to Joseph Hergesheimer shortly after publication: "I would
like this favorite among my books to have another chance
in the crystal light of your taste." Although this "favorite" of
his sold 14,595 copies in three printings in 1934—a respectable figure for the time—Fitzgerald spent his last six years
concerned about what he considered its failure. The so-
called "Author's Final Version," putting the novel in chronological order, which Fitzgerald hoped might answer some
of the novel's critics, was edited by Malcolm Cowley for
Scribners in 1951 in the early stages of the Fitzgerald
revival.

Since the 1950s, *Tender Is the Night* has achieved the status that Fitzgerald hoped that it would, not in the Cowley
revision, which was out of print in America and England
by 1995, but in the 1934 version, a work of genius that is
now rightfully ranked as one of the great American novels
of the Twentieth Century. Although other criteria are more
important, and this list has its critics, the editors of the Modern Library ranked it twenty-eight in their 1998 list of the
100 best novels in English in the last 100 years.

Perhaps the most telling evidence in a study of the reputation and readership of *Tender Is the Night* is the sales statistics. Charles Scribner III and Phyllis Westberg of Harold
Ober Associates provided the following figures (rounded
off) for the United States sales of the Scribner Library quality paperback edition of *Tender Is the Night.*

1961 – 22,000	1981 – 20,000
1962 – 24,000	1982 – 20,000
1963 – 21,000	1983 – 29,000
1964 – 28,000	1984 – 27,000
1965 – 22,000	1985 – 29,000
1966 – 46,000	1986 – 21,000
1967 – 51,000	1987 – 35,000
1968 – 42,000	1988 – 45,000
1969 – 45,000	1989 – 34,000
1970 – 43,000	1990 – 31,000
1971 – 54,000	1991 – 27,000
1972 – 50,000	1992 – 20,000
1973 – 50,000	1993 – 22,000
1974 – 60,000	1994 – 15,000
1975 – 45,000	1995 – 24,000
1976 – 28,000	1996 – 17,000
1977 – 25,000	1997 – 23,000
1978 – 25,000	1998 – 26,000
1979 – 22,000	1999 – 28,000
1980 – 20,000	2000 – 28,000
	2001 – 19,000

In the past forty years, *Tender Is the Night* has sold, in this edition, 1,263,000 copies. Some thirty other editions have been
published worldwide.

–Marvin J. LaHood

V. S. Pritchett

what he (or rather his reviewers) called his 'fatal facility'. They are less facile than they look. If he had not succeeded so early and had not wished to live like a rich boy he would not have had to write them. The prose of most of the fatally facile work done by good writers for magazines in order to earn money is rarely as liquid and free from dead conjunctive phrases as Fitzgerald's is. His generation had discovered an indigenous American prose which may have tired itself out since, but which was fresh in his time. The other selection, made and introduced by Mr J. B. Priestley, contains *The Great Gatsby, The Last Tycoon,* the bitter confession called *The Crack Up,* the very clever Wells-Wodehouse fantasy *A Diamond as Big as the Ritz,* and *Crazy Sunday* which might be a try-out for his posthumous novel of the Hollywood studios. These are the best of Fitzgerald; for all its good things, *Tender is the Night* is ruined by the failure of structure. Mr Mizener speaks of its thoughtful and philosophical tone—and Fitzgerald did intend a sort of *Vanity Fair* about Paris and the Riviera—but Mr Priestley is right when he says, in a general judgment, that the weakness is

a lack of thickness, solidity, in what might be called the middle distance of his panorama of narrative. Every surface detail is right, and the depths are won-

The essence of Fitzgerald's talent is in the last sentence. It is closer to him than the usual astonishment at his dual nature, the being innocently involved and at the same time cool and observant: few writers lack that duality. Fitzgerald's novels and stories are collections of suspended minutes and the sadness of watching them melt one into the other, as if he saw us all living on the pained white face of an indefatigable little watch. Writers with that temperament probably begin to feel they are losing their youth, that time is passing through their fingers, once they get out of the pram. At fourteen Fitzgerald certainly had it; at twenty it was a settled state of mind that he would never lose.

There are two new Fitzgerald collections. One is a selection of uncollected stories and essays, *Afternoon of an Author,* made by his excellent biographer and critic, Arthur Mizener. It includes some of the early Basil Duke Lee tales about dates, girls, and lovely fast cars and rich boys in his pre-Princeton days; the harder epilogue to them, twenty years on, in the tales of Pat Hobby, the broken-down film writer; and magazine articles like *Afternoon of an Author, How to Live on $36000 a Year, News of Paris Fifteen Years Ago* and many others. They come out of

---

Incest as a Motif

In his concluding paragraph, Robert Stanton summarizes the argument of his essay "'Daddy's Girl': Symbol and Theme in 'Tender Is the Night.'"

The incest-motifs, as we have seen, help to unify the novel on several levels, as well as to show how those levels are interrelated. First, these motifs function literally as one result of Dick's relationship to Nicole; they are symptoms of his psychological disintegration. Second, they both exemplify and symbolize Dick's loss of allegiance to the moral code of his father. Finally, by including such details as *Daddy's Girl* as well as Dick's experience, they symbolize a social situation existing throughout Europe and America during the Twenties. Fitzgerald's ability to employ this sort of device shows clearly that he not only felt his experience intensely, but *understood* it as an artist, so that he could reproduce its central patterns within the forms and symbols of his work. His experience transcends the historical Fitzgerald who felt it and the historical Twenties in which it occurred, and emerges as art.

—Modern Fiction Studies, 4 (Summer 1958): 142

derfully suggested, but there is an uneasy suggestion of emptiness between them, so that when we are not captivated or moved we begin to think the story he is telling is too thin, too brittle. It is as if Fitzgerald for all his sense of time and place did not know quite enough about the world and person he is describing.

We come back to that phrase about loving life terribly for a minute. Fitzgerald's art is lyrical, instantaneous and, in a self-protective way, egoistical. It has knowledge of the infinite particles of illusion and reality that are like dust picked out in the sun. It is also romantic. He is hurt when the sun goes in and dust becomes dust. Gatsby and Stahr are heroes of the dream of fortune and power. They are the human being considered as his own fiction, as his collection of illusions. The reality that Gatsby is a bootlegger, familiar with crime, and that Stahr is a tycoon drugging the public, is barely conveyed. Their significance in the society they have risen from is ignored.

The detail is everything in Fitzgerald's work and it is set down by a dedicated artist. There is the well-known scene in *The Last Tycoon,* where Stahr gives a recalcitrant highbrow writer a talk on the writing of stories for the films. Stahr is describing a stenographer coming into an office. She takes off her gloves, opens her purse and empties it out on a table:

'She has two dimes and a nickel—and a cardboard matchbox. She leaves the nickel on the desk, puts the two dimes back into her purse and takes her black gloves to the stove, opens it and puts them inside. There is one match in the match-box and she starts to light it kneeling by the stove. You notice that there's a stiff wind blowing in the window—but just then the telephone rings. The girl picks it up, says hello—listens—and says deliberately into the phone, "I've never owned a pair of black gloves in my life". She hangs up, kneels by the stove again, and just as she lights the match, you glance around very suddenly and see that there's another man in the office, watching every move the girl makes—.'

Stahr paused. He picked up his keys and put them into his pocket.

'Go on,' said Boxley, smiling. 'What happens?'

'I don't know,' said Stahr. 'I was just making pictures.'

Boxley felt he was being put in the wrong.

'It's just melodrama,' he said.

'Not necessarily,' said Stahr, 'in any case, nobody has moved violently or talked cheap dialogue or had any facial expression at all. There was only one bad line, and a writer like you could improve it. But you were interested.'

'What was the nickel for?' asked Boxley evasively.

In his review of the revised version of Tender Is the Night *in the 15 November 1951 issue of* The New York Times, *Charles Poore wrote that the "quality of splendor, sometimes strained, always somehow thinly golden, runs through all his books—particularly 'Tender Is the Night.'"*

John O'Hara to Charles Poore, 23 October 1958

Poor Scott was, I sometimes believed, suspicious of me when I told him how good TENDER IS THE NIGHT was. As you know, I read proof for him when he could no longer look at the words and lines and pages. I believe he died without ever knowing how good it was. The atmosphere was hostile when that book was published. It was the time for Odets and Steinbeck and, to some extent, me, although I came in for some of the same kind of hostility toward the kind of people Scott and Phil Barry were writing about. The Theatre Guild became the Group Theater, and I declare Ina Claire became almost a public enemy. The people who bought books and went to plays, and who wrote about the books and plays, developed a mass bad conscience that was a miniature social revolution but like many revolutions, came from unworthy origins for unpraiseworthy reasons. The handy victims were Vanity Fair, the Pierce-Arrow, the Hangar Club, and F. Scott Fitzgerald. Scott should have been killed in a Bugatti in the south of France, and not to have died of neglect in Hollywood, a prematurely old little man haunting bookstores unrecognized (as he was the last-but-one time I saw him). I am immodest enough to believe those who have told me that my preface to the Viking Portable Fitzgerald started the revival that would have started anyway, later or much later. I therefore feel involved in the revival as I always felt involved with the living man, even before I ever laid eyes on him.

—Selected Letters of John O'Hara, pp. 278–279

'I don't know,' said Stahr. Suddenly he laughed. 'Oh yes—the nickel was there for the movies.'

The two invisible attendants seemed to release Boxley. He relaxed, leaned back in his chair and laughed.

'What in hell do you pay me for?' he demanded. 'I don't understand the damn stuff.'

'You will,' said Stahr grinning, 'or you wouldn't have asked about the nickel'.

Fitzgerald always asks about the nickel. His eye never misses the important fact on that level or any other. It may be a judgment of character:

She was variously described as a nymphomaniac, a virgin, a pushover, a Lesbian and a faithful wife.

Without being an old maid, she was like most self-made women, rather old maidish.

Or notes on motor cars:

The big limousine seemed heavy with remembered conferences and exhausted sleep–

and:

Leaving the studio, he was still tense, but the open car pulled the summer evening up close, and he looked at it.

Or:

They were northwest of Sunset, climbing one of the canyons through the hills. Lighted bungalows rose along the winding road, and the electric current that animated them sweated into the evening air as radio sound.

Or a night scene at the studios:

Under the moon the back lot was thirty acres of fairyland–not because the locations really looked like African jungles and French chateaux and schooners at anchor and Broadway at night, but because they looked like the torn picture-books of childhood, like fragments of stories dancing in open fire.

The word 'torn' in that paragraph is wonderful.

Yet Fitzgerald's prose is not diamond-stuffed with *mots justes*. He has an eye living easily in the present. It swivels from point to point in his story-telling, unstiffened by literary memories in its naturalness of movement. His account of one of Stahr's story conferences in *The Last Tycoon* is one of a score of easy seizures of reality; there is no farce, no satire, no comment—no poker face either—and nothing flat, but an intent, buzzing along with the minute. He knows what talk to put in, what to leave out, when to move from words to gestures, when to catch the blinking of eyes, where to snap a vanity, a jealousy, an hypocrisy or a panic. To write of the surface like this is a very rare gift, commoner in American and Russian literature than our own, where we are weighed down by the judgments of our inherited culture and are very conscious of our own brains. Of course, in these two literatures, we do find the two dangers that accompany surface writing: sentimentality and a drift towards self-pity. When so much living goes into the surface, there is less to go in beneath it. We do not feel in *Tender is*

the Night that Fitzgerald has told us very much about the rich after all, except that time hangs on their hands and that they are afraid, in the long run, of any society beyond their own. True, a hundred years have passed but they have thin and apathetic lives compared with the lives of Balzac's rich. Fitzgerald was sentimental about them because he thought being rich meant being superb and being able to buy everything; he conceived wealth as a spendthrift might. The real rich put in a twenty-four-hour day hanging on to what they have got.

The notebooks for *Tender is the Night* and *The Last Tycoon* are packed with small observations (Mr Mizener has told us), for behind the ease of Fitzgerald's writing lies enormous, patient labour. (*Afternoon of an Author* is a detailed and appallingly true study of a writer's day; for any writer it is sheer misery to read it.) He also left a long summary of the complex plot which he had planned for *The Last Tycoon*. It is so complex, so ambitious that one doubts Fitzgerald's capacity to deal with it. He had understood his personal deficiencies as an architect. In addition to this, he was sensitive to the attacks made on his work by the critics of the Marxist Thirties who had abused him, with the usual stupidity, for his choice of material; and it looks as though, in planning to describe the labour troubles and the crises of management in Hollywood, he was trying to meet them. With his usual acumen, he had spotted the coming issue: the relation of the individual to the huge organisation. With self-control, health and an emotional rebirth, Fitzgerald's plan might have succeeded for, like Diver in *Tender is the Night,* he had put too much energy into trying to reclaim the irreclaimable in private life; on the other hand, the plan might have ended in one more disastrous attempt to write 'the great American novel' which has left so many abandoned epics in the dust bowl. As Mr Priestley shrewdly says in his introduction, Fitzgerald was running already into trouble with his narrator. It is natural to speculate, but we have in our hands the lyric master of the string of small scenes, and the minutes running into an hour or two. And if we are looking for a Fitzgerald who knew how the rich get their money and whom they destroy to get it, *A Diamond as Big as the Ritz* ought to satisfy us. There is such a thing as short-breath documentation, thank heavens, and Fitzgerald understood it.

* * *

Before assessing the greatness of Tender Is the Night, *Friedrich finds fault with its original structure and asserts that Fitzgerald "fell into the old trap of ascribing his own experiences to largely unrelated causes that he provided for the sake of the plot." His praise for Fitzgerald's novel derives in part from his recognition of the author's development of Anthony Patch in* The Beautiful and Damned *to Dick Diver.*

F. Scott Fitzgerald: Money, Money, Money
Otto Friedrich
American Scholar, 29 (Summer 1960): 401–402

Yet in spite of its faults, *Tender Is the Night* is unquestionably a great novel. While *The Great Gatsby* represents Fitzgerald's most perfectly expressed insight into the fraud of his own dream of success, *Tender Is the Night* combines that new insight with a new understanding of how and why the dream disintegrates. Disillusion was Fitzgerald's first and most deeply felt sense of the world, long before he had anything to be disillusioned about. But the similarities between *The Beautiful and Damned* and *Tender Is the Night* are less striking than the differences. The disasters in the early novel are melodramatic and even silly because they represent no inherent necessity but only Fitzgerald's self-titillating forebodings. He was not only terribly vulnerable to suffering, he almost courted it. Like Mark Twain and Jack London, Fitzgerald enjoyed vast talent and vast success, but felt some need to dissipate both. When Nicole Diver remarks that "so many smart men go to pieces nowadays," Diver retorts that "smart men play close to the line because they have to." Although the game was emotional, Fitzgerald usually described it in terms of money—emotional capital, emotional bankruptcy—and yet his whole relationship toward wealth had gradually changed. Anthony Patch went to pieces because he lacked wealth. Dick Diver went to pieces despite his wealth, even because of it.

In his youth, Fitzgerald had virtually equated money with success. Both meant "mobility and grace," as well as pretty girls. Fitzgerald rarely thought much about how money was made—or even

---

John O'Hara wrote to Gerald Murphy, Fitzgerald's model for Dick Diver, after a profile of the Murphys, "Living Well Is the Best Revenge," was published in the 28 July 1962 issue of The New Yorker.

John O'Hara to Gerald Murphy
30 July 1962

Dear Gerald:

I imagine you and Sara will be getting a lot of letters about the New Yorker piece—and this is one of them. As far as I'm concerned, the piece told a few things about you both that I never knew, and left out a fair number that I thought should have been in. But it was respectful, and literate, and appreciative, and needed to be written, so I give it high marks.

I am writing you because I feel the need to sound off on the subject of the *roman a clef,* which can be pretty disturbing to me. A byproduct of my sounding off may be that you and Sara will feel a little better about TENDER IS THE NIGHT, which I love. You see, I understand exactly what Scott did, although I never discussed it with him.

. . . .

Now as to Scott and the Murphys, he did what all your writing friends wanted to do, which was to write about Gerald and Sara and their life. But Scott didn't have my method to guide him, and he had only the superficials to work with, with the result that Dick and Nicole were never you or Sara. Hoytie?—well. And some of the minor characters, yes. But you two, no. Scott wrote the life, but not the lives. And that is true partly because Scott was always writing about the life. Sooner or later his characters always came back to being Fitzgerald characters in a Fitzgerald world. He was really quite shocked by BUTTERFIELD 8, because no matter what his own conduct was, it did not seem to belong in the Fitzgerald world. He was our best novelist in spite of this limitation. Tarkington, with a worse case of the same limitation, without it would have been much, much better than Scott. They had a fastidiousness that in my opinion should be no part of an author's equipment, at least if it makes him cheat even a little bit. The old thing about no omelet without breaking eggs, no surgery without letting blood.

But we all have our limitations and restrictions, and the lucky ones know them, and this is no criticism of Scott, really. If I had known the Murphys and been compelled to write about them, I would have started by putting them in, say, Santa Barbara, if only to get away from the very things that Scott most wanted to write about. The life, the way of life. And of course as he moved along, he got farther away from any resemblance to the real Murphys. Dick Diver ended up as a tall Fitzgerald, and you could almost see that coming a third of the way through the novel. And the sadness I felt, the pity for this great waste, was finally the real success of the novel, over and above my delight at the writing, the observations, the heat of the sun, the flowers, the nervous fun and the brutality. (To me, GATSBY is greasy kid stuff compared to TENDER IS THE NIGHT.) I'm sure Scott's dissatisfaction with TITN was due to his failure to present the Murphys, but he got his novel anyhow.

—Selected Letters of John O'Hara, pp. 401, 402

In his article "Sherwood Anderson—F. Scott Fitzgerald—Ernest Hemingway" for the second volume of Major Writers of America *(1962), edited by Perry Miller, critic and novelist Mark Schorer warmly praised* Tender Is the Night.

Much more complex that *The Great Gatsby,* the new novel, in spite of the tortured circumstances of its composition, is probably Fitzgerald's greatest achievement. A story of 'emotional bankruptcy', it depicts not only the dissolution of a life but of a way of life. It is a story of breakdowns. The hero, Dick Diver, an ambitious and charming young man who wants to become the best doctor in the world, marries Nicole Warren, his patient, in part to help her recover from her breakdown. The large action of the novel shows Nicole's slow recovery of health, and the discovery of an identity, at which point she abandons Dick, and, contrapuntally, his slow disenchantment, disintegration, and final loss of identity, at which point he disappears, in the literal sense of *dissipation* on which Fitzgerald had remarked: something turning into nothing. Breakdowns in the self, then, but also in marriages, in friendships, even in a way of life. It is the elegy of the 1920s, the allegory of a dream that Fitzgerald himself tried to make of reality and the dissipation of that dream. It is, quite simply, one of the most moving novels in all American fiction. And the reviews were lukewarm, obtuse, the sales trivial. It was Fitzgerald's greatest defeat.

Connolly commented on Fitzgerald's novel, number 79 on his list, for his 1965 survey The Modern Movement: One Hundred Key Books from England, France and America 1880–1950.

This novel is over-praised. Fitzgerald wrote the last part in a great hurry and some of it when drunk so that it becomes little more than an undigested diary. The beginning however is a wonderful evocation of the second phase of American expatriates ensconced in glittering villas on the Riviera in contrast to the home-spun tipplers of *The Sun Also Rises.* The break-down of a marriage in which the doctor-husband, having fulfilled his healing role, makes it inevitable that his wife should leave him, is described with flashes of genius by an expert in self-destruction, and there is a haunting account of Fitzgerald's own pet drunk, the story-teller Ring Lardner (Abe North) and of the predicament of 'grace under pressure' from too many parties and too much money.

—pp. 75–76

what money really is, society's payment for time, work and ideas, rather than God's gift to the young and beautiful—but when he did, he assumed that it came from something vaguely unpleasant, like Gatsby's shadowy bootlegging. Sordid commercial work was done as pure necessity, a subject not worth treating in literature, and Fitzgerald seems never to have understood that some men might enjoy making or selling shoes more than they might care about the money involved. But he did learn from his own career, as did Theodore Dreiser, that real success involves doing something rather than having money. If this was still uncertain in *The Great Gatsby,* the uncertainty disappeared by the time Fitzgerald wrote *Tender Is the Night.* Unlike Gatsby, Diver depends not on his money for self-respect but on his career, a career that he has sold on the installment plan. It is the final loss of that career—a loss made specific when his pedestrian Swiss colleague decides to buy out Diver's share in their clinic—that heralds Diver's complete disintegration in the last section. In fact, it is the cause of that disintegration.

The real greatness of *Tender Is the Night* depends on two things that go beyond all analysis. The first is mood, an evocation of time and scene, the Riviera, the late twenties and a society in search of excite-

ment. But it is more. One need never have known Paris or the twenties to feel the sense of the physical goodness of life, and the sense of nostalgia at a man's loss of that life. The other intangible is the character of Dick Diver. Fitzgerald committed so much passion to his creation that he achieved a kind of magnetic effect on the reader's emotions. The final shock, the realization that Diver's ruin is really happening and cannot be stopped, achieves its overwhelming force not by exact detail but by the very vagueness with which Fitzgerald ends. "His latest note was post-marked from Hornell, New York, which is . . . a very small town; in any case he is almost certainly in that section of the country, in one town or another."

This novel is a vision in art of an era in American history, of the failure of a society and of an individual who embodied its graces and its weaknesses. In *Tender is the Night* Fitzgerald created a work of fiction rare in American literature, a novel uniting romantic beauty and also historical and social depth; and he proved by his creation that his art, and his identity as an artist, could survive the death of the society which had nurtured him.

—Robert Sklar, *F. Scott Fitzgerald: The Last Loacoön,* p. 292

By the Numbers:
Critical Studies of *Tender Is the Night*

The first critical book devoted to *Tender Is the Night* was Matthew J. Bruccoli's 1963 *The Composition of Tender Is the Night* (University of Pittsburgh Press). The second appeared in 1969–*Tender Is the Night: Essays in Criticism,* edited by Marvin J. LaHood (Indiana University Press). Other books devoted entirely to *Tender Is the Night* include *Critical Essays on F. Scott Fitzgerald's Tender Is the Night,* edited by Milton Stern and published in 1986 (Hall); the 1996 *Reader's Companion to F. Scott Fitzgerald's Tender Is the Night* by Bruccoli with Judith S. Baughman (University of South Carolina Press); and Stern's 1994 *Tender Is the Night: The Broken Universe* (Twayne).

Eight doctoral dissertations on *Tender Is the Night* have appeared, the first in 1961, two in the Seventies, and five in the Nineties. From 1940 to 2002, of the 122 master's theses on Fitzgerald, thirty-six have treated *Tender Is the Night*–seven were written between 1949 and 1969, twelve in the Seventies, six in the Eighties, eight in the Nineties, and one in 2002.

In the Thirties seventy periodical articles on *Tender Is the Night* were written, sixty-seven in 1934 and all essentially reviews, and three in 1935, 1936, and 1937. Only one article on the novel was written in the Forties; during the Fifties, eight such articles appeared. Since 1960 sixty-three articles on *Tender* have been published in journals, including twenty-eight since 1990, and another forty-seven in the following six collections:

Tender Is the Night: Essays in Criticism, ed., Marvin J. LaHood, Indiana University Press, 1969;

Fitzgerald/Hemingway Annual, ed., M. J. Bruccoli, Microcard Editions, 1969–1979;

Critical Essays on F. Scott Fitzgerald's Tender Is the Night, ed., M. R. Stern, Hall, 1986;

New Essays on F. Scott Fitzgerald's Neglected Stories, ed., J. R. Bryer, University of Missouri Press, 1996;

Readings on F. Scott Fitzgerald, ed., K. deKoster, Greenhaven, 1998;

French Connections: Hemingway and Fitzgerald Abroad, C. J. Kennedy and J. R. Bryer, eds., St. Martin's Press, 1999.

There were also eleven articles published separately in eleven collections in which each is the only essay on *Tender Is the Night.*

–Marvin J. LaHood

Translations of *Tender Is the Night*

As Linda C. Stanley notes in the introduction to The Foreign Critical Reputation of F. Scott Fitzgerald: An Analysis and Bibliography *(1980), "Fitzgerald has never been as highly regarded in Europe as in America, either in the 1920s when, for the only period during his lifetime, he enjoyed great popular and critical success, or during the 1950s and 1960s when his American reputation was again steadily advancing." Fitzgerald's foreign reputation has risen since the late 1960s, however.*

Bibliographic information on translations from twenty-one countries is presented in this section.

Bulgarian
Nežna e noštta, trans. Dimitri Ivanov. Sofija, Bulgaria: Nar. kultura, 1967.

German
Zärtlich ist die nacht, trans. Grete Rambach. Berlin: Blanvalet, 1952, 1968.

Greek
Trypheri einai e nykta, trans. Mina Zographou. Athens: Galaxias, 1961.

Japanese
Yoru wa yasashi, trans. Rikuo Taniguchi. Tokyo: Kadokawa shoten, 1960.

Polish
Czuta jest noc, trans. Maria Skroczynska and Zofia Zinserling. Warsaw: Czytelnik, 1967.

Portuguese
Suave é a noite, trans. Lígia Junqueira. Rio de Janeiro: Civilização Brasileira, 1964. (Original version).

Serbo-Croatian
Blaga je nóc, trans. Bora Glišić. Subotica, Yugoslavia: Minerva, 1956, 1958. (Revised version).

Turkish
Geceler güzeldir, trans. Azize Erten Bergin. Istanbul: Tifdruk Matbaacilik Sanayii A. Ş. Marbaasi, 1962.

Yabanciya gönül verme, trans. Semih Yazicioğlu. Istanbul: Çelikcilt Matbaasi, 1962.

Afrikaans edition, translated by Jan Vorster. Johannesburg: Boek Mosaiek, 1968. "Author's Final Version" (Bruccoli Collection of Fitzgerald, Thomas Cooper Library, University of South Carolina).

Catalan edition, published in 1987, translated by Ramon Terenci Moix. Originally published, Barcelona: Edicions 62, 1968. "Author's Final Version" (Bruccoli Collection of Fitzgerald, Thomas Cooper Library, University of South Carolina).

Czech edition, translated by Lubomír Dorůzka. Praha: Odeon, 1968. "Author's Final Version" (Bruccoli Collection of Fitzgerald, Thomas Cooper Library, University of South Carolina).

Danish edition, translated by Helga Vang Lauridsen and Elsa Gress. Kopenhagen: Wangel, 1954; Skrifola, 1961 (Bruccoli Collection of Fitzgerald, Thomas Cooper Library, University of South Carolina).

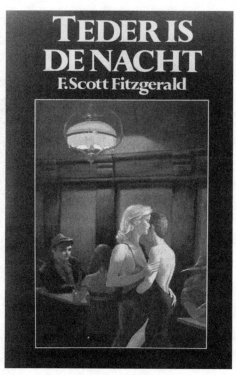

Dutch edition, published in 1982, translated by H. W. J. Schaap. Originally published, Amsterdam: Contact, 1969. "Author's Final Version" (Bruccoli Collection of Fitzgerald, Thomas Cooper Library, University of South Carolina).

French edition, translated by Marguerite Chevalley. Paris: Stock, 1951; reprinted, Paris: Delamain et Boutelleau, 1951; Brussels: Les Éditions Biblis, 1953; Lausanne: Ed. Rencontre, 1965; Paris: Stock, 1967; Paris: le Livre de poche, 1969 (Bruccoli Collection of Fitzgerald, Thomas Cooper Library, University of South Carolina).

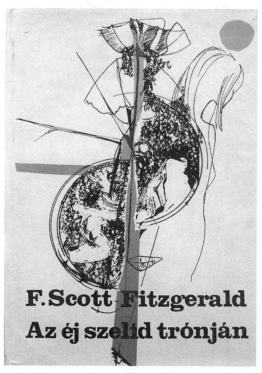

French edition, published in 1985, translated by Jacques Tournier. Paris: Belfond, 1985 (Bruccoli Collection of Fitzgerald, Thomas Cooper Library, University of South Carolina).

Hungarian edition, published in 1972. Budapest: Europa Kvonyvkiado, 1972. "Author's Final Version" (Bruccoli Collection of Fitzgerald, Thomas Cooper Library, University of South Carolina).

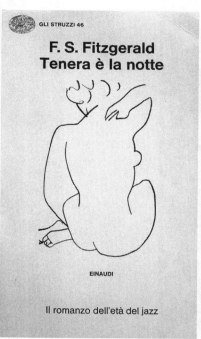

Italian edition, translated by Fernanda Pivano. These covers are from 1958, 1973, and 1978. Torino, Italy: Einaudi, 1949;
reprinted, 1957. Milano-Verona: Mondadori, 1958; Milano: Mondadori, 1967 (Bruccoli Collection of Fitzgerald,
Thomas Cooper Library, University of South Carolina).

Portuguese edition, translated by Cabral do Nascimento. These covers are from 1962, and 1987. Lisbon: Portugália
Editôra, 1962 (Bruccoli Collection of Fitzgerald, Thomas Cooper Library, University of South Carolina).

*Slovak edition, translated by Tatjana Ruppeldtová. Bratislava,
Czechoslovakia: SVKL, 1965. "Author's Final Version"
(Bruccoli Collection of Fitzgerald, Thomas Cooper
Library, University of South Carolina).*

*Dust jacket of the Spanish edition, published in 1972, translated by
Marcelo Cervelló. Originally published, Barcelona: Plaza & Janés,
1963. "Author's Final Version" (Bruccoli Collection of Fitzgerald,
Thomas Cooper Library, University of South Carolina).*

*Dust jacket and cover for Spanish movie tie-in editions, published in 1963 and 1978. "Author's Final Version"
(Bruccoli Collection of Fitzgerald, Thomas Cooper Library, University of South Carolina).*

Swedish edition, translated by Arne Hägglund. Stockholm:
Wahlström & Widstrand, 1952 (Bruccoli Collection of
Fitzgerald, Thomas Cooper Library,
University of South Carolina).

Dust jacket for the Swiss edition, published in 1982, translated by
Walter E. Richartz and Hanna Neves, Zurich: Diogenes, 1982.
"Author's Final Version" (Bruccoli Collection of Fitzgerald,
Thomas Cooper Library, University of South Carolina).

The 1962 Movie

David O. Selznick, who had fired Fitzgerald as a screen-writer for Gone With the Wind *in 1939, owned—but did not produce—*Tender Is the Night. *The movie rights were sold by the Fitzgerald Estate to Vanguard Films in 1946; Vanguard assigned rights to Loew's, Inc. in 1948; Loew's assigned the rights to Selznick in 1953. He wanted to make the movie with his wife, Jennifer Jones; but a British theatre boycott of Selznick's production was threatened because he had sold his backlist to British television. Selznick assigned the* Tender *movie rights to 20th Century-Fox in 1956; Fox reassigned the rights to Selznick in 1960; and he reassigned them to Fox in 1962, retaining certain rights of approval and consultation. The movie was produced by Henry Weinstein, who had never produced a movie. The extensive correspondence among Selznick and the people involved in making the movie is in the Bruccoli Collection of Fitzgerald, Thomas Cooper Library, University of South Carolina.*

In the following 7 August 1956 letter to Robert Chapman and Sidney Carroll, producer Selznick discusses the difficulties of making a movie from Fitzgerald's novel.

I hope that by this time one or the other or prefer-ably both of you have read the original Fitzgerald manuscript, because I continue to feel that the story that Fitzgerald was trying to tell did not appear within book covers, and to hope that what we are looking for and what we must have was written by Fitzgerald. I say this because I feel that the outline still gives no promise of telling the story effectively. We have the results of what went on, but not the cause. We see that Nicole is better and finally well, but we don't know why. We see that Dick is sliding downhill, to his ultimate destruc-tion, but we don't know sufficiently why. I make this distinction between Nicole and Dick because at least we have the superficial aspects of Dick's destruction in the company they were keeping and the life they are lead-ing, and in the destructive results of excessive wealth that is put to no proper use; and in Dick's case we at least have the agonies and the results of Nicole's jealou-sies and of Dick's infatuation with the empty-headed film star. But even in Dick's case we don't know or see the very essence of the story—which is the equivalent of his life for Nicole, despite all the proper and sadly accu-rate warnings of his fellow psychiatrists.

If TENDER IS THE NIGHT is to be any-thing, as a film, and is to be more successful as a film than it was as a book, it must be a smart-set story of human bondage.

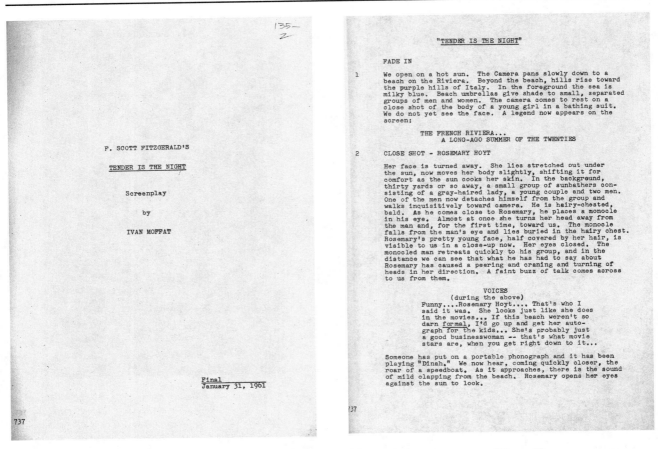

135—
2

F. SCOTT FITZGERALD'S

TENDER IS THE NIGHT

Screenplay

by

IVAN MOFFAT

Final
January 31, 1961

737

"TENDER IS THE NIGHT"

FADE IN

1   We open on a hot sun. The Camera pans slowly down to a
    beach on the Riviera. Beyond the beach, hills rise toward
    the purple hills of Italy. In the foreground the sea is
    milky blue. Beach umbrellas give shade to small, separated
    groups of men and women. The camera comes to rest on a
    close shot of the body of a young girl in a bathing suit.
    We do not yet see the face. A legend now appears on the
    screen:

            THE FRENCH RIVIERA...
            A LONG-AGO SUMMER OF THE TWENTIES

2   CLOSE SHOT - ROSEMARY HOYT

    Her face is turned away. She lies stretched out under
    the sun, now moves her body slightly, shifting it for
    comfort as the sun cooks her skin. In the background,
    thirty yards or so away, a small group of sunbathers con-
    sisting of a gray-haired lady, a young couple and two men.
    One of the men now detaches himself from the group and
    walks inquisitively toward camera. He is hairy-chested,
    bald. As he comes close to Rosemary, he places a monocle
    in his eye. Almost at once she turns her head away from
    the man and, for the first time, toward us. The monocle
    falls from the man's eye and lies buried in the hairy chest.
    Rosemary's pretty young face, half covered by her hair, is
    visible to us in a close-up now. Her eyes closed. The
    monocled man retreats quickly to his group, and in the
    distance we can see that what he has had to say about
    Rosemary has caused a peering and craning and turning of
    heads in her direction. A faint buzz of talk comes across
    to us from them.

            VOICES
            (during the above)
        Funny....Rosemary Hoyt.... That's who I
        said it was. She looks just like she does
        in the movies... If this beach weren't so
        darn formal, I'd go up and get her auto-
        graph for the kids... She's probably just
        a good businesswoman -- that's what movie
        stars are, when you get right down to it...

    Someone has put on a portable phonograph and it has been
    playing "Dinah." We now hear, coming quickly closer, the
    roar of a speedboat. As it approaches, there is the sound
    of mild clapping from the beach. Rosemary opens her eyes
    against the sun to look.

737

*Title page and first page of the script that was produced in 1962 (Bruccoli Collection of Fitzgerald,
Thomas Cooper Library, University of South Carolina)*

TENDER IS THE NIGHT has frustrated the attempts at adaptation of some very able men. It has attracted great film makers like Willy Wyler and Fred Zinnemann, but each of them has recognized the enormous problems of getting it into screenplay form, precisely as I do. I mention this now to keep you from being discouraged: it's not going to be licked easily; and before we lick it, we are going to have to realize more throughly just where the problems lie. Certainly it is somewhat easier (although that is small comfort) to adapt it for screen purposes than for the stage because it is more narrative than dramatic in form and because it does not break easily into the pattern of conventional and traditional dramatic construction. While this may seem inapropos, I make the point only because I think we must all recognize that the basic rules of dramatic construction are not all going to apply in this case. This is not a story of a few dramatic climaxes; rather it is, like Maugham's OF HUMAN BONDAGE, a story of intimate and subtle human relationships, and of the processes by which people become enslaved to each other. Discerning critics and a limited audience read

into this book, perhaps Fitzgerald's masterpiece because he felt it more keenly than anything else he ever wrote, what he did not put on paper—and perhaps even partially because they, this limited group, read into it what they knew of the relationship between Fitzgerald and Zelda. We too are among this small company that read into it what we know of this relationship. But 99% and more of the reading public did not "get" it, and the book failed—and I think it would be self-deceptive to argue that it failed solely because readers of that period looked down their noses at stories about the idle rich. Just so, 99% and more of our picture audience will not "get" it unless they see and hear what Fitzgerald knew and lived through, in this kind of enslavement, instead of seeing only the results, and only hints at the full revelation of the truth.

I suppose I was the first producer to insist upon faithfulness to great and successful works of fiction. I think I learned out to give the illusion, to readers of a great book, that they had seen all of the book, picturized, although of course they saw only a fraction of it, for to photograph a book like DAVID COPPER-

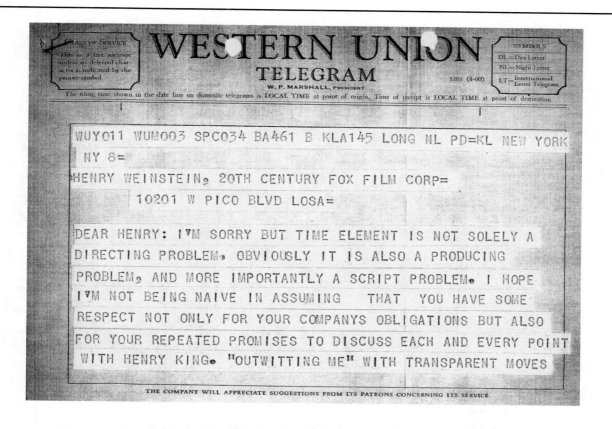

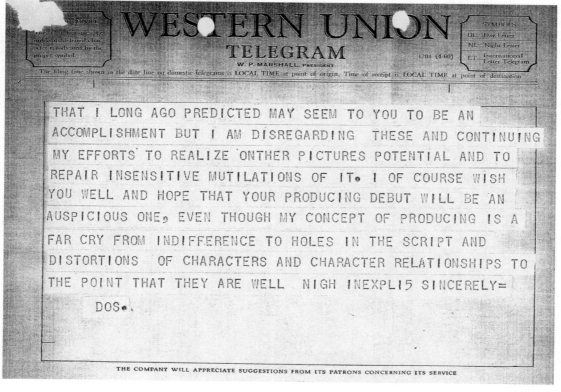

A 1961 cable from David O. Selznick to Henry Weinstein, who produced Tender Is the Night *for 20th Century-Fox (Bruccoli Collection of Fitzgerald, Thomas Cooper Library, University of South Carolina)*

CAST

Nicole Diver	Jennifer Jones
Dick Diver	Jason Robards, Jnr.
Baby Warren	Joan Fontaine
Abe North	Tom Ewell
Tommy Barban	Cesare Danova
Rosemary Hoyt	Jill St. John
Dr. Dohmler	Paul Lukas
Mrs. McKisco	Bea Benaderet
Mr. McKisco	Charles Fredericks
Dr. Gregorovious	Sanford Meisner
Colis Clay	Mac McWhorter
Louis	Albert Carrier
Francisco	Richard de Combray
Mrs. Hoyt	Carole Mathews
Pardo	Alan Napier
Topsy Diver	Leslie Farrell
Lanier Diver	Michael Crisalli
Piano Player	Earl Grant
Sir Charles Golding	Maurice Dallimore
Mrs. Dunphrey	Carol Veazie
Governess	Arlette Clark

CREDITS

Produced by	Henry T. Weinstein
Directed by	Henry King
Screenplay by	Ivan Moffat
Based on the novel by	F. Scott Fitzgerald
Music by	Bernard Herrmann
Song—"Tender Is The Night" by	Sammy Fain and Paul Francis Webster
Jennifer Jones, Joan Fontaine, and Jill St. John Dressed by	Pierre Balmain
Director of Photography	Leon Shamroy, A.S.C.
Art Direction	Jack Martin Smith and Malcolm Brown
Set Decorations	Walter M. Scott and Paul S. Fox
Costumes Designed by	Marjorie Best
Film Editor	William Reynolds, A.C.E.
Assistant Director	Eli Dunn
Make-up by	Ben Nye
Hair Styles supervised by	Helen Turpin, C.H.S.
Miss Jones' Hair Styles created by	George Masters
Special Photographic effects by	L. B. Abbott, A.S.C. and Emil Kosa, Jnr.
Sound	Bernard Freericks and Warren B. Delaplain
Main Title by	Pacific Title

Colour by De Luxe

A 20th CENTURY-FOX

CinemaScope PICTURE

JENNIFER JONES · JASON ROBARDS JR.

JOAN FONTAINE · TOM EWELL

IN

F. SCOTT FITZGERALD'S

TENDER IS THE NIGHT

Colour by De Luxe

Co-Starring CESARE DANOVA · JILL ST. JOHN · PAUL LUKAS

Produced by HENRY WEINSTEIN   Directed by HENRY KING

A 20th CENTURY-FOX **CinemaScope** PICTURE

STORY

On an exclusive beach on the French Riviera, Dick Diver (Jason Robards, Jr.) and his wife, Nicole (Jennifer Jones) are an attractive couple, rich, apparently happy and very much in love. With them are their house guests, Abe North (Tom Ewell), a composer who has pretty well drowned his talent in whiskey, Tommy Barban (Cesare Danova), a handsome soldier of fortune who makes no secret of his affection for Nicole, and the Divers' two small children.

Realising it is Independence Day, Dick impulsively decides to give a party for the Americans on the beach, among whom is the beautiful young film star, Rosemary Hoyt (Jill St. John). The party at the Divers' luxurious Villa Diana proceeds charmingly except that Rosemary seems to be fascinated by Dick. Suddenly Nicole disappears and Dick finds her in the bathroom suffering a temporary mental derangement, the main symptom of which is hostility to Dick and suspicion of his intentions towards Rosemary.

In the early hours of the morning, having comforted Nicole, Dick wanders sleeplessly through the house. His mind flashes back a few years . . .

Dick is a promising young psychiatrist at a clinic in Zurich and Nicole is his patient. Through her sister, the rich and arrogant Baby Warren (Joan Fontaine), Dick discovers the terrible secret behind Nicole's mental trouble and able now to cure her, proceeds to do so.

In the course of the treatment, however, they fall in love and Dick's mentor, Dr. Dohmler (Paul Lukas) is forced to point out that for a psychiatrist to marry his patient is both unethical and dangerous. Dick acknowledges this and takes leave from the clinic to work on a book.

Several months later, however, fate reunites him with Nicole, now completely cured. The old fires are rekindled and they marry. Dick wants to return to his work but Nicole has never really lived and with the family money paving the way, is determined to see the world. Dick's conscience is stifled in Nicole's need of him and the fact that he is thoroughly enjoying himself . . .

Nicole's relapse convinces Dick he must resume his professional life and he returns to the clinic at Zurich. But Dr. Dohmler is dead and his successor wants Dick only for the money his wife can supply towards the clinic. Disgusted, Dick meets Nicole in Paris where they form a gay group with Rosemary, Abe North and Tommy Barban. Rosemary's passion for Dick remains unabated and unrequited while Tommy waits patiently, confident that Nicole's marriage must eventually fail.

Arriving home from an all-night party, Dick and Nicole find their daughter critically ill through having drunk from half-filled liquor glasses. Almost immediately after, they learn that Abe North, whom they have left drunk in the street, has been killed in a brawl. Dick realises they must call a halt to their futile mode of living and reluctantly accepts the bargain at the Zurich clinic.

However, Dick's impatience with certain of his wealthy, bigoted patients who, he feels are depriving the needy of his services, precipitates a violent quarrel with his associate and Dick resigns.

Sending Nicole back to the Riviera, Dick visits Baby Warren in Rome in the hope of obtaining funds to start a free clinic. Unsuccessful, he starts drinking and, meeting Rosemary unexpectedly, decides to experiment with her. His old magic is gone, however, and he masks his humiliation with insults. Thrown out, Dick provokes a fight and is knocked down at the feet of Rosemary, a scene which makes the front pages.

The disgraced Dick returns to the Riviera and Nicole. On Baby Warren's huge yacht, Dick overhears a conversation between his wife and Tommy, in which Nicole infers that she has lost all feeling for Dick except gratitude. Tommy persuades Nicole that she must leave Dick.

Refusing to discuss the question of a divorce with Tommy, Dick also turns down the offer of a cash settlement by Baby Warren. Realising now that there is nothing to save his marriage, Dick returns to his home town in America, leaving Nicole to determine which course her life shall take,

Plot synopsis and credit list from the British pressbook for the 1962 movie (Bruccoli Collection of Fitzgerald, Thomas Cooper Library, University of South Carolina)

The Movie that Might Have Been

The following 3 January 1962 letter from David O. Selznick, addressed to Spyros P. Skouras, head of 20th Century-Fox, and carbon copied to Peter Levathes, was labeled "DON'T SEND." It was written after the movie was made but before it was released.

Dear Spyros:

I hope that, like myself, you and Pete are hopeful for the best on *Tender Is the Night,* but are prepared for the worst. I have steeled myself, I have attempted to steel Jennifer, and I now would like to try to steel you against what may be an onslaught by the critics against what they may conceive to be a mutilation of their favorite author's most beloved work. . . .

I hope you will remember what the picture might have been, had I been listened to—and this regardless of whether or not it delivers satisfactorily or better. . . .

I just think of what the picture might have been had it been made the way I visualized it: Jane Fonda as Rosemary—and she was desperate to play the role, and even volunteered to make a test for it, before the moles at the studio destroyed the character of Rosemary with unauthorized script cuts (and you would have had enormously valuable options on Jane Fonda for the future). . . . Imagine Fred Astaire, or Monty Clift, or any one of the dozen other actors that I tried to sell the studio on for the role of Abe—instead of Tom Ewell. Imagine my suggestions of Peter Ustinov or Joseph Schildkraut in the role in which they cast [Sanford] Meisner . . . not that Meisner is not a good actor, but obviously he does not have the personality. And so it went through all the casting, right down to the minor roles, which destroyed utterly the party sequence—thus resulting in its having to be cut to ribbons. And most of all, I hope you remember my urgings of Richard Burton or Peter O'Toole for Dick, only to be told that Burton was "poison," and that nobody knew O'Toole; and what could have been done with the role of Tommy, with someone like my first choice, Louis Jourdan, or my final attempt, Marcello Mastroianni. . . .

Of course the script cuts made the whole difference in more ways than the casting. These cuts included all of the

showmanship with which I had loaded the picture. . . . Even promises that were made during the shooting were not kept—none of them. . . .

Even on the music, I failed. . . . The score is completely unnostalgic, and hence another great element of showmanship was thrown away. On the underscoring, further errors were made: actually some of the best scenes in the picture were infinitely better in the picture's rough cut, because they did not suffer the destructive underscoring—notably in the film's best scenes. . . .

The damage was further compounded with one of the worst and most wasteful habits of Hollywood studios—the dubbing of scenes that were perfect in their original recording. Scene after scene is about half as good as it was originally, because the Sound Department has to justify itself, and its needlessly and foolishly expensive attempts to "perfect" sound, without regard to the quality of the original performances. This is one of the various fields in which European productions are getting better and better, by comparison with Hollywood's output, because they do not have the money to squander on these alleged "improvements," which actually break the hearts of the performers and the director, and damage scenes immeasurably, even when they are good. . . .

Even the main title is a disgrace—and the danger with the critics has been aggravated by the insult of giving Fitzgerald a credit . . . equivalent to that given to the hairdressers and the makers of the main title! And the foreword which I had written, out of Fitzgerald's own language and best-known phrasing, to at least get the picture started on the right note, was also disregarded. . . .

All of this is water over the dam. It is literally true that I worked harder and longer on this film than I did on *Gone With the Wind*—the difference being that it took five times as much time and effort to have only a fraction of my ideas listened to than it did to actually do them, down to the last detail, in *Gone With the Wind,* and in all the other pictures that I have made. To me, it is heartbreaking. . . .

—Memo from David O. Selznick, pp. 466–467

FIELD or A TALE OF TWO CITIES or GONE WITH THE WIND would mean a film running hundreds of hours. But I also learned the folly of being faithful to a book that had failed, however much I might personally be in love with that book. Hence, while I insisted upon and literally enforced faithfulness to the wildness of Dickens' coincidences—and they worked in films exactly as well as they did in his great novels—and while similarly I insisted upon other allegedly bad things in great books being adhered to (and invariably successfully, for a combination that works in a successful novel also works in a successful film). I think it would be foolish of me and would deny the experience of myself and others not to be equally

insistent on trying to figure out why a book that superficially appears to be superb failed with the public. I must produce <u>successfully</u> for mass audiences, or I can't produce at all. The writer of a novel has the advantage that there is no investment but his own precious time, plus some paper and pencils. The investment of millions in a film is quite another thing. I want to try to keep everything of Fitzgerald that has made all three of us love the book; but I want to try to find what it is that has always been missing from the book. I hope that this is in the original manuscript.

* * *

*Advertisement for the first movie production of Fitzgerald's novel (Bruccoli Collection of Fitzgerald,
Thomas Cooper Library, University of South Carolina)*

Review of *Tender Is the Night*

Paul V. Beckley

New York Herald Tribune, 20 January 1962, p. 6

In "Tender Is the Night," all of the awkward-nesses of F. Scott Fitzgerald's novel and none of its graces have been assembled in a nearly two-and-a-half-hour film that rarely escapes a sort of jejune air, like children "dressing up" as adults, in which form is confused with substance.

Jason Robards Jr., plays the role of Dick Diver, Fitzgerald's romantic psychiatrist who marries a wealthy patient for the sake of love. What can one think seeing the man who was so persuasive on stage in "Long Day's Journey Into Night" shuffling about staring, and looking as though a half dozen words of dialogue were not quite clear to him? One can only conclude that he is finding it hard to make out just what kind of a man lurks under the hide of

Fitzgerald's hero, half psychiatrist, half adolescent, who seems as influenced by the Edgar Allan Poe of "Annabelle Lee" as by Freud. Jennifer Jones has it a little easier with the character of Nicole, who is meant to seem incomprehensible because psychotic, but she looks most comfortable in the last half hour when some shred of a sane dilemma confronts her.

Most of the film is given over to postures rather than to people, and a great deal has been made of the opportunity to indulge in a fashion show of gowns of the period, which in spite of an occasional touch intended to rouse a nostalgic giggle are largely modified with an eye for splendor. Technically speaking, the camera has been held almost static in most of the scenes—the actors move about but the camera rarely does. Sequences are held long after their point has been made.

After all, it isn't really possible to portray the illusions of American expatriates in Europe after World

316

Jason Robards Jr. as Dick Diver (Bruccoli Collection of Fitzgerald, Thomas Cooper Library, University of South Carolina)

War I by pretending that the illusions are reality. Whatever these people may have thought they were doing, we should be able to see what they were actually about. The shortcomings of the naive among sophisticates ought to be apparent or else the film itself must end by seeming to us as naive as its characters.

Actually, the only character who seems to give an occasional glimpse of the spirit of the time is that played by Tom Ewell, who has virtually all of the film's best lines, but he isn't intended to throw much light on the basic issues of the story. To sum it up, Robards marries Miss Jones's wealthy psychotic and in order to soothe her disturbed nature, gives up his career and self respect, finally becoming dependent on her as she started by relying on him. It might have been believable if everything had been focused on that, but with the script and camera continually running off into side issues, the basic drama evaporates into no more than mawkish pretense. Not alone will fans of Fitzgerald be irritated but those who see it without having read one Fitzgerald line are likely to find it unendurably vapid.

* * *

Lobby card (Bruccoli Collection of Fitzgerald, Thomas Cooper Library, University of South Carolina)

*Robards as Diver and Jill St. John as Rosemary (Bruccoli Collection of Fitzgerald,
Thomas Cooper Library, University of South Carolina)*

Review of *Tender Is the Night*
Brendan Gill
The New Yorker, 37 (27 January 1962): 83–84

It is only fair to mention that "Tender Is the Night" is one of my favorite novels and that my heart sank when I heard it was going to be screened. It is also only fair to mention that the picture is described as "based" on the novel, and "based" is a word that can be very loosely construed. Now I find my worst fears confirmed, and the reason, oddly, isn't that Twentieth Century-Fox took too many liberties with the text but that it took too few. The picture is flagrantly unlike the book but at nearly every moment conscientiously seeks to be accepted as its twin. Again and again, with honorable intentions, and therefore rather touchingly, it attempts a likeness and achieves parody; one hears phrases, and even whole sentences, of dialogue that one has cherished for upward of thirty years, and for the first time they ring false, they have gone stone dead. Still, how could anyone have hoped to turn the delicacy and anguish of Fitzgerald's mind into so many CinemaScope images? Far better to have salvaged only his title and to have made a picture such as the present one often threatens to become—a boffo about a drunken songwriter named Abe North who can't quite finish a certain item of popular music on which he has long been working and is killed in a brawl with a young Negro whose fault has been to sit down at a piano in a Paris night club and courteously show North how to melt his grand block. Deplorable as such a picture would have been, it would have justified the tiresomely reiterated theme song and would have left comparatively unblemished our memories of the Divers, Rosemary, Baby Warren, and the rest.

As if to make a hard task doubly sure of failure, the producer has chosen a cast that is in nearly every case ideally unsuitable. The chief objection to

Cover of the sheet music for the movie theme song, which did not become a hit (Bruccoli Collection of Fitzgerald, Thomas Cooper Library, University of South Carolina)

be made to them is that they're all too old—in the novel, Nicole is twenty-four, Dick is just past thirty, and Rosemary isn't quite eighteen, and much of the pathos of the story lies in their extreme youth. Jennifer Jones works hard at being Nicole but cannot embody her, and Jason Robards, Jr., is Dick Diver in neither age nor temperament nor appearance. As for Rosemary, whom Fitzgerald presents as so warm and full of promise, she is played by Miss Jill St. John, who looks like every Miss Rheingold that ever was and acts accordingly. Equally miscast are Tom Ewell as Abe North and Joan Fontaine as Baby Warren. Only Paul Lukas, as Dr. Dohmler, and Carole Mathews, as Rosemary's mother, seem to fit comfortably inside their roles. To conclude this

extended lament, let me utter a protest against one of the settings. In the novel, Fitzgerald describes the Divers' villa in the ancient hill village of Tarmes as "made out of a row of peasant dwellings that abutted on the cliff," and continues, "The exterior walls were untouched so that from the road far below it was indistinguishable from the violet gray mass of the town." In the movie, the villa becomes an enormous yellow *palazzo,* leaping up against the sky in the worst possible taste. Why? If one knew the answer to that, one would know a lot about why Hollywood bungles even the things that it ought to do best.

The Text of the Novel

Novelist and writing teacher George Garrett discussed his admiration for the opening of the novel at a discussion at the Fitzgerald centenary celebration held at the University of South Carolina, which was published in DLB Yearbook: 1996.

George Garrett on the Opening

George Garrett: I'm going to read two paragraphs—the first two paragraphs—of *Tender Is the Night*, which were the first two paragraphs of F. Scott Fitzgerald that I ever read. The purpose there, as he knew very well—and, thank goodness, we got away from that revised Malcolm Cowley edition, which ruined this—the purpose is to hypnotize the reader, and a whole series of things works hypnotically to do that: Some of the same things that you heard in Dick's reading about the trains in the Midwest, where a series of sensory-affective details bring this to life in a certain tone and exactness. There's one great moment in the second paragraph. Many of you have heard readings by Jim Dickey, and some of you remember how when a good line was coming up he'd warn you in advance: "It's comin'! It's comin'! Here it is! Wow, we'll be wreckage forever!" This passage has one, and I will print it out in neon when we get there, because it's just remarkable—it's that moment of genius in the middle of an otherwise spellbinding performance.

On the pleasant shore of the French Riviera, about half way between Marseilles and the Italian border, stands a large, proud, rose-colored hotel. Deferential palms cool its flushed façade, and before it stretches a short dazzling beach. Lately it has become a summer resort of notable and fashionable people; a decade ago it was almost deserted after its English clientele went North in April. Now, many bungalows cluster near it, but when this story begins only the cupolas of a dozen old villas rotted like water lilies among the massed pines between Gausse's Hôtel des Étrangers and Cannes, five miles away.

The hotel and its bright tan prayer rug of a beach were one. In the early morning the distant image of Cannes, the pink and cream of old fortifications, the purple alp that bounded Italy, were cast across the water and lay quavering in the ripples and rings sent up by sea-plants through the clear shallows. [*Here comes the moment—.*] Before eight a man came down to the beach in a blue bathrobe and with much preliminary application to his person of the chilly water, and much grunting and loud breathing, floundered a minute in the sea. When he had gone, beach and bay were quiet for an hour. Merchantmen crawled westward on the horizon; bus boys shouted in the hotel court; the dew dried upon the pines. In another hour the horns of motors began to blow down from the winding road along the low range of the Maures, which separates the littoral from true Provençal France.

I love that man coming out; I don't think anybody else would have thought of it—to suddenly humanize the scene. And then, if you were doing it in shots—which is one way he thought; he really was a very visual writer; no wonder he liked working with film—moving out to a big, panoramic view with boats in the distance. But in order to do that, he set that little man in the blue bathrobe; it's just wonderful.

Garrett also praised the opening in his collection Going to See the Elephant: Pieces of a Writing Life *(2002).*

I loved all that I read, especially *Tender Is the Night*. Even as a young man, a green kid, I could admire *Gatsby*. But I loved *Tender Is the Night*. How could I not love it, when it took me directly to the Riviera, to the "bright tan prayer rug of a beach," and in less than a page was showing me a sun-glittering and wholly glamorous world as witnessed by Rosemary "who had magic in her pink palms and her cheeks lit to a lovely flame, like the thrilling flush of children after their cold baths in the evening"? Cowley's later revised edition aside, this is the only place and the only way to begin that particular story. It is illuminated by youthful witnessing and means so much more that way. It is so much more credible and moving because of the unforgettable impact of its powerful first impressions. It was only much later that I would come to recognize and to understand the technical skill of the author and the extraordinary capacity he possessed for evoking honestly and exactly the world of youth—of adolescence. It is something not at all easy to do without stumbling or pratfalls.

* * *

In the following excerpts Stark analyzes the opening of Fitzgerald's novel. He refers to two other critics who have examined the author's style: Elizabeth Wells, "A Comparative Statistical Analysis of the Prose Styles of F. Scott Fitzgerald and Ernest Hemingway," Fitzgerald/Hemingway Annual *(1969): 47–67; and Arthur Mizener, "The Voice of Scott Fitzgerald's Prose,"* Essays and Studies Collected for the English Association, *16 (1963): 56–67.*

The Style of *Tender Is the Night*
John Stark
Fitzgerald/Hemingway Annual (1972): 89, 90–93

Fitzgerald's style has rarely been analyzed, possibly because it at first seems less interesting and distinctive than some of his contemporaries'. One analysis, and a good foundation for discussion of his style, is an article by Elizabeth Wells. She does a statistical analysis of his style and Hemingway's, showing their essential differences and making some interesting generalizations. Fitzgerald's style is quite complex and artful, worth being analyzed more often as Mrs. Wells has analyzed it. Like most novels, *Tender Is the Night,* in its first published version, begins with a meticulously composed passage, so here—the first [two] paragraphs—is a good subject for stylistic analysis.

Arthur Mizener is almost the only critic who has discussed the style of this passage. He, of course, is informative, but his comments take up less than a page in an essay about Fitzgerald's style in general. He mentions the social values inherent in this passage and points out Fitzgerald's sense of delight and spoiled delight. His comments on the shifts in time could be expanded, because he mentions only the past and the "future" that has already happened. He lists three examples of "fanciful" writing—one thesis of his essay is that Fitzgerald wrote less fancifully as his career developed and his dreams were shattered— but there seem to be other examples as well. His essay is a good first step toward understanding these paragraphs, but more steps can be taken.

In this passage Fitzgerald adroitly uses the smallest unit of style, sound. He repeats one suffix— "notable and fashionable"—and uses many alliterative phrases: "flushed facade," "ripples and rings," "beach in a blue bathrobe," "beach and bay," "bus boys," "dew dried." Five of these examples occur in the second paragraph. His description late in that paragraph of horns blowing is, because of its deep "o" sounds, onomatopoeic. These effects are important because they suggest that Fitzgerald's imagination is quite poetic; that is, he frequently orders experience by organizing the sound of words that describe it.

The most important part of Fitzgerald's diction is his use of adjectives, partly because of their frequency here, which is in contrast with their relative scarcity in some of his other work. Mrs. Wells points out that only 11% of the substantive words in the opening of "The Rich Boy" are adjectives, a smaller percentage than in the Hemingway passage she analyzes. Nearly all his nouns are modified in the opening of *Tender Is the Night,* however, many by two or three words. Thus, his style, like his themes, shows the great importance he attaches to the qualities of objects. Among his adjectives, ones describing color predominate: "rose-colored," "flushed," "pink," "tan," "cream," "purple," "blue," "ash blond," "gold." His adjectives, like his fanciful reference to "deferential palms," sometimes suggest the social

class of an object's owner. In general, Fitzgerald's diction seems a little more ornate than Mizener says it is. Some of this ornateness reflects the European setting; for example, the Italian "cupola" and the British "villa." Although his diction is poetic, this passage is not over-written, for its touch of ornateness suits the kind of society that he describes.

His images and figures of speech play a prominent role in this section. Some of his images make a moral point. For example, by claiming that the villas rot but the bungalows do not he implies that large, gaudy dwellings do not endure as long as small, unpretentious ones. Some of his figures of speech function in the same way. He personifies some objects, like the "flushed facade," and, conversely, he describes in animal terms the man in the blue bathrobe: with "much grunting and loud breathing [he] floundered a minute in the sea." This dehumanization is striking since it immediately follows a somewhat lofty description of the same man making "preliminary application to his person of the chilly water." This mixture of personification, dehumanization and loftiness gently reinforces Fitzgerald's point that his characters' values are askew, particularly in regard to the relative worth they ascribe to the human and nonhuman realms.

Perhaps the slyest aspect of this section's prose is its allusiveness. The name of the hotel, Gausse's Hôtel des Etrangers, alludes to Christian Gauss, who was a professor and later a dean at Princeton. Fitzgerald, during his college years, had been an enthusiastic disciple of Gauss and wrote to him until at least 1935. In fact, the hotel's name sounds like the socially ill-at-ease Fitzgerald's conception of Princeton when he was an undergraduate. More relevant to the novel is the allusion in "a dozen old villas rotted like water lillies," which probably derives from the last line of Shakespeare's sonnet 94: "Lilies that fester smell far worse than weeds." This line would make a fitting epigraph for *Tender Is the Night* since it states one of the novel's major themes.

Another striking figure of speech metaphorically transforms a scene into a painting, thereby logically concluding Fitzgerald's painterly interest in color: "in the early morning the distant image of Cannes, the pink and cream of old fortifications, the purple Alp that bounded Italy, were cast across the water and lay quavering in the ripples and rings sent up by sea-plants through the clear shallows." Because, as Fitzgerald states at its beginning, this brief passage describes not a scene but a scene's *image,* it is like a description of a painting. In fact, this play of light and color on a French waterscape is reminiscent of an Impressionist painting.

The next larger stylistic unit, the sentence, is not used by Fitzgerald to imply an attitude toward rationality, as it is by two of his contemporaries. Faulkner's yoking of disparate elements in long, complex sentences imitates thought. Hemingway's dependence on simple and compound sentences implies that logical relationships between ideas are irrelevant or impossible. Fitzgerald's style, however, seems neither to imitate, nor to deny the possibility of, thought but to be a product of the imagination. That is, his mind connects images or sounds rather than ideas or sentences. His sentences are neither inordinately long nor short, twenty-seven words being about the average, according to Mrs. Wells. One significant attribute of the sentences in this passage is that they are for the most part complex: Mrs. Wells has discovered that this is typical. The penultimate one in the second paragraph is notable because, atypically for *Tender,* it is logically ordered. Its clauses are linked not only by parallelism but also by a movement from the sea to the shore to the hills.

Fitzgerald's paragraphs are interesting because of the strong contrast between their beginnings and endings. One reason for this is their length, quite a bit longer in the opening of *Tender* than the average for his descriptive paragraphs found by Mrs. Wells. But also this quality conveys a meaning. His first paragraph starts like a travelogue: "on the pleasant shore of the French Riviera, about half way between Marseilles and the Italian border." But it ends with the allusions to Gauss and Shakespeare. Similarly, the second paragraph opens with the exotic reference to the "prayer rug of a beach" but closes with an almost scientifically precise geographical description. Fitzgerald does not organize these paragraphs by sweeping his eye methodically over the scene; rather, he jumps around, juxtaposing details that resonate with each other in his imagination. These qualities of paragraph construction, like many other aspects of his style, suggest that he composed imaginatively, not rationally. Specifically, he denies the reader the logical matrices of space and, as Mizener briefly points out, of time. There are three distinct times in each paragraph. In the first paragraph, the temporal settings are "a decade ago," "now," and then "when this story begins." The times in the second paragraph are closer together and not quite as confusing: an indeterminate early morning hour, another time "before eight," and then "in another hour." Spatially and temporally disoriented, the reader must respond imaginatively.

* * *

The following excerpt is adapted from a German scholar's article titled "Teaching Fitzgerald's Tender Is the Night: *The Opening and the Closing Chapters of a Great Novel."*

On the Ending
Horst Kruse
Literatur in Wissenschaft und Unterricht, 31 (1998): 251–267

The ending of the novel is—justly—famous, a true match of the novel's complex opening . . . and a true match also of the ending of *The Great Gatsby.* Fitzgerald himself repeatedly discussed it, defended its method, identified its sources, and explicitly referred to it as a "dying fall," while critics commend the "haunting understatement" of the final paragraph.[1] In a letter of 1 June 1934 to Ernest Hemingway Fitzgerald identifies three "sources" which prove helpful for an interpretation of the ending while at the same time they indicate the deliberation that went into its planning and writing. The author points out that the theory behind it derives from Joseph Conrad. In the preface to his novel *The Nigger of the Narcissus* Conrad states that, unlike in oratory or in philosophy, "the purpose of a work of fiction is to appeal to the lingering after-effects in the reader's mind," not, apparently, to provide a definite conclusion.[2] A second source is an argument that Fitzgerald and Hemingway carried on over the ending of *A Farewell to Arms.* In the first version of it that Fitzgerald saw, Hemingway had given "a sort of old-fashioned Alger book summary of the future lives of the characters" (175).[3] Fitzgerald had disapproved of it and suggested that the novel end more dramatically. But Hemingway had been "against this idea because [he] felt that the true line of a work of fiction was to take the reader up to a high emotional pitch but then let him down or ease him off" (175). Though he had given no aesthetic reason for this, Fitzgerald had been won over by his argument. A final contribution to the ending, "a third piece of burglary," as Fitzgerald calls it, was the result of his "admiration of the dying fall" in David Garnett's novel *Lady into Fox:* "I imitated it as accurately as it is humanly decent in my own ending of *Tender,* telling the reader in the last pages that, after all, this is just a casual event, and trying to let *him* come to bat for *me* rather than going out to shake his nerves . . ." (175). The ending of Garnett's 1922 novel as it actually reads can be used to assess Fitzgerald's enormous improvement of the dying fall: "For a long while his life was despaired of, but at last he rallied, and in the end he recovered his reason and lived to be a great age, for that matter he is still alive." If this is "magnificent," as Fitzgerald calls it, then what shall we call the ending of *Tender Is the Night?*

The best way to understand and to assess Fitzgerald's achievment in closing his novel is to try to identify the means that he uses to produce the lingering after-effects. An obvious answer is: through direct identification with the views, the ideals and the feelings of Dick Diver in his life and in his eventual plight. For almost all of the 406 pages of the book (going by the numbering in the first printing), the reader has been sharing the vicissitudes of his career, vicariously living his life while simultaneously being exposed to the author's subtle guidance in the evaluation of all of Diver's thoughts and deeds. But the present interpretation and its implicit suggestions for teaching the opening and the closing paragraphs of *Tender Is the Night* are based on the supposition that no reading of the novel has taken place and that no reading is necessary to recognize Fitzgerald's achievement in writing these paragraphs. It is safe to assume that, going by what little information has been given about Dick Diver and the characters in the novel, readers will still be able to experience the lingering after-effects. What is it then that helps to produces them?

The key to an answer to this question lies in the author's narrative strategy. Full appreciation of Fitzgerald's achievement in *The Great Gatsby* implies a clear recognition of the function of first-person narration and the role that Nick Carraway plays in actually telling the story of Gatsby. First-person narration as practiced in the earlier novel can be used as a foil for recognizing and appreciating the omniscient disembodied narrative voice in the introductory paragraphs of *Tender Is the Night*. What we learn about the history of Gausse's Hotel, the man in the blue bathrobe, and the arrival of Mrs. Speers and her daughter one June morning in 1925 is not presented as an eyewitness account, but as omniscient narration. When we turn to the dying fall ending of the novel, however, we readily realize that at this point the disembodied narrative voice is anything but omniscient. Nearly all the information given about Dick Diver's doings after his return to America, which are the ostensible subject of the ending, is channeled, as it were, through the perspective of his former wife Nicole, now married to Tommy Barban and still living in France. While we do not have her own syntax, but the syntax of the narrative voice ("Nicole kept in touch with Dick after her new marriage . . ."), we occasionally seem to have her words and also enough of her syntax ("Dick opened an office in Buffalo, but evidently without success." / "Perhaps . . . his career was biding its time . . .") to be able to follow her thoughts and her reactions to what she learns or gathers about her former husband. But he is far away, and there are no reliable and no objective sources; we do not even learn what sources, other than his own missives, there are ("she heard . . ."/ "By accident she heard . . ."). In an earlier version of the manuscript, in the Diver holograph of 1932, Fitzgerald toyed with the idea of using an identifiable go-between, but his decision not to be

specific contributes to the blurring and the general obfuscation that are important to the effect produced by the ending.[4] Even Diver's own communications to his former wife are not at all likely to present objective information, focusing, as the do, on business matters and the children. His initial expectation to have his children come and see him in America, for instance, would induce him to present his circumstances in a favorable light. What information Nicole does get, moreover, she herself is likely to access (and actually to put into words) in a manner that will keep it from upsetting her, even though again she may not be aware of it or want to admit this to herself. Although her frequent assertion "I loved Dick and I'll never forget him" does seem somewhat automatic, her interest in him continues. She goes to the trouble of looking up Geneva in an atlas and seems to be pleased to find that "it was in the heart of the Finger Lakes section and considered a pleasant place." The same impression results from the sentence that follows this: "Perhaps, so she liked to think, his career was biding its time, again like Grant's in Galena." Despite her seeming interest in her former husband, there is a definite suggestion here as well as in the last sentence of the novel, that, quite in accordance with her egotism, Nicole is lying to herself about the true circumstances of Diver's life and that in doing so she is trying to absolve herself from all guilt in the matter. For actually it is quite clear that she and the world that she represents are wholly responsible for Diver's dying fall and that there will be no recovery for him.

Summarizing these various observations, we realize that (except for the presence of an identifiable first-person narrator with his own syntax) we have a situation very similar to that in *The Great Gatsby*. Our interest focuses on what is actually being told (the circumstances of Dick Diver's life in America) as much as on how and why it is told (the reactions of Nicole Warren to what she learns about her former husband). As in *The Great Gatsby*, though for different reasons and in different measure, there are gaps in the story, and we are thus left to infer what really happens. Although there is an omniscient voice, probably the same voice as in the opening paragraphs, it deliberately chooses not to make use of its omniscience. But gaps, plausible gaps which in *The Great Gatsby* as much as in *Tender Is the Night* result from a carefully chosen narrative technique, in the story of a protagonist whose life the reader has vicariously participated in over an extended period of time are disquieting, irritating, annoying. As a consequence he begins to speculate, to read between the lines, to interpret what evidence there is on his own. The particular quality of the text thus causes a passive reader to become an active interpreter, it induces him to proceed to make his own text, as it were. It is precisely this what Fitzgerald had intended to do and what he had in mind when he explained and justified his adaptation of Garnett's ending in his letter to Hemingway: ". . . telling the reader in the last pages that, after all, this is just a casual event, and trying to let *him* come to bat for *me* rather than going out to shake his nerves, whoop him up, then leaving him rather in a condition of a frustrated woman in bed" (174). The implication of this is that the observant reader, the congenial reader, unlike Nicole, the totally inadequate reflector of her former husband's fate, will come to see that the totally inadequate reflector of her former husband's fate, will come to see that Diver's dying fall is not just a casual event, but a tragedy of major proportions. In other words: Fitzgerald's narrative strategy will induce the reader to examine and reject the deficient story as it is actually told in the final chapter and to attempt to replace it by the true story such as he himself (re)constructs it from faulty and incomplete evidence. This process can never be wholly complete, and one of the lingering after-effects that Fitzgerald strove for is an awareness of this deficiency: Is Diver still "in that section of the country, in one town or another"? Is he, like Garnett's protagonist, "for that matter . . . still alive"?

. . . .

The difficulties that have been discussed in ascertaining and assessing the facts of Dick Diver's doings in his life in various upstate New York towns after his return to America are a definite part of Fitzgerald's realization of the dying fall. They result from the fact that Diver has been moved to the very fringe of the world that has conquered him. Nicole Warren with her riches, her particular morals and her new husband, barbarian Tommy Barban, now determines where the center is. It is appropriate, therefore, that she should serve as a reflector who distorts the truth as it might emerge from omniscient narration. The very scarcity of the facts relating to Diver, along with their distortion, is a measure of what little attention he now commands in the circles whose brilliant center he once was. This decline in the estimation of other people as expressed through Nicole's role as reflector in the author's narrative strategy is matched by the actual facts about Diver's life as they emerge from the account. It is in the particular circumstances of his moves in upstate New York that the dying fall is most clearly charted.

Fitzgerald uses a maximum of information in a minimum of space by resorting to symbols and suggestive detail, and he achieves all the compression of a tightly structured short story. There is a sequence of details that suggest Diver's professional decline, there is sequence that suggests his moral decline, and there is also a sequence that suggests his social decline. It is obvious, however, that these separate sequences affect each other. Diver first opens an office in Buffalo, then moves to Batavia, then to Lockport, then to Geneva, then to Hornell and possibly to still another town in the Finger Lakes section of the state of New York. The places can be charted on a map (a task that is not without interest as an assignment), and while information about the actual sizes of their population do not bear out the suggestion that this is a steady downward movement,[5] the movement as such betokens aimlessness, loss of direction and of purpose. A professional decline would seem to emerge from Diver's first opening an office in Buffalo (a city with a population in 1930 of more than half a million), apparently a psychiatrist's office, then opening offices in Batavia and Lockport, specifically as a general practitioner, as Nicole learns from sources other than Diver himself. That this detail should be important emerges from the fact that when in his last letter to Nicole Diver tells her that he is now practicing in Geneva, he does not specify in what particular capacity. While no reasons are given for Diver's lack of success in Buffalo and for his removal from Batavia, his leaving Lockport is obviously due to either malpractice or some illegal business, and perhaps also to his having become entangled with a woman of low social status, "a girl who worked in a grocery store." Fitzgerald deliberately rejected the idea of having the girl be a minor and thus saves his protagonist from outright disgrace.[6] It is in Lockport that he is still lionized and admired by the ladies, and also still has a manuscript on his desk, but while the unidentified source of this information, as well as Nicole herself, seems to interpret these details as positive, the reader knows how far down from former glory the dying fall has taken Diver in actuality even at that point. It is important to note that after the Lockport affair and the lawsuit he "didn't ask for the children to be sent to America and didn't answer when Nicole wrote asking him if he needed money." Fitzgerald clearly has him retain a degree of self-respect: by refusing money from a source whose enormous wealth had corrupted him[7] as well as by avoiding the questions that would have been asked had he insisted on having his children visit him. There is some ambiguity, however, about Nicole's supposition "that he had settled down with someone to keep house for him." It must be remembered that in 1930 the kind of living together suggested by the wording was definitely still frowned upon and certainly considered disgraceful for a professional. But it is not clear if Nicole's assumption is correct.

The dying fall is also obvious in the decline of the correspondence carried on between former husband and wife: there is a last "letter" from Geneva, and after that just a "note" mailed from Hornell. Hornell, last in the sequence of Diver's moves, is called "a very small town." It has been pointed out that this is not borne out by the census figures for 1930. In view of what has been said about Nicole's way of dealing with information about Diver, however, this can also be assumed to be a mistake that she makes. It could well reflect (subconsciously, not admitted to herself, perhaps) her growing view of his career as a dying fall. After all, while his preceding stay in

Geneva had still induced her to think of Grant's biding his time in Galena, and thus to entertain hope for his recovery, Hornell must have suggested to her another move on a downward scale.

The reference to Grant—and we must assume this to be Nicole's, even though the earlier reference to Grant that justifies the "again" is definitely that of the omniscient narrator, who in chapter 1 of Book II provides a survey of Diver's early career—once more demonstrates the complexity and ambiguity of Fitzgerald's text. It is one of a number of such references which in various ways serve to establish historical parallels and relate individuals and their experiences to the American nation and events in its history. Ulysses S. Grant, the Civil War general and 18th President of the United States, after graduating from the U.S. Military Academy and serving during the War with Mexico and later in California and Oregon, resigned from the army and eventually clerked for some years in his father's leather store in Galena, Illinois. It was there that he was biding his time, as it were, awaiting his destiny as an important figure in the history of the United States. Similarly, Dick Diver, from the conclusion of his studies up to his discharge from a neurological unit in 1919, was biding his time, equally "ready to be called to an intricate destiny" (155). No doubt the first reference to Grant is meant to suggest something positive about Diver. Bruccoli finds that the second reference to Grant, the one in the final chapter, "reinforces the connection between Diver and Grant as representative American figures."8 But while Nicole would indeed seem to use it in a positive sense once more, Dick Diver's very situation indicates that it is probably another aspect of Grant's career that prompts the author to introduce the comparison at this point (and at the same time to undercut Nicole's judgment yet again). It is well known that after his service in the Mexican War, Grant "hated the routine of soldiering [and] took to solitary drinking," and that during his Presidency, though he was personally honest, "his administration was one of corruption and graft; he was overawed by men of wealth and social station, and was a poor judge of human nature."9 All of this also holds for Diver, who had allowed himself to be corrupted by the money of the rich and was disappointed by the very people he had served, and who had turned to alcohol as a solace. The second reference to Grant then would indeed seem to be designed to undermine the validity of Nicole's views.10 It shows her to be an incompetent judge of the plight of her former husband, unable also to face up to what his situation really is, and an unreliable reflector deliberately to be used by the author in conjunction with the narrative voice to create the charged ambiguity of the closing chapter of the novel in its superb rendition of the dying fall theme.

Notes

1. Matthew J. Bruccoli, *Some Sort of Epic Grandeur: The Life of F. Scott Fitzgerald* (New York: Harcourt Brace Jovanovich, 1981), p. 374.

2. FSF to EH, 1 June 1934, in Matthew J. Bruccoli, *Fitzgerald and Hemingway: A Dangerous Friendship* (New York: Carroll and Graf, 1994), p. 174. All subsequent references to this letter are to this reprinting and will be identified parenthetically in the text.

3. The implicit evaluation of Horatio Alger novels testifies to Fitzgerald's more than casual acquaintance with the work of the popular writer of success stories and its propagation of the American myth of success. In Alger's best-known book, *Ragged Dick* (1867), the success hero proves to be a competent swimmer.

4. It is highly instructive and useful in assessing Fitzgerald's narrative and stylistic achievement in the final version to have students compare the first brief paragraph of the printed text to the 1932 Diver holograph version and its emendations. The holograph version reads as follows: "Nicole kept in touch with Dick after her <insert: new> marriage through letters on business matters and through the recurrent problems that faced them about the children—who tended to gravitate toward her as she grew better and stronger." (*F. Scott Fitzgerald Manuscripts, Tender Is the Night*, vol. IVb, Part 2, p. 614. Page references in footnotes 26 and 27 are to this volume.)

5. Bruccoli gives the actual 1930 census figures and concludes that they "do not jibe with Fitzgerald's intention. Batavia was not 'a little town,' and Hornell was not 'a very small town.'" (*Reader's Companion*, p. 151).

6. In the manuscript that part of the sentence still reads, "but he became entangled with a sixteen year old girl in a grocery store . . ." (p. 615). In the First and Second Typescripts he had reduced the age of the girl to fifteen before deleting the specific reference altogether.

7. Once more a comparison of the text with its manuscript version can be used for instructional purposes. Again, the manuscript is more explicit, while the printed version leaves things unsaid and works with understatement, a method of foreshortening also typical of the short story: ". . . but he answered with a sharp letter when Nicole wrote asking him if he needed money" (p. 615).

8. *Reader's Companion*, p. 151.

9. *The Reader's Companion to American Literature*, ed. by Max J. Herzberg (New York: Crowell, 1962), s.v. "Grant, Ulysses S[impson]."

10. As if to make sure that the reader did not miss the negative implications of the Grant-Diver comparison at this point, Fitzgerald had included a reference to Grant's drinking in the drunken speech of Abe North at the end of chapter 24 of Book I, preceding the two Grant in Galena references. In fact, he had Abe North, whose looks and whose first name relate him to Abraham Lincoln, allude to Lincoln's response to reports about Grant's drinking. (See also Bruccoli, *Reader's Companion*, p. 101.)

The 1985 Television Production

Schulberg wrote this reminiscence of Fitzgerald on the occasion of the 1985 BBC TV broadcast.

Lost in Paradise
Budd Schulberg
Radio Times, 21–27 September 1985, pp. 99–100

Early in 1939, when I was labouring on a conventional college movie predictably titled *Winter Carnival,* producer Walter Wanger called me in to say he thought I needed a collaborator. 'I've just hired Scott Fitzgerald,' he said. '*Scott Fitzgerald!* I thought he was dead.' 'He's in the next room, reading your script.'

In the adjoining office I met Fitzgerald for the first time. His complexion was manuscript white and, though there was still a light brown tint to his hair, the first impression he made on me was of a ghost–the ghost of the Great Novelist Past who had sprung to early fame with *This Side of Paradise,* capped his early promise at age 29 with what many critics hailed as the great American novel, *The Great Gatsby,* and then had taken nine years to write and publish the book most of the same critics condemned as 'disappointing', *Tender is the Night.*

Five years later, one mean and practical reason I thought Fitzgerald literally dead is that his once-vaunted reputation–the greatest writer of his day, the spokesman for his generation, the veritable creator of the Jazz Age–had died with the critical and financial 'failure' of his last completed novel, the aptly titled, poetically conceived *Tender is the Night.*

Early in our friendship, which was to survive the cinematic catastrophe of *Winter Carnival* and continue until the (December 1940) dying of the light, still in awe that I was actually in the presence of the living Fitzgerald, I tried to tell him how much his work had meant to me–not just *Gatsby,* and the vibrant short stories, but especially *Tender.* He was childishly pleased and vulnerable: 'I'm really surprised that you're even aware of it, much less have read it.'

This was the end of the 'Red', or Popular Front decade, when most thinking young men considered themselves 'Marxists' and read Steinbeck, James T. Farrell, and Dos Passos's *USA.* Fitzgerald, although strongly influenced politically by Edmund Wilson, Malcolm Cowley and other social-minded critics, had come to be identified with his subject matter, the playboys, the parasites, the idle rich.

Reviewers, with pinked preconceptions, had dismissed *Tender is the Night* as superficial and, in those years of social struggle, irrelevant. Even his old chum and competitor Ernest Hemingway had come down hard on poor Fitzgerald, charging that he had not really written a novel at all but simply a thinly disguised version of Scott's and his tragic wife Zelda's relationship with the famously rich Gerald and Sara Murphy on the Riviera.

As Fitzgerald went on about the 'failure' of *Tender,* he seemed to rub salt in wounds still open. The Hemingway dig hurt, for Ernest would–almost pathetically–remain a hero to Scott. In the now clichéd but still telling exchange between them, Scott had observed with his wry double-vision that 'I talk with the authority of failure–Ernest with the authority of success. We could never sit across the table again.'

The Fitzgerald of 1939 listed for me the 'failure' of the book he had hoped would restore both his literary and financial standing. It had sold a mere 12,000 copies, a modest sale for 1934, but a slap in the face for the best-selling prodigy of the 20s, whose explosive first novel had sold three times that many, and had been adopted by his so-called 'Lost Generation' as its Bible, its credo, its celebration of post-war youth.

Nowhere does the roller-coaster of success climb higher, only to plunge lower, than in America. The young Fitzgerald, seemingly, had had it all, but, to cop a Hemingway title, *Winner Take Nothing,* for here was my defeated Scott Fitzgerald of 1939, still mindful of the downward economics, still complaining that Bennett Cerf and his prestigious Modern Library had rejected *Tender* as a modern classic, almost masochistically convinced that he and his work were out of step with the new generation and therefore condemned to oblivion.

A dedicated writer with a sensitive skin and a stubborn sense of craft, Fitzgerald obviously had been brooding and puzzling over the failure of *Tender* to meet his high material and artistic standards. And he had come to the conclusion that the novel was wrongly constructed, 'broken in two' so to speak, since in the original version it opened on the French Riviera, where the protagonists, Dr Dick Diver, a young psychiatrist, and his wealthy, vivacious wife Nicole, seem to be at the top of their game, an American pair of 'beautiful people' surrounded by fun-loving admirers in a romantically hedonist world.

This world, wondrously described, is seen in the first section of the book, through the young and innocent eyes of a Hollywood *ingénue* who falls in love not only with Dick as a charismatic figure but with the irresistible Divers as co-stars in their own mythic movie, the American Dream. Only at the end of Book One, with startling dramatic effect, is it revealed that this lovely world of the rich and glamorous may be rotten at the core.

The cast of the 1985 television production of Tender Is the Night: *Peter Strauss (center) as Dick Diver and,
left to right, John Heard, Sean Young, and Mary Steenburgen as Abe North, Rosemary Hoyt,
and Nicole Warren Diver (Bruccoli Collection of Fitzgerald, Thomas Cooper Library,
University of South Carolina)*

Book Two flashed back from Antibes to wartime Zurich where Nicole is revealed as beautiful but insane. Dr Dick both treats and falls in love with her, and so we have the seeds of tragedy, heralded by Nicole's tough-minded sister Baby Warren who admits that her indecently wealthy family plans to 'buy a doctor' for her. What the guileless Rosemary saw on the Riviera were the Divers in mid-passage, for Nicole was to grow stronger as Dick Diver, a kind of Gatsby in psychiatric clothing, finds himself increasingly, and finally hopelessly, entrapped in a life-style directly at cross-purposes with his once serious ambition to become a great psychiatrist.

In the novel's own words, 'Naturally Nicole, wanting to own him, wanting him to stand still forever, encouraged any slackness on his part, and in multiplying ways he was constantly inundated by a trickling of goods and money.'

As the novel moves on to its inevitable 'dying fall' or slow fade-out, purposely understated climax, Nicole grows more relaxed and happy, 'almost complete', while Dick Diver recedes into a nondescript America, to live out his lost life as a small-town doctor.

Fitzgerald was a master at sublimating his own personal agonies and using them as materials, as a great artist mixes paints. If wrong in denigrating the novel as thinly disguised fact, Hemingway was right in reading Dick and Nicole as Scott and Zelda. The young, romantic, vulnerable author became the ambitious Zurich psychiatrist, and the Southern belle whose youthful flamboyance was cosmetic protection for genuine madness was recreated as the granddaughter of a self-made American capitalist and a German count, whose world is described by Fitzgerald in a memorable passage that makes his social message clear:

Nicole was the product of much ingenuity and toil. For her sake trains began their run to Chicago and traversed the round belly of the continent to California; chicle factories fumed and link belts grew link by link in factories; men mixed toothpaste in vats and drew mouthwash out of copper hogsheads; girls canned tomatoes quickly in August or worked rudely at the Five-and-Tens on Christmas Eve; half-breed Indians toiled on Brazilian plantations and dreamers were muscled out of patent rights in new tractors—these were some of the people who gave a tithe to Nicole . . .

Half a century ago I–and friends like John O'Hara, Dorothy Parker and Nathanael West–found it possible to applaud the best of 'proletarian' fiction without having to disown Fitzgerald, as did too many fair-weather critics. Re-reading *Tender is the Night* today, and still preferring the original version to Fitzgerald's (and Malcolm Cowley's) chronological revision, it is easier to see what so many reviewers missed, that Fitzgerald, while writing an intensely emotional and personal novel, was also making his own statement about the corruption and false values of an aristocracy without roots, tradition or responsibility, founded on the power of money alone.

Here is a story of disintegration as haunting as anything I have read in American fiction. I was fortunate to have an opportunity to tell the author this face to face when he was down, but (*vide The Last Tycoon*) not quite as out as his finely drawn, tragically penned Dick Diver.

If there *is* a far side of paradise, and Scott Fitzgerald made it, there must be an ironic smile on his face as he sees all of his books back in print, and finds himself an even more profound cult hero in the 80s than he was in the 20s. And this time around, the positive response to the once maltreated *Tender is the Night* is virtually unanimous. More power to the BBC for bringing it now to a new and wider audience.

* * *

Showtime's new 'Tender' a little tough to take
Clifford Terry
Chicago Tribune, 25 October 1985, p. 5:5

When F. Scott Fitzgerald wrote that "there are no second acts in American lives," he might have added that there should be no second chances in American literature.

Attempts to adapt 20th-Century novels and stories to the big and small screen have largely resulted in disaster, from Hemingway's "The Sun Also Rises" to Cheever's "The Swimmer."

In 1962 Hollywood turned out a version of "Tender Is the Night," Fitzgerald's 1933 novel about '20s dissolution, but despite the pairing of Jason Robards Jr. and Jennifer Jones, it never came off.

Now comes a six-hour, five-part cable-television version, as Showtime presents its first-ever mini-series [starting at 7 p.m. Sunday and continuing for four consecutive Tuesdays beginning Nov. 5], starring Peter Strauss as the psychiatrist trying to

write the great scientific treatise and Mary Steenburgen as his "poor butterfly" of a wife.

Fitzgerald's story of the fragile, frenetic marriage of Dick and Nicole Diver was a composite of the real-life relationships of the writer and his mentally anguished Zelda and their friends, the American expatriates Gerald and Sara Murphy, who brought their legendary sparkle and charm to the south of France.

As in the original, the storyline bounces between the sunshine of the Riviera and the musty gloominess of the Swiss sanitorium where Diver has taken charge of the poor little rich girl, who is suffering from the acute schizophrenia triggered by an incestuous episode with her father [played here by Ed Asner]. Trying to transform "hysterical despair into normal unhappiness," he brings his own strength to her broken places, only to eventually find that the roles have been reversed.

The series was directed by Robert Knights, who periodically creates some fine moments, particularly in his conveying through bouncy music, colorful costumes and tinkling glasses the scintillation of the '20s–a time of flappers and philosophers, of "pretty bubbles in the air." But for most of the six hours, it is plodding and stolid.

In the major supporting roles, Sean Young combines smashing, Joan Hackett-like looks with a nicely curious blend of sensitivity and vapidity as the movie starlet Rosemary Hoyt, who eases into an affair with Diver. But as Abe North–the cynical, boozing songwriter whose talent has been shelved for seven years [the actual prototype was writer Ring Lardner]–John Heard lacks the necessary bite to turn the self-described "decomposer" into a kind of precursor of Oscar Levant.

The biggest problem, though, is in the casting of the leads. Steenburgen, who has displayed an admirable, off-beat looniness in the films "Goin' South" and "Melvin and Howard," simply lacks the dazzling looks and center-stage quality of the Ophelia/Isadora Duncan character that Fitzgerald describes as "dramatic," "inspiring" and "formidable," although her performance is often quite moving as she tries to come to grips with "the arrows that fly in the twilight."

Conversely, Strauss ["Rich Man, Poor Man," "Masada"] has the perfect classically chiseled, Van Heusen shirt-handsomeness for a Fitzgerald protagonist, but turns the hard-drinking, "serious and brilliant" doctor into–like Robert Redford's Gatsby–a bloodless character. Dashing and debonair, he fails to convey the torment of a man who, like the author himself, was in the midst of physical and creative disintegration. Instead of its being 3 o'clock in the morning in the dark night of Dick Diver's soul, Strauss plays it as high noon.

* * *

Kemp reviewed two television productions that were broadcast on BBC 2: The Other Side of Paradise *and* Tender Is the Night.

The flight of the rocket
Peter Kemp
TLS, 15 November 1985, p. 1292

The most interesting fact to emerge from *The Other Side of Paradise—Bookmark*'s profile of Scott Fitzgerald—was that the first word he wrote was "Up". Aiming high was his primary urge. But, along with his impulsion to climb—into the world of the rich, the headlines, a high-income bracket, literary celebrity—went a contrary leaning towards collapse. Played out against the 1920s boom and the 1930s depression, Fitzgerald's life follows a legend-like trajectory from euphoria to decline; so did the plots of his novels. One after another, his protagonists slump from promise to waste, charm to seediness, energy to lethargy, alertness to befuddlement. It's apt that a projected title for his second book, *The Beautiful and Damned,* should have been *The Flight of the Rocket.* Icarus-like, Fitzgerald's heroes regularly plummet from some glittering height. Monroe Stahr, in his final, uncompleted work, *The Last Tycoon,* was to have undergone the most literal and lethal instance of this: dying in a plane crash.

As if in unfortunate homage to this pattern in Fitzgerald, *The Other Side of Paradise* started promisingly, then nose-dived into the banal. Ian Hamilton's opening commentary offered perceptive pointers into Fitzgerald's work, but none of these was followed up: occasional glances towards the novels scarcely penetrated beyond close-ups of their dust jackets; *The Beautiful and Damned* didn't even get direct mention. Instead, the programme opted for a trudge over familiar ground. The main milestones in Fitzgerald's life, from Princeton to Hollywood, were plodded past. Morley Callaghan and Malcolm Cowley—"two survivors of the lost generation", as the *Radio Times* billed them—re-aired musty reminiscences, as did other veteran Fitzgerald familiars. Jerky bits of home movie and clips from period newsreel alike failed to get much animation into things. Far and away the most compulsive footage in the programme, in fact, comes from BBC 2's recent dramatization of *Tender is the Night.* Vibrant with atmosphere and intelligence, extracts from this provided a reminder of its distinction and flair.

Following the revised version of the novel, where events are narrated chronologically, Dennis

Cover for the 1985 television tie-in edition of the novel (Bruccoli Collection of Fitzgerald, Thomas Cooper Library, University of South Carolina)

Potter's adaptation of *Tender is the Night* streamlines the story. The Divers' children—never closely integrated into the book: Nicole thinks of them as "orphans"—are removed; so is Mary North's reappearance as Mary Minghetti. This means that some lively scenes are lost: Mary's break-up with the Divers, her *matelot* antics with Caroline Sibley-Biers, the eerie garish episode where Nicole runs amok in a fairground. And there are a couple of moments where Potter's pruning shears clip damagingly into the dialogue. The announcement of Abe North's death after being beaten up in a speakeasy gets cut from "He just managed to crawl home to the Racquet Club to die" to "He just managed to crawl home to die"—thus losing the full bleakness of his end. Nicole's reflection, "better a sane crook than a mad puritan," is unaccountably abbreviated to the unlikely, too crude-sounding "better a crook than a puritan."

Such cavils aside, though, this is an adroit and imaginative adaptation whose discreet additions, tidyings-up and splicings-together never stop it catching the spirit of Fitzgerald's book. Robert Knight's direction of it stylishly combines lushness and astringency. Visually, the film is handsome, moving out from the damp greens and greys of Switzerland to the hot colours of the Riviera, then on to the chic tints and creamy luxury of Paris in 1925. Opulent with period detail—women slithering from square-topped cabs in a shimmer of shiny headbands, silk stockings and flapper skirts, men sleek from their trilbies to their two-tone shoes—the production reflects Fitzgerald's fascination with glamour without ever softening into mere goggling at gorgeousness.

As appealing as the look of the film is its soundtrack. Potter's script, as might be expected, makes widespread use of period music—something Fitzgerald, who once wished he'd been a creator of musicals like Cole Porter or Rodgers and Hart—would surely have relished. Twenties melodies—some mentioned in the book, some not—underscore what's happening. Saxophones sob out "Poor Butterfly" and other tunes about transience—"I'm Forever Blowing Bubbles," "Glow, Little Glow Worm." When Dick and Rosemary finally make love—too late and in a mood of feverish pleasure-grabbing rather than passion—"Let's Misbehave" cynically hums in the background. There's an especially good early scene in which a wind-up gramophone emits the scratchy jauntiness of ragtime as Nicole—shakily lively—starts to manoeuvre Dick into becoming her partner.

Mary Steenburgen's dark Nicole isn't physically accurate: she should have "very blonde hair", highlighting her resemblance to Zelda who was, Dorothy Parker noted, "very blonde". She also looks slightly too old—as does Sean Young's Rosemary Hoyt, another blonde darkened in this film. Where Sean Young's Rosemary misrepresents the character, though—giving her a moody, Pre-Raphaelite-seeming sophistication that is at odds with the immaturity the book insists on—Mary Steenburgen is perfectly cast as regards Nicole's personality. Adept at chameleon-quick flickering from one emotion to another, she conveys with uncanny immediacy the darting fluctuations of response Nicole is at

first subject to, then gives a convincing picture of the ominous recovery. Beginning with the portrayal of a trepidant, suddenly radiant, flutteringly predatory creature, she shows the character hardening into tough-knit egotism, clinching her outbursts of verbal aggression with a mean little nod of assertiveness, narrowing her remarkable eyes into glinting slits of animosity.

Peter Strauss also makes telling use of his eyes—even managing to convey the sudden flash of blue from his gaze that Fitzgerald attributes to Diver. Like Mary Steenburgen, too, he gives a riveting performance of a split personality. Torn between his roles as doctor and husband, between an initial desire to explore human depths through psychiatry and his eventual restriction to the surface world of charm, he has to encompass a wide span. That Diver never really convinces as a psychiatrist—despite the production's investment in white coats and a tome-lined study adorned with Freud's photograph—is due not to Strauss but to Fitzgerald, who never gives sufficient substance to these sections of the story. Where Strauss shines is in his transmission of Dick's charm, and his depiction of the man's final leached-out collapse. The "low painful fire of intelligence" you never quite believe in when you hear of its being devoted to pioneering psychological treatises flares out in acute sarcasms as he tries to kick away the vacuous socialites he has sustained for so long.

Kate Harper's Baby Warren—a Bette-Davis-like performance of rich bitchery—is outstanding as an instance of that money-varnished repulsiveness Dick finally turns against. And, elsewhere too, the production is strong in its subsidiary roles: John Heard's Abe North, sodden with alcohol and bitterness at his own futility; Jurgen Brugger's Franz Gregorovius, a splendid rendering of pursed, pussy-footing resentfulness. As a terminally ill patient—fastidious speech emerging from behind a mask of bleeding tetters of eczema—Joanna David gives a moving, brief performance. Timothy West, as the father of a young alcoholic—Australian in the book, here from the Midlands—gusts through one scene with hilarious sour bombast. Lastly, applause is due to the trio of inmates who, at the psychiatric clinic's *matinées musicales,* flailingly and unfailingly saw out Suppé's *Light Calvalry Overture* with discomposing zest.

The Novel on Stage

Tender Is the Night, *as dramatized by Simon Levy, was produced for the Fountain Theatre in Hollywood, opening for a monthlong run on 2 March 1995.*

Review of *Tender Is the Night*
Polly Warfield
Drama-Logue, 23–29 March 1995

Golden is the glamor, bittersweet is the romance, and potent is the magic of F. Scott Fitzgerald's classic Jazz Age novel *Tender Is the Night,* brought lyrically and luminously—and, yes, tenderly—to the stage in this sensitive dramatization by Simon Levy.

Gilded by the Mediterranean sun, lulled by sounds of surf and mewing gulls, its opening tableau of giddy merrymakers in suspended motion on a French Riviera beach captures the tone and sets the scene. Like some other landmark eras, 1920s' Flaming Youth epoch was both the best and worst of times: like their real life counterparts Scott and Zelda, Dick and Nicole Diver gloriously personify the best and worst of it.

In a marvelous casting coup, we have a Dick and Nicole (a Scott and Zelda) so convincing we can accept starlet Rosemary's rapt tribute: "You are both so—so—*perfect!*" As heartbreaker Nicole (heartbreaker in more ways than one) Tracy Middendorf bursts unheralded upon us in her first local stage outing. Her Nicole is created of moonbeams, stardust, jonquils and jazz; she is enchanting, diaphonous, impish—and, unfortunately, crazy. The actress inhabits Nicole in all her childlike simplicity and hidden complexity, and we haven't seen hands, fingers, total being used so eloquently since Michael Crawford's Phantom. She's sound of mind and free of spirit, but Nicole is tortured by a shattered psyche. We learn why. This is an extraordinary performance. If it were in a movie it would deserve an Academy Award.

Larry Poindexter's Dick Diver is her worthy partner and perfect complement. Dick and Nicole's meeting and mating as if is fated and, in a sense, fatal. The two are drawn together as if by magnets, and by the chemistry we feel in their scenes together. Poindexter creates a character who can charm without trying, whose love for Nicole is manifest, and whose inability to rescue her from her demons all but destroys him. Handsome and an

Cover of the program for the premiere of the first stage adaptation of the novel (Bruccoli Collection of Fitzgerald, Thomas Cooper Library, University of South Carolina)

accomplished actor, Poindexter is a compelling Dick Diver and the Fountain's answer to Warren Beatty.

Philip Abrams is the sardonic, wryly amusing (Oscar Levant-inspired) Abe North, who plays a mean piano and drinks himself to death. Jill Holden is his good-natured, earthy wife Mary. Lisa Robin Kelly is Wampus baby star Rosemary Hoyt, with Mary Pickford curls, who has a terrific crush on Dick. (Fitzgerald's *roman a clef* bases Rosemary on Hollywood starlet Lois Moran, who shared a real-life fling with Scott.) Rosemary's film, in a nice bit of irony, is titled *Daddy's Girl*. Nicole's daddy, Mr. Warren, an aristocrat and plutocrat, is smoothly played by David Beckett; Nicole, tragically, was indeed "daddy's girl." Beckett also appears as a flamboyant Russian prince. Don Winston is appealing as Rosemary's smitten swain Collis Clay. Susan Marie Brecht is obstreperous, silly American tourist Violet McKisco, always trying to get into "the plot." Robert Stephen Ryan is her even sillier husband Albert, another perennial outsider. In a tour de force change of persona, Brecht appears later as an exotic vamp who might have been painted by Matisse. Her seductive, tipsy tango with Dick ends in a roll on the floor and a barroom brawl. Ryan, also transformed, is a combative Italian waiter and Maximillian Mastrangelo is an Italian taxi driver quick with his fists, as well as a bohemian-type Count.

Cinematic scenes under Heidi Helen Davis' astute direction flow rhythmically as style and substance unite to create magic. Robert W. Zentis' set of graceful curves and black and gold adornment is elegantly art deco. Doc Ballard's lighting warms it with sunlight and washes it with moonlight. Ben Decter's sound is enhancing. Jeanne Reith's Erte-esque costumes—cloche hats, "headache bands," egret plumes, maribou, lots of sequins—are downright dazzling. Everyone looks wonderful in them. Bill and Deborah Bartlett choreographed the delightful, well-performed period dances—Charleston, Black Bottom, tango. Jay Alan Quantrill composed the original music.

Playwright Levy and the Fountain's ensemble capture the novel's heady, lyric quality. Harmonious blend of many talents, the essence of the dramatic art, makes this a magical, exciting theatre experience.

Dennis Potter, the British playwright, adapted Tender Is the Night *for the BBC in 1985.*

Later Critical Views

Introduction to the Folio Society Edition
Dennis Potter

Fitzgerald was puzzled, hurt, and scared to the bone by the relative commercial failure of *Tender is the Night* in America, where stories about failure always threaten to taint the native dream of the proper order of things. He did not try to apportion any blame, but he might well have wondered what had happened to the once so eager throngs of admiring readers. *Tender is the Night,* after all, was the novel which had come the hardest to him, bearing his most vivid hopes, and which, in shape and detail, had been the closest to his own marrow.

He had worked and picked at it, on and off, for a considerable part of his maturity. Piling up the words, cutting them, adding, cutting again. Shifting and sifting, putting aside, and going back to with differing resolves, and perpetually brooding upon it as the events and people around him seemed to partake of the stuff of his own text. When Fitzgerald at last delivered it up—perhaps better say, let it go—he demonstrated the sort of exhaustion which has the disconcerting habit of masquerading as triumph.

One particular image for all this can be excavated from a few sentences in the book. Dick Diver, the spiri-

Frontispiece and title page for the Folio Society edition (Bruccoli Collection of Fitzgerald, Thomas Cooper Library, University of South Carolina)

tually doomed hero of the novel, is shown to us—and to the watching eyes of a beautiful young film actress—raking the sand on the exclusive stretch of beach in front of the basking, suitably rose-coloured hotel where money speaks to money across the marbled spaces. He is wearing a jockey cap, and moving the rake gravely, up and down, 'ostensibly removing gravel and meanwhile developing some esoteric burlesque held in suspension by his grave face.'

The manner, the action, for me irresistibly suggest the picture of Fitzgerald himself, raking over his own prose. Rills and ridges on both the white page and tan-coloured beach, waiting to take the imprint of golden bodies, languorous and indolent, but calling across to each other. And then, when the sun has gone down in the tide of its own vermilion, or inspiration has momentarily withdrawn, and a wind stirs and frets

from across the now darkening sea, the obdurate sand of grainy imagining needs to be raked all over again.

Years he worked upon it, this stretch at the rim of his talent, until the words heaped themselves up against the breakwater in almost unmanageable drifts. Long after it was supposedly finished, by now half-submerged in the tepid channels of its initial reception, Fitzgerald continued to nag himself about the novel's structure.

As first published (and in this edition), *Tender is the Night* opens on that dazzling strand between the rose-coloured hotel and Cannes, five swanking miles away. 'Now, many bungalows cluster near it, but when this story begins only the cupolas of a dozen old villas rotted like water lilies among the massed pines . . .' The cork is pulled on a richly seductive vintage, and the senses cannot but respond at once to the especial bouquet. But there is also something else at work, drawn from deeper down, mingling with that first fine savour, threatening the taste of dankness, and redolent of that which has already faded. You are gradually made aware of premonitions and echoes, or, rather, of a sort of stealthy tension silkily stretching between the two. A sense of mystery is gathering itself together like mere wisps and tatters of cloud far out over the glistening bay, by no means certain to move inland, and not yet much of a threat to these first few figures disporting themselves on the fringe of the golden land.

Dick and Nicole Diver—the one to fall, the other to rise—are glimpsed at an angle and at one remove in the full flush of their strangely hypnotic charm. A happy and entrancing couple, it seems, with their due retinue of admirers and the excluded outer-ring of the fascinated and envious. The witness—soon to be drawn in—is the newcomer to the beach, the young actress Rosemary Hoyt.

Rosemary falls asleep in the sun, and her valuable young skin begins to broil. When she awakes—and it happens in at least one fairy tale—the beach is deserted, except for Dick Diver. Everyone has gone in to luncheon, with its blaze of silver and flashes of white linen, and even the rake has been stowed away in a rock crevice. 'It's not a bad time,' he says to her. 'It's not one of the worst times of the day.' The phrasing, the style, not

much to go on, are nevertheless instantly the man. Dick Diver has stepped out of the haze—and she falls for 'the bright blue worlds' of his eyes as quickly as she would in one of the plots of her silly films. Indeed, there are always disconcerting moments in any Fitzgerald story which seem to belong in a bad movie: one of the reasons why other writers feel so fondly about his work.

When people call into question the true quality of Fitzgerald as a writer, and falter upon this or that reservation before venturing any genuinely confident measure of his stature, I would point to an ample number of exceptionally compelling or at times almost magically luminous passages in *The Great Gatsby* and *Tender is the Night*. Sumptuous prose not quite holding back more febrile anxieties. One such passage is this opening sequence on the beach, which so deftly uses a predilection for the baroque and the romantic to do and to reveal so many more things than the purely functional one of setting the time and place.

'—when this story begins . . .' chimes the cadence in the first few lines, an old manner of implying a properly chronological narrative. Years later, though, Fitzgerald was at pains to persuade himself that he had put this opening paragraph in the wrong place. The *true* beginning—to use his own emphasis—sits much further on in the novel: Book Two, in fact, at the psychiatric clinic near Zurich,

---

An Enduring Novel

Wilfrid Sheed, a member of the editorial board of The Book-of-the-Month Club, recommended Tender Is the Night *in* The Well-Stocked Bookcase: Sixty Enduring Novels by Americans Published Between 1926–1986 *(1987), a BOMC publication.*

Tender Is the Night has always suffered the fate of being compared to its handsome little brother, *The Great Gatsby*. Outside of the author's name, there is no serious comparison. *Gatsby* is short and perfect, and—at least in the case of books—it's a lot easier to be perfect if you're short. *Tender* is big, rich and, all right, flawed. F. Scott Fitzgerald poured so much of himself into it that he couldn't always keep the shape straight, and his lyrical prose sometimes bursts into lushness. These are minor offenses in view of the book's achievements, because Fitzgerald also pulls off the near-impossible: he manages to translate his own private torments with Zelda and alcohol into a totally convincing fable about two quite different people.

The story concerns a brilliant psychologist who saves a patient from madness, falls in love with her and

pours his strength into her, only to lose both her and his strength. It is all so authentically *felt* that a psychiatrist friend of mine used to read the book once a year and imagine himself into the soul of Dr. Dick Diver and wind up doing crazy tricks on an actual diving board to prove he hadn't lost his strength after all. And it's a rare novel that can do that to *anyone*.

But the Divers' story represents more than just one man's crack-up. Fitzgerald also gives us perhaps the best portrait we have of a whole doomed community: the fun-loving expatriates of the '20s, still frolicking gamely on the Riviera in the shadow of Depression and war. By following his rich patient-wife into that world, Dick Diver has bought into both the fun and the doom. In a haunting climactic scene the once-masterful doctor winds up bestowing a boozy papal blessing over the crowd on the beach before departing alone for the United States. Fitzgerald, who had once celebrated the decade and who helped to invent it, is telling us, and himself, that the party is over.

—pp. 65–66

F. Scott Fitzgerald

TENDER IS THE NIGHT
A Romance

Text established by Matthew J. Bruccoli

London: Samuel Johnson, 1995

*Title page for the corrected text of the novel that reproduces a marked
copy of the 1934 edition (Bruccoli Collection of Fitzgerald,
Thomas Cooper Library, University of South Carolina)*

where young Doctor Richard Diver meets impossibly rich Nicole Warren for the first time.

We already know when we reach this place, going forward in pagination but backward on the calendar, that there is something wrong with the magical couple. The high-gloss glamour of the Divers and the charm of their company, their good looks and money and grace and magnetism, are threaded with other things, and threatened. An unknown or undefined darkness, even an evil, lies coiled in waiting, ready to seep into all the crystalline spaces between the laughter, the brittle chatter, the tinkling tunes and the chink of the glasses. Certain warning asides and a few bizarre incidents, graphic but nevertheless puzzling and ominously incomplete, have opened up alarming fissures in the glittering surfaces. Unease is quickening the nerve of the story. The innocent eyes of the first observers cannot remain the dominant perspective. We are to be pulled back to the source of the mystery, to probe at last at the suppurating root of the ache.

It is 1917: a wise time to be in Switzerland. The world beyond the clean mountains is bloodily engulfed by more than the usual quota of madness. The young doctor, who has a different sort of glory in his sights, laughs off the idea that the carnage is a threat to him. He enjoys 'the illusion of eternal strength and health, and of the essential goodness of people'. The muffled note of bitterness is a later comment, an 'editorial' interjection. Such overt interventions are rare, and oddly unsettling. Whenever they occur, the portrait of Dick Diver momentarily blurs then re-forms as a reflection of Scott Fitzgerald at one of the times when he was awash with depression, anxiety, or weariness.

Dick goes off to the war, clad in a spankingly new American uniform that makes him feel like a fraud. As he leaves the haven of the clinic, there is a chance encounter with a young girl who is 'about the prettiest thing I ever saw'. And yet this crucial first encounter between Dick Diver and Nicole Warren virtually takes place in a gap between paragraphs, so to speak. It is all but thrown away in the form of later and reported speech. The echoes of the way Scott Fitzgerald met Zelda in the country club are deadened a little: but the prettiest thing he ever saw, author and fictional creation both, flitting so briefly across a few spikes of conversation on the page, is a wounded creature, wife and fictional creation both. 'Poor Butterfly', as the song has it, with a blue sob on the saxophone. We are tipped, then, into the notes for a psychiatric case study: a shift in style which can hardly be accidental.

The perpetual re-workings of the novel, as well as the many opposing moods or ambitions which prevailed during the separated bursts and crawls of its composition, have undoubtedly left their scars. Even the most generous critic, to say nothing of the patient reader, would have to concede that there is upon occasion a feeling of incompleteness about particular scenes. A doubt which hangs over more than just the chronological structure of the book.

So marked a characteristic is this, indeed, that one is perversely tempted into the fond exasperation of asserting that *Tender is the Night* is a great novel because rather than in spite of such an apparent failing. You get the sense, while reading it, that there are cupboards or even rooms in the edifice, or places just off the page, into which you are invited to look and then almost absentmindedly not shown. The decorators are still around, the pastel-dipped brushes are still soaking in the pot, and the plaster needs to be replaced in that far, dark corner.

Far from being damaging, the effect is to draw us into the feelings of ambivalence and tension in a way that stays open and unresolved in the mind. As Dick Diver loses his glory, he appears to recede from the centre of the narrative. Nicole's growing strength is taken directly from him, it seems: and yet this is also shown not to be the case.

William Maxwell, a novelist and an editor at
The New Yorker *for forty years*

A Centenary Tribute

William Maxwell's remembrance of reading Tender Is the Night *was published in* F. Scott Fitzgerald . . . Centenary Tribute *(Columbia: Thomas Cooper Library, University of South Carolina, 1996).*

I wish I had written *The Great Gatsby*. Those diaphanous curtains blowing into the room from the windows. The sad wisdom.

Reading *Tender Is the Night* when it first came out (in, I think, *Scribner's*) brought on a disaster. I was trying to write, and living on the kindness of friends, and I had learned to do without money. I was so moved by the ending of the novel that, with my eyes blinded by tears, I pulled my sweatshirt over my head, forgetting that I had my glasses on. They were rimless, and flew across the room and broke. I reread the novel not long ago and was struck by how prophetic it was.

The romantic prose, brilliant in its evocations, bumps against hidden reefs. It almost flounders. The struggle and the sadness reach out beyond the style and the structure of the narrative. The reader who is prepared to acknowledge this, and to use a responding concern or imagination, will be rewarded at deeper levels than is usual in the literature of our times.

Such a response, if given, will also allow a more direct access to the author himself, who in later years was reduced to insisting in a humiliating emphasis to a Hollywood director that he was, really was, a good writer. *Tender is the Night* is about waste, but never about indignity of this order. A wise reader, perhaps, will permit himself at least one small shudder of recognition to temper the many beauties offered by the flowing sentences.

It would not only be vulgar in the bad, wet-mouthed way, but also factually incorrect to draw out too close a symmetry between F. Scott Fitzgerald and the subsequently troubled Zelda, and Dick Diver with the dazzling young schizophrenic, Nicole. But such proper scruples cannot allow one to deny that *Tender is the Night* takes on an extra poignancy when laid against the turmoils of Fitzgerald's own life. The man himself casts first a long, then a shortening, and then once again a lengthening shadow across the page. The reader comes to feel like a solitary walker whose shoes ring on the stones as he approaches, comes alongside, and then passes the fluttering glow of a single street lamp. But shine it does. Oh, yes, it shines.

Tender Is the Night in the Rare-Book Market

Matthew J. Bruccoli

One measure of a novel's stature and influence is what people are willing to pay for a copy of the book as it was first published. This is not the best test, but it backs literary judgment with money: a meaningful act in the realm of promiscuous opinion. A $10,000 book is not twice as good as a $5000 book—or 1000 times as good as a $10 book. Nonetheless, the collector who pays $10,000 for a book declares his confidence in his taste and his commitment to the work. What you spend money on defines you. This rule extends to the speculators and conspicuous consumers who buy books for the wrong reasons, but they are buying books—not yachts. The right reason is love of the work.

There are connections between the auction and dealer prices of a rare book and its literary reputation; but the connections are complicated by factors of rarity, condition, and collector fashion. *The Great Gatsby* has always been the star F. Scott Fitzgerald work in the auction room and in the class room. It has become the prime desideratum of Gatsbyesque buyers, who have bid it up to $163,500.[1] *Tender Is the Night* has been offered in dealers catalogues at the peak figure of $50,000. *Tender* is a rarer book than *Gatsby*: 7,600 copies of the *Tender* first printing, and 20,870 copies of *Gatsby*.

The presence of the dust jacket is the key factor in determining the price of a modern first. The jacket is usually worth more than the book. Thus

American Book Prices Currents (ABPC), which reports auctions, records for 2000 an unjacketed *Tender Is the Night* for $300 and a copy in the "2nd state of dj" at $5250. *Bookman's Price Index* (BPI), which reports material offered in dealer catalogues, lists a copy of *Tender* in the "first issue dust jacket" offered at $50,000 in 2001–the top asking price for an uninscribed copy.

The BPI listings indicate that dealers did not identify the "state" or "issue" of *Tender* jackets before 1998. Dealer and auction catalogues are notoriously untrustworthy in the application of the terms "state" and "issue." There are no states or issues of the *Tender* jacket. There is the first printing of the jacket with front-flap blurbs by T.S. Eliot, H.L. Mencken, and Paul Rosenfeld; a later printing of the jacket replaces these with blurbs by Mary Colum, Gilbert Seldes, and Marjorie Kinnan Rawlings.

Inscriptions drive auction prices to record levels. "Inscription" is another abused term: it means that the author of the book wrote something in it that is more than a signature. "Inscription" does not mean "dedication." The dedication copy of *Tender*–the one inscribed to the Murphys–has not been found. In 2000 a *Tender*

in "worn and chipped first issue dust jacket" inscribed to Harold Ober brought $26,000 at auction and was subsequently catalogued by a dealer at $85,000 in 2001; an unjacketed copy inscribed to Barbara Trego Ballantyne brought $30,000 at auction in 2001. A copy in unidentified jacket, with a routine inscription to Donald Ogden Stewart, set the auction record for *Tender* in 2002 at $119,500.[2] Inscribed copies are not comparable. The survey of *Tender* prices provided here excludes inscriptions, except for illustrations.

The record of *Tender* prices replicates the rise of the novel's literary standing. It was a slow starter in the critplace and the marketplace, but it has moved up rapidly in the past decade. Most of the evidence in this survey is drawn from ABPC and BPI, supplemented by catalogues in the Bruccoli Collection of F. Scott Fitzgerald at the Thomas Cooper Library, University of South Carolina.

F. Scott Fitzgerald died on 20 December 1940. A copy of *Tender* was not sold at auction until 1951, when it brought $22. (APBC inconsistently noted dust jackets, which weakens the evidence.) The first copy stipulated as in jacket was auctioned for $18 in 1957. *Tender*

Inscription to the wife of Fitzgerald's Princeton friend Howard Ballantyne. Christie's (22 May 2001), #233.
The pre-sale estimate was $15,000–$20,000; this copy without jacket reached $30,000.

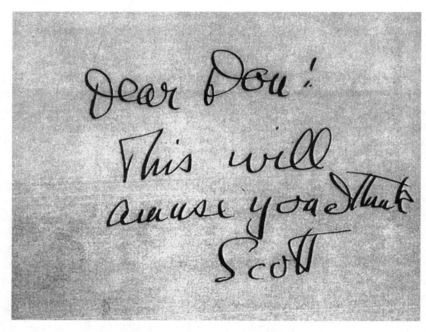

*Inscription to Donald Ogden Stewart. Christie's (11 October 2002), #91. The pre-sale estimate
was $30,000–$40,000; this copy with jacket reached $119,500.*

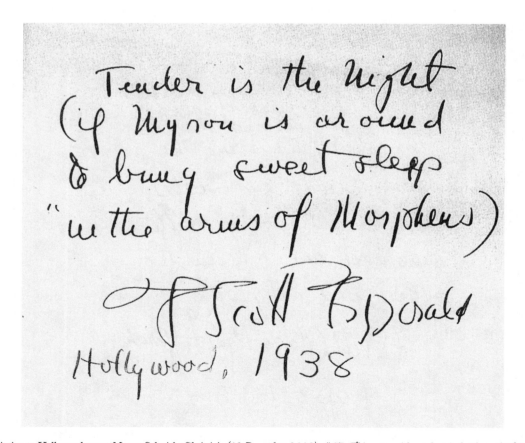

Inscription to Hollywood agent Myron Selznick. Christie's (13 December 2002), #97. This copy without dust jacket brought $12,000.

broke three figures in 1964, when a jacketed copy reached $130 at auction. This was the top price until a jacketed copy was catalogued by a dealer for $225 in 1973. Between 1978 and 2002 *Tender* prices climbed from $400 (BPI) to $850 (BPI 1983) to $1200 (BPI 1984) to $2400 (ABPC 1992) to $4500 (BPI 1994), to $5250 (BPI 2000) to $50,000 (BPI 2001), and then down to $37,500 in a 2002 dealer's catalogue. At the end of 2002, Between the Covers catalogue 98 listed a copy in the "first issue dustwrapper" at $50,000 with a copy of the "Second edition" (meaning the second printing) in a "second printing dustwrapper" for $7500. Fifty grand is much more than Fitzgerald made from *Tender* during his lifetime.

An undetermined number of *Tender* advance copies in wrappers were distributed—the only Fitzgerald book so treated during his lifetime—of which perhaps six survive. These should be the most desired copies of *Tender* in terms of precedence and scarcity, but buyers prefer the first printing in jacket. The first of the advance copies sold at auction brought $800 in 1975. Subsequent auction prices reached $4200 (ABPC 1996); a dealer catalogued a copy at $13,500 in 1991.

Christie's New York auctioned a set of *Tender* proofs on 20 November 1992 (#183). These proofs were set in book-page format from the serial installments, apparently in an attempt to expedite production of the book; but Fitzgerald revised and rewrote his novel between serialization and book publicaiton, rendering these proofs useless. They sold for $6000 to a non-institutional bidder and have not been traced.

The Brits have been slow to embrace *Tender Is the Night*. The first London auction price was £38 in 1968. Thereafter fourteen copies of the American first printing were catalogued by English dealers, with the top price of £110 (jacket not specified) in 1975. There is no sales record for the British first edition.

Young readers and collectors fall in love with *The Great Gatsby;* then they grow up to *Tender Is the Night*, which is not a novel for kids or cowards.

Notes

1. Poe's *Tamerlane*—a great rarity—brought $180,000 at auction in 1988 and $150,000 in 1990. Melville's *Moby-Dick*, a scarcer book than *Gatsby* currrently brings $10,000–$20,000, depending on condition; *The Whale* (3 volumes) brings $50,000–$100,000.

2. At this auction an uninscribed *Gatsby* in dust jacket reached the record price of $140,000. Hemingway's first book, *Three Stories and Ten Poems* (1923) brought $100,000.

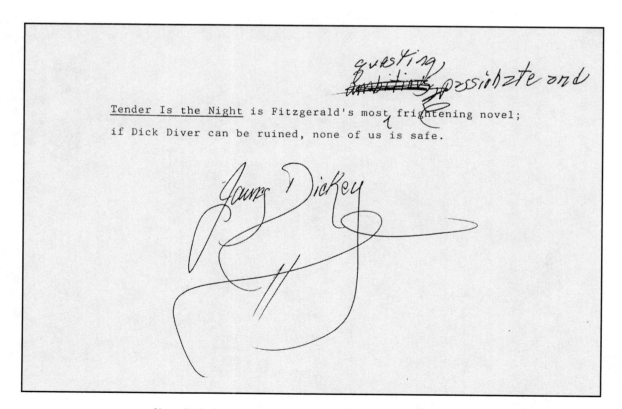

questing,
~~ambition~~ *passionate and*

Tender Is the Night is Fitzgerald's most frightening novel; if Dick Diver can be ruined, none of us is safe.

James Dickey

James Dickey's statement on Fitzgerald's greatest novel (Bruccoli Collection of Fitzgerald, Thomas Cooper Library, University of South Carolina)

Fitzgerald's Publications

This primary bibliography is reprinted from the "Checklist of Further Reading," prepared by Mary Jo Tate and Lisa Kerr and published in DLB 219: F. Scott Fitzgerald's The Great Gatsby.

Books

Fie! Fie! Fi-Fi! Cincinnati, New York & London: The John Church Co., 1914. Seventeen song lyrics.

The Evil Eye. Cincinnati, New York & London: The John Church Co., 1915. Seventeen song lyrics.

Safety First. Cincinnati, New York & London: The John Church Co., 1916. Twenty-one song lyrics.

This Side of Paradise. New York: Scribners, 1920; London: Collins, 1921. Novel.

Flappers and Philosophers. New York: Scribners, 1920; London: Collins, 1922. Stories.

The Beautiful and Damned. New York: Scribners, 1922; London: Collins, 1922. Novel.

Tales of the Jazz Age. New York: Scribners, 1922; London: Collins, 1923. Stories.

The Vegetable. New York: Scribners, 1923. Play.

The Great Gatsby. New York: Scribners, 1925; London: Chatto & Windus, 1926. Novel.

All the Sad Young Men. New York: Scribners, 1926. Stories.

John Jackson's Arcady, arranged for public reading by Lilian Holmes Strack. Boston: Baker, 1928. Story.

Tender Is the Night. New York: Scribners, 1934; London: Chatto & Windus, 1934. *Tender Is the Night,* "With the Author's Final Revisions." Ed. with intro. by Malcolm Cowley. New York: Scribners, 1951; London: Grey Walls, 1953. Novel.

Taps at Reveille. New York: Scribners, 1935. Stories.

The Last Tycoon. Ed. with intro. by Edmund Wilson. New York: Scribners, 1941; London: Grey Walls, 1949. Unfinished novel. With *The Great Gatsby* and 5 stories.

The Crack-Up. Ed. with intro. by Edmund Wilson. New York: New Directions, 1945; Harmondsworth, U.K.: Penguin, 1965. Essays, selections from the notebooks, and letters.

The Stories of F. Scott Fitzgerald. Ed. with intro. by Malcolm Cowley. New York: Scribners, 1951.

Afternoon of an Author. Ed. with intro. by Arthur Mizener. Princeton, N.J.: Princeton University Library, 1957; New York: Scribners, 1958; London: Bodley Head, 1958. Stories and essays.

The Pat Hobby Stories. Ed. with intro. by Arnold Gingrich. New York: Scribners, 1962; Harmondsworth, U.K.: Penguin, 1967.

The Apprentice Fiction of F. Scott Fitzgerald, 1909–1917. Ed. with intro. by John Kuehl. New Brunswick, N.J.: Rutgers University Press, 1965.

Dearly Beloved. Iowa City, Iowa: Windhover Press, 1970. Story.

Three Hours Between Planes. Agincourt, Ontario: The Book Society of Canada Limited, 1970. Story.

F. Scott Fitzgerald In His Own Time: A Miscellany. Ed. with intro. by Matthew J. Bruccoli and Jackson R. Bryer. Kent, Ohio: Kent State University Press, 1971.

The Basil and Josephine Stories. Ed. with intro. by Jackson R. Bryer and John Kuehl. New York: Scribners, 1973.

Bits of Paradise. Selected by Scottie Fitzgerald Smith and Matthew J. Bruccoli, with foreword by Smith and preface by Bruccoli. London: Bodley Head, 1973; New York: Scribners, 1974. Stories by Fitzgerald and 10 stories by Zelda Fitzgerald.

F. Scott Fitzgerald's Preface to This Side of Paradise. Ed. John R. Hopkins. Iowa City, Iowa: Windhover Press/Bruccoli Clark, 1975.

The Cruise of the Rolling Junk. Intro. by Matthew J. Bruccoli. Bloomfield Hills, Mich. & Columbia, S.C.: Bruccoli Clark, 1976. Three travel articles.

F. Scott Fitzgerald's Screenplay for Three Comrades by Erich Maria Remarque. Ed. with afterword by Matthew J. Bruccoli. Carbondale & Edwardsville, Ill.: Southern Illinois University Press, 1978.

F. Scott Fitzgerald's St. Paul Plays, 1911–1914. Ed. with intro. by Alan Margolies. Princeton, N.J.: Princeton University Library, 1978.

The Price Was High. Ed. with intro. by Matthew J. Bruccoli. New York & London: Harcourt Brace Jovanovich/Bruccoli Clark, 1979; London: Quartet, 1979. Stories.

Poems 1911–1940. Ed. Matthew J. Bruccoli; intro. by James Dickey. Bloomfield Hills, Mich. & Columbia, S.C.: Bruccoli Clark, 1981.

Babylon Revisited: The Screenplay. Intro. by Budd Schulberg. New York: Carroll & Graf, 1993.

Letters, Diaries, Notebooks

The Letters of F. Scott Fitzgerald. Ed. with intro. by Andrew Turnbull. New York: Scribners, 1963; London: Bodley Head, 1964.

Thoughtbook of Francis Scott Key Fitzgerald. Intro. by John Kuehl. Princeton, N.J.: Princeton University Library, 1965.

Dear Scott/Dear Max: The Fitzgerald-Perkins Correspondence. Ed. with intro. by John Kuehl and Jackson R. Bryer. New York: Scribners, 1971; London: Cassell, 1973.

As Ever, Scott Fitz–. Ed. with intro. by Matthew J. Bruccoli and Jennifer M. Atkinson, with foreword by Scottie Fitzgerald Smith. Philadelphia & New York: J. B. Lippincott, 1972; London: Woburn, 1973. The Fitzgerald/Harold Ober correspondence.

F. Scott Fitzgerald's Ledger: A Facsimile. Intro. by Matthew J. Bruccoli. Washington: NCR Microcard Books/ Bruccoli Clark, 1978.

The Notebooks of F. Scott Fitzgerald. Ed. with intro. by Matthew J. Bruccoli. New York & London: Harcourt Brace Jovanovich/Bruccoli Clark, 1978.

Correspondence of F. Scott Fitzgerald. Ed. with intro. by Matthew J. Bruccoli and Margaret M. Duggan, with Susan Walker. New York: Random House, 1980.

F. Scott Fitzgerald: A Life in Letters. Ed. with intro. by Matthew J. Bruccoli, with Judith S. Baughman. New York: Scribners, 1994.

Editions and Collections

The Portable F. Scott Fitzgerald. Ed. Dorothy Parker; intro. by John O'Hara. New York: Viking, 1945.

The Bodley Head F. Scott Fitzgerald, 6 vols. London: Bodley Head, 1958–1963.

The Stories of F. Scott Fitzgerald, 5 vols. Harmondsworth, U.K.: Penguin, 1962–1968.

F. Scott Fitzgerald on Writing. Ed. Larry W. Phillips. New York: Scribners, 1985.

The Short Stories of F. Scott Fitzgerald. Ed. with preface by Matthew J. Bruccoli. New York: Scribners, 1989; London: Scribners, 1991.

The Cambridge Edition of the Works of F. Scott Fitzgerald. Cambridge: Cambridge University Press, 1991– .

The Great Gatsby, ed. with intro. by Matthew J. Bruccoli, 1991; *The Love of the Last Tycoon: A Western,* ed. with intro. by Bruccoli, 1993.

Tender Is the Night. Ed. Matthew J. Bruccoli. London: Samuel Johnson, 1995. Facsimile of Bruccoli's emended copy of the first printing.

Tender Is the Night, Centennial Edition. Ed. with intro. and notes by Matthew J. Bruccoli. London: Everyman, 1996.

F. Scott Fitzgerald on Authorship. Ed. Matthew J. Bruccoli, with Judith S. Baughman. Columbia: University of South Carolina Press, 1996.

F. Scott Fitzgerald: The Jazz Age. Intro. by E. L. Doctorow. New York: New Directions, 1996.

Facsimiles

The Great Gatsby: A Facsimile of the Manuscript. Ed. with intro. by Matthew J. Bruccoli. Washington: Bruccoli Clark/NCR Microcard Books, 1973.

F. Scott Fitzgerald: Inscriptions. Columbia, S.C.: Matthew J. Bruccoli, 1988.

F. Scott Fitzgerald Manuscripts. Ed. Matthew J. Bruccoli. New York & London: Garland, 1990–1991. 18 vols.: *This Side of Paradise, The Beautiful and Damned, The Great Gatsby* galleys, *Tender Is the Night, The Last Tycoon, The Vegetable,* stories, and articles.

Fie! Fie! Fi-Fi! Intro. by Matthew J. Bruccoli. Columbia: University of South Carolina Press for the Thomas Cooper Library, 1996. Music score and previously unpublished acting script.

Trimalchio. Ed. with intro. by Matthew J. Bruccoli. Columbia: University of South Carolina Press, 2000.

Stories and Plays

First periodical appearance and first publication in a Fitzgerald collection.

"The Mystery of the Raymond Mortgage," *The St. Paul Academy Now and Then,* 2 (October 1909), 4–8; *Apprentice Fiction.*

"Reade, Substitute Right Half," *The St. Paul Academy Now and Then,* 2 (February 1910), 10–11; *Apprentice Fiction.*

"A Debt of Honor," *The St. Paul Academy Now and Then,* 2 (March 1910), 9–11; *Apprentice Fiction.*

"The Room with the Green Blinds," *The St. Paul Academy Now and Then,* 3 (June 1911), 6–9; *Apprentice Fiction.*

"A Luckless Santa Claus," *The Newman News,* 9 (Christmas 1912), 1–7; *Apprentice Fiction.*

"Pain and the Scientist," *The Newman News* (1913), 5–10; *Apprentice Fiction.*

"The Trail of the Duke," *The Newman News,* 9 (June 1913), 5–9; *Apprentice Fiction.*

"Shadow Laurels," *The Nassau Literary Magazine,* 71 (April 1915), 1–10; *Apprentice Fiction.*

"The Ordeal," *The Nassau Literary Magazine,* 71 (June 1915), 153–159; *Apprentice Fiction.*

"The Debutante," *The Nassau Literary Magazine*, 72 (January 1917), 241–252; *The Smart Set*, 60 (November 1919), 85–96; *Apprentice Fiction*.

"The Spire and the Gargoyle," *The Nassau Literary Magazine*, 72 (February 1917), 297–307; *Apprentice Fiction*.

"Tarquin of Cheapside," *The Nassau Literary Magazine*, 73 (April 1917), 13–18; *Apprentice Fiction*. Revised and expanded as "Tarquin of Cheapside," *The Smart Set*, 64 (February 1921), 43–46; *TJA*.

"Babes in the Woods," *The Nassau Literary Magazine*, 73 (May 1917), 55–64; *The Smart Set*, 60 (September 1919), 67–71; *Apprentice Fiction*.

"Sentiment—And the Use of Rouge," *The Nassau Literary Magazine*, 73 (June 1917), 107–123; *Apprentice Fiction*.

"The Pierian Springs and the Last Straw," *The Nassau Literary Magazine*, 73 (October 1917), 173–185; *Apprentice Fiction*.

"Porcelain and Pink (A One-Act Play)," *The Smart Set*, 61 (January 1920), 77–85; *TJA*.

"Benediction," *The Smart Set*, 61 (February 1920), 35–44; *F&P*.

"Dalyrimple Goes Wrong," *The Smart Set*, 61 (February 1920), 107–116; *F&P*.

"Head and Shoulders," *The Saturday Evening Post*, 192 (February 21, 1920), 16–17, 81–82, 85–86; *F&P*.

"Mister Icky The Quintessence of Quaintness in One Act," *The Smart Set*, 61 (March 1920), 93–98; *TJA*.

"Myra Meets His Family," *The Saturday Evening Post*, 192 (March 20, 1920), 40, 42, 44, 46, 49–50, 53; *Price*.

"The Camel's Back," *The Saturday Evening Post*, 192 (April 24, 1920), 16–17, 157, 161, 165; *TJA*.

"The Cut-Glass Bowl," *Scribner's Magazine*, 67 (May 1920), 582–592; *F&P*.

"Bernice Bobs Her Hair," *The Saturday Evening Post*, 192 (May 1, 1920), 14–15, 159, 163, 167; *F&P*.

"The Ice Palace," *The Saturday Evening Post*, 192 (May 22, 1920), 18–19, 163, 167, 170; *F&P*.

"The Offshore Pirate," *The Saturday Evening Post*, 192 (May 29, 1920), 10–11, 99, 101–102, 106, 109; *F&P*.

"The Four Fists," *Scribner's Magazine*, 67 (June 1920), 669–680; *F&P*.

"The Smilers," *The Smart Set*, 62 (June 1920), 107–111; *Price*.

"May Day," *The Smart Set*, 62 (July 1920), 3–32; *TJA*.

"The Jelly-Bean," *Metropolitan Magazine*, 52 (October 1920), 15–16, 63–67; *TJA*.

"The Lees of Happiness," *Chicago Sunday Tribune* (December 12, 1920), Blue Ribbon Fiction Section, 1, 3, 7; *TJA*.

"His Russet Witch," *Metropolitan Magazine*, 53 (February 1921), 11–13, 46–51; in *TJA* as "'O Russet Witch!'"

"The Far Seeing Skeptics," *The Smart Set*, 67 (February 1922), 48.

"The Popular Girl," *The Saturday Evening Post*, 194 (February 11 & 18, 1922), 3–5, 82, 84, 86, 89; 18–19, 105–106, 109–110; *Bits*.

"Two for a Cent," *Metropolitan Magazine*, 55 (April 1922), 23–26, 93–95; *Price*.

"The Curious Case of Benjamin Button," *Collier's*, 69 (May 27, 1922), 5–6, 22–28; *TJA*.

"The Diamond as Big as the Ritz," *The Smart Set*, 68 (June 1922), 5–29; *TJA*.

"Winter Dreams," *Metropolitan Magazine*, 56 (December 1922), 11–15, 98, 100–102, 104–107; *ASYM*.

"Dice, Brass Knuckles & Guitar," *Hearst's International*, 43 (May 1923), 8–13, 145–149; *Price*.

"Hot & Cold Blood," *Hearst's International*, 64 (August 1923), 80–84, 150–151; *ASYM*.

"Gretchen's Forty Winks," *The Saturday Evening Post*, 196 (March 15, 1924), 14–15, 128, 130, 132; *ASYM*.

"Diamond Dick and the First Law of Woman," *Hearst's International*, 45 (April 1924), 58–63, 134, 136; *Price*.

"The Third Casket," *The Saturday Evening Post*, 196 (May 31, 1924), 8–9, 78; *Price*.

"Absolution," *The American Mercury*, 2 (June 1924), 141–149; *ASYM*.

"Rags Martin-Jones and the Pr-nce of W-les," *McCall's*, 51 (July 1924), 6–7, 32, 48, 50; *ASYM*.

"'The Sensible Thing,'" *Liberty*, 1 (July 5, 1924), 10–14; *ASYM*.

"The Unspeakable Egg," *The Saturday Evening Post*, 197 (July 12, 1924), 12–13, 125–126, 129; *Price*.

"John Jackson's Arcady," *The Saturday Evening Post*, 197 (July 26, 1924), 8–9, 100, 102, 105; *Price*.

"The Baby Party," *Hearst's International*, 47 (February 1925), 32–37; *ASYM*.

"The Pusher-in-the-Face," *Woman's Home Companion*, 52 (February 1925), 27–28, 143–144; *Price*.

"Love in the Night," *The Saturday Evening Post*, 197 (March 14, 1925), 18–19, 68, 70; *Bits*.

"One of My Oldest Friends," *Woman's Home Companion*, 52 (September 1925), 7–8, 120, 122; *Price*.

"The Adjuster," *Redbook*, 45 (September 1925), 47–51, 144–148; *ASYM*.

"A Penny Spent," *The Saturday Evening Post*, 198 (October 10, 1925), 8–9, 160, 164, 166; *Bits*.

"Not in the Guidebook," *Woman's Home Companion*, 52 (November 1925), 9–11, 135–136; *Price*.

"The Rich Boy," *Redbook*, 46 (January & February 1926), 27–32, 144, 146; 75–79, 122, 124–126; *ASYM*.

"Presumption," *The Saturday Evening Post*, 198 (January 9, 1926), 3–5, 226, 228–229, 233–234; *Price*.

"The Adolescent Marriage," *The Saturday Evening Post*, 198 (March 6, 1926), 6–7, 229–230, 233–234; *Price*.

"The Dance," *Redbook*, 47 (June 1926), 39–43, 134, 136, 138; *Bits*.

"Your Way and Mine," *Woman's Home Companion,* 54 (May 1927), 7–8, 61, 64, 67–68; *Price.*

"Jacob's Ladder," *The Saturday Evening Post,* 200 (August 20, 1927), 3–5, 57–58, 63–64; *Bits.*

"The Love Boat," *The Saturday Evening Post,* 200 (October 8, 1927), 8–9, 134, 139, 141; *Price.*

"A Short Trip Home," *The Saturday Evening Post,* 200 (December 17, 1927), 6–7, 55, 57–58; *TAR.*

"The Bowl," *The Saturday Evening Post,* 200 (January 21, 1928), 6–7, 93–94, 97, 100; *Price.*

"Magnetism," *The Saturday Evening Post,* 200 (March 3, 1928), 5–7, 74, 76, 78; *Stories.*

"The Scandal Detectives," *The Saturday Evening Post,* 200 (April 28, 1928), 3–4, 178, 181–182, 185; *TAR; B&J.*

"A Night at the Fair," *The Saturday Evening Post,* 201 (July 21, 1928), 8–9, 129–130, 133; *B&J.*

"The Freshest Boy," *The Saturday Evening Post,* 201 (July 28, 1928), 6–7, 68, 70, 73; *TAR; B&J.*

"He Thinks He's Wonderful," *The Saturday Evening Post,* 201 (September 29, 1928), 6–7, 117–118, 121; *TAR; B&J.*

"Outside the Cabinet-Maker's," *Century Magazine,* 117 (December 1928), 241–244.

"The Captured Shadows," *The Saturday Evening Post,* 201 (December 29, 1928), 12–13, 48, 51; *TAR; B&J.*

"The Perfect Life," *The Saturday Evening Post,* 201 (January 5, 1929), 8–9, 113, 115, 118; *TAR; B&J.*

"The Last of the Belles," *The Saturday Evening Post,* 201 (March 2, 1929), 18–19, 75, 78; *TAR.*

"Forging Ahead," *The Saturday Evening Post,* 201 (March 30, 1929), 12–13, 101, 105; *B&J.*

"Basil and Cleopatra," *The Saturday Evening Post,* 201 (April 27, 1929), 14–15, 166, 170, 173; *AOAA; B&J.*

"The Rough Crossing," *The Saturday Evening Post,* 201 (June 8, 1929), 12–13, 66, 70, 75; *Stories.*

"Majesty," *The Saturday Evening Post,* 202 (July 13, 1929), 6–7, 57–58, 61–62; *TAR.*

"At Your Age," *The Saturday Evening Post,* 202 (August 17, 1929), 6–7, 79–80; *Price.*

"The Swimmers," *The Saturday Evening Post,* 202 (October 19, 1929), 12–13, 150, 152, 154; *Bits.*

"Two Wrongs," *The Saturday Evening Post,* 202 (January 18, 1930), 8–9, 107, 109, 113; *TAR.*

"First Blood," *The Saturday Evening Post,* 202 (April 5, 1930), 8–9, 81, 84; *TAR; B&J.*

"A Nice Quiet Place," *The Saturday Evening Post,* 202 (May 31, 1930), 8–9, 96, 101, 103; *TAR; B&J.*

"The Bridal Party," *The Saturday Evening Post,* 203 (August 9, 1930), 10–11, 109–110, 112, 114; *Stories.*

"A Woman with a Past," *The Saturday Evening Post,* 203 (September 6, 1930), 8–9, 133–134, 137; *TAR; B&J.*

"One Trip Abroad," *The Saturday Evening Post,* 203 (October 11, 1930), 6–7, 48, 51, 53–54, 56; *AOAA.*

"A Snobbish Story," *The Saturday Evening Post,* 203 (November 29, 1930), 6–7, 36, 38, 40, 42; *B&J.*

"The Hotel Child," *The Saturday Evening Post,* 203 (January 31, 1931), 8–9, 69, 72, 75; *Bits.*

"Babylon Revisited," *The Saturday Evening Post,* 203 (February 21, 1931), 3–5, 82–84; *TAR.*

"Indecision," *The Saturday Evening Post,* 203 (May 16, 1931), 12–13, 56, 59, 62; *Price.*

"A New Leaf," *The Saturday Evening Post,* 204 (July 4, 1931), 12–13, 90–91; *Bits.*

"Emotional Bankruptcy," *The Saturday Evening Post,* 204 (August 15, 1931), 8–9, 60, 65; *B&J.*

"Between Three and Four," *The Saturday Evening Post,* 204 (September 5, 1931), 8–9, 69, 72; *Price.*

"A Change of Class," *The Saturday Evening Post,* 204 (September 26, 1931), 6–7, 37–38, 41; *Price.*

"A Freeze-Out," *The Saturday Evening Post,* 204 (December 19, 1931), 6–7, 84–85, 88–89; *Price.*

"Six of One–," *Redbook,* 58 (February 1932), 22–25, 84, 86, 88; *Price.*

"Diagnosis," *The Saturday Evening Post,* 204 (February 20, 1932), 18–19, 90, 92; *Price.*

"Flight and Pursuit," *The Saturday Evening Post,* 204 (May 14, 1932), 16–17, 53, 57; *Price.*

"Family in the Wind," *The Saturday Evening Post,* 204 (June 4, 1932), 3–5, 71–73; *TAR.*

"The Rubber Check," *The Saturday Evening Post,* 205 (August 6, 1932), 6–7, 41–42, 44–45; *Price.*

"What a Handsome Pair!" *The Saturday Evening Post,* 205 (August 27, 1932), 16–17, 61, 63–64; *Price.*

"Crazy Sunday," *The American Mercury,* 27 (October 1932), 209–220; *TAR.*

"One Interne," *The Saturday Evening Post,* 205 (November 5, 1932), 6–7, 86, 88–90; *TAR.*

"On Schedule," *The Saturday Evening Post,* 205 (March 18, 1933), 16–17, 71, 74, 77, 79; *Price.*

"More Than Just a House," *The Saturday Evening Post,* 205 (June 24, 1933), 8–9, 27, 30, 34; *Price.*

"I Got Shoes," *The Saturday Evening Post,* 206 (September 23, 1933), 14–15, 56, 58; *Price.*

"The Family Bus," *The Saturday Evening Post,* 206 (November 4, 1933), 8–9, 57, 61–62, 65–66; *Price.*

"No Flowers," *The Saturday Evening Post,* 207 (July 21, 1934), 10–11, 57–58, 60; *Price.*

"New Types," *The Saturday Evening Post,* 207 (September 22, 1934), 16–17, 74, 76, 78–79, 81; *Price.*

"In the Darkest Hour," *Redbook,* 63 (October 1934), 15–19, 94–98; *Price.*

"Her Last Case," *The Saturday Evening Post,* 207 (November 3, 1934), 10–11, 59, 61–62, 64; *Price.*

"The Fiend," *Esquire,* 3 (January 1935), 23, 173–174; *TAR.*

"The Night before Chancellorsville," *Esquire,* 3 (February 1935), 24, 165; *TAR.*

"Shaggy's Morning," *Esquire,* 3 (May 1935), 26, 160.

"The Count of Darkness," *Redbook,* 65 (June 1935), 20–23, 68, 70, 72.

"The Intimate Strangers," *McCall's,* 62 (June 1935), 12–14, 36, 38, 40, 42, 44; *Price.*

"The Passionate Eskimo," *Liberty,* 12 (June 8, 1935), 10–14, 17–18.

"Zone of Accident," *The Saturday Evening Post,* 208 (July 13, 1935), 8–9, 47, 49, 51–52; *Price.*

"The Kingdom in the Dark," *Redbook,* 65 (August 1935), 58–62, 64, 66–68.

"Fate in Her Hands," *American Magazine,* 121 (April 1936), 56–59, 168–172; *Price.*

"Image on the Heart," *McCall's,* 63 (April 1936), 7–9, 52, 54, 57–58, 62; *Price.*

"Too Cute for Words," *The Saturday Evening Post,* 208 (April 18, 1936), 16–18, 87, 90, 93; *Price.*

"Three Acts of Music," *Esquire,* 5 (May 1936), 39, 210; *Price.*

"The Ants at Princeton," *Esquire,* 5 (June 1936), 35, 210.

"Inside the House," *The Saturday Evening Post,* 208 (June 13, 1936), 18–19, 32, 34, 36; *Price.*

"An Author's Mother," *Esquire,* 6 (September 1936), 36; *Price.*

"'I Didn't Get Over,'" *Esquire,* 6 (October 1936), 45, 194–195; *AOAA.*

"'Send Me In, Coach,'" *Esquire,* 6 (November 1936), 55, 218–221.

"An Alcoholic Case," *Esquire,* 6 [7] (February 1937), 32, 109; *Stories.*

"'Trouble,'" *The Saturday Evening Post,* 209 (March 6, 1937), 14–15, 81, 84, 86, 88–89; *Price.*

"The Honor of the Goon," *Esquire,* 7 (June 1937), 53, 216.

"The Long Way Out," *Esquire,* 8 (September 1937), 45, 193; *Stories.*

"The Guest in Room Nineteen," *Esquire,* 8 (October 1937), 56, 209; *Price.*

"In the Holidays," *Esquire,* 8 (December 1937), 82, 184, 186; *Price.*

"Financing Finnegan," *Esquire,* 9 (January 1938), 41, 180, 182, 184; *Stories.*

"Design in Plaster," *Esquire,* 12 (November 1939), 51, 169; *AOAA.*

"The Lost Decade," *Esquire,* 12 (December 1939), 113, 228; *Stories.*

"Strange Sanctuary," *Liberty,* 16 (December 9, 1939), 15–20.

"Pat Hobby's Christmas Wish," *Esquire,* 13 (January 1940), 45, 170–172; *PH.*

"A Man in the Way," *Esquire,* 13 (February 1940), 40, 109; *PH.*

"'Boil Some Water—Lots of It,'" *Esquire,* 13 (March 1940), 30, 145, 147; *PH.*

"Teamed with Genius," *Esquire,* 13 (April 1940), 44, 195–197; *PH.*

"Pat Hobby and Orson Welles," *Esquire,* 13 (May 1940), 38, 198–199; *PH.*

"Pat Hobby's Secret," *Esquire,* 13 (June 1940), 30, 107; *PH.*

"The End of Hate," *Collier's,* 105 (June 22, 1940), 9–10, 63–64; *Price.*

"Pat Hobby, Putative Father," *Esquire,* 14 (July 1940), 36, 172–174; *PH.*

"The Homes of the Stars," *Esquire,* 14 (August 1940), 28, 120–121; *PH.*

"Pat Hobby Does His Bit," *Esquire,* 14 (September 1940), 41, 104; *PH.*

"Pat Hobby's Preview," *Esquire,* 14 (October 1940), 30, 118, 120; *PH.*

"No Harm Trying," *Esquire,* 14 (November 1940), 30, 151–153; *PH.*

"A Patriotic Short," *Esquire,* 14 (December 1940), 62, 269; *PH.*

"On the Trail of Pat Hobby," *Esquire,* 15 (January 1941), 35, 126; *PH.*

"Fun in an Artist's Studio," *Esquire,* 15 (February 1941), 64, 112; *PH.*

Elgin, Paul [pseud.]. "On an Ocean Wave," *Esquire,* 15 (February 1941), 59, 141; *Price.*

"Two Old-Timers," *Esquire,* 15 (March 1941), 53, 143; *PH.*

"Mightier Than the Sword," *Esquire,* 15 (April 1941), 36, 183; *PH.*

"Pat Hobby's College Days," *Esquire,* 15 (May 1941), 55, 168–169; *PH.*

"The Woman from Twenty-One," *Esquire,* 15 (June 1941), 29, 164; *Price.*

"Three Hours Between Planes," *Esquire,* 16 (July 1941), 41, 138–139; *Stories.*

"Gods of Darkness," *Redbook,* 78 (November 1941), 30–33, 88–91.

"The Broadcast We Almost Heard Last September," *Furioso,* 3 (Fall 1947), 8–10.

"News of Paris—Fifteen Years Ago," *Furioso,* 3 (Winter 1947), 5–10; *AOAA.*

"Discard," *Harper's Bazaar,* 82 (January 1948), 103, 143–144, 146, 148–149; *Price.*

"The World's Fair," *The Kenyon Review,* 10 (Autumn 1948), 567–568.

"Last Kiss," *Collier's,* 123 (April 16, 1949), 16–17, 34, 38, 41, 43–44; *Bits.*

"That Kind of Party," *The Princeton University Library Chronicle,* 12 (Summer 1951), 167–180; *B&J.*

"Dearly Beloved," *Fitzgerald/Hemingway Annual* (1969), 1–3; *Bits.*

"Lo, the Poor Peacock!" *Esquire,* 76 (September 1971), 154–158; *Price.*

"On Your Own," *Esquire,* 91 (January 30, 1979), 55–67; *Price.*

"A Full Life," *The Princeton University Library Chronicle,* 49 (Winter 1988), 167–172.

Articles and Essays

First periodical appearance and first publication in a Fitzgerald collection.

"S.P.A. Men in College Athletics," *The St. Paul Academy Now and Then,* 3 (December 1910), 7.

Untitled news feature about school election, *The Newman News* (1912), 18.

Untitled news feature about school dance, *The Newman News* (1913), 18.

"Who's Who—and Why," *The Saturday Evening Post,* 193 (September 18, 1920), 42, 61; *AOAA.*

"Three Cities," *Brentano's Book Chat,* 1 (September–October 1921), 15, 28; *In His Own Time.*

"What I Think and Feel at Twenty-five," *American Magazine,* 94 (September 1922), 16, 17, 136–140; *In His Own Time.*

"How I Would Sell My Book If I Were a Bookseller," *Bookseller and Stationer,* 18 (January 15, 1923), 8; *In His Own Time.*

"10 Best Books I Have Read," *Jersey City Evening Journal* (April 24, 1923), 9.

"Imagination—and a Few Mothers," *Ladies' Home Journal,* 40 (June 1923), 21, 80–81.

"The Cruise of the Rolling Junk," *Motor,* 41 (February, March, April 1924), 24–25, 58, 62, 64, 66; 42–43, 58, 72, 74, 76; 40–41, 58, 66, 68, 70.

"'Why Blame It on the Poor Kiss If the Girl Veteran of Many Petting Parties Is Prone to Affairs After Marriage?'" *New York American* (February 24, 1924), LII-3; *In His Own Time.*

"Does a Moment of Revolt Come Sometime to Every Married Man?" *McCall's,* 51 (March 1924), 21, 36; *In His Own Time.*

"What Kind of Husbands Do 'Jimmies' Make?" *Baltimore American* (March 30, 1924), ME-7; *In His Own Time.*

"How to Live on $36,000 a Year," *The Saturday Evening Post,* 196 (April 5, 1924), 22, 94, 97; *AOAA.*

"'Wait Till You Have Children of Your Own!'" *Woman's Home Companion,* 51 (July 1924), 13, 105; *In His Own Time.*

"How to Live on Practically Nothing a Year," *The Saturday Evening Post,* 197 (September 20, 1924), 17, 165–166, 169–170; *AOAA.*

"Our Young Rich Boys," *McCall's,* 53 (October 1925), 12, 42, 69; *In His Own Time.*

"How to Waste Material: A Note on My Generation," *The Bookman,* 63 (May 1926), 262–265; *AOAA.*

"Princeton," *College Humor,* 13 (December 1927), 28–29, 130–131; *AOAA.*

"Ten Years in the Advertising Business," *The Princeton Alumni Weekly,* 29 (February 22, 1929), 585; *AOAA.*

"A Short Autobiography (With Acknowledgments to Nathan)," *The New Yorker,* 5 (May 25, 1929), 22–23; *In His Own Time.*

"Girls Believe in Girls," *Liberty,* 7 (February 8, 1930), 22–24; *In His Own Time.*

"Echoes of the Jazz Age," *Scribner's Magazine,* 90 (November 1931), 459–465; *CU.*

"One Hundred False Starts," *The Saturday Evening Post,* 205 (March 4, 1933), 13, 65–66; *AOAA.*

"Ring," *The New Republic,* 76 (October 11, 1933), 254–255; *CU.*

"Introduction," *The Great Gatsby.* New York: Modern Library, 1934; *In His Own Time.*

"My Ten Favorite Plays," *New York Sun* (September 10, 1934), 19; *FSF on Authorship.*

"Sleeping and Waking," *Esquire,* 2 (December 1934), 34, 159–160; *CU.*

"The Crack-Up," *Esquire,* 5 (February 1936), 41, 164; *CU.*

"Pasting It Together," *Esquire,* 5 (March 1936), 35, 182–183; *CU.*

"Handle with Care," *Esquire,* 5 (April 1936), 39, 202; *CU.*

"Author's House," *Esquire,* 6 (July 1936), 40, 108; *AOAA.*

"Afternoon of an Author," *Esquire,* 6 (August 1936), 35, 170; *AOAA.*

"Early Success," *American Cavalcade,* 1 (October 1937), 74–79; *CU.*

"Foreword," *Colonial and Historical Homes of Maryland,* by Don Swann. Baltimore: Etchcrafters Art Guild, 1939; *In His Own Time.*

"The High Cost of Macaroni," *Interim,* 4, nos. 1–2, (1954), 6–15.

"My Generation," *Esquire,* 70 (October 1968), 119, 121, 123; *Profile of F. Scott Fitzgerald.*

Works about *Tender Is the Night* and Fitzgerald

This secondary bibliography is adapted from the "Checklist of Further Reading," prepared by Mary Jo Tate and Lisa Kerr and published in DLB 219: F. Scott Fitzgerald's *The Great Gatsby.*

Selected Works about *Tender Is the Night*

Bibliographies

Lewis, Christopher D. "*Tender Is the Night* and the Critics: From 1982 to the Present." *Bulletin of Bibliography,* 58 (June 2001), 109–124.

Wenke, Joseph. "*Tender Is the Night:* A Cross-Referenced Bibliography." *Critical Essays on F. Scott Fitzgerald's Tender Is the Night,* ed. by Milton R. Stern. Boston: Hall, 1986, 247–269.

Concordance

Stebbins, Todd Harrison. "*Tender Is the Night*': The Last Love Battle, with a Newly Generated Concordance (Volumes I–IV)." Dissertation. University of South Carolina, 1993.

Critical Studies

Bruccoli, Matthew J. *The Composition of Tender Is the Night.* Pittsburgh: University of Pittsburgh Press, 1963. Critical study of the writing of the novel.

Bruccoli, with Judith S. Baughman. *Reader's Companion to F. Scott Fitzgerald's Tender Is the Night.* Columbia: University of South Carolina Press, 1996. Critical study.

Metzger, Charles R. *F. Scott Fitzgerald's Psychiatric Novel: Nicole's Case, Dick's Case.* American University Studies 24. American Literature. Volume 13. New York: Peter Lang, 1989.

Stern, Milton R. *Tender Is the Night: The Broken Universe.* Boston: Twayne, 1994. Critical study.

Collections of Essays

LaHood, Marvin J., ed. *Tender Is the Night: Essays in Criticism.* Bloomington: Indiana University Press, 1969.

Stern, Milton R., ed. *Critical Essays on Tender Is the Night.* Boston: Hall, 1986.

Book Sections and Articles

Anderson, George Parker. "F. Scott Fitzgerald, Emile Zola, and the Stripping of 'Jacob's Ladder' for *Tender Is the Night.*" *The Professions of Authorship,* ed. by Richard Layman and Joel Myerson. Columbia: University of South Carolina Press, 1996, 169–183. Critical study of the writing of the novel.

Beaver, Harold. "*Tender Is the Night:* Fitzgerald's Portrait of a Gentleman." *Scott Fitzgerald: The Promises of Life,* ed. by Robert A. Lee. London: Vision; New York: St. Martin's Press, 1989, 69–73. Critical article.

Berman, Jeffrey. "*Tender Is the Night:* Fitzgerald's 'A Psychology of Psychiatrists.'" *The Talking Cure: Literary Representations of Psychoanalysis.* New York: New York University Press, 1985. Freudian interpretation.

Boker, Pamela A. "Beloved Illness: Transference Love as Romantic Pathology in F. Scott Fitzgerald's *Tender Is the Night.*" *Literature and Medicine,* 11 (1992), 294–319. Psychoanalytic interpretation.

Bradbury, Malcolm. "Historian of Interlocking Worlds." *Readings on F. Scott Fitzgerald,* ed. by Katie Koster. San Diego: Greenhaven, 1998, 42–52. Critical article.

Brand, Dana. "Tourism and Modernity in *Tender Is the Night.*" *F. Scott Fitzgerald: New Perspectives,* ed. by Jackson R. Bryer, Alan Margolies, and Ruth Prigozy. Athens: University of Georgia Press, 2000, 130–141. Critical article on imagery in novel.

Buehrer, David. "Diving into the Wreck, Again: The Psychological Fragmentation of Character in Fitzgerald's *Tender Is the Night.*" *Journal of Evolutionary Psychology,* 13 (1992), 281–295.

Callahan, John F. "'France was a Land': F. Scott Fitzgerald's Expatriate Theme in *Tender Is the Night.*" *French Connections: Hemingway and Fitzgerald Abroad,* ed. by Gerald J. Kennedy and Bryer. New York: St. Martin's Press, 1999, 173–186. Critical article.

Collins, Angus P. "F. Scott Fitzgerald: Homosexuality and the Genesis of *Tender Is the Night*." *Journal of Modern Literature*, 13 (1986), 167–171. Critical article on the Melarky drafts.

Comley, Nancy R. "Madwomen on the Riviera: The Fitzgeralds, Hemingway, and the Matter of Modernism." *French Connections: Hemingway and Fitzgerald Abroad*, ed. by Kennedy and Bryer. New York: St. Martin's Press, 1999, 277–296. Biographical and critical article.

Doherty, William E. "*Tender Is the Night* and the 'Ode to a Nightingale.'" *Explorations of Literature*, ed. by Rima D. Reck. Baton Rouge: Louisiana State University Press, 1966, 100–114. Reprinted, LaHood, Stern. Critical article.

Ellerby, Janet M. "Conversation and the Fitzgeralds: Conflict or Collaboration?" *The Text and Beyond: Essays in Literary Linguistics*, ed. by Cynthia Goldin Bernstein. Tuscaloosa: University of Alabama Press, 1994, 156–176. Biographical and critical article.

Fetterley, Judith. "Who Killed Dick Diver?: The Sexual Politics in *Tender Is the Night*." *Mosaic*, 17 (1984), 111–128. Critical article.

Fleming, Robert E. "*The Garden of Eden* as a Response of *Tender Is the Night*." *MidAmerica*, 25 (1998), 84–95. Critical article.

Fryer, Sarah Beebe. "Aftermath of Betrayal: Incest, Madness, and Transference in *Tender Is the Night*." *Fitzgerald's New Woman: Harbingers of Change*. Ann Arbor: University of Michigan Press, 1988, 71–91. Chapter in critical study.

Fryer. "Women on the Threshold of Freedom: Nicole Warren Diver and Alabama Beggs Knight." *Fitzgerald's New Woman: Harbingers of Change*. Ann Arbor: University of Michigan Press, 1988, 57–70. Chapter in critical study.

Gajdusek, Robert E. "The Metamorphosis of Fitzgerald's Dick Diver and Its Hemingway Analogs." *French Connections: Hemingway and Fitzgerald Abroad*, ed. by Kennedy and Bryer. New York: St. Martin's Press, 1999, 297–316. Critical article.

Godden, Richard. "Money Makes Manners Make Man Make Woman: *Tender Is the Night*, a Familiar Romance?" *Literature and History*, 12 (1986), 16–37.

Greenberg, Bruce L. "Fitzgerald's 'Figured Curtain': Personality and History in Tender Is the Night." *Fitzgerald/Hemingway Annual* (1978), 105–136. Critical article.

Haegert, John. "Repression and Counter-Memory in *Tender Is the Night*," *Essays in Literature*, 21 (1994),

97–115. Critical article on the narrative structure of original edition.

Jackson, Timothy P. "Back to the Garden or into the Night: Hemingway and Fitzgerald on Fall and Redemption." *Christianity and Literature*, 39 (1990), 423–441. Critical comparison of Hemingway's *The Garden of Eden* and *Tender Is the Night*.

Kruse, Horst. "Teaching Fitzgerald's Tender Is the Night: The Opening and the Closing Chapters of a Great Novel." *Literatur in Wissenschaft und Unterricht*, 31 (1998), 251–267. Critical article.

Kuehl, John. "Flakes of Black Snow: 'One Trip Abroad' Reconsidered." *New Essays on F. Scott Fitzgerald's Neglected Stories*, ed. by Bryer. Columbia: University of Missouri Press, 1996, 175–188. Examines links between the story and *Tender Is the Night*.

Margolies, Alan. "Climbing 'Jacob's Ladder.'" *New Essays on F. Scott Fitzgerald's Neglected Stories*, ed. by Bryer. Columbia: University of Missouri Press, 1996, 89–103. Examines links between the story and *Tender Is the Night*.

Margolies. "'Particular Rhythms' and Other Influences: Hemingway and *Tender Is the Night*." *Hemingway in Italy and Other Essays*, ed. by Robert W. Lewis. New York: Praeger, 1990. Examines influence of Hemingway on *Tender Is the Night*.

Merrill, Robert. "*Tender Is the Night* as a Tragic Action." *Texas Studies in Literature and Language*, 25, no. 4 (1983), 597–615. Critical article.

Montiero, George. "Last Heroes in Fitzgerald and Hemingway: *Tender Is the Night, The Last Tycoon*, and *Across the River and into the Trees*." *Hemingway Review*, 16 (Spring 1997), 61–72. Examines influence of *Tender Is the Night* on Hemingway.

Nattermann, Udo. "Nicole Diver's Monologue: A Close Examination of a Key Segment." *Massachusetts Studies in English*, 10 (1986), 213–228. Critical article.

Nowlin, Michael. "'The World's Rarest Work': Modernism and Masculinity in Fitzgerald's *Tender Is the Night*." *College Literature*, 25, no. 2 (1998), 58–77. Critical article.

Roulston, Robert. "'The Swimmers': Strokes against the Current." *New Essays on F. Scott Fitzgerald's Neglected Stories*, ed. by Bryer. Columbia: University of Missouri Press, 1996, 151–164. Examines links between the story and *Tender Is the Night*.

Scherr, Barry J. "Lawrence, Keats and *Tender Is the Night*: Loss of Self and 'Love Battle' Motifs." *Recovering Literature*, 14 (1986), 7–17. Critical article.

Silhol, Robert. "*Tender Is the Night* or the Rape of the Child." *Literature and Psychology*, 40 (1994), 40–63. Critical article.

Smith, Felipe. "The Figure on the Bed: Difference and American Destiny in *Tender Is the Night*." *French Connections: Hemingway and Fitzgerald Abroad,* ed. by Kennedy and Bryer. New York: St. Martin's Press, 1999, 187–213. Critical article.

Tavernier-Courbin, Jacqueline. "The Influence of France on Nicole Diver's Recovery in *Tender Is the Night*." *French Connections: Hemingway and Fitzgerald Abroad,* ed. by Kennedy and Bryer. New York: St. Martin's Press, 1999, 215–232. Critical article.

Tavernier-Courbin. "Sensuality as Key to Characterization in *Tender Is the Night*." *English Studies in Canada,* 9 (1983), 452–467. Critical article.

Toles, George. "The Metaphysics of Style in *Tender Is the Night*." *American Literature,* 62 (1990), 423–444. Critical article.

Washington, Bryan R. "Communities of Exiles: *Tender Is the Night*." *The Politics of Exile: Ideology in Henry James, F. Scott Fitzgerald, and James Baldwin.* Boston: Northeastern University Press, 1995, 55–69. Chapter in critical study.

Wexelblatt, Robert. "*Tender Is the Night* and History." *Essays in Literature,* 17 (1990): 232–241. Critical article.

Literary and Social-History Backgrounds

Baughman, Judith S., ed. *American Decades: 1920–1929.* Detroit: Manly/Gale, 1995.

Berg, Scott. *Max Perkins: Editor of Genius.* New York: Congdon/Dutton, 1978.

Bondi, Victor, ed. *American Decades: 1930–1939.* Detroit: Manly/Gale, 1995.

Bruccoli, Matthew J., and Robert W. Trogdon, eds. *American Expatriate Writers: Paris in the Twenties.* Detroit: Bruccoli Clark Layman/Gale Research, 1997. Dictionary of Literary Biography Documentary Series 15.

Bruccoli, Matthew J., ed., with Robert W. Trogdon. *The Only Thing That Counts: The Ernest Hemingway/Maxwell Perkins Correspondence.* New York: Scribners, 1996.

Callaghan, Morley. *That Summer in Paris.* New York: Coward-McCann, 1963.

Cowley, Malcolm. *Exile's Return: A Literary Odyssey of the 1920s.* New York: Norton, 1934. Revised edition, New York: Viking, 1951.

Cowley. *A Second Flowering: Works and Days of the Last Generation.* New York: Viking, 1973.

Cowley. *Unshaken Friend: A Profile of Maxwell Perkins.* Boulder, Colo.: Roberts Rinehart, 1985.

Cowley, Malcolm, and Robert Cowley, eds. *Fitzgerald and the Jazz Age.* New York: Scribners, 1966.

Delaney, John, ed. *The House of Scribner, 1905–1930.* Detroit: Bruccoli Clark Layman/Gale Research, 1997. Dictionary of Literary Biography Documentary Series 16.

Donnelly, Honoria M. *Sara and Gerald.* New York: Times Books, 1982.

Donnelly, Honoria Murphy, and Richard N. Billings. *Sara and Gerald: Villa America and After.* New York: Times Books, 1982.

Hoffman, Frederick J. *The Twenties: American Writing in the Postwar Decade.* Revised edition, New York: Collier, 1962.

LeVot, André. "Fitzgerald in Paris." *Fitzgerald/Hemingway Annual* (1973), 49–68.

Meyers, Jeffrey. *Edmund Wilson: A Biography.* Boston: Houghton Mifflin, 1995.

Reynolds, Michael. *Hemingway: The Paris Years.* Oxford & New York: Blackwell, 1989.

Rood, Karen Lane, ed., with foreword by Malcolm Cowley. *American Writers in Paris, 1920–1939; Dictionary of Literary Biography,* vol. 4. Detroit: Bruccoli Clark/Gale, 1980.

Rubin, William, and Carolyn Lanchner. *The Paintings of Gerald Murphy.* New York: Museum of Modern Art, 1974.

Stewart, Rick. *An American Painter in Paris: Gerald Murphy.* Dallas: Dallas Museum of Art, 1986.

Tomkins, Calvin. *Living Well Is the Best Revenge.* New York: Viking, 1971.

Wheelcock, John Hall. *The Last Romantic: A Poet among Publishers.* Columbia: University of South Carolina Press, 2002.

Wheelock, ed. *Editor to Author: The Letters of Maxwell Perkins.* New York: Scribners, 1979.

Wilson, Edmund. *The Shores of Light.* New York: Farrar, Straus & Young, 1952.

Wilson. *The Thirties: From Notebooks and Diaries of the Period.* New York: Farrar, Straus & Giroux, 1980.

Wilson. *The Twenties,* ed. by Leon Edel. New York: Farrar, Straus & Giroux, 1975.

Yardley, Jonathan. *Ring: A Biography of Ring Lardner.* New York: Random House, 1977.

Selected Works about Fitzgerald

Bibliographies and Catalogues

Bruccoli, Matthew J. *F. Scott Fitzgerald: A Descriptive Bibliography.* Revised and augmented edition. Pittsburgh: University of Pittsburgh Press, 1987.

Bryer, Jackson R. *The Critical Reputation of F. Scott Fitzgerald.* Hamden, Conn.: Archon, 1967.

Bryer. *The Critical Reputation of F. Scott Fitzgerald: Supplement through 1981.* Hamden, Conn.: Archon, 1984.

Bucker, Park S., ed. *Catalogue of the Matthew J. and Arlyn Bruccoli F. Scott Fitzgerald Collection at the Thomas Coo-*

per Library, The University of South Carolina. Columbia, S.C.: MJB, 1997.

F. Scott Fitzgerald Centenary Exhibition. Columbia, S.C.: University of South Carolina Press for the Thomas Cooper Library, 1996.

Stanley, Linda C. *The Foreign Critical Reputation of F. Scott Fitzgerald.* Westport, Conn.: Greenwood Press, 1980.

Biographies and Memoirs

Books

Bruccoli, Matthew J. *Scott and Ernest: The Authority of Failure and the Authority of Success.* New York: Random House, 1978. Revised as *Fitzgerald and Hemingway: A Dangerous Friendship.* New York: Carroll & Graf, 1994; London: Deutsch, 1995.

Bruccoli. *Some Sort of Epic Grandeur.* San Diego: Harcourt Brace Jovanovich, 1981; London: Hodder & Stoughton, 1981. Revised edition, Columbia: University of South Carolina Press, 2002.

Graham, Sheilah. *College of One.* New York: Viking, 1967.

Graham and Gerold Frank. *Beloved Infidel.* New York: Holt, Rinehart & Winston, 1958.

Lanahan, Eleanor, ed. *Zelda, An Illustrated Life: The Private World of Zelda Fitzgerald.* New York: Harry N. Abrams, 1996.

Mellow, James R. *Invented Lives.* Boston: Houghton Mifflin, 1984.

Milford, Nancy. *Zelda.* New York: Harper & Row, 1970.

Mizener, Arthur. *The Far Side of Paradise.* Boston: Houghton Mifflin, 1951. Revised, 1965.

Smith, Scottie Fitzgerald, Matthew J. Bruccoli, and Joan P. Kerr, eds. *The Romantic Egoists: A Pictorial Autobiography from the Scrapbooks and Albums of F. Scott Fitzgerald and Zelda Fitzgerald.* New York: Scribners, 1974.

Turnbull, Andrew. *Scott Fitzgerald.* New York: Scribners, 1962; London: Bodley Head, 1962.

Book Sections and Articles

Hemingway, Ernest. "Scott Fitzgerald," "Hawks Do Not Share," "A Matter of Measurements." *A Moveable Feast,* New York: Scribners, 1964, 147–163.

Lanahan, Francis Fitzgerald. Introduction. *Six Tales of the Jazz Age and Other Stories* by F. Scott Fitzgerald, New York: Scribners, 1960, 5–11.

Meyers, Jeffrey. "Scott Fitzgerald and Edmund Wilson: A Troubled Friendship." *American Scholar,* 61 (Summer 1992), 375–388.

Critical Studies

Baughman, Judith S., with Matthew J. Bruccoli. *F. Scott Fitzgerald Gale Study Guide.* Detroit: Manly/Gale, 2000.

Bruccoli, Matthew J. *"The Last of the Novelists": F. Scott Fitzgerald and The Last Tycoon.* Carbondale & Edwardsville, Ill.: Southern Illinois University Press, 1977.

Callahan, John. *The Illusions of a Nation.* Urbana, Ill.: University of Illinois Press, 1972.

Chambers, John B. *The Novels of F. Scott Fitzgerald.* London: Macmillan / New York: St. Martin's Press, 1989.

Cross, K. G. W. *Scott Fitzgerald.* New York: Grove, 1964.

Eble, Kenneth. *F. Scott Fitzgerald.* New York: Twayne, 1963. Revised, 1977.

Fahey, William A. *F. Scott Fitzgerald and the American Dream.* New York: Crowell, 1973.

Fryer, Sarah Beebe. *Fitzgerald's New Women: Harbingers of Change.* Ann Arbor, Mich.: UMI, 1988.

Gallo, Rose A. *F. Scott Fitzgerald.* New York: Ungar, 1978.

Goldhurst, William. *F. Scott Fitzgerald and His Contemporaries.* Cleveland & New York: World, 1963.

Higgins, John A. *F. Scott Fitzgerald: A Study of the Stories.* New York: St. John's University Press, 1971.

Hook, Andrew. *F. Scott Fitzgerald.* London & New York: Arnold, 1992.

Lehan, Richard D. *F. Scott Fitzgerald and the Craft of Fiction.* Carbondale, Ill.: Southern Illinois University Press, 1966.

Mangum, Bryant. *A Fortune Yet: Money in the Art of F. Scott Fitzgerald's Short Stories.* New York: Garland, 1991.

Miller, James E., Jr. *F. Scott Fitzgerald: His Art and His Technique.* New York: New York University Press, 1964. Revised as *The Fictional Technique of Scott Fitzgerald.* Folcroft, Pa.: Folcroft Press, 1974.

Perosa, Sergio. *The Art of F. Scott Fitzgerald.* Ann Arbor, Mich.: University of Michigan Press, 1965.

Petry, Alice Hall. *Fitzgerald's Craft of Short Fiction: The Collected Stories.* Ann Arbor, Mich.: UMI, 1989.

Piper, Henry Dan. *F. Scott Fitzgerald: A Critical Portrait.* New York: Holt, Rinehart & Winston, 1965.

Seiters, Dan. *Image Patterns in the Novels of F. Scott Fitzgerald.* Ann Arbor, Mich.: UMI, 1986.

Shain, Charles E. *F. Scott Fitzgerald.* Minneapolis, Minn.: University of Minnesota Press, 1967.

Sklar, Robert. *F. Scott Fitzgerald: The Last Lacoön.* New York: Oxford University Press, 1967.

Stavola, Thomas J. *Scott Fitzgerald: Crisis in an American Identity.* New York: Barnes & Noble, 1979.

Stern, Milton R. *The Golden Moment: The Novels of F. Scott Fitzgerald.* Urbana, Ill.: University of Illinois Press, 1970.

Way, Brian. *F. Scott Fitzgerald and the Art of Social Fiction.* London: Arnold, 1980; New York: St. Martin's Press, 1980.

Collections of Essays

Bloom, Harold, ed. with intro. *F. Scott Fitzgerald.* New York: Chelsea House, 1985.

Bruccoli, Matthew J., ed. *Profile of F. Scott Fitzgerald.* Columbus, Ohio: Merrill, 1971.

Bryer, Jackson R., ed. *F. Scott Fitzgerald: The Critical Reception.* New York: Burt Franklin, 1978. Contemporary reviews of Fitzgerald's novels and short-story collections.

Bryer, ed. *New Essays on F. Scott Fitzgerald's Neglected Stories.* Columbia: University of Missouri Press, 1996.

Bryer, ed. *The Short Stories of F. Scott Fitzgerald: New Approaches in Criticism.* Madison: University of Wisconsin Press, 1982.

Claridge, Henry, ed. *F. Scott Fitzgerald: Critical Assessments.* 4 vols. Near Robertsbridge, East Sussex, U.K.: Helm Information, 1991. Contents: 226 essays. Volume I: Fitzgerald in Context, Memories and Reminiscences, Contemporary Critical Opinion; Volume II: Early Writings, *TSOP, B&D, The Vegetable,* and *GG;* Volume III: *TITN, LT, The Crack-Up,* and the Short Stories; Volume IV: General Perspectives, Fitzgerald and Other Writers.

Eble, Kenneth, ed. with intro. *F. Scott Fitzgerald: A Collection of Criticism.* New York: McGraw-Hill, 1973.

Kazin, Alfred, ed. with intro. *F. Scott Fitzgerald: The Man and His Work.* Cleveland: World, 1951.

Lee, Robert A., ed. with intro. *Scott Fitzgerald: The Promises of Life.* London: Vision / New York: St. Martin's Press, 1989.

Mandal, Somdatta, ed. *F. Scott Fitzgerald: A Centenary Tribute.* 2 vols. New Delhi: Prestige, 1997.

Mizener, Arthur, ed. with intro. *F. Scott Fitzgerald: A Collection of Critical Essays.* Englewood Cliffs, N.J.: Prentice-Hall, 1963.

Journals

Fitzgerald Newsletter (quarterly, 1958–1968). Reprinted, Washington, D.C.: NCR Microcard Books, 1969. Includes checklists.

Fitzgerald/Hemingway Annual (1969–1979). Washington, D.C.: NCR Microcard Books, 1969–1973. Englewood, Colo.: Information Handling Services, 1974–1976; Detroit: Gale Research, 1977–1979. Includes checklists.

F. Scott Fitzgerald Collection Notes. Columbia, S.C.: Thomas Cooper Library, University of South Carolina, 1995– .

Book Sections and Articles

Berryman, John. "F. Scott Fitzgerald." *The Kenyon Review,* 8 (Winter 1946), 103–112.

Bewley, Marius. "Scott Fitzgerald's Criticism of America." *Sewanee Review,* 62 (Spring 1954), 223–246. Expanded as "Scott Fitzgerald and the Collapse of the American Dream." *The Eccentric Design* by Bewley. New York: Columbia University Press, 1959.

Bigsby, C. W. E. "The Two Identities of F. Scott Fitzgerald." *The American Novel and the Nineteen Twenties.* ed. by Malcolm Bradbury and David Palmer. London: Arnold, 1971, 129–149.

Bishop, John Peale. "The Missing All." *Virginia Quarterly Review,* 13 (Winter 1937), 106–121.

Cowley, Malcolm. "F. Scott Fitzgerald: The Romance of Money." *Western Review,* 17 (Summer 1953), 245–255.

Cowley. "Fitzgerald: The Double Man." *Saturday Review of Literature,* 34 (February 24, 1951), 9–10, 42–44.

Cowley. "The Scott Fitzgerald Story." *New Republic,* 124 (February 12, 1951), 17–20.

Dos Passos, John. "Fitzgerald and the Press." *New Republic,* 104 (February 17, 1941), 213.

Friedrich, Otto. "Reappraisals–F. Scott Fitzgerald: Money, Money, Money." *American Scholar,* 29 (Summer 1960), 392–405.

Fussell, Edwin S. "Fitzgerald's Brave New World." *ELH,* 19 (December 1952), 291–306.

Geismar, Maxwell. "F. Scott Fitzgerald: Orestes at the Ritz." *The Last of the Provincials.* Boston: Houghton Mifflin, 1943, 287–352.

Gervais, Ronald J. "The Socialist and the Silk Stockings: Fitzgerald's Double Allegiance." *Mosaic,* 15 (June 1982), 79–92.

Harding, D. W. "Scott Fitzgerald." *Scrutiny,* 18 (Winter 1951–1952), 166–174.

Irish, Carol. "The Myth of Success in Fitzgerald's Boyhood." *Studies in American Fiction,* 1 (Autumn 1973), 176–187.

Kuehl, John. "Scott Fitzgerald: Romantic and Realist." *Texas Studies in Literature and Language,* 1 (Autumn 1959), 412–426.

Kuehl. "Scott Fitzgerald's Critical Opinions." *Modern Fiction Studies,* 7 (Spring 1961), 3–18.

Kuehl. "Scott Fitzgerald's Reading." *Princeton University Library Chronicle,* 22 (Winter 1961), 58–89.

O'Hara, John. "On F. Scott Fitzgerald." *"An Artisit Is His Own Fault": John O'Hara on Writers and Writing,* ed. by Matthew J. Bruccoli. Carbondale, Ill.: Southern Illinois University Press, 1977, 135–154.

Rosenfeld, Paul. "F. Scott Fitzgerald." *Men Seen.* New York: Dial, 1925, 215–224.

Savage, D. S. "The Significance of F. Scott Fitzgerald." *Arizona Quarterly,* 8 (Autumn 1952), 197–210.

Schwartz, Delmore. "The Dark Night of F. Scott Fitzgerald." *The Nation,* 172 (February 24, 1951), 180–182.

Trilling, Lionel. "F. Scott Fitzgerald," *The Liberal Imagination.* New York: Viking, 1950, 243–254.

Troy, William. "Scott Fitzgerald—The Authority of Failure." *Accent,* 6 (Autumn 1945), 56–60.

Wescott, Glenway. "The Moral of Scott Fitzgerald." *The New Republic,* 104 (February 17, 1941), 213–217.

Wilson, Edmund. "The Literary Spotlight–VI: F. Scott Fitzgerald." *The Bookman,* 55 (March 1922), 20–25.

Videorecording

Bruccoli, Matthew J. *An Introduction to F. Scott Fitzgerald's Fiction.* Modern American Literature–Eminent Scholar/Teachers Series, Detroit: Omnigraphics, 1988.

Selected Websites

Pioneer Press. *Fitzgerald Childhood Home Tour.* 1996. <http://www.pioneerplanet.com/archive/fitzgerald/stories/fitztour10.htm>.

USC: F. Scott Fitzgerald Centenary Home Page. University of South Carolina. December 1997. <http://www.csd.edu/fitzgerald/index.html>.

Cumulative Index

Dictionary of Literary Biography, Volumes 1-273
Dictionary of Literary Biography Yearbook, 1980-2001
Dictionary of Literary Biography Documentary Series, Volumes 1-19
Concise Dictionary of American Literary Biography, Volumes 1-7
Concise Dictionary of British Literary Biography, Volumes 1-8
Concise Dictionary of World Literary Biography, Volumes 1-4

Cumulative Index

DLB before number: *Dictionary of Literary Biography,* Volumes 1-273
Y before number: *Dictionary of Literary Biography Yearbook,* 1980-2001
DS before number: *Dictionary of Literary Biography Documentary Series,* Volumes 1-19
CDALB before number: *Concise Dictionary of American Literary Biography,* Volumes 1-7
CDBLB before number: *Concise Dictionary of British Literary Biography,* Volumes 1-8
CDWLB before number: *Concise Dictionary of World Literary Biography,* Volumes 1-4

G

Cumulative Index

K

T

ISBN 0-7876-6017-5